Investment Advice Diploma

Investment, Risk & Taxation

Edition 8, July 2017

This learning manual relates to syllabus version 8.0 and will cover examinations from **31 Oct 2017 to 30 Oct 2018**

APPROVED WORKBOOK

Welcome to the Chartered Institute for Securities & Investment's Investment, Risk and Taxation study material.

This workbook has been written to prepare you for the Chartered Institute for Securities & Investment's Investment, Risk and Taxation examination.

Published by:
Chartered Institute for Securities & Investment
© Chartered Institute for Securities & Investment 2017
20 Fenchurch Street
London
EC3M 3BY
Tel: +44 20 7645 0600
Fax: +44 20 7645 0601

Email: customersupport@cisi.org
www.cisi.org/qualifications

Author:
Anthony Ward BSc, MCSI, FPFS Chartered Financial Planner

Reviewers:
David Smith
Jon Beckett, Chartered MCSI

This is an educational workbook only and the Chartered Institute for Securities & Investment accepts no responsibility for persons undertaking trading or investments in whatever form.

While every effort has been made to ensure its accuracy, no responsibility for loss occasioned to any person acting or refraining from action as a result of any material in this publication can be accepted by the publisher or authors.

All rights reserved. No part of this publication may be reproduced, stored in a retrieval system, or transmitted, in any form or by any means, electronic, mechanical, photocopying, recording or otherwise without the prior permission of the copyright owner.

Warning: any unauthorised act in relation to all or any part of the material in this publication may result in both a civil claim for damages and criminal prosecution.

A learning map, which contains the full syllabus, appears at the end of this workbook. The syllabus can also be viewed on cisi.org and is also available by contacting the Customer Support Centre on +44 20 7645 0777. Please note that the examination is based upon the syllabus. Candidates are reminded to check the Candidate Update area details (cisi.org/candidateupdate) on a regular basis for updates as a result of industry change(s) that could affect their examination.

The questions contained in this workbook are designed as an aid to revision of different areas of the syllabus and to help you consolidate your learning chapter by chapter.

Workbook version: 8.2 (January 2018)

Learning and Professional Development with the CISI

The Chartered Institute for Securities & Investment is the leading professional body for those who work in, or aspire to work in, the investment sector, and we are passionately committed to enhancing knowledge, skills and integrity – the three pillars of professionalism at the heart of our Chartered body.

CISI examinations are used extensively by firms to meet the requirements of government regulators. Besides the regulators in the UK, where the CISI head office is based, CISI examinations are recognised by a wide range of governments and their regulators, from Singapore to Dubai and the US. Around 50,000 examinations are taken each year, and it is compulsory for candidates to use CISI workbooks to prepare for CISI examinations so that they have the best chance of success. Our workbooks are normally revised every year by experts who themselves work in the industry and also by our Accredited Training Partners, who offer training and elearning to help prepare candidates for the examinations. Information for candidates is also posted on a special area of our website: cisi.org/candidateupdate.

This workbook not only provides a thorough preparation for the examination it refers to, it is also a valuable desktop reference for practitioners, and studying from it counts towards your Continuing Professional Development (CPD). Mock examination papers, for most of our titles, will be made available on our website, as an additional revision tool.

CISI examination candidates are automatically registered, without additional charge, as student members for one year (should they not be members of the CISI already), and this enables you to use a vast range of online resources, including CISI TV, free of any additional charge. The CISI has more than 40,000 members, and nearly half of them have already completed relevant qualifications and transferred to a core membership grade. You will find more information about the next steps for this at the end of this workbook.

Asset Classes	1
The Macroeconomic Environment	133
Principles of Investment Risk and Return	195
Taxation of Investors and Investments	257
Investment Products	317
Investment Planning	405
Investment Advice	437
Portfolio Performance and Review	495
Glossary	519
Multiple Choice Questions	527
Syllabus Learning Map	559

It is estimated that this manual will require approximately 140 hours of study time.

What next?
See the back of this book for details of CISI membership.

Need more support to pass your exam?
See our section on Accredited Training Partners.

Want to leave feedback?
Please email your comments to learningresources@cisi.org

Chapter One
Asset Classes

1. Cash and Cash Equivalents	3
2. Fixed-Income Securities	24
3. Equities	67
4. Property	107
5. Other Assets	128

This syllabus area will provide approximately 14 of the 80 examination questions

Asset Classes

1. Cash and Cash Equivalents

Learning Objective

1.1.2 Analyse the main characteristics, risk and returns of cash deposits: liquidity; rates of interest; past returns; real returns; deposit-takers; statutory protection; risks, inflation risk, interest rate risk and institutional risk; credit risk assessment of deposit-taking institutions; foreign currency deposits; costs, charges and penalties; requirement linked accounts, Financial Services Compensation Scheme limits

1.1.5 Analyse the factors to take into account when selecting between different types of cash deposits, accounts and money market funds: entry requirements

1.1 The Role of Cash Deposits

One of the key reasons for holding money in the form of cash deposits is liquidity – the ease and speed with which an investment can be turned into cash to meet spending needs.

- Deposits held in instant access accounts are highly liquid – that is, access can be gained to them immediately, so that they can be used to meet spending needs as and when they arise.
- Even money held on other forms of deposit – eg, seven-day notice accounts – can be accessed reasonably quickly; and certainly more so than some other forms of investment.

We will look at various types of deposit, and consider how easy it is for the investor to gain access to them, in a later section of this chapter. Most investors are likely to have a need for cash at short notice, and so should plan to hold some on deposit to meet possible needs and emergencies, before considering more risky, and less liquid, investments.

The other main reasons are security, as a savings vehicle, and for the interest return that can be earned on them.

- Accounts for holding cash deposits are generally characterised by a high level of security.
- Capital is very unlikely to be lost, at least in money terms. The purchasing power of capital held on deposit will, however, be eroded by **inflation**.
- Against this, there is the reward of any interest receivable, and the rate of interest may exceed inflation, resulting in a real rate of return for the investor.

A cash deposit account can serve as a vehicle for reaching a savings target, for example, when saving for the cost of a major purchase, or for the deposit (part-payment) on a house purchase.

1.2 Interest Rates

Cash deposits generally provide the investor with a return in the form of interest paid regularly, but no capital growth. The exception is accounts which are held chiefly for transactional purposes, such as chequing and **current accounts**: these generally do not earn interest; and we will ignore these for the purposes of this chapter, as they are not generally held for investment purposes.

Interest is normally paid as a percentage of the capital deposited. Generally speaking:

- Deposit-takers will pay higher rates of interest the larger the deposit. An account holding £10 is likely to earn a lower rate of interest than one holding £100,000.
- Deposit-takers will also pay higher rates of interest for longer-term deposits. An account offering instant access is likely to earn a lower rate of interest than one where the money is tied up for a year.

This is not always the case – in some cases the market rate for long-term deposits can actually fall below that for shorter-term ones; but this is relatively unusual, and in most cases the depositor will earn more for having tied their money up for longer. This is known as the inverse cash rate.

Interest rates may be variable or fixed at the outset. For instant access and notice accounts, they are usually variable, and for fixed-term deposits they are usually set for the entire period of the fix.

1.2.1 Gross and Net Interest Rates

If the interest rate quoted is described as gross, this means that it is the contractual rate of interest paid before deduction of income tax.

Until 5 April 2016, UK banks deducted basic rate income tax at source, before crediting interest to a UK resident's account. However, those UK residents who are non-taxpayers – and overseas residents who are not liable for UK tax – could apply to Her Majesty's Revenue and Customs (HMRC) to receive their interest gross on deposits with UK banks and building societies.

If the interest rate was quoted as net, this was the rate the investor would receive after deduction of basic rate tax. This meant that the rate showed what the investor would receive, after the deposit-taker has deducted income tax at the savings rate of 20% on the amount of interest paid.

From 6 April 2016, interest paid on a UK deposit account is paid gross (no tax is deducted at source). The UK government has claimed that this change will mean that 95% of UK adults will not pay tax on their savings income.

1.2.2 Compounding

Historically, deposits have proved to give low returns compared with some other investments; but this is compensated for by a lower exposure to risk.

Investors attempting to compare the interest rates paid by one institution with those paid by another (or to compare the rates earned on a deposit with the returns on other forms of investment), need to take account of timing factors.

Many institutions pay tiered interest rates – meaning that the larger the balance with them, the higher the rate of interest they will pay. But there may also be variations in when interest is paid – eg, monthly, quarterly, annually – and a higher rate of interest may be payable for interest paid less frequently. This may be an important consideration for an investor who is reliant on the interest for an income stream.

It means that, if two accounts have the same nominal historical rate of interest, but Account A credits interest more regularly than Account B, Account A will give the investor a better return (and more frequent income distributions).

Example

Both accounts pay 4% per annum interest; but Account A pays it quarterly and Account B pays it annually. The investor leaves the interest in the account to roll up (ie, they do not take it out and spend it).

For a £10,000.00 account:

Account A pays 1% (ie, a quarter of 4%) at the end of Q1, taking it up to:
£10,000.00 x 101% = £10,100.00.

At the end of Q2, another 1% interest is paid – on the new total of £10,100.00:
£10,100.00 x 101% = £10,201.00.

At the end of Q3, 1% is paid on the total of £10,201.00:
£10,201.00 x 101% = £10,303.01.

At the end of Q4, 1% is paid on the total of £10,303.01:
£10,303.01 x 101% = £10,406.04.

The account has grown by £406.04.

Account B has capital of £10,000 at the end of year 1, and pays interest at 4%:
£10,000.00 x 4% = £10,400.00.

Hint: if interest is paid regularly over several periods in a year, then use the following equation to compare the terminal wealth generated by each account:

$$T = C(1+(I/N))^N$$

C = initial capital deposited in the account.
I = annual rate of interest paid.
N = number of times in the year interest will be paid.
T = terminal wealth of the initial deposit at the end of the period.

Note: the term $(1+(I/N))^N$ is referred to as the compounding factor.

There is a difference of £6.04, or a small advantage with the account that pays interest more frequently at the same nominal rate, with the interest earned being rolled up into the capital.

The improvement has come about because the depositor has earned interest on the interest. The interest credited in the first quarter is added to the capital, on which interest is calculated at the end of the second quarter, and so on. This effect is called compounding.

Of course, if the investor who has Account A does not leave the quarterly interest payments in the account (ie, takes them out and spends them), they will not get the compounding effect: but will get access to income that can be spent earlier than otherwise would be the case with Account B.

So it is clearly very important to look at not just the headline rate of interest, but also how frequently this is calculated and applied to the account – and whether it is a flat or a compound rate.

1.2.3 Comparing Like with Like – the Annual Equivalent Rate (AER)

Clearly, there are different ways in which institutions can show their current and historic interest rates – and this can be very confusing for many depositors and their advisers. So, in the UK, every advertisement for a savings or deposit account should also show the quoted interest rate along with what used to be called the compound annual interest rate (CAR), and is now usually referred to as the **annual equivalent rate (AER)**.

AER is a notional rate that is quoted on the interest paid on savings and investments. The AER provides the depositor with a true rate of return, taking account of how often interest is credited to their account during a 12-month period, and is supposed to show what the return will be if the interest is compounded and paid annually, instead of monthly or quarterly. It therefore lets them compare one account with another on a like-for-like basis. The AER is usually quoted gross, ie, before any tax is deducted, though it can be quoted net too. It means that a depositor can compare two flat rates from different deposit-takers or accounts, without the complication of trying to work out the effect of one deposit-taker applying interest more frequently than another. Accounts that pay interest monthly or quarterly, compared to annually, will have a higher-quoted AER, to reflect the impact of the compounding of interest on interest.

AERs only apply where interest is left to roll-over in the account for the whole period; if the depositor draws it out (for example, to spend) it will no longer be meaningful.

1.2.4 Real Returns

The performance of cash deposits as an investment can be measured as a real rate of return by comparing the nominal interest rate with the expected future rate of inflation in the investment period. A real return is one that the investor expects to earn after allowing for inflation. The headline interest rate is also known as the nominal rate.

The relationship between the nominal, real and inflation rates is described more formally by the Fisher equation. This states that the real interest rate is approximately equal to the nominal interest rate minus the expected future inflation rate in the deposit period.

Approximately:

Nominal rate of interest – rate of inflation = real rate of return

For example, if annual interest is paid at a nominal rate of 5%, and the rate of inflation is 2%, then the real rate of return is approximately 3%. The purchasing power of the cash investment is increasing at 3% per year.

A more accurate definition of the Fisher equation is presented as follows:

$$R = \left[\frac{(1+Ni)}{(1+Infl)} \right] - 1$$

where:

R = real rate of interest.
Ni = nominal rate of interest.
Infl = inflation expected over the holding period.

Note that if the real rate 'R' is calculated using the example above, then:

$$R = \left[\frac{(1.05)}{(1.02)}\right] - 1$$

R = 1.0294 − 1 = 0.0294 or 2.94%.

Interest rates on cash deposits will generally move approximately in tandem with rates of interest on borrowing; deposit-takers obtain income from the difference (the margin) between the deposit rates they pay, and the rates they charge to borrowers. In the **London Interbank Offered Rate (LIBOR)** money markets, where commercial banks transact lending/borrowing transactions between each other every weekday, the difference between the lending and borrowing rates quoted in the market is called the bid-offer spread. It is also called the bid/ask in other asset markets. The lower of the two quotes is the bid, or the London Interbank Bid Rate (LIBID): the deposit rate paid to depositors. The higher quote is the offer rate, or LIBOR: the lending rate paid to a borrower.

1.2.5 Interest Rates on Accounts with Variable Rates

Rates on accounts with variable rates of interest also generally move in line with the short-term base rate of interest, called the Bank rate. It is set by the Bank of England's Monetary Policy Committee (MPC). This rate is set at a level which the MPC believes will help it in achieving its inflation rate objectives. More generally, the central bank's remit recognises the key role of price stability (maintaining low inflation to a target level of 2%), together with its aims to achieve economic stability and to provide the right conditions to promote growth in economic output and employment. More simply, the **central bank** aims for non-inflationary growth that sustains economic growth while maximising employment potential. Conversely, if the economy appears to be overheating due to inflationary growth, with people finding credit and borrowing easy to obtain and afford, interest rates may be raised to discourage borrowing and to moderate economic activity, together with its negative impact on employment.

Deposit-taking institutions are in competition with one another and the interest rates set on different deposit products reflect these competitive market conditions, as well as credit risk profiles and concerns among the deposit-takers.

1.2.6 Costs, Charges and Penalties on Current Accounts

Terms and conditions apply when money is deposited in a bank deposit account. The service is not entirely free and often entails a series of costs, charges and penalties. Individuals and businesses who have deposited money in these accounts need to look at the schedule of charges closely; in a competitive environment these often vary from one bank to another. A deposit account is a current account, savings account, or other type of bank account, at a banking institution that allows money to be deposited and withdrawn by the account holder.

These accounts are recorded on the bank's books. The balances are effectively a liability for the bank, and represent the amount owed by the bank to the customer. Some banks charge a fee for this service, while others may pay the customer interest on the funds deposited. The costs of maintaining such accounts may involve a maintenance fee or a penalty if the account is overdrawn, even for a short period.

Some special current account products have been offered, where the bank pays interest every month. To receive interest or a cashback, the account holder must meet specific account conditions. For example, a minimum payment may be required every month or the customer may have to maintain a minimum balance or arrange for regular direct debits to be set up on that account. The interest may be worked out on a daily balance on the first few thousands of pounds and the interest paid by the bank into the account every month.

There are also similar accounts available to customers who are under 18 years of age or are students. Different terms and conditions apply to these transactions compared with conventional current accounts. The following information, taken from a major UK bank group, clarifies this.

As an example of charges, current account fees charged by a bank may apply as standard account fees. One UK bank charges a fee of £2 per month on a normal current account, but a much larger fee of £5 per month on its international student current accounts. There are also arranged or unarranged overdrafts if the account temporarily has a negative balance. The bank may only allow the overdraft to run continuously for a maximum period (eg, capped at 20 days in each monthly statement period). The bank may not charge interest when the account is overdrawn, but the following fees may apply:

- If a current account is overdrawn, the daily arranged overdraft fee will be £1 a day, up to a maximum of 20 days. If overdrawn on an unarranged basis, the overdraft fee may be £5 a day, possibly limited to a maximum of 20 days, in each monthly statement period.
- In addition to the above schedules, there is a paid item fee and an unpaid item fee. A paid item fee can be £5–£25 for each item. An unpaid item fee is scaled up to £10–£25 for each item, depending on the type of current account held and the arrangements made with the bank.
- Overdrafts will be capped at £95–£150 per month, again depending on the type of account.

1.2.7 Requirement Linked Accounts

Requirement linked accounts are simply bank accounts that offer a higher-than-average headline rate of interest, but with certain conditions. These conditions often take the form of requiring an account holder to retain a certain balance in a separate low-interest-earning current account, or to ensure that a certain amount, eg, £1,000 per month, is paid into it during the first year. The higher interest rate is often guaranteed only for the first year and, in some cases, there may be a limit to the amount that can be paid in.

In these scenarios it is important to pay close attention to the AER, particularly when you have two linked accounts, one paying little or no interest (eg, a current account) and a separate linked deposit savings account paying the higher rate of interest. The requirement to hold a balance in the lower earning account means that the overall rate of interest on the balance held across both accounts will be lower than the headline rate. Therefore, it is vital to calculate the AER when considering whether this is in fact a good deal.

1.3 Deposit-Takers

The principal UK deposit-takers are the banks and building societies.

The Financial Services Authority (FSA) was originally responsible for the supervision and regulation of banks and building societies in the UK, in terms of their financial soundness and the way in which they carried on their business.

The FSA has now been converted into two separate regulatory authorities: the Financial Conduct Authority (FCA) and the Prudential Regulatory Authority (PRA). More details are available in section 1.5. Note that the creation of these two regulatory bodies was formally made on 1 April 2013. The PRA is part of the Bank of England (BoE) and carries the prudential regulatory powers over financial firms, such as banks, building societies, investment and insurance companies.

National Savings & Investments (NS&I), a government agency backed by HM Treasury, is one of the largest saving organisations in the UK that takes deposits. The money saved and invested with the NS&I is 100% secure because it is backed by HM Treasury. There is no overall limit on how much is guaranteed. As a government agency, NS&I is not required to be authorised by the PRA. We will look at NS&I products in section 1.7 of this chapter.

1.3.1 Building Societies

A building society is a mutual organisation, which means that it is owned by its members. The members are the investment account holders and borrowers; as members, they have voting rights in the running of the organisation. Thus, the organisation's customers are also – in the main – its owners. This contrasts with the situation for banks, as we will see in section 1.3.2.

Many former building societies have demutualised and turned themselves into banks, and some have subsequently been bought by banks. On demutualisation or acquisition of the society, members may be entitled to a windfall payment, reflecting a share of the reserves of the organisation that have been built up over its life. However, most of the remaining building societies now require new account holders to waive their rights to such windfall payments, often by signing over the entitlement to charity. This is intended to prevent people opening accounts speculatively in the hope of gaining a windfall. More information is available from the Building Societies Association website (bsa.org.uk).

1.3.2 Banks

Banks are limited companies, owned by their shareholders. Their shares are almost invariably listed on the stock exchange. Thus, a bank customer may also be a shareholder (and, therefore, an owner), although this is by no means always the case.

The rights of account holders are described in the terms and conditions of the account by contract law: effective supervision and regulation by the central bank and corporate governance principles that agents within the banking industry follow. The account holders do not have voting rights over how the bank is operated.

1.4 Risks

Deposits, as money market products, are generally regarded as low-risk investments, but they are not entirely risk-free.

The risks associated with them are:

- **Capital risk** – capital may be lost if the deposit-taker becomes insolvent and defaults (ie, becomes insolvent and cannot repay its depositors).

- **Inflation risk** – if the prevailing rate of inflation exceeds the interest payable on the account. The real rate of interest will be negative as a result. This is the case if the account is a fixed-interest account: while an investor is locked in at fixed interest rates, inflation could accelerate, due to unforeseen economic conditions, and the purchasing power of the investor's capital will be eroded in real terms.
- **Interest rate risk** – the risk that the rate of interest paid on the deposit is less than could be obtained on other low-risk investment products, or the investor is locked in at a fixed rate for fixed terms, when they might otherwise have been able to take advantage of rising interest rates available in the market.
- **Operational risk** – the risk that the bank or building society gives poor service to the depositor, so that they suffer some form of loss because of this. For example, the bank does not move the money on to a fixed-rate account when the account holder has requested this.

1.5 Regulation

In the UK, deposit-taking is subject to supervision and scrutiny. It is a regulated activity, and deposit-takers have to apply for and receive authorisation from the PRA, which was created by the Financial Services Act (2012) and is part of the BoE.

In April 2013, the PRA became responsible for the prudential regulation and supervision of banks, building societies, insurers, credit unions and major investing firms. The PRA is overseen by the Financial Policy Committee. In a 'twin peaks' regime that has now replaced the FSA, responsibility for protecting the consumer interests falls on the FCA. Displacement of the FSA by the PRA and FCA became necessary in the wake of the 2007 crisis that exposed serious shortcomings in the banking system and the mis-selling scandals of the past.

The PRA's roles are defined by two statutory objectives:

1. promote the safety and soundness of firms in the financial services industry
2. secure an appropriate degree of protection provided to savers, investors and policyholders.

These objectives will ensure that the UK financial system maintains its stability and credibility. From a systemic risk mitigation perspective, it is essential for the UK economy to have a robust and stable financial system that has the ability to continue to provide critical financial services under all market conditions without recourse to the support of the UK government and taxpayers, as happened in 2009.

The FCA is responsible for ensuring that markets function properly. Additionally, the authority aims to ensure that consumers get a fair deal from the financial services industry. Its role includes providing protection to consumers, encouraging effective competition in the interest of consumers and further bolstering the integrity of the UK financial system.

1.5.1 Statutory Protections

Depositors can check out the financial strength of UK banks and other deposit-takers by researching their credit ratings. These are independent assessments carried out by credit rating agencies such as Fitch Ratings Inc, Standard & Poor's and Moody's. They show the rating agency's opinion of the deposit-taker's long-term and short-term financial standing, and how likely it is to be able to meet its liabilities to depositors when they fall due. The agencies all have their own rating systems, but they are generally quite similar; typically, a long-term credit rating of AAA or AA is regarded as very strong, with lower ratings of A, BBB, BB, B and C and below reflecting progressively less strong finances. The agencies may use a combination of capital and lower case letters, together with pluses and minuses (eg, AA–, B+) as indications of sub-gradings within a broad sliding scale or rating band.

1.5.2 The Financial Services Compensation Scheme (FSCS)

If a UK deposit-taker fails, the depositor will have recourse to the Financial Services Compensation Scheme (FSCS). The scheme, originally administered by the FSA, is now under the supervision of the new UK regulatory regime. The FSCS deals with all claims against authorised firms and is an independent body set up under the Financial Services and Markets Act (2000). The FSCS has come to the aid of more than 4.5 million people since 2001, and has paid out over £26 billion in compensation.

The FSCS will pay maximum compensation of £85,000 for each account holder who is an eligible claimant, in each of the authorised savings institutions where an account is held, following default by a UK-regulated bank or building society. Retail deposits made by private individuals and small businesses into any authorised firm are protected by the FSCS. All deposit claims will be paid in UK pounds.

The FSCS compensation limits apply:

- only to UK sterling deposits held at a UK branch of the deposit-taker
- to each depositor, and not to each individual account
- separately to each joint account holder; therefore, two joint account holders could each receive up to £85,000 for a joint account, bringing compensation up to £170,000 for the couple
- deposits held in accounts outside the EEA (European Economic Area), the Channel Islands and the Isle of Man are not covered by the FSCS
- deposits held in other currencies are covered, but all claims are paid in sterling.

The FSCS provides a valuable safety net for many depositors, but those with very substantial deposits will not, of course, receive compensation for their full losses. The ceiling on compensation available through the FSCS leads many investors to consider spreading their capital among a number of banks and building societies in order to reduce the overall risk. This may result in their earning a poorer rate of interest – as smaller deposits tend to command lower rates – but nervous depositors may regard this as a small price to pay. The benefit of spreading the risk in this way should be weighed against the disadvantage of less interest being earned, because of the investor missing out on the higher rates offered for larger deposits.

For more details, visit the FSCS website at fscs.org.uk.

1.5.3 The Financial Ombudsman Service (FOS)

If a depositor suffers because the deposit-taker gives them poor service, they may have recourse to the **Financial Ombudsman Service (FOS)**. The FOS acts to resolve complaints against regulated financial services providers, including banks and building societies, if these cannot be sorted out between the customer and the provider directly.

The FOS will investigate the complaint, looking at evidence from both customer and provider, and make a decision, which is then binding on the provider.

The maximum limit of compensation the FOS can award (excluding any interest and costs) is £150,000. If a depositor believes they have suffered losses greater than this, it may be more appropriate for them to take the provider to court instead.

For more information visit financial-ombudsman.org.uk.

1.6 Foreign Currency Deposits

Deposits can be held with many UK deposit-takers in currencies other than sterling. Depositors may choose to hold accounts in foreign currencies for any of the following reasons:

- They have transactional needs in foreign currencies (eg, overseas income from earnings, or overseas spending needs such as on a property abroad) and wish to hold balances as a result.
- More importantly, for the purposes of this text, they may hold them for investment purposes:
  - An investor may choose to hold cash in foreign currency because the interest rates earned on that currency exceed those which they can obtain on sterling. They run the risk, however, that the currency depreciates against sterling and that the additional income they earn is more than outweighed by a loss in capital value when the deposit is converted back to the home currency.
  - Alternatively, they may hold the foreign currency for speculative reasons – ie, they believe that the currency is due to appreciate against the pound, and that they may, therefore, make capital gains. They run the risk, of course, that they are wrong and the currency depreciates against the pound instead.

Currency movements are notoriously difficult to predict, and the risks mentioned above are not trivial. In addition, a UK bank holding foreign currency deposits may apply higher charges because of the greater administrative burden on it, and these may offset some of the additional returns that might otherwise be earned.

1.7 The Main Types of Deposit Account

Learning Objective

1.1.1 Understand the main types of deposit account: current; instant access; National Savings & Investment products; notice; fixed rate; term; money market accounts

Banks and building societies offer a wide range of account types, in which savers and investors can hold their cash. The key elements, in terms of account type and features, are:

- **How money can be paid in** – some types of deposit impose no restrictions on the amount that can be paid in; others have maximum and minimum balances, and minimum amounts that can be added after the account is opened. This might be for commercial reasons; for example, the deposit-taker is aiming at high net worth customers and does not deal with customers of more modest means. With most fixed-term deposits you cannot add a further amount once the deposit has begun; you will need to open a second, separate deposit account.
- **Withdrawals** – most providers will include rules as to when, how easily and how quickly amounts can be taken out. For a current or instant access account, the depositor may be able to take money out at any time – though again there may be minimum withdrawal amounts, so that the provider does not have to administer very small transactions. For notice accounts, the depositor must give a set amount of notice before they can take any money out. This might be anything from one week upwards (so we might talk about a 90-day notice account, which means the depositor has to give around three months' forewarning if they want some or all of their money back). With a fixed-term deposit, usually no withdrawals are permitted until the end date of the fixed period (so if a depositor takes out a one-year fixed deposit, the money is tied in for the whole period). If a depositor realises they have miscalculated, and needs the fixed deposit money back early, the deposit-taker may agree to release the funds – but often only after deducting a substantial penalty for breaking the deposit.
- **How interest is paid** – interest rates may be variable or fixed at the outset. For instant access and notice accounts, they are usually variable, and for fixed-term deposits they are usually set for the entire period of the fix. Many institutions pay tiered interest rates, meaning that the larger the balance held with them, the higher the rate of interest they will pay. There may also be variations as to when interest is paid – eg, monthly, quarterly, annually – and a higher rate of interest may be payable for interest paid less frequently. This may be an important consideration for an investor who is reliant on the interest for an income stream.

The following are some of the key account types available, and their features:

- **Current accounts** are typically used for transactional purposes, and allow the holder to access their money as and when they need it. They may come with a cheque book so that the holder can access their money simply by writing a cheque; alternatively, or additionally, they may come with a debit card for the same purpose. At one time it was common for current accounts to earn interest, and there was some competition between providers on the basis of the interest rate paid; however, many providers have now stopped paying interest on current accounts.
- **Instant access accounts** also allow the holder to get their money when they want, but do not usually provide a cheque book (or, if they do, may limit the number of times it can be used within a given period). Typically, if they earn interest, it is at a variable rate.

- **Notice accounts** require that the holder gives a certain period of notice before withdrawing all or part of their deposit. A 90-day notice account will thus require that the depositor give 90 days' advance warning before they can have their money back. If the deposit-taker allows this to be waived, it may apply a penalty to compensate itself. These generally earn interest at variable rates (ie, the provider will link the interest paid to the base rate).
- **Fixed-rate accounts** earn a set rate of interest over their entire life; they are invariably for fixed terms as well. Interest is generally credited at the end of the term.
- **Term (or fixed-term) accounts** are tied up for a set period – for example, one or three months. They generally earn a fixed rate of interest over their life, which is added to the account at the end of the term, ie, on maturity.
- **Money market accounts**. To understand money market accounts and money market funds, it helps to know the difference between the two. Money market is simply a generic name used to describe the market wherein banks and other financial institutions lend, borrow and trade money, certificates of deposit (CDs) and other financial instruments. We will cover money market funds in section 1.8 of this chapter.

A money market account is basically a premium account, or a high-interest savings account. A money market account should not be mistaken for a money market fund. A money market fund is an investment strategy with larger returns than a premium savings account. A money market account can be opened very simply at almost any bank. The money you keep in such an account will be invested, but the bank or other institution does the investing and collects the return.

Your money is usually put into investments like CDs, **Treasury bills** (T-bills) or other safe financial instruments. Each of these are low-risk, short-term investments. Your reward for allowing the financial institution to use your money is a premium interest rate, which may be up to twice as high as a typical passbook account.

While a money market account makes a decent low-risk investment, keep in mind that, because it is an investment, there are certain restrictions. Your money will not be as liquid as it is in a regular savings account, and a money market account usually requires a minimum deposit, as well as a minimum balance. While you can make withdrawals from a money market account, there is a limit to how many you can make.

1.7.1 National Savings & Investments (NS&I)

National Savings & Investments (NS&I) products are offered by the government and, as such, are regarded as risk-free investments. Details of the current terms and product offerings are available on the NS&I website (nsandi.com/savings).

NS&I is an executive agency of the Chancellor of the Exchequer, and is accountable to the Treasury. It provides deposit and savings products to the investing public, and in doing so raises funds on behalf of the UK government. An investor holding an NS&I product is in essence lending to the government.

NS&I offers a wide range of products, from easy-access savings accounts to longer-term investments and, of course, premium bonds. As the products are underwritten by the government, they are regarded as effectively free from the risk of default. None of NS&I's products are subject to **capital gains tax**, but some products are subject to income tax. The following are its key products.

Savings Accounts

NS&I offers a range of products aimed at savers, including:

- **Investment account** – this is in effect a passbook-style savings account which, as of 21 May 2012, became a postal-only account. Up to this date, savers operated it over the counter at their post office, by mail or by standing order but this has been converted to a post-only method of savings and withdrawals. It pays variable rates, tiered interest rates and has no set term. The minimum deposit is £20 and the maximum is £1 million. Interest is taxable and paid gross.
- **Direct Saver account** – this account offers the convenience of being able to manage accounts online and by phone. Interest rates are variable, taxable and paid gross. The minimum investment is £1 with an upper limit of £2 million per person.

Income-Providing Products

- **Guaranteed income bonds** – NS&I's product aimed at the investor who is seeking interest income. These provide a guaranteed monthly income. The minimum holding is £500 and the maximum total holding £1 million. Offered for terms of one, three and five years, the interest is taxable and paid gross.

Growth Products

NS&I's growth schemes include the following. Although some are not available as new products, they have been included as they are still available for customers with maturing investments:

- **Index-linked savings certificates** – these pay a return which is guaranteed and linked to the inflation rate as measured by the Retail Prices Index (RPI). The minimum holding is £100, and the maximum is £15,000 per issue. Certificates can be bought for terms of either three or five years. Returns are tax-free. There are currently no new index-linked savings certificates available. These are available for customers with maturing investments.
- **Fixed-interest savings certificates** – these pay a fixed rate of return over a period of time, such as two and five years. The returns are guaranteed for the term and are tax-free on maturity. The minimum holding is £100 and maximum is £15,000 per issue. There are currently no new fixed-interest savings certificates available. These are available for customers with maturing investments.
- **Guaranteed growth bonds** – these provide a guaranteed return on an investment. The minimum holding is £500 and maximum is £1 million. Choice of terms are one, three and five years, with access available before maturity subject to a loss of 90 days' interest. Interest is taxable and paid gross. There are currently no new guaranteed growth bonds available. These are available for customers with maturing investments.
- **Investment guaranteed growth bonds** – available on investments up to £3,000 and paying 2.2% AER on a three-year term, these bonds are available until 10 April 2018.
- **65+ bonds** – often referred to in the press as 'pensioner bonds', these are a growth product available to those aged 65 and over. Although not currently available for new investment, existing holders earn interest on their capital for a fixed term, in the same way as guaranteed growth bonds. Interest is earned daily, and added on each anniversary. The minimum investment is £500, the maximum £10,000, and capital can be accessed before maturity, subject to the loss of 90 days' interest. All interest is taxable and basic rate tax is deducted at source. There are currently no new 65+ bonds available. For customers with maturing investments, they can reinvest into a standard guaranteed growth bond.

Tax-Free Products

Some of NS&I's products provide returns free of tax (although the returns on these products are not generally high, reflecting also the fact that they are regarded as very safe). They include:

- **Premium bonds**, which carry no capital risk (the holder can withdraw their capital in full when they wish). Instead of earning interest, bonds are entered into a monthly draw in which they could win their holder up to £1 million (or one of many smaller amounts). The minimum holding is £100 and the maximum is currently £50,000.
- **Direct Individual Savings Account (ISA)** – this account is NS&I's version of the cash individual savings account – a type of scheme whereby the holder can earn a return free of capital and income taxes. For 2017–18, investors can pay a maximum of £20,000 in a tax year into NS&I's direct ISA, earning variable-rate interest on this free of income tax. There are no withdrawal restrictions.
- **Children's bonds** – a child's parent or legal guardian can buy new bonds for them under the age of 16. These run for a period of five years and offer a guaranteed rate of interest (paid daily) from the outset. Returns are tax-free with no tax liability on the parents. The minimum investment per issue is £25 and maximum is £3,000. Access is allowed during the term, subject to the loss of 90 days' interest, and no interest is credited if the bond is cashed in during the first year.

1.8 Money Market Funds

Learning Objective

1.1.3 Analyse the main characteristics, risks and returns of money market funds: cash assets only; near-cash assets; pricing, liquidity and fair value; costs, charges and penalties; constant NAV; low volatility NAV; variable NAV; fees and gates

1.8.1 What are Money Market Funds?

Money market funds are mutual funds that invest in cash assets or near-cash assets, which are generally viewed as low-risk and liquid. Like other types of mutual funds, investors in money market funds are shareholders in an investment pool created by the mutual fund company. Thus, investors have a pro rata claim on this pool of investments.

Near-cash assets include short-term debt instruments, such as commercial paper and government bonds close to expiry (short-term gilts and Treasury bills), while cash assets include short-term bank deposits.

Funds provide the benefits of pooled investment, as investors can participate in a more diverse and high-quality portfolio than they otherwise could individually. Like other mutual funds, each investor who invests in a money market fund is considered a shareholder of the investment pool, a part-owner of the fund. Money market funds are actively managed within rigid and transparent guidelines to offer the safety of principal, liquidity and competitive sector-related returns.

There are two basic types of money market funds: constant net asset value (CNAV) and accumulating net asset value. Shares in constant net asset value funds are issued with an unchanging face value (such as £1 per share). Income in the fund is accrued daily and can either be paid out to the investor or used to purchase more units in the fund at the end of the month. Accumulating net asset value funds, known alternatively as roll-up funds, operate under the same investment guidelines as CNAV funds and income is accrued daily. However, unlike CNAV funds, income is not distributed. Instead income is reflected by an increase in the value of the fund shares.

A low volatility net asset value (LVNAV) money market fund can also display a constant net asset value, but under strict conditions. Authorisations granted to LVNAVs shall, however, cease after five years, at which point, only the CNAV funds may exist. The regulation proposes that LVNAVs would be authorised for a term of five years. It also proposes that the commission should undertake a review of the regulation after four years, and that this five-year licence term should be one of the topics they consider and potentially abolish.

A variable net asset value (VNAV) refers to funds which use mark-to-market accounting to value some of their assets. The NAV of these funds will vary by a slight amount, due to the changing value of the assets and, in the case of an accumulating fund, by the amount of income received.

This means that a fund with an unchanging NAV is, by definition, CNAV, but a fund with a NAV that varies may be accumulating NAV or distributing or accumulating VNAV.

1.8.2 Industry Origins and Regulatory Aspects

Money market funds were first offered in the US in the early 1970s, and now money market funds are widely used across the financial world in both the institutional and retail sectors. Money market funds were first exported to offshore European centres in the late 1980s. The principal providers of money market funds in Europe formed a trade association, the Institutional Money Market Funds Association (IMMFA). IMMFA funds are European money market funds that have a triple-A rating and abide by the IMMFA code of practice. These funds are managed actively, but operate within rigid and transparent guidelines to offer safety of principal, liquidity and competitive returns. All three main credit rating agencies (Moody's, S&P and Fitch) offer money-market fund ratings. The triple-A rating reflects the ability of a fund to preserve the capital invested, rather than guarantee it. In December 2010, assets in triple-A rated funds were around €460 billion. By 2012, the assets under management (AUM) in IMMFA funds had convincingly broken above the €500 billion mark.

Money market funds in Europe are set up as Undertakings for Collective Investment in Transferable Securities (UCITS). They are subject to the requirements in UCITS legislation and any supplemental regulations that may apply in the fund's domicile. Since the end of 2011, these funds have also been expected to respect the guidelines set by the European Securities and Markets Authority (ESMA).

1.8.3 Fund Ratings

Money market funds have the preservation of capital as their primary objective. Liquidity and competitive, sector-related returns are other key objectives. The rating process methodically identifies, assesses and weights each fund in terms of its ability to deliver on these objectives.

The rating criteria broadly comprise four main areas of analysis that systematically address a fund's operating principles: its credit quality, portfolio construction, fund management and regular post-rating inspection. These are described in more detail below.

Credit Quality

Credit quality is evaluated on three levels: what the fund can buy, whom it can do business with (including the exact nature of business) and whom it can appoint to keep its assets safe. The rating criteria, therefore, stipulate the fund's asset range and restrictions (such as quality, type and currency), acceptable **counterparty risk** (for all transaction-based investments) and appropriate choice of custodian.

Portfolio Construction

The most complex part of analysing a money market fund is judging a fund's sensitivity to changing market conditions and, therefore, gauging a measure of its ability to shield investors from adverse market swings. All money market securities (rated or otherwise) are subject to price fluctuations – based on interest rate movements, maturity, liquidity and the supply and demand for each type of security. Quantifying the cumulative effect of these is crucial to assessing overall portfolio performance.

Capital preservation is expressed in terms of the stability or constant accumulation of the fund's net asset value (NAV) per share. As such, both formats are scrutinised for potential deviation in the fund's market value. Determination of market value, or portfolio price exposure, starts with the examination of susceptibility to rising interest rates. A critical component of this is the fund's weighted average portfolio maturity, which is specifically restricted by rating category.

Fund Management

The rating process requires an assessment of a fund manager's operations – in common parlance, the front, middle and back offices. Key areas of interest are the fund manager's level of experience, the stated investment objectives, portfolio management techniques, risk aversion strategies, operating procedures and internal controls, including disaster recovery. Owing to the precision necessary in running a money market fund successfully, every aspect of the fund's management must be able to withstand close scrutiny and demonstrate effective, ongoing integrity of operation.

Portfolio Inspection

Owing to the constraints of the rating criteria and the extremely low margin of error permitted at the level of fund valuation, rated money market funds are contractually obliged to supply all portfolios for periodic rating agency inspection. This is called fund surveillance. Any infringement or potential concern is communicated to the fund and timely rectification is required.

1.8.4 Benchmarks

Money market funds use different benchmarks to compare the performance of each of the funds under management, as demonstrated through short-term indicative interest rates. The main indices are those shown below.

London Interbank Bid Rate (LIBID) and London Interbank Offered Rate (LIBOR)

The London Interbank Bid Rate (LIBID) is the rate at which banks take deposits from each other. Historically it has normally been around one-eighth of a percentage point lower than the London Interbank Offered Rate (LIBOR), the rate at which banks lend to each other. This bid-offer spread reflects the liquidity and depth in the money market on any given day.

ICE LIBOR (formerly known as BBA LIBOR) is a benchmark rate that some of the world's leading banks charge each other for short-term loans and is produced for five currencies with seven maturities quoted for each, ranging from overnight to 12 months, producing 35 rates each business day.

ICE LIBOR is quoted in ten currencies at 15 maturities for each, by inviting 11 to 17 panel banks to confidentially submit their interbank borrowing rates every working day between 11.00am and 11.10am. The rates quoted by each panel bank are submitted to ICE. An average (trimmed arithmetic mean) is calculated from the submissions and then the final fixings are released at around 11.45am on vendor screens.

In July 2012, a LIBOR scandal was uncovered and resulted in an investigation and action to restore market confidence in the reference rate. Hence, with effect from 2 April 2013, oversight of the daily regular LIBOR rate fixes were transferred to the UK regulator. ICE Benchmark Administration (IBA) took over the administration of LIBOR in early 2014.

IBA administers the following benchmarks:

- **ICE LIBOR** – the world's most widely used benchmark for short-term bank borrowing rates.
- **LBMA Gold Price** – the principal global benchmark for daily gold prices.
- **ICE Swap Rate** (formerly known as ISDAFIX) – the global interest rate swap benchmark for swap rates and spreads.

Sterling Overnight Interbank Average (SONIA)

The sterling overnight interbank average (SONIA) is the weighted average rate of all unsecured sterling overnight cash transactions brokered in London between midnight and 4.15pm, with all counterparties, in a minimum deal size of £25 million.

Euro Overnight Interbank Average (EONIA)

The euro overnight interbank average (EONIA) is the weighted average rate of all overnight unsecured lending transactions in the interbank market, undertaken in the EU and European Free Trade Association (EFTA) countries by the Panel Banks. Calculation and publication of the rate is undertaken by the European Central Bank.

SONIA and EONIA are weighted average overnight deposit rates for each business day. Both indices are published at 5.00pm each day. Details of daily SONIA and EONIA rates can be found at wmba.org.uk.

1.8.5 Types of Funds

Triple-A-rated money market funds invest in high-grade money market instruments. Typically these instruments include CDSs, commercial paper, **floating-rate notes**, repurchase agreements, short-term government securities and time deposits. Managers have strict credit criteria applying to their selection of these instruments.

Commercial paper consists of short-term debt issued by a wide variety of corporations, such as domestic and foreign banks, finance companies, and specific issuers of commercial paper. Any commercial paper purchased by a money market fund must have received a high investment grade rating from a credit rating agency, in order for the fund to maintain its triple-A rating.

Prior to the banking crisis, about half of the commercial paper market was made up of asset-backed commercial paper. This is short-term debt backed not by the name and assets of an entire company, but by a designated pool of specific assets, such as credit card debt, car loans and mortgages, including subprime mortgages, of course.

Traditionally, companies have used this paper to finance operations, borrowing cash they need to meet a payroll or buy inventory. They borrowed short-term money because it gave them flexibility and because it was cheaper than long-term debt most of the time. To extend the maturity of this short-term debt, effectively turning short-term debt into long-term debt at short-term interest rates, all they had to do was roll over the debt when it matured. And traditionally, commercial paper was backed by the credit of the entire company.

Asset-backed commercial paper offered big advantages to both the issuers and buyers of debt. It opened up the commercial paper market to a whole new level of companies that had not been creditworthy enough to tap this source of funding before. A company with a credit rating so low that tapping the commercial paper market was difficult could now put together a package of credit card receivables – the debt that card borrowers had run up doing business with the company. Because that paper was backed by a predictable flow of credit card payments, that particular issue of asset-backed commercial paper would find a ready buyer.

For buyers, the advantage of asset-backed commercial paper was very simple: it paid more than traditional commercial paper did. The difference wasn't much, perhaps 0.1 or 0.2 percentage points, but, to managers of money market funds clawing for market share and investors, adding a fraction of a percentage point to a fund's **yield** can make a huge difference.

The closing of the market for some asset-backed securities has placed constraints on the liquidity of some of the money market funds that had holdings of these instruments. This, together with falling market values for these instruments, has led to some funds delivering negative returns. Investors in these funds were often unaware that such incidences could occur.

1.8.6 Costs, Charges and Penalties on Money Market Funds

Investors in a money market mutual fund have to pay the fund's expenses. Some of these expenses reduce the value of an investor's account; others are paid by the fund and reduce the NAV.

These costs can be broadly split into two categories: loads and expense ratios.

Shareholder Fees

Funds that use brokers to sell their shares typically compensate the brokers by paying them commissions. A fee called the sales load is often imposed on investors. Thus, a load is a one-off sales charge; that is a commission paid to the broker by the mutual fund. A front-end load is charged when an investor deposits money into a mutual fund, while a back-end load (also called deferred sales charge or **redemption** fees) is levied when the money is finally withdrawn from the fund at the end of the investment period. There are also no-load funds that do not charge any one-off entry or exit fees. However, the funds recoup these as expenses from another part of the investment and this will lead to a higher expenses ratio of the fund. Essentially, loads exist to support the sales efforts that bring more money into the fund and the investment company that is creating the fund.

Expenses and Expense Ratio

The expense ratio is a crucial piece of information that investors need to find out how much is taken out of the fund's annual earnings. Loads are often not included in expense ratio calculation. It is an annual operating expense that is levied on the investment income and the biggest part of this ratio is the management fee. Recurring fees and expenses are also included in a fund's total expense ratio. As all funds must compute an expense ratio using the same methodology, it allows investors to compare costs across funds.

The management fee is paid to the **fund manager** or sponsor who organises the fund, provides the portfolio management or investment advisory services and normally lends its brand name to the fund. The fund manager may also provide other administrative services. The management fee often has breakpoints, which means that it declines as assets (in either the specific fund or in the fund family as a whole) increase. The management fee is paid by the fund and is included in the expense ratio.

The fund's board of directors reviews the management fee annually. Fund shareholders must vote on any proposed increase in the management. However the fund manager or sponsor may agree to waive all or a portion of the management fee, in order to lower the fund's expense ratio.

Other Expenses

In this category are expenses not included in management fees and those not included in the marketing and distribution expenses. These may include: custodial expenses; legal expenses; accounting expenses; transfer agent expenses; and any other administrative expenses.

1.8.7 Redemptions Fees and Gates

For investors who require access to their cash in times of stress, a fee may be levied in order to pay for that liquidity (ie, investors might be required to pay a fee if they redeem shares during this time). This may be applied at the discretion of the board of directors in the best interests of shareholders of the fund.

A redemption gate is a temporary measure that may be implemented by a fund's board of directors that limits redemptions in a fund for a short period of time (up to ten business days in a 90-day period). Its purpose is to prevent a run on a fund in times of market stress.

1.9 Peer-to-Peer (P2P) Lending

Learning Objective

1.1.4 Analyse the main characteristics, risks and returns of peer-to-peer lending

1.9.1 What is P2P Lending?

The P2P lending market, also referred to as crowdfunding, began in 2005 and has grown significantly in recent years, partly as a result of the low interest rates offered by high street banks and building societies. The market has grown significantly over recent years. In 2016, lenders collectively lent over £3.2 billion to customers and businesses.

P2P lending involves lending money to individuals without using a financial intermediary such as a bank. A number of independent companies have established an online presence to match lenders with borrowers in return for a fee.

1.9.2 Risks

One of the main risks with P2P lending is the potential for an individual to default on repayment. To mitigate this risk, the company acting as the intermediary 'underwrites' each borrower by reviewing their credit history and also verifying their identity.

As some defaults are likely, the company matching lenders with borrowers seeks to reduce this risk by consolidating a number of smaller loans from a group of individuals into the actual loan amount required by the borrower. In this way, the failure of the borrower to maintain the loan does not have a material effect on one lender, rather it is spread across the group that originated the total loan amount. In some cases, the maximum loan from each individual lender may be capped at 2% of the total amount required by the borrower, ie, 50 individual loans required.

1.9.3 How does P2P Lending Work?

Potential lenders open an account with the firm offering the P2P lending services and deposit a sum of money. Borrowers apply to the same P2P firm requesting a loan and the parties are matched. The minimum loan can be as small as £10 and most P2P lending firms have no upper limit. Payments of interest and capital are generally made by the borrower each month over an agreed term, eg, 1–5 years, and in this way, the lender's account balance grows over time.

Although each loan is made for a fixed term, early access options are available to the lender if access to capital is required. In practice, this involves the transfer of the loan to another individual lender, so there is no guarantee of short-term liquidity and a fee is also likely to be charged by the P2P firm for providing the service. It is also possible to have the monthly repayments paid out as an income to the lender.

1.9.4 Returns and Taxation

The returns are typically higher than those offered by high street lenders, reflecting the higher risk of lending directly to individuals. In fact, comparative returns can be twice as much as the equivalent high street rate. The quoted APR takes into account an assumed level of defaults, based on the experience of the P2P firm. The interest received is paid without tax deducted at source, and must therefore be declared in full to HMRC who will calculate the liability. P2P ISAs are available under Innovative Finance ISA rules which commenced on 6 April 2016.

1.9.5 Regulation

The **Financial Conduct Authority (FCA)** has recently taken an interest in this market, given the extent of its growth over a short term, and the increased risk that it presents to consumers. Concerns have also been raised around how these services are marketed. A review by the regulator resulted in changes to how the market operates, and perhaps restrictions on the types of consumer that can lend money through P2P firms. The FCA is currently carrying out a review of the crowdfunding market to identify if change is required. Andrew Bailey, Chief Executive of the FCA, said: *'Our focus is ensuring that investor protections are appropriate for the risks in the crowdfunding sector while continuing to promote effective competition in the interests of consumers. Based on our findings to date, we believe it is necessary to strengthen investor protection in a number of areas. We plan to consult next year on new rules to address the issues we have identified.'*

Consumers who place deposits with P2P lending firms have no recourse to the FSCS for any losses they may incur, and firms that wish to operate in this market will need to be registered with the FCA.

2. Fixed-Income Securities

Learning Objective

1.2.1 Know the main issuing institutions and purposes for issuing fixed-income securities: sovereign states and governments; public authority; corporate; credit institutions; supranational

1.2.3 Analyse the characteristics and differences between the main types of fixed-income securities: fixed-rate bonds; floating rate notes; zero coupon bonds; inflation-linked bonds; other index- and asset-linked bonds; asset-backed securities; convertible bonds; subordinated bonds; perpetual bonds; eurobonds and foreign issuer bonds; CoCos

2.1 General Features

Bonds are fixed-income securities (also known as debt securities). They are a form of loan instrument where a borrower (often a government, supranational authority or a corporate firm) issues a bond in return for investment funds. The person who invests in the bond is the lender or investor, and the organisation issuing the bond is the borrower. The name derives from the original use of the word bond – a tie or commitment (as in the saying *my word is my bond*). A bond is so called because it represents a promise to repay the capital borrowed at some defined point in the future and also, in most cases, a certain amount of interest paid by the issuer to the lender in the intervening period.

At origination, the issue of new bonds may be sold as an open offer for sale directly to a smaller number of professional investors: this is called a private placing. In an offer for sale, a syndicate of banks with one bank as lead manager will buy the bonds en bloc from the issuer and resell them to investors. In this way, they underwrite the issue since, if the investors do not buy, the banks will be forced to keep them. Needless to say, they charge fees for this risk. If the lead bank buys all the bonds and sells them to the syndicate (usually called the bought deal), the syndicate members may themselves then sell the bonds at varying prices. More commonly these days, the lead manager and the syndicate buy the bonds simultaneously and agree to sell at the same price for a period – the fixed price reoffering. This is very common in the US and now in the so-called Euromarkets. Less frequently (apart from the government bonds), there may not be a syndicate but the bonds are sold by competitive **auction**.

There are several types of bond according to the issuer:

- government bonds, also called 'sovereign debt'
- public authorities bonds
- mortgage- and other asset-backed bonds
  corporate bonds
- supranational bonds
- foreign bonds
- covered bonds
- high-yield bonds.

Corporate bonds may also be debentures, or convertibles, and there is a hybrid type of instrument, the **preference share** or participation stock.

There is another denomination for foreign bonds: the domestic issues by non-residents – bulldogs in the UK, yankees in the US, matadors in Spain, samurai in Tokyo and kangaroo bonds in Australia. Notice that these bonds are domestic bonds issued in a local currency; it is only the issuer who is foreign. They should not be confused with international bonds (eurobonds), which are bonds outside their natural market.

To help us become more familiar with some of the concepts associated with bonds, we will now examine some of the most common types.

2.2 Government Bonds

Government bonds dominate the bond markets, with modern governments running a budget deficit which leads to large-scale issues of bonds. Sometimes the secondary market is run on stock exchanges (France, Germany, UK) and sometimes outside stock exchanges (US).

2.2.1 UK Government Bonds

Governments are regular issuers of bonds; it is one of the key ways in which they raise money to pay for the various activities they carry out.

Since 1998, the UK Debt Management Office (DMO) has issued bonds on behalf of HM Treasury. Bonds issued by the UK government are known as gilt-edged stocks – or gilts, for short. This name derives from the fact that, originally, the certificates representing such investments were printed on paper which had a gold (gilded, or gilt) edging, something which was intended to represent the high level of safety associated with the government. Even today, you may hear people talk about a gilt-edged opportunity, meaning something that they perceive as being a very safe bet.

In the case of gilts, the borrower is the UK government, which uses the money raised in this way in order to fund the central government net cash requirement (CGNCR). The CGNCR represents the shortfall between:

- the central government's revenues (what money it takes in, in the form of taxes and duties)
- what it spends on running the country (on things like paying state benefits and infrastructure projects such as road-building).

As such, it is a component of the **public sector net cash requirement (PSNCR)** (see the following box), which we will look at in chapter 2.

> The amount borrowed annually by the UK government is PSNCR (also referred to as the budget deficit). It is equal to the sum of:
>
> - the CGNCR
> - the local government net cash requirement (LGNCR), and
> - the public corporations net cash requirement (PCNCR).
>
> That is the total shortfall for central government, local authorities, and public corporations. Gilts are used to fund the first of these; but local governments and various public corporations can often issue bonds themselves (eg, local authority bonds).

The PSNCR should not be confused with the national debt. This is the total amount outstanding that is owed by the UK government; effectively a sum of all PSNCRs borrowed over successive years to date.

Historically, the UK national debt first began in 1692 when William III engaged a syndicate of City merchants to market an issue of the government debt. This syndicate became the Bank of England.

To provide perspectives in terms of scale, note that we often specify this debt as a proportion of the UK GDP. Historically, we note two major episodes when this debt exploded above 200% of GDP levels. From 1692 to 1815 (end of the Napoleonic wars), the national debt continued to climb from extremely low levels to set a high of 237% of GDP in 1816, following the Battle of Waterloo. After the Napoleonic wars, the national debt started to fall for a century, breaking well below 50% of GDP and ending at a low of 25% of GDP by 1914. The low set did not last and, with the outbreak of World War I, the national debt rose abruptly (up to 135% of GDP in 1919). Following the economic depression of the 1920s, it rose to 181% by 1923 and remained elevated above 150% of GDP in 1937, dipping briefly to 110% of GDP in 1940. Following World War II, it soared again to set another high at 238% of GDP by 1947. Debt then continued its decline to a low of 25% of GDP by 1992. It remained well below 50% up to the recent 2007 global credit crisis, when it moved above the 50% of GDP mark once more.

In money terms, the UK national debt currently stands at historical record levels. As a result of several years of large government deficits, it first broke through the £500 billion mark at the end of 2006 (£504.1 billion), up from £467 billion in 2005. These were the pre-credit crisis levels. General government gross debt was £1,731.4 billion at the end of December 2016, equivalent to 89.3% of **gross domestic product (GDP)**. This was an increase of £65.4 billion on December 2015.

The UK government finances its debt burden by issuing gilts. New gilt issues help the government meet the cost of repaying existing gilts that are due for redemption.

As with any loan, a gilt pays a rate of interest – known as the **coupon**. This may be fixed or variable; when it is variable, it is calculated by reference to a specific index – in this case, the RPI. Such gilts are known as index-linked gilts.

The significant budget deficit that the UK government has run up has to be financed with the issuance of more gilts. In 2014–15, it was estimated that the annual cost of servicing this debt was around 4.9% of GDP (or £88 billion).

As a result of this high level of sovereign indebtedness, on 23 February 2013, the ratings agency Moody's downgraded UK debt by one notch to Aa1 from AAA. This downgrade was the first since 1978. Both France and the US lost their triple rating standard (AAA) in 2012.

The interest paid will depend on the terms of the gilt, and is usually shown in the gilt's title (eg, with a gilt whose title is 4¾% Treasury Stock 2020, the coupon, ie, the nominal interest rate, is 4.75% per annum). In the UK, conventional gilts that make up a large share of the outstanding gilt issues usually pay the coupon rate in two semi-annual instalments.

Thus, interest on most types of gilt is paid out every six months until the bond matures. In some cases, the coupons can be paid quarterly. When the bond matures, the holder receives the final coupon payment and return of the principal (face value of the bond, often set at par).

Gilts are issued by HM Treasury. Since April 1998, they have been issued by the Debt Management Office (DMO), on behalf of HM Treasury. Gilts are usually repayable by the government (ie, the capital is paid back to the holder of the gilt at the time, and the loan ceases) on their **maturity** or redemption date. The redemption date may be:

- **Fixed** – ie, if we look more closely at the 4¾% Treasury Stock 2020, we'd find that the date in full was 7 March 2020. So, on 7 March 2020, whoever is the holder of the gilt at that time can expect it to be redeemed. In the interim, this bond will pay two coupons every year, one in September and one in March.
- **Repayable between two set future dates** (the choice of exactly when being up to the government). Such gilts show the two dates in their titles, and so are called dual-dated gilts. An example is '7¾% Treasury Stock 2012–15'. It is rare for the government to issue dual-dated gilts these days and the final dual-dated gilt was redeemed in 2013.
- **Undated** – ie, there is no fixed redemption date, and the loan continues to run until the government decides it wants to redeem it. Although there is no obligation for the government to redeem, it may do so at its discretion. Again, the government does not issue new gilts of this type any more. The ones that are still running are among the oldest issues, some going back to the late 1800s. Undated gilts do not usually include a redemption date, eg, Consolidated 2½%. However, a few carry the abbreviation 'Aft' (eg, 3% Treasury 1966 Aft). This implies the government has the right to redeem the gilt in 1966 or at any time after. The last undated gilt was redeemed in 2015.

Types and Classifications of Gilts

There are various different types of gilt. At one time, their different titles (such as Treasury, Exchequer, Funding and War Loan) gave an indication of the reason for their being issued; the issues of War Loan, for example, were made in 1914 and 1915 to help the government pay for the costs to the nation of the Great War. Nowadays, most gilts are issued with the name treasury, unless they have some other name reflecting their investment features, eg, conversion. There is a wide range of coupons (nominal interest rates) and redemption dates (the date on which the loan is repaid) from which investors can choose.

This wide choice, coupled with the fact that gilts (being backed by the government) are regarded as very safe, makes them popular investments not only with private investors, but also with institutional ones, such as pension funds, insurance companies and fund managers.

Conventional gilts or a bullet variety of a bond carries a fixed:

- rate of interest, shown in the title of the gilt
- redemption date, the year of which is also shown in the title.

They cannot be encashed before the final redemption date (ie, you cannot ask the government to repay the debt early); but they can be bought and sold on the stock market, or via the government DMO's purchase and sale service, and through a gilt edged market maker (GEMM).

Other gilt types include:

- **Index-linked gilts (linkers)** – both the interest rate and the capital redemption on these gilts is calculated by reference to the inflation rate, as measured at a set point before the pay date. Note that the first ever index-linked gilt (2% Index-linked Treasury stock 1996) was issued on 27 March 1981 in a £1 billion nominal offering. Indexation of the coupons was to the General Index of Retail Prices. All gilt income has been payable gross of tax since 6 April 1998.

    The first index-linked gilt to be issued with a three-month indexation lag was in September 2005. In 2011, the DMO published a consultation paper on the proposed issuance of index-linked gilts where the indexation is based on the CPI measure of inflation, instead of RPI. The RPI measure of inflation runs higher than the CPI measure of inflation. Pension fund investors have requested a new type of gilt issuance where the coupons are linked payments to CPI, to help them hedge their liabilities that are more closely matched to CPI levels of risk exposures.
- **Convertible gilts** – the owner has the right to convert the gilt into predefined amounts of a different gilt at some time in the future. Convertibles are usually short- to medium-term bonds which may be converted into a longer issue at the discretion of the investor. In the *Financial Times*, they are identifiable by the abbreviation 'Conv' in the title.
- **Floating rate gilts** – these are unusual in that they pay variable coupons, and in that they pay four times a year instead of semi-annually. The coupon is set by reference to LIBID at the beginning of each interest payment period (LIBOR – x% may also be used as a reference date), and they tend to trade at around their par (nominal) value. The DMO does not issue floating rate gilts.

Gilts are classified in terms of how long they have to run before they will be redeemed (ie, before the government repays the capital). There are two different conventions used. One, the *FT* method, is probably more familiar to retail investors who may use the *Financial Times* to follow their holdings' prices. The *Financial Times* classifies gilts as:

- shorts: under five years to run to redemption
- mediums: five–15 years to redemption
- longs: over 15 years to run.

However, market convention – ie, that used between gilt dealers on the **London Stock Exchange (LSE)** by the DMO which issues them, and by professionals, is to classify them as follows:

- shorts: one–seven years to run to redemption
- mediums: eight–15 years to redemption
- longs: over 15 years to run.

In 2005, the DMO was given permission to issue a new range of ultra-long gilts (both conventional and index-linked varieties). It has already done so by way of a conventional 50-year issue, Treasury 5.25% 2055, which has widened investor choice even further. The new gilt was, at the time, the longest-dated 'sovereign debt' issued anywhere in the world, and these ultra-long issues are categorised along with the 'longs'; they do not have a separate category all to themselves. Since then, the DMO has maintained its interest to issue more in the sector to ensure that this area of the **yield curve** remains liquid for investors who desire a security with this maturity and duration. Index-linked gilts have also been issued with ultra-long maturities.

In the March 2012 Budget, UK Chancellor George Osborne was mooted to launch a market consultation exercise for a proposal by the Treasury to raise funds via a 100-year, super-long century gilt. Pension funds require long-dated sovereign issues to match their long-dated liabilities. However, an ultra-long issue of this kind has not been released yet. If a new issue of a century bond is made in the near term then it will pave the way for the longest-dated bond issued by a highly rated sovereign issuer. It would also be in line with the UK's tradition of naming perpetuals or super-long securities after Chancellors of the Exchequers. Just after World War II, 'Dalton bonds' took their name from the then-Chancellor, Hugh Dalton. The only other country to have issued a century bond is Mexico.

Century bonds are not entirely a new concept as they have been issued by the corporate sector in the past. Walt Disney and Coca-Cola already have century bonds outstanding. These corporate bonds (or debentures) have a dual-dated feature incorporated in the issue, enabling the issuer to redeem the bonds earlier.

Features and Characteristics of a Gilt-Edged Security

In order to familiarise ourselves further with the features of a gilt, we will take as an example 4¾% Treasury Stock 2020. Look at the following example certificate to see if you can identify the various bits of information on it.

Reference no: 1234 Transfer no: 13/123456 Certificate no: 0001020304.
ISIN code: GB00B058DQ55. Amount of Stock: £1,000.00

HM TREASURY 4¾% TREASURY STOCK 2020
Redemption at par on 7 March 2020
Interest payments half yearly on 7 March and 7 September

MRS CATHERINE TURNER 1 WOODLANDS CLOSE WESTMINSTER LONDON SW1 0XX

THIS IS TO CERTIFY that the above-named is/are the Registered Holder(s) of one thousand pounds

4¾% TREASURY STOCK 2020

Given under the Signature
On 29 March 2005
Secretary to the Treasury

This certificate must be surrendered before any transfer of the whole or part of the shares herein mentioned can be registered. Registrar and Transfer Office: Computershare Investor Services plc, PO Box 2411, The Pavilions, Bristol, BS3 9WX

You can check your holding at www.computershare.com

This is an example of the information on the certificate which evidences your holding, if you hold £1,000 nominal of this stock.

The first thing to note is that every gilt has a name, to distinguish it from other gilts in issue.

The name gives you lots of information about the terms of a gilt, being made up of:

- The **name of the issuer** (in this case the Treasury Department of the UK government, although in fact nowadays the DMO handles the procedures and practicalities of issuing gilts). The name of the gilt serves no purpose other than to act as an identifier. Examples of gilt names include: Treasury, Exchequer, Funding, Conversion, Consolidated, War Loan. All new gilts are now called **Treasury gilts**. In general, gilts are registered securities, with the register of owners being held and maintained by Computershare Investor Services plc.
- The **coupon** – in this case, 4.75%. This is the amount of interest that an investor will earn each year on the **nominal value (nv)** of the gilt. So, in our example, you will earn £4.75 for every £100 nominal you own of the gilt each year. Interest is paid on most gilts half-yearly (ie, in this case half of the £4.75 will be paid to the holder, twice a year).

    The quoted coupon of a gilt represents the annual amount of interest paid per £100 nominal value. The nv is effectively the original amount borrowed by the government, and in the UK it is market convention to talk about gilts in terms of £100 nv when calculating the return on the investment on their price. Coupons are generally paid semi-annually, on fixed days, six months apart. Note, however, that the 2.5% consolidated gilt and floating-rate gilts pay a quarterly coupon.

    Coupons are taxable (subject to income tax for individuals); however, tax is not normally deducted from the coupon payment and this is referred as to being a gross coupon. An individual taxpayer can choose to have income tax at the rate of 20% deducted from the payment of their coupon. This is referred to as electing for withholding tax to be deducted. For instance, if an individual holds £100 nv of the 6.5% gilt and they elect to have tax deducted, their next coupon receipt will be calculated as follows:

    £100 nv x coupon rate x 6/12 (semi-annual coupon) x 80% (to take account of the 20% tax deduction) = next coupon receipt. £100 nv x 6.5% x 6/12 x 80% = £2.60. The gross coupon is £3.25 and the net coupon is £2.60.
- The **interest payment dates** are not in the title of the gilt – but you can find them on the certificate (in this case, they are 7 March and 7 September each year) and, if you are researching a gilt prior to buying it, your stockbroker will be able to provide you with the dates. In addition, interest payment dates for gilts are shown in the *Financial Times*. A few gilts pay their interest quarterly, instead of half-yearly.
- The **redemption date** – in this case, the year 2020. This is the year in which the government will repay the nominal sum held by the investor who holds the gilt at that time, to that investor. In effect, the government is repaying its loan.

    Some gilts show two dates in their title – eg, 12% Treasury Stock 2013–17. This means that the government can choose to repay the gilt at any time from 2013 onwards, by giving three months' notice to investors – but it must repay it by 2017 at the latest. The gilt was actually redeemed in December 2013 and there are currently no double-dated gilts in issue. It is important to bear in mind that the choice of when to repay the gilt is the government's and not the investor's. The government will make this decision based on what interest rates are doing in the market at the time. If the gilt represents cheap borrowing to it, it will likely let it run for as long as it can, but if it can replace it with cheaper new borrowings, it will probably repay it as early as is possible.

The redemption date is the specified date on which the capital is repaid by the DMO. Normally, redemption is at par, ie, £100 for each £100 nv held. All remaining stock must be repaid on the redemption date. The remaining maturity of the gilt is used for categorisation purposes and the time to redemption is calculated from today's date until the maturity date. For instance, a 20-year bond starts off as a long when initially issued, but five years later it becomes a medium, and eight years later a short. Remember that the *Financial Times* classifies shorts as having redemptions up to five years, medium between 5 and 15, and longs as more than 15 years.

- The **nominal value** held (in this case, £1,000). This reflects the face value of the gilts that the holder owns – rather like the number of shares held in a company, or units in a **unit trust**, in that it is different from the value (despite being expressed in pounds and pence). It is also the value that the government will repay to the holder on the redemption, or maturity date.
- The **price** of a conventional gilt in the market must not be confused with its notional par value. It is a market-determined price at which an investor can purchase the bond in the secondary market from a seller. This price (compared to its fixed par value) may be trading above par (at a premium) or below par (at a discount). The market price is based on the market's assessment of the fair value and is set by the supply and demand for the paper in the marketplace. The cash flows that an investor will receive from the bond are capitalised with the market's expectations about the future pattern of interest rates. These rates are referred to as the term structure of the bond.

    The quoted price is called the clean price and this excludes the accrued interest that is due to the seller of the bond. The **dirty price** of the same bond is the total price payable by the buyer and is the clean price plus the accrued interest.

You will also see that the gilt certificate shows the holder's details, and a certificate number and transfer number.

Gilts are marketable securities – so, while you cannot encash one before its redemption date, by going to the government and asking it to repay your loan, you can buy and sell gilts before their redemption dates.

When a conventional gilt is redeemed by the government, you know what you will get back – £100 per £100 nominal – when you buy or sell in the market, you will get the price that is quoted at the time. This may be more than you paid for it, or less – so you could make a profit or a loss on it.

The value of the nominal holding is not the same as the current value of the stock. To calculate this, we need to know the current market price of the stock. This is expressed as an amount per £100 nominal of the gilt. Let us assume that the market price of 4¾% Treasury Stock 2020 is £105.95, so every £100 nominal of the stock is worth £105.95. Therefore, we could also say that for every £1 nominal of the gilt we buy, it will cost us £1.0595.

So an investor wanting to buy £30,000 nominal of this gilt will have to pay (ignoring costs like stockbroker commissions and any accrued interest):

$$£30,000 \times £105.95 / £100 = £31,785.00$$

There are a few conventional gilts that are not priced and quoted in sterling but in euros. We will look at the features of foreign-currency-denominated bonds, including gilts, in section 2.2.2.

Because there is a ready market for gilts, people who want to hold them do not have to wait until the government issues a new one (though they can do this if they wish). Generally, the market for gilts is very 'liquid' – that is, they can be bought and sold quickly and easily at their ruling market price, so they are easy to turn into cash again.

There are a number of specialist firms known as gilt-edged market makers (GEMMs), whose main function is to ensure that there is a liquid market in stock. GEMMs deal with professional investors, such as pension funds and insurance companies, and with stockbrokers (but not generally with personal investors, who will usually deal either with the DMO or through a stockbroker).

It is the GEMMS that ensure that gilts are as easily marketable as they are.

2.2.2 Foreign Government Bonds

There are a wide variety of gilts issued in the UK market by the UK government, but UK gilts and overseas government bonds act in different ways. Government bonds are usually referred to as risk-free bonds because the government could raise taxes or simply print more money to redeem the bond at maturity. Many governments issue inflation-indexed bonds, which protect the investor against inflation risk. The general features of overseas government bonds and the markets they trade in vary from country to country. Some examples are listed below:

- Bonds may be issued by the central bank of the country (US, Germany, France), by the Ministry of Finance (Netherlands, Japan), or by the DMO on behalf of the government (UK, Ireland, Sweden, Portugal, New Zealand).
- The issue may be to specialist dealers (US, UK, France, Germany and Italy) or to syndicates of banks (Switzerland).
- Bonds may be bearer (anonymous, with no register of holders) or registered form (Germany and UK respectively).
- Some markets pay interest semi-annually (US, UK, Italy, Japan), others once per year (France, Germany, Netherlands, Spain, Belgium).
- Bond prices may be quoted in fractions (US, eg, down to 1/32) or decimal (rest of the world).
- Note that in Germany the Bundesbank acts as market maker for **Bunds**.
- US **T-bonds** are all issued in registered dematerialised form, with a life in excess of ten years. All US T-bonds are issued with a coupon. There are no zero coupon T-bonds when first issued and they are issued by Dutch auction.

Examples of government bonds, and the names by which they are often known, include:

- **T-bonds** – the name given to bonds with a maturity of ten years or more, issued by the US and Canadian governments.
- **T-notes** – as for T-bonds, but with a maturity of between two and ten years.
- **Bunds** – issued by the German government, with a maturity of anything up to 30 years.
- **OATs** (Obligations Assimilables du Trésor) – issued by the French government, with a maturity from four to 30 years.
- **BONOs** (Bonos del Estado) – issued by the Spanish government, may have almost any maturity period.

You could think of all of the above bonds as the overseas equivalent of a UK gilt: that is, a bond issued by the government of a country, in its domestic market.

- The **US** and **Canada** have registered T-bonds with a maturity of greater than ten years, T-notes between two and ten years; two-year Treasury notes are sold every month, while five- and ten-year Treasury notes and 30-year Treasury bonds are sold every quarter. They are sold by auction, on regular dates, to some 40 primary dealers.
- **Germany** has bearer Bunds with a maturity of greater than ten years (10–30), and medium-term notes such as Bobls between three to five years and Schatz two years. The ten-year issues are the popular ones (rather than of longer duration) and most are fixed-rate, although there is the occasional floating rate bond. All are issued by the Bundesbank and they are dealt by 70 primary dealers, contrasted with the 40 primary dealers in the US.
- **France** has bearer OATs (Obligations Assimilables du Trésor) with a maturity of 4–30 years and shorter-dated two- to five-year BTAN issues called Treasury bills rather than bonds (Bons du Trésor à Intérêts Annuels). Short-term T-bills are BTF – Bons du Trésor à Taux Fixe. French government bonds (OATs) are sold on a regular monthly auction basis (on the first Thursday in each month) to primary dealers, who have an obligation to support the auction. They must take up 3% of annual bond issuance and trade 3% of secondary market turnover. The primary dealers are Spécialistes en Valeurs du Trésor (SVTs). However, at each auction the offerings are usually more of existing bonds rather than offering new ones each time. BTANs are sold on the third Thursday in each month. In the past, some fixed-rate bonds have been issued which are convertible later into floating rate, and floating rates convertible into fixed. Also in the past, some **zero coupon bonds** called *felins* have been issued (only nine in recent years). Floating rate bonds with the interest paid quarterly and linked to the yield of ten-year OATs are called TEC10 (Taux de l'Echéance Constante).
- **Italy** has bearer variable-dated bonds: BTPs (Buoni del Tesoro Poliennali) if fixed rate with two–ten years in maturity, CCT (Certificati Credito del Tesoro) if floating with a similar maturity. Both are sold by the central bank to 20 primary dealers on fixed dates every month. There are also six-year bonds which buyers can sell back after three years, called CTO (Certificati del Tesoro con Opzione).
- **Spain** has its BONOs (Bonos del Estado) with maturities of three and five years, but the ten-year maturity is called Obligaciones del Estado. The central bank sells these on a regular date each month.
- **Japan** has JGBs or Japanese Government Bonds, which are usually issued with a maturity of ten years, although maturities of 20 years may be available through a superlong bond, and they are sold by the Ministry of Finance. The election of a new Japanese government in 2012 resulted in the introduction of an aggressive economic stimulus policy designed to encourage inflation. This included the repurchasing of JGBs by the Bank of Japan (BoJ) to increase the monetary base at a rate of 7 trillion yen per month. The impact of this action is still being considered, although a number of ratings agencies issued a note of caution to investors during 2014 on the impact that the failure of this policy would have on the value of JGBs.
- The **UK** DMO, **French** Treasury, **Thailand** and the **Chinese** governments have issued ultra-long maturity 50-year bonds in recent years. These 'ultra-long-dated' bonds have been issued to raise cheap funds during economic downturns, when interest rates are low or to meet strong demand from insurance and pension funds for high-duration securities to match their liabilities.

2.2.3 Index-Linked Bonds

We have noted that most bond issues pay interest at rates which are fixed; hence they are known as fixed-interest securities. However, some pay interest rates which fluctuate – floating rate notes (FRNs). Sometimes, this is in relation to a given measure of current market interest rates to reflect the changing interest rate in a particular coupon payment period. However, one other special form of FRN is the index-linked bond: here, interest payments – and indeed the capital repayment at maturity – vary in accordance with changes in inflation rates. A key issuer of index-linked debt securities in the UK is the Treasury, by way of index-linked gilts (or linkers for short). The UK was one of the earliest developed economies to issue a linker to institutional investors. The first UK index-linked issue was launched on 27 March 1981. The sale was restricted at that time to pension funds or similar institutions writing pensions business. Restrictions on ownership in further new issues were removed in March 1982. It is notable that the DMO has also issued an ultra-long 50-year index-linked bond. This was launched on 25 October 2005 in the first auction of a 1.25% index-linked Treasury gilt in a 2055 maturity.

Index-linked gilts pay a rate of interest and a redemption value based on the change in the RPI in the same period. Other governments that offer index-linked bonds are Australia, Canada, Iceland, Israel, New Zealand, Sweden and, more recently, the US and France. The UK linked-sector is much the biggest of these.

- **Retail prices index (RPI)** – this is an index used by the Bank of England to measure the rate of inflation and is discussed in greater detail in chapter 2. The RPI measures changes in the prices of a basket of different goods and services which the average person is assumed to spend their money on.
- **Consumer prices index (CPI)** – the Bank uses this to measure inflation for some purposes (eg, targeting what it wants to keep the level of inflation at). The CPI uses a slightly different basket of goods and services, and is a relatively new index. It was introduced in the UK because it is more in line with the way other countries in the EU measure inflation; as the UK is a member of the European Union (EU), it needs to be able to measure inflation on a like-for-like basis. The government has said, however, that it has no plans at present to switch from using the RPI for calculating payments on index-linked gilts although, in June 2011, the DMO published a consultation document on CPI-linked gilts to consider future possibilities on new issues.

Index-linked gilts, like conventional gilts, are regarded as low-risk instruments, in that they are backed by the government guarantee and have clearly defined terms for interest and redemption payments.

However, they differ in that both interest and redemption payments are protected against inflation, which – as we have already noted – can at times dramatically erode the nominal value of conventional bonds.

As with conventional gilts, investors receive two interest payments a year and they get a final redemption payment based on the nominal or face value of their gilt holding. With linkers, these final payments are also adjusted to take account of what inflation has done since the gilt was issued.

The key points to remember are:

- The coupon quoted is much lower than is the case with a conventional gilt (typically, of the order of 0.125–5%). This is because each interest payment is adjusted upwards to reflect the change in the RPI since the gilt was issued. So the total payment will – almost always – be greater than the nominal coupon, unless the reference index is flat or falls.

- The capital redemption payment made at the gilt's maturity is also adjusted upwards, in a similar manner.
- The yield to maturity of a linker can be considered to be the real yield, in contrast to a nominal yield available from a conventional bond.

For the purposes of calculating interest and capital payments on index-linked gilts, the government measures the RPI with a three-month lag: three months prior to the relevant pay date (eg, for an interest payment due on 1 June, the payment will be adjusted by reference to the RPI, for April that year).

It compares this RPI measure with that which was in place three months prior to the RPI when the gilt was issued – and adjusts the interest payment of the coupon accordingly. So if inflation is strong, a holder's interest payments will rise, protecting their income.

Note: you should be aware that until 2004, the government used to calculate gilt interest and redemption payments by adjusting these payments using the RPI with an eight-month lag prior to the relevant reference date. It has not changed the basis of calculation for old index-linked gilts issued under these terms – but new index-linked gilts have the use of the more up-to-date RPI figures built into their terms and conditions.

Investors need to remember that, since the RPI can go down as well as up, their income payments from an index-linked gilt can fall as well as rise.

Also, there is no deflation 'floor', ie, their final redemption payment could be less than £100 per £100 nominal, if there is a general fall in the level of prices in the UK.

The amount of capital that the investor will get back on redemption will depend on what inflation does up until a point three, or eight, months before the security is redeemed. The amount of capital redemption will then be worked out in the same way.

2.2.4 Treasury Bills

Treasury bills (T-bills), like gilts, are issued by the UK government through its DMO, as part of its work in managing the government's funding and cash management.

They are an example of zero coupon debt securities (see section 2.3.2), and pay no interest, instead, they are issued at a discount to their face value and redeemed at par (that is, £100 per £100 nominal). The investor receives their return by way of the increase in price between the issue price and the eventual redemption price.

This does not mean, however, that an investor cannot lose money if they decide to sell their treasury bill before its maturity date: the price of T-bills fluctuates in the market, as with any tradeable instrument, and could fall to below what they bought it at before rising again to par at maturity.

T-bills can be issued with maturities of:

- one month (approximately 28 days)
- three months (approximately 91 days)
- six months (approximately 182 days)
- in theory, 12 months (up to 364 days), although to date no 12-month tenders have been held.

Members of the public wishing to purchase treasury bills at the tenders must do so through one of the treasury bill primary participants and purchase a minimum of £500,000 nominal of bills.

2.2.5 Local Authority Bonds

These are loan stocks issued by UK local authorities; they are often referred to collectively, especially by those dealing in them on the LSE, as corporation stocks.

They are usually secured by a charge over the assets of the issuing authority – that is, if the local authority cannot repay the interest or capital of the loan as it falls due, from the cash it has available at the time, then those assets can be sold to raise the money – thus securing the borrower's position.

They may also be guaranteed by the Public Works Loans Board (PWLB), giving them extra safety. That said, and while local authorities might seem pretty sound, it is not unheard of for a local authority to go broke. Investing in local authority issues is not quite as safe as investing in gilts, because the local authorities themselves are separate from central government and the issue may or may not be guaranteed.

> The **Public Works Loans Board (PWLB)** is a statutory body which operates within the DMO.
>
> Mainly, the PWLB's job is to lend money from the National Loans Fund to local authorities and other prescribed bodies, and to collect the repayments. In addition, however, it may also guarantee loans being raised direct by those bodies. See the PWLB section of the DMO website dmo.gov.uk if you would like more information.

Interest is paid to investors net of basic rate tax, ie, tax has already been deducted from the interest payment before it is forwarded to the investor, and will be sent to HMRC for them by the local authority.

Local authority issues are divided into:

- **Local Authority Fixed Stocks** – also known as local authority bonds, or sometimes town hall bonds or town hall mortgages. They are fixed-rate investments, whose capital cannot usually be redeemed early by the investor, unless a penalty charge is paid. Interest is paid net of tax at source, but the tax can be reclaimed by non-taxpayers. These stocks are not marketable – ie, once an investor has bought a holding in the initial issue of stock, they cannot sell it on in the market – they must hold it until the maturity date, unless the local authority is willing to redeem early.
- **Local Authority Negotiable Loans (Yearlings)** – also often issued by local authorities. They have a life of no longer than two years, are issued at par, and are marketable. Again, interest is paid net of basic rate tax.

2.3 Corporate Bonds

Corporate (company) loan stock, or corporate bonds, are issued by companies. They may or may not be backed up with security taken over a specific asset, owned by the issuing company.

Interest is paid at specific intervals which will be set out in the bond's terms – for UK corporate loans, this is usually half-yearly. It is paid net of basic rate tax. As with gilts, capital gains tax (CGT) is not chargeable – providing that the corporate bond is a qualifying one. Broadly, a qualifying corporate bond is one which is interest-paying, rather than a convertible.

Some bond issues carry guarantees with them; this means that the issuing company's parent, or occasionally some other third party, is undertaking to repay the capital and interest if the issuer cannot itself meet the repayments.

Corporate loan stocks may also be unsecured (ie, no specific asset is identified which will be sold to meet the repayments if the issuer does not have the money, and there is no separate guarantee).

The corporate bond market is a very strong one too, especially in the US, and growing significantly in Europe in recent years. In Germany there is a big tradition of reliance on bank finance, as opposed to either bonds or **equities**. Very large European corporates may, in any case, find it easier to issue the bond in London as a **eurobond** rather than as a domestic bond. A domestic bond refers to one in which the nationality of the issuer, the denomination of the bond and the country of issue are the same – for example, a sterling-denominated bond issued in London by a UK company.

An international bond is a bond issued in a non-domestic currency – for instance any non-sterling denominated bond issued in London or any non-dollar bond issued in the US.

Debentures are corporate bonds which are backed by security; for example, land or buildings. If the issuer goes into liquidation, these assets must be sold to pay the bondholders. Because they are more secure, however, the rate of interest is less.

A convertible is a bond which is converted later, either into another type of bond (for example, convertible gilts, see section 2.2.1) or into equity. The difference between the implied conversion price of the equity and the market price is called the premium.

2.3.1 Permanent Interest-Bearing Shares (PIBS)

Permanent interest-bearing shares (PIBS) are issued by building societies (which, as you should remember, are not companies). They are a form of fixed-interest security, and are traded on the LSE. As with other interest-bearing securities, they meet the needs of many investors who seek income; they offer a higher return than gilts, but also carry a higher risk.

PIBS have the following features:

- Interest is paid (gross) at a fixed rate, half-yearly. However there is no obligation on the building society to pay the interest in any one year. If it does not pay it, it is under no obligation to roll it over to the next year (ie, the shares are non-cumulative). It is highly unlikely that a building society would not pay the interest, but it could happen in times of severe financial pressure.
- PIBS are irredeemable, and thus have no redemption date. The only time they will be repaid by an issuing building society is on liquidation, in which case the PIBS holders will be the last creditors to be repaid.
- PIBS holders are members of the building society and will normally qualify for distributions on demutualisation.

If a building society demutualises, PIBS are automatically converted into perpetual subordinated bonds (PSBs). The name comes from the fact that they will be low down in the order for payment compared with other loans, if the issuer were to get into financial trouble.

PIBS and PSBs are fairly illiquid, and an investor may find it difficult to trade when they wish. The illiquidity of the market can lead to relatively large spreads (the difference between the buying and selling prices), adding to transaction costs. The market is relatively small, currently worth under £1 billion.

As with all fixed-interest securities, if interest rates rise, the prices of PIBS/PSBs will fall, as the fixed interest they pay becomes less attractive compared with other options.

An ordinary investor in a building society is protected by the FSCS, but PIBS/PSB holders are not.

In the past, PIBS were of interest to so-called carpetbaggers, who held a minimum investment in the hope of a windfall on demutualisation of the building society, because PIBS holders have membership rights.

Interest on PIBS/PSBs is paid gross and is taxable. Tax is collected through the investor's tax assessment. No CGT is paid on sale because the shares are classified as qualifying corporate bonds.

PIBS and PSBs are bought and sold on a stock exchange, and can be traded through a stockbroker. They can only be traded in round amounts varying from 1,000 to 50,000 shares.

2.3.2 Zero Coupon Bonds

Zero coupon bonds pay no interest. Instead, the investor makes their return by virtue of the fact that the bond is issued at a price well below its eventual redemption price (the latter usually being 'par' – another way of saying £100 per £100 nominal). For example, a zero coupon bond might be issued at £60 per £100 nominal, with an eventual redemption price at £100 per £100 nominal.

Thus the return looks, on the face of it, more like a capital gain than an income stream. The bonds are issued at a discount – less than their face value. Thus the holding's value is likely to rise gradually towards the redemption price (face value), as it nears its maturity date. The capital appreciation over this period compared to the initial purchase price reflects the return on this holding.

It should, however, be noted that in most cases, tax authorities will deem the investor to have received a notional amount of income each year and tax them on that, so as to avoid the possibility of investors abusing zeros as a way to obtain the certainty of return of a fixed-interest instrument, without the income tax liabilities.

Zeros have some intriguing properties that are much valued by pension funds and risk managers who use the bonds to get more effective immunisation against interest rate risks, especially in asset/liability management applications. The duration of a zero is the same as its maturity.

2.3.3 High-Yield Bonds

High-yield bonds are those which are regarded as being below investment grade – that is, their issuer has a credit rating of below BBB– or Baa3, and there is a higher probability of their defaulting on either the interest payments, or the capital repayment. Because of this, they tend to trade at lower prices compared to more secure debt issues, and so their yields (assuming the interest payments can be kept up) are high. High-yield bonds tend to have higher coupons. The yields offered on these bonds are significantly greater than comparable maturity bonds with higher credit ratings.

Generally, a bond with a long-term credit rating of BBB– (Fitch Ratings Inc and Standard & Poor's scales) and above are considered worthy of investment grade, and those below as non-investment grade and speculative bonds.

Greece's credit rating migration in recent years is a good example of a solid credit-rated sovereign issuer that has seen its credit status lowered, in a dramatic fashion, to speculative debt. Let us consider Moody's scale as an example, where the Greek sovereign debt was rated A1 on 30 July 2007. An A1 rating is for obligations considered upper-medium grade for a sovereign with low credit risk of defaulting on its payments. At the same time Germany was rated at Aaa, the highest quality, with minimal credit risk.

As Greece's inability to meet its debt obligations increased, so the credit rating agencies placed Greek debt on negative credit watch. The credit rating was lowered a number of times after the euro credit crisis unfolded in 2010–11. It became clear that the Greek government's austerity measures to contain its ballooning debt were not working and the sovereign would not be able to repay its debt without EU help, in the form of bail-out loans from other EU nations. In a protracted crisis in spring 2012, following the restructuring of Greek debt, its sovereign rating stood at C, the lowest rating awarded by Moody's to a class of bonds that are typically in default.

To consider the high-yield nature of the Greek debt, let us look at the bond yield progression over this period. Ten-year maturity Greek bond yields were 4.66% on 30 July 2007, fairly close to the 4.30% for German ten-year maturity yields. The margin over Germany was just 0.36% for Greece. This premium reflected the difference of A1 sovereign rating for Greece against the Aaa rating for Germany at that time. In June 2017, the ten-year Greek yield stood at 6.07% while the German ten-year bond yield stood at 1.74%. The margin was 5.78%.

The Greek debt situation caused concern for world leaders with Greece's position in the EU becoming uncertain due to the possibility of it defaulting on its debt. This led to negotiations between Greece, the European Central Bank (ECB) and the International Monetary Fund (IMF) and Greece remained in the EU.

2.3.4 Convertible Loan Stocks/Convertible Bonds

As well as the straight corporate bonds we looked at above, corporate issuers may also issue convertible loan stocks. These behave, for much of their lives, like ordinary loan stocks, but have the potential to be converted into shares instead. Governments and local authorities do not offer this type of bond, since they are not companies and do not issue shares.

The main features of convertibles are:

- The loan stock itself generally carries a fixed-interest coupon.
- The stock's terms include the right for stockholders to convert their holding into a predetermined number of ordinary shares, on or between set dates in the future.
- The conversion terms are usually expressed in such a way that a set number of shares will be received in return for each £100 nominal of loan stock converted.
- The conversion period may be on a set date, or a series of set dates, or between certain dates: there will usually be an expiry date, after which the stock cannot be converted. If the stock has not been converted, it then reverts to behaving like an ordinary loan stock (a straight loan stock), with the same coupon and maturity dates as were originally attached to it.
- Usually, convertibles are first made available to existing shareholders to give them the opportunity to avoid the dilution of their existing stake in the company.
- The conversion price – the effective price of the shares to an investor who acquires them by exercising their conversion option instead of buying them in the market – can be calculated by dividing the current market price per £100 nominal of the loan stock, by the number of shares that can be acquired for that £100 nominal. If the conversion price is lower than the current market price at the exercise date, then it will make financial sense to exercise it.

Companies issue convertibles for a number of reasons:

- Convertibles are attractive to many investors, because they combine the certainty and predictable income streams of a loan stock with the potential for growth that shares offer.
- Because of their appeal, a company issuing a convertible (instead of a straight bond) may have a better chance of raising capital than it otherwise would.
- Conditions in the market may make it inadvisable, or impossible, to raise capital by way of a **rights issue** – something that we will look at later. A convertible issue may, however, be a better option.
- Interest on a company's loan capital is paid before tax – ie, the company's tax liability is calculated on the basis of the profits after deduction of interest, which makes it a lesser net cost to the company than the payment of **dividends** (which are paid after tax).

2.3.5 Eurobonds

Eurobonds were created following World War II, when companies wished to raise dollar financing outside the US due to legal constraints in the US. The term eurobond does not have anything to do with the euro currency and eurobonds do not have to be denominated in euros. A market was established in Europe allowing companies to issue dollar bonds outside the US. These are commonly known as eurodollars. Yen borrowed outside of Japan are called euroyen borrowings.

A eurobond is therefore defined as a bond issued outside the home country of its issuer, and in a currency other than that of the issuer's home currency. Eurobonds fall outside the regulatory jurisdiction of any one country. Their main features are:

- They can be issued in any major currency.
- They are issued outside the country of the currency in which they are denominated.
- They can be held by investors in almost any country.
- They are available in a very wide range of structures and with varying terms, to suit market conditions and their target investor base.

- They are not subject to withholding tax – ie, interest on them is paid gross to the holders.
- They are issued in bearer form – that is, the investor's name does not appear on a register held by the issuer.

The term eurobond thus covers a wide variety of bonds, which include, among others:

- **Medium-term notes (MTNs)** – typically these have a maturity of between two and ten years (although in practice they are not required to have a truly medium term, and you may come across issues with longer or shorter durations). They are often dealt in, and settled, in a rather different way to other debt securities, being treated for these purposes as more akin to commercial paper.
- **Euro-convertibles** – these are convertible into the equity of the issuer, as with domestic **convertible bonds**.

2.3.6 Supranational Bonds

These are bonds issued by institutions such as the European Investment Bank (EIB) and the World Bank. As with government bonds, they are regarded as the safest bond investments and have a high credit rating.

2.3.7 Floating Rate Notes

A floating rate note (FRN) is a form of security, created in the euromarkets and adopted elsewhere, that carries a variable interest rate which is adjusted regularly (at one- to six-monthly intervals – whatever is preferred by the issuer) by a margin against a benchmark rate such as LIBOR.

Issued for three years or longer, FRNs are popular during periods of increased volatility in interest rates, when lenders may be reluctant to lend funds cheaply, at a fixed period for a fixed rate.

For example, the issuer might agree that their FRN will pay 50 basis points (0.5%) over the rate of LIBOR. So if LIBOR is 6% per annum over a six-month period (it is usually worked out as an average), the FRN will pay 6% per annum plus the 0.5% spread, or 6.5% per annum in total over the six-month period.

2.3.8 Asset-Backed Securities

Asset-backed securities are bonds issued on the security of a stream of specific income flows, eg, mortgage payments to a bank, out of which interest payments are made to investors.

2.3.9 Contingent Convertibles (CoCos)

Contingent convertibles are also known as CoCo bonds, hybrids, CoCos or contingent convertible notes. They are debt instruments that are designed to convert to equity and were first issued by Lloyds Bank in 2009. Conversion to equity is contingent on a specified event occurring, eg, the company share price reaching a certain level for a period of time.

CoCos tend to have higher yields than higher ranked debt instruments from the same issuer, and their spreads are more closely correlated to other forms of subordinated debt than equity. The ability to convert debt to equity in times of financial stress is an attractive feature for banks as they satisfy the regulator's requirements for core capital, without impacting existing shareholders, until such time as the conversion option is exercised (likely to be in times of financial stress).

In general, there are three types of events that will trigger a conversion: capital adequacy concerns; a regulatory mandate; or a market event, eg, movements in equity prices. The event and the level at which conversion may be triggered will influence the yield, and this needs careful consideration. As such, conversion favours the issuer not the holder, and this should be reflected in a higher yield when compared to other similar forms of debt. The market has since stabilised.

2.4 The Investment Returns on Debt Securities

Learning Objective

1.2.2 Analyse the main sources of investment risk and return associated with fixed-income securities: capital return; interest or yield; liquidity; rates of interest; real returns; credit ratings; credit enhancements; duration

The term yield generally refers to the return an investor makes on a particular investment. The income yield is the annualised income return on an investment, expressed as a percentage of the capital invested or current price.

Sometimes, however, it is the total return – the yield to maturity – which is of more interest. This includes the annualised capital growth or loss which will be made on the investment, if it is held to maturity.

Yields may be quoted gross or net of tax. Yields are useful for comparing one investment with another, to see which is more attractive to the investor.

Taking gilts as our example, the yield on a gilt will depend on:

- the gilt's coupon, and
- its market price.

The two main influences on the price of a gilt are:

- interest rates, as set by the Bank of England
- how long the gilt has to run until maturity.

The price of a gilt (and therefore its yield) will also be affected by demand in the market. As with most markets, when there are more buyers than sellers the price will rise; and conversely, when there are more sellers than buyers the price will fall. But, of course, one of the key factors that influences investor demand is the attractiveness of a gilt compared to other investments – and this is why interest rates play a leading role in how much demand there is.

In addition, movements in the sterling **exchange rate** can affect foreign demand. If sterling is weak, UK gilts may look comparatively good value to an overseas investor; and if it is expected to strengthen then they may see a holding of a UK gilt as a good way to reap the currency gain while holding a secure investment.

Let's look at some different ways of assessing a gilt's yield, taking account of its current market price.

2.4.1 Running Yield

The running yield (also known as the interest yield) on a gilt expresses the income received on it, as a percentage of the investor's outlay.

It is calculated by dividing the coupon rate by the market price, and multiplying the result by 100.

$$\frac{\text{Gross coupon}}{\text{Market price}} \times 100 = \text{Interest yield (also known as running yield)}$$

Using as an example 12% Exchequer 2013–20, trading at a price of £114 per £100 nominal, we have:

$$\text{Interest yield} = \frac{12}{114} \times 100 = 10.53\%$$

In other words, for every £100 actual which the investor invests in the above gilt, they will receive £10.53 per annum, gross, by way of interest. The interest yield is usually expressed gross (ie, as a rate before deduction of income tax).

2.4.2 Capital Returns

The running yield does not, however, tell the whole story for the investor. It does not reflect any capital gain or loss that will be incurred.

As the rates in the market change, the prices of the bonds will rise and fall, hence the investor may incur a capital loss or gain if they resell the bond. The investor could, of course, hold until redemption, in which case we know for sure that £100 will be received for every £100 nominal stock. The capital return will depend on the purchase price. If the holding was bought at a price above par – that is, more than £100 per £100 nominal was paid – the investor will incur a capital loss on the sale. If the investor paid less than par, they will make a gain on the sale.

Holding period return = $\dfrac{\text{(Price received at maturity − Price purchased)}}{\text{Price purchased}}$

The annualised capital gain/loss in terms of a return measure can be represented by:

Annualised return from capital gain/loss = $\dfrac{\text{Holding period return}}{\text{Number of years to maturity}}$

An estimate of these capital returns to redemption can be calculated, and incorporated into the overall return the investor will make should they hold the bond until maturity. The redemption yield, which we will look at next, reflects this capital loss, or gain, in addition to the interest payments that will be received.

2.4.3 Yield to Redemption

The **gross redemption yield (GRY)** (sometimes also written as gross yield to redemption or yield to maturity (YTM)) assumes that the investor will hold the bond to its redemption date. The investor will receive this return annually on the bond investment if held to maturity. The assumption is that any coupons received will continue to be reinvested at a rate that is the same as the redemption yield.

To determine an approximate measure of the YTM from the coupon, bond price and the maturity of the bond, we can calculate the return in two parts: the interest yield component of the return, plus the capital appreciation component of the return.

As far as the capital appreciation component of the bond return is concerned, the investor will (generally) make either a capital gain or a loss, depending on whether they bought the holding above par (at a premium) or under par (at a discount).

Clearly, then, to calculate this estimate of the redemption yield from the price and the coupon on a particular bond, we first need to work out the difference between the bond's current price and par, as well as the number of years it has to run. This procedure is outlined in this section.

Having determined the current yield earlier, we now calculate the return due to capital appreciation on the bond by using the formula presented above.

As already stated, the annualised return from capital gain/loss can be represented by:

$\dfrac{\text{Holding period of return}}{\text{Number of years to maturity}}$

If the market price of the gilt is trading at a discount (below the par value of £100) then there will be a positive element of capital gain per annum to be added to the interest yield. If, on the other hand, the gilt is trading at a premium (ie, market price of the gilt is above par) then the resulting return due to capital loss will need to be deducted from the interest yield, to arrive at the approximate redemption yield.

Example

Let us consider the redemption yield that would have applied for 12% Exchequer 2013–20, priced at £114 in the year 2006, which was redeemed in 2013.

1. Recall from section 2.4.1 that the running yield for this bond is 10.53%.
2. The holding period return is (100−114)/114 = −0.1228.
3. The return due to the annualised loss on capital to redemption is −0.1228/7 = −0.0175 or −1.75%.

The return due to the annualised loss on capital to redemption is equal to the holding period return of −0.1228 divided by the number of years to redemption, ie, 2013−2006 = 7 years.

So, the approximate yield to redemption is a combination of yields in 1 and 3:
10.53% (the interest yield, as calculated before) −1.75% = 8.78%.

The approximate yield to redemption stated above is a gross yield, because no account has been taken of the income tax the investor will pay on it. Remember, there is no CGT payable on gains realised on disposals of gilts.

To calculate a figure which shows the yield to redemption after tax – the **net redemption yield (NRY)** – we need to take account of what income tax rate the investor will actually pay.

To do this, the interest yield needs to be adjusted by the investor's applicable tax rate, ie:

- 0% (non-taxpayers)
- 20% (basic rate taxpayers)
- 40% (higher rate taxpayers)
- 45% (additional rate taxpayers).

2.4.4 Volatility and Risk

There is an inverse relationship between the prices of bonds and their yields. The price variability of a particular bond that has some time left to maturity may change, depending on investor outlooks on an issuer's financial health and long-term business prospects. As a result of this uncertainty, interest rate expectations may be changeable, causing prices to remain volatile over an investment period. Rising interest rate expectations increase the redemption yield and push prices of bonds down. Conversely, falling yield expectations lift bond prices.

The variability of each bond price across the maturity range will depend on a number of factors. In general, longer-dated bonds are more sensitive to interest rate changes than their short-dated counterparts. Coupons also modify the variability of the bond. High coupons damp down volatility while low or zeros increase volatility.

The price variability of a bond depends on its coupon and its maturity. Together these bond features give each bond its unique character in terms of its price sensitivity to exogenous and stochastic factors that influence the changes in interest rates. A simple measure that can characterise the risk in a bond is its duration. This risk measure of a bond encapsulates the combined impact of the coupon and maturity effect on price sensitivity. For example, a set increase in yield will lower prices of all bonds. However, a bond with a higher duration will be more sensitive to the same change in yields than a lower-duration bond.

In general, we expect greater price volatility in:

- bonds of a lower credit-quality. Junk (speculative and non-investment grade) bonds are more volatile because of their greater risk and speculative nature as compared to investment grade bonds.
- lower coupon bonds, because a small change in current interest rates represents a proportionately greater change as a percentage of a low coupon than of a high coupon.
- longer-dated bonds, because current interest rate expectations have a relatively greater impact on the overall return to maturity than for shorter-dated bonds.

Duration is a measure that can be used to estimate the price sensitivity of a bond to small changes in yields. The simplest measure for duration is called Macaulay's duration.

$$\frac{\Sigma(\text{Net present value of the bond's cash flows} \times \text{time to cash flow being received})}{\Sigma \text{Net present value of the cash flows to be received}}$$

When it is adjusted by dividing with a yield relative, it is called modified duration.

$$\frac{\text{Macaulay Duration}}{1 + \text{GRY}}$$

Once you have calculated or obtained the duration value of a bond (ie, from a Bloomberg terminal) you can use this to estimate the anticipated price change of a bond, if there is a small increase or decrease in the yield. For example, if there is a small, albeit the same +0.1% rise in yield in two bonds, the bond with a higher duration will show a bigger drop in its price, when compared to a low duration bond. Knowledge of duration is essential for the selection of bonds in investment management and also in managing risks of bond investments in risk management.

$$\% \text{ change in price of bond} = -(\text{modified duration} \times \% \text{ change in the yield})$$

There is an inverse relationship between prices and yields. As a result we have a minus sign attached to the right hand side of the simple formula. The duration of a bond may be affected by embedded options, eg, callable or puttable bonds. The duration measure should be adjusted to reflect the fact that the exercise of these options will influence the expected cash flows. The adjusted measure is referred to as the 'option-adjusted duration'.

2.4.5 The Yield Curve

It can be useful to display graphically the yields available on a series of bonds of differing maturities. A graph showing this, usually based on gilt yields and shown against the time they have left to maturity, is called a yield curve. The yield curve contains valuable imbedded information about the gilt market's expectations about future interest rates and inflation outlooks. The shape of the yield is often analysed in more detail to gain an understanding about this information that is in the market.

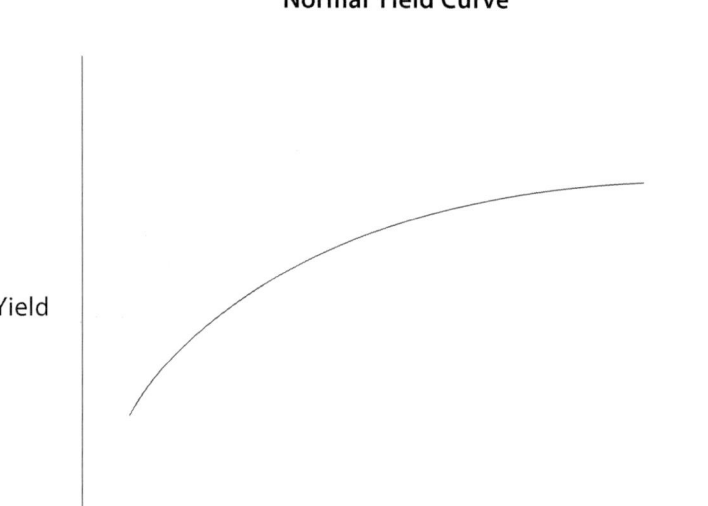

A yield curve must not be confused with a historical time series chart of a yield on a particular bond; instead it is a snapshot of all the yields on a series of different maturity bonds, issued by the same issuer at one point in time.

The shape of this yield curve provides important information to bond market participants about rate expectations in the capital markets. Since interpretation of this is beyond the scope of this book and syllabus, we shall not go into details of the financial theories developed to explain the yield curve or their rate term structures here. Hence a simpler conceptual interpretation is provided at this stage of the learning process. There are three common types of shapes of yield curves observed in practice – normal, flat and inverted. There is also a humped yield curve observed sometimes, which has a combination of these shapes.

A normal yield curve has a positive (upward) slope, reflecting the fact that securities with more time remaining to maturity have a slightly higher yield than shorter-dated securities. Interpretation of the term structure of rates is a specialised activity. However, more broadly, an upward-sloping yield curve depicts the time value of money. Investors will generally require a higher yield, or a premium over shorter-maturity bonds, for tying up their invested capital for longer. This observed term premium is due to greater uncertainty over longer future periods. The yield curve is not static but dynamic, and is continually changing shape over time as new information about future rates arrives and is priced into the market. The emerging news can lead to complex changes in the shape of the yield curve.

At other times, the yield curve may start to look much flatter:

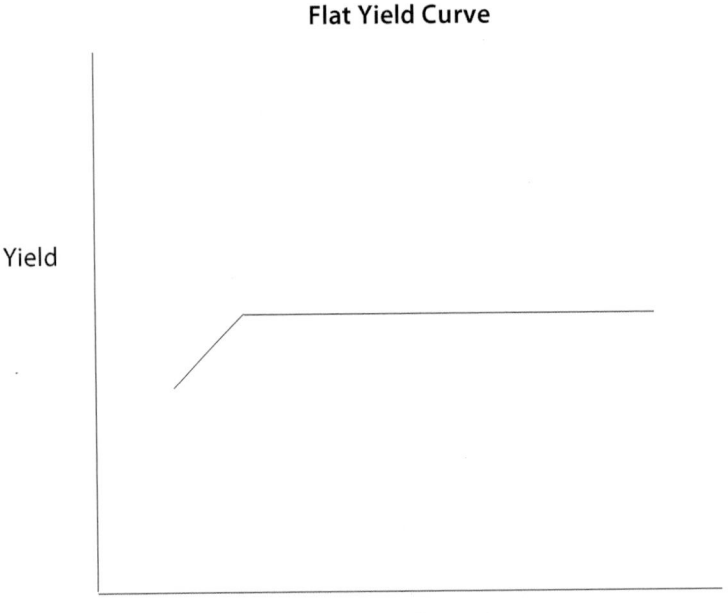

A flat yield curve is characterised by level rates across a range of maturities and this curve may reflect a relatively stable outlook for the economy. Alternatively, this flattening-off (in comparison with the normal yield curve) can reflect expectations of a gradual future decline in interest rates. A curve-flattening development is normally observed during an economic downturn phase in the cycle, also accompanied by moderating inflationary pressures.

When short- and long-term bonds are offering the same yields, investors may choose the bond with the least amount of risk. However, an investor's wish to have the certainty of holding bonds until maturity to meet a long-term obligation may put a high priority on choosing bonds with maturities matching dates when the investor wishes to realise funds.

Asset Classes

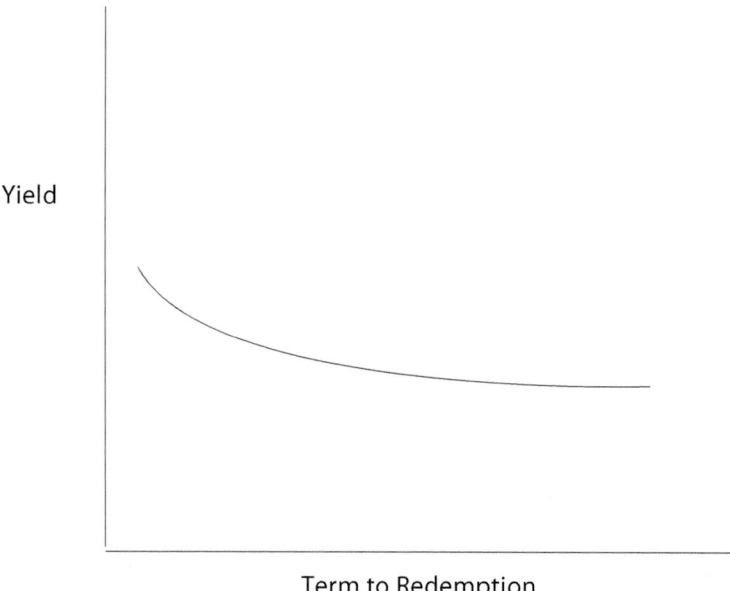

Inverted Yield Curve

Yield

Term to Redemption

The yield curve may also sometimes be **inverted**, with yields on longer-dated securities being lower than on shorter-dated securities.

An inverted yield curve may reflect:

- expectations that interest rates will fall in the future
- expectations that inflationary pressures in the economy will reduce dramatically in the future
- lower supply and higher demand for gilts in the market; for example, a decrease in issuance of gilts by the DMO and/or increased demand from investors for long-dated gilts will cause the longer-dated gilt prices to rise and their yields to fall.

The following graph demonstrates how an actual UK gilt curve may look at different points in time. Here, the UK gilt yield curve is sampled over a number of dates covering the dramatic turn of events over a time period from July 2005 to spring 2012.

In 2005, the UK economy was in a buoyant state and entered a traumatic phase characterised by the 2007–08 global credit crisis. A second wave of this crisis affected the euro region (and beyond) leading into the European debt crisis in the 2010–12 period.

Over these time periods the shape of the UK yield curve has continually evolved to reflect the changing economic and market outlooks. A flat yield curve seen in 2005 had transformed into a downward sloping (inverted) curve just before the 2007–08 credit crisis began. Subsequently, this morphed into an upward-sloping yield curve in 2009, following the credit crisis and the massive government-inspired interventions used to stabilise the banking system and inject liquidity into the real economy. The UK government introduced the quantitative easing programme in spring 2009, combined with aggressive intervention aimed at the recapitalisation of the global banking system. From 2009, the shape of the yield curve remained upward sloping. However, by spring 2012 the whole yield curve had dropped lower to reflect anaemic economic conditions and dampened rate prospects for the European and UK economies.

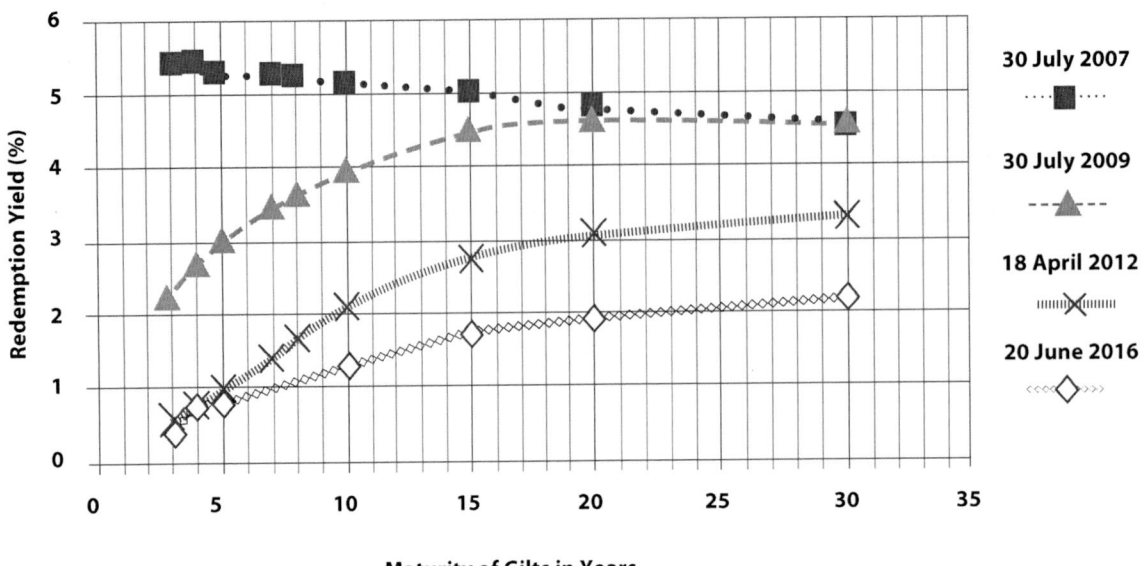

UK Gilt Yield Curves on Different Dates

Source: Bloomberg LP

2.5 Investment Risk and Debt Securities

In the following sections we consider various factors which can affect the riskiness of a debt security, and its performance, including liquidity, interest rates, real rates of return, issuing institutions and credit ratings, and methods of credit enhancement. These factors combine to affect the risk attached to a debt security.

Bonds are, generally, negotiable or marketable securities – that is, they can be bought and sold (although there are, as we have seen, some bonds that cannot be sold prior to maturity, but which have to be held until their redemption dates; these include some local authority issues).

An investor considering holding bonds needs to consider the factors that will influence prices in the bond markets. As with any market this is driven by supply and demand. The following factors affect the supply of, and demand for, bonds in the market:

- Levels of interest rates in the home currency.
- Foreign exchange rates with overseas currencies that bonds are issued in (different to the investor's currency).
- Changes in the credit rating of the issuer.
- Changes in the economic environment – in particular:
  ○ in the UK, the PSNCR has a large effect on the gilt and domestic bond market; in other countries, the local equivalent is also likely to be influential
  ○ levels of gross domestic product (GDP) and gross national product (GNP), seen as barometers of the productivity and economic health of a country
  ○ unemployment figures, since these are also seen as indicative of the health of the economy – and may spark some interest rate movements if the government is trying to take action.
- The coupon and redemption date of the bond.

Sentiment in the bond market often has an effect on equities, as well, in part because the economic events that impact on the one also affect the other, and in part because bonds are often seen as a safe haven when the equity markets are doing badly. This is due to the fact that bond prices are generally much less volatile (less prone to going up and down) than equities, because of their relative certainty of return.

Other factors are considered below.

2.5.1 Liquidity

As with other investments, bonds can carry liquidity risk – the risk that the bond is hard to sell quickly, or can only be sold quickly at a price which does not reflect a fair market value.

Liquidity risk is not a problem for large issues, or issues where there is a guaranteed market such as UK gilts. However, it can be a much greater problem for smaller issues and those where the creditworthiness of the issuer is less sound.

Also, the recession and subsequent regulatory pressures on banks has resulted in lower volumes of trading in certain bond markets. This decline in trading could spell problems for investors looking to trade these securities during times of market stress.

2.5.2 Rates of Interest

Interest rate risk is the risk that market rates rise. The consequence of this for holders of fixed-interest securities is that:

- the coupon becomes comparatively less attractive than it was before, relative to rates in the market
- consequently the price of the bond falls, as demand for it dries up and/or investors sell in order to free money up to lock into higher rates elsewhere.

Thus the investor suffers a 'double hit': they are locked into a bond paying rates which could be bettered elsewhere; and the price of the holding has also fallen, in line with the market.

2.5.3 Real Returns

The returns on fixed-interest securities can, as with the deposit-based investments, be eroded by inflation; indeed if inflation reaches very high levels, the real return on the bond could be negative.

Of course, index-linked bonds – which we looked at earlier in section 2.2.3 – provide protection against inflation risk in that both income and capital are adjusted for changes in the RPI.

As an example, the following graph shows the bond yield curves taken from conventional gilts and index-linked gilts. In the spring of 2012, the UK yield curve was upward sloping with the five-year short-dated gilt yielding 1.03% in nominal terms and the inflation-indexed five-year yield showing a rate of −1.6% in real terms. In the 50-year maturities, the nominal yield was 3.3% against an index-linked real yield of 0%. The spread between the conventional and linker yields shows that in real terms inflation eroded yields and investors were getting little or no value from their investments.

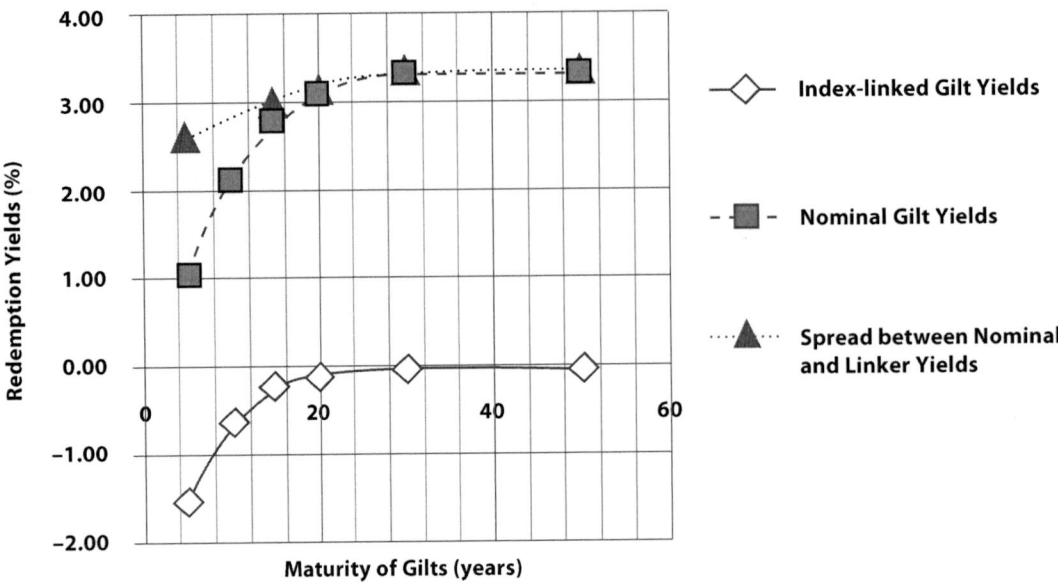

Conventional and Index-Linked Yield Curves

Data courtesy of Bloomberg LP

2.5.4 Issuer Risk

Issuer risk is the risk that the issuer of the bond gets into financial difficulties and cannot keep up the interest payments, or defaults on the capital. Generally speaking, investors regard bonds as less risky than equities, because:

- If the issuer has poor profits (or no profits at all) in a given year, it must still pay interest on its debt. If it cannot, it might have pay lower than required or default on the coupon. Dividends, on the other hand, are paid from profits, so may be at risk in a poor year.
- If an issuer goes into liquidation, then the order of pay-out is such that bondholders will be repaid before shareholders, and, if there are not enough assets to go around, shareholders may therefore get nothing at all. This is because, in the course of a liquidation, assets are sold off to raise the cash to pay off debts – and there is a legally prescribed order in which that cash is distributed. Shareholders are not debtors, but owners of a company, and as such are last in the pecking order for distributions.

That said, of course, much depends on the financial status of the issuer itself. Equities issued by a large, financially sound and well-run company may in fact be a safer investment than debt issued by a company whose finances are in a poor state and which may default on its liabilities.

Still, it is fair to say that when looking at a single issuer, debt instruments issued by it are likely to be more secure than shares issued by it.

The price debtholders pay for this additional security is, of course, the fact that their rewards are limited to the payment of interest and repayment of loan capital, on the terms originally specified. If the company does very well indeed, it will not get any extra profit, whereas shareholders can hope to see their shares rise in price, and to receive rising dividends each year.

The riskiest bond issuers are those falling into the junk category; junk bond issuers suffer a relatively high rate of defaults, for which they are compensated by relatively high yields, providing that the issuer can keep up the repayments. In July 2016, S&P Global Ratings reported that 100 companies had defaulted on debt, 50% more than for the same period in 2015, and the highest level since 2009.

2.5.5 Credit Ratings

A number of issues may affect a bond's safety, in terms of the likelihood of its being repaid. Clearly, an investor in any form of bond is going to be keen to know what the issuer's creditworthiness is, so as to assess whether the returns are worthwhile in light of the risk to their interest and capital.

Generally speaking, bonds issued by governments are regarded as the most secure – although it is not unheard of for governments to default on their debts. In any event, it can be hard for an investor to assess the creditworthiness of either a government or a company. In order to help them do so, a number of specialist agencies provide credit ratings using standardised scales, to bond issues. Among the most well-known agencies are:

- Moody's
- Standard & Poor's
- Fitch Ratings Inc.

If an issuer wishes to be rated (and many do, because some investors will simply not buy debt which does not have an independent credit rating attached to it), then they will invite the rating agency to inspect its financial status and operations. The agencies then assign a rating to the issuer, and often different ratings to individual debt issues from the same issuer, depending on the seniority or otherwise of the specific issue.

The rating agencies consider the following main areas:

- the issuer's current financial strength
- the financial and commercial management of the organisation
- the economic and political background in the environment in which the organisation operates
- competition in the industry in which the organisation operates.

An issuer's rating can change from time to time, with its own fortunes and those of the environment in which it operates. Ratings generally use a series of letters and numbers, which are available for investors to refer to so they can understand what they are seeing.

For example, Standard & Poor's most secure credit rating is 'AAA' (or 'triple-A'), with AA being somewhat less secure, and A and A being progressively less secure yet. The permutations are too numerous to set out here, but you should be aware that (for example):

- AAA-rated debt is more secure than AA-rated debt
- A-rated debt is more secure than B-rated debt
- B-rated debt is more secure than C-rated debt.

2.5.6 Credit Enhancements

In order to make their bond issues more attractive to investors, by reducing the risk of default, many issuers whose finances are not in good shape arrange for another organisation (generally one with very strong finances) to guarantee the debt. This means that, if the issuer cannot pay the interest or capital from its own resources, the 'guarantor' (the organisation issuing the guarantee) will make the repayments.

The investor therefore relies on the creditworthiness of the guarantor, as opposed to that of the issuer, for their security. An example of this is a lesser-known company arranging for its debt to be guaranteed by a major bank or insurance company.

2.5.7 Secured/Unsecured Status of the Debt

The promise given by a bond issuer to pay coupon interest and the final principal on loaned amount together with rights of a bondholder are set out in a written agreement between the issuer and the investor (bondholder). It includes the coupon rate, period to maturity and whether the bond comes with any special features like convertibility or whether it is callable. All bonds must have an indenture and the terms of this are detailed in a bond's prospectus.

Bond issuers can issue debt in secured or unsecured form.

- **Secured debt** involves the identification of certain of the issuer's assets, so that, if the issuer defaults, the bondholders will have a prior legal claim over that asset.
- **Unsecured debt** leaves the investor with no certainty as to the payment of interest or repayment of capital, excepting for the issuer's promise to repay.

If a company which has issued debt goes into liquidation, then any bonds it has issued are ranked in order of seniority.

> **Liquidation** occurs when a company is wound up, with its assets being sold off to repay its outstanding debts, and the surplus (if there is any) is distributed to the shareholders.

This ranking determines the order in which they will be repaid, with those ranking last being at greatest risk of there not being enough money to go round. The ranking will depend on whether the bond is:

- secured or unsecured (if it is secured, then the bondholders can rely on the proceeds of the specific asset designated as security)
- described as subordinated or unsubordinated. Unsubordinated bonds carry an unconditional promise that they will be repaid before the creditor's other obligations. Unsubordinated bonds are also sometimes described as senior debt. Subordinated bonds rank after them for repayment, and are sometimes known as junior debt. An investor in junior debt can find themselves junior in a capital structure by subsequent new issues, after bond has been issued and depending on terms of the respective covenants.

2.6 Dealing in Debt Securities

Learning Objective

1.2.4 Understand how fixed-income securities are traded and settled: primary and secondary markets; decentralised market; retail bond markets; clearing, settlement and safe custody; pricing, liquidity and fair value; coupon; nominal value; market price; clean and dirty prices; redemption date; transaction costs and charges

2.6.1 Costs of Purchase and Sale

Like shares and other stocks, bonds can be bought and sold through a stockbroker. Investors will pay the broker a commission, which may vary from broker to broker and will also depend on the size of the deal. Usually, for larger deals, stockbrokers will charge commissions based on a lower percentage of the deal size. Some brokers will also offer investment advice as to which gilt may suit the investor's needs best, and on conditions in the market.

If an investor buys a bond through a stockbroker, they will pay the current market price; they can, however, give their broker special instructions – for example:

- to buy at best (ie, at the best available price in the market)
- to buy at a limit (ie, not to pay more than a certain amount for the stock; if the broker cannot complete the deal at the limit or better, they will not place it at all).

Gilts can also be bought directly from:

- the DMO's gilt purchase and sale service (operated by Computershare)
- the DMO at gilt auctions.

Directly from the DMO's Gilt Purchase and Sale Service

Since 2003, private investors have been able to deal in gilts which are already in issue, directly with the DMO, on an execution-only basis (that is, no advice is given and the investor must make their own decisions). The service is called the retail gilt purchase and sale service, and it is operated by a firm called Computershare.

To be able to use Computershare, investors must first become approved investors. This is very similar to the anti-money laundering procedures. It is how the DMO and Computershare satisfy the UK anti-money laundering requirements with regard to each investor. Once an investor is approved, they will not have to provide evidence of identity and address every time they want to use the purchase and sale service (nor will they have to do so if they invest via a gilt auction).

Once an investor has been accepted as a member of the approved group, they are able to use the gilt purchase and sale service on an execution-only basis, to buy and sell holdings of gilts. Commission charges on deals made this way (particularly smaller ones) may be less than those levied by stockbrokers and banks for the same sized deals, so this service can be attractive to retail investors.

The investor needs to complete the appropriate dealing form (which they can obtain directly from Computershare). When Computershare sends them the form, it will also include a list of gilts available for purchase. The investor then sends the form, with the appropriate payment (in the case of gilt purchases) directly to Computershare.

The application should show the gilt they want to buy and the amount in money terms they want to invest (ie, **not** the nominal amount of the gilt they want to buy – since they will not know the exact price at which the deal will be carried out when they post their dealing form).

The price at which the deal is done will depend on conditions on the date that Computershare has the form, cleared funds and any other information it needs to proceed; that is, an investor cannot say 'I would like to deal at XX price or better' (as they could if dealing through a stockbroker). They get the prevailing market price, as determined by the DMO, at the time the deal is placed. Thus, the benefit of potentially cheaper dealing costs is to some extent offset by this lack of control.

Computershare sends the contract note setting out all the costs, approximately four days after the deal date.

Direct from the DMO at Auction

Members of the approved group can also deal direct with the DMO to buy gilts at auction. Many large gilt issues are first brought to the market in this way, and it can represent a very cost-effective route for an investor to buy into a new issue, since there is no bid-offer spread to pay, and no stockbroker's commission.

Even though the investor does not know the price at which they will eventually deal, they do at least know that there will be minimal dealing costs.

> **Bid-offer spread** – the difference between the prices at which a share, bond, unit trust or other investment can be bought and sold on the same day.

Example

If a gilt is described as having a price of £118–£118.25, this means that the price at which £100 nominal of that gilt can be **bought** is £118.25. The price at which £100 nominal can be **sold** is £118.00, and the **bid-offer spread** is £0.25 per £100 nominal.

The DMO issues an auction calendar giving details of the gilts which it proposes to auction in the months ahead; this is usually published up to a year in advance, with finalised dates as to which gilts will in fact be auctioned, and on what dates, being announced at the end of each quarter.

Details of the gilt market auctions is provided by the UK DMO at dmo.gov.uk.

Gilts can either be purchased directly from the DMO at its outright gilt auctions or through a secondary market. Bidders at the auctions can choose to participate through a GEMM, who can bid directly by telephone to the DMO on the bidder's behalf or by completing an application form, providing that they are members of the DMO's approved group of investors.

Non-competitive bids – private investors can bid on a non-competitive basis in a gilt auction for a minimum of £1,000 nominal of the particular gilt; the maximum they can bid for is £500,000.

The fact that they bid on a non-competitive basis means that any application will be met in full. That is, the investor gets as much stock as they requested, at the average accepted bid price for that particular auction (ie, the weighted average price paid by successful competitive bidders). So someone sending in a non-competitive bid has to accept that they will be allocated stock at whatever this price turns out to be. They do not know it in advance.

Competitive bids – any application can place a competitive bid submitted through a GEMM stating the price the investor is willing to pay. A bid through a GEMM or from a client bidder must be for one bid at a **clean price**, expressed as a multiple of 0.01 of £1, for at least £1million and for multiples thereof. Investors submitting a competitive bid price which is too low, risk getting no stock, or only a proportion of the amount they originally bid for. Those who bid the highest prices will get as much stock as they have subscribed for, unless the issue is heavily oversubscribed, in which case it may be allocated on a pro rata basis across the highest bidders.

Usually, investors in this category are institutional investors, and sometimes they bid for very large allocations of stock. As we have seen above, it is the competitive bids which are used to determine what price the non-competitive bidders will be allocated stock at.

2.6.2 Retail Bond Markets

Retail bonds are defined as those traded in units of less than £50,000, with a typical value of £1,000, whereas wholesale bonds are those traded in units greater than £50,000. The method of distribution differs between retail and wholesale bonds. Retail bonds are generally offered via intermediaries, ie, wealth managers, whereas wholesale bonds are sold direct to institutions by investment banks sales teams. Retail bonds are an alternative to bank debt, private placements and institutional bonds and generally have terms of between 5–10 years. The LSE's Order Book for Retail Bonds (ORB) received lower issuance in 2015 than in 2014. The main reason for this was the strong return of banks to the lending field, supplemented by institutional direct lenders. The total value traded on ORB corporate bonds in April 2017 was £313.43 million through 4,824 trades.

In 2010, the LSE launched the Order Book for Retail Bonds (ORB) platform as an order-driven trading service providing access to a range of gilts, supranational, and UK corporate bonds, in response to demand from retail investors for an on-screen secondary market in fixed interest securities. The ORB enables issuers to distribute bonds directly to retail investors, stimulating activity and offering wider investment opportunities to private investors. The ORB operates in a similar way to the share trading mechanisms that already exist, and enables market makers to offer two-way prices in fixed interest securities during trading hours. Continuous trading begins at 08.45 and ends at 16.30. The 'tick size' is £0.01 and bonds are traded in the denominations specified in the prospectus. All order book trades are trade reported automatically and published immediately. The ORB has enabled greater flexibility

for issuers in allowing the size of a retail bond to be tailored to meet issuers' requirements. Issue sizes on the ORB have ranged from £20 million to £300 million, which is useful to issuers who do not need a benchmark wholesale bond of £500 million, as it allows the option of issuing in smaller sizes on a more frequent basis.

All trades are executed on a 'clean' basis without accrued interest, and gilts are settled T+1. The standard settlement time for corporate bonds traded on the ORB is **T+2**, which changed from T+3 in October 2014 as part of the harmonisation of EU securities settlement cycles.

2.6.3 Market Prices

Many bond prices, including those of gilts, are quoted in newspapers, such as the *Financial Times*, and online vendors, such as Bloomberg and Reuters.

The prices quoted are:

- the mid-point between buying and selling prices (called the mid-market price)
- clean prices, meaning that they take no account of accrued interest (explained in section 2.6.2).

2.6.4 Clean and Dirty Prices

Interest on a bond is, as we have seen, paid at set periods. However, it accrues on a daily basis – that is, every day an additional 1/365th of the total annual interest becomes due to the owner. So someone selling (for example) a gilt between two coupon periods will be compensated for the interest that was due to them up to the settlement date of the sale, and the person buying it will have to pay for that accrued interest.

So the price paid for the gilt (the market price x the nominal amount being traded) is adjusted by an amount for the accrued interest to date. The accrued interest is calculated up to and including the settlement date of the deal – that is, for gilts, usually one working day after the deal date.

Example

Staying with gilts to illustrate the point, 4¾% Treasury Stock 2020 pays interest on 7 March and 7 September. Someone who bought a holding in it for settlement on 7 April 2015 (that is, a month after the previous coupon payment) is also buying 31 days of accrued interest. Having done this they will then become entitled to the next full interest coupon payment on 7 September.

The price the buyer pays will then (ignoring any stockbroker's commission) be the 'clean' market price for the gilt, plus an accrued interest adjustment of:

Half the coupon (as interest is paid twice yearly) x $\frac{\text{number of days since last payment}}{184 \text{ (ie, days in the coupon period)}}$

or, in the case of our example gilt,

4.75% / 2 x (31 / 184) = £0.400136 per £100 nominal of the gilt.

Seven working days before the interest payment date (or 10 working days in the case of War Loans), the price of a gilt goes **ex-dividend** (also written as xd). This may sound odd, as we usually use the term dividends in connection with shares – it is just a convention, and in the case of gilts refers to the interest that will be paid.

Ex-dividend means 'without the dividend', and it means that anyone buying the gilt between now and the imminent interest payment date won't get that interest, unless they have bought it on special terms, which have been advised to the registrar, so that they know who to make the payment to.

Anyone who holds the gilt on the xd date will get the full interest payment.

Anyone who sells the gilt between the xd date and the pay date (ie, within the xd period) will receive the full interest payment – but will have to pay some of it back to the person who buys the holding, since they will have obtained a couple of days' interest to which they were not entitled.

Sometimes, people dealing in the xd period can agree to ask the registrar to pay the entire forthcoming interest payment to the buyer – even though, as we've seen, this is not the convention. This is called buying cum-dividend – cum is Latin for 'with'.

So, you may see the following adjustments quoted in respect of a gilt deal to ensure that an investor gets the exact number of days' interest that they have held the stock for:

- **Investor buys cum-div** – interest from the last payment date to the settlement date is added to the cost.
- **Investor buys ex-div** – interest from the settlement date to the next payment date is deducted from the cost.
- **Investor sells cum-div** – interest from the last payment date to the settlement date is added to the sale proceeds.
- **Investor sells ex-div** – interest from the settlement date to the next payment date is deducted from the proceeds.

So, as we have seen, interest payments are generally made to the holder who was registered seven business days before the interest payment date. After this date, the stock will be sold without interest (referred to as ex-interest or ex-dividend). The seller of the stock will receive the interest payment, generally for a full six months.

Sales at any time since the last interest payment up to this date are made cum-interest/cum-dividend (with dividend). In this case, the subsequent interest payment will be paid to the purchaser.

Accrued interest is the daily interest earned on the stock since the last interest payment date, which is paid and received at the time of a transaction, in addition to the clean price of the stock, to give the dirty price that the buyer must pay.

If a stock is sold ex-interest/ex-dividend, the buyer will be compensated for the fact that they receive no interest in respect of the time they have held the stock in the current interest period. Thus, the clean price will be adjusted downwards slightly to reflect this interest adjustment.

2.6.5 Redemption Date

Bonds and gilts are issued with a promise that investors' money will be repaid at a set future date – the redemption date. Redemption dates can be set at:

- short-term (within seven years)
- medium (7–15 years)
- long-term (over 15 years).

The investment will then be repaid at the agreed date. Undated gilts, which have no fixed redemption date, are also available.

2.7 Bond Indices

Learning Objective

1.2.5 Understand the purpose and construction of the main bond indices, and the considerations needed for less liquid markets

A bond market index is a composite listing of bonds or fixed-income instruments and provides a statistic that can be used to measure performance in the portfolio management process. Bond indices are relatively new and not widely published. There are many bond indices offered by a number of vendors. However, as mutual funds have continued to experience growth in recent years, so there has been the need to set reliable benchmarks to evaluate performance. Compared to equity indices, it is quite challenging to create and compute a bond market index. There are several reasons for this. First, the universe of bonds is much larger than equities ranging from securities offered in a range of maturities combined with issuers (both from the government and corporate sectors) who have a variety of long-term credit ratings. On top of this, bonds have other clauses such as calls, convertibility or sinking fund features that make it difficult to create a suitable benchmark that can be used to assess all of the bond funds available to investors. Further, as older issues are redeemed, new ones may be issued with characteristics that may differ from the previous issues they have replaced. This means that the universe of securities, from which indices are created, will change more frequently to represent the changed population in the bond universe.

It should be noted that the fixed-income market is more of a dealer market in which dealers buy and sell from their own inventory. Thus, trading individual securities quickly may not be possible if there is less liquidity in the market at any given point in time. Obtaining accurate prices, especially of illiquid securities, may present difficulties.

All of this makes it difficult for bond traders and index providers to replicate a bond benchmark efficiently. Similarly, some bond indices that have illiquid bonds in them may not be investable as easily as the comparable equity indices. Bond ETFs, however, have become increasingly popular with both retail and institutional investors due to their liquidity.

2.7.1　Types of Indices

Bond indices can be categorised based on their broad characteristics, such as whether they are composed of government bonds, corporate bonds, high-yield bonds or asset-backed securities. They can also be classified based on their credit rating or maturity date.

Bond indices are generally total return indices and are used mostly to view performance of a market over time. In addition to returns, bond indices also incorporate the combined yield, duration, and convexity of individual bonds.

Bond indices generally include more individual securities than stock market indices do, and are broader and more rule-based. This allows portfolio managers to predict which type of debt issues will be eligible for each index.

The FTSE global bond index series provides fixed-income professionals with a set of performance benchmarks to include the principal government bond and selected corporate markets. It covers the principal government bond markets and selected corporate markets. The series is organised into four homogeneously constructed bond families: FTSE global government bond indices; FTSE covered bond indices; FTSE corporate bond indices; and the FTSE euro emerging markets bond indices. Barclays, among others, also provide information on fixed income indices.

A popular general index family of global fixed income indices are the Barclays Capital indices. Their database has over 70,000 securities and the global database covers all kinds of fixed income securities. The most recognised Barclays Capital Index is the Barclays Capital US Aggregate Bond Index. The return on this index is a total return: price appreciation plus income as a percentage of the initial holding period market value. This aggregate index includes three major sub-indices: Barclays Capital Government/Credit Bond Index; Barclays Capital Mortgage-Backed Securities Index; and Barclays Capital Asset-Backed Securities Index. To be in this index a bond must be US dollar-denominated and rated at least Baa3 by Moody's.

Merrill Lynch fixed income indices also cover a broad spectrum of fixed income markets. Many are based on the US fixed income securities markets. A primary Pan-Europe broad market index tracks the performance of major investment grade bond markets in the region. The sub-indices in this category include the Sterling Broad Market Index and other government indices.

J.P.Morgan bond indices offer another variation to the long list of bond indices available in the market. They offer a complete list of indices to track global bond markets. The history of some of these indices goes back to 1985, with comprehensive coverage of emerging markets.

J.P.Morgan offers a global government bond index. The sub-indices that emerge from this large index include the government bonds of the following countries: Australia, Belgium, Canada, Denmark, Germany, Italy, Japan, the Netherlands, Spain, Sweden, the UK and the US.

2.7.2 Weighting

Most bond indices are weighted by market capitalisation. Bond indices are usually based on market capitalisation, like the shares indices. If the index is of, say, the top 50 bonds (or companies, in the case of the shares indices), then top means biggest by market capitalisation. Sometimes the index is described as weighted. This simply means that a 1% change in the price of the largest bond/company in the index will have more impact than a 1% change in the price of the smallest. Since the bond/share price is always changing, it follows that all the top bonds/shares are not always the same. There is a provision for removing some bonds/shares and adding others, say, every quarter.

2.7.3 Indices and Passive Investment Management

Bond indices are harder to replicate, compared to stock market indices, due to the large number of issues. Usually, portfolio managers define suitable benchmarks for their portfolios, and use an existing index or create blends of indices based on their investment mandates.

They then purchase a subset of the issues available in their benchmark, and use the index as a measure of the market portfolio's return, against which to compare their own portfolio's performance. Often the average duration of the market may not be the most appropriate duration for a given portfolio. Replication of an index's characteristics can be achieved by using bond futures to match the duration of the bond index.

2.7.4 FTSE Global Government Bond Indices

The FTSE global government bond indices consist of central government debt from 22 countries denominated in the domicile currency, or euros for Eurozone countries. There is a euro aggregate index and the indices are organised by region: Asia Pacific (including China), the Americas and the Eurozone plus a European ex-Eurozone index. The indices are also available at the country level and by maturity band.

2.7.5 FTSE Covered Bond Indices

The FTSE covered bond indices consist of securitised issues from 14 countries, including Jumbo Pfandbrief from Germany. Each issue is comparable in structure and quality to the German Jumbo Pfandbrief market. The indices are available at aggregate, country level and by maturity bands.

2.7.6 FTSE Corporate Bond Indices

FTSE Euro Corporate Bond Index

The FTSE Euro Corporate Bond Index includes euro-denominated issues from global corporate entities. Each bond is classified under the industry classification benchmark (ICB). The index constituents are investment grade debt with a minimum rating of BBB–. Sub-indices are structured by credit rating and maturity band.

FTSE Sterling Corporate Bond Index

The FTSE Sterling Corporate Bond Index consists of sterling-denominated corporate bonds of investment grade quality. Each bond is classified under the ICB. There are 11 industrial sector sub-indices, including telecommunications, utilities and banking. The index has sector rating and maturity sub-indices. Telecommunications and non-financials (ie, the headline index minus financials) are calculated as additional sub-indices.

The FTSE Corporate Bond indices have 14 additional sub-indices besides the maturity sub-indices.

Agency credit ratings have been grouped as follows:

Sub-Indices Rating Definition	Agency Equivalent Ratings		
	Fitch Ratings Inc	S&P	Moody's
AAA	AAA	AAA	Aaa
AA	AA– to AA+	AA– to AA+	Aa3 to Aa1
A	A– to A+	A– to A+	A3 to A1
BBB	BBB– to BBB+	BBB– to BBB+	Baa3 to Baa1

2.7.7 Sub-Indices

All indices have the following five maturity sub-indices:

- one–three years
- three–five years
- five–seven years
- seven–ten years
- over ten years
- over 15 years.

2.7.8 Capital Index

The capital index of all the listed indices is calculated every day. Each capital index is an arithmetically weighted index based on the clean price, and weighted by the nominal amount outstanding.

2.7.9 Total Return Index

A total return index is calculated for all the indices. A total return index reflects the price changes and interest payments of each bond. What does total return mean? When measuring performance, it is the actual rate of return of an investment or a pool of investments over a given evaluation period. Total return includes interest, capital gains, dividends and distributions realised over a given period of time and it accounts for two categories of return: income and capital appreciation. Income includes interest paid by fixed-income investments, distributions or dividends. Capital appreciation represents the change in the market price of an asset.

2.7.10 Additional Calculations

In addition to the capital index and total return index, the following fundamentals of bond indices are also calculated:

- average coupon
- average gross redemption yield
- average time to maturity
- average (Macaulay) duration
- average modified duration
- average convexity
- the sum of the nominal value of all bonds in each index
- the number of bonds in each index
- the weight of the index in relation to its relevant aggregated index (when applicable).

2.7.11 Quality-Controlled Price Sources

The capital and total return indices are calculated using indicative pricing from the key dealer banks in each market. The design of the methodology and availability of the price sources ensures a single price for each bond in the index. The FTSE applies quality controls to ensure each single price in the index is unbiased and representative of the market.

The prices used for the calculation of the indices are based on data and real-time price quotations. To calculate the price, the arithmetic mean between bid and ask quotes (mid-prices) is used in the indices.

2.7.12 Investable Index

These indices enable managers to develop successful investment strategies. The selection criteria of only including constituent securities of bonds which have a bid and ask quote means the indices are an accurate and neutral representation of the market for investors.

2.7.13 Eligibility of Bonds

The following types of bonds are included in the indices:

- all straight bullet bonds maturing in one year or more
- zero coupon bonds
- strippable bonds are included with their total volume and considered as being regular non-stripped bonds.

Excluded from the indices are:

- coupon strips and maturity strips (separated interest and capital repayment securities)
- partly paid bonds
- variable interest bonds (including floating rate bonds)
- index-linked bonds
- callable, puttable and extendible bonds
- convertible bonds
- bonds with no final redemption date.

2.7.14 Historical Data

The indices' base dates are as follows:

- Global government bonds: May 1988.
- Covered bonds: January 1996.
- Euro corporate bonds: July 1999.
- Sterling corporate bonds: March 2004.
- Euro emerging markets bonds: December 1995.

2.8 Selecting Bonds and Bond Funds

Learning Objective

1.2.6 Analyse the factors to take into account when selecting bonds and bond funds: bond characteristics; direct bond strategies; indirect investment; investing in bonds through funds; advantages and disadvantages of investing in bonds and bond funds

2.8.1 Bond Funds

Investment in bonds can be achieved in two ways, directly through a stockbroker (or the DMO), or indirectly through a fund managed by a professional fund manager and marketed to investors by a retail fund management group. Indirect investment is a simple and effective way of investing without getting involved in the effort and costs of buying and selling on your own account.

Money from a large number of investors is pooled and invested in a portfolio of bond stocks. These are selected and managed for the investor by a fund manager. The fund is divided into many small parts known as units. This is why it is often referred to as a unit-linked fund. The price of each unit will depend on the value of the underlying investments. So when you invest, the number of units you receive will depend on how much you invest and the buying price of the units at the time of your investment.

Bond funds are marketed by fund management groups to both private and institutional investors. The funds are managed according to a set mandate by a professional fund manager, who receives a fee for their efforts. A charge is levied for the annual management, and initial charges are applied when new investments are made into the fund. Bond funds will invest in a broad or a tightly focused range of debt securities.

Bond funds can be used to provide access to the underlying securities at a more affordable cost, and to a much broader spectrum of investors. For example, treasury bills are only available to new investments for sums in excess of £500,000, and are out of reach of most private investors.

Bond funds also provide greater liquidity to investors, as they retain an amount of cash within the fund to facilitate any redemption requests.

Using a broad spread of underlying securities can also help to diversify risk away from the investor, and so in this way the risk potential can vary between funds and is dependent on the type and number of securities held.

The performance of bond funds can be compared with sector indices and averages, and against the underlying performance of the individual securities themselves.

Factors to consider when selecting a suitable bond or bond fund for inclusion within a portfolio include the:

- investor's preferences for income or growth
- length of time they are prepared to keep their money invested
- level of access required
- amount of risk that they are prepared to take
- tax consequences on sale.

A number of bond strategies can be employed to deliver income or capital returns to investors, which include duration positioning, yield curve positioning, **asset allocation** and security selection. Qualitative and quantitative market analysis can be used to provide a framework for bond investment decision-making. The investment grade of the debt can be used to determine the risk of capital loss to the investor, while providing opportunities to deliver increased returns over traditional gilts.

2.8.2 Advantages and Disadvantages of Investing in Bonds

Advantages of Bonds

- Bonds pay higher interest rates than savings accounts.
- Bonds usually offer a relatively safe return of principal.
- Bonds often have less volatility (price fluctuations) than stocks, especially short-term bonds.
- Bonds offer regular income.
- Bonds need less careful attention in management than other investments.

Disadvantages of Bonds

- Conventional bonds offer no hedge against inflation, because inflation causes interest rates to rise, which then causes bond prices to fall.
- Even though they are generally less volatile than stocks, bond prices can be quite volatile because market interest rates vary after a bond is issued.
- Bonds over the long term have lower returns than stocks.
- Individual bonds do not compound their interest. However, this is possible with bond funds.
- **Diversification** is hard to achieve unless investing in bond funds.
- Depending on economic conditions and demand, a bond can be difficult to sell and can, therefore, be less liquid than equities.

3. Equities

3.1 What are Equities?

Companies raise their initial capital – the money to carry on their activities – in two ways: through share capital and through loan stock (bonds). In this section, we will consider share capital.

One important contrast to keep in mind is that people who hold loan stock are creditors of the company. The company owes them a debt, which they have to repay, but they have no ownership interest in the company.

On the other hand, the people who own shares in a company are its owners. An individual may only have a few shares out of many thousands (or even millions) issued by the company – nevertheless, that individual still owns a small part of the company and has the rights that attach to that ownership. The term 'equities' refers to the ordinary shares of companies. The directors of the company, who are tasked with running the company, have a duty of care to the shareholders, as they are responsible for looking after their capital.

However, this ownership means that shareholders bear more risk, compared with investors in bonds issued by companies.

Bondholders expect to receive a set sum in interest. (The exception, as you should remember, is where the bond pays a variable rate of interest – but even then the interest is determined by a set formula.) In addition, the bondholder normally expects to receive a nominal amount of capital back on maturity; there is generally no additional profit or gain if the company is doing very well. The only real risk is that of the company running into difficulties so serious that it cannot repay its creditors – thankfully, not a very regular occurrence, though it can happen.

Shareholders, however, generally have a much greater exposure to the financial fortunes of the company they have invested in. If the company does well, they may receive a rising income stream, and the value of their shares can also increase substantially (giving them capital growth); but if a company performs poorly it may, as we shall see, pay falling dividends – or no dividend at all. Its share price may also fall, potentially becoming worthless if the company gets into real trouble.

We will examine this concept in more depth as we progress through the chapter; for now, it is enough to remember that shares are generally characterised by the relative insecurity of both income and capital over the short term (some types more so than others), but they offer a much higher probability of producing real growth over time than, for example, cash and bonds.

There are different types of share in a company, with different rights and investment risks attached to them. We will look at these next.

3.2 The Different Types of Share

Learning Objective

1.3.1 Understand the characteristics and differences between the main types of shareholder equity: ordinary; redeemable; non-voting; preference; convertible preference

3.2.1 Ordinary Shares

As we have noted, ordinary shares are sometimes also called equities, because the people who own them are entitled to the equity in the company which has issued them.

> **Shareholders' funds** is a balance sheet value of the shareholders' interest (or equity stake) in a company. More generally, the shareholders' funds also equals, and represents, all the company's assets (both fixed and current assets) less all the liabilities.
>
> Items within the shareholders' funds are: share capital; reserves; and retained profits. More specifically, the share capital is an accounting number that reveals the issue of ordinary and preference shares in the company. The monetary values of these shares are calculated by taking the par (face values) of the individual shares and multiplying by the number of shares issued to shareholders.

From this it should be apparent that someone holding shares in a company has a stake in that company – they are its joint owner, along with all the other shareholders.

An ordinary shareholder can buy their holding in one of two main ways:

- By buying them as new shares, when the company first issues them (an **initial public offering (IPO)**). A company does this in order to raise money to invest in its business (for example, to buy new premises, carry out new research or expand into new markets). This is called the primary market in shares.
- By buying existing shares which are being traded on the stock market. The shares pass from buyer to seller, and the company does not itself receive any new funds from this activity. This is called dealing in the secondary market.

A company's ordinary share capital is an important part of the way in which it funds its activities – probably the most important part, in fact. It represents the owners' stake in the company and is generally pretty permanent in nature – it will not get repaid (in the way that loan stock will, on its maturity or redemption date) – unless and until the company is wound up, or some other fairly major event takes place.

People who hold shares do so in the hope that the company will do well, and that they will earn a return from them over and above what they originally paid for them. This might be in one of the following forms:

- **Capital growth**, in that if the company does well the price of its shares should go up. The investor hopes they can, eventually, sell the shares for more than they paid for them.
- **Income**, by way of dividends. Many types of company distribute much of the profits they make in any year to their investors (shareholders) by paying a dividend to them. In fact, companies generally pay dividends twice a year – an 'interim dividend' part-way through, and a 'final dividend' once final results are announced.

People who hold ordinary shares also generally have voting rights. These give them a vote over certain issues affecting how the company is run – for example, on things like the appointment of the company's directors and auditors. This does not mean that the ordinary shareholders exercise direct control over the company's day-to-day affairs. (This job is the responsibility of the directors of the company.) The shareholders do, however, have an indirect influence on a company's management – for example, if they are unhappy with the company's performance, they may not support the directors' pay awards, when the time comes to vote on them.

Investing in shares involves risk – both in terms of whether the investor's shares will fall in price, and in terms of whether the company will make enough profits to pay steady, and rising, dividends.

If the company does not do well – or indeed if the stock market as a whole is performing badly – share prices may fall. When this is so, an investor who has to sell their shares at that point may make a loss. Thus, shares are really only appropriate investments for people who can stand the risk of some loss – and who are able to tie their money up for a reasonable period (usually regarded as being five years or more).

If a company is wound up – put into liquidation, with all its assets being sold to pay off its liabilities (debts) – the ordinary shareholders are the last people in line for any pay-out. Thus, there is the possibility there may not be enough money left to give them a pay-out at all: all the money might be spent on paying off the company's creditors (including, of course, its bondholders).

So, just to reiterate, ordinary shareholders suffer from a higher degree of risk than bondholders, in that:

- they rank last for any surplus remaining after liquidation of the company and
- while a share entitles the owner to share equally in any disbursements of profits made by the company – dividends – the company is under no legal obligation to make any such distributions, and, if it does not make decent profits, there may be nothing to distribute anyway.

Their reward for taking on this level of risk is that if the company does very well, they may make handsome capital gains – with (theoretically at least) no cap on how high these could be; and if profits remain strong, they should receive stable and rising dividends.

Companies can issue ordinary shares of different classes, or types. The difference between classes usually relates to the rights their shareholders have compared with one another, and means that each class may appeal to a different type of investor (as they may help them satisfy different investment objectives).

Usually, these distinctions are determined by the voting or dividend rights attached to the share. Holders of 'straight' ordinary shares will have full voting rights, and will be entitled to any dividends declared and paid by the company. A few examples of others are set out below.

Redeemable Shares

A public listed company or even a private company can create a variety of ordinary shares that confer different voting rights on the shareholders. These forms of shares give the company directors more flexibility to make decisions about managing the long-term growth of the firm.

Usually there are two ways that a company can repurchase its shares: buy them back from the market, or retire shares by redeeming shares of a certain class.

Along with ordinary shares, redeemable shares are issued by a company, with an agreement to buy back these issues from the shareholders after a certain date or at some specified future date. These shares cannot be used as a single financing method, and must form part of a package of ordinary shares containing non-redeemables.

Often a company can only issue redeemable shares if its articles of association provide for it. Also, all the details of the redemption, including the date of redemption and the price to be paid for the shares at that date, will be contained in the articles.

The exact nature of such issues is determined by the directors and laid out in the shares' terms of issue. The shares can be redeemed at the directors' discretion from distributable profits or from the issue of new shares to the public. Redeemed shares are retired and reduce the share capital of the firm.

Dual-Class Shares

Redeemable shares should not be confused with dual-class shares. Companies (often newly listed as IPOs) sometimes create another class of common stock that has different voting rights and entitlement to dividends.

Deferred Dividend Shares

Holders of these shares have full voting rights, and rank equally with the other ordinary shareholders if the company is liquidated. However, the payment of dividends to them is deferred until some specified date. Again, these usually trade at a lower price than the 'ordinary' ordinaries; they may also, during the deferral period, suit investors who are more interested in capital growth than income (perhaps because they are higher-rate income tax payers, or because they already have enough income from other sources).

Deferred Ordinary Shares

These are also sometimes called founder shares. Holders of them usually receive no dividend until that paid to the ordinary shareholders has hit some minimum level.

3.2.2 Preference Shares

Preference shares give their holders superior rights and security, over and above those of ordinary shareholders.

The price that holders pay for this additional safety, however, is that the returns a holder can earn are generally limited – whereas in theory, if a company does spectacularly well, there is no limit to the returns the ordinary shareholders might receive.

These additional rights relate mainly to the:

- payment of dividends
- repayment of capital if the company should be wound up (ie, go into liquidation).

Since preference shares are not, technically, equity capital (ie, their holders do not participate fully in the risks of the business), they are not referred to as equities.

The main features of preference shares are as follows (you may wish to compare them with the features of ordinary shares and, where possible, with those of bonds issued by companies:):

- The dividends on preference shares are generally fixed, and are expressed as a percentage of the nominal value of the shares.
- Preference shareholders get priority in the payment of their dividends over the ordinary shareholders. That is, the ordinary shareholders will not get their dividend paid at all unless and until the preference shareholders have received their dividends. If there is not enough profit to go round, the ordinary shareholders may go short.
- Preference shares may be expressed as being cumulative (see below).
- As we have already noted, preference shareholders usually also take priority when the company goes into liquidation. However, all they receive will be the nominal value of their shares (not the market value) and, if there is any surplus to be distributed, it will be distributed to the ordinary shareholders.

The exact rights that a preference share carries will vary from case to case; potential investors should ensure that they have investigated the precise terms and conditions before investing; their stockbroker can usually help them do this.

There are also various different types of preference share (just as there were with ordinary shares), and the type may determine what rights the shareholder has. The main types of preference share are as follows:

- **Cumulative** – if the company has not made enough profit to pay the preference shareholders' dividends in one year, then the unpaid dividend is accumulated and will be paid when the company does have sufficient profits. This may mean the ordinary shareholders have to wait for some time before they receive their dividend – ie, until any arrears on the preference dividends have been 'caught up'.
- **Non-cumulative** – if preference shares are non-cumulative, any unpaid dividend is not accumulated. The shareholder has to wait until the next dividend declaration to receive anything. The ordinary shareholders are therefore in a rather better position, since they do not have to wait until the preference shareholder arrears have been caught up.

- **Participating** – participating preference shareholders receive a fixed dividend (as for traditional preference shares), but they also have the right to participate in surplus profits, along with the ordinary shareholders. The extent to which they participate in this way will vary from company to company.
- **Redeemable** – the company has the right to redeem the shares at some point in the future. This may be on a fixed date, or at a time chosen by the company. When a company redeems shares, the shareholder returns them to the company, which pays the shareholder a sum of money for the shares and then cancels them, so that the company's total issued share capital is reduced.
- **Convertible** – the preference shareholders have the right to convert their shares at some point in the future to a specified number of ordinary shares.

Often, preference shares have a combination of these features – so you might see a share with a name like 'XYX plc £1 Cum. Red. Pref. shares'.

Usually, preference shares are taken to be cumulative unless there is something to the contrary in the title (eg, 'non-cum. Pref. shares').

3.3 Private Equity

Learning Objective

1.3.2 Understand the characteristics and differences between the main types of private equity share capital

The private equity market provides capital to invest in unquoted companies, including public companies that are de-listed as part of the transaction. These investments may take the form of a purchase of shares from an existing shareholder (a buy-out if control is acquired) or an investment in new shares providing fresh capital to the investee company (development capital). Frequently both types of funding are provided in any given transaction.

The term private equity has no consistently applied definition and is increasingly applied to any investor that is not quoted on a recognised financial market. Hedge funds, value funds and active funds and similar institutions have some similarities to private equity, but there are clear organisational and strategic differences that set them apart.

It is increasingly common to see private equity funds investing alongside other types of organisation and combining the industry knowledge of a trade bidder with the transactional and transformational skills of a private equity fund. The private equity market has two distinct components: venture capital, targeted at new and early stage companies, and development capital and buy-outs, targeted at mature businesses.

The most common investment strategies in private equity are **leveraged buyouts (LBOs)**, venture capital, growth capital, distressed investments and mezzanine capital.

3.3.1 Leveraged Buyouts (LBOs)

Leveraged buyouts involve a financial sponsor agreeing to an acquisition without itself committing all the capital required for the acquisition. To do this, the financial sponsor will raise acquisition debt which ultimately looks to the cash flows of the acquisition target to make interest and principal payments. Acquisition debt in an LBO is often non-recourse to the financial sponsor and has no claim on other investment managed by the financial sponsor.

Therefore, an LBO transaction's financial structure is particularly attractive to a fund's limited partners, allowing them the benefits of leverage but greatly limiting the degree of recourse of that leverage. This kind of financing structure leverage benefits an LBO's financial sponsor in two ways: the investor itself only needs to provide a fraction of the capital for the acquisition, and the returns to the investor will be enhanced (as long as the return on assets exceeds the cost of the debt).

3.3.2 Venture Capital

Venture capital is a broad subcategory of private equity that refers to equity investments made, typically in less mature companies, for the launch, early development or expansion of a business. Venture investment is most often found in the application of new technology, new marketing concepts and new products that have yet to be proven.

Venture capital is often subdivided by the stage of development of the company, ranging from early stage capital used for the launch of start-up companies, to late stage and growth capital that is often used to fund expansion of existing business (see section 3.3.3).

Entrepreneurs often develop products and ideas that require substantial capital during the formative stages of their companies' life cycles. Many entrepreneurs do not have sufficient funds to finance projects themselves, and they must therefore seek outside financing. The venture capitalist's need to deliver high returns to compensate for the risk of these investments makes venture funding an expensive capital source for companies. Venture capital is most suitable for businesses with large up-front capital requirements which cannot be financed by cheaper alternatives such as debt. Although venture capital is often most closely associated with fast-growing technology and biotechnology fields, it has also been used for other more traditional businesses.

3.3.3 Growth Capital

Growth capital refers to equity investments, most often minority investments, in relatively mature companies that are looking for capital to expand or restructure operations, enter new markets or finance a major acquisition without a change of control of the business. Companies that seek growth capital will often do so in order to finance a transformational event in their life cycle.

These companies are likely to be more mature than venture-capital-funded companies, able to generate revenue and operating profits, but unable to generate sufficient cash to fund major expansions, acquisitions or other investments. The primary owner of the company may not be willing to take the financial risk alone. By selling part of the company to private equity, the owner can take out some value and share the risk of growth with partners.

3.3.4 Distressed Investments

Distressed, or special situations, is a broad category referring to investments in the equity or debt securities of financially stressed companies.

3.3.5 Mezzanine Capital

Mezzanine capital refers to subordinated debt or preferred equity securities that often represent the most junior portion of a company's capital structure that is senior to the company's common equity. This form of financing is often used by private equity investors to reduce the amount of equity capital required to finance a leveraged buyout or major expansion. Mezzanine capital, which is often used by smaller companies that are unable to access the high-yield market, allows such companies to borrow additional capital beyond the levels that traditional lenders are willing to provide through bank loans. In compensation for the increased risk, mezzanine debt holders require a higher return for their investment than secured or other more senior lenders.

3.3.6 Bridge Financing

Bridge financing is an interim financing option used by companies and other entities to solidify their short-term position until a long-term financing option can be arranged. Bridge financing normally comes from an investment bank or venture capital firm in the form of a loan or equity investment.

3.4 Investment Risk and Shares

Learning Objective

1.3.3 Analyse the main sources of investment risk and return associated with equities: capital return; dividends; liquidity; credit ratings; corporate actions; company liquidation; market conditions

3.4.1 Characteristics, Risks and Performance

Investors generally hold shares in the hope of generating a return on them. However, the pursuit of these returns is not without its risks. These risks can affect:

- the capital the investor has tied up – in that the share price may fall, or fail to rise in line with inflation or with the performance of other, less risky investments
- their income – in that if the company is not as profitable as they had hoped, the dividends it pays may not keep pace with inflation; indeed they may fall or even not be paid at all. This is called passing a dividend.

The past performance of shares can be assessed through reference to the movement in the price of the actual share, and the amount and frequency of the dividend payment. Always remember that past performance is not an indicator of future performance.

In the following sections we will consider various factors which can affect the riskiness of investment in shares, and their performance – including liquidity, growth, volatility and issuing institutions. These factors can combine to affect the risk attached to shares.

3.4.2 Liquidity

In addition to other risks, investors have to consider whether (regardless of how the company has performed, and whether its shares have risen in value) those shares can actually be traded.

Private companies, whose shares are not listed on a stock exchange, may be very difficult to deal in. Further, there may be conditions in the company's constitutional documents (its memorandum and articles of association) which mean that those wanting to sell their shares must first offer them to their co-shareholders, or restrict their ability to sell at an acceptable price. This is in addition to the difficulty in actually determining what is a fair price, since there is no market mechanism to set this.

Even shares which are listed may be illiquid and hard to deal in: some listed shares are not actively quoted and may be dealt in very infrequently. It may be difficult for a broker to find a willing buyer/seller, and then only at a price which is unattractive to the investor.

Liquidity risk is rarely an issue, however, for blue chip companies – eg, those in the **FTSE 100**, where there is a deep and liquid market – that is, many potential buyers and sellers, and no difficulty in dealing quickly at the current market price.

For this reason, investors who are considering investing in the shares of private companies, or those which have small issues or are infrequent dealers, should ensure that they can afford to run the risk of being unable to unload their holding promptly, or at what they see as a current fair market price.

3.4.3 Growth

Many investors' objective in buying shares is to secure capital growth, through an appreciation in the share price. Others invest for income, but usually also hope for this to grow too – so that their income keeps pace with inflation.

But investing for growth involves risk. Will the investor's shares rise (or fall) in price and will the company make enough profits to pay steady and rising dividends?

As covered in section 3.2.1, if a company doesn't do well or if the stock market as a whole is performing badly, share prices may fall and an investor who has to sell their shares at that point may make a loss. Thus, shares are really only appropriate investments for people who can stand the risk of some loss and who are able to tie their money up for a reasonable period (usually regarded as being five years or more).

If a company is wound up, the ordinary shareholders are the last people in line for any pay-out and so there might not be enough money left to give them a pay-out at all.

Ordinary shareholders therefore suffer from a higher degree of risk, in that:

- they rank last for any surplus remaining after liquidation of the company, and
- while a share entitles the owner to share equally in any disbursements of profits made by the company – dividends – the company is under no legal obligation to make any such distributions and if it doesn't make decent profits there may be nothing to distribute anyway.

Their reward for taking on this level of risk is that if the company does very well, they may make handsome capital gains with theoretically at least no cap on how high these could be. If profits remain strong, they should receive stable and rising dividends.

3.4.4 Volatility

Volatility is the term used to describe the degree to which an investment is prone to swings in pricing. Even an investment which appreciates dramatically in price can carry unacceptable levels of volatility, if the investor wants to hold something which performs steadily and does not give them sleepless nights. In recent years, market researchers have noted that there is a stylised aspect to volatility behaviour where dramatic falls in security prices tend to coincide with increases in market volatility. On the other hand, a rising trend in prices tends to coincide with a fall in volatility. Further, they note that volatility clustering can occur over different time periods where volatility remains 'sticky' – ie, contained in a tight range.

It is possible to measure the (historic) volatility of a given share, by looking at the price swings it has undergone in the past. This can then be compared with the returns the share has also historically provided, and these can be looked at against the risk and return of other investments – for example, against the returns available on investments regarded as virtually risk-free. Professional investment managers do this to assess whether the additional returns, which they believe an investment may offer, are worth the additional volatility (risk) to their investors: shares that are volatile are regarded as higher risk because their performance can change, quickly and in either direction, in a short period of time.

Statistically speaking, the key volatility measure includes standard deviation – a statistical measurement of a share's volatility (ie, of that share's tendency to rise or fall in value in a short period of time). The standard deviation of a share measures the average return made on it over a period of time by showing the degree to which its price fluctuates in relation to its mean return.

If share A had given a consistent four-year return of 3%, for example, it would have a mean, or average, of 3%. The standard deviation for share A would then be zero – because its return in any given year had not differed from its four-year mean of 3%.

On the other hand, if share B had, in each of the last four years, returned -5%, 17%, 2% and 30%, it would have a mean return of 11% – on the face of it, more rewarding than share A. It would also have shown a high standard deviation, however, because each year its return differed from the mean return. This share is therefore more risky because the returns fluctuate more widely within the four-year period.

Standard deviation is only one possible way of measuring the volatility of a share – and a share with a relatively stable past performance is not necessarily guaranteed to continue in this way. Unforeseen market factors can influence volatility, and a share that this year has a standard deviation close or equal to zero may behave differently next year.

Investors can compare the returns they are receiving against the volatility of the shares they hold. Of two shares with similar returns, the one with the lower standard deviation will have a better reward-to-risk ratio.

3.4.5 Issuing Institutions

Shares are issued by companies and their performance is linked to the fortunes of those companies. Different companies are subject to different business risks determined by, among other things:

- **The nature of the industry they are involved in** – for example, some companies are established to operate in tried-and-tested fields, and their business model is well established. Others are involved in new areas, such as research and development, where much of their activity is speculative and could result in excellent profits – or in total loss.
- **The cyclicality of that industry** – some companies are involved in providing goods and services which people only want at certain stages of the economic cycle; others, in goods which people want more of in a downturn; and still others in things that people need no matter what the state of the economy.
- **The competence of the management** – no matter how good a company's business model or products, its prospects cannot be good if it is being run by inexperienced or lax management.
- **The financial soundness of the company** – a company which is over-geared can suffer disproportionately if interest rates rise.

3.4.6 Market Conditions

It is not only factors relating to the company itself that can affect the price of its shares; factors affecting the market as a whole will also impact, since an individual share is unlikely to buck the trend (though it may move by a greater or lesser degree relative to the rest of the market). Thus, when conditions are such that the market as a whole is rising strongly, the share prices of even poorly performing companies are likely to benefit to some degree. As one commentator has noted, *'even turkeys can fly in a hurricane'*. Conversely, when the market falls steeply even sound blue chip companies will suffer with it. Factors affecting the market as a whole include:

- The performance of other companies – especially, but not only, those in related or similar industries.
- Political events, especially if a change in government policy will affect conditions for the economy and business.
- Economic news – interest rates, inflation, exchange rates and unemployment are all relevant to sentiment about the market as a whole.
- Price movements on other world stock markets.
- Factors affecting how much investors have in the way of investable funds (eg, changes in interest rates or tax).
- Buying and selling activity on the part of large institutions. For example, one or two large investors moving their asset allocations away from equities and into cash or bonds can have a noticeable impact on the price of the market as a whole.

3.5 Corporate Actions

Learning Objective

1.3.3 Analyse the main sources of investment risk and return associated with equities: capital return; dividends; liquidity; credit ratings; corporate actions; company liquidation; market conditions; activist shareholder

3.5.1 The Impact of Corporate Actions

Corporate actions is the collective term for a range of actions a company can take which affect the holdings, benefits or rights of its shareholders. Many corporate actions have a direct impact on the number and/or value of shares in issue. We will take a look at some of the more common corporate actions here, being capitalisation issues, share splits and rights issues. Dividend payments are also technically corporate actions, but we will look at the impact of these separately later in this chapter.

3.5.2 Capitalisation Issues (also described as Bonus Issues or Scrip Issues)

Sometimes, companies which have their shares listed on the stock exchange want to increase the number of shares in issue without raising new money; one way they can they do this is by issuing new shares and allocating them to existing holders.

Companies do this in part because it may make their balance sheet simpler and cleaner, and in part because having more shares in issue can improve their marketability. We will examine both those reasons in a bit more depth in a moment: first, let's consider what actually happens in practice.

If company ABC plc has a capitalisation issue, the number of its shares in issue will increase – but, as we have said, no new capital will be raised. The new shares are allocated to existing shareholders, on a pro rata basis.

> Pro rata – a Latin term meaning 'in proportion'. Thus shareholders will be allocated new shares in proportion to their previous holdings.

For example, with a 1-for-4 capitalisation issue, the shareholder will be given one new share for every four previously held.

Capitalisation issues have an effect on a company's accounts. Some of the company's reserves (eg, its share premium account, reserves from the revaluation of assets, and retained profits which have not been distributed to shareholders) are converted into share capital, thereby increasing the number of shares in issue. The effect can be to simplify the company's balance sheet.

A before and after example shows what the effect of the 1-for-4 issue we discussed above could be:

	Before cap issue	After cap issue
	£	£
Ordinary shares	200,000	250,000
Share premium reserve account	60,000	10,000
Reserves	140,000	140,000
Net worth (net assets)	400,000	400,000
Number of ordinary shares	400,000 x 50p	500,000 x 50p

The total balance sheet is neither stronger, nor weaker, than it was before, because the total net worth (that is, the net assets) is still exactly the same.

> **Net assets** – the total of a company's assets (everything it owns), less the total of its liabilities (everything it owes).

All that has happened is that there has been a change in the way the shareholders' funds are shown.

The price of the shares in the market after the capitalisation issue (the ex-cap price) will, all things being equal, fall in direct proportion to the increase in share capital. So, in our example, if the company's shares were priced at 250p each before the 1-for-4 **bonus issue**, you could expect to see them fall to around 200p.

400,000 shares x 250p are worth	£1,000,000
100,000 shares are issued free	nil
Thus 500,000 shares are now worth	£1,000,000 + 0 = £1,000,000 or 200p per share

However, certain market factors might also affect the ex-cap price of the shares:

- the lower price per share might make the shares more marketable, since it is easier to deal in them
- capitalisation issues are normally seen as a sign that a company is successful, since it indicates that there are plenty of reserves (such as undistributed profits) to reallocate.

These factors may combine to encourage more investors to want to buy the shares, so the price may rise a little above the expected value.

When a capitalisation issue has been made, the existing shareholders will each receive a renounceable certificate, which shows the number of shares to which they are entitled. If a shareholder wants to sell any of them, all they have to do is sign the reverse. There is no need to also complete a share transfer form (as there normally would be).

3.5.3 Share Splits (also known as Stock Splits)

Share splits occur when a company reduces the nominal (par) value per share of its issued share capital, without altering the value of its total nominal share capital. (Contrast this with what we have seen with capitalisation issues in section 3.5.2.)

The effect of a share split on the market price may, in theory, be the same as for a capitalisation issue. Increased marketability may again cause the share price to settle above the theoretical price, however.

3.5.4 Rights Issues

Very often, a company will need to raise more capital once it is already up and running. It might want to do this in order to:

- pay off existing borrowings, especially if they are at interest rates which look high in comparison with current market rates
- fund expansion
- acquire funding to make new acquisitions (ie, take over other companies).

A company might raise this money by borrowing from the bank, or issuing a bond – but this could be expensive if interest rates are high or the company already has heavy borrowings.

An alternative is for it to ask its existing shareholders to invest more money in the company, by participating in a rights issue. In other words, the shareholders are asked to subscribe for (and pay for) a new tranche of shares.

The term 'rights issue' is used because the existing shareholders have a statutory (ie, legal) right to subscribe for these new shares if they choose to. This protects them from having their interest in the company diluted by other, new shareholders. They do not, however, have to take up these rights if they do not want to.

The main features of a rights issue include:

- New shares carry the same rights – to dividends, votes, etc – as the old shares already in issue. That is, they are described as ranking *pari passu* with the old shares.
- The price to be paid for the new shares (the subscription price) will be below the current market value of the old shares.
- The number of new shares on offer to existing shareholders will depend on the terms of the issue and how much money the company is trying to raise; it is expressed as 'x' number of new shares, for every 'y' number currently held – eg, a 1-for-4 rights issue.

Companies will often arrange to have their rights issue underwritten by an appropriate financial institution, so as to ensure that the issue is successful.

Asset Classes

> **Underwriting** – in the context of a rights issue, a process whereby a specialist financial service organisation (usually a merchant bank, stockbroking house or similar) promises to take up any shares which the existing shareholders do not choose to take up themselves.
>
> The issuing company is thus assured that if the issue is badly received (perhaps because of unexpected and unfavourable conditions in the market) it has not gone to all the expense of arranging the issue only for it to fail to raise any new money. For a fee, the underwriting house undertakes to take up the unwanted new shares at a set price, and it will then hold these shares in its own name. It will try to sell them in the market, preferably for a profit, when conditions improve. The underwriting fee is due to it whether or not the issue is successful; it is the price the issuing company pays for securing a guarantee that the issue cannot fail.
>
> You could think of this as an insurance policy – you pay premiums whether or not you make a claim, in return for the comfort you get that you are covered.

We can calculate the expected market price of the company's old and new shares, after the rights issue; this is known as the theoretical ex-rights price, and it represents the price at which we would expect both old and new shares to start trading at, once the rights issue has been completed and the new shares are fully paid – ie, the investors have paid for the ones they want to take up. The theoretical ex-rights price is calculated as in the following example.

Example

An investor holds 40 shares in ABC ltd, at a current market price of £4.50 each. Thus the total value of their holding is £180.00.

There is a rights issue at £3 on a 1:2 basis (1-for-2).

Thus, the investor can expect rights to 20 new shares to be allocated.

After taking up the rights – 20 new ones at £3 each – the investor now owns 60 shares, total cost value £240.00. This is calculated as follows:

	£180.00	cost of original shares
plus	£60.00	cost of new shares
=	£240.00	

£240.00 divided by the number of shares the investor now owns (60) is £4.

£4 per share is therefore the new level at which all the shares in issue will now trade (other things being equal) – that is, it is the theoretical ex-rights price (TERP).

This also tells us that we can expect:

- the price of the old shares to fall, from £4.50 each, to £4
- the price of the new shares to rise when they start trading, from the £3 they will cost to £4.

The investor will receive a provisional letter of allotment detailing the extra shares they are entitled to receive in accordance with the terms of the rights issue. The letter will advise the investor of the deadline for making a decision; this is usually two or three weeks after it is issued. It will also set out the timetable of events (for example, when any payment will have to be made by).

The investor must then consider what to do – ie, whether to:

- take up the allotment in full
- sell the rights
- split the allotment so that part can be sold to raise money to take up the balance or
- let the rights lapse.

Many investors take professional advice before deciding on what action to take (for example, from their stockbroker). The types of thing they will take into account are:

- the terms of the rights issue
- what the company plans to do with the money – ie, the reason for the issue, and what market sentiment is towards it
- how the company has been performing to date
- how the share price has been performing and what effect the rights issue is expected to have on it in the near term.

We can contrast the effects of a bonus and a rights issue as follows:

Bonus issues:
- raise no new money for the company
- increase the number of shares in issue
- result in a lower share price, which may also make the shares more marketable.

Rights issues:
- raise new money for the company
- increase the number of shares in issue, providing that the issue is successful or is underwritten
- are made at a price below the current market price of the company's shares
- may be used to finance specific activities such as expansion, financing the acquisition of another company (a takeover), or paying off existing debt.

3.5.5 Liquidation

When a company ceases trading it is generally wound up – put into liquidation, and then ultimately dissolved. Part of this process involves turning its assets into cash, so that its debts can be paid off and the surplus paid out to the owners (the shareholders). In some, rare, cases, the shareholders are given assets instead of cash.

Depending on the reasons for the winding-up, there may be enough money to go around – or there may not. If there is not enough money to repay the company's creditors, it is referred to as being insolvent.

On liquidation and winding-up, there is a strict order of priority as to how the assets are distributed. Those first in the order of priority are clearly much more likely to get a full payout. There may well be insufficient money to pay those lower down the list.

Certain creditors take precedence over investors (for example, the liquidator's fees, HMRC). Looking purely at the order in which investors in a company are repaid, the order is as follows:

- secured bondholders and debenture holders stand at the head of the queue, followed by:
- the unsecured bondholders
- the preference shareholders
- the ordinary shareholders.

Within these broad categories, there can be some further subdivisions. For example, there can be different levels of seniority of debt, which determines which of a company's several issues takes precedence, in the event that there is not enough to repay all of the issues.

An announcement that a company is going into liquidation will invariably have some effect on its share price; it is, after all, as major an event as the company can undergo. The market's reaction will depend on whether the company is:

- **solvent** (can pay its debts, and will presumably have some money left over for the shareholders), or
- **insolvent** (unable to pay its debts)

and whether the liquidation is:

- **voluntary** – because the company has carried out the activity it was set up for and is now ready to pay out the proceeds to its owners, or
- **involuntary** – perhaps because the company is insolvent, and its creditors have petitioned the court for it to be wound up.

In cases where a company is insolvent and an order is made for its winding-up, its shares – if they are listed – are likely to have been suspended by the market on which they trade; so investors may find they are 'locked in' to their holdings, and cannot sell even if they wanted to.

3.5.6 Activist Shareholders

An activist shareholder is someone who uses an equity stake in a corporation to put pressure on its management to achieve specific goals, which may or may not be financial, eg, increased value for the shareholder through restructuring or cost savings. Shareholder activism may take the form of shareholder resolutions, proxy battles, publicity campaigns, litigation and negotiation.

3.6 Listing and Trading of Equities

Learning Objective

1.3.4 Understand the issues involved in dealing for clients in equity markets: regulated and designated investment exchanges; multilateral trading platforms; dark pools; organised trading facilities; OTC trading and alternative trading platforms; access to markets; principal and agency trading; listed and unlisted securities; quoted and unquoted securities; admission to trading

3.6.1 Listing of Shares

Companies may seek to list their shares for one of several reasons – for example:

- In order to raise capital for further growth.
- In order to put an objective value on the business.
- To create a market in the company's shares, or increase liquidity in them – so as to give existing shareholders the opportunity to realise the value of their shareholdings (an exit route).
- To allow the company to acquire other companies – both as a result of greater access to the necessary capital to fund the takeover, and being able to issue shares with a market value as a means of funding the acquisition.
- To enhance the company's credibility, which can improve its business prospects.
- To enable the company to provide for employee participation in its ownership, increasing their long-term commitment to the business and improving the recruitment and retention of good staff.
- To improve efficiency. This happens because **listing** requires high levels of disclosure and transparency over the company's affairs, which are likely to lead to improved internal controls and management structure – and, usually, greater operating efficiency for the business as a result.

The term 'listed' means that a company's shares have met a range of criteria which allow them to be traded on a particular stock market. The body which sets these criteria is known as the Listing Authority. The UK's listing authority for the LSE is the FCA.

Not all listed companies' shares are admitted to trading, however; being listed simply means that the company has met the requirements of the listing authority, and its shares are permitted to trade. Where a company's shares are actually available for trading, and prices are available, they are referred to as 'quoted'.

3.6.2 Stock Exchanges

A stock exchange is an organised marketplace for issuing and trading securities by members of that exchange. Each exchange has its own rules and regulations for companies seeking a listing, and continuing obligations for those already listed.

Historically, stock exchanges have operated as national monopolies from a central location, or physical marketplace, mainly catering for the needs of domestic investors and domestic issuers. As mainly mutually owned, or not-for-profit, organisations, many stock exchanges had become bureaucratic, parochial and resistant to change and, ironically, had restricted access to new capital for fund development, investment in new trading and settlement technology and facilitation of expansion into new markets. However, recently, in an attempt to meet the challenges posed by competing trading systems and the globalisation of financial markets in an increasingly price-sensitive and competitive global marketplace, many have sought to become more dynamic and cost-efficient and have striven to create new markets. Indeed, stock exchanges have been taking their lead from the radical changes recently undertaken in the **derivatives** markets. These have included abandoning restrictive mutual ownership by exchange members to become shareholder-owned listed companies, operating as electronic trading networks as the move to electronic trading has gathered pace, and creating new markets through strategic mergers and alliances with other exchanges.

The motivation behind many of these mergers and alliances has been a realisation that financial markets have integrated to such a degree that the shares of most multinational companies, rather than just being listed on their domestic stock exchange, are instead listed on those stock exchanges that best reflect the global distribution and capital requirements of their business. Listing on an overseas stock exchange also enhances the liquidity and marketability of companies' shares and can also build the company's brand. In effect, a global capital market has been created through the globalisation of markets and economies.

3.6.3 The London Stock Exchange (LSE)

The LSE began life in 1773 when traders who regularly met to buy and sell the shares of joint stock companies in Jonathan's Coffee House voted to change the name of the coffee house to that of the London Stock Exchange. The following are some facts and figures available for the LSE:

- There are more than 500 firms worldwide that trade as members of the LSE.
- The LSE claims to be the most international of all stock exchanges, with companies from over 70 countries admitted to trading in its markets.
- The exchange is arguably the largest stock market in Europe.
- In May 2017, the LSE UK orderbook had over 23 million trades with a value of over £120 billion.
- Approximately 2,409 companies are listed on the LSE, with a total market value of $6.43 trillion (USD) (2015).

The LSE is a recognised investment exchange (RIE) and, as such, is responsible for:

- providing a primary and secondary market for equities and fixed interest securities
- supervising its member firms
- regulating the markets it operates
- recording all transactions, or bargains, executed on the exchange
- disseminating price sensitive company information received by its regulatory news service (RNS) and distributed through commercial quote vendors, also known as secondary information providers (SIPs).

The LSE operates both a primary and secondary market for:

- Domestic plcs. These include:
    - companies with a full listing
    - smaller UK plcs admitted to AIM
    - **exchange-traded funds (ETFs)** and other innovative investments on its extraMARK exchange.
- International equities.
- Domestic bonds:
    - gilts
    - local authority fixed-interest securities
    - corporate bonds.

Companies across the world come to the LSE looking to raise money to develop and grow their businesses. The UK markets cater for companies large and small, from start-ups to global brands.

Main Market

The main market is Europe's most prestigious and effective listings venue for established companies, a proven way to raise capital and gain profile.

AIM (Alternative Investment Market)

AIM is the LSE's international market for smaller growing companies. On AIM you will find a wide range of businesses ranging from young, venture capital-backed start-ups to well-established, mature organisations looking to expand. Since its launch in 1995, over 3,500 companies have joined AIM, raising more than £90 billion in the process, both through IPOs and further capital raisings. This capital has helped AIM-quoted companies of all kinds to fund their development and pursue their ambitions. Many companies have made the transition to the exchange's main market following their success and positive experience on AIM.

To join AIM, companies do not need a particular financial track record or trading history. There is also no minimum requirement in terms of size or number of shareholders. This more flexible approach reflects the fact that AIM was designed specifically for smaller growing companies, and has helped AIM to become the leading global growth market.

International Companies

The London Stock Exchange is a global marketplace. Around 350 companies in 70 different countries use a London listing to gain the profile and access to capital they need to grow into truly global companies. Similar markets exist overseas, including **NASDAQ** and the New York Stock Exchange (NYSE) in the US, the Hang Seng in Hong Kong, and the Shenzen in China.

3.6.4 Multilateral Trading Platforms

A multilateral trading facility (MTF) is a trading system that facilitates the exchange of financial instruments between multiple parties. Multilateral trading platforms allow traders to gather and transfer a variety of securities, especially instruments that may not have an official market. These platforms are often electronic systems controlled by approved market operators or larger investment banks. Traders will usually submit orders electronically where a matching software engine is used to pair buyers with sellers.

3.6.5 Dark Pools

This is the name given to a network that allows traders to buy or sell large orders without running the risk that other traders will work out what is going on and increase the price, or decrease it, to take advantage of the order. They have been criticised for their lack of transparency and because the inevitable fragmentation of trading could lead to a less efficient pricing in traditional open stock exchanges. In dark pools, pre-trade prices (the price at which shares are offered for sale) are not visible to anyone, even the participants in them, and the price at which shares change hands is only revealed post trading.

3.6.6 Organised Trading Facilities (OTFs)

MiFID II introduces a new category of trading venue called organised trading facilities (OTFs). An OTF is a multilateral system where multiple third-party buying and selling interests in bonds, structured finance products, emission allowances or derivatives are able to interact in a way that results in a contract. Equities are not permitted to be traded through an OTF.

The introduction of OTFs means that many transactions currently categorised as off-venue will come within a multilateral trading environment. This should increase overall market transparency, reduce the prevalence of opaque market models and products, and increase the quality of price discovery, investor protection and liquidity.

3.6.7 Alternative Trading Systems (ATSs) and Over-the-Counter (OTC)

Alternative trading systems (ATSs) are also known under the Markets in Financial Instruments Directive (MiFID) as multilateral trading facilities (MTFs) and have risen in importance in several financial markets around the world as an alternative to traditional exchanges, or as a complement to voice broking and bilateral over-the-counter (OTC) trading. The UK is host to over 20 ATSs, active in markets for equities, bonds, financial derivatives and commodities. It also hosts a number of firms that are affiliated with overseas-based ATSs. This has allowed market participants to adopt new trading strategies such as posting limit orders or crossing trades.

OTC or off-exchange trading is used to trade financial instruments such as stocks, bonds, commodities or derivatives directly between two parties. This contrasts with exchange trading, which uses facilities constructed for the purpose of trading (ie, exchanges), such as futures exchanges or stock exchanges.

An OTC contract is a bilateral contract in which two parties agree on how a particular trade or agreement is to be settled in the future. It is usually from an investment bank to its clients directly. Forwards and swaps are prime examples of such contracts. It is mostly executed via the computer or the telephone.

3.6.8 Agency and Principal Dealing

When an investor buys a stock from someone who is acting as an agent, it means they do not own the stock that you are buying. Instead, they are buying it from a dealer and then reselling it to the investor.

When the agent buys the stocks, they will pay the dealer's 'mark-up'. However, the agent cannot then pass another mark-up on to the investor. The agent is obliged to get a price for the stock (which is what they have to pay the dealer) and then pass that price on to the investor. However, the agent has to make a living, and they do this by charging a fee for facilitating the transaction.

Buying stocks from someone who is acting as principal means that they have actually purchased the stock themselves and are holding it in their inventory. The principal therefore takes more risk than an agent because, while the principal is holding the stock, they are exposed to any movement in the stock price, and could lose money if the price drops.

The principal does not charge a fee, and instead charges a mark-up. A principal can provide investors with a 'bid' and 'ask' quote. The bid is what they are willing to pay to buy stock from an investor, and the ask is the price they require in order to sell the stock. The difference between the bid and the ask is called the 'spread' or 'mark-up' and represents the profit to the principal.

3.6.9 Unquoted Shares

Shares in some companies, often smaller ones, are not traded on any stock exchange.

Companies might not be quoted (or listed) because they prefer to run their businesses in relative privacy, or because they do not meet the listing requirements, such as minimum market capitalisation; in other words they are too small to join a stock market. The LSE requires companies to have a trading record of three years and sets a minimum market capitalisation.

3.6.10 Admission to Trading

A differentiation is made between the terms listing and admission to trading – the latter takes place without prior listing procedure.

Company	London Stock Exchange Notice
TIDM	
Headline	Admission to Trading – 07/04/2017
Released	08:00 7-Apr-2017
Number	7906J08

RNS Number : 7906J
London Stock Exchange Notice
7 April 2017

> **Notice of Admission to Trading on the London Stock Exchange**
>
> 07/04/2017 08:00
>
> The following securities are admitted to trading on the LSE with effect from the time and date of this notice.
>
> PXP VIETNAM FUND Ltd
>
> 12,000,000   Ordinary Shares of   (B5W0SC0)(KYG7301W1033)
>   USD0.05 each fully paid
>
> If you have any queries relating to the above, please contact Issuer Implementation at the LSE on 020 7797 1614.
>
> This information is provided by RNS, the company
> news service from the London Stock Exchange.

3.7 Dealing in Shares and Share Prices

Learning Objective

1.3.5 Understand how equity securities are traded and settled: liquidity, pricing and fair value; cost of purchase and sale; nominal value; market price; cum- and ex-dividend; transaction costs and charges

3.7.1 Factors Affecting Share Prices

Most investors who buy equity-based products are familiar with warnings such as *'the price of shares can fall as well as rise, and you may get back less than the amount you originally invested'*. Such warnings are required by the regulators, and serve to remind investors that their capital is at risk when they invest in the stock markets.

Memorable stock market crashes, in which share prices fell dramatically and when many investors lost significant proportions of their savings, include the 1987 crash, the worldwide stock market falls that happened in the early part of this century and the more recent financial crisis.

Equity prices have always been volatile – that is, prone to swinging up and down rather than providing steady returns. This is mainly because:

- the value of a share should, all other things being equal, reflect how well a company is doing – and this can vary tremendously, depending on the management's skill, the economic environment, and often a degree of luck
- share prices are driven by supply and demand. If people feel optimistic about a share, or about the stock market or economy as a whole, there will be more buyers than sellers and the price will rise. Conversely, if they are pessimistic, the price will fall.

Even companies which are regarded as stable, well-run and unlikely to suffer badly in an economic downturn (the so-called 'blue chip' stocks) have been known to fall significantly in value – and occasionally to become insolvent. It is this uncertainty that investors have to bear in mind when they are considering buying equities for their long-term growth prospects.

We will next look in detail at one of the main factors that can affect prices.

Supply and Demand

As stated above, the price of shares is driven by supply and demand. In most cases (with the exception of certain collective investment schemes), the number of shares in issue is fixed and the supply of shares must come from people willing to sell their existing holdings (although, as was explained in section 3.5, certain types of corporate actions can also affect supply).

If there are more investors keen to sell their shares than there are new investors looking to buy, the price of the shares will fall; if the converse is true, they will rise.

The appetite of investors to buy or sell a company's shares will depend on a range of factors, including:

- good (or bad) financial results, or indeed expectations of results
- recommendations from stockbrokers to buy/sell a given stock
- rumours that a company may be the subject of a takeover bid or merger
- the skill (or otherwise) of the management team
- the political climate, since government policy can make life harder for some types of company
- the economic climate, including such factors as interest rates, inflation, exchange rates and unemployment
- the price movements on other world stock markets, which can affect global sentiment towards shares
- whether investors have funds available to commit to the markets
- buying and selling activity on the part of large institutions.

3.7.2 Share Dealing

Listed shares and – often – unlisted shares too, are bought and sold through a stockbroker. The broker can deal for the client in one of three ways:

- **Execution-only dealing service** – in this case the stockbroker simply carries out the client's instructions.
- **Advisory or non-discretionary service** – in this case the stockbroker makes recommendations but the client makes the final decision.
- **Discretionary service** – in this case, the stockbroker will have authority to buy and sell without reference to the client. A legal agreement will set out the parameters for the transactions that can be taken on behalf of the client – for example, the amount of risk the client wishes to take or the types of securities they wish to consider.

If the stockbroker is acting on an execution-only basis, this means that the client has agreed that they will not receive advice on their investments. They make their own investment decisions and will give instructions to the broker to buy and sell shares.

The broker placing the deals will generally use either the **Stock Exchange Electronic Trading System (SETS)** or the Stock Exchange Automated Quotation (SEAQ) System.

SETS is the single platform, with an electronic order book, trading constituents of the **FTSE All Share Index**, ETFs and exchange-traded commodities, along with over 180 of the most traded AIM and Irish securities. SETS offers market making in all stocks, including those deemed to be liquid under MiFID. This is an order-driven system, unlike SEAQ which is quote-driven. Investors submit orders to the SETS system via stockbrokers, who are LSE member firms. The information is transmitted electronically, and orders are automatically executed if possible. SETS sends out information (orders, transactions, other messages) via a broadcast public feed.

SETqx (Stock Exchange Electronic Trading Service-quotes and crosses) is a trading service for securities that are less liquid than those on the SETS service.

SEAQ is a non-electronically executable quotation service that allows market makers to quote prices for trading the fixed-interest market and AIM-listed shares not traded on SETS.

The International Order Book (IOB) is a service which enables investors to tap into the world's fastest growing markets through a single electronic order book. It offers cost-effective access to securities via depository receipts from 46 countries, including those in Central and Eastern Europe, Asia and the Middle East and has a similar order of functionality as the SETS. Following a market-wide consultation by the LSE, integrated electronic market making was made available on the IOB from 12 April 2012.

A new International Board trading service is available to trade constituents of the Straits Times Index (STI 30) and the MSCI Singapore Free Index on the LSE. The International Board is the result of a memorandum of understanding which the LSE signed with the Singapore Exchange ltd to allow the largest and most actively traded stocks to be traded by their respective member firms.

The market comprises of market makers and brokers:

- **Market makers** are a type of stock exchange member firm who promise to give buy and sell prices in a given range of securities – so that there is always a market in those securities (hence their name). Market makers are in competition with each other for business, and the broker will choose the best price offered when executing the client's order (the principle of best execution), taking into account a range of factors.
- **Brokers** act as their client's agent, and place deals with the market makers in those securities their clients wish to deal in.

Some firms are allowed to act in dual capacity as market maker and broker, and many large banks do just that.

The settlement system now used for shares in most larger companies is called CREST (Certificateless Registration of Electronic Stock and Share Transfers). The system also allows bondholders to hold assets in electronic (dematerialised) form. UK stocks are held by registrars who are members of CREST and Irish securities and ETFs are also settled directly through CREST members.

International stocks are held as a pool in a local depository where the stocks originate. CREST will then issue a CREST depository interest (CDI) to each holder of the security, which is then transferred into the CREST system like any other UK equity. The CDI is similar to an American depository receipt (ADR) or a global depository receipt (GDR).

The standard market convention is for equity trades to settle on a two-day settlement period (T+2). This means that the proceeds of a sale, or costs of a purchase, and the stock, must change hands within three business days of the deal date. Settlement can be delayed beyond T+3 by agreement between the parties and is commonly seen if private investors sell shares in certificated form – that is, a stock transfer form has to be completed and deposited along with the paper share certificate, which takes much longer, hence the need for a longer time period. Prior to October 2014, the settlement period was T+3, but was adjusted to T+2 in accordance with the Central Securities Depositary Regulation (CSDR), which aims to harmonise securities settlement cycles throughout the EU. Rights issues remained T+1 and the extended settlement time for exchange trades of 20 days also remained unchanged.

3.7.3 Liquidity

Liquidity is the ease and speed with which a holding in a share is turned into cash at the prevailing market price. For the most liquid shares, orders can be quickly executed via SETS at prevailing market prices.

Less liquid shares, or very large deals (outside normal market size) may not be able to be placed so quickly. The broker may only have one or two market makers to choose from. Indeed if the share is unlisted and there is no market maker for it, there may be a considerable delay before a matching buyer can be found.

As we have already learned, the term 'liquidity' refers to the ease with which a company's shares can be turned into cash, ie, sold. Some shares are more liquid than others; those blue chip shares of the very largest companies that make up the FTSE 100 Share Index are the most liquid, as there will generally be a number of market makers willing to set both bid and offer (buying and selling) prices for them.

If shares are less liquid, their prices may be more prone to big swings. They are referred to as being more volatile than other shares.

3.7.4 Costs of Purchase and Sale

The costs of investing in shares can be broken down as follows:

- **Purchase cost** – the purchase cost includes a spread which is the difference between the bid and **offer price** of the share. The spread, from which market makers make their profits, could be 0.5% for a liquid share or 5% or more for a less easily traded share.
- **Broker's commission** – a typical charge will be 1.5% on a deal up to £7,000, with a minimum charge of £25. Execution-only services, including online brokers, are generally cheaper than this, ranging from around £10 per deal upwards.
- **Stamp duty and stamp duty reserve tax (SDRT)** – SDRT of 0.5% is payable on the value of purchases of UK equities settled through CREST, rounded to the nearest penny. Stamp duty of 0.5% is payable on purchases of UK equities not settled through CREST, rounded up to the nearest £5. Stamp duty on stock registered in Ireland is charged at 1.0%.

- **Panel on takeovers and mergers (PTM) levy** – the PTM levy is a flat £1 on either sales or purchases in excess of £10,000.

3.7.5 Nominal Value and Market Price

The number of shares which a company issues is determined by the:

- amount of share capital which is being raised, and
- par or nominal value of the shares.

For example, ABC company may aim to raise £500,000 (to invest in expanding its operations and investing in new premises and machinery). It could do so by issuing:

- 500,000 ordinary shares with a par value of £1 each
- 1,000,000 shares – each with a par value of 50p – to raise the same amount of capital.

The latter option may suit some companies. By making more shares available to potential shareholders, their marketability may be improved.

It is quite possible for companies to sell their shares, when they are initially issued, for more than the stated par value. For example, a company may issue 100,000 ordinary shares of £1 par value, launching them into the market for £1.30. The additional 30p is known as a premium.

> **Premium** – in the context of a share issue, the excess price per share that the company raises, over and above the par value of those shares.

The par, or nominal value of a share, is usually shown in its name. So:

- someone might have a holding of 1,000 £1 ordinary shares in XYZ plc
- but the shares might be trading at £2.30 each on the stock market
- the value of their holding would therefore be £2.30 x 1,000 = £2,300.

We can also talk about the total market capitalisation of a company, by reference to the total number of shares in issue, multiplied by its current share price. If XYZ plc has 1,000,000 shares in issue, then, its total market capitalisation is:

$$1,000,000 \times £2.30 = £2,300,000$$

Nowadays, the regulators in many countries let companies issue shares of no par value (NPV), and you may see this in a share's title: for example, ABC company ordinary shares NPV.

Remember that the price of a company's shares in the market will bear no relation to their par value – and an investor will be more interested in what the market value of their shares is, rather than in what their par value is. The market price of a share need bear no relation to its nominal value; it is determined by supply and demand, based on the various factors – company performance, market sentiment, economic environment – that we have looked at so far.

3.7.6 Cum- and Ex-Dividend Prices

Many UK companies pay dividends twice a year (interims part way through the company's financial year, and then a final dividend when the full-year profits are declared).

Companies which raise money from the public, eg, by issuing their shares on the stock market, are obliged to ensure that the dividends they declare are paid on the due dates. On the declaration date, the company will announce the:

- amount of the dividend
- dividend payment date
- record date.

The record date, is important. To be eligible to receive the dividend, a shareholder must be on the share register, as the registered owner of the shares, as at the record date. The record date usually falls on a Friday.

> **Record date** – this is the cut-off date, selected by the company, to determine which shareholders will receive the imminent dividend payment.

The record date and payment date can, in theory, fall on the same day, but usually the payment date falls sometime after the record date.

Investors who want to buy and sell shares in the run-up to a dividend payment need to be aware not only of the record date, but also of the ex-dividend date.

This date is determined by the stock exchange, and in accordance with guidance issued by the LSE in its dividend procedure timetable, usually falls on the Thursday immediately prior to the record date, giving the company's registrar time to compile an accurate list of eligible shareholders. On this date a company's share price will be quoted with the letters 'xd' after it, to indicate that anyone buying the shares after this point will not be eligible to receive the next dividend.

Because buyers of ex-dividend shares do not qualify for the forthcoming dividend, the opening ex-dividend price falls (by roughly the amount of dividend per share) to reflect this.

A share which is not ex-dividend is described as cum-dividend or cum-div – ie, the buyer buys them with the right to the next dividend to be declared. Shares are assumed to be cum-dividend unless otherwise indicated.

3.8 Equity Indices

Learning Objective

1.3.6 Understand the purpose and construction of the main equity indices, and the considerations needed for less liquid markets

Stock market indices may be classed in many ways. A world or global stock market index typically includes large companies, without regard for where they are domiciled or traded. Two examples are MSCI World and S&P Global 100.

A national index represents the performance of the stock market of a particular nation, and reflects investor sentiment on the state of its economy. The most regularly quoted market indices are national indices composed of the stocks of large companies, listed on a nation's largest stock exchanges, such as the American S&P 500, the Japanese Nikkei 225, and the British FTSE 100. However, it should be noted that, in some cases, such as the FTSE 100, the index may contain a large complement of foreign or multinational companies and, therefore, may not be representative of the national economy. In such cases, it is usual to look at the next level of indices, such as the FTSE 250, as a barometer of 'UK plc'.

The concept may be extended well beyond an exchange. The Dow Jones Total Stock Market Index, as its name implies, represents the stocks of nearly every publicly traded company in the United States, including all US stocks traded on the NYSE (but not ADRs) and most traded on the NASDAQ and American Stock Exchange.

Specialised indices exist that track the performance of specific sectors of the market. The Morgan Stanley Biotech Index, for example, consists of 36 American firms in the biotechnology industry. Other indices may track companies of a certain size, a certain type of management, or even more specialised criteria.

Some indices, such as the S&P 500, have multiple versions. These versions can differ based on how the index components are weighted and on how dividends are accounted for. For example, there are three versions of the S&P 500 Index: price return, which only considers the price of the components; total return, which accounts for dividend reinvestment; and net total return, which accounts for dividend reinvestment after the deduction of a withholding tax.

An index may also be classified according to the method used to determine its price. In a price-weighted index such as the Dow Jones Industrial Average (DJIA), the price of each component stock is the only consideration when determining the value of the index. Thus, price movement of even a single security will heavily influence the value of the index.

In contrast, a market-value weighted or capitalisation-weighted index such as the Hang Seng Index factors in the size of the company. Thus, a relatively small shift in the price of a large company will heavily influence the value of the index.

In a market-share-weighted index, price is weighted relative to the number of shares, rather than their total value.

Traditionally, capitalisation- or share-weighted indices all had a full weighting, ie, all outstanding shares were included. Recently, many of them have changed to a float-adjusted weighting which helps indexing.

A modified market-cap-weighted index is a hybrid between equal weighting and capitalisation weighting. It is similar to a general market cap with one main difference: the largest stocks are capped to a percentage of the weight of the total stock index, and the excess weight will be redistributed equally among the stocks under that cap.

3.9 Measuring the Performance of Shares

Learning Objective

1.3.7 Analyse equity securities and equity funds using the following valuation measures: price earnings (P/E) ratio; earnings per share; dividend yield; dividend cover; gearing; borrowings; net asset and enterprise value; past performance; price-to-cash flow ratios; price-to-book ratio

In this section we will look at some of the key measures that enable investors to compare the performance and value of shares, against each other or against other types of investment.

3.9.1 Earnings Per Share (EPS)

Not all of a company's profits are distributed to its shareholders by way of dividend. Some of them are retained for reinvestment into the business. It is important that this happens, if a company is to grow and remain competitive, and if its share price is to remain strong over the long term.

Investors who are not reliant on their dividend stream to live on may therefore be more interested in a company's overall earnings, instead of just the element it distributes by way of dividend.

Steady growth in a company's earnings should – in theory – ensure that the ordinary shareholders can continue to receive stable and rising dividends in future. So the earnings yield calculation can be a good indicator of one company's comparative strength of earnings against that of another. The formula is as follows:

$$\text{Earnings yield (\%)} = \frac{\text{Earnings per share (gross)}}{\text{Market price of share}} \times 100$$

3.9.2 Price/Earnings (P/E) Ratio and Earnings Per Share (EPS)

The price/earnings ratio (or P/E ratio) of a company is simply the current market price of its shares, divided by the annual earnings per share (EPS):

$$\text{P/E ratio} = \frac{\text{Current market price of share}}{\text{EPS}}$$

Some of the main reasons why the P/E ratio is a useful tool for investors in equities are:

- **Relevance** – it may be more relevant to analyse a share's performance on the basis of its earnings than its dividend record.
- **Comparisons** – P/E ratios can be useful for comparing the shares in different companies, particularly those in similar industries.
- **Risk** – a company's P/E ratio can show how risky the market believes an investment in the company to be:
    - a low P/E ratio may indicate a high perceived level of risk (or poor prospects for profit growth)
    - a high P/E ratio may indicate a relatively low perception of risk, or an expectation of good profits growth.

A company with a P/E ratio which is lower than the average for its sector or industry could, however, have the potential for an upward correction in its price, providing that the market expects its profits to improve in the future (ie, you could regard its shares as 'cheap').

Alternatively, a low P/E ratio could indicate that the company is in difficulties and that prospects for its recovery are seen as uncertain (ie, you could regard its shares as cheap, but for a good reason).

P/E ratios are not without their difficulties as predictors of a company's future share price performance. In part this is because a company's earnings can fluctuate significantly from one year to the next, meaning that reliance on historic figures can be risky. For this reason, P/E ratios can be calculated on a historic basis – or on a projected basis, based on assumptions as to what the company's earnings per share will be in the future.

The EPS is the amount of a company's profits allocated to each outstanding share. It is calculated by dividing the net profit after taxes and preferred dividend by the total number of outstanding shares in the issue.

3.9.3 Dividend Yield

One common comparison is the **dividend yield**. This is the ongoing distribution of profits that investors are receiving from a company. The yield is simply the income earned by the investor on their holding, as a percentage of the prevailing share price.

Gross Dividend Yield

Yields are often calculated on a gross basis (ie, before any tax has been deducted) so that investors can assess them based on whatever their own personal tax rate is.

For UK equities, this is based on the cash dividend paid per share plus any associated tax credit, and the formula is as follows:

$$\text{Gross dividend yield} = \frac{\text{Gross dividend paid in year}}{\text{Current market price of share}} \times 100$$

The gross dividend yield is based on all the dividends paid by the company to the ordinary shareholders in respect of the preceding financial year. It is therefore a historical measurement – ie, it is based on past events which may not, of course, be repeated in the future.

Sometimes, therefore, investors will calculate a prospective yield based on a forecast of what the dividends will be for the current financial year.

When a company declares quarterly or interim dividends, it is usual to continue reporting the dividend yield on the basis of the dividend for the previous year; the dividend is not updated to reflect the current year's part performance to date.

Some Considerations for Investors in Respect of Dividend Yields

Dividend yields on equities generally vary by the type of business the company is in, and the investment risk associated with the company. Companies that are perceived as operating profitably, and with good prospects, usually have lower yields than those in depressed industries or with higher risk factors. This lower return is the price the investor pays for the lower level of risk they are perceived to be taking on.

A company which is not regarded as so secure will tend to have a lower share price. Therefore its dividend yield will be higher as a percentage. This is the investor's reward for the additional risk they are incurring by investing in the company.

A high dividend yield is therefore nearly always an indication of an above-average level of risk.

Investors generally expect their dividends to rise over time, ideally at a rate which exceeds inflation so as to preserve their income in real terms. Of course, if this happens, and healthy dividend growth is seen, share prices will generally also rise, because investors are happy with the company's performance and there is good demand for the shares. However, rising share prices will have an impact on the calculation we looked at above and will, in turn, tend to depress the overall dividend yield of the share – a cyclical effect.

3.9.4 Dividend Cover

Dividend cover is calculated by dividing the total profits attributable to a company's ordinary shareholders by the total amount of dividend actually paid to them.

Profits attributable to ordinary shareholders are the total of profits after tax and preference share dividends have been deducted.

You could think of dividend cover as being a way of showing the number of times that the dividend could theoretically have been paid out to shareholders, from available profits. Thus, shareholders' dividends are safer if there is a high level of dividend cover (there is plenty of money available to pay their dividends). High dividend cover is also a good indication that the company is retaining earnings in the business – which should bode well for the share price in future, too. Dividend cover of 1.5 times or lower is usually considered as low by investors and analysts and could be a cause for concern.

Companies are permitted to (and often do) pay dividends not just from the current year's profits, but also by using previous years' retained profits. This means that a company which has made a loss in the current year may still be able to pay a dividend to its ordinary shareholders. However, when a company pays a dividend which exceeds this year's profits attributable to shareholders, it is described as paying an uncovered dividend.

3.9.5 Gearing

Gearing, also known as financial leverage, is the financial ratio of a company's long-term debt to its equity capital.

A company which has raised a high proportion of its capital through borrowings (as opposed to by issuing shares) is described as being highly geared. Such a company is more vulnerable to business cycle downturns because a company will need to continue to service its debt commitments to its bondholders even when its earnings are depressed. Ideally, a company will not rely too heavily on such sources of funds. This is because:

- A company reliant on borrowings may have problems if its lenders decide not to roll over the debt, and the company cannot easily pay it back.
- The company's business strategies may become distorted, because it has to focus more on the short-term need to generate cash (to make interest payments and repay the capital of the loan) than on longer-term planning.
- If interest rates rise, the company may struggle to find the cash to keep up interest payments – but must do so, even if its profits are poor or non-existent.

The ratio of a company's debt to its equity is known as the gearing ratio. When times are good, highly geared companies may be expected to do better than those of their competitors with little or no borrowings. Their profits will increase, but they are still only committed to the same fixed levels of interest repayments (unless they have issued floating rate debt); thus the surplus profits are available for shareholders. Conversely, however, when times are bad and profits are poor or non-existent, they must still service their debt; and as a consequence will suffer a disproportionately high downturn in profits.

The formula for calculating gearing is:

$$\text{Gearing (\%)} = (\text{Long-term liabilities}/\text{Capital employed}) \times 100$$

Another version of the gearing ratio is the times interest earned ratio. It is calculated as follows:

$$\text{Gearing (\%)} = (\text{Earnings before interest and tax}/\text{Interest payable}) \times 100$$

3.9.6 Net Asset Value (NAV) Per Share

The net asset value (or NAV) of a company is, in essence, everything it owns, less everything it owes – thus:

$$\text{NAV} = \text{assets} - \text{liabilities}$$

We can calculate the NAV per share of a company by calculating the total net asset value of the company and dividing this by the number of shares in issue:

$$\text{NAV per share} = \frac{\text{assets} - \text{liabilities}}{\text{shares in issue}}$$

The importance of the NAV per share of a company depends on the type of business it is in. For those companies whose resources are mainly made up of the people skills they possess (for example, architects' practices, advertising agencies or law firms), most of the value of the business may be tied up in the skills and knowledge their employees possess, and the relationships and ideas they have. There is relatively little in the way of physical or financial assets. For other companies, however, with most of their resources committed to plant, property and equipment, such assets may be more valuable. In this case, an investor who buys a share at 100p may be interested to know that the NAV of the company is 130p, because if the company goes into liquidation there is, in effect, a 30p buffer supporting that share price.

NAV is particularly important for investors in **investment trust** companies, a type of investment company which invests into the shares of other companies.

3.9.7 Enterprise Value

The enterprise value (EV) of a business is a measure of what the market believes a company's ongoing operations are worth and is equivalent to the market capitalisation plus debt, less cash and any cash equivalents. It is not a measure of the company's value, but the value of its business, and is considered a theoretical measure for the cost of takeover.

The EV is calculated as follows:

$$\frac{\text{Market capitalisation} + \text{Debt} + \text{Preferred share capital} + \text{minority interest}}{\text{Less cash} + \text{Cash equivalents}}$$

3.9.8 Past Performance

In assessing whether to invest in a share or not, investors will invariably consider its past performance (despite repeated warnings that past performance may be no guide or guarantee to the future).

However, the past performance of a single share in isolation does not tell the whole story. Investors should consider this in the light of the following factors:

- **The performance of the market as a whole** – for example, by measuring how the share has performed against the performance of the market as a whole. This can be done by looking at the performance of an appropriate benchmark. For example, an appropriate benchmark for blue-chip shares might be the FTSE 100 Index.
- **The share's total return** – that is, not only the capital growth (or loss) that has been obtained, but also the dividends that have been received. This is because a company's share price falls when it declares a dividend in favour of its shareholders, since it is paying away part of its value to those shareholders. Investors should be careful, when comparing one share with another, to consider

the total returns of each; a share that pays out dividends may appear to have performed badly on a purely capital basis, when compared with one that had a policy of paying no dividends to its investors.
- **The volatility of the share** – we have looked at this in section 3.4.4, but in essence it is important to consider not only how well the share has done, but also the bumpiness of the ride the investor has experienced in the process.

3.9.9 Price-to-Cash Flow Ratio (P/CF)

This measure assesses the market's expectations or prospects about a company's financial health. It is similar to a P/E ratio except that this measure utilises the cash flow instead of earnings. Thus, the effects of depreciation and other non-cash items are removed. The ratio is calculated as follows:

$$\text{Price-to-cash flow} = \frac{\text{Share price}}{\text{Operating cash flow per share}}$$

In some cases the free cash flow is used instead of the operating cash flow. Analysts can use this method in the same way as the traditional P/E ratio to determine whether a firm is over-valued or under-valued. The calculated P/CF may be compared to similar companies or peers in a sector (comparables approach). In a relative valuation exercise of this type, the firm's comparables act as a benchmark against which its P/CF is evaluated. A low P/CF ratio is attractive, as it may suggest on further investigation that the price of the firm is low when it is compared to its cash flow. This result may point to an under-valuation of the share. On the other hand, a high P/CF may suggest that a firm is not generating enough cash flow when compared to its peers. Analysts will never place all their bets on just one metric and will use other complementary techniques to investigate the intrinsic value of a share before reaching a final conclusion on its relative valuation.

3.9.10 Price-to-Book Ratio

The price-to-book ratio (p/b) compares the market value of a company's stock to its book value, ie, the value remaining after all assets are liquidated and liabilities settled. The ratio is predominately used when analysing the banking sector.

$$\text{p/b ratio} = \frac{\text{Market price per share}}{\text{Book value per share}}$$

3.10 Selecting Equities and Equity Funds

Learning Objective

1.3.8 Analyse the factors to take into account when selecting equities and equity funds: equity fund strategies – growth, income, market capitalisation, sector, region, customised; growth/dividend prospects; direct versus indirect investment; advantages and disadvantages of investing in equities; cost, turnover, liquidity and ease of trading

To select a suitable equity or equity fund for investment you must first understand the investor's requirements in terms of income or growth, their tolerance and attitude to investment risk, and their need for liquidity and access. Investors may, for example, wish to avoid certain sectors such as utilities or transport, while others may express a wish to invest in a socially responsible or ethical way.

The past performance of the equity or fund and the various performance measurement methods discussed earlier (P/E ratio, dividend cover) should be used to help assess the performance of the equity or fund relative to its peers.

In the case of an equity fund, the experience of the manager and their team should be taken into account. The fund strategy should be assessed to ensure that it matches the investor's needs (income or capital growth) using an active or passive management style.

3.10.1 Growth Investing

Growth investing is a relatively aggressive investment style. At its most aggressive, it simply focuses on those companies whose share price has been on a rising trend and continues to gather momentum as an ever-increasing number of investors jump on the bandwagon. This is referred to as momentum investing.

Growth at a reasonable price (GARP) investing is a less aggressive growth investment style where attention is centred on those companies that are perceived to offer above-average earnings growth potential that has yet to be fully factored into the share price.

True growth stocks, however, are those that are able to differentiate their product or service from their industry peers so as to command a competitive advantage. This results in an ability to produce high-quality and above-average earnings growth, as these earnings can be insulated from the business cycle. A growth stock can also be one that has yet to gain market prominence but has the potential to do so: growth managers are always looking out for the next Microsoft.

The key to growth investing is to forecast future earnings growth rigorously and to avoid those companies susceptible to issuing profits warnings. A growth stock trading on a high P/E ratio will be savagely marked down by the market if it fails to meet earnings expectations.

3.10.2 Income Investing

Income investing aims to identify companies that provide a steady stream of income.

Income investing may focus on mature companies that have reached a certain size and are no longer able to sustain high levels of growth. Instead of retaining earnings to invest for future growth, mature firms tend to pay out retained earnings, as dividends, as a way to provide a return to their shareholders. High dividend levels are prominent in certain industries, such as utility companies.

The driving principle behind this strategy is to identify good companies with sustainable high dividend yields to receive a steady and predictable stream of income over the long term. Because high yields are only worth something if they are sustainable, income investors will also analyse the fundamentals of a company to ensure that the business model of the company can sustain a rising dividend policy.

3.10.3 Value Investing

In contrast to growth investing, value investing seeks to identify those established companies, usually cyclical in nature, that have been ignored by the market but look set for recovery. The value investor seeks to buy stocks in distressed conditions in the hope that their price will return to reflect their intrinsic value, or net worth.

A focus on recovery potential, rather than earnings growth, differentiates value investing from growth investing, as does a belief that individual securities eventually revert to a fundamental or intrinsic value. This is known as reversion to the mean. In contrast to growth stocks, true value stocks also offer the investor a considerable safety margin against the share price falling further, because of their characteristically high dividend yield and relatively stable earnings.

3.10.4 Geographic and Regional Spread

A well-diversified portfolio should include exposure to different stock markets around the world. A global asset allocation will help give weighting to markets that may generate the returns that the investor is seeking, and also provide the right balance of risk and reward to meet their objectives.

3.10.5 Market Sectors

As well as looking at the geographical spread, an adviser or investment manager may also consider specific market sectors that they expect to outperform in a particular economic cycle, eg, banking, oil, pharmaceuticals and telecoms.

3.10.6 Market Capitalisation

Consideration should also be given to the market capitalisation of stocks and further diversity achieved through selecting between large-cap, mid-cap and small-cap stocks.

In stock market terminology, a company's value is measured by calculating how much its shares are worth in total. If a company has 1,000 shares in issue and each is worth 100p, for example, the company is capitalised at £1,000. If the share price rises to 150p, the company will be capitalised at £1,500. This is often referred to as a company's market cap. The biggest companies on the LSE are often known as large caps; those in the FTSE 250 can be described as mid-caps and the smallest shares are known as small caps.

Large caps are sometimes referred to as blue chip shares and many hold certain characteristics. Typically they are more heavily traded than smaller stocks, which make it easier for investors to buy and sell them. Technically speaking, they are more 'liquid', which essentially means they are easier to trade. Smaller company shares, by contrast, can be less liquid, which means their shares are traded less regularly.

3.10.7 Direct and Indirect Investment

Equities clearly have a major part to play in the investment portfolio of all investors; this can be achieved either by direct investment in shares, indirectly through investment funds, or by a combination of both.

Appreciating the need to diversify and having regard to the client's objectives, it is unlikely that a single investment fund or one individual security will meet a client's requirements. As an alternative to direct investment, or to complement direct holdings, investors can also utilise the wide range of equity investment funds or ETFs that are available.

Fund Costs

The direct purchase and sale of equities involves a variety of costs including: dealing transaction costs, commissions, stamp duty, and the PTM levy.

Some investment funds, eg, **open-ended investment companies (OEICs)**, make charges for undertaking the management of the fund and the types of charges that can arise include:

- **Initial charges** – investment funds may impose an initial charge for investing in a fund and that is expressed as a percentage of the amount invested. The range of charges varies widely from fund to fund and depending upon whether the investor deals directly with a manager or uses a fund supermarket or platform. Because of investor dissatisfaction with the high level of initial charges, a number of fund groups have dispensed with these and instead moved to a basis of charging exit fees, if the investor disposes of their holding within a specified period of time.
- **Ongoing charges** – a fund will incur costs and expenses for the running of the fund such as dealing commissions, audit fees and custody fees. The fund management group will also make a charge for the management of the fund, and this is usually expressed as a percentage of the funds under management.
- **Performance charges** – performance fees may also be charged in certain funds over and above the annual fee providing that specified levels of growth over a benchmark have been achieved.
- **Unquoted charges** – funds also contain a number of charges not shown elsewhere, and these include charges for trading costs, bid-offer spreads, slippage costs and research costs.

Charges vary from fund to fund, but the charging structure must be detailed in the fund's prospectus. Institutional investment in funds is clearly going to be significantly larger than any retail investment.

Exchange-Traded Funds (ETFs)

Exchange-traded funds (ETFs) are a type of **open-ended** investment fund that are listed and traded on a stock exchange. They typically track the performance of an index and trade very close to their NAV. Some of their distinguishing features include:

- They track the performance of a wide variety of fixed-income and equity indices as well as a range of sector and theme-specific indices and industry baskets. Some also now track actively managed indices.
- Some ETFs are more liquid, or more easily tradeable, than others depending upon the index they are tracking.
- The details of the fund's holdings are transparent so that their NAV can be readily calculated.
- They have continuous real-time pricing so that investors can trade at any time. They will generally have low bid-offer spreads depending upon the market, index or sector being tracked.
- They have low expense ratios and no initial or exit charges are applied. Instead, the investor pays normal dealing commissions to their stockbroker.

The returns of ETFs include both price movements and any income from the underlying index components. The index can be composed of: equities (developed, emerging, sectors or/and themes), bonds (government bonds, corporate bonds, money market), alternatives (commodities, private equity, hedge funds), or short/leverage (short-term trading/hedging instruments, eg, day trading).

With exchange-traded products (ETPs), a distinction can be made between:

- **ETFs** – exchange-traded funds as a diversified basket of securities, UCITS-regulated
- **ETCs** – exchange-traded commodities as single-commodity or diversified basket of securities, futures or physically backed, typically collateralised
- **ETNs** – exchange-traded notes as single-commodity or diversified basket of securities, typically uncollateralised, issuer credit risk.

ETFs can be used by retail and institutional investors, hedge funds and private wealth managers. In this way, they can work together towards an efficient way to gain index exposure. They can be used by retail and institutional investors for a wide range of investment strategies, including the construction of core-satellite portfolios, asset allocation and **hedging**.

It should be noted that ETFs are available in two forms:

- **Cash-based** – in which case the manager uses the investors' money to purchase the referenced asset (eg, fully replicated or optimised)
- **Synthetic** – in which case the manager retains the investors' money, which may not be segregated, and uses derivatives, such as **futures** and swaps to replicate the return on the referenced asset.

The credit risk of the investor to the two styles of funds may be different. In addition, synthetic ETFs tend to have a slightly worse tracking error than do cash ETFs.

3.11 Advantages and Disadvantages of Investing in Equities

Learning Objective

1.3.8 Analyse the factors to take into account when selecting equities and equity funds: equity fund strategies – growth, income, market capitalisation, sector, region, customised; growth/dividend prospects; direct versus indirect investment; advantages and disadvantages of investing in equities; cost, turnover, liquidity and ease of trading

Advantages

- Equities typically provide the best returns of any asset class over the long term.
- Equities traditionally provide a hedge against inflation.
- It is possible to participate in international as well as domestic opportunities in a broad variety of different industries, helping to achieve a great degree of diversity and reduce risk within the portfolio.
- Equities offer improved liquidity when compared to other forms of investment such as direct property or alternative investments like art, diamonds, gold and vintage cars.

Disadvantages

- Share prices fluctuate, which short-term-orientated investors may find disconcerting.
- Companies may suffer financial problems and possibly even go bust, resulting in the loss of the investor's capital.
- Unlisted or small-cap stocks are potentially riskier and may even prove difficult to trade in certain market conditions.

3.11.1 Turnover

Turnover refers to the rate at which the individual equities within a portfolio, directly or indirectly held, are bought and sold. Whether an investor holds equities directly or indirectly through a fund, the frequency of purchase and sale transactions within the portfolio may impact on the eventual rate of return experienced by the investor, particularly if the level of trading is significant. This is a result of the costs discussed in sections 3.7.4 and 3.10.7.

3.11.2 Liquidity

Unlisted stocks may be difficult to trade in certain market conditions and could, therefore, be termed illiquid. Indirect investment in equities may offer greater liquidity by comparison, due to the ability of the fund manager to repurchase an investor's interest in the fund, using cash held for this purpose.

3.11.3 Ease of Trading

One of the benefits of holding equities directly is that they can be very easy to trade. A number of well-known stockbrokers offer dealing facilities via the internet, allowing retail investors the ability to trade online, at minimal cost, once the account opening process has been completed.

Purchasing indirect equity holdings, through an OEIC for example, usually requires a little more administration. In the past, this would have involved the completion of an application form to purchase 'units' in a particular fund, which would then be submitted to the manager with a cheque for the investment amount. However, it is now possible to open an account with a fund supermarket or platform and buy and sell OEICs in much the same way as direct equities through a stockbroking account. This ongoing development in IT back office systems and their integration with the internet is enabling investors even greater access to investment opportunities, reducing both cost and administration.

4. Property

Learning Objective

1.4.1 Understand the differences, characteristics, risks and returns of the main property markets and sectors: residential; buy-to-let; commercial – retail space, hotel, office, industrial/warehouse

1.4.2 Analyse the main sources of investment risk and return associated with property investment, both direct and indirect: capital growth; yield; location and quality; occupancy rate; tenant creditworthiness, tenancy and rental agreement; term and structure of lease; asset liquidity; market volatility and risk; sector risk

1.4.3 Understand how the direct residential and commercial property markets operate: ownership and lease structures; conveyancing, buying and selling; costs – transactional, management; property valuation; finance and gearing; investment performance measurement and the role of the Investment Property Databank

As an asset class, property has consistently provided positive real-long-term returns, allied to low volatility and a reliable stream of income. An exposure to property can provide diversification benefits, owing to its low **correlation** with both traditional and alternative asset classes.

However, property can be subject to prolonged downturns and, if invested in directly, its lack of liquidity and high transaction costs on transfer only really make it suitable as an investment medium for the long term. The availability of indirect investment, however, makes property a more accessible asset class to those portfolio managers running smaller diversified portfolios.

4.1 Residential Versus Commercial Property

Over the past decade, investment in property has proliferated as people saw the value of properties rise, and has led to greater interest in this asset class. Property has a role to play in a well-diversified portfolio and an investment manager needs to consider whether exposure to the residential or commercial sector is appropriate for the portfolio they are managing. It is therefore important to understand the differences between the two and some of the key differences are shown in the following table:

	Residential Property	Commercial Property
Direct Investment	Range of investment opportunities including second homes, holiday homes and buy-to-let	Size of investment required means direct investment in commercial property is limited to property companies and institutional investors
Tenancies	Typically short renewable leases	Long-term contracts with periods commonly in excess of ten years
Repairs	Landlord is responsible	Tenant is usually responsible
Returns	Largely linked to increase in house prices	Significant component is income return from rental income

4.1.1 Characteristics of the Residential Property Market

The UK has a relatively high level of owner-occupation of residential property, compared with some other countries. Home ownership has been promoted by tax incentives, including exemption from CGT for the taxpayer's own principal private residence. The rented sector also saw the rise of buy-to-let (BTL) ownership by many new private landlords during the 1990s and early 2000s. More easily obtainable mortgage finance, and rising house prices, together with increasing knowledge on the part of private property investors fuelled the BTL boom.

The economic downturn experienced in 2008, and the subsequent lack of high loan-to-value mortgages, reduced demand for new investment properties. However, this lack of suitable mortgage product also meant that individuals who were unable to purchase would instead rent, and so rental demand in certain regions did not diminish significantly.

Inexperienced landlords who bought properties at the top of the market, with the expectation of making a short-term gain, found themselves with an asset that had diminished in value. Coupled with any breaks in letting these properties, many found themselves forced to sell in a less than receptive market. The market has since recovered to pre-crisis levels, although restrictions on mortgage lending is limiting activity.

4.1.2 Characteristics of the Commercial Property Market

Commercial property is divided into three main sectors: retail, offices and industrial. The types of underlying property contained in each sector are:

- **Retail** – shopping centres, retail warehouses, standard shops, supermarkets and department stores.
- **Offices** – standard offices and business parks.
- **Industrial** – standard industrial estates and distribution warehousing, or logistics facilities.

A breakdown of the UK investment market based on mainstream institutional property is monitored by Investment Property Databank (IPD). It covers only the three main sectors and its reports show:

- London and the southeast have the lion's share of commercial property investments.
- Retail property is more evenly distributed across regions than offices or industrial. Shopping centres, retail warehouses, department stores, supermarkets and standard shops are found in most towns of any size throughout the country and, with the exception of standard shops, come in large lot sizes.

- The office market is heavily skewed towards London and the southeast. London alone accounts for more than 66%, with concentrations in the City and West End.
- Industrial property is also concentrated in London and the southeast.

Investment in commercial property has tended in the past to be dominated by insurance companies and pension funds. These institutions may, in the course of their investments, act as property developers and, once a property is built, the landlord. In recent years, more private investors have been making direct investment in commercial property, including wealthy individuals from overseas.

Commercial property is typically let on long leases. In the past this could be as long as 99 years. Now it is likely to be a maximum of 25 years, with three- or five-year rent reviews. Offices, factories and warehouses tend to produce the highest yields in the property sector, and retail typically produces the lowest yields.

The value of commercial property is generally assessed as a multiple of the rental income. For example, a property might be purchased at a price which equates to 20 years' multiple of the annual rent.

The owner of an investment property hopes that the:

- rental income will increase (a rising income return)
- property will increase in value as well (a capital return).

A property price set at a high multiple may reflect expectations of strong future rental growth.

With the exception of auctions, there is obviously no formal public market in commercial property and transactions are agreed between buyers and sellers often using the services of specialised agents. This lack of a formal exchange means that valuers are used to estimate the likely selling price of a commercial property. This process combines financial information about the property with market data to come to a balanced, evidence-supported assessment of its value using the Royal Institution of Chartered Surveyors (RICS) appraisal and valuation standards (known colloquially as the Red Book).

As with other types of property, sales and purchases are both time-consuming and expensive. The costs of buying a property are significant when compared with other assets and can range from 0.54% to 5.15% of the value of the property purchased. This variance reflects stamp duty costs, legal fees and land registry fees faced by a buyer. Stamp duty is the largest contributor as there is a stepped charge based on the value of the property purchased.

The following extract from an IPD Summary Report cites some interesting features of property investments.

> *UK property has delivered positive long-run real returns. However in most cases it is not always a perfect hedge against inflation. Nominal returns may not always keep in line with inflation or inflation expectations. In comparison, equities tend to be a far better hedge against inflation. At the same time, property does hedge against economic growth and, consequently, is useful for matching future assets to liabilities where future liabilities are nominal GDP related (ie, wages).*

The three key factors for property investments in terms of performance are position in the cycle at purchase, GDP growth and inflation, in that order. Inflation is an important driver of nominal returns but not the dominant one. As income provides all of the real total returns over most years and sub-periods, looking at returns in real terms emphasises the need to maintain and protect income.

Total returns to the different sectors and to alternative assets, and their relative volatility, behave differently in the face of changes to inflation and GDP growth.

- **Best scenario for property** – high-growth low-inflation stage of the economic cycle associated with the non-inflationary consistent expansion (NICE) era.
- **Worst scenario** – high-inflation low-growth (stagflation) stage. This implies that cost-push inflation, such as when **commodity** prices are rising faster than retail inflation, is not favourable.
- **Beneficial scenario** – high GDP growth, unless it is also accompanied by high inflation. This means that the demand-pull scenario combination (when strong economic growth causes competition for resources and rising prices) does not imply a higher property allocation, except for investors prepared to take on high risk.
- Property should be preferred to equities when low inflation is expected, except for the low inflation-low growth combination where equities should be preferred.

4.2 Ownership and Lease Structures

In England and Wales, an interest in property can either take the form of a freehold or a leasehold interest.

- **Freehold** – the freeholder of a property has the right to use or dispose of the property as they wish, albeit subject to legislation, local planning laws and any covenants that specifically apply to the property.
- **Leasehold** – the freeholder can create a lessor interest in the property known as a leasehold interest. The leaseholder, or tenant, to whom this interest is conferred, has the right to use the property for a specific period, subject to the terms of the lease and the payment of rent. Unless prevented from doing so under the terms of the lease, the leaseholder can also create a sublease and act as the head lessee to a sub-tenant.

Some leases include break clauses that can significantly impact on the investment value of a property as they can give the landlord and the tenant the option to end the lease before its expiry date. The standard convention is to assume that a tenant's break option will be exercised and that it will negatively impact as the income from the property can change or even disappear at this point.

On the other hand, landlords' break options can have a positive impact, as they give the opportunity to re-let at a higher rent, find a better tenant or refurbish the property. When a commercial property is rented out, a rent review period is agreed between the landlord and the tenant and set out in the terms of the lease. Typically, commercial rents in the UK are reviewed every five years and the revised rent is based on what rents can be achieved in the open market for comparable properties. Leases often provide for upwards-only reviews, where the new rent cannot be lower than the rent that the tenant is currently paying.

Commonhold is a system of property ownership in England and Wales that was introduced in 2004 to remedy a number of problems that have existed in the leasehold system. It involves the indefinite freehold tenure of part of a multi-occupancy building (typically a flat) with shared ownership of and responsibility for common areas and services. It has features of the strata title and the condominium systems, which exist in Australia and the United States respectively. It was introduced by the Commonhold and Leasehold Reform Act 2002 as an alternative to leasehold, and was the first new type of legal estate to be introduced in English law since 1925.

An important difference between commonhold and leasehold is that commonholds do not depreciate in value in the same way that leaseholds do towards the end of their lease terms.

A commonhold consists of both units and common parts. The units are individual freehold properties, such as flats, offices and shops and the owners of freehold units are called unit-holders.

The common parts are any part of a commonhold development which is not a unit. This includes shared facilities such as the roof, stairs and landings. The common parts are owned and managed by a limited company called the Commonhold Association (CA). Membership of the CA is restricted to unit-holders. Therefore, unit-holders have two different interests in commonhold. The first is a direct interest in their unit and the second is an interest in the membership of the CA. The CA is required to manage the commonhold in accordance with the terms of the commonhold community statement (CCS). The CCS sets out the extent of the commonhold properties, the rights and obligations of the CA and unit-holders and procedures for dispute resolution. The CA must be registered at Companies House and have both a memorandum and articles of association. The CCS, memorandum and articles should all be registered at HM Land Registry. The main benefits of commonhold over leasehold are that:

- commonhold does not lose its value over time in the same way as leasehold, as it does not have a diminishing lease term
- there is no need for a landlord – the CA and unit-holders manage the commonhold
- the commonhold documentation is largely standardised, making it easier to identify unit-holders' rights and obligations; and there is only one set of documentation for the whole commonhold.

4.3 Borrowing

Given the substantial value of most properties, and the fact that they can make excellent security for lending purposes, most property investments are made with help from borrowed funds. The investment is geared.

The gearing effect of borrowing for property purchase can be severe if prices start to fall, and negative equity can result if the loan is a high percentage of the property value.

4.4 Returns from Rent

Property which has been let produces an income return, in the form of rent paid by its tenants to the owner (the landlord). This is true both of private residential property lettings to households, and of commercial properties let out to businesses.

Research shows that, over the long run, investment in property has provided real returns ahead of the returns on cash and gilts and slightly below that of equities. The commercial property market has, however, suffered from crashes from time to time; for example, between 1989 and 1992, following a period of significant levels of speculative development in London, some office rent levels halved.

The residential property market tends to move in cycles, which are different from those of the commercial property market, and it is influenced by economic factors such as disposable incomes and interest rates. A major slump in the residential market followed substantial rises in interest rates in the years following 1989. A shortage of building land and planning restrictions contributes to rising prices in some areas, particularly the south of England. The declining affordability of homes for many people means that they have to rent (unless they have some alternative, such as living with parents), and this keeps demand for rental property – and therefore rents – relatively high.

The rental income on property will depend on a variety of factors, including:

- supply and demand
- the quality of the property itself and how appealing it is to the tenant
- the terms that have been agreed. Depending on the nature of the lease or letting agreement, there may be restrictions on how often and by how much the rent can be adjusted.

For residential properties, rental income is taxed as business income. It is treated as a single business, even if the investor has bought and lets out more than one property. A residential property investor who lets out several properties can offset losses from one against profits from another.

Note:

- there are some differences in the tax treatment for residential and holiday lettings
- very low rental income (up to £7,500 pa) under the rent-a-room scheme – where someone lets out a room in their own home – is tax-free.

The rent on commercial property is also treated as business income. Because of this, there are various capital allowances and expenses which can be offset against it, potentially reducing the investor's overall tax burden.

The rental yield from a property investment can be calculated as:

$$\text{Rental yield} = \frac{\text{Gross rent} - \text{expenses}}{\text{Cost of property, including purchase costs}}$$

Gross rent should be adjusted by excluding estimated void periods (ie, times when there is no tenant), which can generally only be estimated in calculating the yield for a future period.

Expenses include agents' charges, buildings insurance (and contents insurance, if furnished) and the cost of renewals of furnishings and appliances. Total expenses are likely to be between 20% and 25% of the gross rent.

Purchase costs include legal fees, the cost of surveys or valuation, **Stamp Duty Land Tax (SDLT)** and the initial cost of furnishings. Agents' fees may be incurred on the transaction if an agent has been employed to search for the property, but usually only the seller incurs agents' fees.

Note that the costs of loan interest have not been included in expenses. The rental yield is the rent after expenses as a proportion of the capital cost of the investment. The rental yield income can be compared with the rate that the investor is paying for a loan to purchase the property.

4.4.1 Quality of Tenants

The quality of tenant in a let property is important to its overall investment return. Poor-quality tenants may:

- not be able to pay their rent. Evicting and replacing them can (depending on the terms of the tenancy) be costly and time-consuming. It may also result in rental voids
- fail to meet their obligations in terms of maintaining the property in good order, resulting in expense to the landlord in bringing it back to lettable standard once they depart.

The ideal tenant is one of good financial standing who is likely to have an interest in maintaining the condition of the property on an ongoing basis.

4.4.2 Occupancy Levels

When the property is unlet (void periods), no income is being earned. A prospective investor should understand the local rental market and what factors influence local levels of demand, in order to estimate what void periods can be expected and build these into estimates of rental income. The location of the property and its overall condition and character can affect the incidence of void periods.

4.5 Capital Returns

Over time, property values can be seen to increase, generally in excess of inflation (providing a real return). However, the property market is cyclical and can fall sharply.

Commercial property, to a greater extent than residential property, can be vulnerable to influences on overseas investment. Factors such as the value of sterling and how foreign investors are taxed on UK commercial property can affect prices. In addition, since much of the commercial property market is owned by large institutional investors, it means it must compete with other asset classes such as equities and bonds.

Effects such as interest rate moves can have a significant effect on the property market, due to the market's leverage through borrowing. This can affect the cost of servicing any debt taken on. Higher rates can have a negative effect, while lower rates can be positive.

4.5.1 Depreciation

Property prices can be affected by the condition of the property. If it is deteriorating and no remedial action is taken, it may depreciate steadily as the costs involved in restoring it continue to rise. Eventually it may fall to a level where the only real value is the land on which it stands – and this must be offset against the costs of levelling the property and rebuilding.

4.6 Costs

4.6.1 Transaction Costs

Property transactional costs are relatively high compared to other financial instruments. This is another reason why property should be seen as a longer-term investment.

- In addition to agents' and legal costs, property purchases are subject to SDLT.
- Often, property transactions are protracted and the vendor may incur expenses during this period.

SDLT is payable on the purchase or transfer of property or land in England, Wales and Northern Ireland where the amount paid is above a certain threshold. SDLT is not applicable to property transactions in Scotland, where the land and buildings transaction tax (LBTT) is levied instead. Various rules apply for working out the amount to be paid. The calculation is based on a value called the 'chargeable consideration' – it can vary depending on whether the land is residential, non-residential, freehold or leasehold. Broadly, this tax is paid as a percentage of the amount paid for property or land when it is bought or transferred. No SDLT is chargeable for transfers on divorce, or for transfers to charities if the land is to be used for charitable purposes. Details of these rates can be found at hmrc.gov.uk under 'Stamp Duty Land Tax'.

SDLT is charged as a percentage of the amount paid for property or land when it is bought or transferred – unless there is a relief or exemption. The amount payable can also vary depending whether the property is being used for residential or non-residential purposes, and whether the property is sold as a freehold or leasehold. The rates for residential buyers are set out in the tables below, and full details of SDLT rates and thresholds can be found at hmrc.gov.uk.

Residential Land or Property SDLT Rates and Thresholds

Purchase price/lease premium or transfer value	SDLT rate
Up to £125,000	Zero
The next £124,999 (£125,001 to £250,000)	2%
The next £674,999 (£250,001 to £925,000)	5%
The next £574,999 (925,001 to £1.5 million)	10%
The remainder above £1,500,001	12%
Over £500,000 (purchased by certain persons including corporate bodies) from March 2014	15%

From 1 April 2016, individuals have to pay 3% on top of the normal SDLT rates if buying a new residential property means they own more than one. However, if an individual is replacing their main residence, they will not pay the extra 3% SDLT if the property they are buying is replacing their main residence and that has already been sold.

If there is a delay selling their main residence, and it has not been sold on the day they complete their new purchase:

- they will have to pay higher rates because they own two properties
- they may be able to receive a refund if they sell their previous main home within 36 months.

Source: HMRC

SDLT is charged at 15% for properties of more than £500,000 for certain non-natural persons. This broadly includes a body corporate, for example, companies, collective investment schemes and all other partnerships with one or more members who are either a corporate or a collection investment scheme.

If the value is above the payment threshold, SDLT is charged at the appropriate rate on each portion of the whole of the amount paid. For example, a house bought for £130,000 is charged at 2% on £130,000–£125,000, ie, £5,000 @ 2 % or £100.

A house bought for £350,000 is charged at as follows:

£125,000 @ 0% = £0
£125,000 @ 2% = £2,500
£100,000 @ 5% = £5,000
Total SDLT = £7,500

Non-Residential Land or Property Rates and Thresholds

Purchase price/lease premium or transfer value (non-residential or mixed use)	SDLT rate
Up to £150,000	Zero
The next £100,000 (the portion from 150,001 to £250,000)	2%
The remaining amount (the portion above £250,000)	5%

Source: HMRC

Note that for the above purpose the annual rent is the highest annual rent known to be payable in any year of the lease, not the NPV used to determine any tax payable on the rent.

When you purchase a new non-residential or mixed use leasehold, SDLT is paid on both the:

- purchase price of the lease (the lease premium)
- value of the annual rent you pay (the net present value).

These are calculated separately and then added together, and the net present value (NPV) is based on the total rent over the life of the lease.

4.6.2 Maintenance Costs

Various costs in maintaining a property, include:

- **Ongoing repairs and maintenance** – these may fall to the landlord or the tenant, depending on the terms of the rental agreement; it is important to factor this in when calculating the net return on the property.
- **Insurance** – which again may fall to the landlord or tenant, depending on terms.
- **Rates and council taxes** are payable on the property. These will vary by local authority.

If the property is commercially let, there may be legal requirements to ensure certain standards of access, security and safety, which can increase costs.

4.7 Conveyancing

Conveyancing is the legal process of transferring property rights from seller to buyer (for a sale/purchase), or switching a mortgage from one lender to another (for remortgaging).

A conveyancing solicitor acts on behalf of either the buyer or seller and represents their interests in the property transaction. They ensure that the terms and conditions of the contract for sale are fair and reasonable and that all financial information is correct. The process differs depending upon whether they are acting for the buyer or the seller.

The seller's conveyancer will first request a copy of the land registry entry for the property. This is sometimes referred to as the office copies. They then prepare a contract for sale, incorporating the land registry plan and details, before forwarding it to the buyer's solicitor.

The buyer's solicitor will apply for the searches from a variety of bodies, including the local authority, and will assess the contract for sale that has been received from the seller's lawyer. Additionally, if the buyer is borrowing money on a mortgage, the solicitor will need to receive a copy of the formal mortgage offer and be satisfied that the buyer has sufficient funds available to complete the transaction.

If there are items in the contract for sale that the buyer's solicitor is not happy with, they will raise a query with the seller's solicitor. Once these have been resolved, the searches have been completed and proof of funds provided, both parties exchange contracts.

Exchange of contracts is the point of no return for both parties and is a legally binding agreement. At any time up until this point, either party can withdraw from the process with no penalty other than any monies incurred to date.

At exchange of contracts a completion date is normally agreed when the transfer will be finalised. On the day of completion the monies are transferred between the parties and ultimately, the keys are handed over.

4.8 Liquidity

Direct investment in property (whether commercial or residential) is generally pretty illiquid:

- Property can take some considerable time to sell.
- It is generally indivisible – if the investor wants to realise a small part of their portfolio, they cannot sell, say, only the bathroom of one of their residential properties. They could perhaps sell one flat in a block of flats they own, but this might be uneconomic in terms of breaking up the value of the block as a whole.
- A number of property funds have recently effected a price swing (normally occurring when the fund moves from offer to bid pricing) and this is the latest sign of changing fortunes for property portfolios. While property funds typically hold double-digit cash weightings in order to preserve liquidity, price swings aim to ensure investors will not suffer from increased transaction costs should assets be sold to meet redemptions.

Collective investment funds holding property are also at risk of illiquidity, particularly when faced with a significant number of redemption requests from investors. Although these funds are required to hold an element of cash, this may not be sufficient to meet demand in times of market stress. A good example of this was seen in 2016 when a number of large UK property funds suspended withdrawals for six months.

Property should not be recommended to investors who have immediate or near-term liquidity needs (see also section 4.12.4).

4.9 Performance Measurement

Performance in the property market is measured by reference to the various indices and analysis offered chiefly by the IPD (now part of the MSCI group).

IPD is a leading provider of property indices and portfolio benchmarks across 32 countries, allowing portfolio managers to gain market transparency and performance comparisons in the real estate market.

The UK Monthly Property Index tracks performance of 3,046 property investments, with a total capital value of £44.6 billion as at February 2017. Results are published 12 times a year, ten working days after month-end. A breakdown of the total UK property market index revealed that the office property sector, the retail property sector, the office sector and the industrial property sector see varied performance depending on the supply and demand across these sectors.

Property is an important asset within a portfolio as it adds diversification and is not directly correlated to equities and fixed-interest investments.

As an asset class, property equities are considered to be investments in shares of companies that have business interests in the real estate market, eg, purchase of shares of Land Securities plc, a FTSE 100 listed stock. Land Securities plc is the UK's largest **real estate investment trust (REIT)** with a commercial property portfolio valued at approximately £14.5 billion (as at 31 March 2016).

Unlike direct property investment (for example, purchasing land or residential property), the distinguishing characteristic of investment in listed property equities is that the asset class draws a regular, attractive income and capital gain made over the medium and longer term from the underlying direct property investment made by the company. Further, there are benefits in terms of liquidity as investors can sell the shares in the property company stock to release capital when required.

4.10 Valuation Measures

Learning Objective

1.4.4 Analyse property and property funds using the following valuation measures: cash flow and average yield; capitalisation rate; rental value, review; reversionary value; comparative analysis; market indices and trends

4.10.1 Cash Flow and Average Yield

Like the economy, the property market goes through cycles: periods of growth leading to oversupply and market weakness, followed by stabilisation, absorption and then growth, leading to shortage of supply and so on.

The simplest yardstick of property value is initial yield. This is the current annual rent divided by the value of the property, including purchase costs. The average initial yield across the whole property market fluctuates over time and may reflect a general economic cycle and/or specific changes in attitude towards property.

4.10.2 Capitalisation Rate

The capitalisation rate or cap rate is a ratio used to estimate the value of income-producing properties. Put simply, the cap rate is the net operating income divided by the sales price or value of a property expressed as a percentage. Investors, lenders and appraisers use the cap rate to estimate the purchase price for different types of income-producing properties.

A market cap rate is determined by evaluating the financial data of similar properties which have recently sold in a specific market. It provides a more reliable estimate of value than a market gross rent multiplier since the cap rate calculation uses more of a property's financial detail. The gross rent multiplier (GRM) calculation only considers a property's selling price and gross rents. The cap rate calculation includes a property's selling price, gross rents, non-rental income, vacancy amount and operating expenses, thus providing a more reliable estimate of value.

In a property transaction, the seller is trying to get the highest price for the property or sell at the lowest cap rate possible, while the buyer is trying to purchase the property at the lowest price possible, which translates into a higher cap rate.

Investors expect a larger return when investing in high risk income properties. The cap rate may vary in different areas of a city due to desirability of location, level of crime and general condition of an area. You would expect lower cap rates in newer or more desirable areas of a city and higher cap rates in less desirable areas, to compensate for the added risk.

In a property market if net operating incomes are increasing and cap rates are declining over time for a given type of property such as office buildings, values will be generally increasing. If net operating incomes are decreasing and cap rates are increasing over time in a given marketplace, then property values will be declining.

4.10.3 Reversionary Value

The reversionary value of a property is the expected value at the end of the term of the lease.

It is in the nature of leasehold tenancy for a property's value to diminish as the lease expires, and a long lease is generally worth more on the open market than a short lease.

In enfranchisement cases, when the enfranchising leaseholders have the opportunity to grant themselves lease extensions, it can generally be assumed that the action will achieve some improvement in the value of the individual properties.

The amount of this improvement will be heavily dependent upon the length of the unexpired term before extension and there are no hard and fast rules as to how much the value will increase. A valuer will assess this and make an estimate, based on research into similar properties in the local area.

If a leaseholder has made improvements to the property that affects its value, these must be disregarded for the purposes of the valuation. If the improvements are substantial, the valuer will have to calculate the additional value they give to the property and then discount this from the estimated present value of the property.

For the purpose of calculating the reversionary value, a value must be ascribed to the property representing what it could be sold for when the current term expires.

Most long leaseholders have statutory protection to revert to assured tenancies on the expiry of their existing leases. In the valuation of leasehold interests subject to protected occupancy, the improved value is sometimes discounted by a percentage to reflect the fact that the landlord will not receive a vacant property on expiry, but a paying tenant.

4.10.4 Rental Value Review

The rent review period is agreed between the landlord and the tenant and set out in the terms of the lease. Typically, commercial rents in the UK are reviewed every five years.

In general, a rent review is decided by negotiation between the tenant and landlord, and by referring to the rents achieved in the open market for comparable properties. Once agreed, the tenant is committed to pay the landlord a rental income which is effectively fixed (subject only to further reviews) until the lease is terminated.

UK commercial leases have traditionally provided for upwards-only reviews. This means that the new rent negotiated on review cannot be lower than what the tenant is currently paying, even if the market rents in the area have fallen below that level. In this case, the tenant and landlord usually agree to continue with same rent the tenant currently pays.

Although upwards-only reviews are traditional, it should be noted that UK leases can specify a different basis for reviewing rents. Leases which spell out an annual amount or percentage by which the rent will increase, or link the increase to the RPI, are becoming more common. In addition, but less frequently, a rent review may state the exact properties to be used as comparables. If the landlord and tenant cannot agree a rent review, they can ask an independent expert or arbitrator (often appointed by the RICS) to decide the matter.

4.10.5 Comparative Analysis, Market Indices and Trends

Commercial property investors need to be able to measure the returns they achieve on their investment and compare performance. The IPD produces objective, reliable property benchmarks and indices for 18 countries and is the world leader in performance analysis for the owners, investors, managers and occupiers of real estate. The IPD started in the UK in 1985 and began to compile data from leading commercial property investors, eventually creating the UK's first reliable index of commercial property returns. The IPD maintains various databases, which hold records of properties owned by investors, managed by portfolio managers, and occupied by businesses and government. They contain detailed financial and descriptive information on each of the individual buildings, leases and tenants. The IPD measures the financial performance of real estate for fund managers and insurance, pension and private investment companies across the world.

However, performance is not measured on the basis of transaction data, but by records from portfolio valuations.

The IPD's annual database is the most comprehensive benchmark of direct property performance in the UK. It monitors 22,985 properties in 288 funds with a total value of £183 billion. These properties are valued annually, but two subsets are valued more frequently.

The quarterly index, launched in 2006, values 9,400 properties (worth £150 billion in September 2016) held in 228 separate funds. The monthly index compiles a database of 51 portfolios (3,485 properties in March 2016). The latter provides a fast-moving indicator of current market conditions. The monthly index covers approximately 15% of the UK investment market, but differs in composition from the annual index. For example, it contains few large portfolios and fewer higher-value assets, such as shopping centres and central London offices. A summary of the end-month results is published in the Companies & Markets section of the *Financial Times*.

The analysis carried out by the IPD enables investment managers to measure the performance of their real estate portfolios and to benchmark themselves against their peers. The various indices and measures available help to highlight the strengths and weaknesses of a property fund's performance.

In 2006, another index series, the FTSE UK Commercial Property Index, was launched. It differs from the IPD indices in several important respects. Most significantly, it is based on the indirect property holdings of a Guernsey-listed real estate fund. This fund is invested in a range of property vehicles and is structured so that its holdings mimic the UK commercial property investment market.

The headline FTSE UK All Property Index has three additional sector indices, giving investors daily performance data on the retail, office and industrial sectors of the UK commercial property market. It is available by subscription.

There are also the UK Pooled Property Fund Indices, compiled by the IPD and sponsored by the Association of Real Estate Funds and HSBC. These measure the quarterly performance of commercial and residential property held by collective investment schemes offering indirect exposure to UK property.

The performance of UK quoted real estate company shares is tracked as part of the FTSE Actuaries All Share Index for UK equities, published daily in the Companies & Markets section of the *Financial Times*.

It is important to understand that property indices are based on valuations and not transaction prices. Therefore, they tend to underestimate the true volatility of the market. Nevertheless, even after adjusting to allow for valuation smoothing and lag, property's volatility is still lower than that of other assets.

4.11 Indirect Property Investment

Learning Objective

1.4.5 Analyse the factors to take into account when selecting property and property funds: property shares, OEICs, REITs, bonds, trusts, funds, fund of funds, limited partnerships; relative merits of investing through open-ended and closed-ended vehicles; property fund strategies; growth/dividend prospects; direct versus indirect investment; pricing, liquidity and fair value; advantages and disadvantages of investing in property; costs and ease of trading

You should be aware that collective investment schemes offer the investor the benefit of indirect exposure to a variety of asset classes.

A number of these can include property – generally commercial, but sometimes also residential. We will take a look at a few of the options available.

4.11.1 Property Company Shares

A variety of property development and property investment companies are listed on the LSE. They invest in a wide variety of properties, some undertaking the development of property projects and some simply seeking to identify and invest in undervalued properties. If the properties are let, the company may pay a dividend income to its investors; others, however, which invest in development opportunities, may pay no income at all.

The price of the shares will move with supply and demand and may diverge from the value of the underlying asset values. **Gearing** (borrowing) by the company can increase the share price volatility.

The share price can be affected by systemic factors affecting the stock market as a whole, as well as factors specific to the company or the property sector.

Compared with direct investment in property, a significant advantage of this means of investing in property is liquidity. The investor can realise their investment in a listed property company easily through a stockbroker, since there are market makers who quote prices for all listed stocks.

4.11.2 Unit Trusts

Originally, unit trusts were prohibited from directly investing in property and could only invest indirectly via property shares. Nowadays, they can invest directly into commercial property. At the launch of such a fund, the manager must be confident that they will attract sufficient funds to make adequate property purchases to establish a well-spread portfolio.

There are, however, restrictions on the proportion of the fund that can be invested in leases with less than 60 years to run, or in unoccupied property. There are also restrictions on holding mortgaged property, which limits gearing. No more than 15% in value of the fund assets can be invested in a single property.

Additionally, there are unit trusts that invest in property company shares.

As with unit trusts and OEICs generally, the investment will be redeemed at NAV. However, if many investors choose to sell at one time, the unit trust or OEIC may need to invoke its right to postpone encashment of units/shares until property can be sold. This possible restriction in accessibility makes property funds potentially less liquid than other funds (though still more liquid than an investment directly into property). This happened during the 2007–08 economic crisis.

There is no CGT charged to the fund itself for unit trusts, OEICs and investment trusts. Investors may be subject to CGT on gains when they sell the units or shares.

Authorised property unit trusts are regulated by the FCA. Like all authorised funds, they can be sold direct to retail investors. They pay corporation tax on their income but do not pay CGT within the vehicle.

There is a wide variety of property unit trusts, from specialist funds (eg, urban regeneration and residential) to general commercial property. Most have a wide commercial property base, thus offering investors a sufficient variety of underlying assets to give them exposure to a diversified portfolio of property investments. There is also a wide range of authorised unit trusts (AUTs) investing into property company shares and real estate investment trusts (REITs), a vehicle which we will look at in section 4.11.4.

Such vehicles can surmount some of the liquidity issues that face investors investing directly in property; for example, if a unit trust holds shares in a listed property fund, it can sell those shares on the stock market to realise cash to meet its investors' redemption needs. Each open-ended property unit trust will have predetermined redemption procedures (which differ from trust to trust), so the investor should ensure that they understand these before investing.

In addition, there is a developing secondary market that allows the transfer of units between investors on a matched bargain basis; in some cases this can provide an exit route, where the individual trust's terms are more restrictive and an investor needs to sell their units promptly.

4.11.3 Property Authorised Investment Funds (PAIFs)

Property authorised investment funds (PAIFs) invest mainly in property, including UK and non-UK REITs, and can elect for a special form of tax treatment.

Under the PAIF regime, rental profits and other related income is exempt from tax in the fund, and is distributed to investors net of basic rate tax, which can be reclaimed by non-taxpayers. Property income is ring-fenced within the fund, and all other taxable income is charged to corporation tax at 20%. Distributions to investors are split into three categories of income: property income, other taxable income (bank interest and non-UK dividends), and UK dividend income.

In order to qualify as a PAIF, the fund must meet a number of conditions, including:

- the fund must be structured as an OEIC
- at least 60% of the net income of the PAIF must be from the exempt property investment business
- the value of the assets involved in the property investment business must be at least 60% of the total assets held by the PAIF
- the shares of the PAIF must be widely held and no corporate investor must hold 10% or more of the NAV of the fund.

4.11.4 Real Estate Investment Trusts (REITs)

REITs are a relatively new investment vehicle in the UK. A REIT is an indirect investment in the property market and can provide investors with tax-efficient and diversified exposure to rental properties. REITs are tax-transparent property investment vehicles. Initially introduced in the US, they have been adopted by other countries including Japan, the Netherlands and France and were launched in the UK in January 2007.

REITs own and manage portfolios of real estate properties. UK REITs have to be resident in the UK and must be listed on a recognised stock exchange.

To qualify as a REIT, they have to offer fully transferable shares, have at least 100 shareholders and have to pay dividends of at least 90% of their taxable income. They must hold at least 75% of the total investments in real estate and derive their gross income from rents and other sources of income that are in line with the business interest of a REIT. This means that REITs can gain exemption from paying capital gains taxes and corporation tax liabilities. Investors, on the other hand, pay tax on dividends and any capital growth from their REIT investments at their marginal tax rates.

UK REITs are listed on the main market of the LSE and may also be registered on any recognised exchange, including AIM. REITs provide the following benefits to investors:

- tax transparency
- potentially high-yield returns
- access to property with minimal outlay
- low/controlled gearing
- portfolio diversification (low correlation to equities and bonds)
- liquidity – easy to sell/buy
- strong corporate governance.

The following further conditions apply for REITs treatment:

- a single company wishing to become a REIT must be UK resident for tax purposes and not dual resident. Its shares must be listed on a recognised stock exchange
- a company must not be a 'close company' – one owned by five or fewer participants
- at least 75% of the company's assets must be represented by at least three different investment properties (which can be residential or commercial and do not have be situated in the UK)
- the value of any one property should not exceed 40% of the total value of investment properties
- at least 75% of the income must be rental income
- the ratio of interest paid on borrowings to fund the tax-exempt business to its rental income should not exceed 1.25:1.00
- at least 90% of the tax-exempt profits must be distributed
- no single shareholder may hold 10% or more of the share capital or voting rights.

A group of companies can join to become a 'Group REIT'. This may consist of a principal company and all of its 75% subsidiaries.

REITs can be held in ISAs and child trust funds (CTFs). A number of UK property companies have chosen to convert to become REITs.

4.11.5 Life Assurance Property Bonds

Life companies offer bonds. These are not a debt security of the type we have already looked at, but rather a type of life policy giving investment exposure to a variety of asset classes. Property is among the range of asset classes to which exposure can be obtained through a life policy or insurance-based pension product. The value of the benefits paid under the life policy is directly linked to the NAV of the properties held. A life fund is not permitted to borrow.

In addition, most 'with profits' funds operated by life companies include an element of property exposure in their portfolios.

Although life products are more liquid than direct investments in property, life companies retain a right to postpone the encashment of units (and therefore the payment of benefits under the policy). This could come into effect if several investors wished to encash their bonds at the same time, necessitating the sale of properties – a process that could take some time. This condition was invoked by several life companies during the crisis in 2008.

Income and capital gains are subject to tax within the fund at 20%. This cannot be reclaimed by non-taxpayers, and both higher rate and additional rate taxpayers will pay further tax. The tax treatment of holdings accessed through a policy is thus different from that for collective investment schemes and listed property shares.

In addition, the policy carries insurance benefits for the policyholder.

4.11.6 Offshore Funds

Many property funds are established in offshore or international financial services centres such as the Isle of Man, Cayman and Dublin. This may provide certain tax advantages, though offshore vehicles are not advantageous for every investor, and some can be positively disadvantageous. In many cases it is because of the more relaxed regulations in those jurisdictions, which may mean that the fund has to comply with fewer rules, in terms of diversification and the levels of liquidity it has to maintain, or in terms of how the assets are held.

4.11.7 Investment Trusts

Investment trusts are listed, **closed-ended** vehicles which are traded on the stock market. A number of these invest in the shares of property companies.

Property investment trusts are, therefore, closed-ended, pooled investments. They are not a direct holding, however, investing in shares of an investment trust can give exposure to direct holdings. They are permitted to borrow, which can increase the risk for the investor as well as the potential return.

The share price of the trust will fluctuate with supply and demand for the shares of the trust and may be at a discount or a premium to the NAV.

4.11.8 Funds-of-Funds

One of the investee funds, in which a fund of funds (FOF) invests, may well focus specifically on the property market. This provides the investors in the FOF vehicle with a measure of exposure, and access to specialist expertise, in this asset class.

4.11.9 Limited Partnerships

In some cases, the fund vehicle for investment in the property market may be established as a partnership vehicle (as opposed to a unit trust or company). Such vehicles are usually aimed at direct investment in the property market, and are targeted at the wealthier or more experienced investor. Their tax treatment is rather different from that of trust or corporate-based vehicles, since the HMRC 'looks through' the vehicle to a greater extent.

4.11.10 Investing in Open- or Closed-Ended Funds

Diversification

These funds usually contain a wide variety of stocks, bonds and other securities issued by companies and governments from around the nation or the world. Investors become part owners of numerous securities and are, therefore, diversifying their holdings. If one stock drops in value, it does not necessarily hurt them much, as one of the other stocks or bonds in the fund may grow in value. In contrast, when investors buy individual securities, their returns depend on just a small number of stocks or bonds.

Professional Management

Investors can manage their own finances by choosing stocks and bonds through online brokerage firms. However, managing money can prove time-consuming, especially if they are not financial experts, in which case they must spend hours carrying out research just to get to grips with their options. Open-ended funds are controlled by fund managers, who are responsible for buying and selling securities. These professionals look for good deals on inexpensive securities, and make money by selling over-priced stocks, bonds and other securities.

Liquidity

These funds are highly liquid. Investors can redeem their shares at any time. When shares or units in the fund are sold, the fund liquidates them at the end of the next business day and within a few days the money is paid to the investors.

4.12 Costs and Ease of Trading

Learning Objective

1.4.5 Analyse the factors to take into account when selecting property and property funds: property shares, OEICs, REITs, bonds, trusts, funds, fund of funds, limited partnerships; relative merits of investing through open-ended and closed-ended vehicles; property fund strategies; growth/dividend prospects; direct versus indirect investment; pricing, liquidity and fair value; advantages and disadvantages of investing in property; costs and ease of trading

4.12.1 Valuation

Auctions aside, there is no public market in commercial property investments. It is primarily a private market, made principally by agents, who seek to match buyers and sellers with buildings. Sellers typically engage an agent to market their property. The buyer will usually recognise the agent's role in introducing the property to them, either by retaining the agent to act on the purchase or simply by paying an introductory fee.

With the advent of e-commerce, many agents now market properties for clients via websites and there are several platforms that seek to create electronic marketplaces. Property auction houses also sell commercial lots for sellers. In recent years the auction market has grown steadily, driven by the growing demand from private investors. Two factors fuelling this demand are that initial yields on properties in the auction room have been higher than finance rates and that there has been a ready supply of debt finance.

4.12.2 Costs

The costs of buying a property are significant when compared with acquiring interests in other assets. In large part, they stem from the fees associated with the necessary due diligence. The market norm reflects fees, plus VAT for the following services:

- Agents' advice on the purchase, which may sometimes, but not always, include fees for valuation, building surveys, environmental audits and mechanical and engineering tests.
- Legal transaction fees.
- SDLT.

See section 4.6.1 for details of SDLT rates.

4.12.3 Pricing and Fair Value

Unlike other financial assets, most commercial real estate does not trade on an exchange with openly quoted prices. Professional valuers are used to estimate the likely selling price of an asset. This process combines financial information about the property with market data to achieve a balanced, evidence-supported assessment of its price. The valuer uses their expert knowledge and experience of the market to make a judgement.

The RICS Appraisal and Valuation Standard is the national valuation practice standard in the UK. It is used by RICS members, who value most of the investment property in the UK, and their clients. But even when these standards are used, the valuation of a property and the price it sells for can be different.

To some extent this reflects the imperfect nature of market information, ie, the seller may know more than the buyer, or vice versa. It can also reflect different views about the future prospects for the property itself and how the market is likely to perform.

4.12.4 Liquidity

Investors often cite a lack of liquidity as a key disadvantage of commercial property. However, research published by the Investment Property Forum (IPF) in 2004 found that the UK market average holding period for an investment was seven years. It also found that the holding period had shortened over time, suggesting steady gains in liquidity.

Nevertheless, turnover is relatively low compared to that in the equities and gilts markets. Two reasons for property's 'stickiness' are that it takes longer and is more expensive to execute a deal. Although the property industry has taken steps to streamline transactions, it can take several months from initial marketing to completion of contracts. This time lapse clearly represents an opportunity cost for investors.

5. Other Assets

Learning Objective

1.5.1 Understand the purpose, characteristics, risks and returns of the main types of alternative investments: gold and other metals; commodities; art; antiques

1.5.2 Analyse the factors to take into account when investing in alternative investments: direct versus indirect investment; investment time horizon; features – quality, durability, provenance; transaction, delivery and ongoing costs; pricing, liquidity and fair value; advantages and disadvantages of investing in alternatives

Alternative investments are those which fall outside the traditional asset classes of equities, property, fixed interest, cash and money market instruments.

They include physical assets, which we will focus on here; you may also hear them referred to as chattels. Chattels are tangible, moveable things. When used for investment purposes, they are sometimes also referred to as collectables.

While assets of this type tend to be popular with collectors, they do also have the potential to appreciate substantially in value. They are not exclusive to wealthy clients and due to the wide variety of options available, even modest investments are possible; many people have a collection of coins or stamps, for example, and can find to their surprise that they have amassed a portfolio of reasonable value over time.

Some chattels can make good investments – they may go up in value. However, there may be disadvantages:

- They often suffer from illiquidity and can be difficult to sell quickly if funds are required for other purposes.
- They can be difficult to value due to the size of the different markets.
- Prices can change rapidly as markets are subject to trends and fashions. The art and antiques markets, for example, can be very volatile and are specialist areas.
- These objects rarely generate income (unless they can be hired out to museums and the like).
- Dealers' charges tend to be quite high.
- Special and secure storage may be required, again at a cost.
- There is the risk of fire, theft, damage or flood to be insured against.
- It may be hard to get a true valuation, as this may be a matter of the valuer's opinion unless and until the object comes to be sold.
- There is little or no regulation in the market for chattels.
- It is usually not possible to buy chattels via an ISA or pension.
- The item may prove to be a forgery, and next to worthless.

Alternative investments include (but are not limited to): jewellery; antiques; books; art; classic cars; autographs; posters; coins.; stamps; comic books; toys (which can eventually be worth four to five times more than their original price, if they are in good condition and in the original packaging); racehorses; fine wine; precious metals; and memorabilia (eg, commemorative items).

Alternative assets are becoming increasingly popular in the UK, and with alternative investments there is fun in choosing your items, such as works of art and items of antique furniture, which can brighten your home as well as providing a potential profit.

As well as the potential for growth, there is the pleasure to be had from owning a rare object. Investment in chattels should generally be seen as an area for specialist or wealthy investors only.

These are high-risk sectors and the value can go down as well as up, as fashions and demand change. Research and careful selection of pieces are a must.

5.1 Art

Investing in art sounds so civilised: perusing the catalogues of the country's best-known auction houses looking for a personal masterpiece, or hunting through flea markets in the hope of hidden treasures. But the world of art is not an easy one for amateurs to navigate. For one thing, it's immense, and knowing what you are looking for can be incredibly difficult, even for experts.

Getting to grips with artists, with movements, with genres and periods is one part of the problem, and becoming competent at choosing where to invest can take a very long time. And it's not just the artists you need to get to know. The subject matter is key to a painting, or indeed a photograph's, value. A brilliantly painted portrait of the artist's wife, for example, could not rival a less impressive portrait of Winston Churchill in terms of value. Similarly, photographs of famous people, places and events will often be more saleable than more obscure, albeit attractive, scenes. Unfortunately, buying a new artist's work and hoping it will be worth more when they hit the big time cannot be directly compared with investing in a small company early and cashing in later.

Young, talented artists will often have a dealer, and that dealer will make sure the prices are set at the right level. Tactics such as driving up the bidding at auction can often make finding a bargain difficult. Fairytale-like stories of paintings being bought at auction for next to nothing and sold on for a fortune make auctions more alluring. But not everyone is that lucky, and buying at auction is expensive, with fees to be paid to the auction house by both the buyer and seller, sometimes at up to 20% of the price. A painting will have to appreciate substantially in value if one is to make money from it.

The main trouble with investing in art is that it is very difficult to get an accurate valuation. At auction, rival bidders who want the same piece can quickly push the sale price beyond all estimations, which can clearly work in an investor's favour if they are the seller.

5.2 Antiques

Antiques are among the most tangible alternative assets, and like works of art they are collected for their aesthetic appeal, as much as their value. Investing in antiques, like investing in art, is a medium-to-long-term venture. The trick is to choose a style and period you like best and stick to it, because collections of similar pieces are more likely to increase in price than a mishmash of items.

Assets should be examples of fine craftsmanship and be in good condition. To maximise profit, investors should seek to acquire items that they feel may become popular in the future, rather than buying items that are already fashionable and expensive.

Indirect investment in art and antiques can be achieved by investing in businesses which operate in these markets.

5.3 Precious Metals

During times when inflation has soared, currencies have weakened, and stock markets have plummeted (such as during the current period of instability), precious metals have been seen as more attractive. The degree of their attractiveness seems to directly correspond to the level of fear in the markets.

Gold, of course, has always been regarded as intrinsically valuable, accepted internationally and negotiable. Many investment portfolios have a small percentage invested in gold. But investing in precious metals can be complex. Gold prices are dependent on the wider conditions of market for bullion. Gold prices can fluctuate due to political and international events and changes in specific countries. They are open to speculation, as well as changes in technologies involving gold, such as usage in the automobile industry. Depending on how the investor chooses to invest in gold, there may be costs of ownership too. Banks, for example, may apply holding charges for precious metals, and there are no dividends to be earned from gold investment per se.

Investment in precious metals is also open to fraud, with investors advised to purchase their precious metals through banks or reputable dealers. Investment in gold can catch out unwary investors, with large quantities being stolen by criminal gangs, involved in fraud or otherwise being of dubious origin or purity. Demand for gold is variable and subject to fluctuations influenced by the factors discussed above.

Because of their volatility, precious metals should represent only a small portion of an investor's portfolio. The most conservative way to go into precious metals is through a unit trust or OEIC fund. This will be professionally managed, diversified and often particularly well suited to new investors. The drawback to holding precious metals is that they increase in value only when the price per ounce goes up. By contrast, stocks and bonds can pay dividends and offer other income sources. If conditions for gold are poor, it can sit for years doing virtually nothing.

There are five principal ways to invest in gold and precious metals: tangible coins and bars; certificates; precious metals mutual funds; stock in mining companies; and gold and metals futures.

5.4 Commodities

For those keen to invest in commodities, there are several options open. They can spread-bet on moves in the relevant index, although this is not for the faint-hearted as potential losses incurred are unlimited and may exceed the initial investment. They can invest in individual companies, eg, Rio Tinto, although, unless they have a lot of money to play with, they are not really going to be able to spread their risk adequately. A UK-listed collective fund specialising in natural resources or commodities may be more appropriate.

Key Chapter Points

- Fixed-interest securities carry more risk than holding money in a deposit account, because their capital value varies. Changes in interest rates and other economic factors can affect bond prices.
- Fixed-interest securities include those issued by governments (called gilts in the UK) and by companies and other corporate bodies (corporate bonds).
- Bonds from lower-quality issuers (companies with poor credit ratings) will have higher yields than those from higher-quality issuers (such as governments), reflecting the different levels of default risk.
- If held to redemption, the investment cash flows of fixed-interest securities are known, assuming that the bond issuer does not default.
- Ordinary shares and preference shares differ in their dividend rights, in the rights they give over control of the company and in their priority of entitlement to assets on a liquidation.
- Buy-to-let is a form of direct investment in residential property. Returns can vary widely between different regions and timescales.
- Property should be selected with care. All costs and possible void periods should be fully evaluated.
- Most property investors invest for capital gains, but gearing means that a downturn in the market could affect equity severely.
- Commercial property is a different market and some exposure may be considered by investors seeking to diversify across various asset classes.
- Indirect or pooled investment in property allows relatively small sums to be invested in a diversified portfolio of properties and there is much more liquidity than with direct investment.
- Offshore life companies also offer a similar range; in addition, some offer portfolio bonds – where the policyholder can tailor the investments to which their benefits are linked – and capital redemption bonds, where there is no life assured.
- A variety of specialist investments, such as collectables, can prove rewarding but are higher-risk, often illiquid or hard to value, and usually only suitable for experts.

End of Chapter Questions

Think of an answer for each question and refer to the appropriate workbook section for confirmation.

1. What rate is used to compare the interest paid on different savings and investments?
   Answer reference: Section 1.2.3

2. What protection is in place for deposit holders in the UK?
   Answer reference: Section 1.5.2

3. What type of gilt pays a variable rate of interest quarterly?
   Answer reference: Section 2.2.1

4. What form of zero coupon debt securities are used to manage the government's cash and funding requirements?
   Answer reference: Section 2.2.4

5. The holders of which form of share rank last for any surplus remaining after the liquidation of a company?
   Answer reference: Section 3.2.1

6. What form of corporate action results in an increased number of shares in issue without raising any additional capital for a company?
   Answer reference: Section 3.5.4

7. What does a low price/earnings ratio imply for the prospects of a share?
   Answer reference: Section 3.9.2

8. When analysing factors for investing in equities, what would a high dividend yield indicate?
   Answer reference: Section 3.9.3

9. How is the rental yield for an investment property calculated?
   Answer reference: Section 4.4

10. What percentage of taxable income must be distributed to investors in order to qualify for REIT status?
    Answer reference: Section 4.11.4

Chapter Two
The Macroeconomic Environment

1. Macroeconomic Trends and Indicators	135
2. Global Trends and Their Impacts	150
3. National Income (NI)	157
4. Economic and Business Cycles	160
5. Key Economic Indicators	163
6. Fiscal and Monetary Policy	171
7. Influences on Asset Classes	184

This syllabus area will provide approximately 6 of the 80 examination questions

The Macroeconomic Environment

1. Macroeconomic Trends and Indicators

Learning Objective

2.1.1 Understand the main long-term global trends and the effects of technological changes/advancements: ageing population; rising living standards; access to education; growth of the service sector; changing patterns of the economy; productivity of capital and labour; wealth and income distribution; growth of developing economies; natural resources

2.3.1 Understand the role of financial investment in the economy: primary markets as introducers of new funds to business and government; secondary markets enabling investors to adjust investments to meet individual needs

1.1 Introduction

This section develops an understanding of the main economic long-term global trends and the effects of technological and other changes and developments. It should be recognised at this stage that along with other exogenous factors (political, social, technological, environmental and legal and regulatory), the macroeconomic dimension has a strong influence on all of the key capital markets and the asset classes that are studied by us, namely: money markets; fixed income; equities and all of the other alternative investments.

We will begin by considering a variety of features relating to the UK population – predominantly, social, demographic and economic factors. These are, of course, interrelated, and the reason that we begin with them is to help us understand people's investment needs, which result from the socioeconomic environment in which they live, and the trends that they may be subject to.

The term 'demography' means the study of populations using statistics, based on numbers collected through census returns and other surveys. In the UK, a full census of the population is carried out every ten years. The latest took place in 2011. The UK government originally conducted its census as a simple head-count of the population; however, more recently, additional information about the population has been obtained.

The UK government publishes various statistics every year. Two examples are:

- the Annual Abstract of Statistics
- Social Trends.

Both contain information on the population as a whole, but Social Trends describes in more detail the way that people live. Summary census information can also be viewed at statistics.gov.uk (as can the entire texts, both of the Annual Abstract and of Social Trends). Some data comparisons from the past and projections into the future are given in the comments below (source: statistics.gov.uk).

The statistics cited may appear to be somewhat out of date, but at the time of drafting were the most up to date available. This highlights the difficulty in collecting, collating and analysing demographic data for an entire population.

1.2 Population Growth and the Ageing Population

The Office for National Statistics (ONS) revealed in October 2011 that the UK population is projected to increase by 4.9 million to 67.2 million over a ten-year period to 2020. This is equivalent to an annual growth rate of 0.8%. If past trends continue, it is estimated that the UK population should reach 73.2 million by 2035.

The figure below shows the age structure and profile of the UK population in mid-2010 and its projected growth across the population age profiles by mid-2035, for males and females. In the shaded area of this diagram, there are three peaks in the population densities, located around the following age groups: 20–30 years, 40–50 years and 65 years. The peak-level longevities are expected to slide upwards across the age spectrum by 2035. The numbers of pensioners are set to increase over this period as the baby-boomers of the 1960s continue to enjoy longer lives.

Estimated and Projected Age Structure of the UK Population from Mid-2010 to Mid-2035

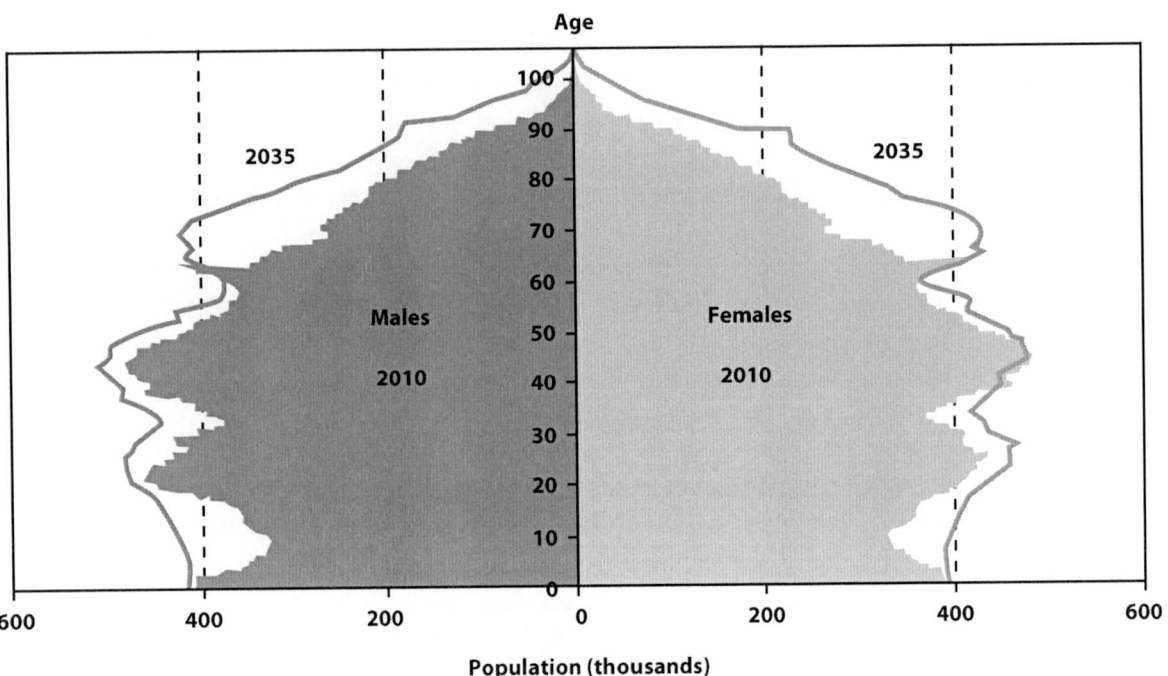

Source: ONS.gov.uk

In common with Europe and other parts of the G7 economies, the UK has an ageing population. The ONS notes that longevity increases in the coming decades will be due to a natural increase (more births than deaths), together with a net inward flow of migrants.

In every year since 1901 (with one exception – 1976) there were more births than deaths. Until the mid-1990s, this natural increase was the main driver of population growth. Since the late 1990s, there has been a continuing natural increase, but net international migration from other countries has also been an increasingly important factor. The population is expected to continue ageing, with the median age rising from 39.7 in 2010 to 39.9 in 2020 and 42.2 in 2035. The number of people of state pension age (SPA) is projected to increase by 28% from 12.2 million to 15.6 million by 2035. This reflects the population of people who were born after the World War II and those born in the 1960s 'baby boom'. There have been longevity improvements in males together with general improvements across the population as advances in medicine, better living standards, housing and nutrition mean that people are living much longer and have higher chances of survival. In 1970 there were just 1,180 centenarians (aged over 100 years) and by 2010 the numbers swelled to a record 12,640. As the figure reveals, this trend is expected to continue further upwards with more super-centenarians (over 110 years of age) emerging as a new class of survivors in the coming decades.

1.3 The Implications of an Ageing Population

Let us consider the impact of ageing population on the economy. This means that there will be a greater percentage of the population over the state pension age (SPA), over 65 years of age. The SPA for women is set to increase from 60 to 65 by 2018, the same as men, and by 2020, the SPA for both sexes will be 66. This means that there will be an increase in the dependency ratio with a smaller percentage of active workers in the society supporting a greater number leaving the workforce.

Generally, it is the working population that has the burden of generating a country's economic wealth. As a greater proportion of the population reaches retirement, there will be an increase in the dependency ratio. The same will, of course, be true in a country where there is a high percentage of people who are so young as to be below working age. The ageing factor means that there will be more people claiming benefits, such as state pension benefits and other age-related benefits if their health deteriorates in old age. At the same time, there will be fewer people working to pay income taxes to service these increased burdens on the state.

Government as a result will have to increase spending on health care and pensions provisions. Those in work will have to continue to pay even higher taxes. This increased level of taxation may create disincentives to work and discourage firms from investing, which would have a negative impact.

Shortages of workers could push wages up leading to wage inflation. Alternatively, firms may have to respond to a worsening labour shortage problem, by encouraging more people to enter the workforce through flexible working practices.

The government has already responded to this demographic challenge by increasing the participation rate in pension savings, and raising the retirement age. The state will also encourage the private sector to share the burden of responsibilities, in terms of pensions provision, health care and education and training of younger people.

In the UK, while the working population as a percentage of the total population has been fairly constant, there has been a shift in the relative proportion of elderly to young dependants. This has been occurring since 1961 and continued into the 1990s. This long-term shift is important for the following reasons:

- Elderly dependants have different needs (for long-term health provision, for example) from younger people, whose main requirements from the state are for education. Planners must take this into account when allocating resources for social provision.
- The elderly, as a market segment, are becoming increasingly dominant. For this category of the population, retirement planning is a key concern.
- The falling numbers of young people will mean that organisations might have to change their recruitment policies or production methods. There will be fewer people of what is currently regarded as working age, and employers will have to compete for them.

1.4 Other Important Demographic and Social Trends

Demographic information is also used to map the social units in which people live (eg, family size) and can impact on the economy in terms of housing needs and other social factors. In social trends surveys, some commonly identified trends in the UK are highlighted below.

As the UK population continues to grow there are notable changes in family and household types.

The ONS families and households survey of 2015 revealed there were 18.7 million families in the UK. Of these, 12.5 million were married or civil partner couples with or without children.

A previous survey covering the period between 2001 and 2011 showed that in 2011 there were 17.9 million families in the UK and of these, 12 million consisted of a married couple with or without children. Since 2001, the number of households has increased by 7%, slightly faster than the 5.3% growth in population and in 2011 there were 26.3 million households in the UK. In 2014, this figure increased to 26.7 million households. This is mainly due to a trend towards smaller household sizes. Between 1961 and 2009, the average household size in the UK fell from 3.1 people per household to 2.4 people. Married couple families are still the common type of family in the UK with the next common type of household in the UK being the one-person household – 7.7 million lived alone in 2011.

Finally on this point, international comparisons of household types reveal that the UK has a much higher average of lone parents with dependent children. Of the 28 EU member states, only Ireland has a higher proportion than the UK. In comparison with the rest of Europe, a slightly lower proportion of households in the UK contain dependent children. Even though fertility is relatively high, a large proportion of women remain childless by the end of their child-bearing years when compared to other European countries.

A number of demographic trends have influenced families and households in recent times and statistics reveal changes in attitudes to marriage and motherhood. For women born in the UK in 1981, only 16% had married by the time they were 25, compared to 71% in 1956.

On education and training, statistics show that there has been a major expansion in early years education. Demand for nursery places for three- to four-year-olds has risen and there has also been an expansion in the further education sector, as more teenagers have continued into full-time education after school. Note that in 1970–71 there were 621,000 continuing on to full-time education compared to 3 million in 2013.

Following the sub-prime crisis in 2008, the UK economy contracted and the proportion of households without work increased. Unemployment rose and also had a negative impact on the savings ratio. The ratio plunged to 1.7% of total resources, when compared to its long-term average of 7.6% over the 1970–2008 period. Further examination of household expenditures revealed a new pattern as households were spending more on housing, water and fuel – 21% of the housing budget was allocated to this expense against 15% in 1970. Spending on services increased, namely: personal care services and products; financial and insurance services products; and transportation.

On health, reports show low infant and neonatal mortality rates. Improvements are traced to better nutrition together with rapid advancement in medicine and allied technologies that have also contributed significantly to increased longevity in the rest of the population. Even though there has been improvement on these fronts, individual behaviour and lifestyle choices in relation to diet and exercise, particularly in the lower income groups, have resulted in increased concerns among doctors and the National Health Service (NHS) over obesity rates. In 2015, 58% of women and 68% of men were deemed to be overweight or obese and obesity prevalence increased from 15% in 1993 to 27% in 2015.

The economic downturn in 2008 also depressed activity in the house-building and home-sales sectors, although this has since recovered to pre-recession levels. Although government initiatives, such as the Help to Buy scheme have been useful for new entrants to the residential property market, first time buyers continue to struggle to get a foot on the ladder. New rules introduced for mortgage lending in April 2014 continue to have an impact on new lending. Historically, the proportion of households aged under 30 buying homes with a mortgage fell from 43% in 1997 to just 29% in 2009, and this trend continues.

On the environmental, energy safety and climatic factors side, the UK government signed up to the EU Renewables Directive in June 2009. The agreement committed the UK to an ambitious target of sourcing 15% of its energy from renewables by 2020, meaning that approximately 35–40% of electricity generated in the UK will have to come from renewable resources. In 2006, renewable electricity accounted for just 4.6% of the gross electricity consumption. So far, the UK has failed to reach its 10% renewable electricity target, returning only 6.5% of electricity from these sources. However, the government is committed to developing a renewables sector, as this is a growth industry where many jobs will be created in the future. In February 2016, Parliament's Energy and Climate Change Committee confirmed the government was set to receive 11.5% of its energy from renewable sources by 2020 unless action was taken.

In the area of transportation, statistics reveal that individuals, particularly children in the UK, have increasingly become reliant on cars as a mode of transport to school.

Finally, on lifestyles and social participation there has been growing popularity in internet usage. In 2014, 74% of the adult population bought or ordered goods and services over the internet. This was the highest percentage of internet usage in any EU country. Websites are also the most popular source of reading among 9–14 year olds. Going on holiday trips remains the most popular activity for UK residents.

1.5 The Effects of Changing Demographics on the Financial Life Cycle

The financial life cycle is a concept that is used when considering what people's financial needs might typically be at various stages in their lives. Although not everyone's life follows this pattern, this generality can still be a useful tool for predicting what products and services will be in most demand as the population's demographic (in terms of age) changes.

Particular products and services can be target-marketed at people who occupy specific stages in the cycle. For example, the following stages might be identified:

- **Childhood** – characterised by dependence for most needs on adult carers. Financial needs are usually few, though a child may have a need for a savings account, and perhaps a cashpoint card.
- **Single young adulthood** – usually at this stage, the person is either in further education or in their first job. Income may still be relatively low, but the individual may also have few financial commitments as yet and a reasonable amount of disposable income. The thought of saving for the future may not be a high priority.
- **Young couple, no children** – at this stage there may be two incomes coming into the household and, with no children, again no major financial commitments. However if the couple are attempting to get on the property ladder, then saving for a deposit will be a priority: if they have already bought, then the right mortgage will be important.
- **Parents with dependent children** – usually in a couple, but, as we have seen, lone parents are becoming increasingly common. At this stage, disposable income is likely to fall: in addition the parent(s) may have less time for leisure activities. Saving for a larger property or for school fees may be a priority.
- **Empty-nesters** – this is the term used for parents whose children have left home and are independent. Such people may suddenly find that they have more disposable income than they have had for a long time. In addition, their careers may be well advanced so that their incomes are reasonably high, and if they are fortunate they may also have paid off a large proportion of their mortgages and be living in a property which has increased in value. However, for many this stage has not been so easy – their property may have fallen in value, and because of the difficulty of getting on the property ladder their adult children may still be living at home.
- **Retired** – an increasing proportion of the population, as we have seen. Retirees who have been in employment or otherwise managed to save for much of their lives may have accumulated a reasonable amount of capital; in addition, if they are homeowners, they may have capital locked up in the value of their homes. Their financial needs may centre on ensuring that this capital generates enough income for them to live on; on provision of long-term care when their health is not so good; and perhaps on how they may best leave any surplus assets to their intended beneficiaries on death.

This traditional pattern is, however, changing – for a variety of reasons:

- Our empty-nesters may find that, rather than caring for their children, they are now caring for their elderly parents – which places an additional financial and time burden on them. This pattern is likely to continue, and indeed increase, as the population ages.
- The increasing longevity of people means that the issue of paying for care into old age is gaining in importance – especially if the adult children of the elderly population are unwilling or unable to shoulder this burden.
- Affordability issues – brought about by the fact that wage inflation has not kept pace with house price inflation – means that many people who would in earlier decades have been on the housing ladder are now renting or – increasingly – remaining in the family home until well into adulthood. This means that would-be empty-nesters may, in some cases, have both their own parents and their adult children living with them.

1.6 UK Living Standards

The standard of living refers to the level of wealth, happiness, comfort, material goods and other necessities available to a certain socioeconomic class in a geographic area. The measure includes factors such as income, quality and availability of employment, class disparity, poverty rate, quality and affordability of housing, hours of work required to purchase necessities, the GDP and a whole host of other factors that improve the quality of life for an individual living in a particular country. Given that living standards also provide an assessment on the quality of life, which is in fact a subjective measure, it is not surprising that economists have trouble in identifying a suitable quantifiable and reliable measure. Such a measure will need to encapsulate all the features of a living standard and quality of life in a single index that is also comparable across all geographic regions of the world.

One common benchmark for measuring the standard of living in a country is to use the real national income per capita; found by dividing the real inflation-adjusted national income (GDP or GNP) by the total population. For cross-country comparisons, the data is nearly always expressed in a common currency (typically US dollars). However, measures of living standards across different countries are difficult to compare. Social and welfare economists have over the years devised a variety of indices to try to get a more accurate representation of this attribute. Other measures that you may find include the poverty rate, access and quality of health care, income growth inequality, the Pareto Index (breadth of income and wealth distribution) and educational standards. Other measures are discussed in the next section where income and wealth distribution is covered.

Clearly some of these factors have subjective elements that may be quite difficult to measure from the macroeconomic statistics that are available from each country. Of course, the assumption is that all countries produce audited data that is transparent and reliable enough for economists and market analysts.

From the statistical information, economists draw inferences about living standards and the quality of life. For example, in an industrialising economy, even though the GDP per capita in an economy may be rising, estimates of pollution levels may point to externalities in terms of increased social costs that deprive individuals of a certain quality of life. In addition, even though the average GDP per capita for an economy may be rising, the numbers of people living at the poverty level may not change, nor draw any benefit from improvements in the economy, while the rich may continue to get richer. As examples, some social welfare statistics that are employed to measure the quality of life are:

- number of patients per doctor and hospital waiting times – a measure of health provision
- infant mortality rates
- literacy rates – measure of educational attainment and provision
- average food intake per person – a measure of nutrition provision
- average educational attainment at different levels
- crime rates
- divorce rates
- corruption rate.

Now let us look at evidence that has been provided about the rising living standards in the UK. As a developed economy, the UK has been experiencing rising living standards for a number of decades.

In 2010, a study conducted by Eurostat (186/2011 13 December 2011) revealed that despite the turbulence in the global economy, created by the 2008 credit crisis, the standard of living in the UK remained the second highest in the EU area; Luxembourg held the top position. They used a measure called the actual individual consumption (AIC) per head to draw this conclusion. The average index is 100 for 27 economies in the EU; Luxembourg had an AIC index of 150 and the UK had one of 121. Bulgaria was lowest with an AIC of 42, 58% below the EU average. In the 2013 study, the UK had dropped to tenth highest with an AIC of 115; Luxembourg remained top with an AIC of 141, and Bulgaria remained the lowest with an AIC of 38.

AIC is often used as a measure of households' standard of living as it incorporates all goods and services that a household consumes, regardless of whether they pay for them.

In contrast to the AIC index, when GDP per capita was used in the Eurostat study, the UK dropped to tenth position in the EU list, where it remains today. In a relative comparison, the UK is indexed at 109 GDP per capita against 257 for Luxembourg. Real GDP per capita per head measures how much individuals spend rather than consume. The disparity between the AIC and the GDP per capita measures is explained by public services, such as health and education, being largely government-funded in the UK.

Another study of UK living standards published by the Institute of Financial Studies (IFS) in September 2011 revealed a different picture with a worsening situation. In the light of the government austerity measures, the IFS study warned that the UK government might have to reconsider their plans for spending cuts in the face of weak economic growth and prospects. Its survey showed that families saw the biggest fall in living standards in 30 years during 2010–11, and household budgets face a ten-year long squeeze on the back of the government's tax rises and austerity measures. The most severe consequences of the recession in UK living standards were just starting to be felt and would continue for many years to come, the survey noted. In 2014, the IFS reported that there was little reason to expect a strong recovery in living standards over the next few years.

In March 2015, IFS projections showed that living standards in 2014–15, as measured by median household income, had reached a level similar to that seen in 2007–08 or prior to the recession. Nevertheless, the recovery in living standards that began in 2011–12 has been much slower than in each of the three previous recessions. In 2017, the IFS predicted real median income to grow by 3.8% between 2017 and 2022, but this projection is highly sensitive to future pay growth.

1.7 Changing Patterns of the Economy

A distinction can be made between the primary, secondary and tertiary sectors of the economy. As we will see, these sectors can change in importance over time (see section 1.7.1 for more information on the structural changes experienced within the UK):

- The **primary sector** of the economy consists of industries that produce raw materials such as crops and minerals. These are sometimes called extractive industries. Over the long term, this is a shrinking sector in the UK.
- The **secondary sector** consists of industries that process raw materials – largely, the manufacturing industry. This sector normally grows rapidly during the early stages of economic development. In the UK, this is also in decline – mainly due to falling manufacturing (the part of the sector most heavily involved in international trade), as opposed to construction, energy and water. The decline in the secondary sector has led to falling employment in this area. This has created some severe unemployment problems in regions which were previously heavily dependent on particular industries.
- The **tertiary sector** is made up mainly of goods distribution and service industries. It is often referred to as the service sector of the economy. This sector has become the predominant provider of employment and output in the UK economy. A major reason for the continuing growth in this sector has been the rapid expansion in the banking, finance and insurance sectors, many of which are well placed to capitalise on recent technological advances (see section 1.10).

1.7.1 The Growth of the Service Sector

In 2008, HM Treasury provided a comprehensive review of the long-term performance and strategic challenges for the UK economy. This report highlighted the structural adjustment that the economy is expected to undergo, as a result of two major developments in the global economy:

- technological advances that have reduced transport and communication costs, offering businesses greater choice in where their operations are located, and
- the integration of emerging markets in the world economy that has seen a rapid increase in trade and investment flows. The emergence of the BRIICS (Brazilian, Russian, Indian, Indonesian, Chinese and South African) economies is described in detail in section 1.11.

Since the 1970s the most noticeable trend in the UK has been the substantial de-industrialisation of the economy. Manufacturing activity has been replaced by a growing services sector. It is important to recognise that the UK is not the only economy to see a switch from manufacturing activity to services in recent decades, but this is typical of the structural changes faced by many other G7 economies.

Industries were responsible for 22.1% of the UK's GDP output in 2010 (20.5% in 2014) and the UK is the sixth largest manufacturer of goods in the world according to the value of outputs. Despite its low contribution to the overall output, the UK manufacturing sector continues to play an important role, in particular in the high value-added areas where the UK continues to have a comparative advantage. Growth in high-technology industries, such as aerospace, pharmaceuticals and computer manufacturing, has outpaced growth in other manufacturing sectors.

Agriculture contributed 1.4% of the UK's GDP in 2010 (0.7% in 2014) and this sector is still considered, both from a historical and traditional perspective, to be an important part of the economy as it delivers 60% of the nation's food needs.

By far the most dominant component of the UK economy is the services industry, contributing 78.9% to GDP in 2014, compared to 66% in 1995 and under 55% in 1975. Within this broad services sector, as a sub-set the finance and banking sector has a prominent role, with the London being a major global centre for financial services.

Tourism is another important service sector in the UK. HM Treasury has noted that over the last decade the shift to services orientation has been much greater in the UK than other G7 economies. In part, this reflects the UK's comparative advantage in financial and other business services and the creative industries.

Within the tertiary (service) sector, the rising share of banking, finance and insurance reflects a number of factors:

- London has built on its reputation as one of the leading financial centres of the world and in many areas (for example, currency trading) it is pre-eminent, despite increasing competition from other centres. The strong position of the City (the London financial community) makes it a large exporter of financial services.
- Increasing affluence and changing social factors (eg, increasing levels of owner-occupation of housing) have increased domestic demand for financial products of various kinds (eg, current accounts, mortgages and insurance products).
- Events such as the abolition of exchange controls in 1979 and the deregulation of financial markets during the 1980s served to widen supply as well as intensify competition in this subsector.

Further, the dynamic forces of change that have spread across the economy in the last decade have highlighted a growing importance of the knowledge economy and of innovation.

The Sainsbury Review of Science and Innovation (October 2007) estimated that the knowledge-intensive sector as a proportion of GDP increased by 5% over the previous decade. Moreover, the creative industries have also played an increasingly important role, growing by an average of 6% a year between the period 1997 and 2005. The creative industries currently contribute 6% of GDP, employ over two million people and export over £16 billion annually.

The Macroeconomic Environment

As the economy has moved towards knowledge-based activity and shifted to the production of high-tech and high value-added services, the importance of skills, high-level training and innovation has increased. The productivity improvements and expansion in the UK services industry has not arisen just through local or domestic demand, but also through a focus on tradeable, knowledge-intensive services with which the other developing low-wage economies with less skilled labour are less able to compete. Apart from the US, the UK has a greater proportion of value-added that has risen from knowledge-intensive services growth. The OECD defines this type of value-added as high-growth services.

1.8 Productivity

Economists identify four factors of production in the economy: land, labour, capital (ie, machinery and plant) and enterprise. These factors are combined in various ways, in order to produce goods and services.

Productivity is a measure of the efficiency with which factors of production are used. It can be calculated as the total output divided by the number of units of a factor of production, for example, the number of persons employed (to measure the productivity of labour) or the number or value of machines used (to measure the productivity of capital).

Substitution between factors of production (for example, between labour and capital) may take place if it is feasible; for example, machines can be made to do work previously carried out by labour, or people can provide labour to do work that would otherwise be done by machines. It is most likely when the price or productivity of one factor of production rises relative to another. If wages go up, the marginal cost of labour will rise and firms will want less labour at this higher cost. Labour will also become more expensive in relation to capital, and there will be some substitution of capital for labour. The net result of an increase in wages is a reduction in the quantity of labour employed, unless the productivity of labour can be increased at the same time, to strengthen the demand for labour.

Increases in productivity create greater economic wealth and boost real household incomes. By producing more with the country's factors of production, there are more goods and services available for people to use and consume.

In general, the service sector has higher profitability than the manufacturing sector; this reflects the fact that the manufacturing sector is more capital-intensive and so involves more capital expenditure on fixed assets.

As productivity is a key determinant of long-term growth together with employment growth, it helps UK residents to enjoy high levels of prosperity. However, the UK has more to do in order to catch up with their comparators in Europe. Based on the *Productivity in the UK* report published by the HM Treasury in November 2007, it has been established that the UK has had a long-standing productivity gap with the US, France and Germany for some time. It has been estimated by other economists that, while the UK used to have the highest levels of GDP hours worked in the world, by 1950 the UK had slipped to fifth position (behind the US and Australia). By 1973, the UK had slipped to 11th position falling behind most EU countries.

Between 2000 and 2010 the UK regained some ground and raised its productivity rate to narrow the gap with its comparators. HM Treasury noted in 2008 that the output per hour productivity growth in the current economic cycle (1997H1–2006H2) averaged 2.4% per year against 1.9% per year in the previous two cycles over the 1978–97 periods. The ONS has recently stated that output per hour worked in the UK was 18 percentage points below the average for the remaining six members of the G7 group of industrial nations in 2014.

The historic productivity gap with comparator countries has also been reduced. It is believed a number of factors have contributed to this improvement, including the UK's policy to open its trade and investment, together with the resilience of the economy to shocks, government policies, macroeconomic stability and the structural shifts and adjustments that have taken place in the economy over the last few years.

1.9 Wealth and Income Distribution

Economists make a clear distinction between income and wealth.

- Income is a flow of factor incomes such as wages and earnings from work. Personal income is the amount received by individuals and households from all sources, including wages and salaries, state benefits, tax credits, pensions and investments (ie, rent from ownership of land and interest and dividends from savings and ownership of shares).
- Wealth is a stock of financial and real assets. Personal wealth is the value of individual and household assets, including property, financial, physical and pension assets.

Income and wealth is not evenly distributed throughout households in the UK: roughly speaking, the top fifth of households are some four times better off, in income terms, than the bottom fifth.

In 2008–09, the original income (that is, income like wages and pensions – before allowing for taxes and benefits) of the top fifth of households in the UK was 15 times greater than that for the bottom fifth (£73,800 per household per year compared with £5,000). However, after this had been redistributed through taxes and benefits, the ratio came down to four-to-one (an average final income of £53,900 compared with £13,600). Before taxes and benefits, the richest fifth of households had an average income of £80,800 in 2013–14; this was 15 times greater than the poorest fifth, who had an average income of £5,500. In 2015–16, households in the bottom 10% of the population have, on average, a disposable (or net) income of £9,644 (this includes wages and cash benefits and is after direct taxes, such as income tax and council tax, but not after indirect taxes, such as VAT). The top 10% have net incomes of almost nine times that of the bottom 10% (£83,875).

The distribution of income and wealth can be measured by using concepts such as the Lorenz curve and the Gini coefficient. The Lorenz curve plots the % income cumulative against the income distribution of households (from poorest to richest). It is a straight line relationship where there is perfect equality in an economy. However, in all economies there is inequality and the resultant Lorenz curve produced is concave.

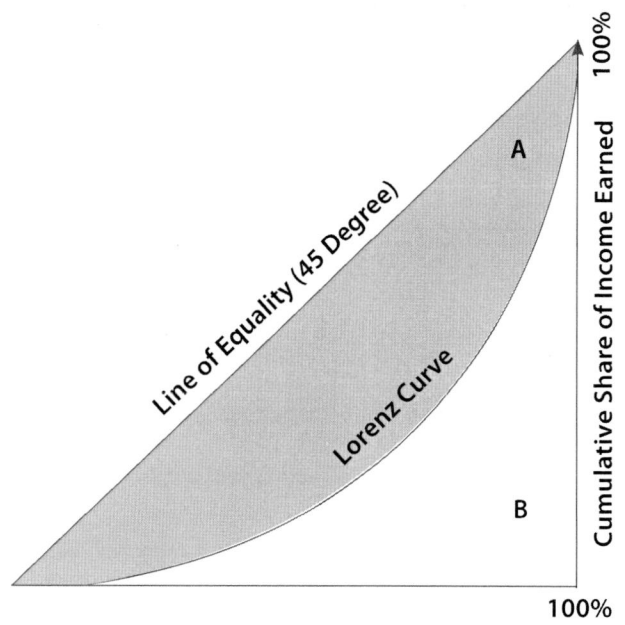

Cumulative Share of People from Lowest to Highest Incomes

In simple terms, the graph above represents the proportion of the income that is distributed between the poorest people, middle-income people and richest people. There will always be rich and poor, but we are interested in determining how evenly wealth in a country or an economy is distributed across the groups. It should come as no surprise that most governments try to ensure that this Gini coefficient is kept as low as possible.

The Gini coefficient ranges between 0 and 100 and is calculated by taking the ratio of two areas:

$$\text{Gini coefficient} = \frac{\text{Area A}}{\text{Area (A+B)}}$$

Area of A represents the region between the straight line (line of equality) and the curve (Lorenz curve). Clearly if this region was zero in terms of area, then A = 0 and Gini coefficient = 0. It means the Lorenz curve is actually the line of equality. In this case, it means there is perfect distribution of income (ie, everyone earns the same amount).

If A occupies a very large area (making B very small), then the Gini coefficient is large (almost 1) and it means there is uneven distribution of income. Countries with a high Gini coefficient are more likely to become unsettled by dissenting masses of poor people who are envious of the wealth and greed of a few rich people.

Economists have long recognised that such inequalities are addressed by taxation of high-income households. Further, the ONS points out that some types of household gain more than others from the redistribution of income through tax and welfare benefits.

Let us now consider some historical perspectives on income. Unlike the 1970s and the 1980s, real household disposable income per head continued to grow almost continuously through the 1990s and 2000s, irrespective of recessions. Seventy-three per cent of household income in 2006–09 was generated from wages, salaries and from self-employed earnings. The household income distribution is uneven:

- Pensioner households reliant on state welfare benefits, together with lone parent households are more likely to be at the lower end of the income spectrum.
- Couples without children are more likely to be at the top of the spectrum.

Cash benefits like income support, pension credit, child benefit, incapacity benefit and the state retirement pension play a big part in reducing income inequality, as they are paid mainly to households with lower incomes.

Visit www.equalitytrust.org.uk/scale-economic-inequality-uk for the most up-to-date picture on income and wealth distribution in the UK.

In 2014, 6.5% of the UK population were in persistent poverty, equivalent to approximately 3.9 million people. Persistent poverty is defined as experiencing relative low income in the current year, as well as for at least two out of the three preceding years.

The 2014 UK persistent poverty rate is one of the lowest in the EU; however, the overall poverty rate of 16.8% placed the UK twelfth highest out of the EU countries.

Explanations for the Scale of Income and Wealth Inequality in the UK

There is a host of reasons to explain the existence of the divide in incomes and wealth in the UK. A majority are of an economic origin, and some have social origins.

a. **Differences in pay in different jobs and industries** – high-growth and knowledge-based high-growth industries have enjoyed above-average increases in pay and earnings. Pay is also better in those areas where skill shortages are apparent, namely: financial; business services; and IT industries. On the other hand, the public-sector service jobs have seen a decline in relative pay levels.
b. **Falling relative incomes of people dependent on state benefits** – state welfare benefits paid to pensioners and lone households with children tend to fall in this category and as these households are reliant on welfare benefits, that are index-linked, their relative pay has fallen over time.
c. **Effects of unemployment** – this is a key cause of relative poverty where real incomes have fallen back as a result of one or more members in the household losing their jobs and some entirely reliant on state welfare.
d. **Changes to the tax and benefits system** – changes to direct and indirect taxes are designed to equalise pay and to address inequalities resulting from externalities, but changes can increase relative poverty as well. The top marginal rate of tax fell from 83% in 1979 to 40% in 1988 where it has remained, although an additional rate of tax (currently 45%) was introduced in 2010 for those with incomes above £150,000. The basic rate has come down from 33% in 1979 to 20% today and these tax deductions allow people in work to keep more of their pay. However the fall in the progressive nature of the UK tax regime has highlighted some inconsistencies where people on above-average incomes have disproportionately gained from the tax ease.

1.10 Technological Changes and Advances

The development of new technology is behind many of the increases in productivity that have helped create economic growth. New technologies can produce significant leaps forward in economic conditions.

For example, the dawn of mass production made possible by the industrial revolution of the late 18th century was fuelled by technological advances – specifically, in the spinning of cotton and the development of steam power. Electrification and the development of motorised transport were further major technological changes.

More recently, computerisation has made major changes to the economy and to how businesses organise their operations. Interconnectedness, by way of the internet and advanced telecommunications, is having a further effect in terms of how information and data are transmitted, how businesses and people communicate and how, when and where people work.

The availability of fast and efficient telecommunications enables a shift to new ways of employing staff resources and of reaching customers. In the past, workers may have had to relocate to where employers delivered their services. Now, a bank, for example, may outsource many staff functions involving communication with customers to overseas centres; extensive branch networks have become a thing of the past for many financial services companies, and many functions have been centralised.

1.11 The Growth of Developing Economies

An exact definition of emerging economies and their markets are difficult to find. However, the term 'emerging markets' (EM) was first coined in the 1980s by the economist Antoine Van Agtamael, then at the World Bank. He originally identified a set of economies that were large and were going through a period of transformation that was characterised by rapid economic growth and industrialisation. These economies were in a transitional phase, from developing into developed.

The acronym used to identify the first four of these economies is BRIC, representing the large EM nations: Brazil, Russia, India and China. By 2006, around 28 emerging markets in the world had been identified, and by 2012 this list had expanded to include a total of 40 or so countries. Still, the eight largest emerging and developing economies by either GDP or GNP are: China, Brazil, Russia, India, Mexico, South Korea, Indonesia and Turkey. These countries do not necessarily share a common agenda, but they are starting to make a significant impact in the world economy and on political platforms. Even today, China and India are fast becoming economic powerhouses, but are still considered emerging economies.

All EM economies are in a transition, meaning that they are in a process of moving from a closed economy to an open economy. Another feature of the big EM is that their countries can often have large populations and/or occupy large land masses where the potential for economic and future development is great, thus presenting G7 nations in particular as trade partners with further opportunities to boost their own trade via exports or investment. EM growth is fuelled in two different directions: through external growth, where strong trade links are established with G7 economies; and also through internal growth that supports domestic demand from their own domestic markets for goods and services. It is this dual nature of growth that provides EM economies opportunities for accelerating their growth when compared to the developed G7 economies. Often, the large EMs back up their economic prowess with emerging political clout. EM economies have a desire to pursue large projects calling for infrastructure developments. These countries have pursued economic policies that lead to faster growth and expanding trade and investment with the rest of the world. They also have aspirations to be future technological leaders.

1.12 Natural Resources

The continued globalisation of economies has led to a more distributed world, where consumption is becoming more widely spread than before. Consumers are gaining greater mobility and middle class society continues to expand. This continued growth and distribution has led to a significant increase in demand for natural resources (both hard and soft commodities), eg, metals, crops, etc. As a result, there is increasing pressure on economies to identify and secure access to these resources in order to remain competitive in the global market. Continued advances in technology are crucial in helping to locate, extract (or preserve), and ultimately exploit the resources. Costs are also a crucial factor and even though these resources may be identified, the cost of extraction combined with environmental factors may be prohibitive. This can lead to a requirement to 'buy in' the resources, potentially at a premium from a competitive economy.

2. Global Trends and Their Impacts

Learning Objective

2.1.2 Understand the impact of the following on global trades and asset classes: international markets; trade agreements; tariffs; protectionism; globalisation of business and finance; market failures

So far, we have thought about the effects of various local factors, such as demographics, on the UK economy. But a country's economy does not exist in isolation; it is also affected by what is happening in the rest of the world. In many ways the effect of world events on countries' local economies and social environments is increasing; we call this effect globalisation.

2.1 International Markets

The financial markets in the UK are regarded by many as the main world markets for dealing in a variety of assets such as securities and derivatives: equities, warrants, fixed income, currencies, money markets, contracts for difference (CFDs), **options**, futures, and other linked investment products. But these UK-based markets face stiff competition from other financial centres, which try to compete for international business by introducing innovative financial instruments, ensuring speedier or more secure settlement, or making dealing cheaper and quicker. However, as competition can improve efficiency and global education, we should regard this as a positive outlook in the long term.

In addition to these longer-term considerations, financial markets in the UK are affected on a daily basis by what is going on overseas. Just as events in other countries affect the UK economy, so they do the UK stock market. Rates of growth in the rest of the world are especially important for economies (like the UK's) that have a large foreign trade sector. If trading partners have slow growth, the amount of exports a country can sell to them will grow only slowly. This limits the country's own opportunities for investment and growth.

Different national economies may be at different stages of the business cycle at any one time. However, with increasing globalisation of trade and investment, there is a tendency for their economic cycles to become increasingly correlated (tied in with one another). In particular, the large size and economic wealth of the economy of the US exerts a significant influence on the economies of other countries, particularly its major trading partners such as the UK.

The importance of the US in the world economy means that investment markets, such as equity and bond markets, often react most closely to what is happening in the economy and markets of the US. If there is an economic recovery in the US, it is anticipated that this recovery will soon affect other economies, as US consumers and companies will demand more goods and services available on world markets. The stimulus to other countries will have knock-on effects in those countries as companies' earnings are boosted and employment rises.

To summarise:

- The price of assets dealt on UK markets is affected by events on foreign markets. If events in the US mean that its stock market falls sharply, then other world markets invariably suffer as a result. (As the old adage has it, if the US stock market sneezes, the whole world catches a cold.) A good example is the 2008 credit crisis and, more recently, the markets' reaction to the suggestion of a reduction in US quantitative easing in May 2013 – the 'Taper Tantrum'.
- Many multinational companies have their shares traded on more than one stock market. Events affecting the shares in one place will affect the prices at which they are quoted in others, through **arbitrage** activity. Arbitrage is activity which aims to take advantage of the different prices at which an asset might be traded on different markets; it has the effect of bringing those prices back into balance.
- Many companies quoted on the LSE have operations around the world – so economic events in other countries affect their value and profitability.
- Events affecting other countries' currencies can (as we will see in section 5.9) have a significant effect on UK markets, through the economy and interest rates.

Because of these and similar factors, the wealth of UK people and businesses, which is tied up in shares or other investments, can be affected by what is happening in the international markets.

As well as monitoring the growth of individual economies, we can measure growth and output for larger regions – and, indeed, for the world as a whole. The International Monetary Fund (IMF) publishes a *World Economic Outlook* twice a year.

2.2 Globalisation of Business and Finance

In terms of business and finance, the term 'globalisation' tends to be used in several ways.

- It is often used to describe the increasingly interrelated and interconnected nature of business and financial systems. Businesses which were once essentially local now increasingly cross borders: banks offer services to people and businesses in many different countries; and businesses find their raw materials, and sell to customers, much farther afield than used to be the case.
- It is also used to describe the way in which various things (products, processes and, in some cases, lifestyles) are becoming more similar around the world – as people and businesses become more mobile, taking their ways of doing things with them, and as international standards are established to make it easier for international trade and activity to take place.

You can probably think of some examples pretty easily: McDonald's is a good example of a retail business which provides a pretty similar consumer experience, wherever you are in the world; and there are few countries without a McDonald's. In the world of finance, HSBC (which provides banking, investment and a host of other services) has some 9,500 offices in 85 countries and describes itself as 'the world's local bank'; perhaps in an attempt to show that, while it may be truly global, it also makes an effort to reflect local business practices wherever it operates. A customer of HSBC, or any other global banking organisation, could probably move from one country to another without having to change the banking group with which they dealt.

The pace at which trade and finance becomes globalised, and the rate of flow of goods, services and money around the world as a consequence, has also been helped by the efforts of governments and many multinational organisations such as the World Trade Organisation (WTO) and the Organisation for Economic Co-operation and Development (OECD).

- The WTO deals with the rules of trade between different nations and among its aims are the liberalisation of trade laws between countries. It provides a forum in which governments can negotiate the basis on which their countries will trade with one another.
- The OECD describes itself as *'an international organisation helping governments tackle the economic, social and governance challenges of a globalised economy'*. Among other things, it aims to help contribute to world trade, and to support sustainable economic world growth.
- Alongside the work undertaken by the WTO in liberalising trade through the use of global multilateral agreements, the development of regional trade agreements (RTAs) has continued to grow and now accounts for over half of all international trade. The OECD considers that the use of RTAs helps to strengthen the existing WTO framework and certain features adopted at regional level actually serve to complement the existing multilateral rules on global trade.

Another international forum working on liberalising trade, this time within a specific block of countries, is the EU, which is covered in section 2.3.

Globalisation is seen by some as good (for example, where it enables poorer countries to participate in international trade) and by others as bad (for example, where it results in the loss of national identities and an increasingly homogeneous world – or where it results in the rise of huge multinationals, which are so big that they are seen as being beyond the control of governments and regulators). Whatever your view, it is an increasing fact of life.

2.2.1 The Impacts of Technology

We have already noted that technology has had a huge impact on the way businesses interact, and on how profitable they are. A number of issues arise from this, in the context of global dynamics:

- As we saw in section 1.10, some businesses – including financial services firms – have found that they can outsource or offshore certain activities (typically call centres and computer programming) to countries where appropriately skilled labour is cheaper, such as India.
- For some types of businesses – including in financial services – the internet has been a key factor in this development; it is easy for buyers and sellers to find one another, and electronic communications – coupled with increasing clarity on the law regarding electronically concluded agreements – has speeded up the pace at which they can do business across borders.
- If one country has access to new technologies which have not yet been adopted, or cannot be afforded, in another, it can give the first country a significant economic advantage.

2.3 European Economic and Monetary Union

The European Union (EU), initially called the European Economic Community (EEC), was set up after the Second World War, with the aim of integrating the various countries and helping them rebuild their economies. The process of European integration was launched on 9 May 1950, when France officially proposed to create *'the first concrete foundation of a European federation'*.

Six countries (Belgium, Germany, France, Italy, Luxembourg and the Netherlands) joined from the very beginning. Today, after several waves of accession, the EU has 27 member states.

The EU works towards single European markets in various trade sectors, finance being one of the most important. The aim is to remove barriers to international trade by, among other things, ensuring that similar regulatory rules are in place throughout the EU. From a financial services perspective this should mean that, in terms of investor protection, it makes no difference to a customer whether they buy a financial product from a provider in their home state, or from a neighbouring state.

Many of the measures by which the EU is working towards this come under an initiative called the financial services action plan, which aims to introduce similar laws and regulations in various areas of financial services. Many of these are already in place, and the UK itself has implemented a number of them. This means that it is easier for UK financial services firms to sell their products into Europe – but also that it is easier for EU firms to sell their products into the UK (meaning more local competition for UK firms).

A further aim of the EU is to achieve monetary union across as many member countries as is possible, through the process of substituting the euro for their existing home currency. Countries have to satisfy certain economic conditions before they can do so, but many believe that the benefits of meeting those conditions are worthwhile.

A referendum was held on 23 June 2016 to decide whether the UK should leave or remain in the EU.

The referendum turnout was 71.8%, with over 30 million people voting, and was the highest turnout in a UK-wide vote since the 1992 general election. The UK voted in favour to leave the EU by 52% to 48%.

England voted to leave the EU by 53.4% to 46.6%, while the leave vote in Wales received 52.5% of the vote. Both Scotland and Northern Ireland voted to remain in the EU. Scotland backed to remain in the EU by 62% to 38%, while 55.8% in Northern Ireland voted to remain.

In order to leave the EU, the UK had to invoke Article 50 of the Lisbon Treaty. Article 50 has only been in force since late 2009 and has yet to be tested, and so how the exit process will work is somewhat unknown territory. On 29 March 2017, the UK triggered Article 50 and started the two-year countdown to the UK leaving the EU.

EU law will continue to stand in the UK until it ceases being a member. As it negotiates a withdrawal agreement and the terms of its relationship with the EU, the UK will continue to abide by EU treaties and laws but will not take part in any decision-making.

2.4 Market Failure

Market failure occurs when freely functioning markets fail to deliver an optimum allocation of resources. This prevents equilibrium – a situation in which demand for products and services does not equate to the quantity supplied and, as a result, economic and social welfare may not be maximised and eventually lead to economic inefficiencies. Under such circumstances, there is a clear economic case for government intervention in markets that is required to redress the economic balance and to restore equilibrium.

Government can justify their interventionist policies by stating that they are acting in the best interests of the public when markets cannot achieve market efficiency. This is especially true if, for example, there is a Pareto sub-optimal allocation of resources in a market/industry.

The main causes of market failure are as follows.

Externalities

This is where private and social costs and/or benefits diverge. The social optimum output or level of consumption diverges from the private optimum. They are defined as third party (or spill-over) effects arising from the production and/or consumption of goods and services for which no appropriate compensation is paid. Externalities can cause market failure if the price mechanism does not take into account the full social costs and social benefits of production and consumption.

Public Goods

The characteristics of pure public goods are the opposite of private goods. In fact, most are services rather than goods. These services are clearly in demand but must be provided collectively by the government for two main reasons:

- **Non-excludability** – goods cannot only be confined to those who have paid for them. However, there is always the problem that non-payers can take a free ride and enjoy the benefits of consumption of the goods.
- **Non-rivalry in consumption** – consumption by one person does not reduce the availability of the same goods to others.

Some examples of public goods/services include police services, flood defence systems, street lighting, public parks and beaches and national defence. Public goods are not normally provided by the private sector in an economy and because of their nature, the private sector is unlikely to be willing and able to provide public goods. The government therefore provides them for collective consumption and finances them through general taxation.

Merit Goods

Merit goods are those goods and services, the provision of which the government regards as necessary to avoid under-consumption. The government feels obliged, therefore, to subsidise or provide the good/service free at the point of use.

Both the public and private sector of the economy can provide merit goods and services. Consumption of merit goods is thought to generate positive externality effects when the social benefit from consumption exceeds the private benefit (for example, health services, education, work training, public libraries, citizen's advice, inoculations).

Monopoly

Agents operating in a market can gain market power, allowing them to prevent other mutually beneficial gains from trades occurring. This can lead to inefficiency due to imperfect competition. Agents may artificially fix prices higher and moderate output when compared to free-functioning competitive markets where there are many suppliers.

Inequality

Market failure can also be caused by the existence of inequality throughout the economy. Wide differences in income and wealth between different groups within the economy can lead to a wide gap in living standards between affluent households and those experiencing poverty. Society may come to the view that too much inequality is unacceptable or undesirable.

In this case, the government may decide to intervene to reduce inequality through changes to the tax and benefits system and also specific policies such as the national minimum wage.

Government intervention may seek to correct the distortions created by market failure and to improve the efficiency in the way that markets operate as follows:

- pollution taxes to correct for externalities
- taxation of monopoly profits (the windfall tax)
- regulation of oligopolies/cartel behaviour
- direct provision of public goods (defence)
- policies to introduce competition into markets (de-regulation)
- price controls for the recently privatised utilities.

2.5 Trade Agreements and Tariffs

Trade agreements are when two or more nations agree on the terms of trade between them. Trade agreements determine the tariffs (taxes and duties) that countries impose on imports and exports.

Below are some of the types of trade agreements:

- **Unilateral trade agreements** are when one country either imposes trade restrictions, or loosens them, and no other country reciprocates. Many developed countries often do this as a type of foreign aid to help emerging markets strengthen certain industries.
- **Bi-lateral agreements** are between two countries. Both countries would agree to loosen or remove trade restrictions to expand business opportunities. They typically involve lowering tariffs and conferring preferred trade status with each other.
- **Multilateral trade agreements** – these are among three countries or more and are the most difficult to negotiate; however, once negotiated, they are very powerful. This is because they cover a larger geographic area, conferring a better competitive advantage on the signatories. All countries in a multilateral agreement give each other most favoured nation status, which means they treat each other equally.

Once agreements move beyond the regional level, they usually need assistance, and this is where the World Trade Organization (WTO) steps in. It is an international body that helps negotiate global trade agreements and, once agreements are in place, the WTO enforces the agreement and responds to complaints. The WTO currently enforces the General Agreement on Tariffs and Trade.

2.6 Protectionism

Protectionism (or trade protection) is the deliberate attempt to limit imports or promote exports by putting up barriers to trade. Despite the arguments in favour of free trade and increasing trade openness, protectionism is still widely practised. Protection of domestic industries may allow them to develop a comparative advantage; for example, domestic firms may expand when protected from competition and benefit from economies of scale. As firms grow they might invest in real capital; and human capital, and develop new capabilities and skills. Once these skills and capabilities are developed there is less need for trade protection, and barriers may be eventually removed. Retaining some self-sufficiency is, however, seen as a sensible economic strategy given the risks of global downturns, and an over-reliance on international trade.

3. National Income (NI)

3.1 National Income, Gross National Product and Gross Domestic Product

The following simple diagram shows how income is generated and circulates in an economy:

- In order to make the goods and services they provide, firms must use labour provided by households. They have to pay those households for the labour they provide, thus providing the households with income.
- Households must pay firms for the goods and services they need. The income of firms is thus the sales revenue from the sale of goods and services.

This creates a circular flow of income and expenditure; income and output are different sides of the same coin. This diagram assumes a closed economy, ie, there is no leakage of income to overseas providers.

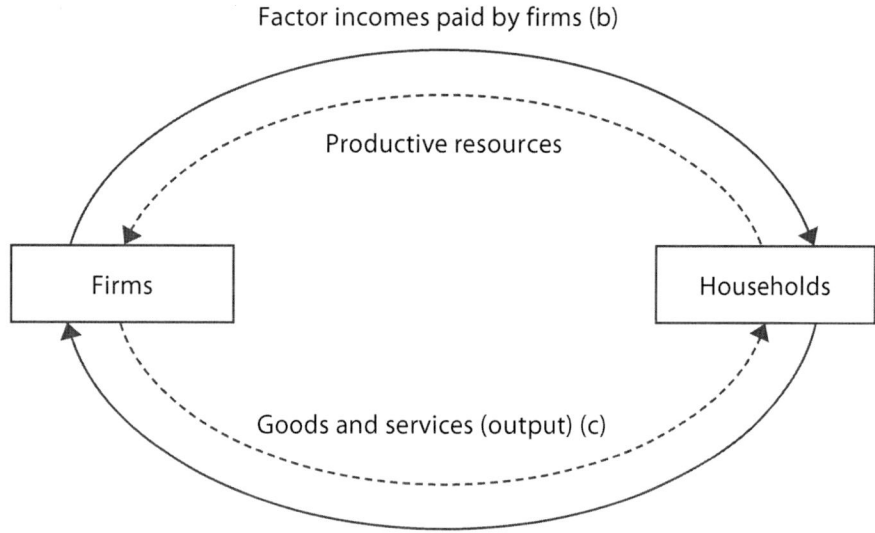

We can measure the activity shown in the above diagram in the economy, in different ways. The measure chosen will depend on which aspect of the above flow we are focusing on. Three key measures of economic activity are:

- national income
- gross national product (GNP)
- gross domestic product (GDP).

3.1.1 National Income (NI)

UK national income is defined as 'the sum of all incomes of residents in the UK which arise as a result of economic activity, from the production of goods and services'. Such incomes, which include rent, employment income and profit, are known as factor incomes because they are earned by the so-called factors of production: land, labour and capital. (Office for National Statistics)

National income is also called net national product. As noted above, the terms income and product are two different aspects of the same circular flow of income around the economy. The term net means after deducting an amount for capital consumption or depreciation of fixed assets from the gross figure.

Although technically national income has a particular definition, generally you will find all of the three measures given above (NI, GNP and GDP) loosely referred to as national income.

Measuring national income is useful for the following purposes:

- measuring the standard of living in a country (national income per head)
- comparing the wealth of different countries
- measuring the change in national wealth and the standard of living
- determining long-term trends
- assisting central government in its economic planning.

3.1.2 Gross Domestic Product (GDP)

National income is largely derived from economic activity within the country itself. Domestic economic activity is referred to as total domestic income or domestic product. It is measured gross. The term GDP refers (in the UK) to the total value of income/production from economic activity within the UK.

3.1.3 Gross National Product (GNP)

As we noted above, the diagram showing the circular flow of income in the economy assumes that it is closed. In reality:

- some of the UK's national income arises from overseas investments
- some of the income generated within the UK is earned by people who are non-residents.

The difference between these items is net property income from abroad. The sum of gross domestic product plus net property income from abroad is the GNP.

We can, therefore, show the relationship between GDP, GNP and national income like this:

	GDP
Plus	Net property income from abroad
Equals	GNP
Minus	Capital consumption
Equals	National income (net)

3.1.4 Injections and Withdrawals

In addition to using total incomes in the circular flow, as a measure for national income, we can use a method that measures total expenditure in the economy.

We add a number of injections to, and withdrawals from, the circular flow. These arise from:

- savings by consumers (a withdrawal from the cycle, since the money is no longer circulating if it is being saved)
- investment flows into firms (an injection, since it represents money the firms can now start using in their economic activity)
- imports (a withdrawal, since the money goes overseas to pay for goods and services bought from abroad)
- exports (an injection, since overseas buyers make payments into the UK to pay for goods and services)
- government spending (an injection, since the government adds to the revenues of firms providing it with goods and services)
- taxation (a withdrawal, since it reduces the income households have available to spend on goods and services).

You should be able to see that we are moving away from – or at least building on – the simplified, closed-economy model that we started this section with.

The gross domestic product is made up of:

$$C + I + G + (X - M)$$

This measure gives us one way of looking at the level of national economic activity. It also shows us that if a government wants to influence levels of activity, it may be able to do so by influencing one or more of the components of the formula above. For example, it could:

- try to increase consumer expenditure – that is, spending by households, or C above
- take steps to increase private investment in firms (I)
- the government (G) increases its own spending
- try to improve the balance of payments (X – M).

From the above you should be able to see that it is possible to measure the amount of economic activity, or output, in a national economy. This is done by aggregating (adding together) all the incomes generated, to give a total figure for national income.

The bigger the national income in a country, the more its average income. A rising level of income means more spending on the output of firms, and more spending means more output of goods and services. Providing that such increases are not simply due to the effects of inflation, then the resulting increases in income should lead to a rise in the standard of living.

Rising national income (economic growth) is an economic policy objective of most governments. It is better if this growth is stable and steady, rather than uncontrolled and erratic.

Most UK national income is derived from economic activity within the UK. The measure of economic activity within the UK is referred to as total domestic income or domestic product. It is measured gross, ie, before deducting an amount for capital consumption or depreciation of fixed assets, to give the GDP, referring to the total value of income/production from economic activity within the UK.

4. Economic and Business Cycles

Learning Objective

2.1.3 Understand the main stages of economic, financial and stock market cycles, including: trade cycles; business cycles; asset price bubbles; economic shocks; difficulty in forecasting national and international trends

4.1 The Trend Rate of Growth

Although there are many sources from which economic growth can emanate, in the long run the rate of sustainable or trend rate of growth ultimately depends on the:

- growth and productivity of the labour force
- rate at which an economy efficiently channels its domestic savings and capital attracted from overseas into new and innovative technology and replaces obsolescent capital equipment
- extent to which an economy's infrastructure is maintained and developed to cope with growing transport, communication and energy needs.

This trend rate of growth also defines an economy's potential output level or full employment level of output – that is, the sustainable level of output an economy can produce when all of its resources are productively employed.

When an economy is growing in excess of its trend growth rate, actual output will exceed potential output, often with inflationary consequences. However, when a country's output contracts – that is, when its economic growth rate turns negative for at least two consecutive calendar quarters – the economy is said to be in recession, or entering a deflationary period, resulting in spare capacity and unemployment.

4.2 The Economic Cycle

Unlike in microeconomics, where the establishment of a market-clearing price in a single market brings supply and demand into equilibrium, in macroeconomics the interaction of individual markets and sectors may cause the economy to operate in a state of disequilibrium, often for significant periods of time. This is considered in sections 6.2 and 6.3. The fact that actual growth fluctuates and deviates from trend growth in the short term gives rise to the economic cycle, or business cycle.

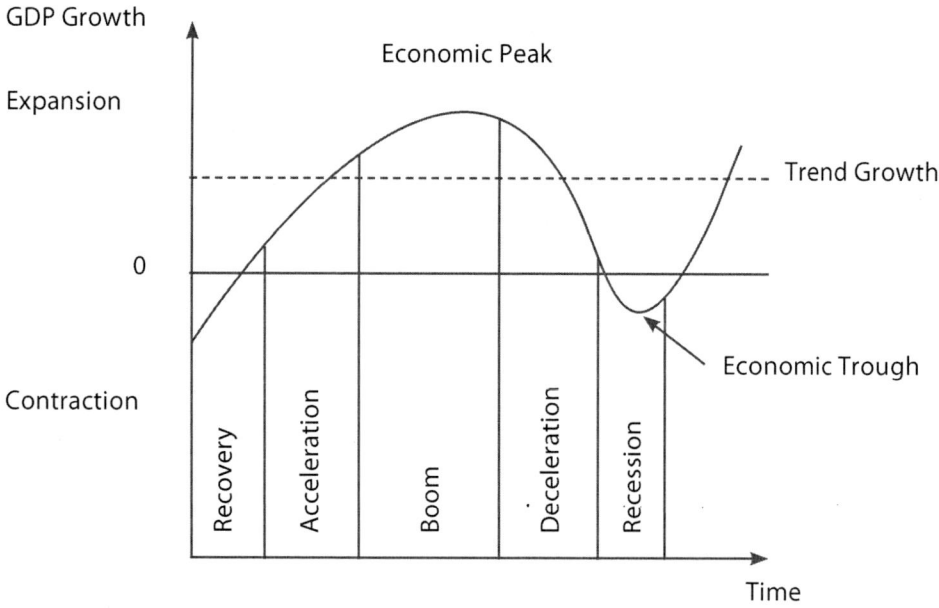

Economic cycles describe the course an economy conventionally takes, usually over a seven- to ten-year period, as economic growth oscillates in a cyclical fashion. The length of a cycle is measured either between successive economic peaks or between successive economic troughs. Although cycles typically assume a recovery, acceleration, boom, overheating, deceleration and recession pattern, in practice it is difficult to identify exactly when one stage ends and another begins, or, indeed, to quantify the duration of each stage.

Where an economy is positioned in the economic cycle also determines the performance of the various asset, or investment, classes (see section 7.2). Finally, empirical evidence shows that if the short-term peaks and troughs of conventional cycles are ignored, economic cycles of 50 years or so pervade economies. These so-called Kondratieff cycles (or super-cycles) flow from the benefits of innovation and investment in new technology.

The economy tends to experience different trends which may feature boom, slump, recession and recovery.

- **Boom** – a period of fast economic growth. Output is high due to increased demand and unemployment is low. Business confidence may be high, leading to increased investment. Consumer confidence may lead to extra spending.
- **Slump/Deceleration** – a period when output slows down due to a reduction in demand. Confidence may begin to suffer.
- **Recession** – a period when economic growth slows down and the level of output may actually decrease. Unemployment is likely to increase. Firms may lose confidence and reduce investment. Individuals may save rather than spend.
- **Recovery/Acceleration** – a period when the economy moves between recession and a boom.

What Happens in a Boom?

- Businesses produce more goods.
- Businesses invest in more machinery.
- Consumers spend more money. There is a high level of consumer confidence.
- Less money is spent by the government on unemployment benefits.
- More money is collected by the government in income tax and VAT.
- Prices tend to increase due to extra demand.

What Happens in a Recession?

- Businesses cut back on production.
- Some businesses may go bankrupt.
- Consumers spend less money. There is a fall in consumer confidence.
- Individuals may lose their jobs.
- More money is spent by the government on unemployment benefits.
- Less money is collected by the government in income tax and VAT.
- Prices start to fall.

4.3 Business Cycles

As explained, over the long term, economies usually display an underlying positive rate of growth, sometimes known as the trend growth rate. This is likely to reflect, among other factors, the average level of investment. Investment also plays a key role in the business cycle, sometimes known as the trade cycle, the pattern of fluctuations around the trend.

A variety of different economic indicators shows cyclical movements of expansion and contraction in economic activity over time. Some of these indicators rise in periods of economic expansion. See section 5 for more on these.

4.4 Asset Price Bubbles

A bubble is *'a sharp rise in price of an asset or a range of assets in a continuous process, with the initial rise generating expectations of further rises and attracting new buyers – generally speculators, interested in profits from trading in the asset rather than its use or earning capacity'* (Charles P. Kindleberger, *The New Palgrave: A Dictionary of Economics*). This definition implies that, in a bubble, the price of the asset deviates from its fundamental value and that a reversal of expectations and a sharp decline in prices (a crash) will usually occur.

4.5 Economic Shocks

An economic shock is defined as an event that produces a significant change within an economy, despite occurring outside it. Economic shocks are unpredictable and typically impact supply or demand throughout the markets. An economic shock may come in a variety of forms. A shock in the supply of staple commodities, such as oil, can cause prices to skyrocket, making them expensive to use for business purposes. The rapid devaluation of a currency will produce a shock for the import/export industry because a nation will have difficulty bringing in foreign products.

4.6 Trend Forecasting

Governments and international organisations try to look forward and influence not only the short-term economic outlook, but also to learn from analysing longer-term trends, and to influence these as well. Even quite small changes in growth, year-on-year, can have a considerable cumulative effect over a longer period.

The UK government, for example, has a stated aim of increasing long-term growth (known as the trend growth rate) – through strategies aimed at increasing employment opportunities and productivity, by promoting economic stability and by way of its wider economic policies.

5. Key Economic Indicators

Learning Objective

2.1.4 Interpret key economic and business indicators: gross domestic product; inflation; interest rates; consumer price and inflation indices; retail sales; unemployment rate; industrial production; stock market indices; money supply changes; foreign exchange indices; leading, lagging and coincident indicators; procyclic, countercyclic and acyclic indicators

A variety of different economic indicators show cyclical movements of expansion and contraction in economic activity over time. Some of these indicators rise in periods of economic expansion. They are known as procyclic indicators and include the rate of growth of consumer spending, job vacancies and investment. An increase in a procyclic indicator such as GDP will be reflected in a strong economy. Conversley, if GDP decreases it means that the economy could be headed for a recession. Other indicators (the so-called countercyclic indicators) fall in periods of economic expansion, such as unemployment and the number of bankruptcies. An acyclic indicator has little effect on the economy.

5.1 Gross Domestic Product

Gross domestic product (GDP) refers, in the UK, to the total value of income/production from economic activity within the UK. Its measurement is important in understanding the growth, and trends, in the UK economy and output.

5.2 Interest Rates

When you hear talk of the BoE adjusting interest rates, it means that the BoE is adjusting the rate at which it lends money to banks, known as the base rate. Usually, other interest rates – such as the rates on a credit card or a variable mortgage – will follow the BoE's adjustments, because banks pass on the extra costs of borrowing to the end consumer.

Investors watch changes in interest rates very closely. An increase in interest rates not only slows down consumer spending, but will also hit the future performance of companies. Higher interest rates make it more expensive for firms to expand their business operations by borrowing money or issuing debt, because they will have to pay a higher interest rate on their loans. High interest rates have a secondary effect of encouraging investors to switch out of equities and into low-risk cash instruments, thereby further depressing share prices.

5.3 Inflation Indices

Inflation is the name given to a general increase in price levels. (Another way of describing a general rise in prices is as a decline in the purchasing power of money.)

Inflation is an important concern for investors, as well as for borrowers; for investors, inflation erodes the value of their investment if the growth in the investment does not keep pace with it.

Inflation is measured by reference to an index, made up of a notional basket of all the things the average person is assumed to spend their money on. However, in reality different people spend their money on different things – so there are several inflation indices, reflecting different ways of calculating the general rise in price levels and the cost of living. These are known collectively as consumer price indices.

They may be used for several purposes – for example:

- as an indicator of inflationary pressures in the economy
- as a benchmark for wage negotiations
- to determine annual increases in government benefits payments.

In the UK, there are a number of different ways of measuring the way prices change. Both the RPI and the CPI are measures designed to track the level and changes of prices over time. The CPI is a recent introduction to UK measures of inflation while the RPI has been around for some years. However, both CPI and RPI come up with different values because there are slight differences in the indices based on the basket of goods and services that are contained in each measure. Secondly, the method of calculation of each index is different.

The RPI is sometimes referred to as the 'headline' rate of inflation. It is the rate often cited by unions as a benchmark for agreeing wage settlements. The CPI measure is the rate of the government's preferred inflation target and is an international comparative measure of inflation.

From an historical perspective, note that in December 2003, the standardised European inflation measure, the harmonised index of consumer prices (HICP), began to be used as the basis for the UK's inflation target. In the UK, it is now more commonly known as the consumer prices index (CPI). The CPI excludes most housing costs. However, pensions and benefits and index-linked gilts continue to be calculated on the same basis as previously, using the RPI.

Let us now look at how the two main measures of inflation are calculated and the differences between them.

Both measures attempt to track the changes in prices of a representative basket of goods and services in the UK. Each month, thousands of prices of the representative basket are analysed to check for changes in their prices. Depending on the measure, some of the items in the baskets may have higher weightings to reflect consumer spending patterns. It is important to note that not all items are common to each index. For example, CPI does not include a number of housing cost items. Moreover, the CPI measure contains a broader range of items than the RPI. It is primarily designed to provide a measure of inflation that is harmonised, and therefore comparable, to the EU CPI measure.

Based on the representative basket, an index is created using a weighted averaging procedure (the method of calculation of the index is not part of this syllabus; those interested in the detailed procedures for determination of the indices and reporting can consult the ONS website (ons.gov.uk)).

Once the index for each measure is determined, the mathematical approach used to calculate the price changes is different: CPI utilises the geometric mean; RPI uses the arithmetic mean.

Effectively, this means that for naturally volatile time series of index values that are taken over successive months, the CPI will always yield a lower rate of inflation than the RPI.

In other areas of investment, the arithmetic mean is used as a point estimate or a forecast of the future index value. The geometric mean is used to represent that actual average for an historic time period. Consequently, it is arguable whether the CPI truly reflects prospects for future inflation.

Until 2003, the UK government targeted a rate of inflation known as RPIX (the same as RPI but excludes mortgage interest payments from the basket). In December 2003, the UK Chancellor announced that the targeting would switch to the CPI with immediate effect. The following reasons were given for the switch to CPI from RPIX:

- the CPI basket offers more realistic patterns of consumer behaviour and consumption
- it is a comparable measure for referencing the rate to international economies for price levels and changes
- it represents international best practices.

The UK government inflation (CPI) target is 2%. Note that this target has been exceeded for a number of years. The BoE pages on inflation targeting has the following statement:

If the target is missed by more than 1 percentage point on either side, the Governor of the BoE must write an open letter to the Chancellor explaining the reasons why inflation has risen or fallen to such an extent and what the Bank proposes to do to ensure that inflation comes back to target.

High levels of inflation can cause problems:

- Businesses have to continually update prices to keep pace with inflation.
- Employees find the real value of their salaries eroded.
- Those on fixed levels of income, such as pensioners, will suffer as the price increases are not matched by increases in income, thus leading to a decrease in living standards.
- Exports may become less competitive.
- The real value of future pensions and investment income becomes difficult to assess, which might act as a disincentive to save.

There are, however, some positive aspects to high levels of inflation:

- Rising house prices contribute to a feelgood factor (although this might contribute to further inflation as house owners become more disposed to borrow and spend).
- Borrowers benefit, because the value of borrowers' debt falls in real terms – ie, after adjusting for the effect of inflation.
- Inflation also erodes the real value of a country's national debt and so can benefit an economy in difficult times.

5.4 Retail Sales

Retail sales are an indicator of household consumption. They are an important economic indicator because consumer spending drives much of our economy. Think of all of the people and companies involved in producing, distributing, and selling the goods you use on a daily basis like food, clothes and fuel. When consumers open their wallets, the economy tends to grow steadily. Retail shelves empty and orders are placed for replacement merchandise. Production increases creating a virtuous cycle so long as inflation is contained.

However, if consumers feel uncertain about their financial future and decide to hold off buying new refrigerators or blue jeans, the economy slows down. This is why politicians may resort to tax cuts to give the economy a boost. By putting cash in consumers' hands, they hope consumer spending will help the economy move out of a recession.

5.5 Unemployment

The unemployment rate measures the number of people available for work and seeking employment. Labour statistics offer a general sense of the state and direction of the economy as a whole. If unemployment is on the rise or few new jobs are being created, it is a sign that companies themselves are not expanding their businesses and the economy may be slowing down. On the other hand, tight labour markets and large-scale job creation indicate a growing, or even overheated, economy.

The reaction of markets to news about unemployment can often seem paradoxical. If the economy is doing well, investors will fear that a fall in unemployment (which you would think would be good news) will be inflationary (more people in work and spending money). Very low unemployment can also be a sign of labour shortages. On the other hand, a fall in unemployment when the economy is in recession is good news for the markets as it suggests an improvement in the overall state of the economy.

5.6 Industrial Production

Industrial production measures the change in output for the industrial sector of the economy. The industrial sector includes manufacturing, mining and utilities. Although these sectors contribute only a small portion of GDP, they are highly sensitive to interest rates and consumer demand. This makes industrial production an important tool for forecasting future GDP and economic performance. Industrial production figures are also used by central banks to measure inflation, as high levels of industrial production can lead to uncontrolled levels of consumption and rapid inflation.

5.7 Stock Market Indices

A variety of different indices are used to measure the performance of stock markets. The main indices are:

- The **FTSE 100 Index** measures the combined performance of the hundred most highly capitalised blue chip companies listed on the LSE. In doing so it represents about 81% of the UK market. It is used extensively by portfolio managers to benchmark their performance, and has been in existence since 1984.
- The **FTSE 250 Index** was introduced in 1992, and is made up of mid-capitalised companies which fall outside the FTSE 100. It represents approximately 15% of UK market capitalisation.
- The **FTSE All Share Index** is the oldest of these three examples, having been introduced in 1962 (it was then known as the FTSE Actuaries All Share Index).

Indices can be calculated using different mathematical formulae – for example, in terms of the weightings given to different shares and their price movements. Some are calculated so that the shares are arithmetically weighted according to capitalisation, ie, the larger the company, the bigger its weighting in the index. Others are calculated using the geometric mean and are unweighted: each share counts equally, no matter what its market capitalisation.

5.8 Money Supply Changes

Later in this chapter (section 6.4) we will look at various ways of measuring the money supply (also known as money stock). This is the total amount of money circulating in an economy. We will also look at narrow money and broad money and at the more formal definitions of **M0** and **M4**. The amount of money in circulation, and changes in that amount, are important to the economy – chiefly because of the impact this is assumed to have on prices (and, therefore, on inflation).

5.9 Foreign Exchange Rates

These are the rates at which one country's currency may be exchanged for that of another country. So an exchange rate is the price of one currency, in terms of another. You may see a foreign exchange rate quoted as a single figure – for example, the rate for US dollars against sterling was quoted by Reuters as $1.2855 (that is, $1.2855 = £1.0000) at the opening of business on 5 June 2017. This price is the mid-price because it is the average rate calculated from the bid and ask closing prices on the day.

The foreign exchange rate quoted by dealers is called a currency pair and represents the value of one currency when expressed against another currency. The currency pair consists of a base currency (usually the more valuable of the two currencies) and a pricing currency. A dealer might quote you a price of 1.5741 to 1.5749 based upon the mid-price in the previous paragraph, in which case:

- the dealer buys from you £1 (the base currency) and sells to you $1.4613 (the pricing currency), or
- the dealer sells to you £1 (the base currency) and requires from you $1.4618 (the pricing currency).

The dealers make their profits by selling (the base currency) to one customer at the ask price and simultaneously buying (the base currency) from another customer at the bid price. The difference between the bid-ask price is the bid-offer spread and is the dealer's profit from the deal. Commissions are additional costs borne by the buyers and sellers, but are unusual in the foreign exchange markets.

A country's currency exchange rate with other countries is important for the health of its economy. For example, we saw that changes in the exchange rate can affect the competitiveness of UK goods abroad, and thus can have a major impact on the balance of payments. For the UK pound sterling, exchange rates with the euro, the US dollar and the Japanese yen are key rates, as Europe, the US and Japan are major trading partners.

The foreign exchange (FX or forex) markets are worldwide and the main dealers are banks. Their customers include companies and individuals who are buying or selling goods and services abroad; they also include investment inflows and outflows, as investors trade currencies in the hope of making a gain on any exchange rate movements, or buy currencies which offer higher rates of interest. However, investors buying a high-yielding foreign currency in the hope of benefiting from the high interest rates earned on it also need to be aware that, if that currency declines in value, they may make a capital loss on the exchange rate.

5.10 Economic Indicators and their Characteristics

In relation to the economic business cycle, each economic indicator can be considered to have one of the following attributes that tracks and responds to changes in an underlying economic factor.

- A **procyclic** economic indicator is characterised by directional movement that moves in step with the overall movement of the economy. GDP is a good example of a procyclic indicator because when the economy is growing, this indicator is also moving up in tandem. At the same time, when the economy is slowing down, or is in a contractionary (or recessionary) phase, GDP moves lower (or enters into negative territory). It is worthwhile noting that two consecutive quarters of negative growth confirm that an economy is in a recession. GDP is often released as a quarterly growth measure, while others such as the CPI are released on a monthly basis. All indicators, especially the GDP, are subject to revisions in subsequent reporting periods.
- A **countercyclic** economic indicator is one that moves in the opposite direction to the economic growth trend. The unemployment rate is such an indicator: unemployment often increases when the economy is in a contractionary phase and drops when economic growth is accelerating.
- An **acyclic** economic indicator is one that has no relation to the up or down growth phases of the economy and is generally of little use as a forecasting or economic sensory measurement tool.

Economic indicators are characterised further by their timing properties in response to developments that may be taking place in the underlying economy. These economic indicators can be leading, lagging, or coincident.

- **Leading indicators** are indicators that usually change before the economy as a whole changes. They are therefore useful as short-term predictors of the economy. Stock market index returns are a leading indicator: the stock market usually begins to decline before the economy as a whole declines and usually begins to improve before the general economy begins to recover from a slump. This is why economists sometimes suggest that the stock index of a country is a barometer of the health of the economy. Other leading indicators include the index of consumer expectations, building permits, and the money supply.
- **Lagging indicators** are indicators that usually change after the economy as a whole does. Typically the lag is a few quarters of a year. The unemployment rate is a lagging indicator: employment tends to increase two or three quarters after an upturn in the general economy before it dips.

- **Coincident indicators** are those which change at approximately the same time as the whole economy, thereby providing information about the current state of the economy. An example is personal income. There are many coincident economic indicators: GDP, industrial production and retail sales are coincident indicators and a coincident index may be used to identify, after the fact, the dates of peaks and troughs in the business cycle.

5.11 Difficulties in Forecasting National and Interest Rate Trends

Forecasting national and economic trends in a single country and on a global scale is a highly specialised and challenging activity for econometricians. With regards to forecasting, cabinetoffice.gov.uk offers the following pointers.

Essentially, forecasting as an activity aims to identify and track past trends and then extrapolate into the future. A series of economic data such as interest rates, economic growth or inflation data is tracked regularly over a historic time period. The data is obtained in the form of a time series that is then projected forward by using statistical/econometric techniques. As well as quantitative (statistical methods), it also includes the use of more qualitative (judgemental) methods.

As looking into the future naturally involves a varying degree of uncertainty, sometimes a distinction is drawn between forecasting and projections. In certain contexts, particularly economic ones, forecasting is used to refer to short-term extrapolations associated with a reasonable degree of certainty. Projections are considered to be longer term, more sophisticated, but also less reliable. This distinction does not always hold true, for example demographic projections can be very reliable over the time span of a generation.

There are two main types of trend analysis – quantitative and qualitative analysis.

5.11.1 Quantitative Analysis

Quantitative trend analysis is probably the most common forecasting method. It relies on the statistical analysis of historical data – in other words it is relatively objective. Quantitative techniques include extrapolation (such as moving averages, linear projections against time or exponential smoothing) and econometric methods (typically using regression techniques to estimate the effects of causal variables). This type of analysis is commonly used to forecast demographic and economic changes when extrapolating over time is believed to have some validity.

Other techniques for short- to medium-term analysis and forecasting include:

- **Modelling** – an extremely useful tool for quantitative analysis.
- **Estimation** – one of the key difficulties in conducting forecasting is a lack of available data. If this is the case, estimation may be suitable.
- **Triangulation** – when developing a model, data is often incomplete or approximate. In other instances you may have several sources of data that conflict. One way of developing a base to work from is to triangulate the available information to develop a defensible average.

5.11.2 Qualitative Analysis

Qualitative trend analysis is more subjective and is concerned mainly with social, institutional, commercial and political themes (ie, things which may not be linearly related to the past). For example, qualitative trend analyses deal with issues such as:

- What is the future of trade unions?
- What is the future of political parties or non-governmental organisations (NGOs)?
- What is the future of the entertainment business?

One of the most common forms of qualitative trend analysis is the identification of 'megatrends' – driving forces which can change society in all spheres, eg, politics, economics, technology, values and social relations. Other tools include scenarios and analogies.

Qualitative analyses can be applied to most areas, but work best when focusing on real change. Megatrends apply to all areas, within the defined time and setting. It is important, though, to be aware that megatrends may themselves produce powerful counter-trends – and that they may interact with each other.

Strengths

- Quantitative forecasts are usually more objective, relatively inexpensive and easy to use (contingent upon some knowledge of statistics).
- Qualitative forecasts can be valuable predictors of new trends by using the creativity and good judgement of experts.

Weaknesses

- Quantitative forecasts can be misleading. The past is not always predictive of the future and such forecasts do not take into account unpredictable changes or discoveries (eg, discovery of new natural resources) or wild cards (eg, unexpected acts of terrorism).
- When using qualitative techniques to identify possible new trends, it will always be the case that some or maybe even all of the results are eventually disproved. It is particularly difficult to distinguish between short-term fads and long-term trends.

6. Fiscal and Monetary Policy

Learning Objective

2.2.1 Understand the role of government and central banks in fiscal and monetary policy: interest-rate-setting process; quantitative easing; unwinding of central bank balance sheets; money market operations; fiscal stance; other interventions

6.1 General Economic Policy Aims

As well as providing a legal and regulatory framework for economic activity, the government plays a role in managing the economy. Among the aims of a government's economic policy may be the following:

- To achieve sustainable growth in national income per head of the population. Growth implies an increase in national income in real terms (remember, 'real' means after stripping out the effects of inflation). National income grows through the expansion of economic activity: more goods and services become available for people to consume. The idea of sustainable growth implies that major fluctuations in the business cycle are avoided, and that output grows on a steady upward trend. This is generally seen as the most important goal of a government's economic policy.
- To control inflation in prices. This has become a central objective of economic policy in many countries in recent years.
- To achieve full employment – the aim for a government is to keep employment as high as possible. In practice there is always some residual or frictional unemployment in an economy as people who lost their jobs will be looking for new opportunities and as new school leavers join the ranks of those seeking long-term jobs and training. Economists have suggested that an unemployment rate of 3% is close to full employment, implying that the economy is functioning close to maximum capacity. Some of the possible conflicts include the possibility that an unusually low level of unemployment may create demand-pull or cost-push inflationary pressures in the economy.
- To achieve a trade balance – the government will also aim to ensure that it continues to improve its trade balance by maintaining an equilibrium position between exports and imports of goods. In the UK a trade deficit is always run because the economy is heavily reliant on imports and the manufacturing base is not wide enough or deep enough to meet local demand for such goods. It is in the interests of an economy for the government to aim for a trade surplus because it is a way to earn the extra amount from exports of the goods it produces.

6.2 Fiscal Policy

Fiscal policy is government policy on taxation, public borrowing and public spending.

- **Direct taxation** is taxation of incomes and, in some cases, wealth (as with inheritance tax).
- **Indirect taxation** is taxation of products and services, for example, VAT.

The amount that the government must borrow each year is now known as the public sector net cash requirement (PSNCR) in the UK. The PSNCR is the annual excess of spending over income for the entire public sector – not just for the central government. Thus, PSNCR is the combined financial deficit of central government + local government + the public corporations. It measures the annual borrowing requirement of the government sector of the economy. When the government is running a budget deficit this means that total public expenditure exceeds revenue. As a result, the government has to fund the deficit through the issue of government debt.

A government might intervene in an economy by:

- increasing its spend on activities that will benefit the economy and paying for this spending by borrowing funds with the issuance of debt
- pursuing a contractionary fiscal policy by increasing taxes but at the same time holding spending steady
- raising extra taxes from one part of the economy and diverting this to another part of the economy.

In extreme economic circumstances, specific packages may be introduced, such as the 'Funding for Lending Scheme' which was introduced in 2012 by the UK government to assist banks with lending to small and medium-sized companies

A government's fiscal stance may be expansionary, contractionary or neutral, according to its overall effect on national income.

- Spending more money and financing this expenditure by borrowing indicates an expansionary fiscal stance. Spending will increase and so national income will tend to rise, either in real terms, or in terms of price levels only; that is, the increase in national income may be real (ie, there is growth even after the effects of inflation are stripped out), or it may be simply inflationary.
- Collecting more in taxes without increasing spending indicates a contractionary fiscal stance. A government may deliberately raise taxation to take inflationary pressures out of the economy.
- Collecting more in taxes in order to increase spending, thus diverting income from one part of the economy to another, indicates a broadly neutral fiscal stance. We saw in section 1.9 that the government can redistribute wealth (as measured through net income) through such activity.

If government raises taxes and spending by the same amount, so that its overall budget remains in balance, there will be an increase in aggregate monetary demand. This is because taxpayers would otherwise have saved some of the money they pay in increased tax; but instead the government spends all of it within the economy. The net effect is that more money gets spent, albeit by a different party (in this case the government itself). This effect is called the balanced budget multiplier.

Since government spending or tax reductions may be inflationary, and higher domestic prices make imports relatively cheaper and exports less competitive in foreign markets, fiscal policy has possible implications for the balance of payments (discussed in section 6.5).

Fiscal policy can also be used in an attempt to reduce unemployment and stimulate employment. For example:

- more government spending on capital projects, on which people are employed to work
- government-funded training schemes
- taxation of companies on the basis of the numbers and pay levels of employees.

Government spending, however, may create inflationary pressures, and inflation tends to create more unemployment. Fiscal policy must therefore be used with care, even if the aim is to create new jobs.

The impact of changes in fiscal policy is not always certain, and fiscal policy to pursue one aim (eg, lower inflation) may create barriers to the pursuit of other aims (eg, employment) for a while. In addition, the effects of fiscal changes can take a very long time to feed through into the economy, by which time other factors may have changed, complicating the overall outcome.

Government planners also need to consider how fiscal policy can affect savers, investors and companies.

- The tax regime, for example, affects different savings instruments and/or property ownership, and this affects investors' decisions.
- Companies will be affected by tax rules on dividends and profits, and tax breaks for certain activities. They may take these rules into account when deciding on dividend policy, or on whether to raise finance through debt (loans) or equities (by issuing shares) and other activities.

One feature of fiscal policy is that a government must plan what it wants to spend, and so how much it needs to raise, either in income (through taxation) or by borrowing. It needs to make a plan in order to establish how much taxation there should be, what form the taxes should take and which sectors of the economy (firms or households, high-income earners or low-income earners) the money should come from. This formal planning of fiscal policy usually follows an annual cycle. In the UK, the most important statement of changes to policy is the budget, which takes place in the spring of each year. The Chancellor of the Exchequer also delivers a pre-budget report each autumn. The pre-budget report formally makes the government's spending plans available for scrutiny.

Because of the annual planning cycle of government finances, and because there is usually a considerable time-lag before businesses and people act upon changes brought about through tax and government spending, fiscal policy is not very responsive to shorter-term developments in the economy. For shorter-term fine-tuning of the economy, the government may need to use monetary policy.

6.3 Monetary Policy

Monetary policy is concerned with changes in the amount of money in circulation – the money supply – and with changes in the price of money – interest rates. These variables are linked with inflation in prices generally, and also with exchange rates – the price of the domestic currency in terms of other currencies. How the supply or stock of money in an economy affects inflation and other economic variables is covered in section 6.4.

Until the 1970s, the tools for implementing monetary policy also included direct controls (exercised through the BoE) on the amount of lending that banks were allowed to undertake. In the 1980s, most monetary policy implementation centred on trying to control the overall supply of money in the economy. Targets were set for the growth of money (notes, coins, bank deposits), and interest rates were varied accordingly. However, measures of the amount of money in the economy did not always prove to be a reliable guide to demand and inflation. As a result, by the mid-1980s monetary policy came to be based on an assessment of a wider range of economic indicators rather than a single measure of money supply growth.

Since 1997, the most important aspect of monetary policy in the UK has been the influence over interest rates exerted by the BoE, the central bank of the UK. The new government at the time gave the BoE independence to set interest rates. This was a major change in the policy framework and means interest rates are no longer set or influenced by politicians. The Bank acts independently of government, though the inflation target is set by the Chancellor. The BoE is accountable to parliament and the wider public.

The Monetary Policy Committee (MPC) of the BoE is charged with the responsibility of setting interest rates with the aim of meeting the government's inflation target of 2% based on the CPI.

The UK inflation objective given to the BoE was initially explained in a letter from the Chancellor. The object was then formalised in the 1998 Bank of England Act. This Act states that the Bank of England is expected '*to maintain price stability and, subject to that, to support the economic policy of HM Government including its objectives for growth and employment*' (Bank of England Act 1998).

The Chancellor restates the inflation target each year. From June 1997 to December 2003, the target was 2.5% for RPIX inflation, the retail price index that excludes mortgage interest payments. The Chancellor, on 10 December 2003 changed this target to 2% of the CPI inflation, the consumer prices index.

If the inflation target is missed by more than one percentage point on either side for three successive months – in other words, if the annual CPI inflation rate is more than 3% or less than 1% – the BoE Governor, as Chairman of the MPC, must write an open letter to the Chancellor explaining why, and what the BoE proposes to do to ensure inflation comes back to the target. So far the Governor has written a series of open letters to the Chancellor. CPI on all these occasions was 1% point above the 2% target.

The MPC influences interest rates by deciding the short-term benchmark **repo rate** – the rate at which the BoE deals in the money markets. This is known as the BoE's base lending rate, or the **base rate** for short. (A repo contract is a sale and repurchase agreement: securities are sold but must be repurchased later.) The base rate affects the commercial rates which financial institutions then set for the different financial instruments they offer or deal in; so when the MPC changes the base rate, commercial banks generally react quickly by changing their own deposit and lending rates.

However, a government does not have an unlimited ability to have interest rates set how it wishes. It must take into account what rates the overall market will bear, so that the benchmark rate it chooses can be maintained.

6.3.1 The Interest-Rate-Setting Process: The Monetary Policy Committee

Setting UK interest rates was once the Chancellor's responsibility. The system was subject to abuse. Chancellors periodically overruled the advice of Treasury experts, especially when an election approached.

For this reason, following Labour's May 1997 election victory, one of the Chancellor's first actions was to de-politicise the rate-setting process. Responsibilities for setting interest rates were assigned to the Monetary Policy Committee (MPC) of the BoE.

The MPC has operated in an extremely able and transparent manner over the last few years. It announces each decision to change rates or keep them unchanged precisely at 12 noon on the day each meeting ends. Gone are the days when sudden and unexpected rate announcements would spook investors.

Composition of the MPC

The Bank's MPC is made up of nine members – the governor, the two deputy governors, the Bank's chief economist, the executive director for markets and four external members appointed directly by the Chancellor. The appointment of external members is designed to ensure that the MPC benefits from thinking and expertise in addition to that gained inside the BoE. Members serve fixed terms, after which they may be replaced or reappointed. Compared to other government rate-setting agencies in Washington and Brussels, the MPC is a model of openness.

Each member of the MPC has expertise in the field of economics and monetary policy. Members do not represent individual groups or areas. They are independent. Each member of the committee has a vote to set interest rates at the level they believe is consistent with meeting the inflation target. The MPC's decision is made on the basis of one person, one vote. It is not based on a consensus of opinion. It reflects the votes of each individual member of the committee.

A Treasury representative attends meetings to ensure that the MPC is fully briefed on fiscal management policy. The Treasury representative can discuss policy issues, but is not allowed to vote. The MPC is fully briefed on fiscal policy developments and other aspects of the government's economic policies and the Chancellor of the Exchequer is kept fully informed about the proceedings.

It is important to understand the background and reasons why a government representative is on the MPC.

The interest level set by the MPC has a significant impact on the UK economy as a whole, and it also influences exchange rates, inflation, market rates, asset prices and the expectations and confidence of the overall market.

In 1997, the BoE was given the power to set interest rates. This new power was formalised in the Bank of England Act in 1998, which also created the MPC on a statutory basis. The Act required the Bank to *'maintain price stability, and subject to that, to support the economic policy of HM Government including its objectives for growth and employment'*.

This change represented a transfer of power that had been vested with the government. The decision to move the monetary policy-setting powers to the MPC was not without its share of concerns. Opponents claimed that the separation of control between the monetary policy and fiscal policy objectives could potentially lead the MPC to overly focus on inflation targets at the expense of others, such as the exchange rate. In response to these concerns, a Treasury representative has been appointed to keep the MPC informed about the government's plans in relation to its fiscal policy and, further, to act as a reminder that the Treasury has the ultimate veto if it feels that rates should be set at a different level.

MPC Meetings

The MPC meets eight times a year to set the interest rate. In the weeks between each meeting, the MPC receives extensive briefing on the economy from BoE staff. This includes a half-day meeting – known as the pre-MPC meeting – which usually takes place on the Friday before the MPC's interest-rate-setting meeting. The nine members of the committee are made aware of all the latest data on the economy and hear explanations of recent trends and analysis of relevant issues. The committee is also told about business conditions around the UK from the bank's agents. The agents' role is to talk directly to business to gain intelligence and insight into current and future economic developments and prospects.

The monthly MPC meeting itself is a two-day affair. On the first day, the meeting starts with an update on the most recent economic data. A series of issues is then identified for discussion. On the following day, a summary of the previous day's discussion is provided and the MPC members individually explain their views on what policy should be. The governor then puts to the meeting the policy which they believe will command a majority and members of the MPC vote. Any member in a minority is asked to say what level of interest rates they would have preferred, and this is recorded in the minutes of the meeting. The interest rate decision is announced at 12 noon on the second day.

Public Accountability: Explaining Views and Decisions

The MPC goes to great lengths to explain its thinking and decisions. The minutes of the MPC meetings are published two weeks after the interest rate decision. The minutes give a full account of the policy discussion, including differences of view. They also record the votes of the individual members of the committee. The committee has to explain its actions regularly to parliamentary committees, particularly the Treasury committee. MPC members also speak to audiences throughout the country, explaining the MPC's policy decisions and thinking. This is a two-way dialogue. Regional visits also give members of the MPC a chance to gather first-hand intelligence about the economic situation from businesses and other organisations.

In addition to the monthly MPC minutes, the Bank publishes its Inflation Report every quarter. This report gives an analysis of the UK economy and the factors influencing policy decisions. The Inflation Report also includes the MPC's latest forecasts for inflation and output growth. Because monetary policy operates with a time-lag of about two years, it is necessary for the MPC to form judgements about the outlook for output and inflation.

The MPC uses a model of the economy to help produce its projections. The model provides a framework to organise thinking on how the economy works and how different economic developments might affect future inflation. But this is not a mechanical exercise. Given all the uncertainties and unknowns of the future, the MPC's forecast has to involve a great deal of judgement about the economy.

6.3.2 Money Market Operations

The BoE's framework for its operations in the sterling money markets is designed to implement the MPC's interest rate decisions while meeting the liquidity needs of, and so contributing to the stability of, the banking system as a whole.

The BoE is the sole issuer of sterling central bank money, the final risk-free settlement asset in the UK. This enables the bank to implement monetary policy and makes the framework for the bank's monetary operations central to liquidity management in the banking system as a whole and by individual banks and building societies.

The Bank's market operations have two objectives, stemming from its monetary policy and financial stability responsibilities as the UK's central bank. They are to:

- Implement monetary policy by maintaining overnight market interest rates in line with bank rate, so that there is a flat risk-free money market yield curve to the next MPC decision date, and very little day-to-day or intra-day volatility in market interest rates at maturities out to that horizon.
- Reduce the cost of disruption to the liquidity and payment services supplied by commercial banks. The bank does this by balancing the provision of liquidity insurance against the costs of creating incentives for banks to take greater risks, and subject to the need to avoid taking risk on to its balance sheet.

The framework has four main elements: reserves-averaging scheme, operational standing facilities, a discount window facility and open market operations.

Operational Standing Facilities

Operational standing deposit and (collateralised) lending facilities are available to eligible UK banks and building societies. They may be used on demand. In normal circumstances, the lending/deposit rates are 25 basis points higher than bank rate and 25 basis points below bank rate respectively.

The purpose of the operational standing facilities is to stabilise expectations that overnight market interest rates will be in line with bank rate; and, to that end, to give banks a means to manage unexpected 'frictional' payment shocks that could otherwise take their reserves accounts either below zero or to a level where they will otherwise be unremunerated. The Bank will seek to satisfy itself that use of the facility is consistent with these purposes.

On each day in a monthly maintenance period, the rate charged on the operational standing lending facility is 25 basis points above bank rate; and the rate paid on the operational standing deposit facility is 25 basis points below bank rate.

The operational standing deposit facility is uncollateralised. The operational standing lending facility is for overnight reverse repo against eligible collateral. The operational standing facilities are available all day, subject to operational constraints arising from deadlines in payments and securities settlement systems.

The Discount Window Facility (DWF)

The purpose of the DWF is to provide liquidity insurance to the banking system. The DWF is not intended for firms facing fundamental problems of solvency or viability. Eligible banks and building societies may borrow gilts, for up to 30 days, against a wide range of collateral in return for a fee, which will vary with the collateral used and the total size of borrowings. Institutions eligible to participate are banks and building societies that are required to pay cash ratio deposits (CRDs) and which otherwise meet the requirements for eligibility, as determined by the Bank, for the Bank's sterling monetary framework facilities.

Open Market Operations (OMOs)

OMOs are used to provide to the banking system the amount of central bank money needed to enable reserve-scheme members, in aggregate, to achieve their reserves targets. OMOs comprise short-term repos at bank rate, long-term repos at market rates determined in variable-rate tenders, and outright purchases of high-quality bonds.

Short-term OMOs are held weekly, with an overnight-maturity fine-tune on the final day of the maintenance period. The size of the weekly OMO is varied to offset expected weekly changes in banknotes in circulation and other sterling flows across the Bank's balance sheet (so-called autonomous factors). Day-to-day, reserve averaging absorbs the short-term fluctuations that occur across the Bank's balance sheet. The Bank currently provides long-term financing to the banking system through long-term repos at market rates determined in monthly OMOs; and through monthly OMOs to purchase conventional gilts. The Bank plans in due course to inject reserves via the purchase of high-quality foreign currency bonds, with the cash flows swapped into sterling (outright purchases).

In normal circumstances, the Bank's weekly short-term OMOs take place on Thursdays and have a maturity of one week. They are conducted at bank rate. On the days when the MPC makes scheduled interest rate decisions, the Bank undertakes its weekly short-term OMO at 12.15pm, in order to follow the MPC's noon announcement. On days when there are no scheduled interest rate announcements, the Bank undertakes its weekly, short-term OMO at 10.00am. Short-term OMOs are settled same day.

The Bank conducts, as a matter of routine, an overnight-maturity fine-tuning OMO at the end of each reserves maintenance period (ordinarily the Wednesday preceding the Thursday MPC decision) to ensure that the banking system's net need for central banking money, taking into account the amount required for reserve-scheme banks to achieve their aggregate reserve targets, is provided as precisely as possible. These operations take place at 10.00am. They are for same-day settlement. The Bank is prepared either to provide or drain central bank money at the Bank's official rate in this operation and both are equally likely on the assumption that errors in the Bank's liquidity forecast are unbiased.

The bank conducts long-term repo OMOs monthly, usually at 10am on a Tuesday mid-month. The bank may lend at three-, six-, nine- and 12-month maturities. These OMOs are variable-rate tenders open to the bank's OMO counterparties. The Bank is therefore a price-taker and allocates the funds offered to successful bidders at the rate(s) that they tender. Settlement of long-term repo operations takes place on the day following the OMO (T+1). The Bank conducts OMOs to purchase gilts monthly, normally on a Monday towards the end of the month. These are likewise competitive tenders in which the Bank is a price-taker and buys gilts from those making successful offers at the price they offer.

6.3.3 Fiscal Stance and Other Interventions

Macroeconomic fiscal stance is usually assessed by looking at the scale of the public deficit – the gap between the state income and expenditure. The term is used to describe whether fiscal policy is being used to actively expand demand and output in the economy (a reflationary or expansionary fiscal stance), or conversely to take demand out of the circular flow (a deflationary fiscal stance).

It is important to also note that both fiscal policy and monetary policy cannot be seen in isolation. Even though the BoE has independence to set interest rate policies, the decisions are taken with full knowledge of the government's fiscal stance. The government lets the MPC know about decisions taken in the budget.

When traditional fiscal and monetary combinations do not work very well, especially during extreme market shocks, then further interventions may be necessary. During the credit crisis of 2007–08, a dramatic series of interest rate cuts ended up with the UK base rate at 0.5%, its lowest level in the BoE's history. Still, commercial banks were not inspired by these low rates and were not keen to lend money to borrowers in the real economy, putting the recovery at risk. This lack of availability of funds to consumers and firms prompted the BoE to intervene further by rolling out an aggressive quantitative easing (QE) programme. QE is a way of pouring money into a cash-starved banking system. The banks get cash in exchange for government bonds, helping them to build up their liquidity – and the hope is that they then lend some of it out to families and businesses to revive consumer spending and economic growth.

During the 2007–08 global credit crisis, the US was the first country in recession to turn to QE to unblock the credit freeze in the banking sector and the wider economy. To stimulate economic growth and to encourage banks to lend to the retail sector the US federal funds rate (a key US reference rate) was slashed. By December 2008 the Fed funds rate stood at 0.25% (compared to a cycle high of 5.25% in September 2007). Ben Bernanke, chairman of the Federal Reserve, followed this rate cut move with QE in the spring of 2009 by purchasing billions of dollars' worth of assets, including mortgage-backed assets.

QE is not new and was used by Japan when it faced deflation – a period of falling prices – from 2001 until 2006. Along with the US Fed, the UK BoE also actioned the QE programme. In March 2009, the MPC announced that, in addition to setting the base rate at 0.5%, it would start to inject money directly into the economy in order to meet the inflation target and to ward off the dangers of deflationary pressures. In a bold move, the instrument of monetary policy shifted towards the quantity of money provided rather than its price (bank rate). QE had never been tried out in the UK before.

Significant reductions in bank rate to a record low of 0.5% provided the large stimulus to the economy that the Bank wanted. With interest rates not far from zero, the MPC needed to provide additional stimulus to support demand in the wider economy. So the MPC boosted the supply of money by purchasing assets like government and corporate bonds. Thus, the Bank supplied extra money directly into the economy to unfreeze the credit markets – but this did not involve printing more banknotes. Instead, the Bank paid for these assets by creating money electronically and crediting the accounts of the banks it bought the assets from. This extra injection of billions of pounds was intended to support more lending by the banks and, therefore, more spending in the economy.

The effect of the record low base rate set by the MPC, combined with QE, was to boost the UK stocks markets and reduce medium- and long-dated gilt yields.

6.3.4 Unwinding of Central Banks Balance Sheets

Many central banks have undergone a programme of buying bonds to stave off a complete collapse in the financial system. For example, the Federal Reserve in the US started large-scale purchases of government bonds and mortgage-backed securities in 2008 and, as a result, the Fed has an estimated US$4.5 trillion of these assets on its balance sheet.

Central banks now face the challenge of trying to normalise balance sheets and this can be done in one of two ways; selling securities or by choosing not to reinvest maturing securities. Either way, when central banks undertake this unwinding of their balance sheets, it will have an impact on the markets, not only in relation to how they undertake this exercise, but in the pace of the unwinding and how this is communicated to the market.

6.4 The Money Supply and its Effects

Learning Objective

2.2.2 Understand how the money supply affects: inflation, deflation, disinflation; interest rates; exchange rates; relationship between money supply, inflation and employment

The term money supply is used to describe the total amount of money circulating in an economy – and, as with many concepts in economics, there are different ways of measuring it. For example, economists often talk about narrow money and broad money.

- **Narrow money** – describes the total sum of all financial assets (including cash) which meet a pretty narrow definition of money; for example, they must be very liquid and available to finance current spending needs. A deposit which was fixed for a long period would not, therefore, meet this definition.
- **Broad money** – describes the total sum of a wider range of assets, including some which are not as liquid as those falling within the definition of narrow money. It may include, for example, money held in savings accounts which are not instant-access accounts.

When governments attempt to affect the economy, one of their tools is the money supply. This is measured by reference to the monetary aggregates – of which there are four, all published by the BoE.

The most important of the four are known as M0 and M4:

- **M0** is the measure of notes and coin in circulation outside the BoE, plus operational deposits at the BoE. (This is, therefore, quite a narrow definition of money.)
- **M4** is the measure of notes and coin in circulation with the public, plus sterling deposits held with UK banks and building societies by the rest of the private sector. (This is thus a broader definition.)

6.4.1 How Money Supply Affects Inflation, Deflation and Disinflation

Inflation measures the general rise in prices in an economy. As we saw in section 6.3, the BoE is charged with taking steps to keep inflation within a certain range. Interest rates are the main, and most effective, tool it has at its disposal for doing this; but the money supply is also a factor. In this section we will look at why this is so.

If money is regarded as being held mainly for transactional (spending) purposes; an excess of money will mean that more money is chasing the same amount of assets, and therefore pushing their prices up. Conversely, if there is less money in supply, there is less to be spent – so asset prices will fall correspondingly. This theory works better in some economic environments than in others.

Deflation describes a general fall in the level of prices, and disinflation is a reduction in the rate of inflation (ie, a slowing of price growth – as opposed to a fall in prices). Using the quantity theory of money, price growth can, in theory, be slowed (disinflation) or even reversed (deflation) through changes to the money supply.

6.4.2 How Money Supply Affects Interest Rates

Money supply is also important to interest rates.

We can think of interest rates as being the price of money. If a bank lends us money it is the price we are willing to pay that bank for the use of its cash (and the price the bank is willing to accept for having to forgo the opportunity to use the money for other, potentially more lucrative, activities). Conversely, if we place our cash on deposit with a bank, the interest we earn on it is what the bank has agreed to pay us.

Monetary economic theory states that interest rates are largely determined by the demand and supply of loanable funds. That is, if the money supply increases, and there is no increase in the demand for money (eg, for investment purposes) then this increases the amount of loanable funds available (eg, for savings). As there is more money available for savings this acts to depress interest rates.

6.4.3 The Relationship between Money Supply, Inflation and Employment

The monetarist explanation of inflation operates through the Fisher equation.

$$MV = PT$$

where:

M = money supply
V = velocity of circulation
P = price level
T = transactions or output

There is a direct relationship between the growth of the money supply and inflation, as monetarists assume that V and T are fixed. The mechanisms by which excess money is translated into inflation are examined below. Individuals can also spend their excess money balances directly on goods and services. This has a direct impact on inflation by raising aggregate demand. The more inelastic the aggregate supply in the economy, the greater the impact on inflation.

The increase in demand for goods and services may cause a rise in imports. Though this leakage from the domestic economy reduces the money supply, it also increases the supply of pounds on the foreign exchange market, thus applying downward pressure on the exchange rate. This may cause imported inflation.

If excess money balances are spent on goods and services, the increase in the demand for labour will cause a rise in money wages and unit labour costs. This may cause cost-push inflation. Cost-push inflation occurs when there is a reduction in aggregate supply. This inflation is bad news, as it means that real national income will fall and prices will rise.

Inflation can be bad for businesses: their costs will rise because the amount they have to pay for goods will go up. Their sales may fall as consumers will not want to buy as much because the prices have gone up. Exports will fall as UK prices rise in comparison to other countries' prices. Inflation can also cause a disruption of business planning; uncertainty about the future makes planning difficult and this may reduce the level of investment. Budgeting becomes a problem as businesses become unsure about what will happen to their costs. This may have a knock-on effect on employment.

However, it is possible that some businesses will benefit from inflation as consumers carry on buying their good or service at the higher price. This will lead to an increase in the business revenue.

6.5 The Balance of Payments

Learning Objective

2.2.3 Understand the impact of surpluses and deficits on business and the economy

2.2.4 Understand the composition of the balance of payments, and the factors behind and benefits of international trade and capital flows: current account; imports; exports

The balance of payments in an economy measures the payments between that country and others. It is made up of the country's exports and imports of goods, services and of transfers of financial capital. It measures all the payments received, and money owed, from overseas parties, less all the payments made, and debts owed, to people overseas.

6.5.1 Current and Capital Accounts

The accounts used to measure the UK's balance of payments are:

- the current account
- the **capital and financial account**.

The balance of payments figures also include a 'balancing item' to correct any statistical errors and to make sure the accounts 'balance'.

The current account measures flows in relation to trade in goods and services, income from investment and compensation of employees and current transfers (eg, private sector gifts to people overseas, or government aid to abroad). The current account balance is usually seen as the most important component of the balance of trade, because it has the greatest impact on other economic factors such as output and employment.

The capital and financial account measures inward investment, foreign investment, foreign currency borrowing by, and deposits with, UK banks, and changes in official reserves.

The balancing item is included to deal with errors and omissions in the accounts; if more currency flows into the UK than is recorded in actual transactions, then the balancing item will be positive, and vice versa.

6.5.2 The Impact of Imbalances on Exchange Rates

The balance of payments between the UK and other countries is important for a number of reasons, not least the impact that it may have on UK exchange rates (and therefore on the competitiveness of UK exports and of imports into our economy).

A deficit on the current account means that the country is not matching its overseas expenditures with its current overseas income. How much this matters depends on the size of the deficit and on how persistent it is. A small negative balance, or one which only persists for the short term, may not be regarded as too serious. It can be financed by the country running down its reserves, or capital inflows. However, a deficit lasting longer has to be financed. A country's reserves are not infinite, so cannot be run down indefinitely. The alternative is to increase overseas borrowing to finance the deficit. To do this to too great an extent is not in the country's interests either, since the larger the UK's debts to the outside world, the greater are the servicing requirements (repayment of interest and capital) on that debt.

One method of correcting a current account deficit may be to allow sterling to fall in value against other currencies. This tends to make foreign goods and services more expensive for UK buyers and so will encourage consumers to buy British instead. In addition, it makes UK goods and services cheaper for overseas customers, helping UK exports. Both these factors will help to restore a positive current account balance.

However, if the current account is also being financed by raising overseas debt, this can create concerns about the stability of the economy, which may lead to government action to raise interest rates (so as to prevent an outflow of investment funds). You should remember that higher interest rates can encourage foreign investors to invest in sterling assets – pushing up the exchange rate as they buy sterling to do so. Rising interest rates may well lead to a strengthening of the currency – which is clearly at odds with the strategy outlined above, of trying to manage the current account through a low exchange rate.

Persistent surpluses and deficits on the balance of payments can create a considerable headache for a government and can impact on exchange rates, interest rates and consequently other activity in the economy.

7. Influences on Asset Classes

Learning Objective

2.3.1 Understand the role of financial investment in the economy: primary markets as introducers of new funds to business and government; secondary markets enabling investors to adjust investments to meet individual needs

7.1 Market Behaviour

The economy as a whole has a big influence on the financial markets.

- In a recession and at the start of a recovery, inflation and interest rates are typically low or falling. Low short-term interest rates mean that the yields on longer-term fixed-interest securities will look relatively attractive, so investors will be prepared to pay higher prices for such securities, so long as they believe that inflation will remain subdued.
- Conversely, the higher interest rates generally seen in a boom period will result in lower prices for fixed-income securities. That is, investors will not be willing to pay a high price to secure the fixed coupon attached to the security if more attractive opportunities exist in, for example, the equity market. (We will look at this idea in section 7.2.2.)

The prices of equities (company shares) also tend to reflect market sentiment about prospects for the economy and so are influenced by the stages of the economic cycle. The main share price indices, such as the FTSE 100 Index in the UK and the S&P 500 Index in the US, serve as barometers for the market.

Share prices can be sharply influenced by changes in sentiment, and these themselves can happen quickly – for example, because of news that a particular economic indicator has been announced as being significantly different from what was expected. If there is a new expectation of an economic recovery, for example, share prices may rise in anticipation. People will expect that the recovery will mean better prospects for companies, higher profits, and therefore increasing share prices and dividends. Investors will be prepared to pay a premium for those shares – and the expected rise in prices becomes self-fulfilling.

A situation of persistently rising share prices is often called a bull market. If expectations about economic recovery are dented – for example, because there are reports of rising unemployment or bankruptcies – share prices may drop back again. If an economy is booming, higher interest rates or concerns that it might be coming to an end can reverse the general direction of share prices. A persistent downward trend in equities prices is often called a bear market.

In the long run, share prices benefit from a steadily growing economy, with rising output, where corporate earnings grow.

7.1.1 Primary Markets

The term primary market refers to the market for new issues of shares or other securities (for example, debt instruments).

Companies and governments need capital in order to carry on their activities (for example, to buy premises and invest in machinery). In order to raise this capital they may issue securities such as shares, bonds or loan stock. It is worth remembering that:

- shares represent a share in the ownership of a company. Investors buy them in the hope of capital appreciation (the value of the company, and therefore the price of the share, goes up); or income (the company earns profits and pays them to its investors in the form of dividends).
- debt instruments represent borrowings by the issuer, which must be repaid at some time. They therefore have a capital repayment value to the investor and (usually) a coupon, which represents the interest that will be paid periodically to the investor. An example of a debt instrument issued by a company is a bond or debenture; an example of a loan issued by the UK government is a gilt.

In order to raise the money it needs, whether it be by way of share capital or debt capital, the issuer will offer the new securities on the primary market.

Primary markets are important both for new ventures – eg, a company which is just being established – and for existing ventures which are expanding and raising new capital, or which have been in existence for a while but are just introducing their existing shares to the public market for the first time.

For a new company, listing its shares for the first time, the LSE acts as a primary market: the market through which it reaches its initial investors and raises a new tranche of capital.

The process of introducing shares, bonds or loan stock on to the market for the first time is known as listing them. Issuers have to meet certain standards before they can list their securities on the exchange:

- the size of the company
- the value of securities they are introducing on to the market
- the information available to potential investors in order to decide whether to invest
- on an ongoing basis, the information companies must disclose to the market about activities or shares.

7.1.2 Secondary Markets

Once an investor has bought a holding in shares or debt instruments in the primary market, they may need to sell or reduce it due to a change in their circumstances or those of the company. They may need their money back, their investment objectives may change, or substantial capital gain can be realised.

The secondary markets offer a mechanism for them to do this and to invest in other listed securities.

The LSE acts as a secondary market in securities, among other exchanges. The secondary market is not capital raising but allows for trading of existing issues.

7.2 Macroeconomic Influences on Asset Classes

Learning Objective

2.3.2 Analyse the impact of macroeconomic influences on each of the following asset classes: fixed income; commodities; cash; property; equities

In arriving at a suitable investment strategy it is worth considering the impacts of the wider economy on the individual asset classes. Armed with this information, it is possible to position a portfolio to potentially benefit from changes in the macroeconomy.

In addition to using a suitable asset allocation model in order to diversify the portfolio and reduce risk by limiting exposure to any one sector or asset, the investment manager also needs to assess the macroeconomic indicators and the position of the economy in the business cycle in arriving at a decision over when to make the individual investments within each asset class. As we will see in the following pages, each asset class may respond differently to changes at the macroeconomic level.

The investment clock below describes the interrelationship between the economic cycle and various sectors:

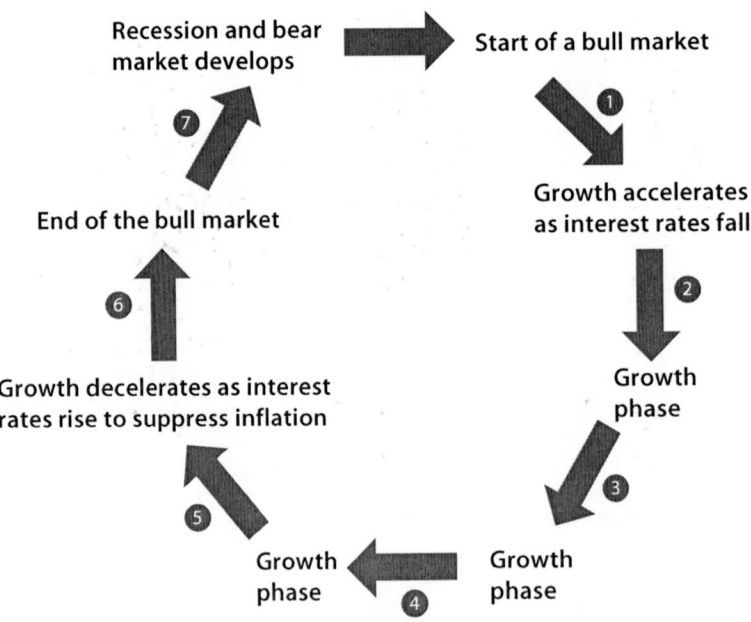

Sectors which may be in favour with investors at each point in the economic cycle include:

1. Bonds, interest-rate-sensitive equities – banks, house buildings.
2. Exchange-rate-sensitive equities – exporters, multinationals.
3. Basic industry equities – chemicals, paper, steel.
4. Cyclical consumer equities – airlines, automobiles, general retailers, leisure.
5. General industrial and capital spending equities – electrical, engineering, contractors.
6. Commodities and basic resources.
7. Cash; defensive equities – food, retail, pharmaceuticals, utilities.

However, the clock assumes that the portfolio manager knows exactly where in the economic cycle the economy is positioned and the extent to which each market sector is operationally geared to the cycle. Moreover, the investment clock doesn't provide any latitude for unanticipated events that may, through a change in the risk appetite of investors, spark a sudden flight from equities to government bond markets, for example, or change the course that the economic cycle takes. Each economic cycle is different, and investors' behaviour may not be the same as that demonstrated in previous cycles.

7.2.1 Cash

The returns achieved on traditional cash deposits are influenced by regional and international macroeconomic factors such as inflation. Cash deposits, along with other money market instruments (such as T-bills and commercial paper) are an asset class having maturities of less than 12 months. These products provide investors with liquid investments that meet short-term needs.

Along with cash deposits, the returns provided by these investments also depend on the issuers' industry and firm-specific factors. The nominal rate of return on cash is made up of the real rate plus the inflation rate. Inflation erodes the value of capital and, if the real rate of interest being earned on the capital is less than the rate of inflation, then the value of a cash investment will diminish over time. Although interest rates may be increased by the BoE to control excessive inflationary growth in the economy, any investors holding time deposits will have to wait until the deposit matures in order to benefit from any changes in rates.

7.2.2 Fixed-Income Securities

Any changes that are made to interest rates as a result of macroeconomic influences will also affect the value of fixed-income securities. These assets often have maturities of more than one year. An issuer of a fixed-income security raises funds from capital markets and, in return, an investor in this asset class receives regular coupon interest on the long-term loan that they have provided to the issuer, plus a redemption of the principal value of the investment at the maturity of the longer-term loan.

Yield to maturity (YTM) is a term used to identify the dynamic annualised return or rate that is provided to the investor for the entire period of the loan. There is an inverse relationship between the level of yield and the price of a bond. The yield on a particular bond is not static, but reacts instantaneously to fresh news as underlying factors or drivers start to influence market expectations. Typically, bond investments lose value when the whole interest rate cycle turns upward.

As an example, let us consider macroeconomic influences on bonds. At the top of the growth phase in a normal economic cycle, inflationary pressures are likely to be increasing at an unacceptably high rate. Thus, interest rates may be increased. This rate increase will be necessary in order to control and moderate near- or long-term inflationary excesses in the economy. An increase in short-term rates can be transmitted across the whole yield curve, affecting bonds of longer maturities. This effect will diminish the value of existing fixed-interest holdings within the portfolio.

Alternatively, as the economy declines and begins to enter recession, interest rates may be reduced to stimulate the economy and to encourage consumption and spending. Falling money market interest rates and bond yields will lead to an increase in the prices and value of fixed-interest assets.

In the case of higher quality corporate bonds, credit spreads need to be taken into consideration. If the market believes that a company has become less creditworthy, it will increase the credit spread applied to that company's debt causing the price to fall, even if there has been no change in interest rates. Conversely, if the market believes that a company has become more creditworthy, it will decrease the credit spread causing the price to rise.

7.2.3 Equities

As an asset class, equity prices are affected by both macroeconomic and company-specific factors. The price of a share is directly influenced by economic considerations. News that helps to boost company prospects, stimulate sales and lower costs of production and distribution will clearly be beneficial. Hence share prices increase on activity that translates into higher company cash flows and also raise expectations of higher dividends. When the economic growth cycle turns upward, investor confidence grows on expectations that increased spending and consumption in the economy will revive business activity. If this business confidence translates into visibly higher cash flows that strengthen a company's position in the marketplace, then increased investor demand for a company's shares will continue to lift share prices. Therefore, whereas bond returns measured in nominal terms are negatively impacted by rising inflation pressures, equities are seen as moderately good hedges against inflation.

7.2.4 Property

As an asset class, property or real estate is often considered to be a special type of alternative investment. Real estate provides access to tangible assets; often this is in commercial or retail property. This asset class has some unique features that are not common to equities or bonds. First, it is investment in a fixed immovable object, ie, land or property located in a certain space. Second, one property is only approximately comparable to another, hence it is not fungible with another and presents challenges for valuers. Property is also not divisible, which makes it unique, and, finally, a property is illiquid due to its immovability and indivisibility.

In the last few years there has been increased interest from money managers to strategically include property in their portfolios. In addition to return opportunities, the asset allows managers to reduce risks through diversification and to provide inflation protection. Within a contemporary portfolio of bonds and equities, property provides good diversification benefits because of its lower correlations with other financial asset classes. As a result of this benefit it has become a common investment vehicle for pension funds and insurance companies worldwide.

Returns from property come from two sources: rental yield, and capital appreciation of the underlying property stock.

As with the common types of financial asset classes (money market, equity and bonds), the intrinsic value of real estate is affected not only by the key macroeconomic factors (eg, GDP growth, inflation, interest rates and employment), but also by other asset-specific factors relating to the rental yields available to investors, the possibilities for capital appreciation, the availability of land, EU migration patterns, bank lending policy and taxation benefits and subsidies.

As an example, we can examine the impact of the response of the UK housing market to particular macroeconomic events. During much of the earlier 2007 boom, the strength in the property market coincided with relatively low interest rates, strong equity market performances, high levels of consumer confidence, high employment rates across Europe, and loose credit card and bank lending policies. However, the onset of the mortgage crisis in the sub-prime mortgage market in the US in the autumn of 2007 triggered the first wave of a two-stage crisis. Combined with the ensuing credit crunch in the global capital markets, the resulting global economic recession and sharp drop in investor confidence lasted up until March 2009, when QE began. The outlook for growth was dampened not only by the drying up of credit by banks in the crisis, but also by outlooks for poor GDP growth in wider G7 economies.

Liquidity had dried up and a sharp credit squeeze in the commercial and the retail property market by banks triggered foreclosures in the US housing market. The contagion spread across the world, leading to the prominent bankruptcy of Lehman Brothers in the autumn of 2008 that further escalated the banking and housing market crises. The crisis was partially alleviated by large-scale central bank and government intervention in spring 2009. The co-ordinated intervention took the form of maintaining record low base rates in the UK and US, the part nationalisation of selected banks, monetary support to recapitalise the global banking system and further injections of liquidity via quantitative easing. All of these interventions were designed to stabilise the banking system, reduce the impact on the real economy and to stimulate and encourage the ailing banks to lend funds to households and companies.

The overall housing market performances as measured by the UK Nationwide Housing Price Index stood at 9738.6 in September 2007, its highest level since the quarterly index was created on 31 December 1952. The housing market plunged during the crisis of 2007–08 to set a cycle dip by March 2009, and this reflected a housing market drop of 21% over an 18-month period.

This co-ordinated action at government level pump-primed the banking system and stabilised the capital markets. Stock markets recovered and, along with a moderating credit-squeeze, the property market regained composure, again stimulated by strong recoveries in the BRIC economies. Low historic interest rates and QE policies continued to drive modest improvements in the commercial and retail property markets. However, during 2010 and early 2011, the rise was tempered by high levels of unemployment across Europe, sluggish economic growth and tight government fiscal policy and record levels of budgetary deficits in some EU economies that have hampered recovery in the property markets.

Whereas the retail property market is more sensitive to employment conditions and the general health of household accounts, the commercial property market is not only dependent on economic drivers but also on external dependencies linked to global markets. In addition, most reputed developers prefer the leasing model and then to sell the leased-out property to investors. These are good options to buy, as they give the buyer a return on investment from the very beginning.

Real estate is a complex investment with its own unique benefits and disadvantages that each investor weighs differently. The possible benefits are as follows:

- Tax subsidy law allows commercial mortgage interest, property taxes and other expenses to be tax deductible.
- Mortgage loans allow property borrowers to utilise more financial leverage than is available on shares or bonds. The loan-to-value (LTV) on a property in the UK has stabilised around the 75-80% mark even after the 2007–08 credit crisis.

- Property investors have opportunities to add value to their property through renovation and restoration. This flexibility is not available to investors holding shares in companies.
- Multiple property investments in a portfolio with different geographical locations can provide diversification opportunities.
- Property can provide a good inflation hedge, because there is positive correlation between inflation and property prices.

7.2.5 Commodities

Even though households have been investing in gold and diamonds for centuries, commodities have found a useful place in the money manager's portfolio. The low correlation of these assets with financial assets such as equities and bonds has generated strong interest in these securities. Their appeal is based on the notion that commodities (ranging from gold to oil to wheat) are not financial investments but have intrinsic value that is dependent on other forces. These forces are not necessarily affected to the same extent by macroeconomic conditions as financial assets. Their low correlation with other financial investments makes them useful as effective hedges against inflation.

Gold bullion, physical silver and oil have all received significant coverage in the press in recent years. Even before paper money existed, gold and silver were the currencies of choice as their portability and durability proved to be useful as a medium of exchange. Their scarcity value and safe-haven status during economic and political strife has proved that they deserve a strategic role in the institutional portfolio in order to stabilise returns.

In terms of macroeconomic influences on commodity markets, a number of research studies have been published in this area. The scope is wide and we have provided a brief outline of some key impacts of macroeconomic and other related factors on commodity prices in general. We have focused mainly on energy and metals, although there are others, such as grains, softs and livestock, which are not discussed in this section.

US studies reveal that over the period from 1950–2012 there has been a link between real interest rates (US three-month T-bill rate) and real commodity price index, measured in dollars using the Moody's Commodity Price Index. The results show a statistically significant relationship between the two. There is an inverse relationship between commodity prices and the real interest rate – over periods when interest rates were low, real commodity prices were higher.

Before we discuss some other influences, commodity products range from energy resources through to metals. Consequently, given the breadth of products in the asset class, there can be a series of individual factors that can have specific influential impacts on each commodity. Space does not allow for a detailed examination of all the factors for each commodity in this section. Readers who wish to look at a single commodity in more detail are advised to consult information sources that are more closely related to their areas of interest.

The Macroeconomic Environment

Surveys reveal that, in general, crude oil, natural gas, coal and uranium fuel prices tend to be strongly affected specifically by changes in demand/business cycles and supply/production constraints. The anticipated future demand from two of the most important energy consuming economies (US and China) are monitored closely by commodities traders. In actual fact, there are also significant influences on metals prices based on expected demand from China and other emerging nations, especially the industrial metals such as aluminium, copper and steel. To assess how energy and metal prices may be affected by supply considerations, traders also monitor the supply/demand situation in individual commodity markets to identify potential bottlenecks. Interestingly, government trade policies and linkages to the foreign exchange rates (dollar) are not as important to these types of commodity markets.

Although industrial metals have relatively weaker links to the dollar, gold and silver are more sensitive to changes in the foreign exchange rate. In addition, they are influenced by actions taken by investment funds. A reason for this is that funds have incorporated these metal assets as part of their portfolios to mitigate the effects of increased market uncertainties and volatilities.

The price of gold (US$/oz) and the US dollar index (measured against a broad range of currencies) reveals an interesting relationship. Traditionally, gold has been considered a long-term hedge against dollar weakness. A negative relationship between the two has been observed. This relationship is accentuated by episodes when the dollar has been weakened by concerns over the US economy or its public debt. However, some of these long-term macroeconomic influences have been temporarily ignored during heightened periods of political strife or geopolitical risks. Both gold and the dollar have moved up on safe-haven trade plays.

Please refer to chapter 1 for more on the asset classes above.

Key Chapter Points

- The UK population is increasing. In aggregate, the age structure is shifting towards a higher proportion of elderly people (though immigration is slowing this trend, to a degree).
- There is an increase in single person households, though most people still live as part of larger units.
- With more older people, and also more young children, the proportion of the population that is working reduces, and the proportion that is non-working, and dependent on the working population, increases.
- Living standards rise when incomes increase by more than the rate of inflation.
- The value of property is a significant part of personal sector wealth in the UK.
- Productivity is a measure of how much output is produced by factors of production. Factors of production are land, labour, capital and enterprise. Increases in productivity, for example those produced by technological developments, create economic wealth and enhance household incomes and therefore living standards.
- A major factor behind the growth in the tertiary (service) sector of the economy has been the rapid expansion of the banking, finance and insurance sectors – and of technology.
- A number of international factors influence UK markets and the local economy.
- Globalisation is an increasing factor, both in business and finance.
- The UK is part of the EU, but has not yet joined into monetary union with the euro. There are advantages, and disadvantages, to doing so.
- Fiscal policy is the government's policy on taxation, borrowing and public (government) spending.
- Monetary policy is concerned with measures which affect the amount of money in the economy (the money stock or money supply) and the price of money (ie, rates of interest).
- A central bank acts for a government and typically has various functions, such as the issuance of banknotes, management of government finances, dealing in the money markets to set interest rates and acting as lender of last resort to the banking system. The BoE is the UK central bank, and the MPC its interest rate-setting body.
- Economies go through cycles with identifiable phases and characteristics; governments try to stabilise the volatility of these cycles through various forms of intervention.
- The primary markets are the markets on which new funds are made available to enterprises and to government. Instruments are subsequently traded in secondary markets.
- Countries can suffer from trade imbalances when they import significantly more than they export, and vice versa.
- There are a number of economic and market measures or indices which can be used to gauge the direction and strength of changes in the economy, or of a market.

End of Chapter Questions

Think of an answer for each question and refer to the appropriate workbook section for confirmation.

1. Identify and explain the factors of productivity in the economy.
   Answer reference: Section 1.8

2. What are the pro-cyclic indicators?
   Answer reference: Section 5

3. Describe what the public sector net cash requirement is.
   Answer reference: Section 6.2

4. How is the setting of interest rates managed in the UK?
   Answer reference: Section 6.3

5. What is the purpose of the discount window facility (DWF)?
   Answer reference: Section 6.3.2

6. What is the definition of broad money?
   Answer reference: Section 6.4

7. Describe what is meant by the term 'disinflation'?
   Answer reference: Section 6.4.1

8. In the context of the UK economy, describe what is meant by a current account deficit?
   Answer reference: Section 6.5.2

9. How are share prices affected in both bull and bear markets?
   Answer reference: Section 7.1

10. At what point in an economic cycle are investors likely to favour commodities?
    Answer reference: Section 7.2

Chapter Three
Principles of Investment Risk and Return

1. The Time Value of Money — 197
2. Investment Risk and Return — 210
3. Models of Investment Theory — 237

This syllabus area will provide approximately 6 of the 80 examination questions

Principles of Investment Risk and Return

1. The Time Value of Money

1.1 Compound Interest

Learning Objective

3.1.1 Understand the effects of compound interest and the time value of money

In finance, we often face decisions concerning the determination of how much we need to save today (the present value or PV) for consumption in the future (its future value or FV). Alternatively, we may need to find out what a future payment of money will be when it is converted to PV terms. To carry out these tasks easily we need to understand the mathematics of time value problems. The time value of money is a concept where today's cash flow (PV) is converted to an equivalent value to any point in the future (FV). Understanding the time value concept is an essential skill for any finance practitioner. See section 1.4 for further details.

The time value concept tells us that the £1 we have in our pocket today is worth more now (higher purchasing power) than the same £1 we will have in the future. Thus, money loses its value the further we move into the future. If we know the PV of a cash flow, we can determine its FV by compounding a PV with an interest rate over the time. Conversely, if we know the FV of a cash flow, we can determine its PV by discounting.

The idea of compound interest and the effect it can have on an investment takes account of the additional growth that arises when an investor leaves their interest invested with the main deposit (the principal) instead of withdrawing it to spend: they begin to earn interest on that interest, and their investment rolls up all the faster for it.

Example

Suppose that £2,000 is invested at 10% interest which reflects the deposit rate for this saving. After one year, the original principal plus interest will amount to £2,200.

	£
Original investment	2,000
Interest in the first year (10%)	200
Investment at end of one year	2,200
Interest in the second year (10%)	220
Total investment at the end of two years	2,420

The second-year interest of £220 is made up of 10% earned on the original investment, and 10% earned on the interest earned in the first year. The PV of the original investment was £2,000. With interest rates steady over two years at 10%, this amount increases to generate a terminal value at the end of two years (FV) of £2,420. FV was obtained by discretely compounding the PV at a given interest rate over a series of intervals.

Instead of performing the calculations shown above, we can easily calculate the future value (FV) of an investment using a standard formula, as follows:

$$FV = PV(1 + r)^n$$

where:

PV = the original sum invested – its present value.
r = the interest/return rate, expressed as a proportion (so 10% is written as 0.10).
n = the number of periods over which we are compounding.
FV = the sum invested after n periods.

Compounding effects may appear to be minimal over one or two periods, but over a long time they can make a considerable difference to the growth of an investment.

The term $(1+r)^n$ is the compounding factor that is applied to the original amount invested.

In the previous example, interest has been calculated annually, but this isn't always the case. Interest may be compounded discretely over smaller intervals of time: daily, weekly, monthly or quarterly or even continuously.

If r, the annual rate of interest is given, along with the n total period that the amount will be invested for, then the compounding factor can be easily determined for payments of interest based on any frequency: daily, weekly, quarterly, etc.

In this case, be sure to use the following general expression to work out the compounding factor (CF) first. Then multiply this CF with the present value (amount originally invested):

General form where r is the annual rate of interest quoted and n are periods in number of years over which the investment is made: compounding factor= $(1+(r/j))^{nj}$

j in this case is the frequency or number of interest payments made in one year. For example, if interest is paid quarterly (four times in one year), then j is 4. Similarly, if interest is paid daily, then j = 365 or 366 in a leap year.

This compounding factor is then multiplied by the PV to determine the FV.

We have set up an example below to demonstrate application of this formula. Note that when interest is being paid continuously, then the general formula of the compounding factor changes and is given as follows:

Continuous compounding: compounding factor = e^{RT}

where:

R = the annual rate of interest paid (not the same as r, the discrete rate used in the previous formula).
T = the total time period of investment in number of years.
e = the mathematical Napier's constant – approximately equal to 2.71828.

Continuous compounding is, broadly, the same as interest paid daily.

Principles of Investment Risk and Return

Example

Suppose that you have £100 to invest over a five-year time period. The interest will be 5% per annum. Determine the future value of this investment if the annual interest is paid in the following manner: annually, semi-annually, quarterly, monthly, weekly, daily and continuously.

To solve and evaluate this problem we use the first equation below to determine the compounding factor for discrete interest payments. This is then multiplied by the £100 invested.

Finally, we use the second equation when interest is paid continuously over the year to determine the compounding factor. Then we multiply this CF by £100 of the original investment.

CF, Compounding factor based on discrete interest payments = $(1+(r/j))^{nj}$
CF, Compounding factor based on continuous interest payments = e^{RT}
Assume R is the same as r, namely: 5% annual interest.

Assume you will invest £100 for five years at an annual interest rate of 5%:

	Notation used	Value
Amount invested today (£)	PV	100
Annual interest rate	r	0.05
Term of investment (years)	n	5

Payment of interest	Frequency of Interest payments in one year, j	Compounding factor (CF)	Future value of investment
Annual	1	1.2763	127.6282
Semi-annual	2	1.2801	128.0085
Quarterly	4	1.2820	128.2037
Monthly	12	1.2834	128.3359
Weekly	52	1.2839	128.3871
Daily	365	1.2840	128.4003
Continuously		1.2840	128.4025

The results of this exercise show clearly that over the entire five-year investment period, the final terminal wealth or the future value of the investment is sensitive to the frequency of interest payments in a year.

In general, note that the terminal wealth (FV) will always increase as the frequency of payments increases, reaching a maximum limit when the frequency of interest paid gets infinitely large (continuous).

This effect applies to any interest rate and any term of the holding period. The impact on the future value is greater if the annual interest rate (r) increases and/or the term of investment (n) increases.

If interest rate frequency is daily or continuous, it may be easier to use the second equation that utilises the Napier constant, e.

1.2 Present Value

Learning Objective

3.1.2 Calculate the present value of: lump sums; regular payments

The calculation of present value (PV) is used to determine how much to invest today, given a known rate of interest and frequency of payment, in order to achieve a required amount in the future (FV). The methods used to calculate present value are known as discounted cash flow techniques (DCF). The rate of interest that is to be received is known as the discount rate, and the amount that is required to be achieved is known as the terminal value or future value.

1.2.1 Present Value of a Future Sum Cash Flow

The amount that needs to be invested today in order to obtain a targeted future sum is determined through discounting. The procedure is a reverse process to compounding. Thus, the future amount required by the rate of interest earned over the period is calculated by rearranging the formula for compound interest as follows:

$$PV = \frac{FV}{(1+r)^n}$$

where:

PV = present value (or value of sum invested).
FV = future value (or value at end of compounding period).
r = interest rate expressed as an integer (eg, 5% = 0.05).
n = number of periods being compounded (eg, five years).

We will use data from the compound interest formula to illustrate this. How much needs to be invested today at 5% per annum to generate £127.63 (to two decimal points) after five years?

The formula is:

$$PV = \frac{£127.63}{(1+0.05)^5}$$

$$= \frac{£127.63}{(1.05)^5}$$

$$= \frac{£127.63}{1.2763}$$

$$= £100$$

This can be proved by entering into a calculator 127.63 ÷ 1.05^5 and can be checked in reverse using the compound interest formula: 100 x 1.05^5 = 127.63.

As the present value formula expresses future cash flows in today's terms, it allows a comparison to be made of competing investments of equal risk, which have the same start date but different payment timings or amounts.

1.2.2 Present Value of an Annuity

The PV of an annuity refers to a series of equal cash payments that will be received over a specified period of time. As before, the PV of an annuity is calculated by discounting the future cash flows to today's value. The same formula can be used for regular payments.

We will first consider where payments are made in arrears. If we expect to receive payments of £100 over each of the next three years, we can calculate their PV assuming interest rates remain at 5%, using the formula above.

Year	Cash Flow	Discount Rate	Formula	Discount Factor	Present Value
1	100.00	5%	100.00 ÷ 1.05	0.9524	95.24
2	100.00	5%	100.00 ÷ 1.05^2	0.9070	90.70
3	100.00	5%	100.00 ÷ 1.05^3	0.8638	86.38
Total					272.32

So the PV of those future payments totalling £300.00 is actually £272.32. The table also shows how this converts into a discount factor, that is, by how much the future value is discounted in decimal terms.

Instead of calculating each PV, this can be calculated by using another formula:

$$\text{PV of an annuity} = £ \times \left[\frac{1 - (1+r)^{-n}}{r} \right]$$

where:

£ = the amount of the annuity paid each year.
r = the rate of interest over the life of the annuity.
n = the number of periods that the annuity will run for.

Using the example above, the calculation is as follows:

$$\text{PV of an annuity} = 100 \times \left[\frac{1 - (1+0.05)^{-3}}{0.05} \right]$$

$$= 100 \times \left[\frac{1 - (1.05)^{-3}}{0.05} \right]$$

$$= 100 \times \left[\frac{1 - (0.86384)}{0.05} \right]$$

$$= 100 \times \left[\frac{0.13616}{0.05} \right]$$

$$= 100 \times \left[2.7232 \right]$$

$$= £272.32$$

The PV of an annuity can be used for calculating such things as the monthly repayments on a mortgage and it can also be used in investment appraisal.

1.2.3 Present Value of Perpetuities

A perpetuity is a series of regular cash flows that are due to be paid or received indefinitely, which in practice is defined as a period beyond 50 years.

It is simply calculated using the following formula:

$$\text{PV of a perpetuity} = \frac{A}{r}$$

where:

A = amount of periodic payment.
r = interest rate.

Although a perpetuity really exists only as a mathematical model, it can be used to approximate the value of a long-term stream of equal payments by treating it as an indefinite perpetuity.

So, for example, if you have a commercial property that generates £10,000 of rental income and the interest rate is 8%, then the formula can be used to calculate its PV by capitalising those future payments into its PV of £125,000.

$$\text{PV of a perpetuity} = \frac{£10,000}{0.08} = £125,000$$

Perpetual Bond Calculations

A perpetual bond is a bond with no maturity date. Hence it pays coupons indefinitely and the bond is not redeemed. It is irredeemable. They are also known as consols. Some of the historically notable perpetual bond issues were made by the UK Treasury to pay off loans related to the Napoleonic wars (1814). There exist eight undated gilts, which make up a very small proportion of the UK government's debt. They have no fixed maturity date. These gilts are very old. The redemption of these bonds is at the discretion of the UK government, but because of their age, they all have low coupons, and there is therefore currently little incentive for the government to redeem them.

Perpetual bonds are priced using the following expression:

$$P = \frac{C}{Y}$$

where:

P = price of the bond.
C = annual coupon rate.
Y = yield to maturity of the bond.

Preference Shares and Calculations

Preference shares are equity instruments that are often considered to be a hybrid; having similar characteristics to a bond and a share. The shares pay a constant dividend indefinitely. Hence, as with a perpetual bond, they can be considered as securities offering fixed income indefinitely.

Preferred equity is priced by using the following expression:

$$P = \frac{D}{K}$$

where:

D = constant dividend set for the security.
K = return expected by the holder of the share.

1.3 Future Value

Learning Objective

3.1.3 Calculate the future value of: lump sums; regular payments

1.3.1 Future Value of Lump Sums

Future value refers to the future value of an amount invested now at a given rate of interest. We effectively already looked at future value when we considered compounding interest in section 1.1. We saw that the future value of £100 deposited today at 5% per annum for a period of years was:

Year	Balance at the start of the year	Interest for the year at 5% per annum	Balance at the end of the year
1	100.00	5.00	105.00
2	105.00	5.25	110.25
3	110.25	5.51	115.76
4	115.76	5.79	121.55
5	121.55	6.08	127.63

To calculate future value, use the following formula:

$$\text{Future value (FV)} = \text{Present value (PV)} \times (1 + r)^n$$

So to calculate the value in five years' time and invested today at 5% per annum, we would enter this into a calculator as 100 x (1.05 ^ 5) = 127.63.

where FV is to be calculated given:

PV = £100.

r = 5% or 0.05.

n = 5 years.

If interest is paid more frequently, the formula is adjusted. If interest is instead paid half-yearly it becomes:

$$FV = PV \times (1 + r/2)^{2n}$$

$$£100 \times (1 + (0.05 \div 2))^{2 \times 5} = £100 \times 1.025^{10} = £128.00845$$

In the example above the rate of interest for the half-year has been calculated first; namely, half of 5%, which is then expressed as a decimal, ie, 1.025. The term is then converted into the number of periods on which interest will be paid, in other words ten half-yearly interest payments.

1.3.2 Applying Compound Interest to Regular Payments

So far we have concentrated on establishing the final value of invested lump sums when compound interest is applied. We now move on to looking at how final values are established when a series of equal payments are invested either at the start or the end of each year. The former payments are known as being made in advance, while the latter are termed as being made in arrears.

If investing at the start of each year, then the following formula may be used:

$$FV = \text{Payment} \times \left[((1 + r)^n - 1)/r \right] (1 + r)$$

where:

FV = future value.

r = interest/return rate.

n = number of payment periods.

Principles of Investment Risk and Return

Example

£100 is invested at the start of each year for five years at a fixed rate of interest of 6% per annum compounded annually. What will the accumulated value of these series of payments be at the end of the five-year period?

Solution

$$\begin{aligned}
FV &= £100 \times [((1.06)^5 - 1)/0.06](1.06) \\
&= £100 [((1.06)^5 - 1)/0.06](1.06) \\
&= £100 [(1.34 - 1)/0.06](1.06) \\
&= £100 [(0.34)/0.06](1.06) \\
&= £100 [5.6371](1.06) \\
&= £563.71(1.06) \\
&= £597.53
\end{aligned}$$

The FV is £597.53.

We can check these figures using the following table.

Year	Deposit Paid	Future Value			
		Balance at Start	Interest Rate	Interest Earned	Balance at End
1	100	£100.00	6%	£6.00	£106.00
2	100	£206.00	6%	£12.36	£218.36
3	100	£318.36	6%	£19.10	£337.46
4	100	£437.46	6%	£26.25	£463.71
5	100	£563.71	6%	£33.82	£597.53

If investing at the end of each year, then the following formula may be used.

$$FV = \text{payment} \times \left[((1 + r)^n - 1)/r \right]$$

Example

£100 is invested at the end of each year for five years at a fixed rate of interest of 6% per annum compounded annually. What will the accumulated value of these series of payments be at the end of the five-year period?

Solution

FV = £100 x [((1.06)^5 – 1)/0.06]

= £100 [((1.06)^5 – 1)/0.06]

= £100 [(1.34 – 1)/0.06]

= £100 [(0.34)/0.06]

= £100 [5.6371]

= £563.71

The FV is £563.71.

We can check these figures using the following table.

			Future Value		
Year	Deposit Paid	Balance at Start	Interest Rate	Interest Earned	Balance at End
1	100	£0.00	6%	£0.00	£100.00
2	100	£100.00	6%	£6.00	£206.00
3	100	£206.00	6%	£12.36	£318.36
4	100	£318.36	6%	£19.10	£437.46
5	100	£437.46	6%	£26.25	£563.71

Note: The difference between this and the earlier example, ie, (£597.53 – £563.71 = £33.82) is solely accounted for by one earlier payment being invested over the entire five-year period, ie, £100 x (1.06^5 – 1) = £33.82.

1.4 The Time Value of Money

Both investor and adviser need to appreciate the implications of holding investments over a period of time, and the effect of inflation during the time period on returns from investments.

When considering the passage of time, understanding the compounding effects we have just considered is critical. The principle of discounting is rather like compounding in reverse, as it allows us to calculate, among other things, what rate of interest or return will produce a specific sum at a future date.

Principles of Investment Risk and Return

If a person has a choice between (A) £1,000 now, and (B) £1,000 in one year's time, then they will prefer (A). If you have £1,000 now, you can invest it and earn interest, so that you will have more at the year-end. You might alternatively have other uses for the money.

This example shows that money has a time value. The option of having money now is of more value than the option of having money at a date in the future, because we can make it work for us from an earlier point. Interest can be seen partly as the return required by the lender to compensate for the time value of money that the lender is supplying to the borrower.

The formula we use to calculate the effects of compounding is, you will remember, that if we invest £PV now for n years at r% interest per annum we should obtain $£PV(1 + r)^n$ in n years' time. Thus, if we invest £10,000 now for four years at 10% interest per annum, we will have a total investment worth £10,000 × $(1+10\%)^4$ = £14,641 at the end of four years (that is, at year 4 if it is now year 0).

The principle of discounting is that if we wish to have £FV in n years' time, we need to invest a certain sum now (year 0) at an interest rate of r% in order to obtain the required sum of money in the future.

Example

If we wish to have £14,641 in four years' time, how much money would we need to invest now at 10% interest per annum? (You could think of this as being a bit like the reverse of the compounding calculations we have already looked at.)

Using our compounding formula, $FV = PV(1 + r)^n$

where: PV = the original sum invested.
r = 10%.
n = 4.
FV = the sum we want to achieve = £14,641.

£14,641 = $PV(1 + 0.1)^4$
£14,641 = PV times 1.4641
so X = $\dfrac{£14,641}{1.4641}$ = £10,000

We can see that £10,000 now, earning interest at 10% per annum, is the equivalent in value of £14,641 after four years. We can therefore say that £10,000 is the present value of £14,641 at year 4, at an interest rate of 10%.

1.5 Inflation and Investment Returns

Learning Objective

3.1.4 Calculate real and inflation-adjusted returns: nominal returns; real or inflation-adjusted returns; total returns

The nominal return on an investment is the return it gives, unadjusted for inflation. Thus, a bank account paying 4% interest annually has a nominal return of 4%. The real return is the return it provides an investor after stripping out the effects of inflation.

Thus, if inflation is running at 3% per annum, the above bank account is providing a real return calculated as follows:

Nominal return − Rate of inflation = Real return

4% − 3% = 1% real return

This estimation is useful for giving an approximation of the investment's real rate of return – but if we need a more accurate measure of the real return, it is a little more complicated. To get a completely accurate figure, the relationship between the rate of inflation, the real rate of return and the nominal rate of return is as follows, with rates expressed as a decimal (eg, 5% is expressed as 0.05):

(1+ real rate of return) × (1+ inflation rate) = 1+ nominal rate of return

In a similar fashion:

$$(1 + \text{real rate of return}) = \frac{(1 + \text{nominal rate of return})}{(1 + \text{inflation rate})}$$

$$\text{Real rate of return} = \left[\frac{(1 + \text{nominal rate of return})}{(1 + \text{inflation rate})}\right] - 1$$

Note that if we add 1 to the return (1 + r), or to the inflation rate (1 + inflation rate), as in the brackets above, then the terms in the brackets may be referred to as the **return relative** or the **inflation relative**.

Example

If the nominal rate of return is 12% per annum and the annual rate of inflation is 8% per annum. The real rate of return is the return earned after allowing for the return needed just to keep pace with inflation.

We rearrange the equation to find the real rate of return:

$$\frac{1 + \text{nominal rate}}{1 + \text{inflation rate}} = 1 + \text{real rate}$$

$$\frac{1.12}{1.08} = 1.037$$

Thus, the real rate of return is 3.7%.

Principles of Investment Risk and Return

It is not unusual for people to use the approximate measure we looked at first, however – ie, real return as the difference between the nominal rate of return and the rate of inflation. In our last example, this would be 12% – 8% = 4%.

It is possible for a real return to be negative; in the example above, if inflation were to run at 6% per annum but a bank account continued to pay 4% per annum, then the real return on it would be around –2%. Put another way, the purchasing power of a deposit held in that bank account would be falling at 2% a year.

This is important, because investors need to keep the effects of inflation in mind when planning their financial affairs. Even quite low levels of inflation can erode the purchasing power of someone's wealth over time.

You may also see the term total return. This means the return on an investment both from its income production, and any capital gains (or losses) it generates. The total return on an investment may be important to an investor when comparing one investment with another; but it may also be important to them to strip out the elements of that return into two elements: a return coming from the capital gain/loss, and a second generated from the income portion of the investment. Individual elements of this total return may be treated differently for tax purposes.

You should remember that we looked at methods of calculating the redemption yield on a fixed-interest security in chapter 2. The redemption yield takes account of both the interest to be paid, and any gain/loss if the security is held to maturity. It therefore calculates the annualised total return on that security, assuming it is held to maturity.

Also with a share investment, the total return is composed of the capital appreciation (depreciation) element and the dividend income portion.

Similarly, with a bond investment, the total return will include the capital gain on the investment, together with the portion of the income from bond coupons over the holding period.

2. Investment Risk and Return

2.1 Risk Premium

Risk and reward are important aspects of investment decisions. It is true that low-risk investments generally generate a low return. To believe, however, that taking on a high level of risk is a sure way to produce higher returns is to misunderstand the meaning of risk. Risk is present when there is a possibility of poor performance. A risky investment can offer the possibility of relatively high rates of return, but the other side of the coin, from which the riskiness arises, is that the return might instead be low or negative.

We can say that risk and potential reward are generally positively correlated; investments with a higher potential return generally carry a higher risk.

Both financial advisers and their clients need to understand clearly the connection between risk and return:

- High-risk investments generally have the potential for a higher reward, plus a greater possibility of loss.
- Low-risk investments generally have a lower reward, with a lower possibility of loss.

An investment strategy that provides a way to invest money to produce the optimum rate of return for a given level of risk would clearly be valuable. The aim of a fund manager (or an individual investor) is to achieve higher returns than others, without incurring greater risks.

While it is almost impossible to avoid risk entirely, a holding in a UK government security (a gilt) is regarded as being virtually free from risk of default by the government. It is therefore used to give a benchmark for what is described as the risk-free rate of return. If we hold a gilt from now up to its redemption date, or if it is an undated gilt which will never be redeemed, then we know exactly what return we will get if we continue to hold it. The risk-free rate of return will vary through time, just as interest rates generally vary.

The government's 4% Consolidated Stock, an undated or perpetual gilt, can be used for these purposes. There is no preset date for redemption at par, and the instrument is effectively a government promise to pay the owner £4 for each £100 of the stock each year, indefinitely. For example, when the stock is priced at around £80, it will give a yield of 5% indefinitely – which can be regarded as a virtually risk-free rate of return if we simply hold on to the stock. The yield on this undated stock indicates the market's view of the long-term interest rate.

The rates of return on other investments (such as shares, commodities and property) will differ from the risk-free rate, reflecting the additional return that is required by investors to compensate them for taking on the risk of those investments. This additional return is the risk premium.

The idea of risk premium is relevant in various contexts:

- An individual may find that such a premium is required from them when taking out a mortgage, for example. The housebuyer seeks an investor (lender) from whom to borrow money. If the individual's mortgage proposal carries higher than average risk, they may find that they have to pay a higher rate of interest than if the risk were lower. If the individual's credit rating is below average, or if

the amount to be borrowed is a relatively high percentage of the value of the property, then the individual may find that some lenders will not offer their most favourable terms. Thus, the borrower is effectively paying a risk premium in order to borrow the money.
- For companies seeking finance, the principle is the same. For example, loans to companies with relatively low credit ratings will generally carry higher rates of interest (carrying a risk premium relative to the interest rates that are available to companies with higher credit ratings).

For academics in finance, another key measure of the risk premium that is monitored over time is the equity risk premium. It is a key driver of future equity returns and is also used by corporate financiers who are concerned about raising new capital for new projects, to work out the overall costs of capital to a firm.

Extensive studies of this risk premium have been conducted in the US. By using a long historical database spanning from 1928 to 2010, Ibbotson has estimated that US stocks have earned an average premium of 4.31% over US long-term government bonds. In a separate study, the academic has shown that in the period from 1926 to 2010, the average yield on large capitalisation stocks was 9.9% against 5.5% for US bonds. The equity risk premium calculated from this finding for the US is 4.4% in nominal terms. Also, it is important to note that for small capitalisation US stocks, the rate of return over the same period was 12.1%, resulting in an equity risk premium for small-cap stocks of 6.6% in nominal terms.

In the UK during the 20th century, equities produced a return 5.6% per annum higher than the return from gilts, on average. This can therefore be treated as the risk premium from investing in equities. Equity holders run the risk that they may receive much lower returns – even below the rate on risk-free assets. The risk premium from investing in shares compensates them for taking that risk.

2.2 Types of Risk

Learning Objective

3.2.1 Analyse and explain the main types of risk and the implications for investors: systemic risk; systematic risk; market risk – asset price volatility, currency, interest rates, foreign exchange rates, commodity price volatility; concentration and diversification; long-term investment risk; liquidity, credit risk and default; gearing; country risk; counterparty and institutional risk; market timing; corporate governance risk

Almost all investments carry a certain level of risk. As we worked through different asset classes in chapter 2, we considered the different risk levels attached to different types of investment.

However, a large element of the risk attached to any one investment can be mitigated (reduced) through appropriate diversification. It is necessary to take a certain level of risk if you want to achieve any form of reward. There is a trade-off between increasing levels of risk, and the potential rewards your investment may give you.

You might think that some investments are not risky at all – in particular, the liquid and interest-bearing elements of a portfolio. Indeed, we even describe some investments as being risk-free, for comparison purposes. Even these investments, however (which include bank deposits and investments like gilts), carry some risk. They are subject to:

- **Interest rate risk** – the risk that interest rates move against the investor. For example, they invest in an asset with a fixed interest rate of 4% over three years. Meanwhile, interest rates move up to, say, 8%, but they are still locked into the low rate. Or, they invest in a bank deposit paying a variable rate of interest and rates are reduced – so their income falls.
- **Inflation** – a general rise in the level of prices, which means that a fixed sum of money won't buy as much at the end of the year as it did at the start – it's worth less because inflation has eroded its purchasing power.

To protect capital against these risks, people often invest in equities. The hope is that the companies will do well and their shares will go up in value, providing capital growth for the investor. However, shares can go down as well as up; when companies do very badly, their shares may even fall to a **nil** value. So this part of the portfolio may be considerably riskier than the liquid and interest-bearing elements.

Companies pay a large portion of their annual profits out to their shareholders in the form of dividends. If they do well, and make more profits each year, dividends will go up, so the investor gets rising income as well as capital growth. But again there is an element of risk. Falling profits could mean falling dividends, and sometimes companies do so badly that they pay no dividend at all.

So, to limit the risk involved in investing in equities, the investor needs to diversify by spreading their equity holdings across a number of different companies.

2.2.1 Systemic and Systematic Risk

A systemic risk must not be confused with systematic risk as it is used in capital markets theory. In finance and economics, systemic risk is often discussed in connection with the risk of collapse of an entire financial system or entire market, as opposed to risk associated with any one individual entity, group or component of a system. It can be defined as '*financial system instability, potentially catastrophic, caused or exacerbated by idiosyncratic events or conditions in financial intermediaries*'. Systemic risk tends to be associated more with interlinkages and interdependencies in a system or market, where the failure of a single entity or cluster of entities can cause a cascading failure, which could potentially bankrupt or bring down the entire system or market.

In capital markets theory, systematic risk is one which affects the financial system as a whole – as opposed to any individual share that harbours unsystematic, specific or unique risks. Thus, systematic or the market risk is likely to affect pretty much all investments. Sometimes systematic risk is plainly called market risk or the aggregate risk. It is the risk that is inherent in the aggregate market that cannot be mitigated and removed by diversification. **Systematic risks** tend to be outside the power of most investors to predict, and often of the investment manager to protect against; however some types of investment are more vulnerable to systematic risk than others. They tend to be of the following types:

- **Liquidity** – the term can mean both the amount of cash in a portfolio, or, in connection with a given investment, how easily it can be converted into cash. If a specific type of investment or market is

- **illiquid** – ie, it is hard to sell the investment quickly for a fair price – there is little that can be done. Problems of illiquidity can be normal for a particular investment class (eg, property can be hard to sell in poor markets) – or they can arise suddenly, because of a particular event. For example, if one large bank were to fail, and other banks were owed a lot of money by it, there could be a liquidity problem in the banking industry.
- **Interest rates** – the outlook for interest rates, and the length of time at which they stay at a given level, has a great effect on most types of investment – certainly on fixed-interest securities and shares. If interest rates are high, businesses find it expensive to borrow to fund any expansion of their activities; even if they have additional funds, they may find it more profitable to put this on deposit and earn high rates of interest, instead of using it to trade. If economic activity is affected by recession as in recent years, some shares prices may fall, and vice versa. In addition, consumers are affected by high interest rates – their credit card or mortgage bills are likely to be higher – so they spend less, reducing the profits that companies can make from their consumer activities. Also, when interest rates are high, the prices of fixed-interest securities fall as their fixed-interest element becomes less attractive compared to current market rates.
- **Inflation** – a general rise in the level of prices (and so also a general fall in the purchasing power of money). The level of inflation in an economy is a big indication of its overall health, and of the steps that are being taken by the government to tackle issues such as unemployment, and growth.

High levels of inflation are often associated with high interest rates, and vice versa. If inflation is higher than the level of interest being earned on a deposit account, then that account is in effect worth less to its owner at the end of the year than it was at the start. Inflation can thus erode the real value of capital, even where investments are making reasonable returns.

Currently we are seeing inflation at what are, historically, very low levels. There are many who can remember inflation levels in the mid-teens during the 1980s (and interest rates to match). A gradual reduction in inflation, in the UK and other countries, over the past 15–20 years has led to the current environment of low interest rates, and has, to a degree, encouraged investors to seek higher returns by investing in stock markets rather than keeping their money on deposit with banks and building societies.

- **Currency** – currency risks apply to a range of investments. It might seem obvious that a sterling-based fund holding shares in a US company, priced in US dollars, carries some currency risk; but there is some currency risk if an investor holds shares in a UK company quoted in sterling.

This is because most major UK companies have some exposure to foreign currencies themselves; either because they have branches and subsidiaries abroad, earning profits in foreign currency – or perhaps because they buy their raw materials abroad or sell their goods overseas. Thus movements in the price of one currency against another can have an effect on their profits, when translated back into sterling.

A strong pound sounds like a good thing on the face of it. But it usually creates problems for those UK companies that export a lot of what they manufacture. This is because, as the pound gets stronger (and the foreign currency correspondingly weaker), it costs the overseas buyer more in their home currency to buy the sterling-priced goods. It has not cost the UK company any more to make the goods in sterling terms but they cost the buyer more in US dollars, euros or any other home currency. The foreign buyer may well decide to buy from another supplier, in another country.

Similarly, UK companies that import their raw materials from overseas will suffer if the pound is weak. When they sell sterling to buy the foreign currency they need to pay their overseas suppliers, they will get fewer units of the foreign currency per £1. So it will cost them more, in sterling, to buy their raw materials – which means that either they must raise their prices (which may make them uncompetitive in sterling terms) or they earn lower profits. In terms of the stock market, currency can have an impact. If the pound falls, the price of shares on the LSE may be relatively cheap to foreign buyers, when translated into their home currencies – so there may be an increase in overseas buying.

2.2.2 Capital Risk

This is the risk that the investor's capital falls in value (or fails to grow at an acceptable rate). Some investments, such as equities, carry significant capital risk; others carry virtually none. An investor who cannot tolerate any loss of capital at all should opt for an investment in the latter class. An example, for a retail investor, might be one of the products offered by National Savings & Investments; for an institutional investor it would include UK gilts bought at or below par and held to maturity. In both cases this is because the issuer is the UK government, and the risk of the government defaulting on its debts is regarded as very low.

This capital security should, however, be weighed against the low returns to be obtained from such investments. In addition, inflation may still erode the real value of the investor's capital unless they have selected an index-linked option.

2.2.3 Income Risk

This is the risk that the income from an investment falls, or does not rise in line with inflation, or in some cases the investment ceases any payouts. Examples are:

- a fixed-income security defaulting on an interest payment
- a company suffering falling profits and paying lower or no dividends for a given year.

An investor requiring absolute certainty of income might be well advised to consider an investment such as:

- a bank deposit paying interest at frequent periods, and/or
- a gilt.

In both cases, however, they should consider the impact of inflation on their long-term returns.

2.2.4 Currency Risk

Currency risk arises from fluctuations in the value of currencies against one another. A UK resident who buys foreign stocks or bonds faces currency risk.

Suppose that a UK investor buys shares in a US company which does most of its trading in the US.

- The share price in US dollars fluctuates on the US stock market; this is market risk.
- Additionally, the value of sterling fluctuates against the US dollar; this is currency risk.

The sterling value of the investment will fluctuate in time as a result of two effects; the changing dollar share price, and the changing US dollar/sterling exchange rate.

Some companies hedge their foreign exchange earnings or their foreign raw materials costs, to give them greater certainty about future earnings and to reduce currency risks. The term hedging means undertaking transactions to protect against a certain event – in this case, an adverse currency movement. This may be done, for example, by entering into forward currency contracts, a type of agreement which fixes the value of future currency inflows at the time of transaction.

2.2.5 Inflation Risk

Rising prices can reduce the purchasing power of an amount of capital, or income. By investing money in assets which may not keep up with inflation, the investor may be risking loss in the purchasing power of their portfolio over the life of the investment.

Some economies suffer deflation in prices. Japan has done so for most of the last two decades. If prices are falling, buying goods today bears the risk that those same goods could have been purchased for less later. There is then a strong incentive for people to save, since the purchasing power of cash, even if no interest is being earned, will increase over time. This is one reason why deflation can be an economic problem. If people have a strong incentive to save, demand for goods and services may suffer.

2.2.6 Interest Rate Risk

Interest rate risk means that interest rates move against the investor. For example:

- they invest in an asset with a fixed interest rate of 4% over three years. Meanwhile, interest rates move up to, say, 8% but they are still locked into their lower rate or
- they invest in a bank deposit paying a variable rate of interest, and rates fall – so their income falls accordingly.

Interest rate risk can also affect an investor's capital, since the price of fixed-interest securities tends to vary inversely with the direction of interest rates.

Financial gearing is a term used to describe the relationship between the amount of debt (or long-term loans) taken out by a firm to finance its business activities, as a proportion of financing from its shareholders. Total financing is made up of debt plus shareholder funds and debt as a proportion of the total financing is a measure of a financial gearing ratio.

A highly geared company usually has a sizeable amount of financing raised through long-term debt issuance. Regular interest has to be paid on debt taken out by the company and this payment takes precedence over dividends paid to shareholders. Financial risk increases as gearing rises because if a company's earnings are volatile, under difficult business conditions it may not be able to meet its obligations to its debt holders.

2.2.7 Issuer Risk

This is the risk that the issuer of a security defaults – cannot repay the capital, or (in the case of a fixed-interest security) the interest, as it falls due. A review of an issuer's credit rating can give some comfort as to the likelihood of this, but is not an absolute guarantee.

Financial crime is any kind of criminal conduct relating to money or to financial services or markets involving:

- fraud or dishonesty
- bribery or corruption
- false accounting
- misconduct in, or misuse of information relating to, a financial market
- money laundering/terrorist financing
- handling the proceeds of crime
- financial sanction breaches.

It arises from the risk that a company may fail to comply with financial crime legislation and industry laws on anti-money laundering, may suffer losses as a result of internal or external fraud, or may fail to ensure the security of personnel, physical premises and its assets. Fraud is one form of financial crime that can also be a significant threat to the earnings, capital and reputation of a company or organisation, particularly when associated with a failure to comply with a core regulatory requirement or expectation. In the UK, the FCA has a statutory objective to reduce the extent to which it is possible for a financial business to be used for a purpose connected with financial crime.

With financial crime having been on the rise in recent years, companies, especially those in the financial services sector, have established protocols that assess the implications of all emerging legal and regulatory requirements that impact them. They establish and operate risk control frameworks in respect of anti-money laundering, terrorist financing, sanctions and bribery and corruption crimes.

2.2.8 Non-Systematic Risk

Non-systematic risks can also be known as specific risks or unique risks.

Non-systematic risks are those which relate to a particular business, investment or share. They can usually be reduced through diversification. We will now look at some examples of non-systematic, or specific, risks.

- **Business risks** – these are risks which are associated with the nature of a company's profits and dividends – they include factors such as:
    - product design
    - labour relations
    - the costs of raw materials
    - the strength of the company's balance sheet.

    We could think of these things as internal business risks.

- **Industry risks** – these include:
    - tariffs and barriers to trade
    - industry-wide strikes

- changes in consumer taste
- seasonal factors.
- **Management risks** – these are risks that relate to the calibre of management of a company – are the managers good enough to plan and manage the company effectively, or are they out of their depth and unable to cope with challenges?
- **Financial risk** – any risk associated with the nature of the financing options selected by a firm. For example, a company's assets may be financed through a mixture of debt and equity. Thus it is directly related to its capital structure. A firm which is 100% equity-financed has no financial risk. Incorporation of debt financing in the capital structure brings with it financial obligations to repay the coupons and principal on the debt at various stages.

2.2.9 Counterparty Risk

Counterparty risk (also referred to as credit risk or default risk) is the risk that your counterparty in a transaction cannot honour its obligation to you. For example, you have bought a corporate bond from company XYZ, expecting to receive coupon payments and the nominal value of the bond at maturity. Under this transaction, you are exposed to the risk that XYZ cannot pay you the coupons and principal at the agreed point in time.

Another example is an equity **put option** bought on the OTC market. If markets plunge, as they have done in recent times, the mark to market value of the put option increases sharply, introducing significant counterparty risk to the buyer of the put option. Similar risk exists in swaps, swaptions, and inflation-linked swaps.

2.2.10 Mitigating Risk by Diversification

Sectors

It is possible to mitigate the risk of investing into any one stock by buying shares in several companies. Ideally, they will not all be stocks in the same sector. This is diversifying across different sectors; for example, a well-diversified portfolio of shares might include holdings in the banking sector, the manufacturing sector, the retail sector and so on. Diversification can be thought of as 'not having all your eggs in one basket'.

Research shows that a portfolio of shares is well diversified if it has roughly equal amounts invested in 15–20 different holdings across different sectors. Very big portfolios (such as those operated by the big fund companies) often hold over a hundred different shares.

Markets

Just as it increases risk to be exposed to any one company or sector, so it may be risky to be exposed only to one market. For example, the UK stock market as a whole may suffer if there is an announcement of poor economic figures. The types of factors that can affect the market were examined in chapter 1.

While different world markets are rather more closely correlated in their performance than was once the case, they do not usually move in tandem for long periods; one country's economy may be booming while that of another is struggling, and their markets will reflect the economic backdrops. So an investor with sufficient assets to do so may well wish to diversify their exposure by holding some investments in their home market and some in the other major (and perhaps also emerging) markets of the world.

Asset Classes

The factors that affect one asset class may affect another in quite a different way – or even not affect it at all. It may therefore also be important to diversify across asset classes, to ensure that a portfolio includes elements of:

- liquidity (cash)
- interest-bearing investments (eg, bonds)
- equities.

This will reduce the risk associated with any one of these – ie, interest rate risk, inflation risk and stock market risk. This is asset class diversification.

2.2.11 Market Timing and Timescale

Timing and **timescale** are also important factors in investing. Ideally, in terms of timing, an investor would be able to put their money into the stock market just as it begins a strong rise (and would manage to take their money out just before it fell); however, market timing is very difficult to predict, and sudden events can cause stock market falls. So, while over the long term it can be shown that shares generally deliver better returns than other, less risky asset classes, in the short term they can also go up and down (they are more volatile).

For this reason a sensible investor will accept the fact that stock markets are prone to rises and falls, and be prepared to tie their money up over the long term to ride out the volatility.

Nonetheless, there are times when waiting to invest can pay off. It may be prudent to keep some available cash liquid, and invest it as and when opportunities arise.

2.2.12 Corporate Governance Risk

In recent years, corporate governance (CG) has received a lot of attention because of high-profile scandals involving the abuse of corporate power and, in some cases, alleged criminal activity by corporate officers. This is an increasingly complex area that has a multidisciplinary scope, where a number of professionals from a variety of fields are involved. The emerging regulation in CG is continuing to change as policymakers continually revise and update regulations to cope with moral hazard: risks that impact largely on the economy (contagion) or on shareholder and corporate stakeholder interests. In essence, CG is being directed to cope with emergent or nascent moral hazard risks in corporations. Moral hazard arises if there is a principal–agent problem, when one party, called an agent (senior management in a company), acts on behalf of another party, called the principal (shareholders). The agent usually has more information about their actions or intentions than the principal does, because the principal usually cannot completely monitor the agent. The agent may have an incentive to act inappropriately (from the viewpoint of the principal) if the interests of the agent and the principal are not aligned.

Thus, regulation is mostly directed at senior management in firms. In essence, CG is also aiming to reduce adverse selection problems, improve the corporate image and firm-level performances. Further, given that over the last two decades investor sentiment has been affected badly by corporate scandals, abuses of power and the banking crisis, CG aims to redress the imbalance so that confidence is restored.

An integral part of an effective CG regime includes provisions for civil or criminal prosecution of individuals who conduct unethical or illegal acts in the name of the enterprise. According to the Cadbury Committee (1992), CG is a system by which companies are directed and controlled. It involves a set of relationships between a company's management, its board, its shareholders and other stakeholders; it deals with prevention or mitigation of the conflict of interests of stakeholders. Ways of mitigating or preventing these conflicts of interests include the processes, customs, policies, laws, and institutions which have impact on the way a company is controlled. An important theme of corporate governance is the nature and extent of accountability of people in the business, and mechanisms that try to decrease the classic principal–agent problem and to reduce the impact of corporate failure or mismanagement risks to shareholders' and stakeholders' wealth and livelihoods.

Although this is not a new topic, in the UK, initial CG developments can be traced back to the late 1980s when corporate scandals such as Polly Peck and Maxwell rocked the corporate world. The resulting Cadbury Report in 1992 outlined a number of recommendations that called for: a separation of roles between a firm's chief executive officer and chairman, balanced composition of the board, selection processes for non-executive directors, transparency of financial reporting and policies and calls for sound internal controls to manage risks. The report included a code of best practice that was subsequently incorporated in the listing rules of the LSE.

Then in 1995, following shareholder concerns about firm directors' pay and share options, the Greenbury Report recommended disclosure of director's remunerations in the annual report and suggested that a remuneration committee be also set up to monitor pay at board level. It was recommended that the committee should be comprised of non-executive directors. The majority of these points were included in the stock exchange listing rules as well.

To gauge the extent of the adoption of the Cadbury code and implementation of the recommendations made by the Greenbury Report, there was the publication of the Combined Code on Corporate Governance issued in 1998. This report had a broader remit and covered areas relating to the structure and operations of the board, director's remuneration, accountability and audit, relations with institutional shareholders and the responsibilities of institutional shareholders. The 1998 Combined Code was designed to apply to all listed companies from 31 December 1998. The code was revised in 2003 and this time it required that companies explicitly make specific statements in their annual report about whether they had complied with the code and the extent to which the provisions laid out in the code had been followed or adopted.

Further regulation followed in which directors were expected to show that they had adequate internal controls, structures and financial reporting procedures in place in order to comply with section 404 of the Sarbanes-Oxley Act (SOX). Roles and conduct of auditors were also included in the CG revisions that followed. This Act had become necessary following the Enron scandal in 2001 in which one of the world's largest accountancy firms, Arthur Andersen, was implicated in the biggest audit failure in American history at that time. Enron was bankrupt and left employees and shareholders with losses – billions were lost in pensions and share prices. Enron's $63.4 billion loss in its assets made this the biggest corporate bankruptcy in US history at the time. However, a year later this record was broken with a chapter 11 filing, bankruptcy of Worldcom's loss of assets of $103.9 billion. Worldcom had misrepresented its financial statements by inflating profits and fell into disrepute after improper accounting practices were uncovered.

In the UK, more regulation on corporate governance and practice has continued to be introduced to provide shareholders with more power to have a bigger say on directors remuneration and to increase transparency and communications between parties. Dislocations in the principal–agent relationship were being addressed again to mitigate moral hazard risks.

All this led to a combined code on CG that set out standards of good practice in relation to issues such as board composition and development, remuneration, accountability and audit and relations with shareholders. All companies incorporated in the UK and listed on the main market of the LSE are required, under listing rules, to report on how they have complied with the Combined Code in their annual reports and accounts. In turn, the FRC has pointed out that *'investors are encouraged to sign up to the Stewardship Code, which sets standards for monitoring and engaging with the companies in which they invest.'*

Since 2010, the Financial Reporting Council (FRC) has consulted on changes to the Combined Code and a new version called the UK Corporate Governance Code (2010) was introduced. FRC notes that *'The Codes are normally updated every two years to ensure they stay relevant. Any changes are subject to extensive consultation and dialogue with the market. The most recent editions of both codes were published in September 2014.'* Readers may wish to consult the FRC website under the 'UK Corporate Governance Code' for more details on recent changes (frc.org.uk).

2.3 Return

Learning Objective

3.2.2 Understand the main risk and return measures, and how they are used within asset and portfolio evaluation, and their purposes: holding period return; total return and its components; standard deviation; volatility; covariance and correlation; risk-adjusted returns; benchmarking

2.3.1 Holding Period Return (HPR)

When comparing the returns on one investment with another, in the context of their relative degrees of risk (measured by **standard deviation**; see section 2.3.3) we should remember to include all the total holding period returns. The total holding period return (HPR) on an investment is made up of:

- the income earned on it (ie, any dividends or interest paid)
- any capital gain or loss over the period
- the current yield and the capital appreciation yield.

$$HPR = \frac{(P1 - P0 + I)}{(P0)}$$

where:

P1 = the price at the end of the holding period.
P0 = the price at beginning of the holding period.
I = the sum of all income received from the investment over the holding period.

2.3.2 Total Return

An investor needs to know about the success of their investments. This means that an accurate way must be found to determine investment performance that can in turn provide a foundation for further analysis.

Total return is a measure of investment performance that includes the change in price of the asset plus any income (dividends and interest). It is assumed that all income is reinvested. The calculation of total return is expressed as a percentage of the purchase value.

In an investment management context there are three different methods used to measure portfolio performance:

- holding period yield – sometimes referred to as total return
- money-weighted rate of return (MWRR)
- time-weighted rate of return (TWRR).

Money-Weighted Rate of Return

The money-weighted rate of return is used to measure the performance of a fund that has had deposits and withdrawals during the period of investment. More simply, this method takes account of the timing and amount of all money flows into and out of the portfolio over a review period. It is also referred to as the internal rate of return (IRR) of the fund. The standard money-weighted return measurement used in the UK is the Modified Bank of America Institute (BAI) method. It is also called the linked internal rate of return method.

Essentially, the formula for calculating the return takes the beginning and the end values of the portfolio, together with the timing and size of any interim cash flows.

We wish to determine the overall growth rate of the fund over its holding period, identified in the equation below with the letter 'r'.

The BAI equation takes the beginning value of the fund as V_0 and the ending value as V_1. Multiple cash flows made or received into the fund during this period (cash injections, withdrawals or even income) are C_k, where C is the cash flow and the subscript k (1, 2, 3, etc) denotes the timing in days from the initial investment.

All are connected through the following ending-value equation:

$$V_1 = V_0(1+r) + \sum C_k(1+r)^{Wk}$$

- r is the rate we are trying to determine and it is the IRR that satisfies the above ending value expression.
- Wk is the fraction of which a particular cash flow applies. More precisely:

$$Wk = (TD - D_k)/TD.$$

where:

TD = the total number of calendar days in the period.
D_k = the number of days from the beginning of the period for the cash flow at k. Note k is related to each of the cash flows 1, 2, 3....k.

The objective is to determine r from this equation. However, this may not be a straightforward task and r has to be determined by trial and error. A simple calculation can be set up on an Excel spreadsheet to solve r using an iterative procedure.

Example

Consider a simple case where the investment is worth £200 million at the beginning of a time period. At the end of the period the investment is £250 million, the whole time period between the start and end dates is 31 days and a cash inflow of £20 million is made ten days into the beginning of the holding period. Determine the return from this investment.

Note that r is the linked internal rate of return for the investment we have to determine. A simple equation is set-up using the expression given earlier.

$W_1 = (31-10)/31 = 0.677$

$250 = 200(1+r) + 20(1+r)^{0.677}$

By using trial and error method the return is 14.1% over this holding period.

Conceptually, note that the terminal value of the fund is equated to: appreciation of initial capital invested, plus a sum of all of the future values of the individual income or payment streams.

Time-Weighted Rate of Return (TWRR)

The time-weighted rate of return removes the impact of cash flows on the rate of return calculation. This is a preferred method in the investment management industry. The term 'time-weighted' refers to the fact that returns are averaged over time. The TWRR is established by breaking the whole investment period into a series of sub-periods: monthly, quarterly or another time period. A sub-period is created whenever there is a movement of capital into or out of the fund. Immediately prior to this point, a portfolio valuation must be obtained to ensure that the rate of return is not distorted by the size and timing of the cash flow. Calculate the holding period return of each sub-period. Then, link all of the sub-period returns together. The TWRR is calculated by compounding the rate of return for each of these individual sub-periods, applying an equal weight to each sub-period in the process.

For each sub-holding period, the rate of return is determined by using the following formula:

$$R_t = (V_t / V_{t-1}) - 1$$

where:

V_t = ending period value.
V_{t-1} = beginning period value.

The geometric return of all the holding period returns of sub-periods is determined. This is known as unitised fund performance. The formula for time-weighted rate of return is:

$$TWRR = [(1 + RSP1)(1 + RSP2)........(1 + RSP_n)] - 1$$

where:

SP_n = the percentage return during a sub-period. Adding 1 to each sub-period return converts it to return relatives, so that negative returns in any period can be handled properly.

Principles of Investment Risk and Return

Example

A portfolio is valued at £1,000 at the beginning of October and grows in value to £1,100 by 15 October. It receives a cash inflow of £215 on 16 October and at 31 October is valued at £1,500.

Using TWRR, a percentage return is calculated for each separate period as follows:

Period 1: r = 1,100/1,000 − 1 = 0.10

Period 2: r = 1,500/(1,100 + 215) − 1 = 0.141

TWRR = [(1 + 0.10)(1+0.141)] − 1 = 1.2551 − 1 = 25.51%

In many cases, the differences between the MWRR and the time-weighted rate of return will be relatively small, but in certain circumstances wide variations can occur. As a result, the TWRR is more widely used.

2.3.3 Variance and Standard Deviation

There are various ways in which risk can be measured. Usually, these measure risk in terms of the degree of fluctuation, or volatility, that an investment has shown historically. We can see the variability, or volatility, of different assets' investment values by looking at graphs of daily share prices or share indices over a period of time. The standard deviation is a square root of the variance of the dispersion.

The volatility in the value of an investment can be quantified statistically by calculating the standard deviation of the values. Standard deviation measures how widely the value of an investment is dispersed around its mean or average. The more volatile the value of an investment is, the greater its standard deviation.

- An investment with returns that do not vary much from its average return has a low standard deviation. Low standard deviation implies lower risk.
- An investment with returns that do vary greatly from its average return has a high standard deviation. High standard deviation implies higher risk.

The standard deviation is calculated on the basis of past data.

Knowing the standard deviation can help us to understand the range of returns we may expect from an investment.

For example, suppose that an investment has an average annual return of 9% and a standard deviation of returns of 4%. We can expect that, if we make the investment:

- there is a chance of 2/3 that the annual return will be between 5% and 13%
- there is a chance of 1/3 that the annual return will be below 5% and above 13%.

The volatility of a share, or holding in a fund, can be compared with a benchmark – a standard against which its performance can be compared. This might be the volatility of the index which relates most closely to that share or fund (for example, a blue chip share's standard deviation might be benchmarked against that of the FTSE 100 index); or for a fund, against other funds in the same sector.

Investments with high volatility involve higher risk; there will be a greater variation in returns than for a lower-volatility investment. Rational investors should be particularly interested to hold investments that produce higher than average returns but with low volatility.

The variance is a single measure of portfolio returns that are observed for a security in a historical time series. It can be determined by using the following equation:

$$\text{Variance } (\sigma^2) = \sum \frac{(X_i - \mu)^2}{N}$$

Standard deviation (σ), commonly known as the risk of the security, is the square root of the variance.

$$SD = \sqrt{\text{Variance}}$$

Where the Greek letter sigma (σ) is the standard deviation of the portfolio of returns, X_i is the series of individual returns in each time period, and N is the number of returns sampled over the time period. Greek letter mu (μ) is the average return of the sampled returns. This average return is determined by calculating the arithmetic mean or the geometric mean of the time series.

$$\text{The Coefficient of Variation (CV)} = \frac{\text{Standard Deviation}}{\text{Average Return}}$$

The CV allows us to make comparisons between two investments and it controls for the size of the mean as well. It is a measure of the amount of risk taken with each investment for a 1% unit of return.

Example

Determine the variance and standard deviation (risk) of an investment. The returns over the last three months, in annualised terms are: 5%, 15%, 25%.

Month	Monthly return, X_i (annualised %)	Deviation X_i – mean)	Deviation squared $(X_i$ – mean$)^2$
1	5	–10	100
2	15	0	0
3	25	10	100
Arithmetic mean =	15	Sum =	200

Variance	=	Sum/3	=	66.67
Standard Deviation	=	√Variance	=	8.19

$$\text{Average return or arithmetic mean, } \mu = \frac{(5 + 15 + 25)}{3} = 15\%$$

$$\text{Variance } (\sigma^2) = \left[\frac{(5 - 15)^2 + (15 - 15)^2 + (25 - 15)^2}{3} \right] = \frac{200}{3} = 66.67 \text{ (2 decimal places)}$$

Standard deviation (σ)= √Variance = √67 = 8.19% (2 decimal places)

$$CV = \frac{8.19}{15} = 0.55$$

This means that for 1% of return gained from this investment we are taking 0.55 risk. Investors who are selecting and comparing investment choices will prefer investments that have low risks (low CV values).

2.3.4 Correlation

In investment terms, correlation is the extent to which the values of different types of investments move in tandem with one another in response to changing economic and market conditions.

Correlation is measured on a scale of –1 to +1. Investments with a correlation of +0.5 or more tend to rise and fall in value at the same time. Investments with a negative correlation of –0.5 to –1 are more likely to gain or lose value in opposing cycles. Mathematically, correlation and covariance are closely related statistics that measure the co-movement of returns between two securities. This correspondence between the two statistics means that, if we have information on one of these statistics, we can easily work out the other.

2.3.5 Covariance

Covariance is a statistical measure of the relationship between two variables such as share prices. Technically, it is a product of the movements of each of the two random variables from their means. The covariance is also related to another similar statistic called the correlation coefficient. The correlation coefficient is easier to understand because it is only ever found in a range from –1 to +1. A positive perfect correlation (+1) suggests that two returns are perfectly correlated. If one security goes up, the other matches its move identically. The other extreme is a perfect negative correlation (–1). In this case the co-ordination between a pair of securities is still perfect but they are moving in unison in opposing directions. States of correlation in between show the less than perfect co-ordination of return between pairs.

The covariance between two shares (σ_{AB}) is calculated by multiplying the standard deviation of the first (σ_A) by the standard deviation of the second share (σ_B) and then by the correlation coefficient (ρ_{AB}).

$$\sigma_{AB} = \rho_{AB} \times \sigma_A \times \sigma_B$$

A positive covariance between the returns of A and B means they have mostly moved in the same direction, while a negative covariance means they have mostly moved inversely. The larger the covariance, the greater the historic joint movements of the two securities in the same direction. From these two equations, the following conclusions can be drawn:

1. Although it is perfectly possible for two combinations of two different securities to have the same correlation coefficient as one another, each may have a different covariance, owing to the differences in the individual standard deviations of the constituent securities.

2. A security with a high standard deviation in isolation does not necessarily have a high covariance with other shares. If it has a low correlation with the other shares in a portfolio then, despite its high standard deviation, its inclusion in the portfolio may reduce overall portfolio risk.
3. Portfolios designed to minimise risk should contain securities as negatively correlated with each other as possible and with low standard deviations to minimise the covariance.

If we have historical data of annual returns for two securities over the same period, we can determine the statistical relationship between them by calculating their covariances and their correlations.

The formula for the covariance between security A and security B is given as:

$$\text{Covariance (A,B)} = \frac{\sum(X_i - \mu_A).(Y_i - \mu_B)}{N}$$

- X_i is the return of A in a given time period, with Y_i the corresponding return on B.
- μ_A and μ_B are the average means of each time series.
- N is the total number of values in the time series.

Example

An investor has data on two investments: security A and security B. Over the last three months, the annualised returns for each one of these securities is given in the table below. Use this data to determine the covariance and correlation between A and B. Comment on the significance of these results.

Month	Monthly return on A X_i, annualised (%)	Monthly return on B Y_i, annualised (%)	Deviation of A (X_i − mean of A)	Deviation of B (Y_i − mean of B)	Product of deviations A&B
1	2	3	4	5	4x5
January	5	40	−10	25	−250
February	15	10	0	−5	0
March	25	−5	10	−20	−200
Arithmetic mean	15	15		Sum	−450
				Covariance = Sum/3	−150

Covariance between A and B	−150
Variance of A	= [(−10 x −10) + (0 x 0) + (10 x 10)] / 3 = 66.67
Standard deviation (SD) of A is the square root of the variance of A	= 8.16
Variance of B	= [(25 x 25) + (−5 x −5) + (−20 x −20)] / 3 = 350
Standard deviation (SD) of B is the square root of the variance of B	= 18.71
Correlation = Covariance/(SD of A x SD of B)	= −150 / (8.16 x 18.71) = −0.98

Note that both A and B have the same returns: 15%. However, security B has a higher standard deviation than A. The coefficient of variation (CV) of A is 0.54, against the CV of B of 1.25. Clearly, B is more risky than A.

The covariances of the returns over the last three months are negative, which corresponds to a correlation of −0.98. This means that there is near perfect and negative (inverse) relationship of the performances between securities A and B. Since the correlation can only take a range from −1 to +1, this correlation is close to −1.

This means that in the long run, when the return of A is moving up, the corresponding return on security B will move down. A negative correspondence of returns between securities in a portfolio can help investment managers to diversify their risks.

2.4 Risk-Adjusted Returns

Having calculated how a portfolio has performed, the next stage is to compare its performance against the market as a whole or against other portfolios. This is the function of risk-adjusted performance measurements, of which there are four traditional methods in use:

- Sharpe ratio.
- Treynor ratio.
- Jensen measure.
- **Information ratio**.

2.4.1 Sharpe Ratio

The Sharpe ratio measures the return over and above the risk-free interest rate from an undiversified equity portfolio for each unit of risk assumed by the portfolio: risk being measured by the standard deviation of the portfolio's returns.

The ratio is expressed as follows:

$$\text{Sharpe ratio:} \quad \frac{(R_p - R_f)}{\sigma} \quad \text{or} \quad \frac{\text{(return on the portfolio} - \text{risk-free return)}}{\text{standard deviation of the portfolio}}$$

The higher the Sharpe ratio, the better the risk-adjusted performance of the portfolio and the greater the implied level of **active management** skill. This performance measure allows the investor to assess the amount of excess return (risk-adjusted) obtained from the portfolio for a unit (1%) of total risk taken.

Sharpe's measure is meaningful when it is compared either to other competing portfolios or the market portfolio. A high Sharpe ratio suggests that this portfolio dominates another with a lower value.

2.4.2 Treynor Ratio

The Treynor ratio takes a similar approach to the Sharpe ratio but is calculated for a well-diversified equity portfolio. As the portfolio's return would have been generated only by the systemic risk it had assumed, the Treynor ratio, therefore, divides the portfolio's return over and above the risk-free interest rate by its capital asset pricing model (CAPM) **beta** (see section 3.3).

The ratio is expressed as follows:

$$\text{Treynor ratio} = \frac{(R_p - R_f)}{\beta_p} \text{ or } \frac{\text{(return on the portfolio - risk-free return)}}{\text{beta of the portfolio}}$$

Once again, the higher the ratio, the greater the implied level of active management skill.

2.4.3 Jensen Measure

The Jensen measure of risk-adjusted equity portfolio returns is employed to evaluate the performance of a well-diversified portfolio against a CAPM benchmark with the same level of systematic risk as that assumed by the portfolio. That is, the CAPM benchmark beta is the same as that of the portfolio.

The ratio is expressed as follows:

$$\text{Jensen measure} = R_p - R_{capm} \text{ or return on the portfolio - return predicted by CAPM}$$

The Jensen measure establishes whether the portfolio has performed in line with its CAPM benchmark and, therefore, lies on the security market line (SML; see section 3.3) or whether it has out- or underperformed the benchmark and is, therefore, positioned above or below the SML. The extent of any out- or underperformance is known as the portfolio's **alpha**.

2.4.4 Information Ratio

The information ratio compares the excess return achieved by a fund over a benchmark portfolio to the fund's tracking error. Its tracking error is calculated as the standard deviation of excess returns from the benchmark. The tracking error gives us an estimate of the risks that the fund manager takes in deviating from the benchmark.

The ratio is expressed as follows:

$$\text{Information ratio} = \frac{ER}{\sigma_{ER}} \text{ or } \frac{\text{arithmetic mean of excess returns}}{\text{standard deviation of excess return from the benchmark}}$$

A fund's performance may deviate from the benchmark due to the investment manager's decisions concerning asset weighting. If the fund outperforms, the ratio will be positive, and if it underperforms it will be negative. A high information ratio is therefore a sign of a successful fund manager.

2.5 Benchmarking

If the performance of an investment fund or investment manager is to be assessed, then the first issue to address is how to measure that performance. Investment performance is usually monitored by comparing it to a relevant benchmark.

There are three main ways in which portfolio performance is assessed:

- Comparison with a relevant bond or stockmarket index.
    - An index comparison provides a clear indication of whether the portfolio's returns exceed that of the bond or stock market index that is being used as the benchmark return.
    - As well as the main stock market indices that are generally seen, many sub-indices have been created over the years which allow a precise comparison to be made.
- Comparison to similar funds or a relevant universe comparison.
    - Investment returns can also be measured against the performance of other fund managers or portfolios which have similar investment objectives and constraints.
    - A group of similar portfolios is referred to as an investment universe.
- Comparison to a custom benchmark.
    - Customised benchmarks are often developed for funds with unique investment objectives or constraints.
    - Where a portfolio spans several asset classes, then a composite index may need to be constructed by selecting several relevant indices and then multiplying each asset class weighting to arrive at a composite return.

2.5.1 Alternative Benchmarking Methods

Rather than use an established index to benchmark portfolio performance, a peer group average is often employed. World Markets (WM) is a worldwide independent investment information services company which provides, among other services, performance measurement services to pension funds and other investing institutions. Combined Actuarial Performance Services (CAPS) ltd is an independent investment performance measurement service for the UK, covering over 1,800 pension funds. CAPS was set up as a joint venture by firms of consulting actuaries.

Most pension funds adopt cautious investment policies, and the guidance and benchmarks they set for fund managers mean that most schemes keep their asset allocation close to the CAPS or WM averages. Both create universes which are an aggregation of funds or portfolios with similar investment briefs or types of owner and are used for peer group comparisons. There are many specialist sub-groups of universe groupings to cater for a wide range of fund structures and investment management styles to provide a relevant and accurate relative comparison.

Global investment performance standards (GIPS) are not a way of benchmarking performance, but are global standards for calculating and presenting performance figures. As such, they represent a great leap forward for the performance measurement industry. Originally established in 1999 by the Chartered Financial Analyst (CFA) Institute, GIPS were significantly enhanced in 2005 and have been voluntarily adopted by industry representative organisations in over 20 countries in order to help promote best standards.

2.5.2 Performance Attribution

Performance attribution analysis attempts to explain why a portfolio had a certain return. It does so by breaking down the performance and attributing the results based on the decisions made by the fund manager on asset allocation, sector choice and security selection.

2.6 Measurement of Portfolio Performance

Learning Objective

3.2.3 Apply the theory of investment and risk and return to the measurement of portfolio performance: holding period return; relative return; standard deviation; risk-adjusted returns

2.6.1 Holding Period Return of a Two-Security Portfolio

We have learnt from the previous sections about how to determine the returns and risks of individual securities. We have also learnt how to calculate the correlations between two securities on a pair-wise fashion. We now move on to portfolio theory, where we can learn about determining the overall return and risk on a portfolio that is created from two securities. In advanced practice, this idea is extended to incorporate a portfolio of many securities and asset classes. However, the mathematics and extension to a multi-security portfolio is beyond the scope of this syllabus.

First, let us look at the return of a portfolio that involves combining investment A with investment B. If we take the same data for investments A and B that we provided in sections 2.3.3 and 2.3.5, we note that the return of security A was 15% and that of security B was 15%.

Assume you have £100 to invest. You could buy some of A and some of B. The proportion invested in each security is called the allocation. It is expressed in percentage terms. Thus, 60% of your money (£60) could be invested in A and the remainder (40% or £40) in B. The return on this combined portfolio is unlikely to vary with allocation because both of the underlying security returns are 15%. A general equation to work out the weighted average return of a portfolio P composed of A and B, given expectations of the holding returns of A and B is given by the Markowitz formula for return as follows:

$$Rp = (W_A \times R_A) + (W_B \times R_B)$$

where:

Rp = the overall return on the portfolio composed of securities A and B.

RA = the return on security A.

WA = the % allocated in A.

RB = the return on security B.

WB = the % allocated to B.

Note: WA + WB = 100%.

Example

An investor invested £1,000,000 in two securities. They allocated £600,000 of this money to a mutual fund P, and the rest (£400,000) to another mutual fund Q. The holding period return over the last year in fund P was 15% and that for fund Q was 20%. Determine the return they got from a portfolio created from the two funds.

Use the Markowitz formula for portfolio return:

Rp = (WP x RP) + (WQ x RQ)

Substituting values into this expression:

Allocation in P is 0.6 (£600,000 / £1,000,000)

Allocation in Q is 0.4 (£400,000 / £1,000,000)

Note both allocations sum up to 1.

R_p = (0.6 x 15) + (0.4 x 20)

= 17%.

The weighted average returns of the individual components of the portfolio provide a combined return to the portfolio of 17%.

The relationship is linear. As more is allocated (weighting increased) to the higher return constituent Q, the overall return on the combined portfolio increases in a linear fashion.

2.6.2 Relative Return

The returns we have in an investment is normally stated in absolute terms. For our portfolio PQ we received a return of 17% in an absolute sense. This return tells us very little about the performance of the fund when we compare it against another fund manager, however. Thus, it is normal to express an absolute return in relative terms. Relative return is obtained by subtracting the absolute return on a fund from the return on an appropriate benchmark. For example, a fund manager who is concerned about building a portfolio of large UK stocks can calculate their relative return by taking their return away from the FTSE 100 Index return. The index now acts as a large capitalisation equity benchmark.

Assuming that fund PQ returned 17% over the last year, and the FTSE 100 index as a benchmark returned 15% over the same period, then the relative return on fund PQ is 2%: the difference between the fund and the benchmark returns. The relative return of one manager can be compared against another so that we can get a better idea about the performances of each.

2.6.3 Standard Deviation of a Portfolio

The standard deviation (SD) of a portfolio composed of two securities can be calculated by using the Markowitz risk equation. This is probably one of the most mathematically challenging concepts that we have introduced in this book. However, time spent in understanding it thoroughly will be extremely useful.

The risk on a portfolio that is comprised of fund P and Q is calculated from the variance and then expressed as an SD. The famous portfolio risk equation in finance was presented by Harry Markowitz in 1952 for which he later gained the Nobel prize:

$$\sigma^2_{PQ} = W^2_P \sigma^2_P + W^2_Q \sigma^2_Q + 2W_P W_Q \text{Cov}_{PQ}.$$

Where:

σ^2_{PQ}	=	Variance of portfolio composed of securities P and Q. Its squared root is the SD.
W^2_P	=	Weight or allocation in P squared.
σ^2_P	=	Variance of security P. It is the SD of P squared.
W^2_Q	=	Weight or allocation in Q squared.
σ^2_Q	=	Variance of security Q. It is the SD of Q squared.
$\text{Cov}_{PQ}.$	=	Covariance of the returns between security P and security Q.

The covariance is also connected to the correlation (ρ_{PQ}) as mentioned in section 2.3.5.

$$\text{Cov}_{PQ}. = \rho_{PQ}.\sigma_P.\sigma_Q.$$

Conceptually, the main point that is made in this equation is: when two securities (or more) are combined to form a portfolio, the resulting variance and its standard deviation (risk) is in practice often less than a weighted average of the risks of the constituents.

This effect is most potent when the correlation between two securities is less than perfect: that is correlation is less than +1. This is why clients are advised to have a diversified portfolio. As the expression states: 'don't put all your eggs in one basket'.

The next question that arises is how many securities should we have in a portfolio to provide good diversification? In terms of a share portfolio, as a rough guide, a portfolio of shares with around 25–30 or more, should diversify the specific risk of each share.

However, the full impact of diversification is not achieved unless the share portfolio has at least 100 shares. This is why funds that are constructed to mimic the FTSE 100 and the US S&P 500 (or any other large country index), are considered to be diversified funds.

Now, let us consider how the risk on a two-security portfolio can be calculated if we have obtained information about the model inputs.

Example

An investor invested £1,000,000 in two securities. They allocated £500,000 of this money to a Mutual Fund P, and the rest (£500,000) to another Mutual Fund Q. The holding period return over the last year in Fund P was 15% and that for Fund Q was 20%. The weighted average return they got from a portfolio created from the two funds was 17.5%.

Determine the risk of the portfolio if your analyst provides you with the following model inputs: SD risk of P is 20% and that of Q is 30%. The correlation between Securities P and Q is 0.5.

Use the Markowitz formula for portfolio risk:

$\sigma^2_{PQ} = W^2_P \sigma^2_P + W^2_Q \sigma^2_Q + 2W_P W_Q \text{Cov}_{PQ}$.

Weight in P, squared = 0.5 x 0.5 = 0.25.

Weight in Q, squared = 0.5 x 0.5 = 0.25.

Variance of P = 0.2 x 0.2 = 0.04

Variance of Q = 0.3 x 0.3 = 0.09.

Covariance PQ = 0.5 x 0.2 x 0.3 = 0.03.

Substituting values into this expression:

Variance of PQ = (0.25 x 0.04) + (0.25 x 0.09) + 2(0.5)(0.5)(0.03) = 0.0100 + 0.0225 + 0.0150 = 0.0475.

SD of PQ = 0.2179 or 21.79%.

Portfolio PQ delivers an absolute return of 17.5% with risk of 21.79%. Its coefficient of variation is 1.245.

If the correlation between P and Q was perfect (+1), instead of the +0.5 used in this example, then the risk on the portfolio P and Q would simply be an average of the two risks of P and Q in portfolio PQ: that is 25%. You will note that the risk we have in our portfolio calculation of 21.79% is lower than this average of the two. It will always be the case for any portfolio where the correlation is not perfect (ie, less than +1).

This is due to the fact that risk in a portfolio is not linearly dependent on the allocations of P and Q. Instead, the risk will vary with allocation in a non-linear fashion. This is because the Markowitz risk formula suggests that there is a quadratic form to the equation. The correlation or its covariance plays a key role in this behaviour. The diversification impact is greatest where two securities have perfect negative correlation (−1).

2.6.4 Risk-Adjusted Returns of a Portfolio

We consider applications of the risk-adjusted returns we discussed in section 2.4 to portfolios in this section.

Risk Premium

The risk premium (also called the excess return) of a portfolio of securities is the difference between its absolute return and the return on a security that is considered to be risk-free. In practice, the risk-free security is the return on a three-month Treasury bill, because they are issued by a government or a sovereign and considered to be default–free issues. Bonds by the same issuer are not used because there are term premia (time value) considerations that increase the returns and risks of longer-dated securities.

In the example below we see how two risk-adjusted return measures are used to evaluate performances. Sharpe and Treynor ratios are used in the example.

Example

A performance analyst is preparing a report on a couple of funds that their company is monitoring. they have obtained the risk and return information of the funds, together with a FTSE 100 Tracker fund that is a proxy for a diversified benchmark index. The risk-free rate is 5%.

On the basis of Sharpe and Treynor performance indices, evaluate the following results:

	Fund R	Fund S	FTSE 100 Index Tracker Fund
Mean Return %	10.78	12.02	13.46
Standard Deviation %	10.03	13.17	13.33
Beta	0.64	0.85	1

Use the Sharpe and Treynor formulae to determine the index values for each fund first.

Sharpe Ratio = (Fund Return – Risk-Free Rate) / Risk of the fund

$S_R = (10.78 - 5) / 10.03 = 0.576$.

$S_S = (12.02 - 5) / 13.17 = 0.533$.

$S_{Benchmark} = (13.46 - 5) / (13.33) = 0.635$.

With the Sharpe index, results show that both funds R and S fail to outperform the Benchmark. Fund R has a higher ratio than S. Hence, fund R outperforms fund S.

For the data in the table we now calculate the Treynor ratios for the funds.

Treynor ratio = (fund return – risk-free rate) / Beta risk of the fund

$T_R = (10.78 - 5) / 0.64 = 9.031$.

$T_S = (12.02 - 5) / 0.85 = 8.259$

$T_{Benchmark} = (13.46 - 5) / 1.0 = 8.46$.

With the Treynor ratio, the excess return is divided by beta as a measure of the risk. Beta risk assumes that the portfolios are already diversified. With Treynor, the excess return is adjusted only to the market (systematic risk). The residual specific or **unsystematic risk** is totally ignored in this calculation because the model assumes that this element of the risk can be diversified by investors, simply by holding a larger portfolio of diverse and uncorrelated securities.

The benchmark has a T-value of 8.46. Portfolio S has a T-value of 8.26, underperforming the benchmark. Portfolio R outperforms both the benchmark and the portfolio S with a T-value of 9.03.

Now when we compare the results from both Sharpe and Treynor, the benchmark has once again outperformed fund S and the benchmark remains the dominant fund, in performance terms.

Moving on to a comparison between R and the benchmark, even though Sharpe indicates the benchmark was better than R, Treynor suggests otherwise. There is now a conflict that is apparent between the two performance measures about whether R is better, or the benchmark is better. How can this difference in results between the two measures be resolved?

We know the benchmark is a totally diversified fund – in the total risk of the security, only systematic risk is present and the unsystematic risk is zero. Fund R, on the other hand, must have both the unsystematic and the systematic risks present in its standard deviation. The beta measure excludes unsystematic risk and as a result, with Treynor the performance of R is overstated. The lack of diversification present in fund R is ignored by Treynor, but is included in Sharpe.

This simple analysis reveals to us that one performance measure cannot be used in isolation and when combined with others they all provide a much better assessment of performances.

Measuring Diversification

Funds may have different levels of diversification. Hence, our next question is – how can diversification be measured in practice?

A statistical approach is taken. The returns over a series of discrete periods are correlated with returns obtained from a benchmark index. A regression coefficient called the coefficient of determination (R-squared) is used to denote the extent of the diversification present in a portfolio. An R-squared value of 1 tells us that the fund is fully diversified. The fund return behaviour will then be completely explained by the benchmark index.

If the R-square for a particular fund is less than 1, then some of the returns of that fund are not attributable to the benchmark, and may be explained by other factors. This points to the fact that there is unsystematic risk(s) present in the fund.

Application of the Measure

Next we use the same data provided in the earlier example to demonstrate application of this measure. In section 2.4.3, we provided the formula for the Jensen's ratio. We rewrite the formula below:

$$\text{Jensen measure} = R_p - R_{capm} \quad \text{or return on the portfolio - return predicted by CAPM}$$

Jensen's uses the CAPM model to frame the behaviour of securities. CAPM states that a fair return we should get from a portfolio is: the risk-free rate (R_f) plus a market risk premium ($R_m - R_f$), adjusted by the beta sensitivity factor.

$$R_{capm} = R_f + \beta(R_m - R_f)$$

However, in practice the actual return we get from the portfolio is Rp. Hence, the difference between this return and the fair return calculated with the CAPM formula is called the alpha (α) or Jensen's return measure. We apply this knowledge in the example to determine Jensen's alpha for each one of the two funds: R and S.

Example

Determine Jensen's alpha for funds R and S, given the following return information together with the fund betas. The risk-free rate is 5%.

	Fund R	Fund S	FTSE 100 Index Tracker Fund
Mean Return %	10.78	12.02	13.46
Beta	0.64	0.85	1

Fund R-CAPM Return

$R_{capm} = 5\% + 0.64(13.46 - 5) = 10.41\%$

$R_{Actual} - R_{capm} = 10.78\% - 10.41\% = 0.37\%$

Jensen's alpha for R is + 0.37%

Fund S-CAPM Return

$R_{capm} = 5\% + 0.85(13.46 - 5) = 12.19\%$

$R_{Actual} - R_{capm} = 12.02\% - 12.19\% = -0.17\%$.

Jensen's alpha for S is –0.17%

Jensen's alpha is used to identify superior performances. A positive alpha denotes superior performance that exceeds a fair return that is predicted by CAPM. A negative alpha denotes inferior performance against the model.

Interpretation of these results can only be done properly by further detailed analysis. However, based on Jensen's alpha, R has a positive residual return and is clearly superior to the negative alpha return generated by Fund S.

Superior and inferior return can result from the following two sources:

1. The portfolio manager has been successful in identifying undervalued securities consistently to generate a portfolio that meets the market forecasts. We say that the manager is demonstrating selection skills.
2. The portfolio manager has been able to time market turns, by varying the composition in accordance with the rise and falls in the market. We say that the manager is demonstrating timing skills.

Principles of Investment Risk and Return

3. Models of Investment Theory

The study of how markets behave, in terms of sentiment, is known as the study of market psychology. In essence it is the study of the collective behaviour of all the investors – both buyers and sellers – making up a market.

3.1 The Efficient Market Hypothesis (EMH)

Learning Objective

3.3.1 Understand the main propositions and limitations of the efficient markets hypothesis (EMH): strong form; semi-strong form; weak form; assumptions and shortcomings

One of the key theories used in the study of market psychology is the efficient market hypothesis (EMH). This theory states that because information about companies is generally freely available and known to investors/potential investors, it will lead to their shares (or other securities) being correctly priced, providing that:

- the securities are freely traded (so that the pricing mechanism can work efficiently) and
- the markets themselves are operationally efficient (so that supply and demand will lead to the price reflecting investors' informed viewpoints).

There are three versions of the EMH, depending on how efficient you believe the market actually is. They are as follows:

- The weak form assumes that the market price of shares currently reflects all relevant information implied in historic share prices.
- The semi-strong form of the theory assumes that the market currently reflects all publicly available relevant information.
- The strong form assumes that the market price of a share currently takes into account all publicly and privately available relevant information.

3.1.1 Assumptions and Shortcomings

Each version is similar, in that it assumes that because information is available it will have been used by investors in arriving at their decisions (and therefore be reflected in current share pricing).

The validity of the theory is hotly debated among market practitioners and theorists; those who argue against it point out that just because information on a share is available, that does not mean that it will have been discovered – or taken into account – by an investor. Further, it does not take account of the fact that some investors (particularly large institutions) have a long, drawn-out decision-making process – so the fact that they have information available to them and are using it does not mean that it has yet been reflected in a share's price, through their buying and selling decisions.

Some other assumptions used in the EMH are that:

- a large number of competing profit-maximising participants analyse and value securities, each independently from the others
- new information regarding securities comes to the market in a random fashion
- the competing investors attempt to adjust security prices rapidly to reflect the new information (security prices adjust rapidly because numerous profit-maximising investors are competing against one another).

3.2 Modern Portfolio Theory (MPT)

Learning Objective

3.3.2 Understand the main principles of modern portfolio theory, the capital asset pricing model (CAPM), its application and limitations: risk-free rate of return; risk premium; cost of capital and return on capital; excess returns; correlation measures; systematic and unsystematic risk; risk and diversification; efficient frontier, portfolio optimisation and leverage; assumptions and shortcomings

You can find a trio of modern portfolio theory statistics on most fund company fact sheets. So what does this all mean, if anything? To start, you need to have a brief understanding of the basic assumptions of Harry Markowitz's modern portfolio theory (MPT), which was thought to be at the forefront of portfolio analysis in the 1950s but has come under scrutiny more recently.

The underpinnings of the theory are twofold. First, it assumes that rational investors will demand a higher rate of return to invest in a riskier asset than they will to invest in a less risky asset. Second, the cornerstone of the theory is that diversifying your portfolio by adding securities (or funds) which do not behave in the same way reduces its overall risk, even if those securities individually are higher-risk.

Investors probably keep the above in mind while building their portfolios without always realising it. Your asset allocation is the direct result of your time horizon, risk tolerance and financial goal, and to achieve that goal in a timely way you take on a certain level of risk.

Furthermore, you may mix different investments that are weakly correlated with the aim of protecting the value of your portfolio under different market conditions. For example, stock and bond markets don't typically move in the same direction. For most investors, the risk from holding a stock is that the returns will be lower than expected.

Modern portfolio theory states that the risk for individual stocks consists of:

- **Systematic risk** – these are market risks that cannot be diversified away.
- **Unsystematic risk** – this is the risk associated with a specific stock and can be diversified away by increasing the number of stocks in a portfolio. So a well-diversified portfolio will reduce the risk that its actual returns will be lower than expected.

Principles of Investment Risk and Return

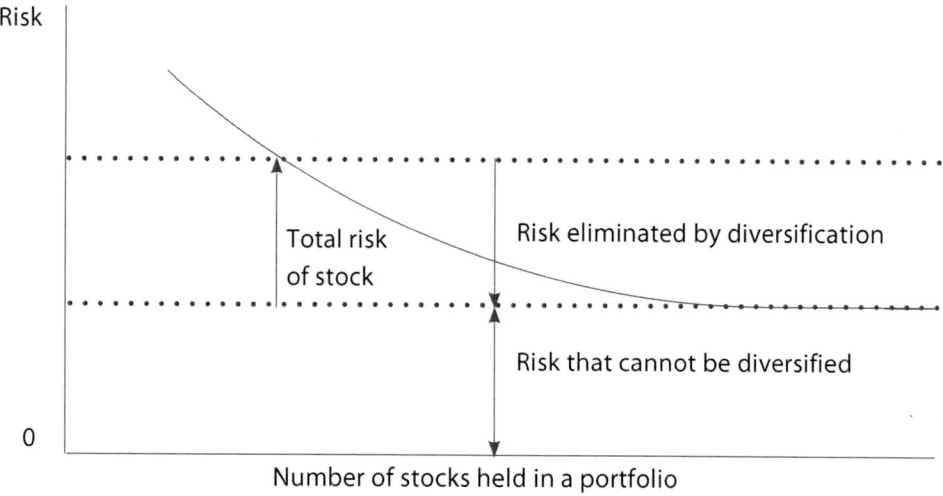

This then leads on to how to identify the best level of diversification. This is described by the efficient frontier.

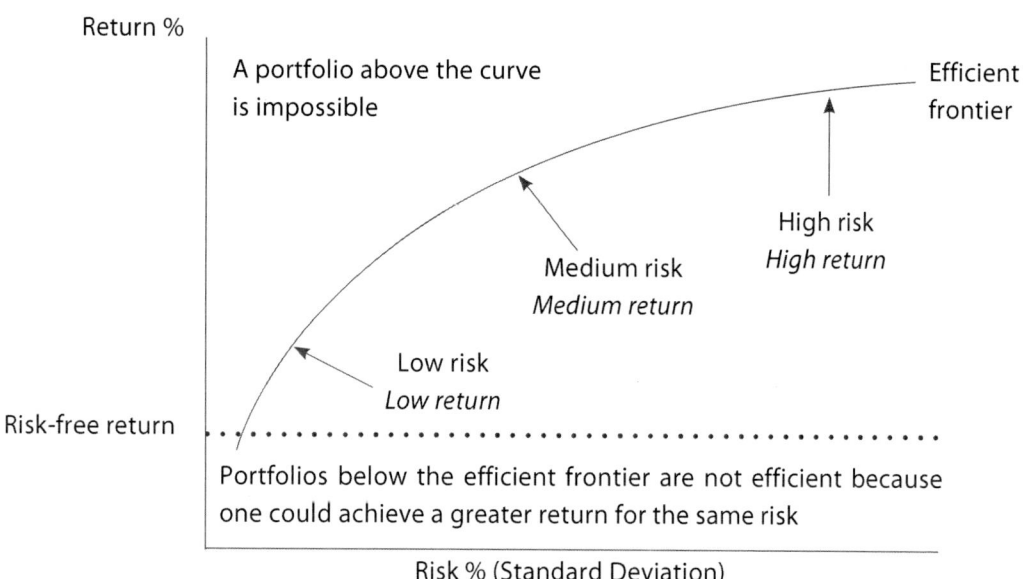

The chart shows that it is possible for different portfolios to have different levels of risk and return. Each investor decides how much risk they can tolerate and diversifies their portfolio accordingly. The optimal risk portfolio is usually determined to be somewhere in the middle of the curve because, as you go up the curve, you take on proportionately higher risk for lower incremental returns. Equally, positioning a portfolio at the low end of the curve is pointless, as you can achieve a similar return by investing in risk-free assets.

Since its origins in the early 1950s, this basic portfolio selection model has been developed into more sophisticated models, such as the **capital asset pricing model (CAPM)** in the mid-1960s and arbitrage pricing theory (APT) in the late 1970s. However it remains the backbone of finance theory and practice.

CAPM and APT are considered in sections 3.3 and 3.4.

3.3 Capital Asset Pricing Model (CAPM)

Learning Objective

3.3.2 Understand the main principles of modern portfolio theory, the capital asset pricing model (CAPM), its application and limitations: risk-free rate of return; risk premium; cost of capital and return on capital; excess returns; correlation measures; systematic and unsystematic risk; risk and diversification; efficient frontier, portfolio optimisation and leverage; assumptions and shortcomings

The capital asset pricing model or CAPM says that the expected return on a security or portfolio equals the rate on a risk-free security plus a risk premium (see section 2.1), and that, if the expected return does not meet or beat this required return, then the investment should not be undertaken.

CAPM has some built-in assumptions:

- All market participants borrow and lend at the same risk-free rate.
- All market participants are well-diversified investors and specific risk has been diversified away.
- There are no tax or transaction costs to consider.
- All investors want to achieve a maximum return for minimum risk.
- Market participants have the same expectations about the returns and standard deviations of all assets.

Using those assumptions, CAPM is used to predict the expected or required returns to a security by using its systematic risks, ie, its beta. Systematic risk is assessed by measuring beta, which is the sensitivity of a stock's returns to the return on a market portfolio, and so provides a measure of a stock's risk relative to the market as a whole.

Beta is calculated by constructing a scattergram of returns achieved by the stock against the market as a whole. By using regression analysis, a line of best fit is then drawn and the gradient of the line represents the stock's beta:

- If the stock's beta is 1, then the stock has a similar volatility to and moves in line with the market as a whole.
- If it has a beta of greater than 1, then the stock is more volatile than the market as a whole. If a stock has a beta of 1.5, then it has 50% greater volatility than the market portfolio.
- If it has a beta of less than 1, the stock is less volatile than the market as a whole, so a stock with a beta of 0.7 has 30% less volatility.

We can use a stock's beta in conjunction with rate of return on a risk-free asset and the expected return from the market to calculate the return we should expect from a stock. The CAPM formula is usually expressed as:

Required return: risk-free rate + (market rate – risk-free rate) x beta

By using the CAPM equation, it enables what is termed the security market line to be presented graphically. If a graph is plotted depicting the expected return from a security against its beta, then the relationship is revealed as a straight line.

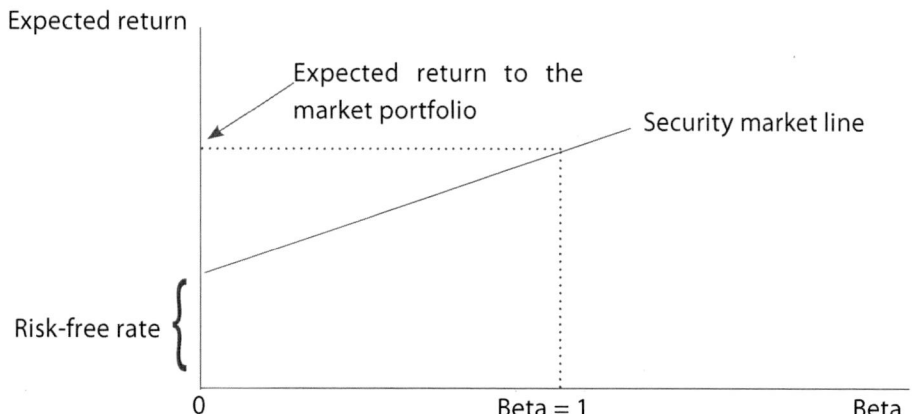

The security market line shows that the higher the risk of an asset, the higher the expected return. The market risk premium is the return an investor will expect over and above the risk-free rate, as a reward for taking on the additional market risk.

We can use the CAPM formula to calculate the return we should expect from a stock. For example, if the current risk-free rate is 5% and the expected return from the market is 10%, what return should we expect from a security that has a beta of 1.5?

The beta of the individual stock tells us that it carries more risk than the market as a whole, and the CAPM formula tells us that we should expect a return of:

Expected return = 5% + (10% – 5%) x 1.5 = 12.5%

CAPM, by providing a precise prediction of the relationship between a security's risk and return, therefore, provides a benchmark rate of return for evaluating investments against their forecasted return.

3.4 Arbitrage Pricing Theory (APT)

Learning Objective

3.3.3 Understand the main principles behind arbitrage pricing theory (APT), its application and limitations: factor structure and analysis; macroeconomic and market factors; arbitrage theory and mechanics; relationship with CAPM; assumptions and shortcomings

Arbitrage pricing theory was developed in the late 1970s in response to the CAPM's main limitation that a single market beta is assumed to capture all factors that determine a security's risk and expected return. APT, rather than relying on a single beta, adopts a more complex multi-factor approach by:

- seeking to capture exactly what factors determine security price movements by conducting regression analysis
- applying a separate risk premium to each identified factor
- applying a separate beta to each of these risk premiums, depending on a security's sensitivity to each of these factors.

Examples of factors that are employed by advocates of the APT approach include both industry related and more general macroeconomic variables, such as anticipated changes in inflation, industrial production and the yield spread between investment grade and non-investment grade bonds. The underlying assumptions of APT include:

- Securities markets are price-efficient.
- Investors seek to maximise their wealth, though do not necessarily select portfolios on the basis of mean variance analysis.
- Investors can sell securities short. Short-selling is selling securities you don't own with the intention of buying them back at a lower price in order to settle and profit from the transaction.
- Identified factors are uncorrelated with each other.

APT is attractive in that it:

- explains security performance more accurately than CAPM by using more than one beta factor
- uses fewer assumptions than CAPM
- enables portfolios to be constructed that either eliminate or gear their exposure to a particular factor.

However, APT's shortcomings include a reliance on:

- identified factors being uncorrelated with each other
- stable relationships being established between security returns and these identified factors.

3.5 Behavioural Finance

Learning Objective

3.3.4 Understand the principles of behavioural finance: loss aversion; price reaction and price trends; barriers and biases – practical and psychological; relationship with EMH; assumptions and shortcomings

Behavioural finance picks up where modern portfolio theory leaves off, completing the circle. It describes how investors actually behave, rather than how they should behave. It recognises that we sometimes act in our own best economic interests, and sometimes don't. Assuming that modern portfolio theory largely correctly describes the way markets operate, behavioural finance describes how we might best profit from that knowledge.

Behavioural finance is a field of study that has evolved which attempts to better understand and explain (through the use of psychology and other social sciences) how emotions and cognitive errors influence investors and the decision-making process.

The key observations from the study of behavioural finance are that:

- people often make decisions based on approximate rule of thumb, not strictly rational analysis
- people do not appear to be consistent in how they treat economically equivalent choices if the choices are presented in significantly different contents, which is referred to as the framing effect
- there are explanations for observed market outcomes that are contrary to national expectations and market efficiency, which include mispricing, non-rational decision-making and return anomalies.

From these observations it is clear that judgements can be systematically wrong in various ways. Systematic errors of judgement are called biases. Financial decisions are made in situations of high complexity and high uncertainty that preclude reliance on fixed rules and compel the decision-maker to rely on intuition.

3.5.1 Biases

Loss Aversion

Loss aversion refers to people's tendency to strongly prefer avoiding losses to making gains. Some studies suggest that losses are twice as powerful, psychologically, as gains. This leads to risk aversion when people evaluate a possible gain. Conversely, people strongly prefer risks that might possibly mitigate a loss (called risk seeking behaviour). Loss aversion implies that a person who loses £100 will lose more satisfaction than another person will gain satisfaction from a £100 windfall.

Confirmation Bias

Confirmation bias suggests that an investor is more likely to look for information that supports their original idea about an investment rather than seek out information that contradicts it. As a result, this bias can often result in faulty decision-making, because one-sided information tends to skew an investor's frame of reference, leaving them with an incomplete picture of the situation.

Hindsight Bias

Hindsight bias tends to occur in situations if a person believes (after the fact) that the onset of some past event was predictable and completely obvious, whereas in fact the event could not reasonably have been predicted. Many events seem obvious in hindsight. Psychologists attribute hindsight bias to our innate need to find order in the world by creating explanations which allow us to believe that events are predictable. While this sense of curiosity is useful in many cases (in science, for example), finding erroneous links between the cause and effect of an event may result in incorrect oversimplifications.

Cognitive Biases

A cognitive bias is a pattern of deviation in judgement that occurs in particular situations, Many of these biases are studied for how they affect belief formation, business decisions, and scientific research.

- **Bandwagon effect** – the tendency to do (or believe) things because many other people do (or believe) the same. Related to groupthink and herd behaviour.
- **Base rate fallacy** – the tendency to ignore available statistical data in favour of particulars.
- **Bias blind spot** – the tendency not to compensate for one's own cognitive biases.
- **Choice-supportive bias** – the tendency to remember one's choices as better than they actually were.
- **Congruence bias** – the tendency to test hypotheses exclusively through direct testing, in contrast to tests of possible alternative hypotheses.
- **Contrast effect** – the enhancement or diminishing of a weight or other measurement when compared with a recently observed contrasting object.
- **Denomination effect** – the tendency to spend more money when it is denominated in small amounts (eg, coins) rather than large amounts (eg, bills).
- **Distinction bias** – the tendency to view two options as more dissimilar when evaluating them simultaneously than when evaluating them separately.
- **Endowment effect** – the fact that people often demand much more to give up an object than they would be willing to pay to acquire it.
- **Experimenter's or expectation bias** – the tendency for experimenters to believe, certify and publish data that agree with their expectations for the outcome of an experiment, and to disbelieve, discard or downgrade the corresponding weightings for data that appear to conflict with those expectations.
- **Focusing effect** – the tendency to place too much importance on one aspect of an event; this causes error in accurately predicting the utility of a future outcome.
- **Framing** – using an approach or description of the situation or issue that is too narrow. Also framing effect – drawing different conclusions based on how data is presented.
- **Hyperbolic discounting** – the tendency for people to have a stronger preference for more immediate payoffs relative to later payoffs, where the tendency increases the closer to the present both payoffs are.
- **Illusion of control** – the tendency to believe that outcomes can be controlled, or at least influenced, when they clearly cannot.
- **Impact bias** – the tendency to overestimate the length or the intensity of the impact of future feeling states.
- **Information bias** – the tendency to seek information even when it cannot affect action.
- **Interloper effect** – the tendency to value third-party consultation as objective, confirming, and without motive. Also consultation paradox, the conclusion that solutions proposed by existing personnel within an organisation are less likely to receive support than from those recruited for that purpose.

- **Irrational escalation** – the tendency to make irrational decisions based upon rational decisions in the past or to justify actions already taken.
- **Just-world phenomenon** – the tendency to rationalise an inexplicable injustice by searching for things that the victim might have done to deserve it.
- **Mere exposure effect** – the tendency to express undue liking for things merely because one is familiar with them.
- **Money illusion** – the tendency to concentrate on the nominal (face value) of money rather than its value in terms of purchasing power.
- **Moral credential effect** – the tendency of a track record of non-prejudice to increase subsequent prejudice.
- **Need for closure** – the need to reach a verdict in important matters; to have an answer and to escape the feeling of doubt and uncertainty. The personal context (time or social pressure) might increase this bias.
- **Negativity bias** – the tendency to pay more attention and give more weight to negative than positive experiences or other kinds of information.
- **Neglect of probability** – the tendency to completely disregard probability when making a decision under uncertainty.
- **Normalcy bias** – the refusal to plan for, or react to, a disaster which has never happened before.
- **Not Invented Here** – the tendency to ignore that a product or solution already exists, because its source is seen as an enemy or as inferior.
- **Omission bias** – the tendency to judge harmful actions as worse, or less moral, than equally harmful omissions (inactions).
- **Outcome bias** – the tendency to judge a decision by its eventual outcome, instead of basing the judgement on the quality of the decision at the time it was made.
- **Planning fallacy** – the tendency to underestimate task-completion times.
- **Post-purchase rationalisation** – the tendency to persuade oneself through rational argument that a purchase was good value.
- **Pseudocertainty effect** – the tendency to make risk-averse choices if the expected outcome is positive, but make risk-seeking choices to avoid negative outcomes.
- **Reactance** – the urge to do the opposite of what someone wants you to do out of a need to resist a perceived attempt to constrain your freedom of choice.
- **Restraint bias** – the tendency to overestimate one's ability to show restraint in the face of temptation.
- **Selective perception** – the tendency for expectations to affect perception.
- **Semmelweis reflex** – the tendency to reject new evidence that contradicts an established paradigm.
- **Status quo bias** – the tendency to like things to stay relatively the same (see also loss aversion, at the start of section 3.5.1, and endowment effect, above).
- **Wishful thinking** – the formation of beliefs and the making of decisions according to what is pleasing to imagine instead of by appeal to evidence or rationality.
- **Zero-risk bias** – preference for reducing a small risk to zero over a greater reduction in a larger risk.

3.5.2 Behavioural Finance and the EMH

In finance, the efficient market hypothesis (EMH) asserts that financial markets are efficient and implies that investors cannot consistently achieve returns in excess of average market returns on a risk-adjusted basis. Investors and researchers dispute the EMH both empirically and theoretically. Behavioural economists attribute the imperfections in financial markets to a combination of cognitive biases such as overconfidence, overreaction, representative bias, information bias, and various other predictable human errors in reasoning and information processing.

3.5.3 Assumptions and Shortcomings of Behavioural Finance

If we assume that financial markets are efficient and investors are rational, then why are there so many studies about investors' psychology?

Investment managers seek to make money for themselves and their clients. That is the reason they care about the psychology factor of financial markets as well as investors.

The behaviour of investors is not always rational, so investment managers do not forget how the psychology factor of a person plays a substantial role in the behaviour of financial markets.

But, modern finance theories have almost completely ignored the role of the complex motivational and cognitive factors that influence investors' decision-making.

3.5.4 Theories of Behavioural Finance

There are four theories of behavioural finance. They are as follows:

- Prospect theory.
- Regret theory.
- Anchoring.
- Over- and under-reaction.

Prospect Theory

This theory says people respond differently to equivalent situations, depending on whether it is presented in the context of a loss or a gain. Most investors are risk-averse when chasing gains but become risk-lovers when trying to avoid a loss.

Regret Theory

Regret theory is about people's emotional reaction to having made an error of judgement. Investors may avoid selling stocks that have gone down in order to avoid the regret of having made a bad investment and the embarrassment of reporting the loss. They may also find it easier to follow the crowd and buy a popular stock. If it subsequently goes down, it can be rationalised as everyone else owned it.

Anchoring

Anchoring is a phenomenon in which, in the absence of better information, investors assume current prices are about right. People tend to give too much weight to recent experience, extrapolating recent trends that are often at odds with long-run averages and probabilities.

Over- and Under-Reaction

The consequences of investors putting too much weight on recent news at the expense of other data are market over- or under-reaction. People show overconfidence. They tend to become more optimistic when the market goes up and more pessimistic when the market goes down. Hence, prices fall too much on bad news and rise too much on good news. In certain circumstances, this can lead to extreme events.

3.5.5 Conclusion

The field of modern financial economics assumes that people behave with extreme rationality, but they do not. The two common mistakes investors make, ie, excessive trading and the tendency to disproportionately hold on to losing investments while selling winners, have their origins in human psychology. The tendency for human beings to be overconfident causes the first mistake and the human desire to avoid regret prompts the second. So, psychological research teaches us about the true form of preferences, allowing us to make finance more realistic within the rational choice framework.

Behavioural finance is subject to criticism. While all of us are subject to behavioural biases from time to time, traditional economic theorists argue that market forces will always act to bring prices back to rational levels, implying that the impact of irrational behaviour on financial markets is generally negligible and therefore irrelevant.

3.6 Multi-Factor Models, Assumptions and Limitations

Learning Objective

3.3.5 Understand the types and uses of multi-factor models, their assumptions and limitations

A multi-factor model is a financial model that may be used in the analysis of securities when constructing an investment portfolio for a client. The model compares two or more factors in order to help illustrate the relationship between these variables and the level of returns achieved.

There are three broad categories of multi-factor models:

1. Macroeconomic.
2. Fundamental.
3. Statistical.

Macroeconomic models look to compare the returns achieved by a security against factors such as employment statistics, inflation and interest rates, whereas fundamental models compare the returns against underlying factors such as earnings, eg, company profits or dividend ratio, when assessing equities. Statistical models compare the performance of a range of different securities based on the statistics for each individual security.

The following model explains how these factors are compared:

$$R_i = a_i + \beta_{i(m)} R_m + \beta_{i(1)}F_1 + \beta_{i(2)}F_2 + \ldots + \beta_{i(N)}F_N + e_i$$

where:

R_i	=	the returns of security i.
R_m	=	the market return.
$F(1,2,3\ldots N)$	=	each of the factors used.
β	=	the beta with respect to each factor including the market (m).
e	=	the error term.
a	=	the intercept.

In general, multi-factor models are used to assist in the construction of portfolios with certain characteristics, such as a certain level of risk or those designed to track certain indices. The models do have some limitations, however; for example, it can be difficult to decide exactly how many and which factors to include. The models also use historical information, which may be very different from current performance.

The following are two examples of well-known multi-factor models.

- **Capital asset pricing model (CAPM)** – the CAPM is a multi-factor model that expresses a simple relationship between risk and return. It indicates the expected return from holding an asset, based on a risk-free rate of return plus a risk premium.

    The CAPM is usually expressed as: $E(R_i) = R_f + \beta_i (R_m - R_f)$.

    where:

$E(R_i)$	=	the expected return on the risky investment.
R_f	=	the rate of return on a risk-free asset.
R_m	=	the expected return of the market portfolio.
β_i	=	the measure of sensitivity of the investment to movements in the overall market.
$(R_m - R_f)$	=	the market risk premium, the excess return of the market over the risk-free rate.
$\beta_i (R_m - R_f)$	=	the risk premium on the risky investment.

- **Fama & French Model** – Fama & French created a multi-factor model that expanded on the CAPM, through the introduction of factors for company size and value.

3.7 Reducing Portfolio Risk

Learning Objective

3.3.6 Understand how to reduce portfolio risk through diversification and hedging: significance of alpha and beta; correlation and relative risk; principles of asset allocation; hedging and immunisation; active and passive strategies

The following paragraphs discuss methods of assessing and managing risk within a portfolio.

3.7.1 Alpha, Beta and R-Squared

MPT statistics provide a snapshot of the portfolio's returns versus the return of the benchmark index.

Beta is an expression of a fund's sensitivity to movements in the benchmark index. It is thus a measure of volatility, or risk, relative to the index. The beta of the benchmark is by definition 1 (because it is simply measuring the benchmark's volatility relative to itself). So, if beta is greater than 1 then that implies the fund has been more volatile – hence more risky – than the index; a beta of less than one indicates lower volatility.

Alpha measures the difference between a fund's actual returns and its expected performance, given its level of risk (as measured by beta). A positive alpha figure indicates the fund has performed better than its beta would predict. In contrast, a negative alpha indicates a fund has underperformed, given the expectations established by the fund's beta. Some investors see alpha as a measurement of the value added or subtracted by a fund's manager, and it is often cited as such in the media. An alpha that looks at a fund's returns over the risk-free rate, relative to the benchmark's returns over the risk-free rate, is commonly known as Jensen's alpha (see section 2.6.4).

R-squared ranges from 0 to 100 and reflects the percentage of a fund's movements that are explained by movements in its benchmark index. An R-squared of 100 means that all movements of a fund are completely explained by movements in the index.

Thus, index funds that invest only in FTSE 100 stocks will have an R-squared very close to 100. Conversely, a low R-squared indicates that very few of the fund's movements are explained by movements in its benchmark index. An R-squared measure of 35, for example, means that only 35% of the fund's movements can be explained by movements in its benchmark index. Therefore, if you already own a fund with a very high R-squared with the FTSE All Share, you might avoid buying another that correlates too closely to that index.

Use with Care!

As we've seen, MPT statistics can help inform investors about their fund's risks, value-added, and ability to diversify their portfolio. However, one needs to be careful about placing too much faith in them.

First, they are based purely on past performance. Looking at funds with attractive alphas and betas does not imply they will behave the same way in the future. For example, a fund might have had a different manager or strategy during the period over which the statistics were calculated. Further, the market environment could change dramatically.

Also, whenever you use alpha or beta, you need to be aware of the index used and the fund's R-squared with the index. Without getting too technical, these figures all rely on taking a scatter-plot graph of a fund's returns (vertical axis) against the benchmark's returns (horizontal axis) and drawing a straight line through the middle of the scatter that represents the best fit to all the points. The beta is the slope of the line, and alpha marks where the line intercepts the vertical axis, ie, the fund's return when the benchmark's return is zero.

The weak link is the 'fit' of the line to the scatter-plot of returns, which is what R-squared measures. If R-squared is low, it means the points are widely scattered around the line and therefore that beta and alpha are not good estimates of actual fund behaviour. Thus, if you look at alpha and beta without checking R-squared, you may be misled by the results.

Look Beyond the Numbers

MPT statistics can be very useful, subject to the limitations described above. However, investors should remember to look beyond mere past performance when making investment decisions. There are many fundamental risks which may not be apparent from past performance. Credit risk is one notable example. In a strong credit environment, a bond fund laden with poorly rated credits may perform well for years, but if the credit environment changes sharply, as it has recently, the fund could find itself in difficulty.

3.7.2 Correlation

Correlation is the degree of co-movement between two variables determined through regression analysis and quantified by the correlation coefficient. Correlation does not prove that a cause-and-effect or, indeed, a steady relationship exists between two variables, as correlations can arise from pure chance.

3.7.3 Asset Allocation

Asset allocation is the result of top-down portfolio managers considering the big picture first, by assessing the prospects for each of the main asset classes within each of the world's major investment regions, against the backdrop of the world economic, political and social environment. Within larger portfolio management organisations, this is usually determined on a monthly basis by an asset allocation committee. The committee draws upon forecasts of risk and return for each asset class and correlations between these returns.

It is at this stage of the top-down process that quantitative models are often used, in conjunction with more conventional **fundamental analysis**, to assist in determining which geographical areas and asset classes are most likely to produce the most attractive risk-adjusted returns taking full account of the client's mandate.

Most asset allocation decisions, whether for institutional or retail portfolios, are made with reference to the peer group median asset allocation. This is known as asset allocation by consensus and is undertaken to minimise the risk of underperforming the peer group.

When deciding if and to what extent certain markets and asset classes should be over- or underweighted, most portfolio managers set tracking error, or standard deviation of return, parameters against peer group median asset allocations, such as the CAPS median asset allocation in the case of institutional mandates. Remember (see section 2.5.1) that CAPS is one of the performance measurement services that tracks the investment performance of institutional portfolios for comparison purposes.

The decision whether to hedge market and/or currency risks must be taken. Over the long term, recent academic studies conclude that asset allocation accounts for over 90% of the variation in pension fund returns.

3.7.4 Hedging

In finance, a hedge is a position established in one market in an attempt to offset exposure to price fluctuations in an opposite position in another market with the goal of minimising exposure to unwanted risk. There are many different ways to accomplish this, including insurance policies, forward contracts, swaps, options, many types of over-the-counter and derivative products, and, perhaps most popularly, futures contracts.

3.7.5 Immunisation

In finance, interest rate immunisation is a strategy that ensures that a change in interest rates will not affect the value of a portfolio. Similarly, immunisation can be used to ensure that the value of a pension fund's or a firm's assets will increase or decrease in exactly the opposite amount to their liabilities, thus leaving the value of the pension fund's surplus or firm's equity unchanged, regardless of changes in the interest rate.

Interest rate immunisation can be accomplished by several methods, including cash flow matching, duration matching, and volatility and convexity matching. It can also be accomplished by trading in bond forwards, futures, or options.

Other types of financial risks, such as foreign exchange risk or stock market risk, can be immunised using similar strategies. If the immunisation is incomplete, these strategies are usually called hedging. If the immunisation is complete, these strategies are usually called arbitrage.

3.8 Bond Strategies

Just like equities, bonds can be managed along active or passive lines.

3.8.1 Active Bond Strategies

Generally speaking, active-based strategies are used by those portfolio managers who believe the bond market is not perfectly efficient and, therefore, is subject to mispricing. If a bond is considered mispriced, then active management strategies can be employed to capitalise upon this perceived pricing anomaly. Bond switching, or bond swapping, is used by those portfolio managers who believe they can outperform a buy-and-hold passive policy by actively exchanging bonds perceived to be overpriced for those perceived to be underpriced.

Bond switching takes three forms:

- **Anomaly switching** – this involves moving between two bonds similar in all respects apart from the yield and price on which each trades. This pricing anomaly is exploited by switching away from the more to the less highly priced bond.
- **Policy switching** – when an interest rate cut is expected but not implied by the yield curve, low-duration bonds are sold in favour of those with high durations. By pre-empting the rate cut, the holder can subsequently benefit from the greater price volatility of the latter bonds.
- **Intermarket spread switching** – when it is believed that the difference in the yield being offered between corporate bonds and comparable gilts, for example, is excessive, given the perceived risk differential between these two markets, an intermarket spread switch will be undertaken from the gilt to the corporate bond market. Conversely, if an event that lowers the risk appetite of bond investors is expected to result in a flight to quality, gilts will be purchased in favour of corporate bonds.

Active management policies are also employed if it is believed the market's view on future interest rate movements, implied by the yield curve, are incorrect or have failed to be anticipated. This is known as market timing. Riding the yield curve is an active bond strategy that does not involve seeking out price anomalies but instead takes advantage of an upward-sloping yield curve.

Example

If a portfolio manager has a two-year investment horizon, then a bond with a two-year maturity could be purchased and held until redemption. Alternatively, if the yield curve is upward-sloping, and the manager expects it to remain upward-sloping without any intervening or anticipated interest rate rises over the next two years, a five-year bond could be purchased and sold two years later when the bond has a remaining life of three years. This rate anticipation method may use horizon analysis to project a bond portfolio's expected returns over several time frames, or investment horizons, to arrive at a more realistic expectation of performance from different bond strategies.

Assuming that the yield curve remains static over this period, the manager will benefit from selling the bond at a higher price than that at which it was purchased as its gross redemption yield falls.

3.8.2 Passive Bond Strategies

Passive bond strategies are employed either when the market is believed to be efficient, in which case a buy-and-hold strategy is used, or when a bond portfolio is constructed around meeting a future liability fixed in nominal terms.

Immunisation is a passive management technique employed by those bond portfolio managers with a known future liability to meet. An immunised bond portfolio is one that is insulated from the effect of future interest rate changes. Immunisation can be performed by using either cash matching or duration-based immunisation. Cash matching involves constructing a bond portfolio whose coupon and redemption payment cash flows are synchronised to match those of the liabilities to be met.

Duration-based immunisation involves constructing a bond portfolio with the same initial value as the present value of the liability it is designed to meet and the same duration as this liability. A portfolio that contains bonds that are closely aligned in this way is known as a bullet portfolio. Alternatively, a barbell strategy can be adopted. If a bullet portfolio holds bonds with durations as close as possible to ten years to match a liability with a ten-year duration, a barbell strategy may be to hold bonds with durations of five and 15 years. Barbell portfolios necessarily require more frequent rebalancing than bullet portfolios.

Finally, a ladder portfolio is one constructed around equal amounts invested in bonds with different durations. So, for a liability with a ten-year duration, an appropriate ladder strategy may be to hold equal amounts in bonds with a one-year duration, and a two-year duration, right through to 20 years.

Key Chapter Points

- Money has a 'time value': having it now is better than having a promise of it in the future.
- Inflation erodes the value of money. The 'real rate of return' measures how much is being earned, over and above the rate of inflation.
- Compounding and discounting are key concepts in calculating returns through time.
- Investors face a variety of investment risks.
- In general, seeking a higher return involves taking higher risks. This means that, instead of the higher return hoped for, losses could be incurred instead. Investors in risky investments, such as equities, require a 'risk premium'. The risk premium is reflected in the amount by which the long-term higher average rate of return exceeds the risk-free rate of return on a very safe investment.
- Diversification involves choosing investments in different asset classes, and choosing different investments within a particular asset class.
- Overall risk can be measured from the variability or volatility of investment returns.
- Volatility arises from:
    - the 'systematic' fluctuations in the wider market, which cannot be diversified away, and
    - the 'non-systematic' investment-specific risks of the particular investment.
- Standard deviations of returns from an investment measure their variability.
- Beta factors measure how much returns from an investment vary relative to the market or a sector benchmark.
- Data on past performance has its uses in checking the track record of certain types of investment, but the future performance of risky investments may differ significantly from the past.
- A variety of factors relating to an investor's personal circumstances need to be considered when arriving at a financial plan for them.
- Attitudinal factors and the investor's past experiences may also be a factor.

End of Chapter Questions

Think of an answer for each question and refer to the appropriate workbook section for confirmation.

1. If the nominal rate of return on an investment is 6%, and the current rate of inflation is 2%, what is the real rate of return?
   Answer reference: Section 1.5

2. Explain what is meant by the terms 'systemic risk' and 'systematic risk'.
   Answer reference: Section 2.2.1

3. What risks does corporate governance present and how are these managed?
   Answer reference: Section 2.2.12

4. What is money-weighted rate of return and how is it calculated?
   Answer reference: Section 2.3.2

5. What is time-weighted rate of return and how is it calculated?
   Answer reference: Section 2.3.2

6. In the context of investment risk, what does a low standard deviation imply?
   Answer reference: Section 2.3.3

7. If two equities have negative covariance, how are they likely to perform in a portfolio?
   Answer reference: Section 2.3.5

8. What is the Sharpe ratio and how is it calculated?
   Answer reference: Section 2.4.1

9. What conclusion can be drawn from an investment with a positive information ratio?
   Answer reference: Section 2.4.4

10. Using the CAPM formula, calculate the expected return for a stock with a beta of 1.50, where the risk-free rate of return is 2%, and the expected market return is 6%.
    Answer reference: Section 3.3

Chapter Four
Taxation of Investors and Investments

1. Personal Taxation — 259
2. Taxation of Trusts — 261
3. Taxation of Investment Income — 265
4. National Insurance Contributions — 269
5. Capital Gains Tax — 273
6. Inheritance Tax — 277
7. Residency and Domicile — 288
8. Stamp Duty — 297
9. Value Added Tax — 300
10. Corporation Tax — 302
11. Tax-Planning Strategies — 304

This syllabus area will provide approximately 16 of the 80 examination questions

1. Personal Taxation

Learning Objective

4.1.1 Understand how a private individual's income tax liability is determined using: tax rates; tax rate bands; personal allowances

4.1.3 Understand the application of income tax in respect of: individuals; trusts; charities

The income tax position for a private individual is dependent on the source of income, ie, employment, investments, savings, dividends or a combination of each. The following tax rates, bands and allowances apply to income received in the current tax year (2017–18) as well as previous years.

1.1 Income Tax Rates and Taxable Bands

	Tax Rate	2015–16	2016–17	2017–18
Starting rate for savings	0%	£0–£5,000	£0–£5,000	£0–£5,000
Basic rate	20%	£0–£31,785	£0–£32,000	£33,500
Higher rate	40%	£31,786–£150,000	£32,001–£150,000	£33,501 to £150,000
Additional rate	45%	Over £150,000	Over £150,000	Over £150,000

The rates of tax applicable to dividends are 7.5% basic rate, 32.5% higher rate and 38.1% additional rate.

1.2 Income Tax Allowances

The personal allowance enables individuals to earn a certain amount of income each year without it falling within the income tax net. If an individual does not use up their personal allowance in earned income, then unearned (eg, investment income) may fall within this band.

	2016–17	**2017–18**
Personal allowance for those born after 5 April 1948 (1)	£11,000	£11,500
Income limit for personal allowance	£100,000	£100,000
Blind person's allowance	£2,290	£2,320

Further allowances may be available for married couples born before 1935. Couples born after this date may also be able to transfer a proportion of their own personal allowance between them.

1. The personal allowance is reduced by £1 for every £2 of income over the £100,000 limit and this reduction applies irrespective of age.

Source: HMRC

The following example illustrates how income tax payments are calculated for an employed individual with interest and dividends from savings and investments.

Example

A 35-year-old has employment income of £51,000 in the current tax year (2017–18). In addition, they also receive £500 in gross interest from cash savings held at the bank and £250 in gross dividend income dividends from their holding of shares in XYZ ltd. Their total personal income tax liability is calculated as follows:

Employment income before tax		£51,000
Basic personal allowance	£11,500	
Taxable income	(£51,000–£11,500)	£39,500
Basic rate band	£33,500 @ 20%	£6,700
Higher rate band	(£39,500–£33,500 = £6,000 @ 40%)	£2,400
Interest income	(£500)	£0*
Dividend income	(£250)	£0**
Total income tax		£9,100

* Interest in the example is covered by the personal savings allowance and is therefore tax-free (see section 3.1.2).
** The dividends in this example are covered by the dividend allowance and are therefore tax-free (see section 3.1.1).

If income exceeds £100,000 per annum in 2017–18, then the personal allowance is progressively reduced below the basic amount of £11,500 until it is fully exhausted.

1.3 Taxation of Charities

Registered UK charities qualify for a number of exemptions, reliefs, and allowances against income tax, capital gains tax (CGT), and tax on profits from certain activities. However, in order to qualify for these deductions, the charity must register with HMRC.

In general, most of the income and gains received by charities are exempt from tax as long as the income is used for charitable purposes. Charities can also claim tax relief on donations made by UK taxpayers under the Gift Aid Scheme. Furthermore, charities can register to have bank interest paid gross in the same way as non-taxpaying individuals. However, they are unable to reclaim the tax deducted at source on dividends received from UK companies.

Charities are exempt from paying stamp duty land tax (SDLT) on any property transactions and may be able to reclaim value added tax (VAT) on any goods or services they acquire in the pursuit of their charitable aims.

If charities trade in the provision of goods and services, they may be subject to tax on profits. Also, if the level of income from trading activities exceeds £85,000 in 2017–18, they will need to become VAT-registered and account for VAT in the usual way.

Charities are exempt from CGT as long as the proceeds from the disposal are used for charitable purposes.

2. Taxation of Trusts

Learning Objective

4.1.2 Understand how the income tax liability for a trust is determined based on: trust type; tax rates; tax rate bands

4.1.3 Understand the application of income tax in respect of: individuals; trusts; charities

A trust is a legal arrangement where one or more parties (the trustees) hold assets for the benefit of someone else (the **beneficiaries**). The person introducing the money or assets into the trust is known as the settlor. There are many different types of trust, and these are outlined in section 2.1.

The rules in respect of tax and trusts can be complex, and can merit a whole book in their own right, especially where offshore trusts are concerned.

However, candidates need to be aware of the fact that, because trusts are not separate legal entities (in the way that companies are), in many cases the trustees are assessed on the income and gains earned by the trust.

However, almost invariably they pay the tax liability from the trust's assets. Otherwise, few people would be willing to act as trustees.

There are some exceptions to the rule that liability for CGT falls on the trustees – for example if:

- the settlor, settlor's spouse or civil partner, minor child or step-child can benefit from the trust, then it is the settlor who is liable
- the trust is an offshore trust, any gains may fall to the settlor.

Gains of trustees are taxed at the tax rates applicable for trusts. The rate of CGT for trustees for 2017–18 is 20%.

The capital gains tax allowance in 2017–18 for most trusts is £5,650, ie, half the annual exemption of £11,300 available to individuals. An exception to this is a trust set up for a beneficiary who is disabled. In these circumstances the annual allowance is £11,300.

Trustees may be able to further reduce their CGT liabilities by making a claim for entrepreneurs' relief. If the trustees are eligible to claim entrepreneurs' relief, then any qualifying gains up to the lifetime limit of £10 million will be taxed at the lower rate of 10%.

2.1 Types of Trust

There are four main types of trust:

1. Trusts with an **interest in possession** – where one or more of the beneficiaries has, for the time being, a right to the trust income as it arises or to the use or enjoyment of the trust property.
2. **Discretionary trusts** – where the trustees generally have wide powers over the application of both the trust income and the trust capital.
3. **Accumulation and maintenance trusts** – where one or more of the beneficiaries must become entitled either to the trust income or to the trust capital absolutely by a specified age not exceeding 25. Until then the income must be accumulated or applied for the maintenance, education or benefit of the beneficiary.
4. **Bare or absolute trusts** – where the beneficiary has an immediate and absolute right to both capital and income, which cannot be taken away.

2.2 Taxation of Trusts

2.2.1 Trusts with an Interest in Possession

The Trustees

The trustees are charged basic rate tax (20% for 2017–18) on income arising within the trust fund. Note that for UK equity and dividend income, 7.5% dividend tax is due within the basic rate band.

The Beneficiaries

Beneficiaries entitled to trust income are personally liable to income tax on it, whether they draw the income or leave it in the trust fund. The beneficiaries receive a credit for tax paid by the trustees, unless the income is mandated directly to them, in which case the liability rests entirely with the beneficiary. In general, if the basic rate of tax is 20% and if the trust income for the year is £100 gross, the beneficiary will receive £80 net of basic rate tax. The beneficiary will then be taxed on the full £100 but will receive credit for the £20 paid by the trustees.

If the beneficiary is a basic rate taxpayer, they will have no further liability to tax on the money received. If, however, they are a 40% or 45% taxpayer, then they will be liable for additional tax. If the beneficiary is a non-taxpayer then they can reclaim the tax paid by the trustees. If the trust income is UK savings income, and the beneficiary is a starting rate taxpayer, they can reclaim £10 of the £20 tax credit. If the trust income is UK dividends, the trustees will deduct basic rate tax at 7.5%, and if the beneficiary is a basic rate taxpayer, they will have no further tax to pay. If, however, the beneficiary is a higher or additional rate taxpayer, they will pay tax on their dividends at 32.5% or 38.1% and will therefore be liable for the additional tax due.

2.2.2 Discretionary Trusts and Accumulation and Maintenance Trusts

The Trustees

Trustees are responsible for declaring and paying income tax on income received by the trust.

In both discretionary trusts and accumulation and maintenance trusts, income is taxed at the special trust rates, apart from the first £1,000 of trust income, which is known as the standard rate band. Income that falls within the standard rate band is taxed at lower rates, depending on the nature of the income. This is shown in more detail in the following tables.

If the settlor has more than one trust, the £1,000 standard rate band is divided by the number of trusts the settlor has. If the settlor has more than five trusts, the standard rate band is £200 for each trust.

Trust income below £1,000 per tax year:

Description of Income	Tax Rate (2017–18)
Rental income, savings interest	20%
UK dividend income	7.5%

Trust income above £1,000 per tax year:

Description of Income	Tax Rate (2017–18)
Rental income, savings interest	45%
UK dividend income	38.1%

The Beneficiaries

A beneficiary is taxable only on income paid to them by the trustees or applied by the trustees for their maintenance, education or benefit. Amounts received by the beneficiary are deemed to be net of the special trust rate and a corresponding credit is available. If a beneficiary receives £55, they will be taxable on £100 but a credit of £45 is available. Thus, if the beneficiary is a non- or basic rate taxpayer, some or all of the tax can be reclaimed.

If the settlor of a trust is also a beneficiary or potential beneficiary, the trust income is regarded as theirs for income tax purposes. The trustees remain liable, but if the settlor is not a higher rate taxpayer they may reclaim the balance of tax.

Trustees of a discretionary or an accumulation and maintenance trust have the power to make discretionary payments and therefore need to make sure that they have paid enough tax to cover the tax credit given to the beneficiary. They do this by using a 'tax pool', which keeps a record of all discretionary income payments made by the trustees, and the tax the trustees have paid.

2.2.3 Bare or Absolute Trusts

The tax treatment of these trusts reflects the substantive position. The trust is effectively ignored, with any income tax liability falling on the beneficiary at their own rates, subject to their own personal allowances. The exception to this principle is income arising from assets placed in trust by parents for their own minor children (see section 2.2.4).

2.2.4 Parental Settlements

Minor children have their own personal allowances and starting/basic rate limits. However, if parents create a trust for the benefit of their own minor children, any income paid to the beneficiaries while they are minors and unmarried will be assessed on the parents, unless the total income paid to the beneficiary in any tax year is £100 or less (2017–18 figures).

From 9 March 1999, income generated by bare trusts created by parents for the benefit of their own minor and unmarried children is assessed on the parents, whether or not the income is distributed (subject to the £100 limit).

2.2.5 Trusts for the Vulnerable

Special tax provisions have applied as from 6 April 2004 to any type of trust whose beneficiaries are disabled or relevant minors (such trusts being referred to collectively as trusts for the vulnerable).

- A disabled person is defined as one who is incapable of administering their own property or managing their affairs by reason of mental disorder, or who is in receipt of attendance allowance or disability living allowance.
- A relevant minor is one who is under the age of 18 and has been predeceased by at least one parent.

If a trust has a vulnerable beneficiary, the trustees are entitled to a deduction of tax against the amount they would otherwise pay. The trustees calculate what their trust income tax will be if there is no claim for special treatment, which will vary according to which type of trust it is. They then calculate what income tax the vulnerable person would pay if the income that the trust produced had been paid directly to them as an individual. This takes into account any other income, capital gains and allowances, but ignores any discretionary income payments to the beneficiary. The trustees can then claim the difference between these two figures as a deduction from their own income tax liability.

3. Taxation of Investment Income

3.1 The Income Tax Treatment of Various Asset Types

Learning Objective

4.2.1 Understand the tax treatment of investment income: savings income; dividend income; rental income

3.1.1 Savings Income

Until 5 April 2016, UK banks deducted basic rate income tax at source before crediting interest to a UK resident's account. However, those UK residents who are non-taxpayers – and overseas residents who are not liable for UK tax – were able to apply to HMRC to receive their interest gross on deposits with UK banks and building societies.

From 6 April 2016, all UK banks pay interest gross. If the depositor is a starting rate or basic rate taxpayer, they will pay 20% tax on the interest. If they are a higher rate or additional rate taxpayer, then 40% or 45% tax will be payable to HMRC.

The Personal Savings Allowance

From 6 April 2016, if the depositor is a basic rate taxpayer, they will be able to earn up to £1,000 in savings income tax-free. Higher rate taxpayers will be able to earn up to £500.

This means:

- most people will no longer pay tax on savings interest
- banks and building societies will stop deducting tax from the account interest.

What Counts as Savings Income?

Savings income includes account interest from:

- bank and building society accounts
- accounts with providers like credit unions or National Savings & Investments (NS&I).

It also includes:

- interest distributions (but not dividend distributions) from authorised unit trusts (AUTs), open-ended investment companies and investment trusts
- income from government or corporate bonds
- most types of purchased life annuity payments.

Interest from **Individual Savings Accounts (ISAs)** does not count towards the Personal Savings Allowance as it is already tax-free.

Eurobonds are a type of international bond, and no withholding tax or other taxes are deducted on interest at source. Investors will account for any tax owed in their annual tax return.

3.1.2 Dividend Income

The dividend allowance was introduced on 6 April 2016 and means that individuals do not have to pay tax on the first £5,000 of their dividend income, no matter what non-dividend income they have.

The allowance is available to anyone who has dividend income. Individuals pay tax on any dividends they receive over £5,000 at the tax rate applicable (after deduction of personal allowance/blind person's allowance).

Dividend income falling below the basic rate tax limit	7.5%
Dividend income over the basic rate tax limit and below £150,000	32.5%
Dividend income above £150,000	38.1%

On receipt of the dividend (whether by cheque or direct into their bank account), the investor should also receive a voucher which sets out the sum they have received.

3.1.3 Rental Income

Rental income on residential property is taxed at normal income tax rates: if an individual rents out a residential property, they will be treated as running a business, and should report the rental income on their tax return. (There is an exemption for people renting out a room in their own home, on the rent-a-room scheme, where someone can earn up to £7,500 pa tax-free.) The tax payable will be based on the investor's net income profit from the activity:

- total rental income
- less total allowable expenses.

Allowable expenses include the actual cost of replacing furnishings that have become unusable and have had to be replaced.

All landlords of residential property in or outside the UK are permitted to claim relief for finance costs (eg, mortgage interest) incurred on their let property, giving tax relief at 40% and 45% for landlords paying tax at the higher and additional tax rates respectively. This tax relief will be restricted to the basic rate of income tax only (20%). Implementation will be phased from April 2017 as follows:

- 2017–18 – the deduction from property income will be restricted to 75% of finance costs with the remaining 25% available at the basic rate.
- 2018–19 – 50% of finance costs available for full tax relief and the remaining 50% available at the basic rate.
- 2019–20 – 25% of finance costs available for full tax relief and the remaining 75% available at the basic rate.
- 2020–21 – all financing costs incurred by a landlord will be given as basic rate tax reduction.

Rental profits from commercial property are taxed in the same way as any other rental income. As with residential property, an investor is entitled to a deduction against the rental income for the general costs of running the property (eg, repairs). With commercial property, the investor is entitled to various capital allowances which vary depending on the nature of the capital item involved.

3.2 The Income Tax Treatment of Collective Investments

The tax treatment of distributions from collectives depends on the type of investments in which the scheme invests.

- Funds invested mainly in cash deposits and interest-bearing securities pay out distributions which are mostly made up of interest, and the distribution will be taxed at the applicable rate for savings income.
- Those investing mainly in companies make distributions which are mostly made up of dividends, and the distribution will be taxed at the rate for dividends.

3.2.1 Open-Ended Investment Companies (OEICs), Unit Trusts and Exchange-Traded Funds (ETFs)

Noted below is the tax treatment of OEICs, unit trusts and ETFs. For simplicity, the text only mentions OEICs but you should be aware that it refers to the tax treatment of each.

HMRC taxes investors in OEICs on their dividends, based on what the OEIC is mainly invested in. So dividends from OEICs investing mainly in shares are taxed as dividend income while those from OEICs invested mainly in interest-bearing securities are taxed as interest distributions.

OEICs Investing Predominantly in Shares

If such an OEIC pays a dividend, this will be paid gross and the individual will have to pay tax on this. See section 3.1.2.

OEICs Investing Predominantly in Fixed-Interest Securities

Dividends from such funds are taxed differently from those distributing mainly equity income. Since 6 April 2017, this income is paid gross and individuals will pay any tax due via their tax return.

Equalisation Payments

When an investor first buys units or shares in a fund, they may receive an equalisation payment as part of the next distribution that the fund pays. This equalisation payment is treated differently for tax purposes.

When an investor buys units, the price that they have paid is based on the net asset value (NAV) of the fund, that is, the value of the underlying portfolio plus any income that has been received but not yet paid out. When the next distribution is made, therefore, a part of the distribution that the investor will receive includes this income that they have paid for in the purchase price. It is effectively a return of part of the amount invested, and so is treated differently for tax purposes.

When the distribution is paid, the investor will receive a tax voucher that splits the payment into two parts: the normal distribution and the equalisation payment. As the equalisation payment is a return of the investor's money, it is not liable to income tax. Instead, as it is a return of the amount invested, the payment can be deducted from the cost of the holding when calculating any chargeable gain on an eventual disposal.

Accumulated Income

If a fund does not pay out the income it earns during the year (ie, is a roll-up or accumulation fund), but rolls it up in the fund's unit or share price, the investor has nonetheless earned that income and should receive a tax voucher from the fund manager.

The investor must enter the details on their tax return, and will be assessed on it. HMRC regards this as still being a receipt of income by the investor and will assess them for income tax on the amount accumulated.

3.2.2 Investment Trusts

Investment trusts receiving income from the assets they invest in will pay tax as follows:

- UK dividends are received and the investment trust has no further liability. This is known as franked income.
- Overseas dividends may be received net of foreign withholding tax. The investment trust is liable for corporation tax on the grossed-up income, but, depending on any double taxation agreements, some of the tax already withheld may be offset against this liability.
- The investment trust is liable for tax on other income at the applicable rate of corporation tax.

An **investor** in an investment trust pays tax on the dividends received in the same way as they do for any other share.

- Basic rate taxpayers will pay 7.5% tax.
- Higher rate taxpayers will pay 32.5% tax.
- Additional rate taxpayers will pay 38.1% tax.

3.2.3 Real Estate Investment Trusts (REITs)

Retail estate investment trusts (REITs) are required to pay away at least 90% of the property rental income they receive in a year and these dividends are taxed as property rental income in the hands of the investor (not as ordinary dividends) with tax deducted at source.

So the main benefit of a REIT over a traditional property investment trust or property company is that investors in the latter suffer more tax overall. That is, the traditional property company pays both corporation tax and CGT on its property-related activities; plus, the investor pays income tax on their dividends. REITs, however, do not pay corporation taxes so long as they distribute 90% of their profits.

The investor does, however, as we can see, pay a bit more income tax on their dividend than they will for other sorts of share, because it is classed as rental income. Where they would normally pay 7.5% (basic rate taxpayers), 32.5% (higher-rate taxpayers) or 38.1% (additional rate taxpayers) on dividend income, they will pay 20%, 40% or 45% depending on their personal tax band.

4. National Insurance Contributions

Learning Objective

4.3.1 Understand the basis on which National Insurance contributions (NICs) are levied: employers; employees; self-employed; voluntary

National Insurance contributions (NICs) build entitlement to certain social security benefits, including the state pension. The type and level of National Insurance contributions paid depend on how much people earn and whether they are employed or self-employed. NICs cease in the year an individual reaches state pension age.

4.1 Who pays National Insurance?

NICs are paid by employees and the self-employed aged 16 and over, providing that their earnings are above a certain threshold and they cease at state retirement age. The state pension ages have been undergoing radical changes since April 2010. The changes will see the state pension age rise to 65 for women between 2010 and 2018; and then to 66, 67 and 68 for both men and women.

4.1.1 Employers

Employers are responsible for calculating, deducting and paying Class 1 primary NICs (employees' contributions) to HMRC on behalf of all employees, including directors, earning above the earnings threshold. These must be deducted from their earnings.

Employers (or those treated as the employer if the actual employer is outside the UK) must also calculate and pay Class 1 secondary NICs (employers' contributions) for all employees earning above the earnings threshold.

Employers must keep adequate records showing how NICs were calculated and what payments have been made for each employee.

Rates and Allowances – National Insurance Contributions

National Insurance – Rates and Allowances		
£ per week	2016–17	2017–18
Lower earnings limit, primary Class 1	£112	£113
Upper earnings limit, primary Class 1	£827	£866
Primary threshold	£155	£157
Secondary threshold	£156	£157
Employees' primary Class 1 rate between primary threshold and upper earnings limit	12%	12%
Employees' primary Class 1 rate above upper earnings limit	2%	2%
Class 1A rate on employer-provided benefits (1)	13.8%	13.8%
Married women's reduced rate between primary threshold and upper earnings limit	5.85%	5.85%
Married women's rate above upper earnings limit	2%	2%
Employers' secondary Class 1 rate above secondary threshold	13.8%	13.8%
Class 2 rate	£2.80	£2.85
Small profits threshold	£5,965	£6,025
Special Class 2 rate for share fishermen	£3.45	£3.50
Special Class 2 rate for volunteer development workers	£5.60	£5.65
Class 3 rate	£14.10	£14.25
Class 4 lower profits limit	£8,060 per year	£8,164 per year
Class 4 upper profits limit	£43,000 per year	£45,000
Class 4 rate between lower profits limit and upper profits limit	9%	9%
Class 4 rate above upper profits limit	2%	2%
Additional primary Class 1 percentage rate on deferred employments	2%	2%
Additional Class 4 percentage rate where deferment has been granted	2%	2%

Source: HMRC

4.2 How Much Can Be Earned Without Paying Tax and National Insurance?

4.2.1 Income Tax

Everyone can earn a certain amount each year without paying any income tax. This is called the personal allowance, and in 2017–18 the personal allowance is £11,500.

There are a number of allowances and reliefs available which can reduce the total tax bill, and in some cases mean there is no tax to pay.

4.2.2 National Insurance

It is possible to earn up to £157 a week (2017–18) before paying any National Insurance contributions. This is known as the **primary threshold**. However, as long as earnings are greater than £113 a week (2017–18) it is still possible to build an entitlement to state pension and certain other benefits. This is known as the **lower earnings limit**.

4.3 How Much National Insurance is Payable?

The amount and type of NICs that are payable depend on whether the individual is employed or self-employed and how much they earn. The rates shown below are for the 2017–18 tax year.

4.3.1 Employed

Employees pay Class 1 National Insurance contributions and the rates are as follows:

- Employees pay 12% of earnings between £157 a week and up to £866 a week.
- They also pay a further 2% on all earnings in excess of £866 per week.

4.3.2 Self-Employed

The self-employed pay Class 2 and Class 4 National Insurance contributions.

The rates are as follows:

- Class 2 National Insurance contributions are paid at a flat rate of £2.85 a week.
- Class 4 National Insurance contributions paid as a percentage of annual taxable profits, ie, 9% on profits between £8,164 and £45,000 and a further 2% on profits over that amount.

Self-employed people with profits of less than the small profit threshold (£6,025 for 2017–18) will not have to pay any Class 2 National Insurance contributions. They will not need to claim an exemption in advance.

Class 2 National Insurance Contributions

Class 2 National Insurance contributions are paid at a flat rate of £2.85 a week if earnings are above £6,025 per year (2017–18).

Class 2 contributions count towards certain benefits, like the basic state pension, maternity leave and bereavement benefit. But they do not count towards the additional state pension, statutory sick pay or jobseeker's allowance.

Exceptions to Paying Class 2 National Insurance Contributions

If earnings are less than £6,025 per year, Class 2 National Insurance contributions will not have to be paid. However, it is possible to carry on paying voluntarily to retain entitlement to state pension and other benefits.

Class 4 National Insurance Contributions

The amount of Class 4 National Insurance contributions to be paid in any tax year is based on the profits for that year. 9% is payable on annual profits between £8,164 and £45,000 (2017–18) and 2% on any profit over that amount.

Class 4 National Insurance contributions do not count towards benefit entitlements.

4.4 Voluntary Contributions

Any individuals whose work or personal situation means that they do not currently have to pay National Insurance contributions, or are not entitled to receive National Insurance credits, may still be able to make voluntary contributions to fill in any gaps in their National Insurance record. Voluntary contributions count towards some state benefits and can also increase the amount of benefit they receive.

Voluntary National Insurance contributions are normally Class 3 contributions, but if individuals are self-employed or living abroad they may be able to pay Class 2 contributions voluntarily instead.

4.4.1 Circumstances where Voluntary Contributions may be Payable

Any individual may choose to pay National Insurance contributions voluntarily if they are:

- unemployed and not claiming benefits
- employed but do not earn enough to pay National Insurance contributions and do not get National Insurance credits
- self-employed and have a certificate of small earnings exception that means that they do not have to pay Class 2 National Insurance contributions
- a married woman or widow who cancels her reduced rate election part-way through a tax year
- living abroad.

4.4.2 How Much Do Voluntary Contributions Cost?

If someone wants to pay voluntary National Insurance contributions for the 2017–18 tax year they will pay:

- £14.25 a week for Class 3 voluntary contributions
- £2.85 a week for Class 2 contributions.

If they are self-employed there are some circumstances where they will not be able to pay Class 2 contributions voluntarily. See section 4.4.3.

4.4.3 Voluntary Contributions Choices for the Self-Employed

The self-employed can choose to pay Class 2 voluntary National Insurance contributions even if they do not have to pay them. It's normally better to pay Class 2 contributions voluntarily than to pay Class 3 voluntary contributions. It will cost less and they will receive a wider range of state benefits.

The self-employed may choose to pay Class 2 contributions voluntarily when earnings are low or because they are working outside the UK. However, there are conditions they will need to meet in order to pay Class 2 contributions voluntarily if they are working outside the UK.

5. Capital Gains Tax

Learning Objective

4.4.1 Understand the application of capital gains tax in respect of: individuals; trusts; charities

4.4.2 Understand the application of capital gains tax to the sale of assets, such as: shares; government bonds; corporate bonds; real estate; chattels

Capital gains tax (CGT) is a tax on capital gains made when an asset is disposed of.

A chargeable gain (or an allowable loss) is generally calculated as follows:

	£
Disposal consideration	X
Less incidental costs of disposal	X
Net proceeds	X
Less allowable costs	X

The incidental costs of disposal referred to above may include:

- valuation fees (but this does not include the costs of any appeal against HMRC's valuation)
- estate agency and legal fees
- advertising costs.

These costs should be deducted separately from any other allowable costs.

Allowable costs include:

- the original cost of acquiring the asset
- any incidental costs of acquiring the asset
- capital expenditure incurred in enhancing the asset.

5.1 The Application of CGT to Different Parties

5.1.1 Individuals

When an individual buys an asset and disposes of it at a profit, the difference between its acquisition cost and disposal value is taxed as a capital gain.

Individuals pay CGT on their net chargeable gains – that is, the gains they have made less any losses realised – in a relevant tax year, less unrelieved losses brought forward from previous years and the annual exemption.

Individuals are liable to CGT on their disposal of assets situated anywhere in the world if, for any part of the tax year of disposal, those individuals are either resident, or ordinarily resident, in the UK. Their liability may be affected by any international double taxation agreements.

There is an **annual exemption** for each tax year and for 2017–18 it is £11,300. Gains can be made up to this amount with no taxation payable.

The rate of CGT is currently 10% or 20% depending on the personal income level. Trustees and their representatives are liable for tax on gains at a rate of 20%. Entrepreneurs' relief is also available on lifetime gains of up to £10 million at an effective rate of 10%, which came into effect on 6 April 2011.

In the March 2016 Budget, entrepreneurs' tax relief was extended to long-term investors in unlisted companies. Under these new rules, entrepreneurs are able to access a 10% rate of CGT on newly issued shares in unlisted companies purchased on, or after, 17 March 2016, providing they are held for a minimum of three years from 6 April 2016. These gains will be subject to a separate lifetime limit of £10 million.

Although these are the CGT rates as of 6 April 2016, the CGT rates payable on the sale of residential property are 18% for basic rate taxpayers and 28% for higher rate taxpayers. An individual's main residence remains exempt from CGT.

5.1.2 Charities

A charity is exempt from CGT on any gains when the proceeds of the disposal are applied for, or to be applied for, charitable purposes.

5.1.3 Trusts

There are some exceptions to the rule that liability for CGT falls on the trustees – for example:

- if the settlor, settlor's spouse or civil partner, minor child or stepchild can benefit from the trust, then it is the settlor who is liable
- if the trust is an offshore trust, any gains may fall to the settlor.

Gains of trustees are taxed at the tax rates applicable for trusts, which changed in April 2016 to 20%.

Trusts have an annual CGT exemption which depends on the type of trust in question. For personal representatives of deceased persons and trustees of certain settlements for the disabled it is £11,300. For most others it is £5,650 – half the level for individuals of £11,300.

5.2 Chargeable Assets

Individuals that are resident and ordinarily resident in the UK are known as chargeable persons for CGT purposes. Chargeable persons are potentially liable to CGT on capital gains made on the disposal of chargeable assets regardless of where in the world the capital gain arose.

Most assets are chargeable to CGT including:

- shares in a company
- units in a unit trust
- land and buildings
- higher-value jewellery, paintings, antiques and other personal effects
- assets used in a business, such as goodwill.

There are some exceptions to this, and the following assets are exempt:

- a UK-domiciled individual's nominated main or principal private residence (PPR)
- gilts and qualifying corporate bonds
- jewellery, paintings, antiques and other personal effects that are individually worth £6,000 or less
- savings certificates and premium bonds
- assets held in an Individual Savings Account (ISA)
- **Enterprise investment scheme (EIS)** and **venture capital trust (VCT)** investments subject to being held for a qualifying period
- betting, lottery or pools winnings
- personal injury compensation
- assets held in approved pension arrangements.

CGT arises when a chargeable asset is disposed of. A disposal arises as a result of a transfer of ownership, the making of a gift, the receipt of a capital sum from an asset and even the destruction of an asset. However, a disposal is not potentially chargeable to CGT, or allowable as a capital loss, if made between spouses, made upon death or if the asset is exempt.

5.2.1 Collective Investments

The capital gains tax position for holdings in various collective investments is outlined below.

Open-Ended Investment Companies (OEICs)

- Capital gains made within an OEIC are exempt from tax.
- Capital gains made by a taxpayer on any disposal of the OEIC may trigger a CGT liability depending on whether they have exceeded their annual CGT exemption. If they make a loss, this may be offset against realised gains made elsewhere. Such losses can be carried forward indefinitely if they have no gains to offset in the year they dispose of their OEIC holding.

Investment Trusts

- Providing that they comply with the relevant rules, investment trusts do not pay CGT on internal gains.
- An investor in an investment trust may be liable to CGT on any gains they make on disposal of it. If they make a loss, it may be offset against gains made elsewhere or it may be carried forward to future years.

Real Estate Investment Trusts

- UK Real Estate Investment Trusts (REITs) are not subject to CGT on gains made on the disposal of property, providing that they distribute at least 90% of their profits each year to shareholders as dividends.
- Investors disposing of a holding in a REIT may be liable to CGT on any gains made, as for any other shareholding. Losses may be offset or carried forward.

5.3 CGT Calculation

The following example illustrates how CGT is calculated on disposal of a chargeable asset for a basic rate taxpayer.

Cost	£10,000	
Proceeds	£25,100	
Gain	£15,100	
Allowance	£11,300	
Taxable gain	£3,800	(£15,100 – £11,300)
Tax	£380	(£3,800 x 10%)
Proceeds net of tax		**£24,720**

If the owner also has capital losses carried forward from previous tax years, these are also used to reduce the taxable gain as follows:

Cost	£10,000	
Proceeds	£25,100	
Gain	£15,100	
Losses carried forward	£3,800	
Allowance	£11,300	
Taxable gain	£0	(£15,100 – (£3,800 + £11,300))
Tax	£0	(£0 x 10%)
Proceeds net of tax		**£25,100**

6. Inheritance Tax

Learning Objective

4.5.1 Understand the application of inheritance tax: chargeable transfers; potentially exempt transfers; transfers on death; nil-rate band; exemptions and reliefs; gifts with reservation; valuation of assets; deed of variation

4.5.3 Understand the application of inheritance tax to: transfers into trusts; assets held in trusts; transfers out of trusts

6.1 The Application of Inheritance Tax

Inheritance tax (IHT) is often thought of as a tax which is levied when someone dies, but in fact this is something of a misnomer, as IHT can, in fact, apply when assets are transferred in a variety of ways, for example on death and by gifts. If this were not the case, people would avoid it simply by giving away their assets to their children before they died.

IHT is primarily a tax on wealth. Usually this means wealth that is left to someone else on its owner's death, but it also applies to gifts up to seven years before death and to certain lifetime transfers of wealth.

IHT is different from income tax and CGT.

- For income tax and CGT, the key question is: how much money has the taxpayer made?
- With IHT, the question is: how much have they given away?

It is the amount which the taxpayer has transferred that is taxed. You can also see this as the amount by which they are worse off. Thus if a taxpayer has to pay IHT on a lifetime gift, they will be worse off by the amount of the gift plus the tax; this must be taken into account when calculating the cost of making this gift.

6.1.1 Chargeable Transfers

IHT is a tax on gifts or transfers of value. There are two main chargeable occasions:

- Gifts made during the lifetime of the donor (lifetime transfers).
- Gifts or transfers on death, for example, when property is left to someone in a will (the death estate).

IHT cannot arise unless there is a transfer of value. A transfer of value means any gratuitous disposition made by someone which results in their being worse off – that is, they diminish the total value of their estate.

The sale of an asset at its open market (arm's length) value will thus not give rise to an IHT charge. (It might, however, give rise to a CGT charge if the seller makes a gain on the asset.)

The measure of a gift is always the loss to the transferor (the reduction in value of their estate), not the amount gained by the transferee. In most cases these figures will be the same, but this may not always be so.

IHT arises on any chargeable transfer. A chargeable transfer is any transfer of value not covered by an exemption.

Individuals and trustees of settled property (trust property) are chargeable persons for IHT purposes – that is, they may be liable to IHT.

All transfers of assets (worldwide) made by people who are domiciled in the UK – essentially, people who regard the UK as their permanent home – whether during their lifetime or on death, are capable of being liable for IHT. For individuals not domiciled in the UK, only transfers of UK assets are caught within the IHT 'net'.

6.1.2 Potentially Exempt Transfers (PETs)

A lifetime transfer made by an individual to another individual is known as a potentially exempt transfer (PET). A PET is treated as being exempt from IHT when made – and will remain so providing that the transferor survives for at least seven years after the date on which they make the gift. If the transferor dies within seven years of making the gift, it will become chargeable to IHT.

A lifetime transfer to a discretionary trust is a chargeable lifetime transfer (CLT).

6.1.3 Transfers on Death

When someone dies, the following steps are taken to establish the IHT due:

Step 1 Look back seven years from the date of death to see if any CLTs have been made. If so, these transfers use up the nil-rate band available for the death estate. Work out the value of any nil-rate band still available after this exercise.
Step 2 Calculate the gross value of the death estate.
Step 3 Any part of the death estate covered by the nil rate band is not taxed. Any part of the death estate in excess of the nil rate band is charged at 40%. Deduct any relevant reliefs from the death tax.
Step 4 If relevant, divide the tax due between personal representatives, the person in possession of a gift subject to a reservation and trustees (when applicable).

The Nil-Rate Tax Band

For 2017–18, the first £325,000 of transfers is taxed at 0% (the nil-rate band) and is, therefore, effectively IHT-free. The nil-rate band will remain at £325,000 until 2020–21 when it is then expected to increase in line with the consumer prices index (CPI).

Residence Nil-Rate Tax Band

On 6 April 2017, a residence nil-rate band was introduced. The band was introduced due to growing concern that more people are paying IHT on their estates because of increasing property prices.

This measure introduces an additional nil-rate band when a residence is passed on death to a direct descendant.

The allowance will be brought in in stages as follows:

- £100,000 in 2017 to 2018.
- £125,000 in 2018 to 2019.
- £150,000 in 2019 to 2020.
- £175,000 in 2020 to 2021.

The allowance will then increase in line with the CPI from the tax year 2021–22 onwards, and any unused nil-rate band will be able to be transferred to a surviving spouse or civil partner.

The additional nil-rate band will also be available when a person downsizes or ceases to own a home on or after 8 July 2015 and assets of an equivalent value up to the value of the additional nil-rate band are passed on death to direct descendants.

There will be a tapered withdrawal of the additional nil-rate band for estates with a net value of more than £2 million. This will be at a withdrawal rate of £1 for every £2 over this threshold.

6.1.4 Exemptions and Reliefs

There are various exemptions available to eliminate or reduce the chargeable amount of a lifetime transfer or property passing on an individual's death:

- Some exemptions apply to both lifetime transfers and property passing on death.
- Other exemptions apply only to lifetime transfers (including PETs becoming chargeable on death within seven years).

Transfer of Unused Nil-Rate Band Between Spouses

The Chancellor of the Exchequer's 2007 autumn statement announced that inheritance tax allowances (often referred to as the nil-rate band) were to be transferable between married couples and between civil partners. Thus, for the 2017–18 tax year, a married couple will in effect have an allowance of £650,000 against inheritance tax, while a single person's allowance remains at £325,000. The mechanism for this enhanced allowance is that, on the death of the second spouse, the nil-rate band for the second spouse is increased by the percentage of the nil-rate band which was not used on the death of the first spouse to die.

For example, if in 2017–18 the first married spouse (or civil partner) to die leaves £130,000 to their children and the rest of their estate to their spouse, there is no inheritance tax due at that time and £195,000 or 60% of the nil-rate band is unused. Later, upon the second death, the nil-rate band is increased by the remainder of the unused allowance from the first death, so that if the surviving spouse also died in 2017–18, the first £520,000 (£325,000 x 160%) of the surviving spouse's estate will be exempt from IHT.

This measure was also extended to existing widows, widowers and bereaved civil partners on 9 October 2007, so if their late spouse or partner had not used all of their inheritance tax allowance at the time of their death, then the unused percentage of that allowance can now be added to the single person's allowance when the surviving spouse or partner dies. This applies however long ago the first spouse died, but there are special rules if the surviving spouse remarried.

In a judgement following an unsuccessful appeal to a 2006 decision by the European Court of Human Rights, it was held that the above does not apply to siblings living together. The crucial factor in such cases was determined to be the existence of a public undertaking, carrying with it a body of rights and obligations of a contractual nature, rather than the length or supportive nature of the relationship.

Prior to this legislative change, the most common means of ensuring that both nil-rate bands were used was called a nil-band discretionary trust (now more properly known as NRB relevant property trust). This is an arrangement in both wills which says that whoever is the first to die leaves their nil-band to a discretionary trust for the family, and not to the survivor. The survivor can still benefit from those assets if needed, but they are not part of that survivor's estate.

Exemptions Applying to Lifetime Transfers Only (including PETs)

Small gifts exemption – outright gifts to individuals totalling £250 or less per donee (the person receiving the gift) in any one tax year are exempt. If a gift totals more than £250, the whole of it is chargeable. A donor can give up to £250 each year to each of as many donees as they wish. The small gifts exemption cannot apply to gifts into trusts.

Annual exemption – the first £3,000 of value transferred in a tax year is exempt from IHT (but you cannot use your £3,000 annual exemption and then your £250 small gifts exemption to give the same person a total of £3,250).

The annual exemption is used only after all other exemptions (such as for transfers to spouses/civil partners or to charities). If several gifts are made in a year, the £3,000 exemption is applied to earlier gifts before later gifts. Any unused portion of the annual exemption is carried forward for one year only.

Normal expenditure out of income – IHT is a tax on transfers of capital, not on dispositions of income. A transfer of value is exempt if:

- it is made as part of the normal expenditure of the transferor
- taking one year with another, it was made out of income, and
- it leaves the transferor with sufficient income to maintain their usual standard of living.

As well as covering such things as regular presents, this exemption can cover regular payments out of income under deeds of covenant, and the payment of life assurance premiums on a policy for someone else.

Gifts in consideration of marriage or civil partnership are exempt up to:

- £5,000 if from a parent of a party to the marriage or civil partnership
- £2,500 if from a grandparent or a remoter ancestor of one of the parties to the marriage or civil partnership
- £1,000 if from any other person.

The limits apply to gifts from any one donor for any one marriage or civil partnership.

Exemptions Applying to both Lifetime Transfers and Transfers on Death

Transfers of value between spouses or civil partners are exempt providing that the transferee (that is, the recipient) is domiciled in the UK at the time of transfer.

The exemption:

- applies whether or not the spouses or partners are living together
- ceases to apply on divorce.

Transfers (whether outright or by settlement) to charities which are established in the UK are wholly exempt from IHT. From April 2012, individuals who leave 10% of their net estate (after deduction of liabilities, reliefs, exemptions, and the nil-rate band) to a registered charity may pay a lower rate of inheritance tax of 36% instead of 40% on the amount in excess of the nil rate band. Please see the HMRC website for a worked example (hmrc.gov.uk/inheritancetax/pass-money-property/charity-examples.htm).

Gifts to a qualifying political party are exempt. A political party qualifies if, at the general election preceding the transfer of value, either:

- at least two members were elected to the House of Commons, or
- one member was elected and the party polled at least 150,000 votes.

Gifts for national purposes are also exempt. Eligible recipients include museums, art galleries, the National Trust, universities, local authorities and government departments.

Gifts of land to housing associations are exempt.

Maintenance settlements can be made free of inheritance tax if they are for the upkeep of historic property.

6.1.5 Gifts with Reservation

There are rules to stop people from avoiding IHT by making gifts with reservation – that is, incomplete lifetime gifts when the donor continues to enjoy the 'gifted' asset. If there were not these rules, people would make incomplete gifts so as to escape the charge to IHT. They would then be making a PET; they would also be reducing their estate at death. The value of the assets could in theory thus escape tax entirely, despite the original owner deriving some benefit from them – possibly right up to their death.

An obvious example is a gift of a home to the donor's children – but with the donor continuing to live in it rent-free. Another example is a gift of income-producing assets to someone else, with the income continuing to be received by the donor.

Property given subject to a reservation is property when:

- such property is not enjoyed to virtually the entire exclusion of the donor, or
- possession and enjoyment of the property transferred are not bona fide assumed by the donee.

The term 'to virtually the entire exclusion' will, for example:

- include cases where a donor is allowed occasional brief stays in a house they have given away, without creating a reservation
- not include cases where they spent most weekends in the house. This would create a reservation.

If a gift with reservation is made, it is treated in the same way as any other gift at the time it is made (as a PET or a chargeable lifetime transfer, as appropriate). However, special rules apply on the death of the donor:

a. If the reservation still exists at the date of the donor's death, the asset is included in the donor's estate at its value at that time (not its value at the date the gift was made). So any attempt to 'peg' the value of the assets for IHT purposes at an earlier – and therefore probably lower – value will fail.
b. If the reservation ceases within the seven years before death, then the gift is treated as a PET made at the time the reservation ceased. The charge is based on its value at that time. The annual exemption cannot be used in calculating the value of this PET.

A gift will **not** be treated as being with reservation if:

a. full consideration (ie, payment) is given for any right of occupation or enjoyment retained or assumed by the donor, and the property is land or chattels. For example, an individual might give away their house and continue to live in it, but pay a full market rent for doing so
b. the circumstances of the donor change in a way that was unforeseen at the time of the original gift and the benefit provided by the donee to the donor only represents reasonable provision for the care and maintenance of the donor, being an elderly or infirm relative. This exception only applies to interests in land.

Pre-Owned Assets Tax (POAT)

From 6 April 2005 an income tax charge applies if an individual has the benefit of the free or low-cost use of an asset that they previously owned. The intention behind the charge is to counter schemes which avoid IHT on gifts with reservation. The charging provisions will apply to land (including buildings), chattels and gifts into settlements (trusts) of intangible assets.

The charge for land is based on the rental value. The charge for chattels is calculated by applying a statutory rate of interest to the value of the asset (reduced by any payments made for its use). The charge for intangible assets is calculated by applying a statutory rate of interest to its value, reduced by any CGT payable. There is no charge if the value of the benefit is £5,000 per annum or less.

Transitional provisions allowed individuals to elect for the pre-owned assets tax (POAT) charge not to apply, but this would have had the effect that the property, chattel or intangible asset would be included in the individual's estate for IHT purposes.

6.1.6 Property Valuations

The value of any property for the purposes of IHT is the price which the property might reasonably be expected to fetch if sold in the open market at the time of the transfer.

Quoted Shares and Securities

The valuation of quoted shares and securities is relatively simple. The London Stock Exchange's Daily Official List is a publication which gives the closing bid and offer prices of all quoted securities. Inheritance tax valuations are done on the basis of the 'quarter up rule', taking the bid (lower) price plus a quarter of the difference between it and the offer price. Thus if the closing price for a particular day is 300–304p the inheritance tax valuation is 300 + (304 − 300)/4 = 301p.

The other way of valuing securities is to use the marked bargains price. Each day, certain trades on the stock exchange will be marked, and the valuer may take the average of the highest and lowest marked bargains, ignoring bargains marked at special prices.

The rule for valuation of quoted securities is, therefore, to take the lower of:

- the value on the quarter up basis and
- the average of the highest and lowest marked bargains for the day, ignoring those marked at special prices.

Valuations for transfers on death must be cum-dividend or cum-interest, including the value of the right to the next dividend or interest payment.

Unit Trusts

Units in authorised unit trusts are valued at the managers' bid price (the lower of the two published prices).

Unquoted Company Shares

There is no easily identifiable open market value for shares in an unquoted company. The shares valuation division of HMRC is the body with which the taxpayer must negotiate. If agreement cannot be reached, appeal lies to the special commissioners and then to the courts.

6.1.7 Life Policies

If a person's estate includes a life policy which matures on their death, the proceeds payable to their personal representatives must be included in their estate for IHT purposes. But if a person's estate includes a life policy which matures on the death of someone else, the open market value must be included in their estate.

If an individual takes out a policy on their own life, pays some premiums and then decides to give the policy to someone else by assignment or by declaration of trust, they make a PET.

The value transferred is the greater of the:

- premiums or other consideration paid before the transfer of the policy, and
- the open market value of the policy at the date of transfer.

If an individual writes a policy in trust, or assigns a policy, or makes a subsequent declaration of trust, the policy proceeds will not be paid to their estate but to the assignee or to the trustees, for the trust beneficiaries. The proceeds will, therefore, not be included as part of their free estate at death.

It is common to write policies in trust for the benefit of dependants to avoid IHT. In many cases, these transfers will be exempted as normal expenditure out of income.

6.1.8 Deed of Variation

Sometimes, an individual will inherit under a will but want to change the terms – perhaps because to inherit directly will give them a tax problem, or perhaps because they want someone else to benefit. In these circumstances, it may be possible for a deed of variation to be used. For a deed of variation to be valid, it must:

- relate to a valid will, to an intestate estate or to a trust
- be signed by all the parties who would have benefited had the variation not been made (all of whom must be over 18 and must be of sound mind)
- be executed within two years of the death of the legator (the person who left the money)
- not be made for any consideration (ie, no one should have received money or value as encouragement for them to sign).

The deed must also contain a statement to the effect that it is intended that the inheritance tax effect of the variation will be the same as if the deceased had made that variation themselves.

6.1.9 IHT on Transfers into and out of Trusts and IHT on Trust Assets

The IHT position on transfers of wealth into a trust depends on the nature of the trust itself. In general, transfers of wealth into trusts are treated as PETs, and are therefore excluded from the donor's estate for IHT purposes if they survive seven years from the date of making the transfer. However, a transfer of wealth into a discretionary trust is deemed to be a chargeable lifetime transfer and may be subject to an IHT charge if it causes the individual's IHT allowance to be exceeded at the date the transfer is made.

The position once the assets are in the trust depends on the individual's connection with the trust, ie, settlor or beneficiary. Again, in general terms, the assets do not form part of the estate of the beneficiary unless a distribution of trust capital or income is made to them.

If an asset that has been held within a trust is passed to a beneficiary, it becomes part of their own estate and may create an IHT charge on their own death, if it causes the IHT allowance to be exceeded.

6.2 Estate Administration

The rules as to what happens to the assets and liabilities of an individual upon their death are governed by the laws of succession.

When someone dies, their assets and liabilities still exist and they need to be dealt with. The legal system with regard to succession provides a set of rules governing who will get the assets, and how they must be distributed. The 'who' is determined according to the rules relating to testate and intestate succession (see section 6.3), and the 'how' by the rules relating to the administration of estates.

Administration of the estate of a deceased person is carried out by one or more personal representatives. These may be either:

- executors – in cases where the deceased left a valid will (died testate). The executors will obtain a grant of probate, or
- administrators, where the deceased left no valid will (died intestate). The administrators will obtain letters of administration.

Letters of administration cum testamento annexo (with the will annexed) are needed when a will is left, but, owing to some small defect in it, probate cannot be granted. Both executors and administrators are responsible for putting the deceased's affairs in order and distributing the estate to those entitled to it, either under the terms of the will or under the relevant laws of intestacy.

6.2.1 Personal Representatives – The Charge to Tax

The personal representatives of a deceased person are responsible for:

- settlement of any outstanding income tax liabilities of the deceased in respect of their income up to the date of death
- accounting for tax liabilities arising during the administration period running from the date of death until ascertainment of the residue of the estate.

At the end of the administration period, the residue may pass absolutely to a residuary beneficiary and/or be held in trust under the terms of the deceased's will.

Income During the Administration Period

The personal representatives are liable to income tax at the basic rate on any income arising during the administration period. The income arising is classified in the same way as in accordance with the rules for individuals. Personal representatives are not, however, entitled to personal allowances or the starting rate tax band.

6.3 Intestacy Rules

Learning Objective

4.5.2 Understand how intestacy rules may apply in England and Wales, and the implications of these rules for estate planning

When a person dies without leaving a valid will, their property (the estate) must be shared out according to certain rules. These are called the rules of intestacy. A person who dies without leaving a will is called an intestate person. Only married or civil partners and some other close relatives can inherit under the rules of intestacy. If someone makes a will but it is not legally valid, the rules of intestacy decide how the estate will be shared out, not the wishes expressed in the will.

The Inheritance and Trustees Powers Act 2014 changed the way in which the assets of people who die without wills are shared between their relatives and simplifies the previous complex rules.

Married Couples and Civil Partners

Where a couple is married or in a civil partnership, the intestacy rules differ depending on whether there were surviving issues or not. (Issue are that person's children or if they have predeceased their children).

As you will see, the whole estate passes on intestacy to the surviving spouse/civil partner where there are no children and simplifies the sharing of assets where the deceased is survived by spouse and children.

Intestacy Rules	
Where the deceased dies leaving:	
Issue	<ul><li>Surviving spouse or civil partner entitled to:<ul><li>statutory legacy of £250,000 which is index-linked</li><li>personal chattels</li><li>half of the residue absolutely.</li></ul></li><li>Children entitled to remaining half of the residuary estate at 18</li></ul>
No issue	• Surviving spouse or civil partner entitled to whole estate

Married partners or civil partners inherit under the rules of intestacy only if they are actually married or in a registered civil partnership at the time of death. So, if you are divorced or if your civil partnership has been legally ended, you cannot inherit under the rules of intestacy. But partners who separated informally can still inherit under the rules of intestacy.

The children of the deceased share equally. In the event that a child dies beforehand, leaving children of their own, they take the share that would have belonged to their parent. This also applies where:

- a parent has children from different relationships
- a parent has children but is not married or has not registered a civil partnership
- children are legally adopted children. Stepchildren will receive nothing if there is no will providing for them, unless they have been legally adopted.

Children – if there is no surviving married or civil partner

If there is no surviving partner, the children of a person who has died without leaving a will inherit the whole estate. This applies however much the estate is worth. If there are two or more children, the estate will be divided equally between them. Again, if any have died beforehand, they take the share that would have belonged to their parent.

Intestate dies leaving no surviving married or civil partner or children

In the event that the intestate dies leaving no surviving spouse, civil partner or issue, then closer relatives inherit.

The order in which they inherit is:

- The parents of the deceased – equally if both living
- Brothers and sisters of the whole blood – equally or to their issue if any have predeceased
- Brothers and sisters of half blood – equally or to their issue if any have predeceased
- Grandparents – equally if more than one living
- Uncles and aunts of the whole blood – equally or to their issue if any have predeceased
- Uncles and aunts of half blood – equally or to their issue if any have predeceased
- If there are no surviving relatives, the estate passes to the Crown, the Duchy of Lancaster or the Duchy of Cornwall. When this happens, it is known as bona vacantia.

Bona Vacantia

The Bona Vacantia Division of the Government Legal Department advertises the estates of deceased persons for next of kin to identify their own entitlement. If no heirs to an estate can be found, the assets are realised and the balance is transferred to HM Treasury. The division deals only with solvent estates whose net value exceeds £500.

For assets based in Cornwall and Lancashire, Farrer & Co solicitors deal with bona vacantia on behalf of the Duchy of Cornwall and the Duchy of Lancaster respectively. In both cases, if no rightful owner is found for the assets, the assets legally pass to the respective duchies. Current practice for both is to donate these assets to charity.

7. Residency and Domicile

7.1 Residence and Domicile

Learning Objective

4.6.1 Understand the impact of the rules on residency and domicile and the implications for income tax and CGT

The amount of any UK tax you pay will depend on whether you are deemed to be resident in the UK.

New rules came into effect in April 2013 and are outlined below. For additional detail on this subject, please visit hmrc.gov.uk/international/residence.htm.

7.1.1 Statutory Residence Test

An individual's tax position in the UK will be determined using the statutory residence test and is based on the following:

- The Automatic Overseas Test.
- The Automatic Residence Test.
- The Sufficient Ties Test.

The Automatic Overseas Test

An individual is automatically deemed to be non-UK resident for tax if they meet any of the following criteria:

- they were not present in the UK for all of the previous three tax years, and not present in the UK for less than 46 days during the current tax year
- they were resident in one or more of the previous three tax years, and were present in the UK for less than 16 days
- they work overseas full-time, and
  - work in the UK for no more than 30 days (a work day is classed as any day where an individual does more than three hours' work), and
  - spend no more than 90 days in the UK.

The definition of work includes incidental duties such as training, reporting duties and travel.

The Automatic Residence Test

If an individual does not meet the automatic overseas test, then they are deemed to be UK resident for tax if they meet any of the following criteria:

- They spend at least 183 days in the UK in a tax year.
- Their only home or main home is in the UK (must be available to be used for 91 days and must actually be used for at least 30 separate days (not consecutive)).
- They work full-time in the UK for 365 days.

The Sufficient Ties Test

If an individual's status is not determined by either of these tests, then they must refer to the sufficient ties test, which considers the number of ties the individual has with the UK and factors in the number of days actually spent in the UK into a sliding scale, in order to determine whether the individual is UK tax resident or not.

The ties are:

- **Family tie** – the individual's spouse, civil partner, common law partner or minor children live in the UK. Time spent by minor children to attend school is ignored, and time spent in the UK visiting minor children is also ignored if less than 61 days per tax year.
- **Accommodation tie** – the individual has accessible accommodation in the UK, deemed to be available to use for a continuous period of at least 91 days in a tax year, and they spend at least one night there.
- **Work tie** – the individual has a work tie if they work in the UK for more than three hours a day for a total of at least 40 days per tax year on an employed or self-employed basis.
- **90 day tie** – the individual has spent 90 days or more in the UK in either of the last two tax years.
- **Country tie** – they spend more days in the UK in a tax year than in any other single country – this tie applies to leavers only.

The number of days an individual spends in the UK per tax year will determine the number of ties required to be considered UK resident for tax, as per the following tables.

UK ties needed if a UK resident for one or more of the three tax years before the tax year under consideration:

Days Spent in the UK in the Tax Year Under Consideration	UK Ties Needed
16–45	At least 4
46–90	At least 3
91–120	At least 2
Over 120	At least 1

Source: HMRC

UK ties needed if not a UK resident in any of the three tax years before the tax year under consideration:

Days Spent in the UK in the Tax Year Under Consideration	UK Ties Needed
46–90	All 4
91–120	At least 3
Over 120	At least 2

Source: HMRC

Split-Year Treatment

Under the new statutory residence test, an individual is either UK resident or non-UK resident for a full tax year and at all times for that tax year. However, if during a year they either leave the UK to live or work abroad, or come from abroad to live or work in the UK, then they may be eligible to have the tax year split into two parts:

- a UK part during which they are charged UK tax as a UK resident
- an overseas part in which, for most purposes, they are charged UK tax as a non-UK resident.

HMRC have further rules and guidance on the treatment of different income sources in these circumstances.

Domiciled

Domicile is a general legal concept; it refers to the country which is your permanent home. There are a range of factors that can affect where you are domiciled at any point in your life.

Your domicile status is usually acquired from your father, although you can change it when you become an adult. So if both you and your father were born in the UK, have lived in the UK for all or most of your lives, and do not have strong connections outside the UK, you are domiciled in the UK. Your domicile is only usually relevant if you have income or capital gains outside the UK.

Non-Resident

If you do not meet the requirements to be treated as resident in the UK for income and capital gains tax purposes, you are considered non-resident and therefore unlikely to pay UK taxes. However, as you can see, the actual position can be difficult to determine and in most cases advice needs to be sought from an appropriate tax specialist.

7.1.2 The Tax Implications of Residence and Domicile

If you are resident in the UK you are normally treated as being on the arising basis of taxation. This means that you will pay UK tax on all of your income as it arises and on your gains as they accrue, wherever income and gains are earned in the world. There are some exceptions to this, and these are also outlined in the following paragraphs.

It is possible to be resident in the UK, but not tax resident, or to be resident but not domiciled here. If either of these circumstances applies, then you have a choice of whether to use the arising basis of taxation to account for your worldwide income and gains as they arise/accrue, or to use the remittance basis of taxation.

Broadly speaking, this involves paying tax on income arising and gains accruing in the UK (as with the arising basis), but paying tax on foreign income and gains only as these are brought (remitted) to the UK. Using the remittance basis of taxation is not automatic and, depending on the foreign income and gains, you may have to make a claim if you want to use it by completing the relevant boxes of a UK self-assessment tax return.

When you are taxed on foreign income and/or gains on the arising basis you might find that your foreign income/gains have already been taxed in the country in which they are located. That does not mean that they are not taxable in the UK. You must still declare all of your foreign income and gains. In many cases, relief is given in the UK for foreign tax paid on foreign income and gains under the provisions of the relevant double taxation agreements. Even if no UK tax is payable because it is covered completely by the foreign tax you have paid, you must claim relief under a double taxation agreement by completing a self-assessment tax return.

Remittance Basis

The remittance basis is an alternative to the arising basis of taxation. You can only use the remittance basis of taxation if you are resident in the UK during a tax year and:

- not tax resident in the UK, or
- not domiciled in the UK.

In addition, it applies only if you have foreign income and/or gains during a tax year in which you are resident in the UK. If you are neither of these, then the remittance basis is not applicable for that year.

When you use the remittance basis you will pay UK tax on your UK-source income and gains as they arise or accrue. But you may only have to account for UK tax on foreign income and/or gains when you actually bring (remit) them into the UK.

- If you are resident but not domiciled in the UK, you can use the remittance basis for both foreign income and foreign capital gains.
- If you are resident and domiciled in the UK but are not tax resident, you can only use the remittance basis for foreign income; the remittance basis does not apply to foreign capital gains, which will be taxed on the arising basis.

Even if you are eligible to use the remittance basis, it does not have to be used. You might decide instead to pay UK tax on your worldwide income (and gains if you are not domiciled in the UK) on the arising basis and claim relief from UK tax for foreign tax that you have also had to pay. You might choose to do this rather than lose your personal allowances, as your tax bill could be higher on the remittance basis.

If you decide to use the remittance basis, the impact of these special rules will depend on personal circumstances – how much foreign income and/or gains that arise in a tax year you decide to leave outside the UK, whether or not you are aged 18 or over, and how long you have been resident in the UK. These factors will determine whether to use the remittance basis without having to make a formal claim or if you need to make a claim to use it. They will also determine whether you will need to pay the remittance basis charge (RBC).

If you have less than £2,000 unremitted foreign income and/or gains which arise or accrue in the relevant tax year, you can use the remittance basis without making a claim and retain your entitlement to UK personal tax allowances and the annual CGT exemption.

If you have £2,000 or more unremitted foreign income and/or gains arising/accruing in the relevant tax year and you want to use the remittance basis, you must make a claim for that year. Your claim must be made by completing the relevant boxes of a self-assessment tax return. When you make the claim you will lose your entitlement to UK personal tax allowances and the annual exempt amount for capital gains tax. Depending on how long you have been resident in the UK, you may also be required to pay the RBC.

If you choose to claim the remittance basis and, at any time in the year of the claim, you are aged 18 or over and have been resident in the UK for at least seven of the previous nine tax years, you will have to pay the RBC when you have £2,000 or more unremitted foreign income and/or gains arising/accruing in the tax year. The RBC is an annual charge and is a tax on unremitted foreign income and/or gains. There are rules on how you pay the charge, which is made through the self-assessment system.

If you pay the RBC you will still have to pay UK tax on:

- your UK income and gains (and foreign gains if you are domiciled in the UK but are not tax resident)
- any foreign income and gains which you remit to the UK.

You will also lose your entitlement to UK personal tax allowances and reliefs for income tax and the annual exempt amount for CGT. If you do not wish to pay the RBC, you can choose to pay tax on your worldwide income and gains on the arising basis.

The charges were increased by the coalition government in April 2015, when the charge for those resident in the UK for at least 12 of the past 14 years was increased from £50,000 to £60,000, and a new charge of £90,000 was introduced for those resident for at least 17 of the past 20 years.

In the Summer Budget 2015, the government announced that it will treat any individual who has been resident in the UK for at least 15 of the past 20 tax years as deemed UK-domiciled for tax purposes. From the 16th year, a foreign domiciliary will become deemed UK-domiciled. Once deemed UK-domiciled, an individual will no longer be able to use the remittance basis of tax, nor can they rely on any other rules for people who are not domiciled in the UK. Their foreign and UK assets will be subject to inheritance tax (IHT). The rules took effect in April 2017.

7.2 The Use of Double Tax Treaties

Learning Objective

4.6.2 Understand the use of double taxation treaties

Income tax is payable by UK tax residents. If someone spends a period of time working abroad, they will normally be taxed on their overseas earnings by the country where the income is earned. To prevent those earnings also being taxed in the UK, there exist a number of double taxation agreements (DTAs) with most countries of the world, generally stipulating that the earnings will be taxed only by the country in which they are earned.

Investment income from overseas will be taxed by the UK HMRC at the time the investor becomes entitled to it. If tax is deducted in the overseas country, it will – again depending on any double tax treaties between the UK and the other country – be allowed as a credit against UK tax.

A list of the current tax treaties in force can be viewed at hmrc.gov.uk/taxtreaties/in-force/index.htm

7.3 How Withholding Tax is Applied

Learning Objective

4.6.3 Understand how withholding tax is applied based on: residency; product; tax regime (at source or reclaimable); beneficiary; European Savings Directive; qualified intermediaries scheme

Withholding tax is a tax deducted by the government in one country, when income earned in that country is paid to someone overseas.

The country from which the payment is made, taxes it before it leaves the country to be remitted to the overseas investor, by withholding a proportion of it. The amount withheld is usually somewhere between 10% and 30%.

If there is a double tax treaty in effect, it is often possible to reduce the tax withheld – or to reclaim some or all of the money that was withheld. Further, some recipient countries allow the investor to offset the tax withheld against their domestic tax liabilities.

7.3.1 Residence

An individual's tax residence will be important for determining what rates of withholding tax are deducted by the authorities in other countries. For example, the range of DTAs might mean that if they can show that they are UK resident, they will be liable at a lower rate of withholding tax than if they are resident in a country that does not have a DTA.

7.3.2 Product

Different rates of tax are levied on different forms of income. For example, one country might have a DTA with another, setting out that it will apply withholding tax of one rate of dividend income, another for interest income and yet another for royalties.

7.3.3 Tax Regime

Depending on the nature of the withholding taxes deducted in the country of source of any income, and the terms of any DTA, any reduction of withholding taxes may be effected by:

- relief at source (ie, on notification of the investor's status, the withholding tax is reduced or not applied), or
- reclaim – that is, the withholding tax is deducted, but the investor can submit the appropriate paperwork and reclaim some or all of the sum that was withheld.

7.3.4 Beneficiary

Complications can arise when the entity receiving the overseas income is not the true beneficiary of the investment. In this case, if there are reliefs to be obtained, any DTA should provide that the recipient has a mechanism for reporting to the overseas tax authority on the identity and status of the true beneficiary, and on the relationship between the recipient and the beneficiary, so that an appropriate reclaim/relief at source can be obtained. This could arise if, for example, a financial institution holds shares in overseas companies – registered in its client account name – for its customers' benefit. It could also arise if a trustee holds investments for beneficiaries.

7.3.5 The European Union Savings Directive (EUSD)

An attraction of using offshore bank accounts is the opportunity to receive gross interest, which may be tax-efficient, depending upon the tax rules in the country where the investor is resident.

However, if the investor lives in an EU member state they are likely to be affected by the European Union Savings Directive (EUSD) which came into effect on 1 July 2005. The EUSD was introduced primarily to facilitate the exchange of tax information between member states. Initially some countries chose to withhold tax (retention) instead of exchanging tax information, eg, the Channel Islands and the Isle of Man. However, on 1 July 2011, Guernsey and the Isle of Man withdrew the retention option, and Jersey kept it for existing account holders only. The rate of retention tax was also increased to 35% from 20%.

The tax withheld under this system is in addition to any tax withheld under the territory's domestic legislation. Any investors who continue to receive gross interest will have their details, and the amount of interest they receive, reported to the tax authority in the EU member state where they are resident. It is important to note that the EUSD will only affect the investors who are resident in an EU member state.

7.3.6 Qualified Intermediaries Regime

The US qualified intermediaries (QI) regime is a regime whereby non-US financial intermediaries (including US branches of non-US entities) who generally hold US assets on behalf of investors are required to obtain documentation from the beneficial owners in order to apply the correct level of withholding tax on income (and in certain circumstances capital gains) generated by the assets.

At the end of the US tax year (1 January to 31 December), all income received by the beneficial owners must be reported to the internal revenue service (IRS).

If the financial intermediary chooses to enter into a QI agreement with the IRS and become a QI, these reporting obligations become less onerous: only US persons are reported separately to the IRS (detailing each person's name, taxpayer identification number and income); non-US persons are collectively reported, meaning that person's individual details are not sent to the IRS. Non-US persons for these purposes include overseas corporations that are owned by US persons, and this has been identified as a potential limitation on the effectiveness of the QI regime.

Reportable income broadly includes both dividends and interest income (unlike, for example, the European Union Savings Directive (EUSD) which only includes interest income) and includes corporates and individuals (unlike the EUSD which excludes corporates). In summary, an offshore (to the US) QI entity whose client is a US person is required to report annually to the IRS on the amount of income, and in certain circumstances capital, that the US person received during the past tax year which therefore enables the IRS to police their tax return.

Thus, through the constant obligations of documentation, withholding and reporting, the IRS uses overseas intermediaries to identify and report US persons back to it on an ongoing basis.

7.4 Residence, Domicile and Inheritance Tax

Learning Objective

4.6.4 Know the impact of residency and domicile on the liability to inheritance tax

HMRC refers to the concept of deemed domicile when assessing an individual's liability to IHT following a transfer of assets. Deemed domicile means that HMRC will treat individuals as UK domiciled if, at the date of any transfer of assets, they were:

- domiciled in the UK during the three years before making the transfer, or
- were resident in the UK for at least 15 of the 20 previous income tax years of assessment ending in the year the transfer was made. Prior to 6 April 2017, the rule was 17 of the past 20 years.

Following an announcement in the Summer Budget 2015, from 6 April 2017, anybody who has been resident in the UK for more than 15 of the past 20 tax years will be deemed UK-domiciled for all UK taxes. It is not yet clear exactly how the changes will interact with the existing IHT rule, although they are expected to be aligned following a consultation process.

In general, individuals who are domiciled or deemed to be domiciled in the UK will be subject to inheritance tax on their assets irrespective of where those assets are situated. Individuals who are domiciled abroad will be subject to IHT on their UK assets only. HMRC may also exclude certain assets which they refer to as 'excluded property' from their assessment.

An individual's 'residence' during the tax year has a bearing on their liability to UK income and capital gains taxes, whereas IHT is mostly concerned with the individual's domicile or the country they consider to be their permanent home.

Specific Measures for Those Born in the UK with a UK Domicile of Origin – Formally Domiciled Residents

From 6 April 2017, such individuals will be treated as UK domiciled for all tax purposes, at all times, if they are resident or if they later become resident in the UK subject to a grace period. The grace period apples to IHT only and will mean that such individuals will not be treated as UK domiciled unless they were resident for at least one of the two tax years prior to the tax year in question. The grace period applies to settlors of offshore trusts too.

Any offshore trusts established by these individuals will cease to be excluded from IHT during period the settlor is UK resident.

7.5 International Reporting

Learning Objective

4.6.5 Understand the reporting requirements for: FATCA; CDOT

7.5.1 The Foreign Account Tax Compliance Act (FATCA)

The Foreign Account Tax Compliance Act (FATCA) is a US law designed to combat tax evasion by US persons/entities that fail to report income earned from offshore investments and paying US tax on that income. Implementation of FATCA began on 1 July 2014.

UK FATCA was originally intended to operate from 2014 onwards with no specific end date envisaged. However, following the full implementation of the Common Reporting Standard (CRS) – a multilateral automatic exchange of information regime developed by the Organisation for Economic Cooperation and Development (OECD) – UK FATCA will become obsolete. The CRS is a much broader information reporting regime which is similar, but not identical to, the FATCA regime. Broadly, the CRS provides a framework for jurisdictions to obtain information from their financial institutions and automatically exchange that information with other jurisdictions on an annual basis. Currently, over 90 jurisdictions have committed to exchanging information under the CRS. The CRS has been incorporated into EU law by the European Directive on Administrative Cooperation (DAC) and into UK law by the International Tax Compliance Regulations 2015. Reporting under the CRS was introduced from 2016 with different countries adopting the regime at different times. In the UK, reporting requirements were introduced for financial accounts in existence from 1 January 2016 and financial institutions needed to report specified information to HMRC by 31 May 2017. HMRC would then exchange the relevant information with participating jurisdictions by 30 September 2017.

UK FATCA will be phased out as the CRS is introduced.

7.5.2 Crown Dependencies and Overseas Territories (CDOTs)

UK agreements with its Crown Dependencies (CDs) (Jersey, Guernsey, and Isle of Man) and Overseas Territories (OTs) (Cayman Islands, Gibraltar, Montserrat, Bermuda, the Turks & Caicos Islands, the British Virgin Islands and Anguilla) are in place to improve international tax compliance.

In the UK, CDOT agreements became effective from 1 July 2014 and apply to all new entity and individual accounts opened with financial institutions situated in the UK, CDs and OTs.

The UK and CDOTs agreements apply to financial institutions which include custodians, depositories, investment entities and specified insurance companies situated in the UK, CDs and OTs. It includes legal entities and branches of non-resident financial institutions situated in the UK, CDs or OTs.

Financial institutions situated in the UK and CDOTs have revised onboarding procedures to obtain new mandatory tax documentation in compliance with these agreements.

Self-Certification Forms

- Financial institutions situated in the UK, CDs and OTs are required by law to ask clients to provide information about their tax residence when opening new accounts. Financial institutions can collect this information on a self-certification form. This information will be used for exchanging information with the relevant tax authorities, where clients (individuals or entities) resident in one relevant country open accounts in another relevant country.
- Self-certifications will be validated with anti-money laundering (AML)/know your customer (KYC) records.
- Supplementary acceptable documentation may be required in addition to a self-certification form.

Reporting Requirements

- Reporting requirements are required annually, in May, for the prior calendar year.

Source: http://www.out-law.com/topics/tax/tax-for-entrepreneurs/uk-fatca---the-disclosure-to-hmrc-of-information-about-reportable-accounts-held-by-uk-taxpayers-in-the-crown-dependencies-and-overseas-territories-/.

8. Stamp Duty

8.1 Stamp Duty and Stamp Duty Reserve Tax on Securities

Learning Objective

4.7.1 Understand the application of stamp duty and stamp duty reserve tax (SDRT) to the purchase of securities, including: company shares; share options; unit trusts and open-ended investment companies (OEICs); government bonds; corporate bonds; exchange-traded funds (ETFs)

Stamp duty and Stamp Duty Reserve Tax (SDRT) are taxes paid on the purchase of certain securities, issued by UK-incorporated companies (or by foreign companies which maintain a share register in the UK).

- Stamp duty is the tax payable when there is some paper-based transfer (eg, a stock transfer form).
- SDRT is payable when the transfer is effected electronically (eg, on CREST).

Note: Euroclear UK & Ireland is the central securities depository for the UK markets and Irish stocks. More specifically, Euroclear UK & Ireland operates an electronic settlement system, CREST, which was established in 1996 and is used to settle a vast number of international securities. The company can also physically hold stock certificates on the behalf of customers. By holding securities as well as maintaining an electronic clearing system, CREST can provide for same-day clearing of securities transactions if needed. Its overall ability to provide a fast transfer of title for the securities it handles is its most important advantage to investors.

8.1.1 Company Shares

As discussed in chapter 1, section 3.7.4, there are two forms of duty that an investor of a share will need to pay. The amount paid will depend on whether it is classified as stamp duty or SDRT.

- Stamp duty applies for a paper transaction where the investor uses a stock transfer form to buy shares. The SDRT is a paperless transaction that is settled through CREST.
- SDRT of 0.5% is payable on the value of purchases of UK equities rounded up to the nearest penny.

For a paper transaction, the buyer pays stamp duty and not SDRT. Stamp duty is 0.5% of the consideration value and it is payable on purchases of UK equities not settled through CREST. With paper trading, the duty is rounded up to the nearest £5 for amounts greater than £1,000. However, if shares for any amount of consideration are less than £1,000, then no stamp duty is paid.

Shares that are given to someone for free will pay no SDRT.

Visit www.gov.uk/stamp-duty-reserve-tax-the-basics for further information.

8.1.2 Share Options

Stamp duty is also payable on share options in UK companies, and overseas issuers with a UK register.

8.1.3 Units in Unit Trusts

No stamp duty or SDRT is visibly charged to the buyer of units in a unit trust or shares in an OEIC. However the unit trust or OEIC pays SDRT on the underlying shares in which it invests, and takes this into account when setting the price at which units are sold (eg, with a dual-priced fund, this is allowed for in the spread).

8.1.4 Government Bonds

There is no stamp duty or SDRT on government bonds (gilts).

8.1.5 Corporate Bonds

Generally speaking, there is no stamp duty or SDRT on corporate bonds. However, there is stamp duty or SDRT (as applicable) on convertible loan stocks (that is, corporate bonds that can be converted into shares – whether that conversion right can be exercised either at the time of the purchase, or at a later date).

8.1.6 Exchange-Traded Funds (ETFs)

Stamp duty is not payable on the purchase of exchange-traded funds (ETFs).

8.1.7 Property

There is no stamp duty or SDRT on the purchase of property (though there is, for example, on the purchase of shares in a property company). The tax due on purchase of a direct holding property is, instead, stamp duty land tax (SDLT).

8.2 Stamp Duty Land Tax on Property

Learning Objective

4.7.2 Understand the application of stamp duty land tax (SDLT), including the main reliefs and exemptions, to the purchase of property

Stamp duty land tax (SDLT) is payable by the purchaser on purchases of land and property in the UK. For most residential property, it is calculated as follows:

Purchase Price, Lease Premium or Transfer Value	SDLT Rate
Up to £125,000	0%
On the next £124,999 (£125,001 to £250,000)	2%
On the next £674,999 (£250,001 to £925,000)	5%
On the next £574,999 (£925,001 to £1,500,000	10%
The remainder above £1,500,001	12%
£500,000 and above, purchased by corporate bodies (with effect from 20 March 2014)	15%

Higher Rates for Additional Properties

Since 1 April 2016, individuals pay 3% on top of the normal SDLT rates if buying a new residential property means they own more than one. However, if an individual is replacing their main residence, they will not pay the extra 3% SDLT if the property they are buying is replacing their main residence and that has already been sold.

Further coverage of SDLT can be found in chapter 1, section 4.6.

9. Value Added Tax

Learning Objective

4.8.1 Understand how liability to value added tax (VAT) arises and is charged

Value added tax (VAT) is a tax that is charged on most goods and services that VAT-registered businesses provide in the UK. It's also charged on goods and some services that are imported from countries outside the EU, and brought into the UK from other EU countries.

VAT is charged when a VAT-registered business sells to either another business or to a non-business customer. When a VAT-registered business buys goods or services, it can generally reclaim the VAT it has paid.

There are three rates of VAT, depending on the goods or services the business provides. The current rates are:

- standard – 20%
- reduced – 5%
- zero – 0%.

There are also some goods and services that are:

- exempt from VAT
- outside the UK VAT system altogether.

9.1 What is VAT?

VAT is a tax that is charged on most business transactions in the UK. Businesses add VAT to the price they charge when they provide goods and services to:

- **business customers** – for example a clothing manufacturer adds VAT to the prices it charges a clothes shop
- **non-business customers** – members of the public or consumers – for example a hairdressing salon includes VAT in the prices it charges members of the public.

If a business is VAT-registered, in most cases they:

- charge VAT on the goods and services they provide
- reclaim the VAT they pay when they buy goods and services for the business.

If a business or organisation is not VAT-registered, they cannot reclaim the VAT paid when they purchase goods and services.

VAT-registered businesses add VAT to the sale price of most goods and services they provide.

9.2 Registering for VAT

If goods or services provided by a business count as what is known as taxable supplies, they will have to register for VAT if either:

- their turnover for the previous 12 months has exceeded a specific limit – called the **VAT threshold** (currently £85,000), or
- they believe that turnover will soon exceed this limit.

A business can choose to register for VAT if they wish, even if they do not have to.

9.3 Exempt Items

Some items are exempt from VAT by law. Items that are exempt include the following:

- insurance
- providing credit
- education and training, if certain conditions are met
- fundraising events by charities, if certain conditions are met
- membership subscriptions, if certain conditions are met
- most services provided by doctors and dentists.

Selling, leasing and letting commercial land and buildings are also exempt from VAT.

9.4 Outside the Scope of VAT

There are some things that are not in the UK VAT system at all – they are outside the scope of VAT. They are not taxable supplies and no VAT is charged on them.

Items that are outside the scope of VAT include:

- non-business activities like a hobby – eg, selling stamps from a collection
- fees that are fixed by law – known as statutory fees – for example the congestion charge and vehicle MOT tests.

9.5 The Difference between Exempt and Zero-Rated

If zero-rated goods or services are sold, they count as taxable supplies, but do not add any VAT to the selling price as the VAT rate is 0%.

If goods or services are sold that are exempt, VAT is not charged and they are not taxable supplies. This normally means that VAT on expenses cannot be reclaimed.

Generally, a business cannot register for VAT or reclaim the VAT on their purchases if they sell only exempt goods or services. If some exempt goods or services are sold, they may not be able to reclaim the VAT on all of their purchases.

If a business buys and sells only – or mainly – zero-rated goods or services, they can apply to HMRC to be exempt from registering for VAT. This could make sense if they pay little or no VAT on purchases.

10. Corporation Tax

Learning Objective

4.9.1 Understand how liability to corporation tax (CT) arises and is charged: companies and organisations: trading, non-trading; taxable profits and accounting periods; rates, allowances and reliefs; taxation of franked income

4.10.1 Understand how tax is accounted for and an adviser's duties regarding tax compliance, avoidance and evasion

4.10.2 Understand international disclosure requirements

10.1 How Corporation Tax is Charged

Corporation tax (CT) is paid by limited companies, based on their profits. It is not paid by individuals in business as sole traders (the self-employed), who are taxed on their earnings as income. HMRC lays down rules as to how profits must be calculated for this purpose.

10.2 Different Rates of Corporation Tax

There are two rates of CT, the small profits rate and the standard or main rate. For the financial year commencing on 1 April, the rates are as follows:

	2015–16	2016–17	2017–18
Main rate on all profits except ring fence profits	20%	20%	19%
Special rate for unit trusts and open-ended investment companies	20%	20%	20%

10.3 Capital Allowances

Companies may be given capital allowances – a form of tax allowance on certain purchases or expenses. These enable the company to set such items off, up to a set percentage, against profits before calculating its tax liability – thus reducing the amount of tax it may have to pay. They may be available on such things as plant and machinery, buildings, and research and development. The rate permitted depends on what the item is.

10.4 The Taxation of Franked Income

It is common for one company to hold shares in another, and therefore to receive dividends from that investee company.

If this happens, tax will (in effect) already have been paid out on that dividend (because the investee company has paid it out of its post-tax profits).

For this reason, the dividend paid up to the investor is called **franked income**. Franked income is free of further tax to the receiving company.

10.5 The Legal Requirements Relating to Confidentiality and Disclosure

Financial advisers have a general professional duty to maintain the **confidentiality** of their clients' affairs, including in relation to tax matters; in addition, the **Data Protection Act** imposes obligations on advisers with regard to – among other things – the safekeeping of data on individuals and their affairs. Advisers may thus hold a good deal of sensitive information relating to clients' finances, which should not be disclosed to third parties without proper authority.

In spite of the professional reasons for maintaining confidentiality, there are circumstances in which disclosure of information of clients' affairs is required. The requirement concerns situations in which a financial adviser becomes aware that information held on a client indicates possible breaches of the law. The financial adviser could have disclosure obligations under various pieces of legislation, including the Proceeds of Crime Act 2002 (POCA).

It is a criminal offence under POCA for anyone working in a regulated financial firm not to report any activity that they suspect, or ought to suspect, involves the proceeds of crime. This includes an act of tax evasion by an individual. The report should be made to the firm's Money Laundering Reporting Officer (MLRO). The MLRO must report appropriate cases to the National Crime Agency (NCA).

10.6 International Disclosure Requirements

In today's world of globalisation, individuals and entities work and trade across different countries and tax jurisdictions. Over the last decade there have been numerous efforts by countries to work towards greater transparency when it comes to reporting transactions and paying taxes. See section 7.5 for details of FATCA and CDOTs.

11. Tax-Planning Strategies

11.1 Basic Investment Tax Planning

Learning Objective

4.11.1 Apply the key principles of investment tax planning: use of personal allowances; spouses' personal allowances; children's tax position; pension contributions; use of tax wrappers; use of capital gains tax exemptions; tax deferral; use of life assurance bonds

Tax planning refers to the process of organising one's affairs so as to take best advantage of tax rules.

The practice of organising one's affairs so as to minimise tax liabilities, within the constraints of the law, is sometimes called tax avoidance or tax mitigation, and it is perfectly legal. To make changes to one's affairs in order to avoid tax that one might otherwise have to pay is a permissible activity, providing that no tax rule is being breached. However, caution is necessary with some of the more complex ways of taking advantage of tax rules; the HMRC may raise objections to schemes whose main objective is tax avoidance.

Tax evasion, on the other hand, is illegal. Tax evasion means failing to disclose one's affairs fully to the tax authorities, or breaching tax rules in other ways so as to evade the payment of tax. Penalties can be severe, and conviction for tax crimes could carry a prison sentence.

11.1.1 Use of Personal Allowance

The personal allowance enables individuals to earn a certain amount of income each year without it falling within the income tax net. If an individual does not use up their personal allowance in earned income, then unearned (eg, investment income) may fall within this band.

11.1.2 Spouse or Partner's Personal Allowance, Dividend Allowance and Personal Savings Allowance

A married couple and those in civil partnerships, are taxed as separate people. If spouses or civil partners jointly own income-generating property, it is assumed that they are entitled to equal shares of the income.

If, in fact, the couple are not entitled to equal shares in the income-generating property (other than shares in close companies) they may make a joint declaration to HMRC, specifying the proportion to which each is entitled. These proportions are used to tax each of them separately, in respect of income arising on or after the date of the declaration.

If one's spouse's or civil partner's marginal rate of tax (the rate on the highest part of their income) is higher than the other's marginal rate, they can choose to transfer income-yielding assets to the individual with the lower rate. If that spouse earns no other income, then the income from the transferred asset may thus be free (to the extent of the allowance) of tax altogether.

11.1.3 Children's Tax Position

The law prevents the parent of a minor child from transferring income to that child in order to make use of the child's personal allowance, and the child's starting and basic rate tax bands. Income which is directly transferred by the parent, or is derived from capital so transferred, remains income of the parent for tax purposes.

This applies only to parents, however, and tax savings are therefore possible through gifts from other relatives. Even if a parent is involved, the child's income is not treated as the parent's if it does not exceed £100 a year.

This legislation is concerned with gifts from a parent to a child. It is possible to use the child's personal allowance and starting and basic rate bands if the child is employed in the parent's trade (but it should be remembered that there are rules on the hours which children are allowed to work).

11.1.4 Pension Contributions

Since pensions simplification (also known as 'A-Day', which took place on 6 April 2006), investors can now save up to certain limits into a pension scheme. The rules for claiming tax relief on their pension contributions are more flexible, though tax charges will apply if the investor contributes amounts in excess of certain allowances.

The investor will receive income tax relief on their pension contributions up to an equivalent of 100% of their earnings (salary and other earned income) each year, subject to an annual allowance above which tax will be charged at the individual's marginal rate, whether made by them and/or their employer. The annual allowance for the tax year 2017–18 is £40,000. If an investor exceeds the annual allowance, they will need to declare the extra pension savings and pay an annual allowance charge through their income tax self-assessment.

Investors may also carry forward unused annual allowances from the previous three tax years capped at £40,000 per year. The rules around carry forward are complex. However, investors may in fact invest up to £160,000 in a single tax year, if they have sufficient earnings, have been a member of a registered pension scheme for the previous three tax years, and have not made any prior contributions.

The Tapered Annual Allowance

From 6 April 2016, individuals who have an adjusted income in any given tax year greater than £150,000 will have their annual allowance restricted for that particular tax year.

For every £2 of adjusted income above £150,000 the annual allowance will be reduced by £1.

Adjusted income includes not only income but the value of any pension contributions made by the individual, their employer or a third party.

However, where an individual has an income of £110,000 or less (excluding pension contributions) they cannot be subject to the annual allowance restrictions regardless of the level of their adjusted income.

The maximum reduction to the annual allowance will be £30,000, so anyone with adjusted income of or above £210,000 will have an annual allowance of £10,000.

Money Purchase Annual Allowance (MPAA)

An individual's annual allowance will be replaced by the money purchase annual allowance (MPAA) should they access their pension funds in any of the following ways:

- via uncrystallised funds pension lump sum (UFPLS)
- receiving income above the maximum limit for capped drawdown members
- accessing a flexible annuity
- once income has been taken from a flexi-access drawdown plan.

The MPAA is currently £10,000. Furthermore, the carry-forward of unused annual allowances will not be available where a MPAA applies.

There is also a lifetime allowance, above which a tax charge will apply. The value of any pensions savings above the lifetime allowance will be subject to a lifetime allowance charge; this will apply in addition to the usual income tax due on pension payments. The lifetime allowance limit for 2017–18 is set at £1,000,000 having reduced from £1,250,000 in April 2016, from £1,500,000 in April 2014 and from £1,800,000 in April 2012.

These limits notwithstanding, contributions to a pension fund can be tax-effective, particularly for the higher-rate taxpayer; and, again, contributions to a spouse's scheme can also be helpful if an investor is close to the limits on their own contributions.

An individual with no earnings may also contribute up to £3,600 per annum.

11.1.5 Use of Tax Wrappers

The use of **Individual Savings Accounts (ISAs)** as an investment wrapper is particularly important for individuals who wish to limit their capital gains tax liability.

Higher rate taxpayers also benefit from the fact that they have no further tax to pay on dividends earned from shareholdings within an ISA.

Other wrappers include pensions, SIPPs, investment bonds and junior ISAs. The individual tax benefits will vary depending on the wrapper used.

Lifetime ISA

Lifetime ISAs came into effect on 6 April 2017 and are a tax-efficient savings scheme designed to help people get on the property ladder and/or save for retirement.

Under the terms of the scheme, the government pays in £1 for every £4 saved. The maximum an individual can invest is £4,000 per annum, resulting in the 25% government top-up being worth up to £1,000 a year. The bonus will be added every year; therefore, individuals can earn interest on it thereafter.

The bonus is only paid on contributions made by the account holder until they reach the age of 50. Money in the account can be used at any time to buy a first home or it must remain in the account until the account holder reaches 60.

The total ISA allowance is £20,000 for 2017–18.

11.1.6 Use of CGT Exemptions

Each individual has an annual CGT exemption. An investor with significant investments (outside the tax-free wrapper of ISAs) may choose to plan disposals of investments that are subject to CGT so as to make use of the annual exemption, using the rules set out earlier in this chapter.

11.1.7 Tax Deferral

Various types of tax planning can be aimed at deferring tax, rather than avoiding it altogether. The benefits of a deferral strategy can be:

- cash flow – the money that would have been paid to HMRC stays with the investor for longer, and
- an eventual possibility of legitimate tax avoidance, if the tax becomes payable when the investor has moved to a lower income tax bracket (perhaps because they are no longer earning).

For example, if an investor invests through a collective investment scheme, then the gains made on underlying assets are sheltered within the fund at the point they are realised. The investor is only taxed on the aggregate gains made on the fund as a whole, if and when they eventually come to realise their holding in it.

11.1.8 Use of Life Assurance Bonds

Life assurance bonds can provide the opportunity to combine an element of insurance protection with an investment exposure and some tax-efficiency. For example, an investor may be able to take up to 5% of the value of their policy out on an annual basis, spending it as income, while it is in fact treated as a return of their original capital and therefore is not taxed as income in their hands at the time they take it.

11.2 Criteria for Selecting a Tax-Planning Strategy

Learning Objective

4.11.2 Analyse the criteria for selecting a tax-planning strategy

Any investment strategy should recognise that:

- the after-tax returns from different investments can be affected by tax rules
- taxation should therefore be considered when choosing investments and how they are held.

Favourable tax planning should not, however, be the first priority, over and above the choice of investments appropriate to the individual's risk profile and objectives (that is, possible tax savings should not be used as a reason to choose inappropriate investments).

It should also be remembered that tax legislation is constantly being reviewed and updated; therefore, future charges to taxation rules may render a tax-planning strategy ineffective.

Although not exhaustive, the following points should be considered when selecting a suitable tax-planning strategy:

- What is the client's investment objective eg, income/growth?
- Have all relevant personal allowances already been claimed, eg, income/capital gains?
- If a product wrapper is being used for specific tax benefits, what are the conditions for securing and retaining the tax benefit, eg, minimum five-year holding period for VCTs?
- Are there any ongoing consultations or proposed budget announcements pending that might affect the proposed strategy?
- Are there any anticipated changes to the client's personal circumstances that might affect the strategy in the future, eg, access requirements?
- Is input required from other parties, eg, tax specialists/accountants?
- Are there any additional reporting requirements on the client's tax return as a result of implementing the strategy?

11.3 Key Principles of IHT Planning

Learning Objective

4.11.3 Apply the key principles of IHT planning: lifetime gifts; trusts; transferability of nil-rate band

4.11.4 Apply common tax computations for: an individual's liability to income tax; age allowance; CGT liability on share disposals; IHT liability on lifetime transfers and at death

The key principles of IHT planning are as follows:

- Gifts during the client's lifetime.
- Use of trusts.
- Efficient use of the nil rate band.

11.3.1 Lifetime Gifts

It is possible to make gifts of capital during the course of a client's lifetime, which has the effect of reducing the value of the estate for inheritance tax purposes. Gifts may be made from income or capital and can include physical assets such as property. The type and circumstances of the gift will determine the tax position at the point the transfer is made, and on the subsequent death of the person making the transfer.

Example

John is 70 years old, widowed, in good health and has two children, Mary and Paul. His estate is currently worth £600,000 and includes a property valued at £300,000. John has asked for advice on gifting assets to his family and wishes to mitigate any potential for IHT on death. His wife Eve, passed away five years ago, and her own lifetime allowance (nil rate band) was fully used on death, as assets were transferred to Mary and Paul in line with instructions contained in her will.

The current lifetime allowance (nil-rate band) of £325,000 means that £275,000 of John's estate could be subject to inheritance tax of 40% on his death, ie, a tax liability of 40% on £275,000 = £110,000.

As John has made no gifts previously, he is able to transfer £3,000 each to Mary and Paul in the current tax year, free of any immediate or future IHT liability. He should aim to use this allowance each year going forward. In addition, John has six grandchildren and is able to transfer £250 to each grandchild each year, thereby reducing his estate by a further £1,500 per tax year.

Taking these gifts into account, the amount of John's estate potentially subject to IHT is immediately reduced to £267,500, ie,

2 x £3,000 gifts to Mary and Paul	£6,000
6 x £250 gifts to grandchildren	£1,500
Total	£7,500
Taxable estate before gifts	£275,000
Less total gifts	£7,500
Balance	£267,500

If John wishes, he could transfer the balance of his estate to his relatives now as a potentially exempt transfer (PET). However, if he dies within seven years of making the transfer, then IHT will be levied on a sliding scale. However, in arriving at a decision as to whether to make a PET and at what value, John also needs to consider his own current and future financial needs.

11.3.2 Use of Trusts

In addition to making transfers of wealth direct to relatives, John could also consider setting up a trust and transferring some or all of his wealth into the trust for future distribution to his family.

Example

John decides to create a discretionary trust for the benefit of his family using £200,000 of his remaining capital.

The transfer of assets into a trust created during the settlor's lifetime is a 'chargeable transfer' for IHT purposes. IHT is charged at a rate of 20% on the amount of the transfer that is in excess of the unused nil rate band.

As John has made no previous transfers of wealth, the full nil-rate band of £325,000 is available. As the gift of £200,000 is less than the available nil-rate band, John has no immediate charge to IHT.

11.3.3 Transferability of Nil-Rate Band

It is now possible for married couples to make use of both nil-rate bands and to transfer their allowance to one another. In effect, this means that £650,000 of joint assets may be transferred out of the estate on death without incurring a liability to IHT.

Example

John is 65 and married to Mary who is 63. Their estate consists of a property worth £300,000 and additional assets in savings and investments worth a further £300,000.

Both John and Mary have the use of their own nil rate band of £325,000 and on this basis do not expect to suffer any charge to IHT on death.

Value of estate on death	£600,000
Total nil rate bands	£650,000
Excess nil rate band available	£50,000

Common Tax Computations Example

Kalpesh is 38 years old, married with children, and has gross monthly earnings of £3,800 from employment. Calculate his net monthly pay after income tax.

		Income Tax
Gross income	£3,800.00	
Personal allowance (£11,500/12)	£958.33	£0.00
Taxable income	£2,841.67	
Income taxable at basic rate £0–£33,500/12)	£2,791.67	£558.33
Income taxable at higher rate (£2,847.67–£2,791.67)	£50.00	£20.00
Total income tax payable		£578.33
Net monthly pay	£3,800 – £578.33	= £3,221.67

Example

Caroline is 68 years old, works part-time and earns £14,300 per annum.

Calculate her liability to income tax using 2017–18 allowances.

		Income Tax
Gross income	£14,300	
Personal allowance (2017–18)	£11,500	£0.00
Taxable income	£2,800	
Income taxable at basic rate	£2,800	£560.00
Net annual pay	£14,300 – £560	= £13,740

11.3.4 CGT liability on Share Disposals

There is an annual exemption for each tax year and for 2017–18 of £11,300 and gains can be made up to this amount with no taxation payable. The rate of CGT is currently 10% or 20%, depending on the personal income level. Therefore, an investor with significant investments (outside the tax-free wrapper of ISAs or pensions) may choose to plan disposals of investments that are subject to CGT so as to make use of the annual exemption.

The following example illustrates how CGT is calculated on disposal of a chargeable asset for a basic rate taxpayer who disposes of shares worth £120,000.

Example

Cost	£100,000
Proceeds	£120,000
Gain	£20,000
Allowance	£11,300
Taxable gain	£8,700 (£20,000 – £11,300)
Tax	£870 (£8,700 x 10%)
Proceeds net of tax	£19,130 (£20,000 – £870)

11.4 Tax Planning of Investments and Pensions

Learning Objective

4.11.5 Apply the above principles to basic recommendations relating to the taxation of investments and pensions

The following example highlights some of the issues typically encountered when discussing tax planning on investments.

Example

Scenario

Michael is married to Sarah, and they have two children, James and Anne, who are aged eight and six. Michael and Sarah wish to invest a lump sum of £75,000 now in order to contribute towards the cost of their children's future university education. They do not require access to capital in the short term, and wish to invest the money in the most tax-efficient way possible, as they are both 40% taxpayers. Michael and Sarah agree that they want to retain control over the capital.

Analysis

As Michael and Sarah wish to retain control, the investments should be made in their own names, either individually or jointly. As their objective is to provide a capital sum in the future, the investment strategy should focus on growth rather than income. As such, any tax liabilities arising from investment returns should be subject to capital gains rather than income tax. The benefit from this approach is that they will be subject to capital gains at the 20% rate rather than income tax at the 40% rate. Also, they will both have use of their annual CGT allowances of £11,300 (2017–18) to offset against the gains, whereas their personal allowances are already fully used.

Recommendation

Michael and Sarah should both invest their ISA allowances in the current tax year. The balance of the capital should be invested in a range of suitable collectives in joint names. At the start of each subsequent tax year, sufficient holdings should then be sold within the collective portfolio in order to fund future ISA allowances, while also using some or all of that year's CGT allowances.

Outcome

In this way, the entire capital amount will move to a tax efficient environment over time, while making effective use of both ISA and CGT allowances. The capital remains accessible within the ISA and collective wrappers, and can be used to fund the education costs in the future.

The following example highlights some of the issues typically encountered when discussing tax planning using pensions.

Example

Scenario

Carmel is 42 years old and self-employed. Following successful completion of a recent contract, she received a payment of £100,000 (her only income in the 2017–18 tax year), and would like advice on the most tax efficient method of investing this for the future. She has an existing portfolio of ISAs and a SIPP, which was used to consolidate various pension arrangements in 2007. She tells you that she has no requirement for access to this capital before retirement, and has made no pension contributions since 2009–10.

Analysis

As Carmel is self-employed, she will be required to declare this payment on her next tax return, and should make provision now for the tax liability. However, if she invests this amount in her SIPP instead, then no tax will be payable as she will be entitled to tax relief on the whole amount. The maximum contribution that Carmel can make to pension arrangements during 2017–18 is £40,000 gross. However, pension rules enable her to carry forward her unused allowances for the previous three tax years.

Recommendation

You therefore recommend that Carmel makes a gross contribution to her SIPP in the current tax year using the entire £100,000 and continues to fund ISAs going forward wherever possible.

Outcome

This approach benefits Carmel as she recovers unused pension contribution allowances from previous years, and avoids paying income tax on the £100,000. As she has no immediate need for the money, it is now invested in her SIPP and will grow free of tax until she retires. In retirement, Carmel may be able to supplement the income she receives from her SIPP, using capital withdrawals from her ISA portfolio, and position herself so that her taxable income each year is kept as low as possible.

Key Chapter Points

- Employed and self-employed individuals are liable to pay income tax. Some income is received in full with no tax deducted, while some income has tax deducted at source.
- Various sources of income are aggregated in a personal tax computation. Some income is exempt from income tax and not included in the personal tax computation.
- An individual pays CGT on their net taxable gains in a tax year. There is an annual exemption for each tax year.
- There need to be three things for a capital gain to arise: chargeable person, chargeable disposal, chargeable asset. Disposals between spouses or civil partners are on a no gain/no loss basis.
- Capital losses are deducted against gains in the same tax year. Excess losses are carried forward. Brought-forward losses cannot reduce taxable gains below the annual exempt amount.
- Gilts and qualifying corporate bonds held by individuals are exempt from CGT.
- IHT is a tax on gifts or transfers of value.
- IHT is charged on the decrease in a donor's wealth.
- There are rules to prevent someone making a gift with reservation to avoid IHT.
- Stamp duty or SDRT is payable at 0.5% on the purchase of UK shares.
- A range of planning vehicles allow for legitimate tax avoidance or deferral.
- There are various tax-planning opportunities when an individual's investment strategy is being planned, but the tax tail should not wag the investment dog. In other words, tax considerations should not outweigh proper investment planning.

End of Chapter Questions

Think of an answer for each question and refer to the appropriate workbook section for confirmation.

1. What term is used to describe the person who places property in trust for the benefit of another?
   Answer reference: Section 2

2. Describe the four main types of trust.
   Answer reference: Section 2.1

3. At what rate is dividend income currently taxed in the UK?
   Answer reference: Section 3.1.2

4. How is the equalisation payment treated for tax purposes?
   Answer reference: Section 3.2.1

5. What class of National Insurance contributions do employees pay?
   Answer reference: Section 4.1.1

6. When considering National Insurance contributions, what is the primary threshold?
   Answer reference: Section 4.2.2

7. What is the annual capital gains tax exemption for a discretionary trust?
   Answer reference: Section 5.1.3

8. How is a transfer of capital made during a settlor's lifetime to a discretionary trust treated for IHT purposes?
   Answer reference: Section 6.1.2

9. What is the 'quarter up' rule?
   Answer reference: Section 6.1.6

10. What rate of stamp duty is payable on the purchase of exchange-traded funds?
    Answer reference: Section 8.1.6

Chapter Five
Investment Products

1. Types and Purposes of Collective Investment	319
2. Open-Ended Funds	324
3. Closed-Ended Funds	330
4. The Tax Treatment of Collective Investments	335
5. Common Investment Characteristics of a Fund	338
6. Charges and Pricing of Collective Investment Schemes	342
7. Exchange-Traded Funds (ETFs) and Exchange-Traded Commodities (ETCs)	346
8. Tax-Efficient Savings	350
9. UK Onshore and Offshore Life Assurance Company Products	356
10. Private Equity	361
11. Enterprise Investment Schemes (EISs) and Venture Capital Trusts (VCTs)	366
12. Distributor-Influenced Funds (DIFs)	371
13. Derivatives	373
14. Hedge Funds	384
15. Structured Products	390
16. Retirement Planning	396

This syllabus area will provide approximately 17 of the 80 examination questions

1. Types and Purposes of Collective Investment

Learning Objective

5.1.1 Understand the main types, purposes, common investment characteristics and behaviours of funds, collectives and other products

1.1 Open-Ended and Closed-Ended Funds

Mutual funds are financial intermediaries that combine and pool the financial resources of individuals and companies more efficiently to create a larger diversified portfolio of assets. In addition to the benefits of pooling enjoyed by a large fund, there are economies of scale, such as lower transaction costs and commissions. Inexperienced investors or busy professionals gain from the professional delivery of services in a managed fund by professionals, who have expertise in money management to deliver the superior skills sought by investors.

Some of the first mutual funds were established in Europe; the first mutual fund was created in London in 1868. This fund was the Foreign and Colonial Investment Trust and is now traded as an investment trust on the LSE.

The term mutual fund is usually applied to collective investment schemes that are regulated and offered to the general public. Hedge funds do not belong in this category.

Mutual funds are generally classified by the type of asset classes or principal types of investments that make up the fund. For example, the four main categories of funds are: money market; fixed income; equity; and hybrid funds. They may be passively managed (indexed to a benchmark) or actively managed.

Nowadays, a majority of mutual funds are open-ended funds. Exchange-traded funds (ETFs) belong to this category. The open-ended fund shares are sold to investors at the net asset value (NAV) per share. The investor may have to pay loads (fees for entry or exit into a fund), plus annual management and/or marketing fees. Investors need to consider all the relevant costs to the fund carefully before making an investment decision as these costs will ultimately impact on the return that they receive from each investment. Given that mutual funds are regulated investments, all of the information about each mutual fund is available to the investing public and detailed in the prospectus. Open-ended funds are not traded on organised exchanges – investors buy and sell their shares directly through the investment company at the quoted NAV.

Thus, the total size of the managed fund will vary depending on:

- the amount of money invested by all investors at the inception of the fund
- any further injections of new money or net redemptions of shares made by investors while the fund is operational.

The other type of mutual fund is a closed-end fund, which is so called because it does not accept any new money or redemptions while the fund is being managed. The fund's shares are issued to the public when the fund makes its debut in an initial public offering (IPO). The shares are then listed on a regulated exchange, such as the LSE. Thereafter, investors trade in and out of these shares in the secondary market on the exchange. A unit investment trust is a good example of a closed-end fund.

The growth in the mutual fund industry has been partly explained by the distinct advantages provided by open-ended funds. There are at least five benefits identified for investment made in an open-ended fund:

1. **Liquidity** – there are no penalties for early redemptions. Investors can convert their funds into cash quickly because open-ended funds can be sold at any time and in any amount.
2. **Access to large denomination securities** – small investors gain access to large securities, with a small amount of money. For example, if an investor wanted to buy a money market security in the US, the denominations of such instruments are in $100,000. The small investor can easily invest in this type of security and many others because their funds have been pooled with other investors who have invested in the fund.
3. **Diversification benefits** – risk is lowered depending on how diversified a portfolio of securities is invested.
4. **Cost benefits** – since the fund will buy large blocks of stock, lower transaction costs will reduce the overall cost.
5. **Managerial expertise** – professional money managers have access to a wealth of information and research that ordinary investors do not have. The scope and breadth of the investment company's operations on an international scale offers significant advantages in terms of local knowledge about markets and the selection of international securities. The investor is delegating the portfolio revision responsibility to an expert who is monitoring the fund round the clock.

The money management industry has two sectors: short-term funds and long-term funds. Short-term funds invest in money market instruments and construct a portfolio that delivers to a set of predetermined objectives. Money market funds invest in money market instruments. These funds are suitable for investors who seek high-quality, liquid, short-term investments as alternatives to bank savings accounts. Unlike savings accounts, in the event of a financial intermediary (FI) default, money market funds do not offer the same level of guarantees.

Long-term funds are made up of equity funds, bond funds or hybrid funds (offering a balance of bond and equity securities in their structure). A number of index funds have also been introduced in recent years and have become popular with investors who prefer the relative safety of diversified funds. The fund may be designed to deliver income, capital appreciation or a balance of income and growth.

Bond funds invest in fixed-income securities. The funds may be further sub-classified into: maturities (for example, short-dated; medium-dated or long-dated bonds); investment grade corporates; government/sovereign bonds; high yielders; and so forth. Further, these funds may have specific exposure to one country's currency or they may have an international composition.

Equity funds may be domestic or international in character. They may, as a result, focus on a single country, regions or they may be truly global (world equity funds). If they have a single country exposure, then the funds may be further subdivided into industry sector funds. Style-based equity funds are also incredibly popular and offer the investor choices to match their risk exposure preferences to: small company stocks; middle-sized company stocks; large company stocks; growth company stocks; or value stocks.

Hybrid funds can offer many variations on the themes covered in the above paragraph. Normally these types are presented in bond/equity compositions. There are hundreds of different types of mutual fund products available in the market. Each fund is aiming to capture a set of risk exposure(s) that will meet their client needs and enable that fund to improve its performance over time.

The value of each managed fund will depend on the performance of the underlying securities in the fund. As a result, each investor has a direct investment in the fund; however, the investor is not a direct holder of the underlying securities in the fund.

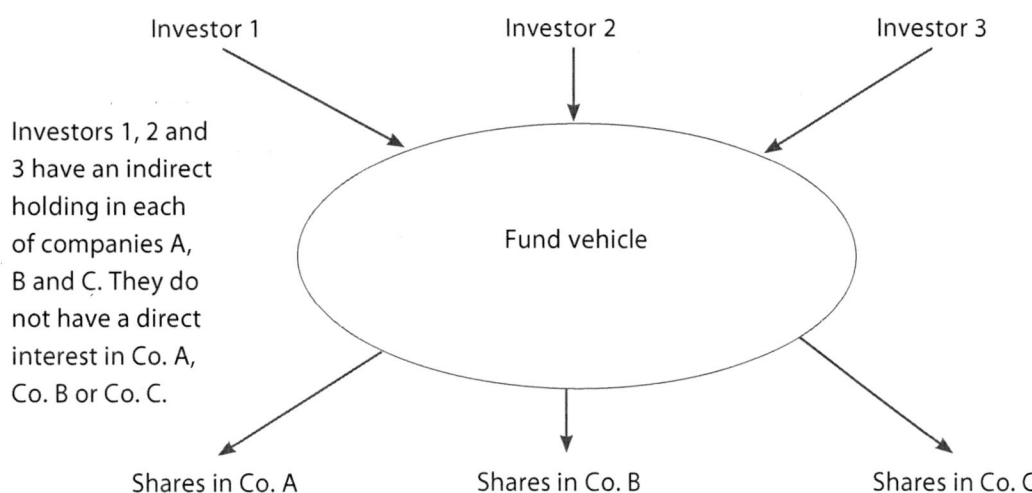

By the nature of an open-ended fund, investors buy their shares/units from, and sell them back to, the fund itself. It allows new investors to buy into the underlying investment scheme without the need to find a matching seller.

When an investor buys shares or units in an open-ended fund, the fund issues new shares/units and fills the purchase order with those new shares/units. As the fund grows, new shares/units are issued by the manager. There is no limit on the number of shares/units a fund can issue to meet investor demand. When investors want to liquidate their holdings, all open-ended funds will stand behind their shares/units and buy them back from the seller. There is never any trading between individual investors. The price fund is based on the NAV of the fund and the number of shares/units in issue.

The definition of NAV per share is:

> **NAV** – the total value of a fund's assets, less liabilities.
>
> **NAV per share/unit** – the total NAV of the fund, divided by the number of shares in issue.

It is calculated at least once a day and represents the value of the underlying securities that are contained in each mutual fund share. Now, we are in a position to consider whether new investments into open-ended funds affect existing investors to any significant degree.

Example

Fund ABC has a portfolio valued at £1 million of assets under management (AUM).

It is made up of 1,000,000 Fund ABC's shares.

Therefore, the net asset value per Fund ABC share is:

£1,000,000/1,000,000 = £1 for each of Fund ABC's outstanding shares.

A new investor has £100,000 to invest.

How many shares of the ABC Fund will this buy them?

Shares are priced at £1 each so it will buy the investor 100,000 shares in the Mutual Fund company.

Two things happen to the fund:

- It gains £100,000 in assets.
- 100,000 more shares are created to give the investor their holding.

The number of shares in the fund is therefore:

- the original 1,000,000 plus 100,000 new shares issued = 1,100,000.

The assets of the fund are:

    £1,000,000 (the original portfolio)

    £100,000 (new cash paid by the investor for their shares)

    = £1,100,000.

The NAV per share is therefore £1,100,000/1,100,000 = £1 per share – ie, unchanged by the introduction of a new investor.

There are different names given to open-ended funds – unit trusts, open-ended investment companies (OEICs) and mutual funds. In some countries, open-ended funds can also be set up as partnerships, or as purely contractual arrangements. In this chapter we will be focusing on unit trusts and OEICs. Also we will contrast the features of open-ended fund vehicles with closed-ended funds.

Closed-ended funds operate with a fixed number of shares outstanding and do not regularly issue new stock. Closed-ended vehicles are limited companies often known as investment trusts. Closed-ended funds have fixed capital and are bought and sold on the stock market just like a stock such as Tesco plc. Like other shares, the price will move in response to supply and demand. Unlike open-ended funds, all trading in closed-ended funds is done between investors in the open market. The fund itself plays no role in either buy or sell transactions.

To form a unit investment trust, a sponsor (brokerage firm) will buy a portfolio of securities. These are deposited in a trust and it then sells increments of the pool of money in the trust as units or shares. These shares are called redeemable trust certificates. More details on this can be found in section 2.1.

Thus, a closed-ended company is in many respects both a common stock (issued on the fund company and listed on a stock exchange), and an investment company offering opportunities for indirect investment.

In summary, candidates need to be aware of the following capital structures:

- open-ended funds, unit trusts and OEICs
- closed-ended vehicles such as investment trusts.

1.2 Multi-Manager and Multi-Asset Funds

Learning Objective

5.1.2 Understand the structure of multi-manager and multi-asset funds

The idea behind multi-manager funds is the recognition that no one fund manager or investment house has expertise in all asset classes, geographic regions and investment styles. Hence by selecting multiple managers, a degree of diversification is obtained and the best managers are selected. They are currently the fastest-growing investment product in the UK. However, the fees associated with these products tend to be higher due to the additional layer of management.

The main types of multi-manager fund categories are: fund of funds (FOFs) and manager of managers (MOMs).

A FOF has one overall manager. It invests in a portfolio of other existing investment funds and seeks to harness the best investment manager talent available within a diversified portfolio. Most funds of funds are managed on an unfettered basis, in that the component funds are run by a number of managers, external to the fund management group marketing the fund of funds.

However, some are managed as a fettered product and are obligated to invest solely in funds run by the same management group as the fund.

By contrast a MOM fund does not invest in other investment schemes. Instead the fund arranges segregated mandates and appoints fund managers who they believe are the best in their sector to manage each pool. One disadvantage is that the initial investment required is usually substantially higher than that required for a FOF or other collective investment scheme.

Multi-asset funds refers to funds which invest in several asset classes. This includes anything from traditional managed funds which may invest in equities (shares), bonds, property and cash, to the new breed of managed funds which invest in a greater variety of assets such as commodities.

Multi-asset funds invest in assets which tend to have different performance characteristics. This increases the diversification of the fund, reducing exposure to the market gains and losses of just one asset class. Multi-asset managers are creating the potential for capital growth and the conditions in which the better performers may offset the poorer performers.

2. Open-Ended Funds

Learning Objective

5.1.1 Understand the main types, purposes, common investment characteristics and behaviours of funds, collectives and other products

2.1 Unit Trusts

Unit trusts are, as the name suggests, constituted as trusts: that is, they have a trust deed and the fund's assets are held by a trustee on behalf of the beneficiaries (investors). Each unit trust will have a manager who makes the investment decisions. The way in which the fund operates is set out in a trust deed.

Unit trusts that are authorised by the FCA, can be marketed direct to the public in the UK; to obtain authorisation, they have to meet certain criteria, both in their set-up and day-to-day management.

These rules include:

- how the unit trust is set up and the contents of its constitutional documents (in this case, the trust deed)
- the types of investment a unit trust can hold
- the fact that these investments must meet certain rules in terms of their liquidity and ease of valuation/trading (eg, the types of markets on which they must be listed and the maximum that may be invested in unlisted investments)
- the maximum amount that can be held in the securities issued by any one issuer (thus ensuring that the fund limits its exposure to a single issuer).

The rules are intended to protect investors in unit trusts to improve their safety relative to less diversified and liquid investments.

UK unit trusts are subject to proper regulation and are often regarded as a comparatively safe investment from the point of view of governance and investor protection.

Some points to remember are:

- Unit trusts are a common form of collective investment scheme, both in the UK and in many offshore centres.
- Like other types of fund, individual investors' assets are pooled together in a centrally managed fund, which is then invested on a collective basis.
- The assets are valued on a NAV basis, and investors buy and sell units at a price determined by the NAV per unit.
- Each unit is equal, representing a fraction of a large portfolio.
- Unit trusts pay distributions periodically – equivalent to paying a dividend to shareholders in a company.
- Because unit trusts have an open-ended capital structure, new units can be created when new investments are made and redeemed when investors dispose of their holdings.
- Unit trusts have a manager, who is responsible for the management of the fund itself, and a trustee, who holds and is responsible for the oversight of the fund.

2.2 Open-Ended Investment Companies (OEICs)

OEICs are also described as investment companies with variable capital (ICVCs).

In the UK until 1997, only open-ended collective investment schemes structured as unit trusts were authorised by the regulator to be offered for sale to the general public. There were no alternative open-ended collective investment schemes which could be authorised. However, since the introduction of new laws permitting companies set up as regulated collective investment schemes to also have open-ended structures, OEICs have been competing with UTs for popularity as an investment vehicle. Legislation permitting funds with OEIC structures to be authorised in the UK was only introduced in January 1997 by introduction of the Open-Ended Investment Companies (Investment Companies with Variable Capital) Regulations 1996 (the ECA Regulations).

An OEIC has many features in common with a unit trust. However, the legal structure is that of a company, not a trust. The OEIC is constituted by an instrument of incorporation (instead of a trust deed), and the OEIC has shareholders and a board of directors.

For UK-authorised OEICs, the management of the fund is carried out by the authorised corporate director (ACD) instead of a manager (in most offshore jurisdictions, however, this function is still carried out by a manager). In addition, the role of the trustee is replaced by a custodian – but the custodian carries out much the same activities, holding and safeguarding the assets and checking that the fund is being run in accordance with the rules.

Again, the assets of the OEIC are managed with the aim of maximising investment returns. Some points to remember are:

- As with a unit trust, individual investors' assets are pooled together in a centrally managed fund, which is then invested on a collective basis. The assets are valued on a NAV basis and the price of the shares will be related to that NAV.
- Similar investor protection rules apply in terms of the types of assets that the OEIC can hold, to those applicable to authorised unit trusts (AUTs).

- The investors' interests are represented by shares in the fund company, instead of – but operating in quite a similar way to – units in a unit trust.
- OEICs pay dividends (not distributions), because they are established as companies, not trusts.
- The capital of the company is open-ended, so, as with a unit trust, net sales and repurchases by investors are met by corresponding increases and decreases in the company's share capital and assets. Shares are created and redeemed to meet demand.
- Shares in an OEIC are bought and sold (and created and redeemed) by the ACD.
- OEICs are common in many offshore jurisdictions; Jersey, Guernsey and the Isle of Man have had OEICs for many years, although they differ in some ways from the OEICs regime in the UK.

2.3 UCITS Funds, including UCITS III and UCITS IV

UCITS stands for undertakings in collective investments in transferable securities. These schemes were established and authorised under a harmonised European Union framework under a UCITS 1 Directive in 1985. A UCITS fund that is established and authorised in one EU member state can be sold across the border into any of the other EU member states, without a requirement for any further authorisation. This 'European passport' for the fund in a UCITS package allows the creators of the fund flexibility to market the product to all investors in the EU region. Thus, financial intermediaries (FIs) who develop and market their fund in one country do not have to re-design or adjust the fund for another country's jurisdiction. Hence, the product is more accessible to all EU investors.

The term 'transferable securities' in the UCITS acronym is defined as:

1. shares in companies or other securities that are treated equivalently to shares in companies
2. bonds and or other forms of securitised debt securities
3. any other negotiable securities carrying the right to acquire such securities by subscription or through an exchange.

These funds have increased in popularity over the years and have become a gold standard EU-based investment product that is recognised as such in the EU and abroad. It was primarily designed as an open-ended diversified product and all types of investors are eligible to purchase these products. Initially it offered investment in permitted classes having high levels of liquidity and borrowing restrictions for the fund that were backed by EU law.

The product continued to gain credibility and UCITS products have evolved over the years. The permitted classes were broadened and more robust governance followed as the product continued its evolution. There have been a number of UCITS directives, progressively building a framework for retail funds within the EU.

This allowed a collective investment scheme established in one EU state, and meeting all the requirements in terms of permitted investments, to be registered for sale in other EU member states after a simple notification process.

Several new directives have since been introduced, modifying UCITS I; they are collectively known as UCITS III and were followed, more recently, by UCITS IV in 2012; they will be modified further by UCITS V which came into force in 2016.

Under UCITS III the concept of the European passport was maintained, but the range of investments in which a fund could invest, while qualifying as a UCITS, was extended. Under UCITS I, funds were restricted to investing primarily in listed securities (ie, mostly listed shares and bonds); the products directive extended this to include:

- liquid transferable securities
- cash
- money market instruments
- their funds (both UCITS and non-UCITS)
- derivatives.

It also allowed for tracker or index funds to qualify as UCITS funds.

As well as expanding the range of assets in which UCITS could invest, the products directive also extended the restrictions on concentration of investment applied to transferable securities to money market instruments as well. It introduced an issuer restriction so that UCITS could now invest up to a maximum of 10% of its NAV in the securities of any one issuer, which included investment trust companies (with some exceptions).

It also introduced the concept of the group. The impact of this was that a UCITS had not only to comply with the various restrictions set out, but it also had to ensure that the aggregate of its exposures to transferable securities, deposits and money market instruments, issued by members of any one corporate grouping, and of OTC derivatives if a member of that corporate grouping was a counterparty, did not exceed 20% of the fund's NAV.

UCITS IV, introduced in 2012, is mostly aimed to make cross-border distribution easier by harmonising regulatory frameworks across the single European market. UCITS IV also introduced the key investor information document (KIID) as a replacement for a fund's simplified prospectus in order to increase transparency and aid the investor.

Some other notable amendments relating to specific types of fund were:

- **UCITS FOFs** – under UCITS I, only 5% of a UCITS could be invested in other funds; under UCITS III this limit had been lifted completely, enabling FOFs to be established. However, the funds themselves had to be UCITS, or subject to similar regulation.
- **UCITS tracker funds** – the products directive made tracker funds more possible than they were under UCITS I. Under UCITS I, there were difficulties if one of the shares which a tracker fund needed to buy accounted for a sizeable proportion of the index; the fund could only invest in the securities of any one issuer to a maximum of 10% of its NAV, but occasions would arise when a share accounted for more than 10% of the index of which it was a constituent. Under the products directive, this limit was raised to 20% of the securities of any one issuer for a tracker UCITS (and in some cases 35%).
- **UCITS investing in derivatives** – under UCITS III, funds had a stated investment policy on derivatives – providing that they abided by specified rules to limit the risk to investors.
- **Money market UCITS** – UCITS funds could now invest in money market instruments (these included instruments such as certificates of deposit and Treasury bills).
- **UCITS investing in cash deposits** – under UCITS III a fund could now invest directly in cash deposits. Prior to UCITS III, cash could only be held for ancillary purposes – eg, the maintenance of 5% or so of the fund's NAV to meet investor redemptions. The UCITS fund could invest no more than 20% of its assets in the deposits of any one institution, or with institutions that are subsidiaries of the same group.

Details of the changes introduced through UCITS V in 2016 are available at www.fca.org.uk/firms/firm-types/fund-authorisation-and-supervision/ucits-v.

Index funds are designed to mimic the movements of a particular equity index such as the FTSE 100 or the US S&P 500 equity index. This tracking is achieved by replicating the make-up of the securities that are in the benchmark indices, with the securities the fund manager has selected for investment in their index fund. The performance of the replicated fund to the benchmark index is monitored closely to ensure that the variability between the index fund and its benchmark is minimised. A measure of this variability is the tracking error that reveals how closely the fund is matched to the equity index. Unacceptably large tracking errors are corrected by adjusting the composition of the index fund. Some studies by Morningstar, which monitors mutual funds, showed that tracking errors averaged 38 basis points in 2003. For a passively managed fund of this variety, a tracking error that is less than 0.5% or lower is normal. Active managers in search of alpha, whose mandates allow them flexibility to create funds that add value to normal index funds can have tracking errors to the benchmark index in excess of 3%.

Costs incurred by a mutual fund include, for example, management expenses, sales commissions, administration costs and transaction costs. To pay for all these costs and to make a profit, funds charge fees to investors. Depending on the fund, some may charge a fee at the beginning (front-end load), while others may charge the same fee when the fund is redeemed (deferred or a back-end load). All funds will charge an annual fee. Additionally there may be other fees to cover, such as management expenses and distribution costs.

A research study was conducted on mutual fund fees around the world and published in March 2009 (Khorana, Servaes and Tufano, Review of Financial Studies). As shown in the table below, in general, equity fund fees were higher than bond funds to reflect the higher costs of using the specialist skills of equity analysts.

Mutual Fund Fees as % of Assets

Country	Bond Funds	Equity Funds
Australia	0.75	1.41
Canada	1.84	3.00
France	1.57	2.31
Germany	1.48	2.29
UK	1.73	2.48
US	1.05	1.53

Source: *Khorana, Servaes and Tufano, Mutual Fund Fees Around the World, Review of Financial Studies*

Following the introduction of the Retail Distribution Review (RDR), it is expected that mutual fund fees will begin to see a degree of compression in the future as platform rebates and trail commission payments cease and the costs associated with managing the fund become more obvious to investors.

2.4 Exchange-Traded Funds (ETFs)

Exchange-traded funds (ETFs) are a relatively new type of open-ended fund having been in existence in the US since 1993 and since 1999 in Europe. They have proved popular in the US, and are increasing in popularity in the UK/EU. Like tracker funds, they follow the performance of an index closely (though some divergence – a percentage or so – can arise). Since these funds are designed to track an index, they offer an alternative to the index fund managed by a mutual fund. Essentially, an ETF offers the convenience of a stock combined with the diversification that comes with a mutual fund-type investment.

An increasing range of ETFs is available, tracking a variety of indices – for example, general share price indices (eg, the FTSE 100 Index in the UK, or the S&P 500 Index in the US) or indices for sub-sectors of the market (eg, pharmaceuticals, or energy stocks).

The fact that ETFs have prices quoted in real time – ie, throughout trading hours, and not a single price based on the previous day's market performance – sets them apart from other types of index-tracking fund. In addition, they have relatively low charges and are not subject to stamp duty. Shares in ETFs can be bought and sold throughout the trading day, enabling investors to speculate on movements in the index within a given day.

Essentially, ETFs are a form of depository receipt that give investors a pro rata claim on the underlying securities held on deposit by a FI that has issued the certificate. The portfolio of securities created for the ETF by the FI is placed in a trust, on which a series of creation units are issued and later sold off as shares enabling investors to hold a claim to the underlying securities. See section 7.1 for more details on the ETC.

2.5 SICAVs and FCPs

Société d'investissement à capital variables (SICAVs) are commonly used in many European countries, such as Luxembourg and France – but UK investors may come across them as the institutions that sell them may be permitted to market them in the UK, since they can be established to comply with UCITS requirements. A SICAV is an open-ended scheme – rather like an AUT or an OEIC – and is established as a company.

Fonds commun de placement (FCPs) are, like SICAVs, commonly established open-ended collective investment vehicles in Europe (typically France and Luxembourg).

FCPs are established by way of contract rather than as a trust or a company. In other respects, they are very similar to the UK's unit trust or open-ended investment company vehicles.

2.6 Dublin-based ICVC

The Irish OEIC is very similar to the UK OEIC, and also the Luxembourg SICAV. The fund will have a board of directors and may have a separate management company, either of which must be based in Ireland in order for the fund to be UCITS-compliant.

3. Closed-Ended Funds

Learning Objective

5.1.1 Understand the main types, purposes, common investment characteristics and behaviours of funds, collectives and other products

5.3.1 Understand the main types, purposes, common investment characteristics and behaviours of: onshore closed-ended funds and investment companies; investment trusts; real estate investment trusts; offshore closed-ended funds and investment companies

5.3.2 Understand when and why borrowing/gearing is used by closed-ended funds, and the benefits or risks associated with it.

5.3.3 Analyse the relative merits and limitations of investing in closed-ended funds and investment companies compared with other forms of direct and indirect investment, in terms of: risk; return; tax treatment; premiums and discounts; turnover, liquidity and access; expenses – transaction and administration; management and administration

3.1 Investment Trusts

Investment trusts are among the oldest form of collective investment; the first UK-based trust was created in the 1860s. The name is misleading as it is a public company not a trust, and is listed on the LSE (though many offshore investment trusts are listed on other exchanges, such as the Channel Islands Stock Exchange or in Dublin). Some points to remember are as follows:

- An investment trust has a capital structure like a company; this means that it has a fixed number of shares in issue at any one time.
- Its principal activity is to invest the funds it controls, according to its stated investment objectives.
- Investment trusts are also subject to some rules on the type of investments they can hold, and the concentration in the securities of any one issuer – but these rules are more relaxed than those for open-ended schemes (unit trusts and OEICs).
- As they are traded on a stock exchange, the price of the investment trust's shares fluctuates according to supply and demand.
- As with unit trusts and OEICs, a NAV is calculated for investment trusts – but this is not used for the share price.
- Shares are generally bought and sold through a broker, not from the fund's manager.
- Like unit trusts or OEICs, investment trusts can be a suitable investment for small investors.
- An investment trust is run by its board of directors; the directors may undertake the investment management of the investment trust themselves (in which case it is called a self-managed investment trust). In practice, however, the board will commonly employ a fund manager to manage the investments and to provide other services, such as administration, registration and accountancy.
- Since the introduction of Retail Distribution Review (RDR) there has been a resurgence of interest in the use of investment trusts. In terms of cost, these now appear attractive when compared to their open-ended counterparts, which were often favoured for their ability to pay trail commissions to advisers. Their closed-ended structure also makes them less susceptible to capacity issues and from becoming too large to manage effectively, both of which are issues that have been seen to affect open-ended funds in recent years.

3.1.1 Share Classes

Investment trusts offer different classes of shares, each offering different rights and benefits. These investment trusts are known as split capital investment trusts or splits. We will look briefly at some of the different types of share class typically issued.

Split capital investment trusts usually have a limited lifespan and their various share classes are intended to appeal to different types of investor.

- Some classes are made up of shares which provide pure capital growth, in forms that range from the safe to the very risky.
- Some classes may provide relatively high levels of income.

On an agreed date, the split investment trusts may be wound up and the assets divided according to a set formula. With some split investment trusts, there is a provision for the shareholders to vote on whether or not to wind up the investment trust. A typical example is a split investment trust set up for an initial life of ten years, but with the provision to extend it by three years at a time.

Basic structure – with an ordinary (non-split capital) investment trust, the ordinary shares are normally entitled to all the income and capital of the investment trust (after any borrowings have been repaid). However, a simple form of split capital investment trust, of the kind which originated in the 1960s, is made up of two classes of shares:

1. **Income shares**, which pay out broadly all the income received by the investment trust. The shareholders of this class will receive the nominal capital value when the trust is wound up.
2. **Capital shares**, which pay no income at all. The shareholders of this class benefit from the bulk of the assets on wind-up of the investment trust, after prior-ranking shares have been paid.

Normally, the income shares are purchased by investors who find income convenient and tax-efficient; the capital shares are bought by investors who find capital gains more tax-efficient and who do not require a regular income stream to live on.

Since their origins in the 1960s, splits have become significantly more sophisticated and offer a wide range of different types of shares. We will now take look at a few different types of share class:

- **Income shares** – there are, in fact, several different types of income shares, with significant differences in capital entitlement. It is important to distinguish between these, because certain shares can give rise to substantial capital losses at redemption – so investors considering buying them should ensure that they understand the terms of investment or take advice before investing.
    - Traditional income shares give a right to the income earned by the investment trust (paid out in the form of regular dividends). They have a fixed redemption price, subject to there being sufficient assets left in the investment trust at the date of its winding-up, after repayment of any debts and other preferred classes of shares.
    - Many of the more recent split capital issues have included income shares which are rather closer to an annuity; an annuity is a product which pays a set, or contractually agreed, regular level of income. Such shares may pay a high level of income, but only a nominal redemption amount (eg, 1p for every 100p share).
    - Some income share issues sit halfway between the above two examples, combining an element of fixed redemption price with a certain share of any remaining capital at redemption.

- **Capital shares** – these are the counterpart of the income shares, and they act as a kind of mirror image. In most cases they pay no income whatsoever.
  - Investors receive the bulk of the assets of the investment trust when it is finally wound up.
  - These shares are highly geared and tend to be very volatile (ie, their price can go up and down dramatically).

Some less common share types which may be encountered are as follows:

- **'A' shares** – these are ordinary shares, but they carry no voting rights; they will often have dividend rights over and above those of ordinary shares.
- **Zero dividend preference shares** or **zeros** – zero dividend preference shares pay no income but offer a predetermined rate of return when the investment trust is finally wound up.
  - Zero holders have first call on the investment trust's assets, when it is wound up, after any bank loans are repaid.
  - The return on zeros is not guaranteed (there may be insufficient assets left at wind up, after all) but there is a very strong likelihood that the return will be paid because of their prior claim on the investment trust's assets. Other classes of shares receive nothing until the zeros have been paid.
  - The final redemption value of the zero at the liquidation date is predetermined, subject to the investment trust actually having enough assets to cover this at that date. Zeros are, therefore, issued at a price which usually rises by a compound growth rate to the final value.
  - The returns on zeros are taxed as capital growth rather than income, and they are particularly attractive to investors who are not subject to CGT – or to those who are able to use their CGT exemption.
- **Stepped preference shares** – these have an income entitlement which grows at a predetermined rate; they also carry a predetermined maturity value. They are not particularly common, but can appeal to investors who need certainty of future income and capital returns.
- **Income and residual capital shares** – income and residual capital shares were formerly called highly geared ordinary shares and are designed to give a highly geared return in terms of both capital and income. They are more volatile because the investment trust has significant levels of borrowings, which must be serviced before these shareholders can receive their benefits. These are also sometimes known as ordinary income shares or highly geared shares.
- **Packaged units** – some of the more recent investment trust issues have bundled together packages of capital, income and zero preference shares to create what is almost the equivalent of an ordinary share. The aim of the units is to reduce or eliminate the discount which may apply to the ordinary share alone.
- **'C' shares** – these were created in the 1990s, as a way of allowing an investment trust to increase its capital base without some of the apparent drawbacks of a traditional rights issue – these drawbacks being that:
  - existing holders may not choose to take up the rights and may feel their investment is being diluted by the new inflow of money
  - the existing shareholders have to bear the costs of the rights issue
  - the investment trust may wish to bring in new shareholders for strategic reasons.

  C shares allow the investment trust to raise new capital in the following way. Money received from a new issue is initially allocated to a temporary class of C shares. These are then converted in due course, and at a price determined by their NAV, into the existing class of shares, once the new capital has been invested. The two portfolios are merged, and so are the share classes. This approach avoids flooding the existing portfolio with cash, which could unfairly dilute the short-term performance of the existing shares – to the disadvantage of the existing shareholders.

- **'S' shares** – these are a means of launching a new investment trust with a strategy which is close to, but not quite the same as, that of an investment trust already in existence:
  - The shares form a distinct and different portfolio which remains separate throughout the life of the investment trust.
  - They have separate price quotes and net asset values.
  - Speed and cost are the main advantages of launching S shares over launching a new investment trust. Shares have been described as perpetual C shares, because they aren't eventually merged into the original share class.
- **Convertibles in investment trusts** – like other companies, investment trusts can issue convertible loan stocks. Some points to remember are as follows:
  - Convertibles offer investors the right to convert their fixed-interest loan stock in the investment trust into a set number of the issuing company's ordinary shares.
  - One attraction for investors is that convertibles usually offer a higher **running yield** than the ordinary shares of the issuing company.
  - In rising markets, convertibles tend to be valued on a basis that takes into account the value of the ordinary shares into which they can be converted. But if the stock market falls below the conversion price, the stock is still valued as a fixed-interest security on the basis of its yield and chances of redemption.
  - Investors must make sure that they convert before the final conversion date, if appropriate, since after that date the stock generally falls in value and is valued simply as a fixed-interest security.

3.2 Real Estate Investment Trusts (REITs)

REITs are another fund innovation with their roots in the US; they were introduced in early 2007 in the UK, as a way of enabling investors to gain exposure to the property market. Investors have – for a long time – been able to do this via property unit trusts, and property investment trusts, but REITs offer a potentially more tax-efficient way to do so. Indeed, a number of property-based investment trusts have already converted to REIT status, or announced their intention to do so. The regime allows companies carrying on a property rental business to benefit from exemptions from corporation tax on property-related income and gains, providing that they meet certain conditions.

Shares in REITs are bought and sold in the same way as for any listed share (ie, the investor bears stockbroking commissions and the usual dealing costs, but not the initial fees associated with some open-ended funds).

Under current law, the holding company of a REIT group must be UK-resident and listed on a recognised stock exchange. REITs are required to distribute at least 90% of their tax-exempt income profits to investors.

REITs can be very tax efficient, as the property company pays no corporation or capital gains on the profits made from property investment.

The major UK REITs are many times larger than most property unit trusts and, as they are subject to continual market scrutiny, are very transparent. As REITs are all listed property companies, investments in them are generally very liquid.

From an investor's point of view there are some factors that need to be considered when investing in REITs. Shares in listed property companies are significantly more volatile than direct property investments or unit trusts, and perform more like equities than property. However, in the long term, their performance is more closely correlated with property than equities.

From a tax perspective, the tax issues include the fact that dividends from REITs are treated as income to the investor, and are taxed accordingly. Purchasing a REIT investment has lower transaction costs where the investor only has to pay a 0.5% stamp duty on shares instead of up to 5% stamp duty land tax (SDLT) on the direct purchase of a property investment.

Distributions are subject to a withholding tax at basic rate income tax, except for certain classes of investors who can register to receive gross rather than net payments. These include charities, UK companies, and pension funds. REITs can also be held in ISAs and child trust funds (CTFs), and the managers of these can receive gross distributions, making these highly tax-efficient.

3.3 Gearing

Learning Objective

5.3.2 Understand when and why borrowing/gearing is used by funds, and the benefits and risks associated with it

An important distinction between open-ended and closed-ended funds (ie, investment trusts) is that the latter has the power to borrow against the fund's assets. Authorised open-ended funds can generally only borrow in certain, limited circumstances. Investment trusts (ie, closed-ended vehicles) have much wider borrowing powers.

Any restrictions on a fund's power to borrow for investment purposes is generally controlled by its internal rules and offering documents. For closed-ended funds there are rarely any regulatory limitations. This means that they have the ability to gear portfolios. Only certain categories of open-ended fund can gear.

The benefits and risks are as follows. A fund which borrows, say, 50% of the value of its portfolio and invests this additional borrowed capital in the market has the following possibilities:

- If it invests well and the new investments gain in value, it stands to make greater gains than a fund which did not borrow; it has geared up its performance. The additional gains made on the extra investment will boost performance, even after it has repaid the capital of the loan and paid the interest due on it.
- If, on the other hand, the portfolio falls in value, the fund must be able to repay the loan when it falls due – and the interest on an ongoing basis. Thus, as well as falling due to the poorly performing investments, the portfolio is suffering from outflows to service the borrowings. The fund will do worse than a similar fund without gearing.

This ability to gear means that investment trusts have both the potential for greater gains than their open-ended peers – and the potential for greater losses. For this reason, investment trusts with borrowing powers should be seen as potentially higher-risk (but also potentially higher-reward) than unit trusts and OEICs.

4. The Tax Treatment of Collective Investments

Learning Objective

5.1.3 Understand the tax treatment within the fund and for UK investors of income arising from collective investments: open-ended investment companies (OEICs); investment companies with variable capital; unit trusts

The tax treatment of distributions from collectives depends on the type of investments in which the scheme invests:

- Funds invested mainly in cash deposits and interest-bearing securities pay out distributions which are mostly made up of interest, and the distribution will be taxed at the applicable rate for savings income.
- Those investing mainly in companies make distributions which are mostly made up of dividends, and the distribution will be taxed at the rate for dividends.

4.1 OEICs, Unit Trusts and ETFs

Noted below is the tax treatment of OEICs, unit trusts and ETFs. For simplicity, the text only mentions OEICs, but you should be aware that it refers to the tax treatment of each.

4.1.1 Capital Gains Tax (CGT)

- Capital gains made within an OEIC are exempt from tax.
- Capital gains made by a taxpayer on any disposal of the OEIC may trigger a CGT liability depending on whether they have exceeded their annual CGT exemption. If they make a loss, this may be offset against realised gains made elsewhere. Such losses can be carried forward indefinitely if they have no gains to offset in the year they dispose of their OEIC holding.

4.1.2 Income Tax

HMRC's website provides details on savings income taxation aspects on UK-authorised investment funds (AIFs) and OEICs. The authority taxes investors in OEICs on their dividends, based on what the OEIC is mainly invested in. So dividends from OEICs investing mainly in shares are taxed as dividend income; those from OEICs invested mainly in interest-bearing securities are taxed as interest distributions. Additionally, investors have to pay capital gains tax on realised gains from an OEIC. It works as follows:

OEICs Investing Predominantly in Shares

OEICs receive dividend income from the underlying securities, paid net of corporation tax. Individuals pay tax on any dividends they receive over £5,000 at the following tax rates:

- 7.5% (basic rate taxpayers).
- 32.5% (higher rate taxpayers).
- 38.1% (additional rate taxpayers).

OEICs Investing Predominantly in Fixed-Interest Securities

Dividends from such funds are taxed differently from those distributing mainly equity income. Since 6 April 2017, income from these funds is paid gross, with individuals paying tax at their marginal rate via their tax return.

4.1.3 Equalisation Payments

When an investor first buys units or shares in a fund, they may receive an equalisation payment as part of the next distribution that the fund pays. This equalisation payment is treated differently for tax purposes.

When an investor buys units, the price that they have paid is based on the NAV of the fund; that is, the value of the underlying portfolio, plus any income that has been received but not yet paid out. When the next distribution is made, therefore, a part of the distribution that the investor will receive includes this income that they have paid for in the purchase price. It is effectively a return of part of the amount invested and so is treated differently for tax purposes.

When the distribution is paid, the investor will receive a tax voucher that splits the payment into two parts, the normal distribution and the equalisation payment. As the equalisation payment is a return of the investor's money, it is not liable to income tax. Instead, as it is a return of the amount invested, the payment should be deducted from the cost of the holding when calculating any chargeable gain on an eventual disposal.

4.1.4 Accumulated Income

If a fund does not pay out the income it earns during the year (ie, it is a roll-up or accumulation fund), but rolls it up in the fund's unit or share price, the investor has nonetheless earned that income and should receive a tax voucher from the fund manager's appointed administrator.

They must enter the details on their tax return and will be assessed on it. HMRC regards this as still being a receipt of income by the investor and will assess them for income tax on the amount accumulated.

4.2 Investment Trusts

4.2.1 Capital Gains Tax

- Investment trusts, providing that they comply with the relevant rules, do not pay CGT on internal gains.

- An investor in an investment trust may be liable to CGT on any gains they make on disposal of it; if they make a loss, this may be offset against gains made elsewhere or it may be carried forward to future years.

4.2.2 Income Tax

Investment trusts receiving income from the assets in which they invest pay tax as follows:

- UK dividends are received gross and the investment trust has no further liability. This is franked income (see chapter 4, section 10.4).
- Overseas dividends may be received net of foreign withholding tax (see chapter 4, section 7.3). The investment trust is liable for corporation tax on the grossed-up income, but depending on any double taxation agreements (see chapter 4, section 7.2) some of the tax already withheld may be offsettable against this liability.
- The investment trust is liable for tax on other income at the corporation tax rate applicable.

An investor in an investment trust is taxed on dividends paid by it in the same way as they would be for any other share.

Individuals pay tax on any dividends they receive over £5,000 at the following tax rates:

- 7.5% (basic rate taxpayers).
- 32.5% (higher rate taxpayers).
- 38.1% (additional rate taxpayers).

4.3 Real Estate Investment Trusts (REITs)

4.3.1 Capital Gains Tax (CGT)

- UK REITs are not subject to CGT on gains made on the disposal of property, providing that they distribute at least 90% of their profits each year to shareholders as dividends.
- Investors disposing of a holding in a REIT may be liable to CGT on any gains made, as for any other shareholding. Losses may be offset or carried forward.

4.3.2 Income Tax

- REITs are required to pay away at least 90% of the property rental income they receive in a year.
- These dividends are taxed as property rental income in the hands of the investor (not as ordinary dividends). This tax is deducted at source.

So the main benefit of a REIT over a traditional property investment trust or property company is that investors in the latter suffer more tax overall. That is, the traditional property company pays both corporation tax and CGT on its property-related activities; furthermore, the investor pays income tax on their dividends. REITs, however, do not pay corporation taxes so long as they distribute 90% of their profits. Property investment trust companies hold shares in property companies, not the direct asset itself.

The investor does, however, as we can see, pay a bit more income tax on their dividend than they would for other sorts of share – because it is classed as rental income. If they would normally pay 7.5% (basic rate taxpayers), 32.5% (higher rate taxpayers) or 38.1% (additional rate taxpayers) on dividend income, they will pay 20%, 40% or 45% depending on their personal tax band.

5. Common Investment Characteristics of a Fund

Learning Objective

5.1.7 Analyse the relative merits and limitations of investing in a collective investment fund compared with other forms of direct and indirect investment, in terms of: risk; return; tax treatment; turnover, liquidity and access; expenses – transaction and ongoing; management and administration

Collective investment schemes (CISs) can provide a useful alternative to direct investment, for those investors without:

- the time to manage their own investments
- the large sums of money required to get adequate diversification
- the expertise to assess investments
- sufficient money that would enable a fund manager to offer a segregated portfolio.

The advantages of investing via a fund include:

- economies of scale (transaction sizes that ensure commissions and other costs may be set at competitive levels)
- a greater degree of diversification (spread of risk) than the investor might be able to achieve investing a relatively small amount of money directly
- access to specialist investment expertise
- eliminating administrative burdens
- many funds are regulated, which can be a big comfort to some investors
- the investor may gain access to foreign/specialist markets not always open to private individuals, but only to institutional investors
- in some cases, offshore funds can act as a tax shelter – since the investor does not pay CGT on gains made on the underlying investments as they arise. Instead, CGT will be paid on the sale of the fund-holding, and this may be at a time when the investor falls into a lower tax bracket.

The disadvantages of investing via a fund include:

- costs, as there is usually an initial charge along with ongoing management costs and fees
- no guarantee of performance. Specialist investment expertise does not guarantee good performance
- the investor has no choice in the investments – a fund will not suit an investor who likes to make their own investment decisions
- tax (again). Some offshore funds are not ideal for UK investors from a tax perspective, because of their unfavourable treatment by the UK taxman. Also, some funds may be liable to withholding taxes on underlying investments which cannot be reclaimed. Investment managers should seek to minimise the impact of such taxes.

5.1 Offshore Funds

Learning Objective

5.1.4 Understand the main types, purposes, common investment characteristics and behaviours of: onshore collective investment funds; offshore collective investment funds

5.1.5 Understand the tax treatment of UK investors investing in offshore funds, including: differences between reporting funds and non-reporting funds; taxation of offshore funds

An offshore fund is an investment that is based in a foreign country, usually a country that has favourable taxation regulations. These funds which are established and run outside the UK jurisdiction, usually in low tax areas, are more generally referred to as offshore funds. Jurisdictions where they are commonly found include the Channel Islands, the Isle of Man, the Cayman Islands, Hong Kong and Bermuda. In recent years, Luxembourg and Dublin have also become important tax havens within the European Union (EU).

According to HMRC, the definition of an offshore fund is limited to 'mutual funds' which take one of three forms and which are resident in, or based in, a territory outside the United Kingdom. The meaning of the term 'mutual fund' is given by section 40B of the Finance Act (FA) 2008, but, broadly, the definition is applied to a company, trust or any other vehicle or arrangement that meets the following characteristics:

- It is not UK tax-resident.
- It exists to enable participants to take part in the benefits arising from acquisition, holding, managing, or disposing of assets of any description.
- The participants do not have day-to-day control of the management of the property whether or not they have the right to be consulted or give directions.
- A reasonable investor would expect to be able to realise any investment based entirely or almost entirely by reference to the net asset value of the assets under management or, alternatively, by reference to an index of any description.

The three forms of mutual funds that fall within the definition of an offshore fund are:

- a mutual fund constituted by a body corporate resident outside the UK
- a mutual fund under which property is held on trust for the participants by trustees resident outside the UK
- a mutual fund constituted by other arrangements that create rights in the nature of co-ownership where the arrangements take effect by virtue of the law of a territory outside the UK.

Certain types of foreign partnerships that do not meet the requirements are specifically excluded from the meaning of an offshore fund given by section 40A(3) FA 2008.

Many offshore funds are run by companies associated with large UK unit trust groups, and most of the countries involved now have their own regulatory framework. Since 1979, when UK exchange controls were abolished, it has become relatively easy for a UK resident to invest money abroad in equities, bonds or pooled investments, such as bonds, Undertakings for Collective Investment in Transferable Securities (UCITS) and OEICs.

There may be income and CGT advantages for UK expatriates who are non-UK resident. In general terms, there will be no tax paid by an offshore fund; however, there may be withholding tax, which may not be reclaimable by the fund. In addition, a fund may be subject to a small amount of local tax. Jersey funds are subject to a flat-yearly corporation tax and Luxembourg funds to a tax on the asset value each year. The expenses of an offshore fund cannot be offset against its income.

However, investment in offshore funds may be not be as advantageous for UK residents as they may think, particularly from a tax point of view. In most cases, the tax benefit is limited to a possible deferral of tax payments resulting from income being paid gross. There can even be tax disadvantages, particularly if the offshore fund invests in UK shares.

The UK regulator recognises the following offshore pooled investments:

- Funds categorised as UCITS are constituted in other European Economic Area (EEA) member states. These funds are automatically recognised by the regulator and can be marketed freely in the UK.
- Funds authorised in designated territories, that is, non-EU territories such as the Channel Islands, Bermuda and the Isle of Man, may not be automatically recognised by the Financial Conduct Authority (FCA). However, the FCA recognises that certain countries in which investments are based offer a similar regulatory authority and investor protection to that afforded to the UK investor onshore. These regulatory authorities are: the Bermuda Monetary Authority, the Guernsey Financial Services Commission, the Isle of Man Financial Supervision Commission, and the Jersey Financial Services Department.
- The regulator also provides for the recognition of overseas schemes on an individual basis.

Non-regulated and non-recognised funds are subject to severe marketing restrictions in the UK. Prospectuses and details can only be forwarded to investment professionals such as stockbrokers and independent financial advisers (IFAs).

There are two categories of offshore funds: reporting funds and non-reporting funds.

5.1.1 Reporting Funds

An offshore entity that meets the definition of an offshore fund (under section 40A(2) Finance Act 2008) can, on meeting certain conditions, apply to be a reporting fund. The relevance of reporting fund status for UK investors is that gains realised on disposals of investments in reporting funds will, in most circumstances, be subject to tax on chargeable gains, whereas gains realised on disposals of investments in non-reporting funds will be subject to less favourable treatment as they will be charged to tax on income.

Reporting funds must prepare accounts in accordance with an acceptable accounting policy and provide reports of their 'reportable income', which is the accounts figure for the total return of the fund adjusted in accordance with certain rules set out in the Offshore Funds (Tax) Regulations 2009. They must provide reports to both HMRC, to include a computation showing their reportable income, and to participants (investors) that show their proportionate share of that income. In addition, reporting funds must make certain information available to HMRC when requested to do so.

Funds may apply for reporting fund status in advance or in arrears, subject to certain time limits. A fund, once granted reporting fund status, may rely on that status going forward subject to continued compliance with the reporting funds rules, which include making reports as described above for each period of account. A fund may exit the reporting funds regime on giving notice and there are rules that permit HMRC to exclude a fund from the regime for serious breaches or a number of minor breaches, subject to an appeals process.

There is a list of funds that come within the definition of an offshore fund and have successfully applied for reporting fund status on HMRC's website. The list is updated on a monthly basis and can be found at hmrc.gov.uk/collective/reportingfundlist.pdf.

5.1.2 Non-Reporting Funds

A non-reporting fund is any offshore entity that falls within the definition of an offshore fund but has not obtained reporting fund status (or has left or been excluded from the reporting fund regime) – that is to say, an offshore fund to which Part 3 of the Offshore Fund (Tax) Regulations 2009, which deals with reporting funds, does not apply.

Non-reporting funds are under no obligation to provide information to HMRC but it is likely that such a fund will be obliged by local law or by its constitution to provide information to investors in respect of income arising to the fund. Although it is expected that they would provide details of distributions as a matter of routine to UK investors, it is the responsibility of investors to otherwise obtain and record such information.

5.1.3 Taxation of Offshore Funds

Offshore funds assume one of two structures. The taxation of the individual investor, who has an interest or stakeholding in an offshore fund, will depend upon the status of the fund, known as reporting and non-reporting funds respectively.

Offshore investment fund companies mainly market open-ended equity, fixed-interest, money market and currency funds. The main European offshore centres are Luxembourg, Dublin, the Channel Islands and the Isle of Man.

Offshore funds are either reporting or non-reporting funds.

The Uses and Tax Benefits of Offshore Funds

Offshore pooled investments may be useful for those who require a wider choice of funds than is available onshore. Offshore funds are particularly attractive to investors who wish to use currency funds or hedge funds.

A fixed-interest fund with reporting status may be useful for a non-taxpayer. Earnings will be invested in a fixed-interest fund which is rolling up tax-free and the investor will receive a gross dividend. In the case of a non-reporting fund, the taxpayer will pay no tax while the income is rolling up.

If a higher rate taxpayer can take encashment when their status will have fallen to basic rate status, the postponement of the encashment will provide a clear tax advantage.

The non-reporting fund may be useful for a UK resident who is anticipating retiring abroad. The investor can 'roll up' the investment tax-free and then encash it when no longer a UK resident and subject to UK tax. The tax treatment of the encashment needs to be examined in relation to the tax code operating in the country in which residence is established.

6. Charges and Pricing of Collective Investment Schemes

Learning Objective

5.1.6 Analyse the charges and pricing of collective investments: initial, annual, exit and performance fee charging structures; single pricing; bid/offer pricing; dilution levies; forward pricing

6.1 Initial, Annual, Exit and Performance Fee Charging Structures (Open-Ended Funds)

All of the parties involved in the operation of a fund will seek payment for their services. Payment may be on the basis of a percentage of the size of the fund, per transaction, a fixed fee per annum or on the basis of expenditure claimed for specific work undertaken.

Before moving on to how a fund is priced, we will briefly look at those fees charged by the manager (unit trust) or **authorised corporate director (ACD)** of an open-ended fund. Remember that other parties – custodians, advisers and the like – will also be levying fees.

The manager/ACD is entitled to:

- the **initial charge** (also sometimes known as the front-end load, or preliminary charge) – this is applied to subscriptions for shares or units by investors and may be added to the NAV per share or included in the unit subscription price

- the **exit charge** – taken from investors when they sell their units or shares. This may also be called a back-end load. This charge is generally levied instead of an initial charge. It is used as an incentive to encourage investors to stay in the fund. Exit charges are deducted from the bid price of the shares/units, and paid by the investor at sale. Exit charges are usually staggered and are often reduced for every year that the investor remains invested in the fund – eg, 5% if the investor sells in the first year, 4% for the second year, and so on
- the **annual management charge** or **management fee** – deducted periodically from the value of the fund and usually a fixed percent of its net asset value. A typical figure might be between 0.5% and 1.5% per annum of the value of the fund. For example, if a fund is valued at £25 million the quarterly management fee will be:

$$£25m \times 1\% \times 13/52 = £62,500.00$$

In addition, certain types of fund – typically those aimed at the more sophisticated and/or wealthy investor – may carry additional performance fees. These reward the manager or adviser with an additional percentage-based fee if they outperform a specified benchmark. Performance fee structures can be complicated and there are a variety of ways of calculating them – each fairer to the investor in certain circumstances. In addition, they are usually stated to be payable only on net new highs – that is, the manager will not be rewarded if the fund falls in value and their 'outperformance' consists of simply regaining ground that was lost. This is often referred to as the 'high-water mark'.

Before the RDR, repeat or trail commissions were becoming increasingly commonplace. This allowed agents to be rewarded for giving their clients ongoing investment advice and, potentially, keeping them invested in a management group's funds, rather than simply receiving introductory commissions when monies are introduced. The manager paid this to the introducing agent out of their annual management fee. The trail commissions were of the order of 0.5% of the value of the investment fund and were usually paid by the provider.

The Retail Distribution Review (RDR) came into effect on 31 December 2012 and it addressed the long-standing problem of bias in advice given by financial advisers to their retail clients. The most significant reform introduced by the RDR is the ban on commission paid by product providers to advisers in exchange for distributing their financial products. Hence, trail commission and initial fees were phased out with the implementation of the RDR. The adviser commission-based charging system was replaced by a fee-based advisory charges system.

Post-RDR, there can now be no commission paid to advisers of UK retail clients. Every authorised retail financial adviser needs to have in place a charging structure that will need to be clearly understood and agreed by a UK retail client. From 2013, adviser payment for advisory services must be agreed and met directly by clients without any influence from product providers. The UK regulator calls this 'adviser charging'. The sorts of charging structures can take a number of forms from a fixed fee or hour rate to a proportional fee based on the percentage of amount invested. These up-front fees, together with ongoing charges (monthly or annual fees), are permissible if the adviser is offering an ongoing service.

As a consequence of the RDR impact, many UCITS and other retail funds produced 'RDR-ready' share classes. A common feature of these products was that the management fee had been reduced to remove the expense of the commission charges that were originally paid to advisers on tied products. Typically, 0.75% is the new lower management fee charged on such funds.

In this regard, there is EU-wide legislation where the payment of commissions by fund providers to advisers is subject to changes as well. The Markets in Financial Instruments (MiFID II) Directive aims to widen the scope and ban firms that provide investment advice on an independent basis or which provide portfolio management services from receiving third party commissions linked to these types of services. The MiFID II Directive covers services provided to both professional clients as well as retail clients.

The MiFID II Directive was approved (in a revised form) by the European Parliament on 26 October 2012. It bans acceptance of commission in relation to advice or portfolio management services, but only when the firm has informed the client that the advice given is on an independent basis. The draft directive moves to the European Council for approval and is expected to be fully implemented by 3 January 2018.

6.2 Pricing

6.2.1 Single Pricing (Open-Ended Funds)

Open-ended funds may be single-priced or dual-priced.

For single-priced funds, the manager/ACD will calculate a single price for the shares/units, which will apply to all transactions in that dealing period. The UK regulator lays down rules as to how this should be carried out, and the manager/ACD must abide by these rules and any additional rules that it sets out in the fund's offering documents.

It does this by valuing the fund net of liabilities and dividing this figure by the number of shares in issue to give the NAV per share.

For many single-priced funds, the manager may apply an initial charge to compensate for the costs of administration.

6.2.2 Dual Pricing (Bid/Offer Prices) (Open-Ended Funds)

As an alternative to single pricing, open-ended funds may be dual-priced – that is, the manager shows a bid and an offer price for shares/units in the fund. Again, the FCA lays down rules for authorised funds on how this must be done.

The bid price is the price which investors will receive if they sell their units/shares back to the fund. It is based on the NAV of the fund.

The offer price is the price investors will have to pay if they buy units/shares. It is also based on the NAV of the fund.

The difference between the bid and the offer price is known as the bid-offer spread.

Investment Products

6.2.3 Dilution Levies (Open-Ended Funds)

The dilution levy is also known as the dealing charge. It is a charge which may be imposed by the manager to cover dealing costs. Dilution describes the reduction in the capital of a fund due to dealing costs, including market spread of the underlying investments. Dilution only affects single-priced funds since the dual-price system includes dealing costs and spreads in the calculation of the bid and offer prices.

The dilution levy might be better known as an anti-dilution levy; it represents an amount that the fund manager may decide to charge on the purchase or disposal of shares. It is designed to ensure that existing investors do not suffer costs associated with inflows/outflows resulting from other investors subscribing for or redeeming shares. The manager will assess the costs and will estimate what, if any, levy is applicable. They are not obliged to apply a dilution levy, but the policy must be stated in the fund documentation so that investors know what to expect.

The important factor is consistency – application to all deals, those above a certain value or portion of the portfolio. Typical levies are in the order of 0.2%.

6.2.4 Forward and Historic Pricing (Open-Ended Funds)

Open-ended funds are dealt in at prices based on their NAV – but the NAV as calculated at what point, exactly? This can matter a great deal, since the prices of the underlying investments of the fund may themselves be very volatile. This could mean that the price of units/shares in a fund is very different at the start of the day and at the close of business.

Consequently, fund managers may have a policy to value funds on a forward pricing basis – and a policy on the cut-off time – or on a historic pricing basis (and again what the relevant cut-off times are).

Forward pricing – a forward basis means that orders are taken from investors, and the prices at which they deal are determined at the next valuation point. This may mean that the investor is dealing blind as they do not know the actual price at which they are dealing.

Historic pricing – here the managers will deal the last valuation price. The main benefit is that investors know the price they are dealing at. There are, however, circumstances in which the unit trust managers who normally deal on a historic basis may choose to deal on a forward basis. These are:

- the managers believe that the fund value has moved by more than 2% in either direction
- the investor requests a forward price
- the managers may choose to deal on a forward basis on large deals.

Under the FCA's COLL 6.3.3 *'the authorised fund manager must carry out a fair and accurate valuation of all the scheme property in accordance with the instrument constituting the fund and the prospectus'*.

Fund managers are, therefore, required to document the methodology they use to determine the value of the underlying assets, including their 'fair value' when no market valuation is available.

6.2.5 Premiums and Discounts (Investment Trusts Only)

Remember, shares in investment trusts are not priced directly in relation to the fund's NAV; rather, because they are traded on the stock market, they are priced in accordance with investor demand.

NAV is calculated as an open-ended fund but an investment trust will trade at either a premium (above NAV) or a discount (below NAV) depending on the performance of the share price. This is shown in newspapers alongside the share price to give investors full disclosure.

The discount or premium is calculated as a percentage so the investor can see how much the investment trust's current share price is as a percentage of the investment trust's actual NAV per share.

7. Exchange-Traded Funds (ETFs) and Exchange-Traded Commodities (ETCs)

Learning Objective

5.2.1 Understand the main types, purposes, underlying structure, common investment characteristics and behaviours of: exchange-traded funds (ETFs); exchange-traded commodities (ETCs)

5.2.2 Analyse the relative merits and limitations of investing in exchange-traded funds (ETFs) or exchange-traded commodities (ETCs) compared with other forms of direct and indirect investment, in terms of: risk; return; physical v synthetic; tax treatment; turnover, liquidity and access; expenses – transaction and ongoing; management and administration

7.1 Exchange-Traded Funds (ETFs)

Exchange-traded funds (ETFs) are a relatively new type of open-ended fund. They have proved popular in the US, and are increasing in popularity in the UK. Like tracker funds, they follow the performance of an index closely (though some tracking error may occur). An increasing range of ETFs is available, tracking a variety of indices. For example, they may track a general share price index (eg, the FTSE 100 Index in the UK, or the S&P 500 Index in the US) or sub-sectors of the market (eg, pharmaceuticals, or energy stocks).

ETFs are quoted in real time – ie, traded throughout the day in line with the underlying index. This sets them apart from other types of index-tracking fund. In addition, they have relatively low charges and are not subject to stamp duty.

ETFs are equally available to all investors, that is to say smaller individual investors and large institutions alike. There is not usually any leverage within an ETF. This means that the fund cannot borrow to increase its exposure to the marketplace. Accordingly, £100 invested will typically represent £100 value of equity exposure.

The liquidity of an ETF relates to the liquidity of the underlying basket of shares. Large orders will usually often be transacted within the visible market price even when volume is low.

The ETF trades at a price that is very close to the exact value of the underlying stocks. The mechanism for creating new shares and redeeming old shares will prevent sustained premiums and discounts from occurring. Unlike other collective investment schemes, exchange-traded funds do not include charges within their secondary market pricing mechanism. The share price will reflect the underlying value of stocks and market movement.

Furthermore, since most funds are registered offshore, an investor will not be liable to pay stamp duty under current regulations. The costs involved within an ETF are exceptionally low. The costs of passive management are small and the administration/custodial charges are available to large funds at very competitive rates. Much of the expense of the investment process is external to the fund – ie, broker commission and savings plan costs.

To fully appreciate the risks associated with ETFs, it is necessary to understand the difference between the two forms: physical and synthetic. Although both track the performance of a security or basket of securities, physical ETFs own the underlying assets whereas synthetic ETFs do not.

Synthetic ETFs gain their exposure using derivative contracts, such as total return swaps, which they negotiate with third party investment banks or counterparties. The ETF provider uses investor cash to purchase securities and create a collateral basket. It then offers the return earned on this collateral to the counterparty, in exchange for a payment equal to the return achieved by the securities that it wishes to track. This strategy presents two risks to investors: the ability of the third party to fulfil their financial obligations, and the quality of the collateral held in the basket. Failure of the counterparty in this scenario would affect their ability to make the required payments to the ETF, while holding poor quality or illiquid securities as collateral could prevent the ETF provider from returning capital to investors.

Although physical ETFs may imply greater security, the low margins earned by most ETF providers have led to an increase in stock-lending activities, when the ETF lends out its underlying securities to counterparties in exchange for a fee. Fees earned in this way represent an additional return to the ETF which is then shared between the provider and the investor, thereby boosting the return for all. However, stock lending introduces similar counterparty and collateral risks to those discussed earlier. Failure of the counterparty in this example would affect the ability of the ETF to recover the stock that had been lent. The ETF would then be forced to call on collateral offered by the counterparty in order to access capital equal to the value of the securities borrowed. Again, if the quality of the collateral is poor or illiquid, investor capital may be at risk.

ETF arbitrage using high-frequency trading strategies exploits the price differential between the ETF shares and the price of the underlying securities. It is a key aspect of how ETFs function and this form of arbitrage serves to keep ETF share prices close to the price of the underlying securities. The increase in ETF arbitrage using high-frequency trading strategies has also meant that the decision over whether to opt for synthetic ETFs over fully replicated, or vice versa, is no longer as clear cut.

	Price	Dealing
Unit Trusts	Advantage Subscribers buy units of scheme assets at around the NAV	Disadvantage Historic pricing/paper processing/administration in hands of single counterparty/slow settlement
Investment Trusts	Advantage Dealing and settlement are transparent, electronic and customer-friendly – effectively they trade like stocks	Disadvantage Investors do not buy in or sell out at prices that directly reflect the value of the scheme assets due to premiums and discounts
ETFs	Advantage Easy to deal just like a stock except no stamp duty	Disadvantage Narrow range of investments compared to mutual funds

Let us consider the underlying structure of an ETF closely. ETFs are investment products created by institutional investors. Barclay's Global Investors have long been a market leader in the ETF market using the brand name iShares, which has operated under the Blackrock name following a merger with Barclays in 2009. The firm provides a wide array of ETFs in equities, bonds and some commodity asset classes and for more information on full product listings offered by the provider, visit iShares.com.

Unlike traditional mutual funds, ETFs do not sell or redeem their shares at the quoted NAV (priced only once every day at the close). Like ordinary shares, ETFs can be traded continuously through the day. Further, ETFs can be sold short or purchased on margin. ETFs are considerably cheaper than mutual funds and do not have the same complexities related to loads and expenses as in mutual funds. Investors buy and sell their ETF shares via a broker and not directly through the fund provider. Broker fees will be paid, but this will be considerably less than the management fee levied in a mutual fund. Consequently, the expense ratios of ETFs are much lower than mutual funds.

Let us first examine the role of the ETF, the large institutional investor and creation units. Assume that we wish to create an ETF that is a FTSE 100 Index tracker. First an institutional investor will deposit a basket of their transferable securities with an ETF. This basket of securities will represent part or a whole portion of stocks coming from the FTSE 100 Index. Other institutional investors will also deposit their securities until the scope of this ETF fund is broad enough to mirror the composition of the FTSE 100 index. In exchange for the basket of securities deposited by the institutional investors, the ETF will provide to each institutional investor, depository receipts in the form of a large block of creation units (often 50,000 units, for example) written under the ETF's name. Each creation unit's performance will effectively mimic the performance of the basket of securities the large investor has placed in trust with the ETF (FTSE 100 index in our example).

Next let us look at the role of the creation unit and an ETF share in the secondary market. Some or all of the ETF's creation units that the institutional investor holds are then sold off on the stock exchange in secondary market trades as ETF shares. This now permits other investors to have opportunities to purchase individual ETF shares that represent a pro rata ownership of the underlying securities that the ETF company holds in trust.

Investment Products

Investors who want to sell their ETF shares have two options:

1. Sell their shares to other investors in the secondary market for cash.
2. Sell the creation units back to the ETF. Institutional investors who wish to redeem their creation units will not receive cash but will instead get back on a pro rata basis their entitlement to the pool of underlying basket of securities held by the ETF. Further the institutional investors can also acquire more creation units if they want by depositing more securities with the ETF.

ETFs like any other investment company will have a prospectus. Investors who purchase creation units will receive a prospectus. Before purchasing shares in an ETF, investors should carefully study all of the available information on that ETF product. ETFs have annual operating expenses and any other shareholder fees that may be relevant disclosed in the prospectus.

7.1.1 Primary Versus Secondary Market

The ETF structure enables authorised participants in the ETF to create new units in the fund at NAV whenever necessary. This is done in large size, typically worth more than £1 million, with a creation basket usually to satisfy demand. The equities within this basket are in the precise proportions of their existing weight in the index. New ETF units are thereby created and available to investors within the secondary market. ETFs generally trade at a price very close to their NAV, eliminating opportunities for arbitrage.

7.2 Exchange-Traded Commodities (ETCs)

An exchange-traded commodity (ETC) is like an ETF except that it tracks the performance of an underlying commodity or basket of commodities.

ETCs work on exactly the same principle as ETFs – with the ETC tracking the performance of a single underlying commodity or a basket of commodities.

ETCs offer investors a number of advantages over both shares and futures – without the associated vagaries of trading an individual stock or the dramatic risk inherent in futures trading. Benefits include:

- **direct exposure to the commodities markets** – where the value of the investment will rise and fall in direct proportion to the price of the underlying commodity
- **liquidity** – ETCs are open-ended securities, which are created and redeemed on demand. This means that the supply of ETCs is unlimited and that price changes will accurately mirror developments in the price of the underlying commodity
- **stamp duty and CGT** – ETCs are generally registered offshore, so trades are exempt from stamp duty. Furthermore, ETCs can be traded within ISA accounts, allowing investors to shelter profit from CGT. They are generally considered as having distributor status coming under CGT rules
- **low dealing costs** – ETCs are traded on the regular stock exchange, making them both accessible and affordable
- **portfolio diversification** – ETCs give broad representation across individual or collective commodity types.

8. Tax-Efficient Savings

Learning Objective

5.4.1 Analyse the key features, restrictions and tax treatment of ISAs, junior ISAs and child trust funds (CTFs): eligibility; eligible investments; subscriptions and additional subscriptions; transfers; withdrawals; use in investment and tax planning

8.1 Individual Savings Accounts (ISAs)

ISAs are tax-assisted savings vehicles. They are not strictly investments in their own right. Providing that the rules are complied with, all returns generated within an ISA are free of CGT and income taxes. This means that gains generated within the ISA roll up at a faster rate than they would for a similar investment not held within an ISA.

ISAs can hold cash in the form of UK and European bank deposits; building society deposits; cash unit trusts; or stocks and shares, such as unit trusts (other than cash unit trusts); shares in investment trusts; shares listed on a recognised stock exchange; and bonds and gilts.

The annual ISA investment allowance for the 2017–18 tax year is £20,000 and can be invested in a cash ISA, a stocks and shares ISA, an Innovative Finance ISA, or any combination of these.

- Those aged between 16 and 18 are restricted to cash only, and can invest up to £20,000 in 2017–18. It is also possible to transfer cash ISAs to stocks and shares ISAs and vice versa.

ISAs are only available to people who are UK-resident and ordinarily resident (see chapter 4). In order to subscribe, the investor must be:

- aged 18 years or over (stocks and shares)
- aged 16 years or over (cash).

ISAs, once established, can usually be transferred from one provider to another; however, there are generally charges involved. In addition, not all providers cater to all the classes of underlying investment, so the investor should check that they will be able to maintain their investments before initiating a transfer.

Junior ISAs are individual savings accounts for children. The accounts offer parents a tax-free way of saving for children who do not have a child trust fund (CTF). They were launched on 1 November 2011. Children can have a junior ISA if they are under 18 years of age, live in the UK and do not already have a CTF. For CTFs see section 8.2. Each child can have one cash and one stocks and shares junior ISA at any one time.

Anyone can put money into a junior ISA and the total limit is £4,128 per year. There is no tax to pay on interest or gains. The money belongs to the child and they can't take this out until they are 18 years of age. If investment in the junior ISA is continued beyond the age of 18, then it will convert to a conventional ISA.

8.1.1 Lifetime ISAs

In April 2017, Lifetime ISAs were introduced.

Individuals are able to save up to £4,000 a year into the lifetime ISA either as a lump sum or by saving on a regular basis. At the end of the tax year, HMRC will add a 25% bonus on top. So, if £1,000 is saved, the individual will have £1,250, and if the full £4,000 is saved, the individual will have £5,000. This is before interest or growth.

Important rules to consider:

- The bonus is paid until the individual reaches age 50.
- The bonus is paid annually at the end of each tax year and, once in the individual's account, will count as the individual's money. Therefore, individuals will be paid interest on it too.
- The maximum bonus an individual could receive is £32,000 (unless the rules change). To do this, an individual will need to open a lifetime ISA on their 18th birthday and continue contributing the maximum of £4,000 each year until the age of 50.

Savings and the bonus can be used towards a deposit on a first home worth up to £450,000 across the country.

Accounts are limited to one per person rather than one per home – so two first-time buyers can both receive a bonus when buying together.

Individuals with a help to buy ISA can transfer those savings into the lifetime ISA in 2017, or continue saving into both – however, individuals will only be able to use the bonus from one to buy a house.

After a 60th birthday, individuals can take out all the savings tax-free. The money can be withdrawn at any time before turning 60, but the government bonus (and any interest or growth on this) will be lost. A 5% charge will also be payable.

8.1.2 Flexible ISAs

A flexible ISA offers the ability to withdraw and replace money in an ISA. As with all tax-related products, there are rules that must be followed.

Replacement payments will not count towards the annual subscription limit (unless you pay in more than previously withdrawn). This flexibility will be available in relation to both current year and earlier year ISA savings where provided for in the terms and conditions of a flexible ISA, but will be subject to conditions, in certain cases, regarding which ISA providers can accept replacement amounts. ISA providers can offer this flexibility for cash ISAs and also for cash that is held in stocks and shares ISAs.

8.1.3 Help to Buy ISAs

A Help to Buy ISA for first-time buyers became available from 1 December 2015 and offers a government bonus when investors use their savings to purchase their first home. They count as a type of cash ISA and if used, investors forgo their right to subscribe to a cash ISA.

- For every £200 that a first-time buyer saves, there will be a £50 bonus payment up to a maximum of £3,000 on £12,000 of savings. The maximum initial deposit will be £1,000 and the maximum monthly saving thereafter will be £200.
- The bonus will be available for purchases of homes of up to £450,000 in London and up to £250,000 elsewhere. The bonus will only apply for home purchase.
- Savers will have access to their own money and will be able to withdraw funds from their account if they need them for any purpose.

The Help to Buy ISA will be open for new savers until 30 November 2019, and open to new contributions until 2029.

8.1.4 Innovative Finance ISAs

In April 2016, the Innovative Finance ISA was introduced. This ISA covers P2P lending, where lenders are matched with borrowers so each enjoys better rates and will mean those lending through P2P platforms will be able to get their interest tax-free.

The Innovative Finance ISA is available to any UK taxpayer aged 18 or over and individuals are only permitted to hold one Innovative Finance ISA account each tax year.

Investors can invest can invest any amount up to the £20,000 limit (2017–18). Although investors can invest more than £20,000 into the P2P lending sector, only the first £20,000 per year will be eligible to be in an Innovative Finance ISA.

8.2 Child Trust Funds (CTFs)

Child trust funds (CTFs) are discontinued, although minors and adolescents holding the accounts can continue to invest in these accounts until they reach 18 years of age. They were originally created to encourage parents to save for their child's future. The government's intention was that when the child reached 18, they would have some money to give them a start to life as an adult. At 18, they could carry on saving or use the money for other things – such as driving lessons or training courses.

As of 1 January 2011, all government contributions to CTFs were stopped. Babies born after this date were ineligible to open CTF accounts and their savings were directed into junior ISA investments Although no new accounts could be opened after that date, existing accounts were allowed to continue until the beneficiaries reached their 18th birthday. This meant that further contributions would continue to be allowed by parents, family and friends into the account subject to a maximum limit of £4,128 per annum per account. Since April 2015, it has been possible to transfer CTFs to junior ISAs.

The main characteristics of CTFs were as follows:

- CTFs were a long-term savings and investment account that was available to children born on or after 1 September 2002.
- Money invested in a CTF belonged to the named child and savings could not be withdrawn until the child turned 18.
- CTFs had the same tax rules as cash ISAs – there was no tax liability on any interest or gains made on the money/savings and accrued interest held in the CTF.

- At 16, the child was able to manage their CTF account, for example by deciding to change provider or type of account.
- At 18, young people with CTF accounts were able to decide for themselves how best to use the money.
- CTFs were treated in the same way as ISAs in respect of tax benefits.

Providers offered up to three forms of CTF account: a savings account, an account that invested in shares, or a stakeholder account. The savings account was a deposit account and offered a secure type of investment, but one whose value was affected by inflation. The accounts that invested in shares offered the potential for growth, but carried the risk of falling values. The stakeholder accounts invested in shares, but the government had set certain rules to reduce risk – in particular, when the child reached the age of 13, the money started to be moved from shares into safer investments.

Other types of account were also available, such as Sharia'a accounts and ethical accounts.

The first CTF accounts will mature in 2020, and if the child does not take the money out it will automatically roll over into an ISA on maturity. The aim is to encourage young people to maintain a savings habit into adulthood.

8.3 Investment Bonds

The range of investment options to which investment bonds can be linked is as broad as what the insurance company is willing to offer. For the types of bonds available, see section 9.

Investment bonds are not a type of tax wrapper in the way that ISAs are; they are a product in their own right, being an insurance product with investment benefits, which happens to have tax benefits owing to the way insurance policies are treated.

Gains on these policies are subject to income tax at the policy owner's marginal rate and are calculated at the point of what is deemed to be a chargeable event, ie, full and partial surrenders, the death of the assured, or the maturity of the policy.

The insurance fund in which the premiums are invested is subject to tax – levied on the life company, currently at a rate of 20%. In this way, the taxation of the product differs from that of many other investments; since the life company has already paid tax, there is no personal liability for basic rate taxpayers to income tax or CGT on any gains arising from investment in the policy.

Policyholders can withdraw up to 5% of their original premium annually (and this is cumulative – ie, if it is not used one year it can be carried forward to later years) for the first 20 years – that is, until 100% of the premium invested has been returned to the policyholder. This is treated as a return of capital.

For higher rate and additional rate taxpayers, there may be a liability to tax on withdrawals or encashment. This liability is calculated by reference to the chargeable gain on the policy. Chargeable gains are calculated as follows:

- If partial withdrawals have been made from the policy, then the chargeable gain is calculated as at the end of the relevant policy year, at the point when they can be totalled. The chargeable gain is the sum by which the total withdrawals in the period exceed the allowance available (ie, 5% for the current year plus any unused allowances from previous years, carried forward).

- When the policy is finally encashed, the total value at that point is added to the total of any withdrawals made previously. From this sum the initial premium invested is deducted, plus any previous chargeable gain. The net result is the final chargeable gain.

This sum is taxable as if it were an addition to the policyholder's income. However, since the life company has already paid income tax on the life fund, it is given a tax credit as though basic rate tax had already been withheld. Thus, it is only higher rate or additional rate taxpayers (or basic rate taxpayers whose income is taken into the higher rate bracket by the chargeable gain) who have any further liability.

If the latter happens, and the addition of a chargeable gain to a policyholder's income takes them over the threshold into the higher rate band, then a principle known as top slicing can be used to mitigate the ensuing tax liability. With top slicing, the chargeable gain is divided by the number of relevant years, to produce an average gain. This is treated as the top slice of income in the tax year in which the gain actually arises. If any tax is payable on that top slice, it is then multiplied by the number of relevant years, and the result is the total arising income tax liability.

In the 2016 Budget, the government announced that it would carry out an evaluation of the taxation of life assurance bonds in an effort to simplify their taxation.

8.4 National Savings & Investments

Learning Objective

5.5.1 Analyse the key features, restrictions and tax treatment of National Savings & Investments, premium bonds and investments: use in investment and tax planning

As covered in chapter 1, section 1.7.1, National Savings & Investments (NS&I) products are offered by the government and, as such, are regarded as risk-free investments. Some NS&I products are available through post offices.

NS&I is an executive agency of the Chancellor of the Exchequer, and is accountable to the Treasury. It provides deposit and savings products to the investing public, and in doing so raises funds on behalf of the UK government. An investor holding an NS&I product is in essence lending to the government.

NS&I offers a wide range of products, from easy-access savings accounts to longer-term investments and, of course, premium bonds. As the products are underwritten by the government, they are regarded as effectively free from the risk of default. None of NS&I's products are subject to CGT, but some products are subject to income tax.

As covered in chapter 1, the following are a few of its key products:

Savings Accounts

NS&I offers a range of products aimed at savers, including the following:

- **Investment account** – from 21 May 2012, this became a postal-only account. Originally, it was a 'passbook'-style savings account. The authority will keep investors informed by sending transaction records and an annual statement. It pays variable rates, tiered interest rates and has no set term. The minimum deposit is £20 and the maximum £1 million. Interest is taxable and paid gross.

- **Direct saver account** – this account offers the convenience of being able to manage accounts online or by phone. Interest rates are variable, taxable and paid gross. The minimum investment is £1 with an upper limit of £2 million per person.

Income-Providing Products

NS&I's products aimed at the investor who is seeking interest income include:

- **Guaranteed income bonds** – these provide a guaranteed monthly income. The minimum holding is £500 and the maximum total holding £1 million. The bonds are available for one-, three- and five-year terms. Interest is taxable and paid gross.
- **Income bonds** – these pay monthly income, and have no set term: the holder can withdraw their money without notice. Interest is variable, tiered, taxable and paid gross. The minimum holding is £500, and the maximum £1 million.

Growth Products

NS&I's growth schemes include the following. Although some are not available as new products, they have been included as they are still available for customers with maturing investments:

- **Index-linked savings certificates** – these pay a guaranteed return linked to the inflation rate as measured by RPI. The minimum holding is £100, and the maximum £15,000 per issue. Certificates can be bought for terms of either three or five years. Returns are tax-free. There are currently no new index-linked savings certificates available. These are available for customers with maturing investments.
- **Fixed-rate savings certificates** – these pay a fixed rate of return over a period of time, such as two and five years. The returns are guaranteed for the term and tax-free on maturity. The minimum holding is £100 and maximum £15,000 per issue. There are currently no new fixed-interest savings certificates available. These are available for customers with maturing investments.
- **Guaranteed growth bonds** – these provide a guaranteed return on your investment. The minimum holding is £500 and maximum £1,000,000. There is a choice of terms of one, three and five years, with access available before maturity subject to a loss of 90 days' interest. Interest is taxable and paid net. There are currently no new guaranteed growth bonds available. These are available for customers with maturing investments.
- **Investment guaranteed growth bonds** – available for investments up to £3,000 and paying 2.2% AER on a three-year term, these bonds are available until 10 April 2018.
- **65+ bonds** – often referred to in the press as 'pensioner bonds', these are a growth product available to those aged 65 and over. Although not currently available for new investment, existing holders earn interest on their capital for a fixed term, in the same way as guaranteed growth bonds. Interest is earned daily, and added on each anniversary. The minimum investment is £500 and the maximum £10,000 and capital can be accessed before maturity, subject to the loss of 90 days' interest. All interest is taxable and basic rate tax is deducted at source. There are currently no new 65+ bonds available. Customers with maturing investments can reinvest into a standard guaranteed growth bond.
- **Guaranteed equity bonds** – these also provide a guaranteed return on investments, linked to the performance of the FTSE 100 Index over a set term. If the FTSE 100 Index grows over the term, the investor will benefit from that growth. If it falls, they will still get back 100% of their original investment. As the FTSE 100 Index measures share prices only, the investor will not receive dividends. This may mean the investment may not achieve as high a return as a direct stock market investment. The returns on guaranteed equity bonds are subject to averaging and are liable to UK income tax on maturity. Although the capital is fully guaranteed, inflation may erode the real value of funds invested.

Tax-Free Products

Certain of NS&I's products provide returns free of tax. However the returns on these products are not generally high, also reflecting the fact that they are regarded as very safe. They include the following:

- **Premium bonds** – these carry no capital risk (the holder can withdraw their capital in full when they wish). Instead of earning interest, bonds are entered into a monthly draw in which they could win their holder up to £1 million (or one of many smaller amounts). The minimum holding is £100 (or £50 if investment is made by standing order) and the maximum is £50,000.
- **Direct ISA** – investors can pay a maximum of £20,000 in the 2017–18 tax year into NS&I's direct ISA, earning variable-rate interest on this free of income tax. There are no withdrawal restrictions.
- **Savings certificates** – NS&I offers a range of savings certificates, some paying fixed interest and others variable-rate interest.
- **Children's bonus bonds** – these run for a period of five years and offer a guaranteed rate of interest (paid daily) from the outset. The returns are tax-free with no tax liability to the parents. The minimum investment per issue is £25 and the maximum £3,000. A bonus payment is made on the fifth anniversary. Access is allowed during the term subject to loss of the bonus payment, and no interest is credited if the bond is cashed in during the first year.

9. UK Onshore and Offshore Life Assurance Company Products

Learning Objective

5.6.1 Analyse the key features, relative merits and limitations of investing in onshore and offshore life assurance-based investments compared with other forms of direct and indirect investment: risk; return; tax treatment (offshore, onshore); turnover, liquidity and access; expenses – transaction and ongoing; management and administration

It might seem odd to include financial products such as insurance policies and pensions in a chapter addressing investments. A professional investment manager would not generally use insurance and pensions products in a client's portfolio.

However, certain insurance and pensions products are regarded as investments, for technical and regulatory purposes. Further, if we are to consider investment planning for the private individual, we should certainly take account of the different investment risks of such products. For information on the tax treatment of investment bonds, see section 8.3.

We will consider those insurance policies and pensions which fall into the domain of investments.

9.1 The Main Types of Onshore Investment Bonds

9.1.1 Single Premium/Regular Premium Bonds

Life companies offer a wide range of products which can be used to provide protection benefits (ie, a payout if one or more particular individuals, the life assured, die). These are life assurance products, or life policies. Many of their products also fulfil other financial needs (providing a payout on the death of a policyholder). They may provide this return:

- at a set date (or earlier, if the life assured dies before this date), or
- they may simply run until either the individual dies or the policyholder redeems their policy.

Such policies may be single premium, or regular premium. With a single premium policy the policyholder (the investor) pays a one-off premium to the life company. Top-ups may be allowed depending on the terms of the policy.

Regular premium policies are paid for with a series of periodic premiums. These may be monthly, quarterly or annual. They may be the same sum or revised from time to time, again depending on the terms of the policy.

When applying for the policy, the policyholder will – if they are also the life assured – have to provide the life company with information about themselves, their lifestyle and health. (If someone else is to be the life assured, then their details will also be required.) This enables the life company to assess the risk of the life assured. It can then decide on what terms to issue the policy, what premium to ask for and indeed whether to proceed at all. This process of assessing the risk is called underwriting.

The benefits paid out on the death of the life assured, or maturity of the bond, or on encashment at the policyholder's request, will depend on the value of the policy at that time. Some policies pay out a guaranteed death benefit, but the maturity proceeds or early encashment value will depend on the value of the investments within the policy. It is therefore very important that the policyholder understands what sort of policy they have purchased. In this section you will see the word bond used; it does not have the same meaning as debt securities. It is, however, a promise to pay, on the part of the life company.

9.1.2 Unit-Linked Bonds

Here the premiums paid by the policyholder buy units in a fund run by the life company, or by an external institution with whom the life company has an arrangement (eg, a unit trust or OEIC). The value of the policy is measured in terms of the total number of units allocated to it, and the value of these units depends on the performance of the underlying investments.

The value of the bond generally fluctuates in line with the underlying investments. Generally, life companies offer a range of unit-linked options, with different risk profiles. These may include gilt or fixed-interest funds, UK equity funds, an international equity fund and other variants. In many cases the policy has no minimum maturity value; rather, its value is linked directly to the underlying funds.

In some cases the investor will need a minimum sum assured – for example, if the policy is being used as the repayment vehicle for an interest-only mortgage, a lender will require that the borrower covers the principal of the loan. This can be arranged through the purchase of appropriate life cover as a part of the policy. Unit-linked policies thus have no inherent basic sum assured; life cover is generally a built-in add-on to the policy.

In practice how this works is that the policyholder pays a monthly premium to the life company. The life company uses this to purchase units in the relevant underlying fund(s); and will also, on a monthly basis, cancel sufficient units to pay for any life cover needed. Life companies do not pay bonuses on unit-linked policies (as they do on with-profits policies); the maturity value is linked solely to the value of units, which may fall as well as rise in value. There can thus be the risk that the policy does not pay out as much as was hoped; for example, it may not repay any associated mortgage loan at the end of its term. If this looks likely, the policyholder can increase their monthly premiums, or perhaps switch to a more appropriate linked fund.

9.1.3 With-Profits Bonds

With-profits endowments also offer a benefit payable at some future maturity date, or on the earlier death of the policyholder, or on encashment by the policyholder. The policyholder pays single or regular (usually monthly) premiums to the life company, which invests them in the markets with the aim of generating sufficient capital to pay the death/maturity benefits.

To achieve a return, the life office invests the premiums received from its many with-profits policyholders in the mix of investments it thinks is most appropriate. These include equities, debt securities, property and cash: in some cases it can also include other assets, such as holdings in hedge funds, foreign currencies and other alternative investments. The portfolio is generally constructed so as to avoid too high a degree of risk.

The policyholder receives a basic sum assured plus a share in any investment profits made by the life company. These profits are shared by way of bonuses: reversionary bonuses, which are added each year and which, once paid, cannot be withdrawn, and terminal bonuses, which are awarded on maturity or earlier death. The policy provides built-in life cover (which can be used to assure repayment of a mortgage in the case that the policyholder dies).

The return (by way of bonus) on a with-profits bond is 'smoothed' by the life company. That is, in years when the underlying portfolio performs well, the company will hold back some of the gains, and will allocate them to policyholders to boost their returns in years when performance is poor. Policyholders should experience lower volatility than with a regular investment.

With-profits policies may be unitised. Unitisation simplifies the life office's communication of performance, since a unit price can be published, so policyholders can monitor the growth in their investment. In addition, bonuses can be added by adding new units to a policyholder's account.

9.1.4 Distribution Bonds

Unit-linked bond funds generally do not treat income and capital separately. Returns from invested income are added to the price of units. If income is required, this can be provided by the regular encashment of units. However, distribution bonds do separate income and capital. In order to produce income, a distribution bond will invest in a mixture of gilts, fixed-interest securities, convertibles and high-yielding equities.

The difference between a distribution bond and an ordinary bond is that a distribution bond has a separate fund into which the income from the main fund is placed. The income in the separate fund can be distributed regularly, eg, quarterly or half-yearly. The advantage of this is that it allows investors to encash units representing just the income portion of the bond. All encashments, whether from income units or the main fund, are deemed by HMRC to be a return of the policyholder's original capital.

9.1.5 Tax Treatment of Onshore Bonds

Investment bonds have a different tax treatment to other investments. This can lead to some valuable tax planning opportunities. The fund that has issued the life assurance bonds has already been subject to tax at the basic rate. This means that fund income that is not already taxed in the UK, such as interest or property income, is taxed at the fund level at 20%. Similarly, capital gains are also subject to the same level of tax. Hence, any further proceeds from the bonds to investors do not carry personal liability to capital gains tax or income tax.

Essentially, note that an investor can withdraw up to 5% each year of the amount paid into the bond without paying any tax on it. This allowance is cumulative and any unused portion of the limit can be carried forward to the future. The maximum limit to this carry-over allowance is 100% of the amount paid into the bond. Higher rate taxpayers are liable for tax above the basic rate, but they can defer their withdrawals of up to 5% to a time when they retire and have a lower tax position.

However, advisers should bear in mind that certain events during the life of the bond may trigger a potential liability. Tax liability can arise if any of the following changeable events occur:

- Death.
- Transfer of legal ownership.
- Withdrawal of more than 5% of the annual allowance or cashing in part or the full value of the bond.

9.2 The Main Types of Offshore Investment Bonds

The following assets may be held within an offshore bond wrapper:

- cash deposits and money market funds
- equity, fixed interest or bond funds, but not direct equities
- capital guaranteed investments, or alternative investments such as hedge funds.

The main benefits of an offshore bond are:

- Income and growth accumulate within the bond free of income and capital gains tax.
- Withdrawals of up to 5% per annum may be made without incurring an immediate tax liability.

- The 5% allowance is cumulative and, if unused, may be carried forward to future years (and, therefore, may be taxable on redemption).
- Bonds may be gifted without crystallising a tax charge.
- Upon encashment of the bond, gains are subject to income tax only.
- Income tax is levied only at the investor's marginal tax rate in the year of encashment, potentially lowering the tax liability.
- They are suitable for an individual with a long-term investment horizon and a possible need for regular distributions.

Offshore bonds are offered in locations such as the Isle of Man, Dublin and Luxembourg. Offshore life companies may offer some variants such as the following:

9.2.1 Portfolio Bonds

These products are usually offered to wealthier investors. A personal portfolio bond allows a policyholder to select their own underlying investments, or perhaps to choose a particular fund manager to run the portfolio rather than buying units in the insurance company's various funds. In some cases, they may be able to use an existing portfolio of shares as the premium for the bond, although this may give rise to a charge to CGT.

The personal portfolio bond operates in all other respects exactly like a normal bond. However, the benefits paid on maturity, death or encashment depend on the value of the portfolio, rather than the value of units in which the bond is invested. Portfolio bonds are now rarely used by UK investors, as they are no longer tax-efficient. However, they are still available and used by investors resident overseas.

9.2.2 Capital Redemption Bonds

Capital redemption bonds are life company products without an insurance element – ie, there is no life assured. Instead they are used purely for investment purposes, and so they only pay out on the expiry of the bond or an early encashment by the policyholder.

9.2.3 Offshore Investment Bonds – Tax Treatment

As discussed in section 9.1.5, the tax on onshore bonds is already paid by the fund, but higher rate taxpayers may have a tax liability above the basic rate of tax. Offshore bonds are located in offshore locations such as Dublin or in the Channel Islands. These products offer growth on their funds that is largely free from any tax.

10. Private Equity

Learning Objective

5.7.1 Understand the main types, purposes, structures, tax treatment and investment characteristics of private equity funds

Private equity funds typically invest in companies which are not listed on a stock exchange. Investors are typically more sophisticated and/or wealthy and can accept the additional risks of this type of investment.

Typically, private equity fund managers take an active role in the management of the companies they invest in – perhaps having a majority shareholding and/or a seat on the board. They look to add value for their investors by transforming the way the investee company is managed, and may aim to make their money by floating the company on the stock market again after a few years, once the company's performance has been improved.

There is a wide spectrum of activities carried out by a private equity firm. They can invest in early stage ventures, such as seed capital and start-ups, and expansion of early-stage investments and buyouts. Venture capital investment is more speculative than buyouts because buyout targets are established with firms with a track record of operating in fairly well-defined markets.

The basic types of private equity and venture funds include:

- bootstrap funding
- venture capital
- leveraged buyouts (LBOs)
- mezzanine finance
- growth
- crowdfunding
- secondaries
- equity co-investment.

Financial bootstrapping is a term used to cover different methods for avoiding using the financial resources of external investors. Bootstrapping can be defined as a means to minimise the amount of outside debt and equity financing needed from banks and investors. The use of private credit card debt is the most known form of bootstrapping, but a wide variety of methods are available for entrepreneurs. While bootstrapping involves a risk for the founders, the absence of any other stakeholder gives the founders more freedom to develop the company.

Venture capital (also known as VC or venture) is typically provided to early-stage, high-potential, growth companies in the interest of generating a return through an eventual realisation event such as an initial public offering (IPO) or trade sale of the company. Venture capital investments are generally made as cash in exchange for shares in the invested company. Venture capital typically comes from institutional investors and high net worth individuals and is pooled together by dedicated investment firms.

A venture capitalist is a person or investment firm that makes venture investments. These venture capitalists are expected to bring managerial and technical expertise as well as capital to their investments. A venture capital fund refers to a pooled investment vehicle (often a limited partnership or limited liability company) that primarily invests the financial capital of third-party investors in enterprises that are too risky for the standard capital markets or bank loans.

Venture capital is most attractive for new companies with limited operating history that are too small to raise capital in the public markets and are too immature to secure a bank loan or complete a debt offering. In exchange for the high risk that venture capitalists assume by investing in smaller and less mature companies, venture capitalists usually have significant control over company decisions, in addition to a significant portion of the company's ownership (and consequently value).

Leveraged buyouts involve financial sponsors or private equity firms making large acquisitions without committing all the capital required for the acquisition. To do this, a financial sponsor will raise acquisition debt which is ultimately secured upon the acquisition target and also looks to the cash flows of the acquisition target to make interest and principal payments. Acquisition debt in an LBO is therefore usually non-recourse to the financial sponsor and to the equity fund that the financial sponsor manages. Furthermore, unlike in a hedge fund, where debt raised to purchase certain securities is also collateralised by the fund's other securities, the acquisition debt in an LBO has recourse only to the company purchased in a particular LBO transaction.

Therefore, an LBO transaction's financial structure is particularly attractive to a fund's limited partners, allowing them the benefits of leverage but greatly limiting the degree of recourse of that leverage. This kind of acquisition brings leverage benefits to an LBO's financial sponsor in two ways: the investor itself only needs to provide a fraction of the capital for the acquisition, and, assuming the economic internal rate of return on the investment (taking into account expected exit proceeds) exceeds the weighted average interest rate on the acquisition debt, the returns to the financial sponsor will be significantly enhanced.

Mezzanine capital, in finance, refers to a subordinated debt or preferred equity instrument that represents a claim on company's assets that is senior only to that of the common shares. Mezzanine financings can be structured either as debt (typically an unsecured and subordinated note) or preferred stock. Mezzanine capital often is a more expensive financing source for a company than secured debt or senior debt. The higher cost of mezzanine capital is the result of its place as an unsecured, subordinated (or junior) obligation in a company's capital structure (ie, in the event of default, the mezzanine financing is less likely to be repaid in full after all senior obligations have been satisfied).

Additionally, mezzanine financing, which is usually a private placement, is often used by smaller companies and may also involve greater overall leverage levels than issuers in the high-yield market and involve additional risk. In compensation for the increased risk, mezzanine debt holders will require a higher return for their investment than secured or other more senior lenders.

Growth capital (also 'expansion capital' and 'growth equity') is a type of private equity investment, most often a minority investment, in relatively mature companies that are looking for capital to expand or restructure operations, enter new markets or finance a significant acquisition without a change of control of the business.

Companies that seek growth capital often do so to finance a transformational event in their life cycle. These companies are likely to be more mature than venture capital-funded companies, able to generate revenue and operating profits but unable to generate sufficient cash to fund major expansions, acquisitions or other investments. Growth capital can also be used to effect a restructuring of a company's balance sheet, particularly to reduce the amount of leverage (or debt) the company has on its balance sheet.

Growth capital is often structured as either common equity or preferred equity, although certain investors will use various hybrid securities that include a contractual return (ie, interest payments) in addition to an ownership interest in the company. Often, companies that seek growth capital investments are not good candidates for additional borrowing, either because of the stability of the company's earnings or because of its existing debt levels.

In finance, the private equity secondary market (also often called private equity secondaries or secondaries) refers to the buying and selling of pre-existing investor commitments to private equity and other alternative investment funds. Sellers of private equity investments sell not only the investments in the fund but also their remaining unfunded commitments to the funds. By its nature, the private equity asset class is illiquid, intended to be a long-term investment for buy-and-hold investors. For the vast majority of private equity investments, there is no listed public market; however there is a robust and maturing secondary market available to sellers of private equity assets.

Driven by strong demand for private equity exposure, a significant amount of capital has been committed to dedicated secondary market funds from investors looking to increase and diversify their private equity exposure.

An equity co-investment (or co-investment) is a minority investment, made directly into an operating company, alongside a financial sponsor or other private equity investor, in a leveraged buyout, recapitalisation or growth capital transaction. In certain circumstances, venture capital firms may also seek co-investors. Private equity firms seek co-investors for several reasons. The most important of these is that co-investments allow a manager to make larger investments without either dedicating too much of the fund's capital to a single transaction (ie, exposure issues) or sharing the deal with competing private equity firms. Co-investors bring a friendly source of capital.

Typically, co-investors are existing limited partners in an investment fund managed by the lead financial sponsor in a transaction. Unlike the investment fund however, co-investments are made outside of the existing fund and, as such, co-investors rarely pay management fees or carried interest on an individual investment. Co-investments are a typically passive, non-controlling investment, as the private equity firm or firms involved will exercise control and perform monitoring functions.

For large private equity funds of funds and other investors, co-investments are a means of increasing exposure to attractive transactions and making investments that have a higher return potential because of the lower economics paid to the general partner. As a result, many private equity firms offer co-investments to their largest and most important investors as an incentive to invest in future funds.

Private equity firms are legally structured with limited liability partnerships (LLPs), made up of two classes of partners:

1. **General partners (GPs)**, or managing partners, have a great deal of technical experience and manage the entire private equity investment process, including the day-to-day management of the assets under their management. For specialist advice and services, GPs retain the services of advisory consultants for a fee. Typically, GPs will receive an annual management fee of about 1.5–2.5% per annum of the value of the fund. Further, they will charge an incentive fee of 20% of carried interest or profits made by the fund. The fee structure is often referred to as the 2–20 charges. The incentive fee will come in when the fund makes a profit that is greater than a hurdle rate.
2. **Limited partners (LPs)** are the investors in a private equity structure. Commit to providing funds on call, pay the annual management fee, and receive their share of the carried interest. They may be high net worth individuals, corporate investors, life assurance companies and pension funds who provide the pooled funding that is needed in a fund partnership.

The private equity funds raised from the LPs are invested by the GPs in a range of investment projects. Funds have a finite life of around ten years, which may be extended for another three years and at maturity, the fund is liquidated. LPs will receive their original principal investment plus the share of the profits that has not already been distributed over the life of the fund.

The private equity market has become crowded by hundreds of firms. To get in on the lucrative deals, hedge funds have also been visible in this expanding area of activity and in recent years, sovereign wealth funds (SWFs) have become an important source of private equity investment. SWFs are set up by governments of countries that have accumulated huge surplus reserves.

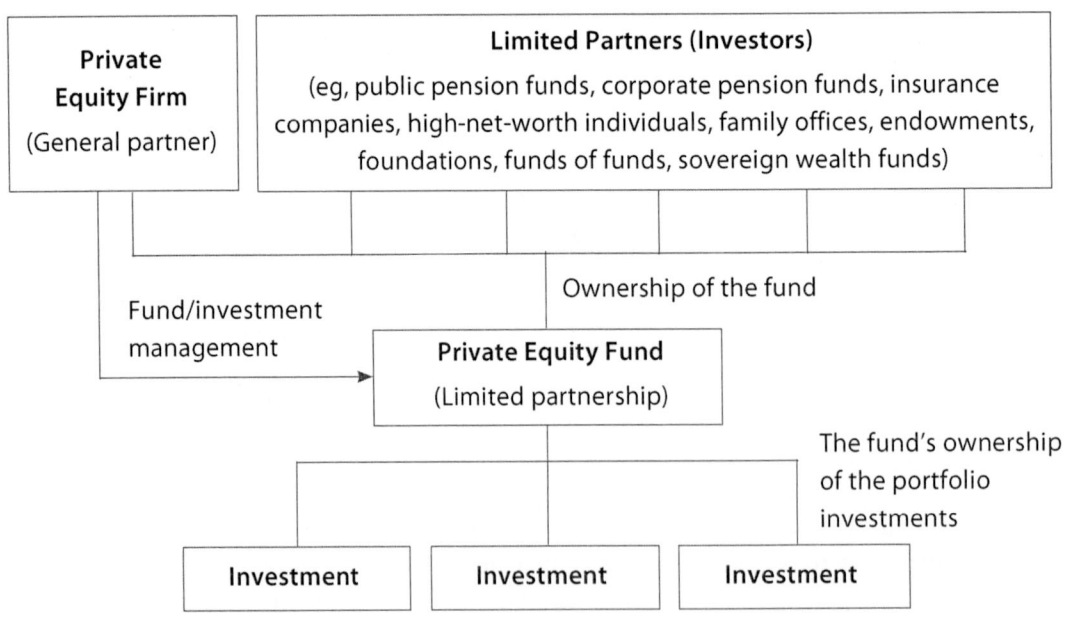

Source: upload.wikimedia.org/wikipedia/commons/a/a3/Private_Equity_Fund_Diagram.png

It should also be noted that within the UK, the management of an alternative fund or a private equity firm may operate under a different partnership setting. More specifically, the Limited Liability Partnerships Act 2000 (the 'Act') introduced a new entity called the English limited liability partnership in April 2009. Over time this has rapidly become the vehicle of choice for the UK-based managers of alternative funds. The LLP arrangement combines the flexibility of a partnership with separate legal personality and a favourable UK tax treatment.

An LLP is a hybrid form of business entity where the key managerial players in the organisation are identified as the members. It combines certain characteristics of a company (eg, limited liability and the status of a body corporate) with those of a partnership (eg, organisational flexibility, privacy and tax transparency).

LLPs are often used as joint venture vehicles, as the management vehicle for UK managers of private equity funds (and hedge funds) and increasingly as the most common structure for UK professional services firms.

An LLP has a legal personality separate from that of its members. An LLP has members rather than shareholders, directors or partners and the Act provides that each member of an LLP has power to bind the LLP.

An LLP has a number of advantages, including tax transparency, the status of a body corporate and the ability of members to take part in management of the business of the LLP.

There is the requirement for an LLP to file annual accounts at Companies House. Each member has limited liabilities under the LLP. In the ordinary course of business, the liability of a member of an LLP is limited to its contribution to the LLP. This contrasts with a general partnership, where each partner has unlimited liability for the debts and obligations of the partnership. This is the main reason for LLPs being popular among accountancy and legal firms which have previously traded as English general partnerships.

11. Enterprise Investment Schemes (EISs) and Venture Capital Trusts (VCTs)

Learning Objective

5.8.1 Analyse the key features, relative merits and limitations of investing in venture capital trusts (VCTs) and enterprise investment schemes (EISs) and seed enterprise investment schemes (SEISs) compared with other forms of direct and indirect investment: partners/investors; investment management; tax characteristics; past performance in terms of risk and returns; discounts; premiums; secondary market liquidity

11.1 The Enterprise Investment Scheme (EIS)

The enterprise investment scheme (EIS) is designed to help smaller, higher-risk trading companies to raise finance, by offering a range of tax reliefs to investors who purchase new shares in those companies. Companies who wish to issue shares under the scheme have to follow a certain number of rules regarding the kind of company it is, the amount of money it can raise, how and when that money must be employed for the purposes of the trade, and the trading activities carried on.

An investor receives tax advantages when investing in EIS companies, providing that they invest in fully paid ordinary shares that carry the full risk of ordinary shares and carry no preferential rights that protect the investor from the normal risks of investing in shares.

Income tax relief is given on investments in an EIS-qualifying company, subject to a maximum of £1 million. The relief is 30% of the cost of the shares, which can be set against the individual's income tax liability for the year in which the investment was made. The shares must then be held for a minimum period of three years; otherwise, the income tax relief is withdrawn. An investor may carry back part or all of the amount invested and claim tax relief for the previous year subject to the limits for relief for that year.

EIS shares can also qualify for relief from CGT providing that they have qualified for income tax relief and that has not been withdrawn. If they have qualified for relief, then any disposals after the minimum three-year period are free from CGT. If a gain is made, the payment of tax can be deferred if the gain is invested in shares of another EIS-qualifying company within a period of one year before or three years after the gain arose. If a loss is made instead, then the amount of the loss less any income tax relief can be set against the income of the year in which they were disposed of or the previous year, instead of being set off against any capital gains.

EISs are only available to individuals who invest in shares in an EIS-qualifying company (though they can invest via a nominee). There are various reliefs available under the scheme as follows:

- **Income tax reliefs** – the investor is eligible for relief of 30% of the cost of the shares, to be set against their income tax liability for the tax year in which the investment was made. Relief can be claimed up to a maximum of £1 million invested in such shares, which means a maximum tax reduction in any one year of £300,000 (assuming the individual had a big enough income tax liability to cover this). The relief cannot be set off against dividend income, as the tax credit attached to a dividend is not recoverable.

Investors can also carry back up to £1 million of their investment to the previous tax year for the purposes of income tax relief. This does not affect an individual's current tax year entitlement, thereby enabling a maximum investment of £2 million per individual in any tax year. Relief cannot be carried forward to a later year.

The shares must be held for a certain period or income tax relief will be withdrawn. Generally, this is three years from the date the shares were issued.

Income tax relief can only be claimed by individuals who are not connected with the company.

- **CGT relief** – if an investor has received income tax relief on the cost of the shares, and the shares are disposed of after they have been held for a set period, any gain is free from CGT.
- **Loss relief** – if the shares are disposed of at a loss, the investor can offset the loss, less any income tax relief given, against income for the year in which they were disposed of, or for the previous year, instead of being set off against any capital gains.
- **CGT deferral relief** – this is available to individuals and trustees of certain trusts. The CGT on a capital gain can be deferred if the gain is invested in shares of an EIS qualifying company. The gain can arise from the disposal of any kind of asset, but the investment must be made within the period one year before, or three years after, it arose. There are no minimum or maximum amounts for deferral, and in this case it does not matter whether the investor is connected with the company or not. Unconnected investors may claim both income tax and CGT deferral relief. There is no minimum period for which the shares must be held; the deferred capital gain is brought back into charge whenever the shares are disposed of.

EIS qualifying companies must be unquoted when the relevant shares are issued. They can, later, become quoted without the investors losing relief – but only if there were no arrangements for them to become quoted in existence when the shares were issued.

The company must not be controlled by another company, nor must there be any arrangements in existence for this to happen, at the time the shares are issued.

Any subsidiaries must all be qualifying subsidiaries – ie, the company has more than 50% of the ordinary share capital of the subsidiary, and it is not controlled by another company. If the EIS company has a property management subsidiary that must be at least a 90% subsidiary.

The EIS company must be a small company, in terms of the gross assets test. Since April 2012, the gross assets of the company – or of the whole group if it is the parent of a group – cannot exceed £15 million immediately before any share issue and £16 million immediately after that issue. It must either carry on a qualifying trade, or be the parent company of a qualifying trading group.

The rules about not being controlled by another company, qualifying subsidiaries and the company carrying on the trade must be followed for a stated period, otherwise the investors will lose their reliefs.

The following changes were confirmed at the Summer Budget 2015, and took effect from 18 November 2015:

- A lifetime limit for the issuing company was introduced to cap the maximum amount that a company can raise under the venture capital schemes. This limit is £12 million for most companies, but there will be an enhanced £20 million for 'knowledge-intensive' companies.

- EIS relief will not be available for share issues in companies that have been trading for more than seven years (ten for knowledge intensive companies), unless:
  - there has been a previous issue of shares under EIS/VCT/SEIS
  - there has been a fundamental change in the nature of the business.
- The maximum number of employees has increased to 499 (previously 249) for 'knowledge-intensive' companies.
- EIS/VCT will no longer be able to be used to fund the acquisition of an existing company or trade.

11.2 Seed Enterprise Investment Schemes (SEISs)

April 6 2012, saw the launch of the seed enterprise investment scheme (SEIS). It complemented the EIS scheme and was predominantly designed to stimulate entrepreneurship and to help small, early-stage companies to raise equity finance. The measure supported the coalition government's growth agenda by helping smaller, riskier, early-stage UK companies, which may face barriers in raising external finance, to attract investment, making it easier for these companies to become established and grow. It applies to smaller companies, under two years old, with 25 or fewer employees and assets of up to £200,000, which are carrying on or preparing to carry on a new business.

It enables individual investors opportunities to receive a range of tax reliefs by investing in new shares of companies in the SEIS. The scheme makes available tax relief to investors who subscribe for shares and have a stake of less than 30% in the company. The relief applies to investments made on or after 6 April 2012. Investors can get up to 50% tax relief in the tax year the investment is made, regardless of their marginal tax rate.

For the first year of the new scheme, the government offered a CGT holiday – 100% of gains realised on the disposal of assets in 2012–13 that were invested through SEIS in the same year were exempt from CGT. In 2013–14, this CGT relief was extended such that 50% of the reinvested gains were free from CGT, and this was then made permanent in the 2014 Budget. Taxpayers can roll up their chargeable capital gains from previous SEIS investments back into SEIS companies, without paying any CGT. Investors need not be UK residents.

SEIS investors can put in up to £100,000 in a single tax year and this investment can be spread over a number of SEIS-eligible companies.

Any one company cannot raise more than £150,000 in total via the SEIS investment. The company must be a UK company that is permanently established in the UK and the company must be an approved company and not in finance or from the investment sector.

A qualifying company can follow a share issue under SEIS, with further issues of shares under EIS, or investment from a venture capital trust (VCT).

A company cannot issue shares under a SEIS scheme if it has already gained finance from prior investment in a VCT or issued shares in respect of which it has provided an EIS compliance statement.

11.3 Venture Capital Trusts (VCTs)

Venture capital trusts (VCTs) are companies listed on the LSE and are similar to investment trusts. They are designed to enable individuals to invest indirectly in a range of small higher-risk trading companies, whose shares and securities are not listed on a recognised stock exchange, by investing through VCTs.

Investment in VCTs attracts special tax advantages and so the companies need to gain HMRC approval to be treated as such. Once approved, VCTs are exempt from corporation tax on any gains arising on the disposal of their investments. Investors may also be entitled to various income tax and capital gains tax reliefs.

As noted, VCTs are structured so as to provide investors with preferential tax treatment in a number of ways; this is intended to encourage individuals to provide capital to smaller, start-up companies which might otherwise be unable to find the funding to grow – and to do so through a vehicle which provides the investor with:

- some incentives (the tax relief), and
- a measure of protection (the diversification of a collective investment).

The tax reliefs are only available to individuals aged 18 years or over, and cannot be claimed by trustees or companies (although there is nothing to stop such investors from holding shares in a VCT).

In terms of income tax, investors benefit from the following:

- Exemption from income tax on dividends from ordinary shares in VCTs (dividend relief).
- Income tax relief at the rate of 30% of the amount subscribed for shares. The shares issued must have been new ordinary shares, and must not carry any preferential rights. They must be held for at least five years.
- The relief for dividend income and gains applies whether the shares were acquired at issue or subsequently via a stock exchange trade. The income tax relief is only available for initial subscriptions.

This tax relief at 30% can be set against any income tax liability that is due, whether at the lower, basic or higher rate.

There are two CGT reliefs from which investors can benefit:

- There is no CGT on any gain made when the investor disposes of their VCT shares. This is called 'disposal relief'.
- If an investor subscribed for VCT shares issued on or before 5 April 2004, they could defer a capital gain on the sale of other assets by using the proceeds to subscribe for shares in a VCT, and thereby defer the gain to a later date. This is called, deferral relief, but is not available for VCT shares issued after 5 April 2004. EISs do, however, continue to offer deferral relief.

Deferral relief is not available in respect of investments in shares issued after 5 April 2004. Dividend relief and disposal relief are available on both newly issued shares and second-hand shares (ie, those bought on the stock exchange – the secondary market). Income tax relief (and, for shares issued before 6 April 2004) deferral relief, can be claimed only for purchases of new shares. Conditions have to be met, and the reliefs can be lost or withdrawn if they are not.

11.3.1 Performance Characteristics (Risk versus Reward)

VCTs can provide very rewarding opportunities for investors – in part because start-up and developmental/growth companies can, in the right conditions, produce significant growth, and in part because the gains and income are not subject to the same tax drag as less favourably treated investments.

However, because of their nature they also involve a high level of risk. For example:

- The companies in which VCTs invest are not listed and so it may be difficult for the VCT to sell them, in order to take advantage of better opportunities. There is a liquidity risk.
- These smaller companies may be more vulnerable to downturns in the markets or the economy. Their share prices may be disproportionately affected by market sentiment. They may also (especially if they have high levels of borrowing) be very sensitive to changes in interest rates.
- In some, but not all, cases they may have relatively young and inexperienced management teams and their lack of track record may mean that the best decisions are not always made.

11.3.2 Discounts and Premiums

As with ordinary investment trusts, shares in VCTs are traded on the stock market and their prices are thus determined by supply and demand. Their prices will therefore trade at a discount or premium to the VCT's net asset value, as based on a valuation of the holdings in its underlying portfolio.

12. Distributor-Influenced Funds (DIFs)

Learning Objective

5.9.1 Analyse the key features, relative merits and limitations of investing in a distributor-influenced fund compared with other forms of direct and indirect investment: roles and responsibilities of underlying parties; fee structure; expenses and commissions; tax characteristics; investment performance and risk; other risks – distributor power and expertise, conflicts of interest, suitability; secondary market liquidity; requirements on avoiding conflicts of interest.

12.1 Distributor-Influenced Funds (DIFs)

12.1.1 Purposes and General Characteristics

Distributor-influenced funds (DIFs) are funds created by an adviser firm for its client base and in which the firm has a role in fund governance but when fund management and administration are outsourced to third parties. They could be designed on a bespoke basis for the distributor or they could be set up using an existing fund that is tailored for the distributor. Fund administration and management is outsourced to other firms but the distributor may have a degree of influence over the fund (short of day-to-day asset selection).

It may be, for example, that the distributor is able to:

- influence the hiring (or removal) of the delegated investment manager
- create accountability of the investment adviser by attending investment committees, or
- appoint (or remove) the ACD.

They are commonly arranged as OEICs (when they may be known as broker OEICs or distributor-owned funds) and are often multi-manager funds, but they may also take other structures (like insurance funds). We have chosen to refer to them as distributor-influenced funds in this workbook, as this term covers the full range of possible structures.

They come somewhere in the fund spectrum between broker funds and independent, third-party funds.

12.1.2 Types

These are created for the clients of a particular distributor, typically an adviser firm or network. There are a variety of types available and funds could be designed on a bespoke basis for the distributor or they could be set up using an existing fund that is tailored for the distributor.

These products present risks that are different from those to which distributors and their customers are ordinarily exposed.

12.1.3 Structure and Arrangement

Fund administration and management is outsourced to other firms but the distributor may have a degree of influence (short of the day-to-day management on asset selection). Given that these funds may have unique risks, the UK regulator expects firms to put in place robust systems and controls to ensure that the use of these products is in the best interests of each client and does not simply increase complexity and costs without providing new services and good value for money. DIFs have come under closer scrutiny by the regulator. The regulator is keen to ensure that they are designed to ensure customers are treated fairly and should not prevent advisers from offering their own portfolio-style collective funds.

12.1.4 Tax Treatment

One of the often-cited reasons for selecting a DIF over an independent vehicle is that it can mitigate clients' CGT liabilities. DIFs can provide a range of tax advantages, but the exact nature of the benefit derived from these products will depend on the tax position of each investor and the type of bespoke product that is constructed and offered within a DIF setting.

12.1.5 Regulatory Requirements on Avoiding Conflicts of Interest

The FCA circulated a fact sheet providing guidance to distributors with their own range of DIFs or those planning to introduce one. The FCA recognises that DIFs are distinct from the operations of fund managers, collective investment scheme operators and private client wealth managers, for whom investment management is central to the business proposition. The FCA considers DIFs to be different from these types. It recognises that DIFs are organised by firms that have decided to outsource to professionals as their preferred route. Some may not have permission to manage investments or operate a fund.

The FCA's key concerns over these investments lie with the potential conflicts of interest that arise from the arrangement. It wants to make sure that controls to ensure compliance with its disclosure rules and safeguards to mitigate risks in their investments are in place.

Inherent conflicts of interest may already be present in DIF structures: between the firm and its advisers and between advisers and their clients. These areas will need to be managed properly. RDR requires all adviser firms to set their own charges. As a brief guide to readers, we have presented a shortened list of some of the recommendations that were made to meet RDR requirements for 31 December 2012:

1. Firms advising on DIFs should only receive an adviser charge or consultancy charge and should no longer receive any other direct or indirect benefit (including a share of the annual management charge) for their role on a distributor-influenced fund governance committee.
2. Adviser charges for recommending a DIF should not vary inappropriately compared to substitutable or competing retail investment products.
3. An independent adviser must provide advice on all of its packaged products. Firms holding themselves out as independents must only make personal recommendations based on a comprehensive and fair analysis of the relevant market that is unbiased and unrestricted.
4. The specific features of the DIF must be suitable for the client. Firms must rigorously assess which product is suitable for each client and record the reasons for their decisions.

5. When communicating with clients, the information presented must be fair, clear, and not misleading.
6. Recommendations include changes to business processes to ensure there are management and controls in place.

13. Derivatives

Learning Objective

5.10.1 Understand the purposes, structure and risk/reward characteristics of the main types of financial derivatives pertaining to each main asset class: futures; forward contracts; options; warrants; contracts for differences

5.10.2 Understand the effects of implementing simple derivatives strategies for the purposes of hedging or speculation in terms of: risk transfer and risk/reward payoff; transaction costs and margin; ease of implementation and unwinding

Derivatives include such instruments as options, futures and contracts for differences (CFDs). They can be used in a variety of ways – both to mitigate risk within an investment portfolio (hedging), and to increase risk by speculating on the direction of the market. Consequently derivatives should be regarded as specialist investments to be used only by experienced clients, when the risks of using them are fully understood and accepted.

Derivatives have a major role to play in the investment management of many large portfolios and investment funds, and are used for hedging, anticipating future cash flows, asset allocation change and arbitrage. Hedging is a technique employed by portfolio managers to reduce the impact of adverse price movements. For example, if a portfolio manager expects to receive a large inflow of cash to be invested in a particular asset, then futures can be used to fix the price at which it will be bought and offset the risk that prices will have risen by the time the cash flow is received. Changes to the asset allocation of a fund, whether to take advantage of anticipated short-term directional market movements or to implement a change in strategy, can be made more swiftly and economically using futures than by adjusting the underlying portfolio.

Arbitrage is the process of deriving a risk-free profit from simultaneously buying and selling the same asset in two different markets, where a price difference between the two exists. If the price of a derivative and its underlying asset are mismatched, then the portfolio manager may be able to profit from this pricing anomaly.

Derivatives are also used for speculation. Since only initial margin, and not the full notional value of the contract, is payable by the counterparties at the point of opening their respective positions, futures provide an ideal means by which to speculate on both rising and falling asset prices in a range of markets.

13.1 Futures

Derivatives are not a new concept – they have been around for hundreds of years. Their origins can be traced back to agricultural markets where farmers needed a mechanism to guard against price fluctuations caused by gluts of produce and drought. So, in order to fix the price of agricultural produce in advance of harvest time, farmers and merchants entered into forward contracts.

These set the price at which a stated amount of a commodity would be delivered between a farmer and a merchant (termed the counterparties) at a pre-specified future time.

These early derivative contracts introduced an element of certainty into commerce and gained immense popularity. They led to the opening of the world's first derivatives exchange in 1848, the Chicago Board of Trade (CBOT).

The exchange soon developed a futures contract that enabled standardised qualities and quantities of grain to be traded for a fixed future price on a stated delivery date. Unlike the forward contracts that preceded it, the futures contract could itself be traded. These futures contracts were subsequently extended to a wide variety of commodities and offered by an ever-increasing number of derivatives exchanges.

It was not until 1975 that CBOT introduced the world's first financial futures contract. This set the scene for the exponential growth in product innovation and the volume of futures trading that soon followed.

13.1.1 Characteristics of Futures

A future is an agreement between a buyer and a seller. The buyer agrees to pay a pre-specified amount for the delivery of a particular quantity of an asset at a future date. The seller agrees to deliver the asset at the future date, in exchange for the pre-specified amount of money. A futures contract is, therefore, a legally binding obligation between two parties for one to buy and the other to sell a pre-specified amount of an asset at a pre-specified price on a pre-specified future date.

Example

A buyer might agree with a seller to pay US$75 per barrel for 1,000 barrels of crude oil in three months.

The buyer might be an electricity-generating company wanting to fix the price it will have to pay for the oil to use in its oil-fired power stations, and the seller might be an oil company wanting to fix the sales price of some of its future oil production.

In the example, the oil quality will be based on the oil field from which it originates (eg, Brent Crude, from the Brent oil field in the North Sea). The quantity is 1,000 barrels, the date is three months ahead and the location might be the port of Rotterdam.

Not all futures contracts require physical delivery of the underlying asset. Most commodity contracts are settled physically, while financial futures are instead settled between the counterparties by cash on the monetary gain or loss to date. These are known as CFDs.

The terms and conditions of a futures contract are standardised so that they can be traded on a derivatives exchange. Standardising the terms allows one investor to sell their future to another and so provide liquidity to the market. These standardised terms are known as contract specifications.

A futures contract, in summary, has two distinct features:

- It is **exchange-traded** – for example on the derivatives exchanges like NYSE Liffe or the Intercontinental Exchange.
- It is dealt on **standardised terms** – the exchange specifies the quality of the underlying asset, the quantity underlying each contract, the future date and the delivery location. Only the price is open to negotiation.

Derivatives markets have specialised terminology that it is important to understand.

- **Long** – the alternative way to describe the buyer of the future. The long is committed to buying the underlying asset at the pre-agreed price on the specified future date.
- **Short** – the alternative way to describe the seller of the future. The short is committed to delivering the underlying asset in exchange for the pre-agreed price on the specified future date.
- **Open** – the initial trade. A market participant opens a trade when they first enter into a future. They could be buying a future – opening a long position, or selling a future – opening a short position.
- **Underlying** – the underlying asset drives the value of the future and is usually referred to as the underlying security or cash asset.
- **Basis** – basis quantifies the difference between the cash price of the underlying asset and the futures price.
- **Delivery Date** – this is the date on which the agreed future transaction takes place and so represents the end of the future's life.
- **Close** – the buyer of a future can either hold the future to expiry and take delivery of the underlying asset or sell the future before the expiry date. The latter is known as closing out the position.

Staying with the example above, the buyer of the contract to purchase 1,000 barrels of crude oil at US$75 per barrel for delivery in three months is said to go long of the contract, while the seller is described as going short. Entering into the transaction is known as opening the trade and the eventual delivery of the crude oil will close out the trade.

Most futures that are opened do not end up being delivered; they are closed out instead.

An opening buyer will avoid delivery by making a closing sale before the delivery date. If the buyer does not close out, they will pay over the agreed sum and receive the underlying asset. This may be something the buyer is keen to avoid, for example, because they are actually a financial institution simply speculating on the price of the underlying asset using futures.

13.1.2 The Risk/Reward Profile of Futures

As we saw above, the buyer of the future is described as going long. In other words, the buyer is agreeing to take delivery of the underlying asset and hopes that the price of the underlying asset will rise.

As the following diagram shows, the long futures position makes money in a rising market and loses money in a falling market.

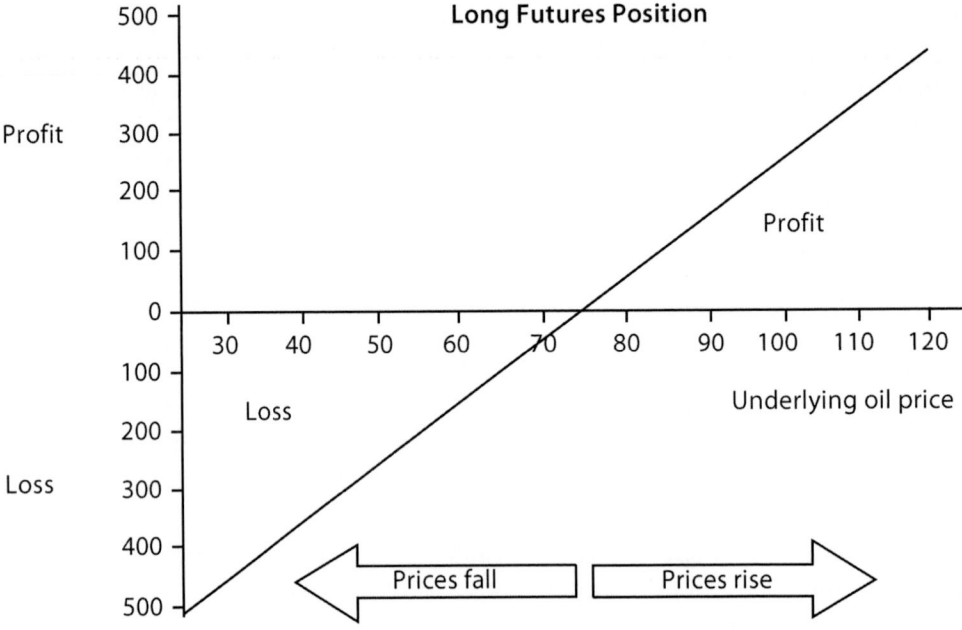

The seller of the future on the other hand is taking a short position. In other words, the seller is undertaking to make delivery of the underlying asset and hopes that the price of the underlying asset will fall. As the following diagram shows, the short futures position hopes to make money in a falling market and loses money in a rising market.

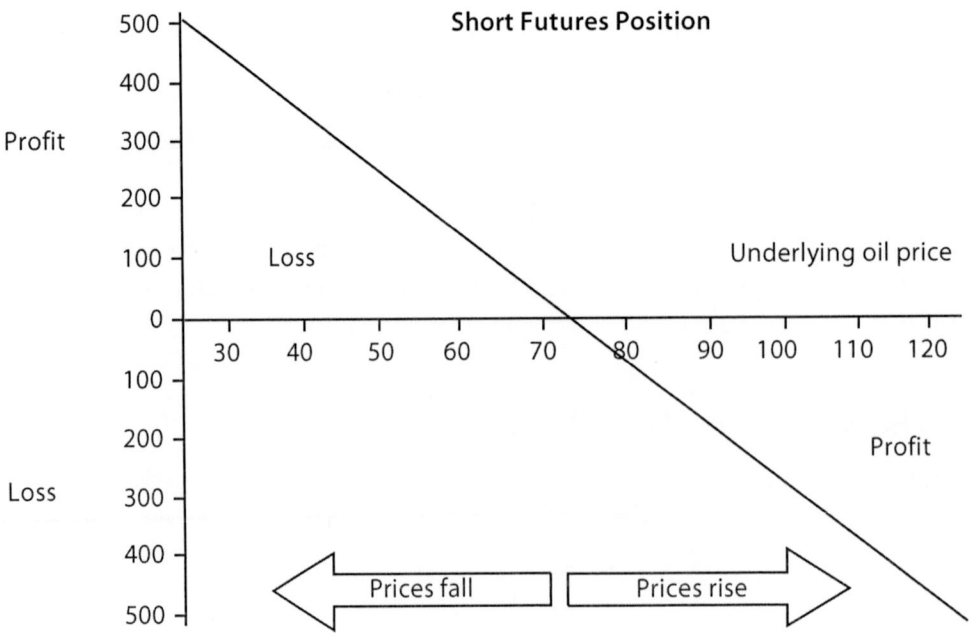

As you can see, the long and short positions are mirror images of each other, so that if the long position gains then the short position loses. For this reason, futures contracts are often referred to as a zero sum game.

Given that futures are highly geared instruments, if the market moves against the speculator, losses can mount up very quickly. Indeed, following several high-profile disasters involving derivatives, most non-practitioners tend to think of futures solely as speculative instruments, used in the pursuit of making quick profits, despite evidence to the contrary.

Whatever the perception, speculation per se should not be discouraged as, apart from adding to market liquidity, or brisk two-way trade, in futures contracts, without speculators, those wishing to use futures to hedge risk would be unable to do so.

13.2 Options

The growth of options can be traced to the work of two US academics – Fischer Black and Myron Scholes – who produced the Black–Scholes option-pricing model in 1973.

Until then, options contracts could not easily be priced, which prevented them from being traded. This model, however, paved the way for the creation of standardised options contracts and the opening of the Chicago Board Options Exchange (CBOE) in the same year.

This in turn led to an explosion in product innovation and the creation of other options exchanges, such as LIFFE. Options can still be traded off-exchange, or over-the-counter (OTC), in much the same way as forward contracts, where the contract specification determined by the parties is bespoke.

13.2.1 Characteristics of Options

An option gives a buyer the right, but not the obligation, to buy or sell a specified quantity of an underlying asset at a pre-agreed exercise price, on or before a pre-specified future date or between two specified dates. The seller, in exchange for the payment of a premium, grants the option to the buyer.

As with futures, options have their own terminology that it is important to understand:

- **Call option** – an option that gives the buyer the right, but not the obligation, to buy an underlying asset.
- **Put option** – an option that gives the buyer the right, but not the obligation, to sell an underlying asset.
- **Holder** – the term used to describe the buyer of the option, ie, the person who has bought it. It is also referred to as the long position.
- **Writer** – the term used to describe the seller of an option. It is also referred to as the short position.
- **Premium** – the term used to describe the price paid for an option.
- **Strike price** – the price at which the underlying asset may be bought or sold. Also referred to as the **exercise price**.
- **At-the-money** – a call option whose strike price is the same as the current price of the underlying asset.

- **In-the-money** – a call option whose strike price is below the current price of the underlying asset and which could therefore be exercised for a profit.
- **Out-of-the-money** – a call option whose strike price is above the current price of the underlying asset and so, if exercised, will result in a loss.
- **Expiry date** – the last day of the option's life.
- **European style** – an option that may be exercised on its expiry date only.
- **American style** – an option that may be exercised at any time during its life up to and including the expiry date.

The two parties to an options contract are the holder and the writer. The writer confers the right, rather than the obligation, to the holder to either buy or sell an asset at a pre-specified price in exchange for the holder paying a premium for this right. This premium represents a fraction of the cost of the asset or the notional value of the contract. Options, therefore, differ from futures in that a right is conferred in exchange for the payment of a premium.

As the holder is in possession of a right, rather than an obligation, the holder does not have to exercise this right if the transaction ultimately proves not to work in their favour. The option can simply be abandoned with the loss of the premium paid. The writer, however, is obliged to satisfy this right if taken up, or exercised, against them by the holder. Potentially the writer has an obligation to deliver the asset to the holder of a call option at the exercise price if the option is exercised. Alternatively, the writer could be required to take delivery from the holder of a put option if exercised.

All the holder can lose is the premium paid. As a result, only the writer is required to make initial and variation margin payments to the clearing house.

Most exchange-traded financial options are cash-settled rather than physically settled. Therefore, if exercised, the cash difference between the exercise price of the option and that of the underlying asset, rather than the asset itself, passes from the writer to the holder.

13.2.2 At-the-Money, In-the-Money and Out-of-the-Money

The definition of the above terms was considered in section 13.2.1. We will expand on this by looking at how this relates to a call and a put option.

Call Option

Assume an investor buys a call option on ABC shares at a premium of 10p and an exercise price of 100p and has an intention to buy the underlying share when the option expires.

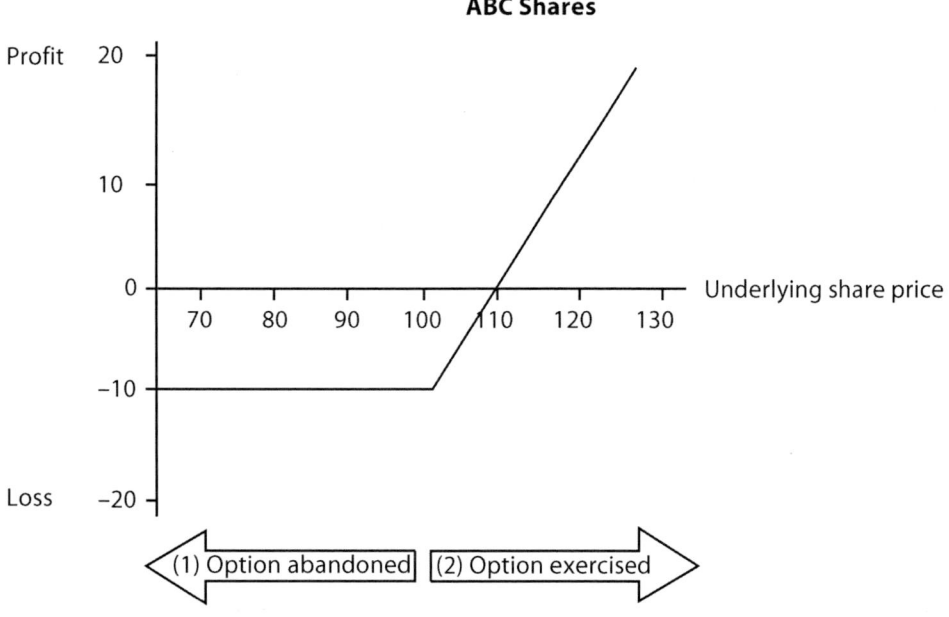

1. **Out-of-the-money** – if the underlying share price is below 100p, the holder will abandon the option and lose the 10p premium. Instead, they can buy the shares at a cheaper price.
2. **In-the-money** – if the underlying share price is above 100p, the holder will exercise the option to buy the shares at 100p.
3. **At-the-money** – the underlying share price is the same as the exercise price.
4. **Break even** – if at expiry the underlying share price is 110p, the holder will break even as it costs 100p to buy shares plus the premium of 10p.

Put Option

Assume an investor buys a put option on ABC shares for a premium of 60p which can be exercised at 200p. They hold a share and have the intention to sell it in the future when the option expires. The position will instead look as follows:

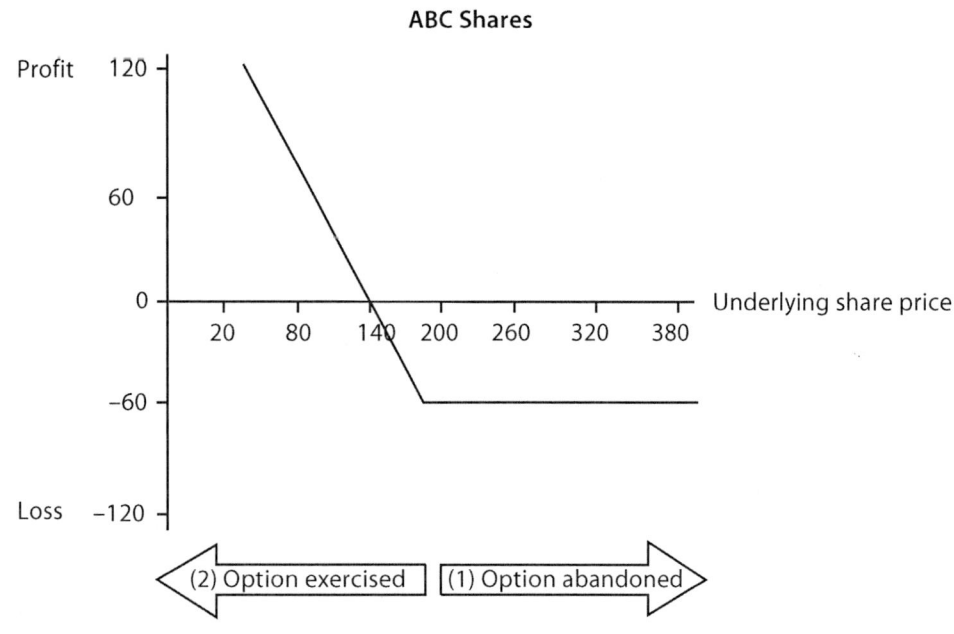

1. **Out-of-the-money** – if the underlying share price is above 200p, then the holder will abandon the option. Instead, they can sell their share at a higher price in the market.
2. **In-the-money** – if the underlying share price is less than 140p, the holder can exercise their option to sell at 200p.
3. **At-the-money** – the underlying share price is the same as the exercise price.
4. **Break even** – if, at expiry, the underlying share price is 140p, the holder can buy the shares in the open market and exercise the option to sell at 200p. Profit of 60p is offset by premium of 60p.

13.2.3 Option Strategies

In this section, we will consider four basic option strategies by looking at a call and put option from the perspective of the holder and the writer (seller).

Call Options

Buyers of a call option take a long call position, while the writer of the same option takes the opposite short call position. Using the same example as before, the buyer of a call pays a premium of 10p for the right to buy the underlying shares at expiry.

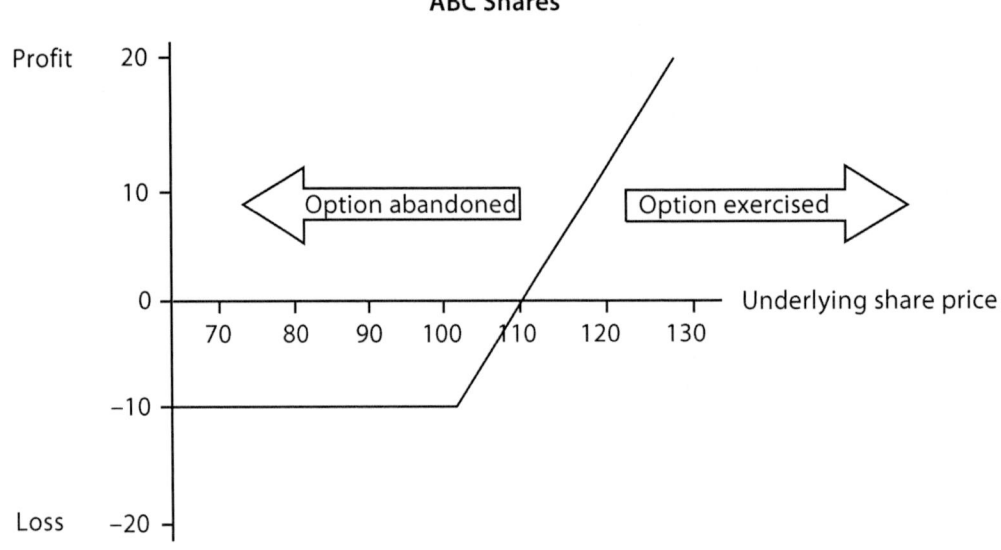

The higher the price of the underlying shares, the more profit the buyer will make and vice versa. The potential risks and rewards for the long call position are:

- The maximum profit is unlimited.
- The maximum loss for the buyer is limited to the premium paid, as they can simply abandon the option.

The writer of the option clearly has a different perspective on the transaction. In return for writing the option, the seller of the option receives the premium and is hoping that the underlying share price will not rise and so the holder will not exercise the option but instead abandon it, leaving the writer with the premium.

The higher the price of the underlying asset, the more loss the writer of the option will make. As a result, potential risks and rewards for the short call position are:

- The maximum profit is the premium.
- The maximum loss for the writer is unlimited.

Put Options

Buyers of a put option take a long put position, while the writer of the same option takes the opposite short put position. With a put option, the buyer pays a premium for the right to sell the underlying asset on expiry if they wish. The more the price of the underlying asset falls, the more profit the buyer will make.

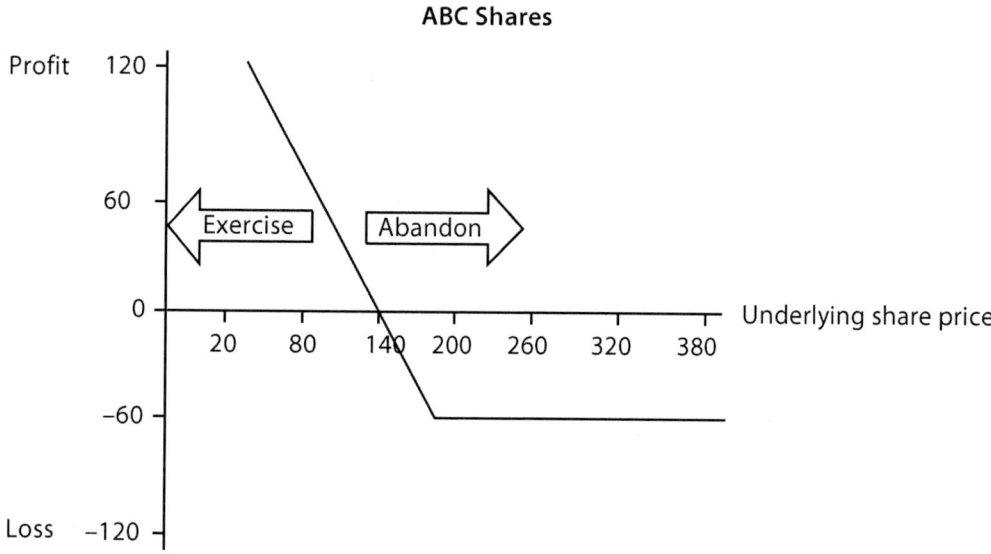

The potential risks and rewards for the long put position are:

- The maximum profit is the strike price less the premium paid.
- The maximum loss for the buyer is limited to the premium paid as they can simply abandon the option.

The seller of the put option will receive the premium but takes on the obligation to buy the underlying asset at expiry. From the perspective of the writer, therefore, they are hoping that the share price will not fall as expected and so the buyer will abandon the option, leaving them with the premium. As a result, potential risks and rewards for the short put position are:

- The maximum profit is the premium.
- The maximum loss for the writer is the strike price less the premium.

13.2.4 Option Premiums

The premium for an option is made up of its intrinsic value and its time value.

- **Intrinsic value** – this is the difference between the exercise price and the current share price.
- **Time value** – an option with a long time to expiry will have a greater amount of time value incorporated into its price, so that the longer the period, the greater will be the time value.
- **American-style** options can be exercised at any time before the contract expires while **European-style** options can only be exercised after the contract expires. As a result of this flexibility in exercise awarded, American-style options are more expensive than European options.

We can consider this by looking at a simple example.

Example

A call option with the right to buy at 90 is trading at 30 when the underlying is trading at 100. The intrinsic value is 10 and the time value is the remaining 20.

In practice, the option premium will be affected by many factors including:

- **The underlying asset price** – the higher the asset price, the more valuable are call options and the less valuable are put options.
- **The exercise price** – the higher the exercise price, the less valuable are call options and the more valuable are put options.
- **Time to maturity** – the longer the term of the option, generally the greater the chance of the option expiring in-the-money; therefore, the higher the time value and the higher the premium.
- **Volatility of the underlying asset price** – the more volatile the price of the underlying asset, the greater the chance of the option expiring in-the-money; therefore, the higher the premium.

There are two other factors that will affect the option premium: the income yield on the underlying asset, and short-term interest rates. It should be noted that their effects on option prices are fairly minor in relation to the other factors.

- **Income yield of the underlying asset** – the greater the income yield of the underlying asset, the greater the sacrifice being made by the call option holder by not holding this asset, but the greater the benefit to the put option holder. Therefore, the higher the income yield, the more valuable the put option and the less valuable the call option.
- **Short-term interest rates** – the higher the short-term rate of interest, the greater the interest income received by the call option holder on the cash not committed to buying the underlying asset. This makes call options more valuable. However, the outlay on a put option not earning this higher rate of interest makes put options less valuable.

13.3 Warrants

13.3.1 Characteristics of Warrants

Warrants are negotiable securities issued by companies which confer a right on the holder to buy a certain number of the company's ordinary shares at a preset price on or before a predetermined date.

Warrants are issued on a stand-alone basis and so, unlike convertible loan stock or preference shares, the conversion right contained within the warrant is traded separately.

Although these are essentially long-dated call options, they are traded on the LSE and, if exercised, result in the company issuing additional equity shares. The warrants market is relatively small.

Given the terms of the warrant issue, the conversion premium or discount can be calculated. The basis for calculating the conversion premium follows the same principles as we considered in chapter 1 for convertible preference shares and convertible bonds.

13.3.2 Covered Warrants

Covered warrants are warrants in a company's shares issued by an organisation other than the company itself – they are also called securitised derivatives. Issuers cover their issues by either shares in the company or warrants issued by the company. Investment banks usually issue covered warrants in a different denomination or a different currency from the underlying share.

When the holder of a covered warrant exercises their right to buy the shares, they are exercising it against the issuer of the covered warrant rather than the company itself. Covered warrants are well established in most international markets but have only been available in the UK since 2002 and are traded on the LSE.

A covered warrant gets its name from the fact that when issued, the issuer will usually buy the underlying asset in the market, ie, they are covered if they should need to deliver the underlying shares, and not exposed to the risk of having to buy them in the market at a higher price.

Covered warrants are issued by a number of leading investment banks and can be based on individual stocks, indices, currencies or commodities. They can be either leveraged, as with individual stock options, or unleveraged, as with commodities.

As with an option, a covered warrant gives the holder the right to buy or sell an underlying asset at a specified price, on or before a predetermined date. There are both call and put warrants available.

A covered warrant does not carry an obligation to buy or sell, so that an investor's maximum loss is restricted to their initial investment. Investors can buy and sell either call or put warrants daily on the LSE.

13.4 Contracts for Difference (CFDs)

In a wider sense, contracts for difference (CFDs) refer to derivatives contracts that are cash-settled. As mentioned earlier, not all futures contracts require physical delivery of the underlying asset. Most commodity contracts are settled physically, while financial futures are instead settled between the counterparties by cash on the monetary gain or loss at the settlement date. These are known as CFDs.

The underlying may be designated in any asset class. The term has also been associated with another type of contract termed as 'retail contracts for differences'. They are created and marketed to individual investors, along with futures and options contracts on a range of indices.

An investor normally enters into CFDs with a derivatives broker who is the counterparty authorised under the Financial Services and Markets Act 2000. The investor can open a trade by either going long or short a CFD. Ultimately this investor will be cash-settled on that trade when it is closed off with an offsetting trade.

14. Hedge Funds

Learning Objective

5.11.1 Analyse the key features, relative merits and limitations of investing in hedge funds compared with other forms of direct and indirect investment: main types of hedge fund; regulatory environment; investment risk; use of short and long positions; custody and safe-keeping practices; limitations in respect of voting capital; funds of hedge funds (FOHFs)

The term hedge fund is a very wide one, with no precise legal definition. In general it is taken to mean a type of fund which can engage in a wide range of investment strategies, many of them outside the strategies permitted for authorised schemes.

Hedge funds are often unregulated, although their operators (eg, the fund manager) will be authorised by the FCA if they are in the UK. Within the hedge fund universe, there are a variety of recognised strategies – for example, absolute return funds (see section 14.1) are those which aim to provide a positive return, regardless of the direction of the markets. It is quite common for such a fund to have the objective of outperforming one of the risk-free assets we looked at earlier. For example, a fund might have the objective of outperforming the return on three-month Treasury bills by a set percentage.

Hedge funds can have a higher level of risk than traditional assets, but they also have the potential for higher returns. Their performance can often be uncorrelated to other asset classes for long periods of time. However, when a major event or shock occurs in the financial markets the correlation returns to other asset classes and can increase markedly, which was the case during the recent financial crisis.

Many hedge funds have high initial investment sizes so access is effectively restricted to wealthy individuals and institutions. However, investors can also gain access to hedge funds through funds of hedge funds (FOHFs).

The Alternative Investment Management Association (AIMA) is the global representative of the hedge fund industry. Membership comprises over 1,600 firms in more than 50 countries, and includes hedge fund managers, fund of hedge funds managers, prime brokers, legal and accounting firms, investors, fund administrators and independent fund directors. AIMA's members collectively manage more than $1.5 trillion in assets.

14.1 Hedge Fund Characteristics

The common aspects of hedge funds are:

- **Structure** – most hedge funds are established as unauthorised or unregulated collective investment schemes. They cannot be generally marketed to private individuals because they are considered too risky for the less financially sophisticated investor.
- **High minimum investment** – most hedge funds require minimum investments in excess of £50,000; some exceed £1 million.
- **Investment flexibility** – because of the lack of regulation, hedge funds are able to invest in a wider range of assets (subject to compliance with the restrictions in their constitutional documents and prospectus). In addition to being able to take long and short positions in securities, some take positions in commodities and currencies. Their investment style is generally aimed at producing **absolute** returns.
- **Gearing** – many hedge funds use leverage and derivatives with the aim of enhancing their returns.
- **Liquidity** – to maximise the hedge fund manager's investment freedom, hedge funds usually impose an initial **lock-in** period of between one and three years before investors can sell their investments.
- **Cost** – hedge funds typically levy performance-related fees, which the investor pays if certain performance levels are achieved, otherwise charging a fee comparable to that charged by other growth funds. Performance fees can be substantial, with 20% or more of the net new highs being common.
- **Low correlation to world securities markets** – despite the greater concentration of their portfolio holdings, hedge funds, when combined with conventional portfolios, may provide additional diversification, owing to their lower correlation with world equity and bond markets.
- **Performance-related fees** – hedge funds typically levy an annual management fee of 2%, in addition to a performance-related fee of about 20%, if an absolute performance target in excess of the risk-free rate of return is met or exceeded and previous losses have been recovered. Although, increased competition within the hedge fund industry has recently led to 'fee compression', with managers of new funds now taking different approaches to charging their management fees, in contrast to the usual '2 and 20' approach.
- **Manager investment** – hedge fund managers generally invest some of their own wealth into their funds. This can reinforce the alignment of manager and investor interests.
- **Dealing** – many hedge funds impose an initial lock-in period of between one and three years before investors may deal in the hedge fund's shares. Any dealing that subsequently takes place is then usually only permitted at the end of each month or quarter.
- **Regulation** – hedge funds are usually domiciled in an offshore financial centre such as the Cayman Islands or Dublin, and usually subject to a lighter regulatory regime.

14.2 Hedge Fund Strategies

Each hedge fund strategy aims to take advantage of a particular investment opportunity. Hedge fund strategies are often characterised by an investment style. A brief outline of styles is given below.

- **Equity market neutral** – takes both long and short positions in equities (undervalued and overvalued securities) and thus neutralises the exposure to market risk.
- **Convertible arbitrage** – exploits price anomalies in convertible securities (convertible bonds, warrants and convertible preferred stock). Mispriced securities are identified and then bought or sold. Simultaneously the associated risks are hedged with an offsetting purchase/sale of the underlying stock.
- **Fixed income arbitrage** – a portfolio of fixed-income securities is created from mispriced securities (overvalued and undervalued). Since both long and short positions are created in the fund, the net market direction is then neutralised.
- **Distressed securities** – invest in companies that are close to bankruptcy on the view that the companies will be turned around.
- **Merger arbitrage** – in a deal arbitrage play, after an announcement, the fund manager will create a position that seeks to extract more of a deal premium from a merger and acquisition situation. One common trade is to purchase the target company stock while selling the bidder company.
- **Hedged equity** – also termed long-short funds. Long or net short bets are taken on equities. The long or short exposures are based on the managers' identification of overvalued and undervalued securities. Portfolios are not structured to be direction-neutral as with equity-market-neutral funds. However, based on the positions existing within the portfolio, the net exposure may have a long or short bias.
- **Global macro** – takes views on global macro-trends and concentrates on major market trends. The hedge fund uses derivatives to gain exposure to the trends identified. Managed futures funds are often classified as global macro funds.
- **Emerging markets** – seeks out profitable investment opportunities in emerging or less developed markets. Often the absence of derivatives products and short-selling restrictions mean that the funds in this category are long in the underlying securities.
- **Fund-of-Funds (FOFs)** – the fund invests in a portfolio of hedge funds. The FOF provides some interesting and unique benefits that are not found with other strategies. FOFs were created to allow easier access to smaller investors:
  - **Economies of scale** – a single investment in a hedge fund could cost an investor several hundred thousand pounds. With the same amount of money, indirect investment into multiple hedge funds is possible in a FOF. Further, a hedge fund company may provide their client with access to other hedge funds in their portfolio that are closed to new clients.
  - **Diversification** – since many hedge fund returns are uncorrelated, the investment in a FOF may provide a larger diversified portfolio.
  - **Expertise** – the hedge fund industry is less regulated than the mutual fund industry. Hedge fund managers working in this industry will have specialist skills, expertise and access to vital proprietary information that even professional money managers in traditional mutual fund sectors may not have.
  - **Transparency** – the hedge fund industry is secretive, and for an institutional investor carrying out due diligence in a hedge fund, this process may use up significant resources. Investing in a FOF could overcome this problem as the FOF manager will perform due diligence on each of the hedge funds in its portfolio.

14.3 Hedge Fund Risks

Specific risks of hedge funds include:

- gearing is used widely
- settlement is OTC
- currency risk
- dealing delays
- illiquid investments
- lack of transparency
- fraud
- lack of independent trustee boards.

As shown, hedge funds are reputed to be high risk. However, in many cases, this perception stands at odds with reality. In their original incarnation, hedge funds sought to reduce market risk. That said, there are now many different styles of hedge fund – some risk-averse, and some employing highly risky strategies. It is, therefore, not wise to generalise about them.

The most obvious market risk is the same risk that is faced by an investor in shares – as the broad market moves down, the investor's shares also fall in value.

As an absolute return fund, the hedge fund often uses leverage, especially in arbitrage-style strategies. This form of flexibility essential for amplifying the impact of the strategy can create unique risks. In a hedge fund, leverage may be created through any of the following ways:

- Borrowing funds to create a larger position or sell short more securities than the original capital put into the security.
- Borrowing through a margin account.
- Using derivatives (eg, futures and options) that require initial margins to gain market exposure. The margin posted will be a fraction of the full cost that is required if the underlying security was purchased in the spot market.

14.4 Absolute Return Funds (ARFs)

Learning Objective

5.12.1 Analyse the key features, relative merits and limitations of investing in absolute return funds compared with other forms of direct and indirect investment: structure; income and capital growth; investment risk and return; expenses; capital protection; monitoring performance versus benchmark

An absolute return objective for an investment is a target set to achieve a positive return in a specified time frame, irrespective of market conditions. The return is not referenced to any external benchmark. Traditional mutual funds on the other hand have a relative return objective.

Hedge funds were originally promoted as a genre of absolute return vehicles. As noted from the previous section, given the nature of such investments, their returns cannot be evaluated using conventional benchmark portfolios. This is because the exposure, composition and investment philosophy of the fund is often radically different from conventional mutual funds. For example, hedge funds can use derivatives and even CFDs in their investment portfolios. Their strategies are often characterised by long positions in conventional and unconventional assets, combined with short selling, trading in derivatives, arbitrage, and the use of leverage.

From a historical perspective, Alfred Winslow Jones is credited with forming the first absolute return fund (ARF) in New York in 1949. At that time, the first hedge fund was a long/short hedged equity vehicle. In recent years, the money management industry has embraced the use of absolute return approaches leading to the dramatic growth of hedge funds at the turn of the century. The success of these alternative investments has prompted institutional investors (even pension funds) with conservative attitudes to investment management and policies to include hedge funds as one segment in their diversified portfolios.

ARF funds may be confused with hedge funds, in that their composition and exposures may be modelled on hedge fund products. However, ARFs are not exclusive products, available only to a privileged group of investors, but have recently been rolled out to smaller retail investors. Essentially they are promoted as an alternative to a hedge fund. Unlike hedge funds, they do not have to be domiciled offshore and may be fully UK-regulated.

UCITS III significantly enlarged the range of investment instruments, notably allowing some use of derivatives. This makes possible for some hedge fund managers and ARF managers to launch versions of their strategies in new UCITS III-compliant wrappers, giving more investors access, but within the more controlling UCITS environment. The Investment Association (IA) is conducting a major review (see section 14.4.1) of its sector classifications to take into account the ramifications of the UCITS III and the RDR on a wide range of funds, including the growth of ARFs in the industry. The implication of this reclassification and development of sector classifications that will include derivative products by the trade body is to improve approaches to benchmark construction for monitoring fund performances. Also, following criticism received after the economic crisis where a large number of these funds failed to outperform or deliver an uncorrelated return, the IA changed the name of the Absolute Return Sector to the Targeted Absolute Return Sector. This is to highlight the point that the performance is a target and not a guarantee.

Absolute return vehicles are evaluated relative to cash deposits, the risk-free rate or LIBOR plus a specified rate to reflect the element of alpha risk taken. For example, the returns objective for such a fund may be stated as '*achieve 20–25% regardless of the market conditions*' or '*UK LIBOR plus 10%*'.

The compensation structure is similar to a hedge fund. A typical charge is made up of two parts, the management fee and an incentive fee. The management fee is worked out as a percentage of the NAV per share. For most funds this can be anywhere from 1–2% of the NAV plus an incentive fee (or performance fee) that ranges from 15–30%. On the profits, the incentive fee averages out to 20%. This '2 and 20' structure is a common charge with many funds. A number also have a high water mark. This means that if the fund declined in value in one year, then the hedge fund has to recover the loss before any incentive fee is paid.

For a graphic illustrating the typical fee structure, visit image.slidesharecdn.com/hffhfstructured12-2012-121220104643-phpapp01/95/how-hedge-funds-are-structured-15-638.jpg?cb=1370524211.

14.4.1 Measuring Performance/Benchmarking Funds

The performance of the ARFs is variable at best. A number available in the market have long/short exposures to a selected market index or its sector. Even though two funds may be classified under the same sector, their returns can be quite different. This is due not only to the variations in the make-up of portfolios, but also the directional sensitivities of the funds, due to their exposures to long and short positions. ARFs with a short-selling component were primarily designed to exploit alpha opportunities during market downturns. Such a portfolio does not perform as well in an upward-trending market as a traditional long-only portfolio.

In an effort to classify sectors for use in ARF applications, to improve transparency and performance measurement, the IA undertook a review. It provided the following definition of the absolute return sector (that will be subject to modification as the industry evolves in the aftermath of the UCITS 111, leading to UCITS IV and UCITS V):

Funds managed with the aim of delivering absolute (ie, more than zero) returns in any market conditions. Typically funds in this sector would normally expect to deliver absolute (more than zero) returns on a 12-month basis.

There is no asset-based monitoring for this sector, and the IA noted that performance comparisons are likely to be inappropriate given the diverse nature of the objectives of funds in this sector.

Advisers should note that analysis of historical performances of such funds is a specialised activity and is evolving. The information for interpretation of performances is achieved by accessing information available from the sellers of the managed funds and data providers who specialise in collecting the prices obtained from the funds and fund of funds. Transparency of information and benchmarking issues present problems. In recent years there have been growing calls from investors to provide means to monitor hedge fund performances, in the same manner that traditional mutual funds are tracked. In coming years, regulation on ARF products will improve, and this will increase transparency. Issues of benchmark selection and construction and measurement are likely to persist for a lot longer, however.

As a genre of alpha generation products, advisers should note that there are several biases that they need to be aware of when interpreting the performance data of ARFs.

As this industry does not have to adhere to a regulated performance presentation standard, biases in the historical data can make it difficult to compare the relative merits and performances of candidates, leading to a distortion of data existing in the public domain. The fund performances are overstated by biases. Further the issue is complicated by the fact that disclosure of this vital investor information by fund managers is voluntary. There are no mandatory reporting standards in place, creating three main biases:

1. **Self-selection bias** – given that disclosure of information is not mandatory, managers can decide themselves whether they wish to disclose their results to a particular service that keeps historic records. Clearly, funds performing badly may not participate and will not disclose details to a public database. Poor performers will want to keep their information out of the headlines; at the same time, high-performing and large funds may not want publicity that makes them stand out from their peer grouping.

2. **Backfill bias** – some funds joining a database may not present a complete record of their past time series of performances. Fund managers may, as a result, decide to start reporting only when their results reach a level that makes a positive impression on their investors. This problem is being addressed by vendor services, but can still be a source of bias for analysts trying to create a true and fair assessment of each fund manager's performance.
3. **Survivorship bias** – in the industry, unsuccessful funds disappear and are dropped out of indices. Only successful funds remain and present their records over a longer time period. This history of results gives the wrong impression about fund performances into the future.

15. Structured Products

Learning Objective

5.13.1 Analyse the key features, relative merits and limitations of investing in retail structured products and investment notes compared with other forms of direct and indirect investment: structure (structured deposits and products); income and capital growth; investment risk and return; expenses; capital protection; American and European soft protection; counterparty risk.

'Structured products' is a generic term used to loosely cover a diverse and a varied range of savings and investment products. They can be separated into two categories: structured deposits and structured investments.

In general all structured products share the following features:

- offer income or growth, but not both
- have defined returns and defined risks
- returns linked to a defined external measure such as FTSE 100 Index, gold prices, oil prices
- a defined term, typically from five to seven years.

All of these products are designed to run up to maturity, at which point the issuer of the product will aim to return the initial investment/deposit amount, along with the underlying linked asset's gain.

These products can be separated into three main categories: structured deposits; principal protected investment products; and capital at risk investment products (or buffer zone investments).

Structured deposits are cash-based products but can only be offered by banks which are able to accept deposits. They are designed to return at least the initial amount deposited at the end of the product's life. Depositors have more protection over their money than normal investments. UK investors in these types of deposit-based products benefit from the FSCS's deposit insurance scheme. This key aspect differentiates this form of structured product from investment-based products. The underlying asset in structured deposits is a cash deposit and the returns may be linked to the performance of another asset such as the FTSE 100 Index or the gold price performance between the date when the fund is set up and its end date.

A structured investment product is generally a pre-packaged investment, which is based on derivatives, a single security, a basket of securities, options, indices (including dual indices), commodities, debt issuances and/or foreign currencies, and, to a lesser extent, swaps. They are primarily innovations designed to fulfil highly customised return/risk objectives. The variety of products just described is demonstrative of the fact that there is no single, uniform definition of a structured product. A feature of some structured products is a principal guarantee function which offers protection of the principal, if held to maturity.

These capital-protected structured products are designed to return the original capital even if the underlying linked measure underperforms. Unlike the deposited-based products, the investment-based category of products do not, however, draw any benefit from FSCS protection in the event of counterparty defaults.

Capital at risk varieties of investment-based structured products offer high returns if the linked index measure outperforms. However, they can generate losses at maturity if the underlying linked index underperforms badly. The structured nature of such products also utilises barriers/buffers to cushion some of the losses in the event of larger than expected falls in the linked index measure.

Structured products can be used as an alternative to a direct investment, as part of the asset allocation process to reduce risk exposure of a portfolio, or to ride the current market trend. The risks associated with many structured products, especially those products that present risks of loss of principal due to market movements, are similar to those risks involved with options. Structured product funds have also begun to appear in the market. These enable investors to access a range of strategies through one investment, rather than using separate structured products for each.

Even in the case of a principal-protected product, they are only insured by the issuer, and thus they have a counterparty risk attached to them. Some firms have attempted to create a new market for structured products that are no longer trading. These securities may not be trading, due to issuer bankruptcy or a lack of liquidity to insure them.

15.1 Types of Structured Product

Retail structured investment-based products can be further sub-divided into the following types:

Principal-Protected Investments (Investment Returns without Principal at Risk)

A principal-protected investment may be appropriate for investors unwilling to risk their principal or who have long-term financial obligations. These investments generally offer a return at maturity linked to a broad-based equity index or a qualified basket of stocks. Investors typically give up a portion of the equity appreciation in exchange for principal protection. Maturities often range from five to seven years, and clients should intend to hold the investments to maturity.

Return-Enhanced Investments (Leveraged Upside in a Moderately Bullish Market)

If an investor believes that market returns are likely to be flat to slightly up, over the near term, a return-enhanced investment may be an ideal investment vehicle. In exchange for accepting full downside exposure in the underlying, a return-enhanced investment offers double or triple the equity returns up to a prespecified maximum. Return-enhanced investments tend to have maturities of one to three years.

Income-Based Investments

Other types of income-based investment offer varying degrees of principal protection, and are primarily focused on generating one or more coupon payments during the term of the investment.

Strategic Access Investments

At times an investor may wish to have exposure to a fairly inaccessible index or to a complicated and expensive trading strategy.

Hybrid Investments

Other possible investments include equities, currencies, commodities and fixed income. These innovative investments enable investors to take investment views simultaneously across several asset classes.

The following are examples of how structured products could work in practice.

Dual Index Products

With these structured products the returns are linked to the performance of two indexes, eg, the FTSE 100 and the Eurostoxx 50. The product will offer a return providing both indexes are at or above a predefined level at a point in time.

Constant Proportion Portfolio Insurance (CPPI)

This is a trading strategy that allows an investor to maintain an exposure to the upside potential of a risky asset while providing a capital guarantee against downside risk. The outcome of the CPPI strategy is somewhat similar to that of buying a call option, but does not use option contracts.

Soft Protection

These structures return investors' capital in full at maturity, provided the underlying asset does not fall below a predetermined barrier. This barrier is usually observed either daily throughout the investment term (an American barrier), or on the maturity date only (a European barrier).

Given the American barrier could potentially be breached daily throughout the term, it is higher risk than the European version, therefore, the payoff for a product with an American barrier will usually be higher than a product with a European barrier.

Example – Principal-Protected Investments

Investor A wants to preserve their principal but make money as equity markets rise. Investor A may consider the equity markets too risky for a direct investment, but is comfortable given the added protection of a principal-protected note. Investor A puts £1,000 in a seven-year principal-protected note linked to a broad-based equity index (such as the S&P 500, the NASDAQ 100 or the Dow Jones Industrial Average) with an 80% participation in the index appreciation.

Scenario 1

The index is up 50% at maturity:

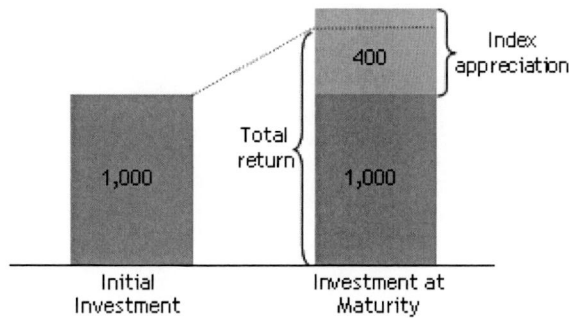

At maturity, the investor will receive their £1,000 principal back, plus 80% of the index appreciation, equal to 40%.

Scenario 2

The index is down 50% at maturity:

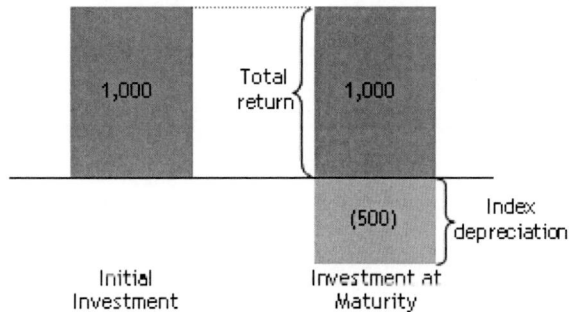

At maturity, because the index has declined, the investor will receive their £1,000 principal back.

Example – Buffer Zone Investments

Investor B is willing to accept a 20% buffer zone, meaning that they will begin to lose their principal if the index has declined more than 20% at maturity, in order to receive 85% participation in the index appreciation over three years. Investor B puts £1,000 in a three-year buffered equity note linked to a broad-based equity index (such as the S&P 500, the NASDAQ-100 or the Dow Jones Industrial Average) with an 85% participation in the index appreciation.

Scenario 1

The index is up 50% at maturity:

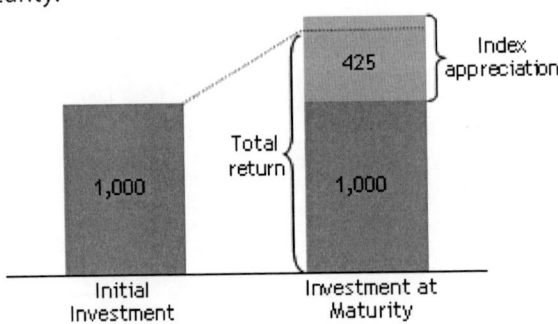

At maturity, the investor will receive their £1,000 principal back, plus 85% of the index appreciation, equal to 42.5%.

Scenario 2

The index is 15% down at maturity:

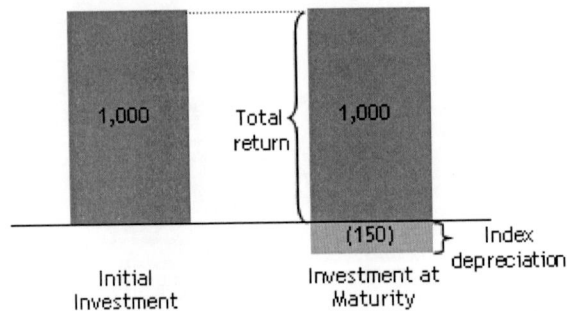

At maturity, the investor will receive their £1,000 principal back because the index is within the buffer zone.

Scenario 3

The index is 45% down at maturity:

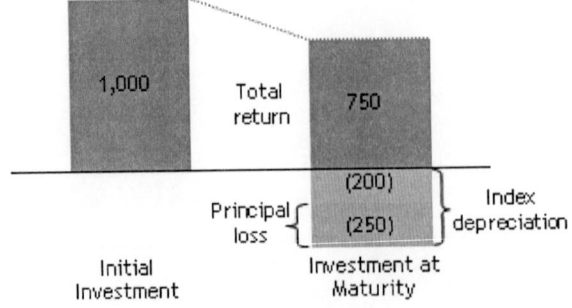

At maturity, the index is 25% below the buffer zone. The investor will lose 1% of their principal for each 1% the index has declined below the buffer zone, or 25% of their initial investment.

Investment Products

Example – Return-Enhanced Investments

Investor C has a flat to moderately bullish market view and would like to achieve a higher return than would otherwise be possible in the current market. With a return-enhanced investment, Investor C will receive twice the appreciation in the underlying equity index as a return, subject to maximum return, or cap of 26%, at the end of two years. If the index has declined at maturity, a 1% loss in principal will occur for each 1% decline in the index. Investor C puts £1,000 in a two-year return enhanced note linked to a broad-based equity index (such as the S&P 500, the NASDAQ 100 or the DJIA).

Scenario 1

The index is up 12% at maturity:

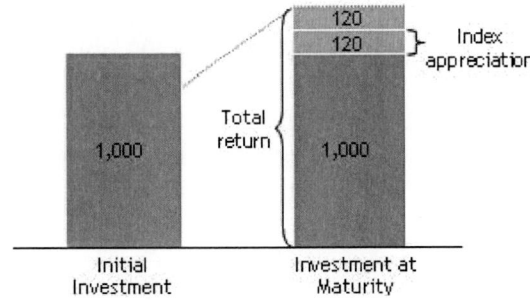

At maturity, the investor will receive their £1,000 principal back, plus double the 12% index return, equal to 24%.

Scenario 2

The index is down 12% at maturity:

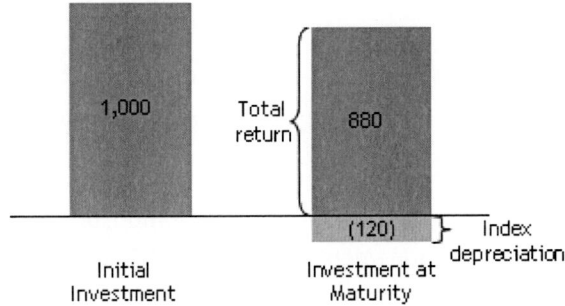

At maturity, the investor will lose 1% of their investment for each 1% decline in the index.

Scenario 3

The index is up 30% at maturity:

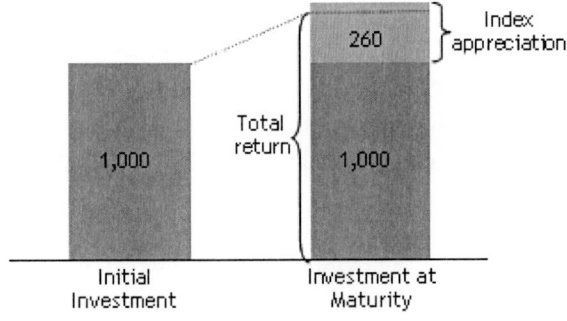

At maturity, because the index is above the 13% upside cap, the investor will receive the maximum return of 26%.

15.2 Counterparty Risks and other Considerations

The returns offered by structured products (even the principal-protected variety) are only as good as the credit quality of the issuer. Even though the cash flows and the principal in a structured product may come from a stable investment (eg, a bond), the products themselves are legally considered to be the issuer's liability. Often the products are created and sold by large global financial institutions and investment banks, whose own credit rating may be less than the underlying assets held. If the issuer goes bust, then the product's principal-protected guarantee may not apply and the capital will be at risk.

Prior to the 2007–08 credit crisis, several firms that issued structured products (including Lehman Brothers) went into administration or bankruptcy during the financial crisis and could not meet their obligations. Investors in structured products had to wait along with bondholders to recover their funds invested with the banks who offered such products.

Regulatory authorities have recognised that counterparty risk is a significant issue in the post-Lehman Brothers collapse and have called for providers to describe the risks in their marketing and sales literature fully.

Structured products can be complex and may have unique characteristics that often cannot be replicated or provided by other issuers. For the investor this product differentiation creates price transparency issues. It is therefore harder to determine the intrinsic values of each competitor product in the market and to compare alternatives offered by each provider.

16. Retirement Planning

Learning Objective

5.14.1 Analyse the main types, purpose, structure and operation, tax treatment and investment characteristics of pension arrangements: defined benefit; defined contribution; personal pensions; self-invested personal pensions (SIPPs); small self-administered schemes (SSASs)

5.14.2 Analyse the key features of pension arrangements: contributions – sources, level and limits; investment selection and performance; how benefits are provided; annual and lifetime allowances

Planning for retirement is an important element of the investment advice process – even for the youngest clients. As people live longer, and (even with rising retirement ages) face the prospect of longer periods of a non-working old age, it is important that they consider the ways in which they may fund their needs as they get older. Pensions and associated products are the main retirement planning tools we will consider.

As of April 2006, a new set of pension rules were introduced which have been refined still further, most recently in April 2015. Despite the complexity in this area, as an adviser you will need to ensure that you are up to date on the rules, or at least in a position to refer clients to a specialist adviser in this area.

Most individual pensions do not start paying an income as soon as an individual retires. Instead, they allow the individual a choice on when and how they wish to start taking the income. This income can be taken from a pension from age 55.

Part of the pension can be taken as a tax-free lump sum, usually around 25% of the value of the pension pot. The remainder can be converted into an income via an insurance provider using an annuity or placed into an alternative retirement product, eg, flexi-access drawdown. The annuity will pay a taxable income to the retiree for the remainder of their life. Once the annuity is set up, the rate is fixed offering a secure lifelong regular income to the pensioner (see section 16.2.1 for more).

Following the changes announced in the March 2014 Budget, which took effect in April 2015, retirees are able to take the balance of their pension fund, after tax-free cash, as a further lump sum taxable at their marginal rate of income tax. In effect, this allows the withdrawal of the entire pension fund, with no requirement to purchase an annuity or to set up a drawdown arrangement. This is referred to as uncrystallised funds pension lump sum (UFPLS).

16.1 Occupational Pension Schemes

Occupational pensions are pensions provided by an employer to its employees. They are either salary-related (also known as defined benefit), or money purchase (defined contribution).

- **Salary-related schemes** pay a pension based on two things: the length of time the employee has been employed, and their salary. Sometimes the salary used as a reference point is their salary on retirement (a final salary scheme); other schemes use the employee's average salary over their time with the company. The scheme assets are looked after by trustees, who should ensure that the employer pays into the scheme regularly. Many defined benefit schemes have been phased out or closed to new members in recent years by employers, and replaced with defined contribution schemes where the risk is borne by the employee. See chapter 6, section 2.5.
- **Money purchase schemes** are not directly based on the employee's salary or years of employment (though this will affect how much is paid in). Instead, an individual pension pot is built up for each employee, through contributions made by the employer and the employee – which the employee uses at retirement to convert into an income, usually by buying an annuity. The value of the employee's salary on retirement will therefore depend on:
    - how much has been paid into the scheme over the employee's working life
    - how well it has performed in investment terms
    - what charges have been deducted, and
    - what conditions are in the market for converting it to an income when the employee retires.

16.2 Personal Pensions

Personal pensions are offered by commercial financial services providers, such as life companies. All personal pensions are money purchase schemes; they may be set up by a client who is arranging their pension privately – a popular option for the self-employed, or those who move between jobs regularly. Some employers also offer access to them and in this case they are not classified as occupational schemes. Personal pensions, self-invested personal pensions (SIPPs), group personal pensions and retirement annuity contracts are all forms of personal pension.

Again, the pension that the client will receive on retirement will depend on:

- how much has been paid into the scheme over the individual's working life
- how well the scheme has performed in investment terms
- what charges have been deducted, and
- what conditions are in the market for converting it to an income when the employee retires.

Stakeholder schemes are a form of personal pension meeting certain requirements, like low charges and accessible minimum contributions; they are designed to make pensions more affordable for those on lower incomes, but have also been popular with other sectors of the population on account of their apparent value for money. Like ordinary personal pensions, they are offered by commercial organisations such as life companies.

16.2.1 Annuities

A member of a defined contribution arrangement (ie, an occupational money purchase scheme, personal pension plan or a stakeholder pension scheme) builds up a 'pot of money' over their working life. On retirement, the member may use all or part of this pot to buy a lifetime annuity. Annuities are available from insurance companies.

For beneficiaries opting to take an annuity, there are a number of options that a financial adviser can recommend.

There are four types of annuity:

- **Lifetime annuity** – a contract between an insurance company and a pension scheme member under which the member hands over all or part of their pension fund. The insurance will now agree to pay an income to the scheme member for the remainder of that member's life. This annuity can either be fixed or it can be index-linked. The annuity can be set up so that it is payable for a minimum of five or ten years, even if the scheme member dies before that period ends. The annuity can then revert to the spouse or civil partner.

    A variation of this is an annuity with a guaranteed period (eg, five years). This is the time period within which the annuity will continue to be paid, even if the pensioner (annuitant) passes away prematurely. After the guarantee period ends, if the pensioner is still surviving, then the regular payment will continue as normal until their death. The maximum guaranteed period for such an annuity is ten years. A reason for taking a guaranteed period annuity is to ensure that a surviving member can benefit from the pension should the annuitant pass away within the period.

    A spouse pension is a feature added on to a regular pension annuity, where a surviving spouse on the death of the annuitant gets the benefit. These types of pensions are selected as 50%, 66% or 100% of the original pension. The regular income provided will be based on the relative ages of the two annuitants.

- **Impaired life annuities** – these pay an annuity in the same way as a lifetime annuity. However, they pay a higher amount to those suffering certain medical conditions on the basis that they have a reduced life expectancy.
- **Enhanced annuities** – normally available to regular smokers, people who are overweight or those who have spent a good proportion of their working lives in hazardous occupations (ie, mining). Note: if a member is accepted under this payment scheme, income will be higher than for a conventional annuity because the provider only expects to pay for a shorter period of time.

- **Deferred annuities** – a pension under an occupational scheme has now been bought out with an insurance product known as a deferred annuity. If the insurance company were to go bankrupt, compensation will be paid out under the **Financial Services Compensation Scheme (FSCS)**.

16.2.2 Small Self-Administered Schemes (SSASs)

An SSAS is a company scheme where the members are usually all company directors or key staff. An SSAS is set up by a trust deed and rules and allows members/employers greater flexibility and control over the scheme's assets.

Contributions paid to an SSAS are subject to the same rules as other registered pension schemes. Consequently there is no limit on the level of member contributions, but tax relief is restricted to the higher of £3,600 or 100% of UK earnings. Tax relief is also limited by the annual allowance.

Contributions made by the employer are also unlimited. Employer contributions are deductible against corporation tax, providing that they are wholly and exclusively for the purposes of the employer's trade. If an employer's contribution is over £500,000 more than the previous year, tax relief may be spread.

Schemes with fewer than 12 members, and where all decisions are made unanimously or have an independent trustee, are exempt from the trustees' knowledge and understanding requirements of the Pensions Act 2004 and the member-nominated trustee requirements. If every member of the scheme is a trustee, the scheme will also be exempt from the internal disputes resolution procedure requirements.

Loans can be made to the sponsoring employer but are subject to certain conditions set by HMRC.

These include:

- The loan should not exceed 50% of the net market value of the scheme's assets.
- The loan should be secured against assets of an equal value by way of a first charge.
- The loan's terms should be no longer than five years.
- Interest of at least 1% above bank base rate should be charged on the loan.

The trustees of an SSAS can invest in a broad range of investments, including:

- commercial property and land
- UK quoted shares, stocks, gilts and debentures
- stocks and shares quoted on a recognised overseas stock exchange
- futures and options quoted on a recognised stock exchange
- OEICs, unit trusts and investment trusts
- hedge funds
- insurance company funds
- bank and building society deposits
- gold bullion.

Shareholdings in the sponsoring employer should not exceed 5%. Shares can also be bought in more than one sponsoring employer, as long the total holdings are less than 20% and shares in any one sponsoring employer are less than 5%.

There is no restriction (apart from the self-investment restrictions above) on the percentage of shares which can be held in one company.

If the scheme is deemed to be an investment-regulated pension scheme (IRPS), tax charges will apply if the scheme invests in taxable property. The definition of an IRPS includes:

- company schemes where there are fewer than 50 members and at least one of them (or a person related to a member) can direct, influence, or advise on investment matters relating to the scheme
- company schemes that do not meet the above conditions but a member (or a person related to a member) can direct, influence or advise on investment matters relating to the member's arrangement.

Taxable property means investment in residential property and tangible moveable property, eg, fine wines and vintage cars.

If investments are made in taxable property, an unauthorised payment charge and a scheme sanction charge will apply. Capital gains can also apply on the sale of a taxable property.

SSASs may borrow to invest and to provide a member's benefit which has become payable. The maximum amount that can be borrowed is 50% of the NAV of the scheme.

16.2.3 Self-Invested Personal Pensions (SIPPs)

Self-Invested Personal Pensions (SIPPs) are a form of do-it-yourself pension plan that permit an investor to put their active investments into a private pension pot. They enable an investor to choose between a variety of investments, unlike other pensions, and in addition they provide the same tax advantages as other pension plans. Recent adjustments to legislation imply that SIPPs are not aimed at those on higher incomes. Initially they were marketed to individuals with a pension fund of £200,000 or even more, but now even people with no steady income source can contribute around £3,600 into a SIPP. It is not possible to draw benefits from a SIPP before the age of 55.

16.3 Pension Contributions and Tax Relief

There are limits on the amount of tax relief that individuals can get. The maximum amount of relief is equal to 100% of all earnings for that tax year. Although individuals can contribute to as many pension schemes as they wish, they only make contributions up to a maximum annual amount, set at £40,000 for the 2017–18 tax year. Contributions made above this limit will be subject to tax at the individual's marginal rate.

The Tapered Annual Allowance

As mentioned previously, from 6 April 2016, individuals who have an adjusted income in any given tax year greater than £150,000 will have their annual allowance restricted for that particular tax year. Please refer to chapter 4, section 11.1.4 for further coverage of the tapered annual allowance.

Money Purchase Annual Allowance (MPAA)

An individual's annual allowance will be replaced by the MPAA should they access their pension funds in any of the following ways:

- via uncrystallised funds pension lump sum
- receiving income above the maximum limit for capped drawdown members
- accessing a flexible annuity
- once income has been taken from a flexi-access drawdown plan.

Please refer to chapter 4, section 11.1.4 for further coverage of the MPAA.

Key Chapter Points

- The NAV of a collective is the value of its assets less its liabilities.
- OEICs pay dividends not distributions.
- Investment trusts have a closed-ended capital structure and therefore have a fixed number of shares in issue at any one time.
- The value of investment trust shares fluctuates, according to supply and demand, whereas the value of the units or shares in a unit trust or OEIC are driven by the value of the underlying assets.
- Zero dividend preference shares pay no income but offer a predetermined rate of return when the investment trust is finally wound up.
- REITs pay no corporation taxes, as long as they distribute 90% of their profits to shareholders as dividends.
- A FOF has one overall manager.
- Authorised open-ended funds can generally only borrow in certain, limited circumstances, whereas investment trusts (closed-ended vehicles) have much wider borrowing powers.
- Collective funds that invest mainly in cash deposits and interest-bearing securities pay distributions that are mostly made up of interest, and the distribution is taxed as savings income. Those investing mainly in companies make distributions that are mostly made up of dividends, and the distribution is taxed as dividend income.
- An equalisation payment is deemed to be a return of the investor's money and so is not liable to income tax.
- Capital gains made within an OEIC are exempt from tax.
- Investment trusts, providing that they comply with the relevant rules, do not pay CGT on internal gains.
- UK REITs are not subject to CGT on gains made on the disposal of property, providing that they distribute at least 90% of their profits each year to shareholders as dividends.
- Reporting funds are funds recognised by HMRC and which distribute at least 85% of their net investment income. Funds with reporting status are treated, for tax purposes, the same as UK-based funds.
- Non-reporting funds are typically those that roll up their capital gains and income. The tax treatment for UK resident investors is different and usually all gains are subject to income tax rather than CGT.
- Open-ended funds may be single-priced or dual-priced.
- The dilution levy is also known as the dealing charge. It is a charge which may be imposed by the manager to cover dealing costs.
- Capital redemption bonds are life company products which have no life assured.
- Income tax relief is given on investments in an EIS-qualifying company, subject to a maximum of £1 million. The relief is 30% of the cost of the shares that can be set against the individual's income tax liability for the year in which the investment was made.
- VCTs are companies listed on the LSE and are similar to investment trusts.

End of Chapter Questions

Think of an answer for each question and refer to the appropriate workbook section for confirmation.

1. Give an example of a closed-ended collective investment fund.
   Answer reference: Section 1.1

2. What is the function of the authorised corporate director?
   Answer reference: Section 2.2

3. What type of split capital investment trust share provides a pre-determined return to investors when the trust is wound up?
   Answer reference: Section 3.1.1

4. How are capital gains taxed within an open-ended investment company?
   Answer reference: Section 4.1.1

5. How are gains on disposals made by offshore reporting funds taxed on the investor?
   Answer reference: Section 5.1.1

6. Explain what is meant by the dilution levy.
   Answer reference: Section 6.2.3

7. What is the current maximum ISA allowance?
   Answer reference: Section 8.1

8. How much can a policyholder withdraw each year from an investment bond without triggering a liability to tax?
   Answer reference: Section 8.3

9. Which NS&I products are liable for capital gains tax?
   Answer reference: Section 8.4

10. How do capital redemption bonds differ from other investment bond policies?
    Answer reference: Section 9.2.2

Chapter Six
Investment Planning

Introduction	**407**
1. **Asset Allocation**	**409**
2. **Investment Selection**	**419**

This syllabus area will provide approximately 5 of the 80 examination questions

Introduction

In investment management, everything is client-driven. The process begins with the formal establishment of a client relationship, hence the starting points for any investment strategy are the client's goals for wealth creation and management, so that they may meet expected or unexpected contingent liabilities. Often a client will complete a risk-assessment questionnaire that will help the investment manager to understand the risk tolerance and to guide investment policy.

The portfolio management process is an integrated set of steps that are taken to create and maintain an appropriate portfolio to meet the client's stated goals. A primary foundation for the process is an investment policy statement (IPS) – a written document that clearly sets out a client's return objectives and risk tolerance over the time horizon, along with constraints such as liquidity requirements, tax position, regulatory requirements and unique circumstances. This plan, combined with capital market expectations, is then executed to deliver the client objectives.

Central to the execution of this plan is the asset allocation decision. The investment manager takes responsibility for this task and then sets about constructing an appropriate portfolio that has a good balance of assets to deliver the desired objectives. This is called the asset allocation decision. Asset allocations can be set over the long term or they can be designed to deliver outcomes over the short term.

A strategic asset allocation is a long-term approach that establishes acceptable exposures to asset classes that are permitted by the IPS, in order to achieve long-run objectives. For example, decisions taken by pension funds are of a long-term nature and asset allocation decisions are designed to meet these objectives. Allocations that are managed continuously over a shorter term and require revisions are tactical asset allocation decisions.

Further, portfolios may be managed passively or actively. A passive approach aims to make the minimum number of adjustments over a planning horizon. Often, performance is monitored so that a selected benchmark or an index is tracked closely; the aim being to minimise the tracking error between the managed fund and the benchmark. Revisions are carried out if there are large divergences between the managed portfolio and the benchmark. An active approach can also utilise the same benchmark but, in this case, the manager aims to beat an index by delivering superior performances; we call this extra return that the manger is trying to achieve, alpha. Money managers who are in search of alpha believe that they have skills, such as security selection or timing skills, that can deliver above average returns to the chosen benchmark.

The IPS will have identified an investor's return requirements. If a benchmark is involved then the returns are assessed in relative return terms. Alternatively, if there is no benchmark included, as is the case of a hedge fund manager, then the expected returns are quoted in absolute terms.

Relative returns are often based on annual spending needs and long-term savings goals, together with wealth requirements. Traditionally, a portfolio was constructed with three components, namely: a money market asset, a bond-like asset and an equity-like asset. Money market instruments provided the liquidity to meet short-term needs or for emergencies. For income-generation, managers relied on the bond component, while long-term growth needs were met by equities. The growth element of the portfolio relies on capital appreciation to deliver outcomes. It would come from any residual income that was not needed to meet short-term liquidity needs and could be reinvested over a longer term to generate higher levels of growth.

Growth or Income

The client's requirements for capital growth or income need to be identified at the outset to ensure the correct mix of assets is used and the most appropriate funds selected. The choice of wrapper and tax consequences will also have a bearing on how the assets are invested. For example, the client's income requirements may be better met through ad hoc withdrawals of capital rather than recurring income payments.

Timescale

The time horizon of the client is also an important consideration. If they only require an income, then the time period may be open-ended, while clients who require capital growth may need to access some or all of their capital at a point in the future. In such circumstances, you will need to consider the liquidity and volatility of the underlying assets.

For example, if the client tells you that they need access to some of their capital in the next six months, then it is likely that an asset class that has daily liquidity and low volatility, to ensure that the capital value is preserved and accessible when needed, will be chosen. In this case, cash deposits are usually preferable.

If the period of time is greater than six months, other fixed-interest assets may be considered.

An investment in equities may only be suitable if access is not required for five years or more. Any earlier and there is a risk that the capital value may have diminished, leaving the client with a possible shortfall.

As property can be illiquid, it should only be used for longer-term investment strategies, ie, ten years plus.

Attitude to Risk

Understanding the client's attitude to risk is a vital part of the investment decision process. A number of different methods may be used to assess how a client feels about investment risk, including questionnaires and bespoke software applications. Question-based assessments generally place clients into one of a number of risk classifications, ie, cautious, balanced, aggressive. See chapter 7 for more details on this.

The combination of the client's objectives, timescale and attitude to risk is a guide to choosing a suitable asset allocation.

1. Asset Allocation

Learning Objective

6.1.1 Understand the purpose and principles of asset allocation: relationship with investment theory; achievement of performance objectives; trade-off between risk and return; stochastic modelling; active and passive management; strategic asset allocation (SAA); tactical asset allocation (TAA)

6.1.2 Understand how investment theory is applied to the process of portfolio construction

Asset allocation divides an investment portfolio among different asset classes, based on an investor's financial requirements. The right mix of asset classes in a portfolio provides an investor with the highest probability of meeting their need. Each asset class selected has a long-term expected return over inflation, known as the real return.

Stocks and bonds are the two classic asset classes used in portfolio construction. Allocation decisions will aim to set the investment amounts in each asset class. For example, do we allocate 25% to bonds and 75% to equities, or settle on a different mix between the two? In practice, investment is carried out in a number of other asset classes, but historically the initial decision was based on division between stocks and bonds. The rationale behind this decision is based on two factors. First, the allocation is based on the expected return that an investor requires to meet their financial objective, and second, it is based on the investor's tolerance of, or capacity, for risk. A successful allocation is one that achieves an investor's financial goals without so much volatility that it causes the investor to make behavioural mistakes.

Asset allocation analysis should include a correlation study between investment types. Correlation analysis shows how the price of one investment has historically moved in relation to the price of another. If two asset classes move in the same direction at the same time, they have positive correlation. If the returns have moved in different directions at the same time, they have negative correlation.

Correlation is not fixed and is time varying – it changes over time and in unpredictable ways. It would be ideal if two asset classes had positive real returns expectations and consistent negative return correlation with each other. Unfortunately, there are no such pairs of investments. Using historical data, it is only possible to forecast the correlation between two asset classes.

Recent studies have shown that, over two decades, cross-correlations between a variety of asset classes have increased. Correlations show wide variations over time, but, during financial crises and increases in volatility, correlations between asset classes increase. During recessions, correlations have shown some tendencies to increase to higher levels. In the recent financial crisis, observers noted that correlations have remained at elevated levels when compared to other historical crises. High correlations also seem to be associated with high volatility.

Modern portfolio theory (MPT) is a theory of investment which tries to maximise return and minimise risk by carefully choosing different assets. Although MPT is widely used in practice in the financial industry, in recent years the basic assumptions of MPT have been widely challenged by fields such as behavioural finance. See chapter 3, section 3.5.

MPT is a mathematical formulation of the concept of diversification in investing, with the aim of selecting a collection of investment assets that collectively has lower risk than any individual asset. This is possible, in theory, because different types of assets often change in value in opposite ways. For example, when the prices in the stock market fall, the prices in the bond market often increase, and vice versa. A combination of both asset classes can therefore have lower overall risk than either individually.

More technically, MPT models an asset's return as a normally distributed random variable, defines risk as the standard deviation of return, and models a portfolio as a weighted combination of assets so that the return of a portfolio is the weighted combination of the assets' returns. By combining different assets whose returns are not correlated, MPT seeks to reduce the total variance of the portfolio. MPT also assumes that investors are rational and markets are efficient.

MPT was developed in the 1950s and was considered an important advance in the mathematical modelling of finance. Since then, much theoretical and practical criticism has been levelled against it. This includes the fact that financial returns do not follow a Gaussian distribution and that correlation between asset classes is not fixed, but can vary depending on external events. There is also growing evidence that investors are not rational and markets are not efficient. See chapter 3, section 3.2 for a more thorough discussion of MPT.

1.1 Risk and Return

MPT assumes that investors are risk-averse, meaning that, given two assets that offer the same expected return, investors will prefer the less risky one. Thus, an investor will take on increased risk only if compensated by higher expected returns. Conversely, an investor who wants higher returns must accept more risk. The exact trade-off will differ by investor, based on individual risk-aversion characteristics. The implication is that a rational investor will not invest in a portfolio if a second portfolio exists with a more favourable risk/return profile – ie, if for that level of risk an alternative portfolio exists which has better expected returns.

1.2 Stochastic Modelling

Stochastic modelling is the use of historical data to model thousands of possible investment return outcomes, for almost all asset allocation combinations. Its application initially started in physics. This method allows actual or theoretical portfolios to be analysed to see their risk/return profiles and determine the likely range of returns, which should be expected. These can then be matched against investors' own risk/return expectations, ensuring portfolios are tailor-made to individual client needs.

There are two approaches to portfolio management:

1. deterministic
2. stochastic.

Investment Planning

Example – The Deterministic Model

Imagine you have to work out how many times you expect to throw heads if you flip a coin 1,000 times. The chance of throwing heads is evens, ie, 50/50. Therefore, the deterministic model of that activity is 1,000 x 50% = 500 heads.

Example – The Stochastic Model

1,000 simulated coin tosses are performed, each of which has a 50/50 chance, and the number of heads is then counted and noted. You might get 487 or 505 or something else close to 500. The more simulations you run, the closer the stochastic result will get to 500, but the number simulated is also a factor that needs to be modelled and brought into account. Where the potential values are 'known' and no other variables are involved, then the outcomes (deterministic or stochastic) are virtually identical, but life and investments are not certain!

1.2.1 So Why Use Stochastic Modelling?

Stochastic modelling comes into its own if the outcomes are what are known as path-dependent.

Example

I am building a portfolio, but also taking constant withdrawals, so the likelihood of my being able to sustain my income levels is not just affected by the impact of stock market movements, but also depends on when those falls happen. There may be a 5% fall in one year, but there is a dramatically different impact on the sustainability of my withdrawals if that 5% fall happens in year one rather than year ten.

In this scenario, the stochastic model runs thousands of trials to chart the frequency of outcomes and thus check the robustness of this drawdown strategy. Potential outcomes are derived from a large number of simulations (stochastic projections) which reflect the random variation in the input(s).

To achieve 20% per annum consistently for 15 years is a goal we would all aspire to. However, you would have to sell and miss the 40 worst days in the last 15 years to achieve this. By simply leaving your money invested for 15 years and not concerning yourself with buying or selling, you will achieve 1.1% per annum. By trying to get it right but actually getting the timing wrong and therefore missing some of the best days, bearing in mind that most of these best days are usually just after a fall (just after the worst days), then you rapidly reduce your annual returns.

Professionals say that trying to guess market timing never pays and these facts go some way to proving that. We should therefore spend most of our time establishing risk rating, based on the following:

- time frame investment
- income or growth required
- attitude to risk
- amount invested.

These factors will determine your risk rating, which in turn determines the asset allocation, ie, the amount required in the different asset classes to fall in line with their attitude to risk. Having established a client's asset allocation, broadly in line with attitude to risk, it is still important to find the best opportunities to benefit from better-performing fund managers in each of the asset classes.

1.3 Strategic Asset Allocation

In strategic asset allocation, the decisions on the portfolio mix are taken from a long-term perspective. Money managers consider long-term client objectives, as well as capital market expectations, to come to this decision. This composition is called a policy portfolio and may be periodically rebalanced to adjust the portfolio to specific weights. It sets the investor's long-term exposures to systematic risk. The interpretation of long-term is vague as it varies with each investor. However, five years is a reasonable minimum reference point.

The policy portfolio is created by considering the long-term behaviour of a set of assets. For example, if stocks have historically returned 10% per year and bonds have returned 5% per year, a mix of 50% stocks and 50% bonds will be expected to return 7.5% per year.

1.4 Tactical Asset Allocation

Over the long run, a strategic asset allocation strategy may seem relatively rigid. Therefore, you may find it necessary to occasionally engage in short-term, tactical deviations from the mix, in order to capitalise on unusual or exceptional investment opportunities. This flexibility adds a component of market timing to the portfolio, allowing you to participate in economic conditions that are more favourable for one asset class than for others.

Tactical asset allocation can be described as a moderately active strategy, since the overall strategic asset mix is returned to when desired short-term profits are achieved. This strategy demands some discipline, as you must first be able to recognise when short-term opportunities have run their course, and then rebalance the portfolio to the long-term asset position.

1.5 Basic Methods of Diversification

Learning Objective

6.1.3 Understand the basic ways to diversify a portfolio: asset class; geographical area; sector; currency; maturity

Diversification within the portfolio can be achieved in a number of ways including exposure to different:

- asset classes
- geographical areas
- sectors
- currencies
- maturities.

Spreading investments across all available asset classes, eg, property, equities, cash and bonds, is the starting point for most portfolio managers. Further diversification can be achieved by spreading the exposure, in a particular asset class, across various geographical areas, eg, UK equities and overseas equities and emerging markets.

Sector diversification such as spreading equity exposure across manufacturing and utilities businesses can help reduce the risk of a downturn in any particular area.

Investing in various currencies can also add to the diversification of a portfolio. This may be particularly useful if the investor is based overseas.

Finally, investing in a series of fixed-interest assets with different maturities can help to limit the effects of inflation or interest rate movements on the whole portfolio. It can smooth out interest rate or investment risk.

1.6 Combinations of Asset Classes

Learning Objective

6.1.4 Analyse combinations of asset classes based on: historical returns; index and benchmark comparisons; correlation of performances between asset classes; advantages and limitations of relying on historical data

1.6.1 Diversification and Correlation

As described in chapter 3, section 2.6.3, correlation is a pair-wise measure of how the returns from two different assets move together over time. It is scaled between +1 and –1. Assets with a high level of positive correlation (close to +1) tend to move in the same direction at the same time. Assets with a low correlation (close to 0) tend to move independently of each other. Assets with strong negative correlations (close to –1) tend to move in opposite directions.

Consider the risk formula we described in chapter 3 again:

$$\sigma^2_{PQ} = W^2_P \sigma^2_P + W^2_Q \sigma^2_Q + 2W_P W_Q \text{Cov}_{PQ}.$$

In this case, the risk on a portfolio based on two asset classes P and Q depends on: the allocation (weighting in each asset), the risk levels of each component and a weighted covariance between the two asset classes.

Assume P represents a low risk and return asset such as a bond, and Q represents a high-risk and high-return asset, such as an equity index. If we allocate more funds in a portfolio to equities (for example from 50% in equities + 50% in bonds to 60/40), the overall risk of a portfolio will increase. The other contributor to risk is covariance between the two assets.

As was also shown in chapter 3, covariance is closely related to correlation. Diversification and risk reduction is achieved by combining assets, whose returns have not moved in perfect step, or are not perfectly positively correlated with one another.

Risk of the portfolio does not change in a linear fashion with the changes in allocations to the higher-risk asset. There can be a significant and beneficial departure from linearity, if the correlation between the two assets starts to move away from a perfect +1 state. Sometimes only a small amount of less-than-perfect positive correlation will help to provide diversification benefits to a portfolio. On a scale from +1 to −1, as correlation gets closer towards −1, diversification benefits in a portfolio combination improve. Clearly, if a fund manager can find two asset classes that are perfectly negatively correlated (−1), then the diversification benefit is maximised. This is because returns in the different assets now move in the opposite direction to one another at all times and in the same proportion. A unique combination of assets with this type of association results in a portfolio that produces a risk-free type security return. Unfortunately, in practice it is difficult to find two assets that are perfectly negatively correlated. Otherwise, everyone would buy into these combinations.

1.6.2 Historical Asset Class Returns

Historical Returns from Different Asset Classes

In Dollar terms 1995–2012	MSCI Equity indices						EFFAS 10+ Sovereign Debt			Property	Commodity	
	World	US	GER	UK	Japan	BRIIC	US Bonds	GER Bonds	UK Bonds	US REIT	Gold	Brent Oil
Return (% Annual)	4.26	6.53	4.59	3.64	−2.34	6.29	8.74	8.90	8.23	10.86	8.47	11.52
Risk (% Annual)	16.08	16.11	24.68	16.32	18.89	30.85	9.86	8.48	7.82	21.74	16.08	36.61
Coefficient of variation	3.78	2.47	5.37	4.48	−8.06	4.90	1.13	0.95	0.95	2.00	1.90	3.18

Theoretically, in the capital asset pricing model (CAPM), a straight line relationship is assumed between returns and risk on assets. This is because over a longer term investors demand a premium (higher return), over a risk-free rate, for any additional risk taken.

However, it is important for investors to recognise that even though high-risk investments offer the potential for higher returns, this return is not guaranteed. It is now dispersed over a much broader range about the expected mean. Compared to a low-risk investment, there is now the possibility for very low or high return outcomes that depends on the nature of a particular state of the world event. This is why, when we say that the risks are higher, we see a broad dispersion in terms of returns about a mean level.

If we consider the empirical results from the table, we can see that bonds occupy the lowest risk position on a scale when compared with equities, property and commodities. Over the 1995–2012 period, the sub-prime crisis in 2007 overshadowed all others. The resultant turmoil impacted badly on stock markets, wiping out all of the strong gains that were made in the previous five years. In dollar terms the UK stock market managed an average annual return of 3.64% over that period, and the world stock index returned 4.26% per annum. The risks of the UK and the world indices were both close to 16%. In coefficient of variation (CV) terms, risk per unit of return and ignoring the Japanese stock market performance, the risks were highest for the German stock market and lowest for the US stock index.

Compared to other asset classes, the CV of the bond indices was lowest of all of the assets. Property and commodities occupied an intermediate position between bonds and equities.

1.6.3 Asset Class Correlation

Given that correlation is a keystone feature of portfolio construction theory, we examine the nature of correlation further in this section.

Assets with a low or negative correlation are incredibly attractive to investors: when one asset is performing badly, the other asset is rising in value. Low correlation (even a value slightly less than +1.0) provides diversification benefits.

Securities with similar characteristics can be classified into groups, called asset classes. Each asset class may be distinguished by considering three factors of investment performance:

- historic level of return that the asset class has delivered
- historic level of risk that the asset class has experienced
- level of correlation between the investment returns of each asset class.

Each asset class can be located in a unique risk/return space. Statistically, it is assumed that individual asset classes are uncorrelated (or have low correlations) with each other. As a result, the explanatory factors responsible for driving performance in each asset class can also be delineated. Investors can use these differences to consider how likely their investments are to meet their objectives and appetite for risk. It can be possible to even out investment performance over time, by spreading investments across different asset classes.

For example, returns from UK equities and other international equity markets are highly correlated, reflecting the increasing globalisation of equity markets. While investors may look to invest overseas, to gain exposure to different industries and companies, most major equity markets now rise and fall together in response to global news and to volatility shocks.

From the table, it is evident that over the period from 1995–2012, in US dollar terms the international stock indices of US, UK and Germany were closely coupled, with correlations coming in range 0.80–0.81. The correlations between Japan/ US and Japan/European stock indices were lower in comparison: 0.47–0.55. This suggests that there have been better opportunities for international diversification for equity-only fund managers in these pairs. However, all equity indices tended to be more strongly correlated during periods of market stress and such events could unravel a diversification strategy.

Overall, bond indices were negatively correlated to equities, reflecting the safe haven properties provided by strong sovereign debt markets during periods when the markets were in a distressed state.

Traditionally, the only three generally recognised asset classes were cash, equities and gilts. In recent years there has been a general trend to include a range of alternative asset classes, so that equity and bond risk factors can be diversified. However, many of these asset classes are either esoteric or not open to most investors. In parallel, commodities and other alternatives have become good candidates over the last few decades and present alternative characteristics to the three historic asset classes. As property has gained in popularity, it has become recognised as a core asset class in its own right.

However, the sub-prime crisis that rocked global markets in 2007–08 somewhat diminished the attractiveness of property as an alternative asset class to equities.

The following table shows the correlation of returns between the major asset classes over the period 1995–2012. In this period the market experienced two booms and busts. The booms were in time periods: 1995–2000, and 2003–07. The busts came into the turn of the century, when the dot-com bubble burst in 2001 first, followed by the lingering waves of crises triggered by the credit crunch in 2007.

The correlations we have in the table have been arbitrarily set to identify investments into broad groups, where a particular risk factor is considered to have a strong influence on each sub-set. We are comparing correlations with equities and have taken this perspective in the analysis. The following points are noted:

- Correlations from 0.66 to 1 demonstrate strong equity to equity relationships, suggesting that a common equity risk factor was responsible for explaining the pair-wise interaction of returns.
- Correlations between 0.33 to 0.66 demonstrate moderate US property index and Japanese equity index relationships with developed equity market indices (US, UK, Germany).
- Correlations between 0 and 0.33 demonstrate zero to low-level relationships between equities and commodity indices oil and gold.
- Correlations below 0 with equities are revealed mainly by sovereign debt indices and corporate bonds.

Investment Planning

	Equity Indices						Bond Indices			Property	Commodity		Corporate Debt
	World	US	GER	UK	Japan	BRIIC	US Bonds	GER Bonds	UK Bonds	US REIT	Gold	Brent Oil	Corp (BAA–AAA)
World	1.00												
US	0.95	1.00											
GER	0.88	0.80	1.00										
UK	0.90	0.81	0.80	1.00									
Japan	0.67	0.53	0.47	0.55	1.00								
BRIC	0.74	0.66	0.66	0.67	0.52	1.00							
US Bonds	−0.22	−0.20	−0.22	−0.23	−0.12	−0.21	1.00						
GER Bonds	−0.19	−0.16	−0.21	−0.20	−0.09	−0.20	0.74	1.00					
UK Bonds	−0.06	−0.05	−0.07	−0.09	−0.03	−0.12	0.73	0.74	1.00				
US REIT	0.60	0.58	0.54	0.56	0.33	0.43	−0.08	−0.11	0.00	1.00			
Gold	0.12	0.03	0.10	0.14	0.22	0.26	0.13	0.01	0.09	0.15	1.00		
Brent Oil	0.24	0.18	0.15	0.23	0.28	0.30	−0.14	−0.19	−0.12	0.11	0.21	1.00	
Corp (BAA–AAA)	−0.24	−0.20	−0.20	−0.27	−0.19	−0.27	0.15	0.13	0.11	−0.26	−0.07	−0.27	1.00

The corporate BAA–AAA debt spread is the difference in yields between the Moody's US corporate BAA rated bond index and the same corporate AAA rated bond index. When yields on lower-rated credit (BAA) rise faster than triple AAA rated corporate debt, the spread increases. There is an inverse relationship between this spread and the US stock market. We have charted this historical spread against the value of the MSCI US Stock Index. An increase in the credit spread occurs when there are concerns about the economy or sector-specific credit-related events. When the spread increases, stock markets sensitised by the 2007 credit events come under selling pressure.

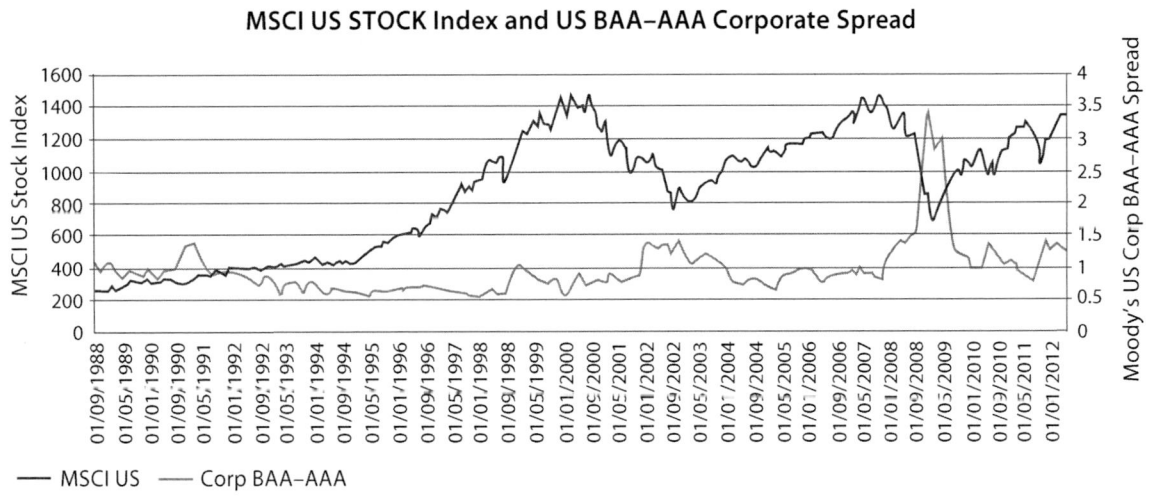

MSCI US STOCK Index and US BAA–AAA Corporate Spread

Data source: *Bloomberg L.P*

1.6.4 Advantages and Limitations of Historical Data

Historical data can be useful when considering the performance of the individual asset classes during the construction of an investment portfolio.

In practice, historical data can provide valuable information to unearth future investment opportunities. If a trend is present, there may be opportunities to apply forecasting techniques to build reliable forward projections. Past data is also useful for performance measurement purposes. It can be used to obtain the key statistical measures of performance, namely returns, standard deviations and correlations. The statistics can then be compared with benchmarks to assess manager performances or to carry out attribution analysis. Many forecasts assume that the return distributions are normal. However, with markets exhibiting great levels of volatility, the investment manager's job has been made even more difficult. Regular presence of skewed distributions and leptokurtosis (fat-tails), and other higher movements continue to present new challenges on the horizon.

In recent years, we have seen dramatic changes in financial markets and in the wider global economy that have never been seen before. For example, over the space of just five years from 2007 to 2012 the financial markets witnessed shocks of mega-proportions. First there was the sub-prime crisis that began in 2007 and led to the collapse of Lehman Brothers in September of 2008. From late 2009, fears of sovereign debt woes developed, embroiling the eurozone in a crisis. Further, the risk of more turbulence has increased, as the whole world markets have been enlarged with the rise of BRIIC nations and many others who are keen to join a growing list of emerging economies. Over this time period, correlations between asset classes have increased, along with volatility, providing investors and managers with restricted opportunities for risk diversification.

The stochastic nature of security prices and difficulties in predicting market behaviours reflect increased complexity in the world if there are rapid changes underway. Hence, as far as forecasting is concerned, developing ex-ante forecasts from historical data sets may not always be possible. This is because there are structural shifts and regime changes under way. Charting the progress of asset classes and their securities in this environment and picking out reliable investment has never been easy. Forecasting is a complex business and utilises high-level mathematical, statistical, economic and financial theory and ideas from many other disciplines, including IT and psychology fields. Even within a controlled markets laboratory setting, it is difficult to know how a growing body of behavioural finance followers will influence market changes in the next decade.

2. Investment Selection

Learning Objective

6.2.1 Understand the aims and characteristics of the main fund management strategies and styles: indexing or passive management; active or market timing; passive/active combinations; cash and bond fund strategies; liability-driven investment (LDI); long, short and geared; sector-specific; contrarian; quantitative, trend and trading strategies

2.1 Passive Investment Management

Passive management is seen in those collective investment funds that are described as index-tracker funds. Index-tracking, or indexation, necessitates the construction of an equity portfolio to track, or mimic the performance of a recognised equity index.

Indexation is undertaken on the assumption that securities markets are efficiently priced and cannot, therefore, be consistently outperformed. Consequently, no attempt is made to forecast future events or outperform the broader market.

Indexation techniques originated in the US in the 1970s but have since become popular worldwide. So much so, in fact, that some of the largest mutual funds in the world today are actually passive index trackers, eg, SPDR S&P500 TR.

Indexed portfolios are typically based upon a market-capitalisation-weighted index and employ one of three established tracking methods:

1. **Full replication** – this method requires each constituent of the index being tracked to be held in accordance with its index weighting. Although full replication is accurate, it is also the most expensive of the three methods so is only really suitable for large portfolios.
2. **Stratified sampling** – this requires a representative sample of securities from each sector of the index to be held. Although less expensive, the lack of statistical analysis renders this method subjective and potentially encourages biases towards those stocks with the best perceived prospects.
3. **Optimisation** – optimisation is a lower-cost, though statistically more complex, way of tracking an index than fully replicating it. Optimisation uses a sophisticated computer-modelling technique to find a representative sample of those securities that mimic the broad characteristics of the index tracked.

The advantages of employing indexation are that:

- Relatively few active portfolio managers consistently outperform benchmark equity indices.
- Once set up, passive portfolios are generally less expensive to run than active portfolios, given a lower ratio of staff to funds managed and lower portfolio turnover.

The disadvantages of adopting indexation, however, include:

- Performance is affected by the need to manage cash flows, rebalance the portfolio to replicate changes in index-constituent weightings and adjust the portfolio for index promotions and demotions.

- Most indices assume that dividends from constituent equities are reinvested on the ex-dividend (xd) date, whereas a passive fund can only invest dividends when received, usually six weeks after the share has been declared ex-dividend.
- Indexed portfolios cannot meet all investor objectives.
- Indexed portfolios follow the index down in **bear markets**.

Smart beta funds have grown in popularity in recent years and combine the passive approach of an index tracker fund with a degree of active management. The objective of smart beta funds is to overcome the main drawback of passive funds, which automatically follow the market up and down, and cannot avoid exposure to any troublesome holdings. Smart beta achieves this by creating their own benchmark consisting of stocks that exhibit certain behaviours, ie, low volatility and consistent strong dividends. The creation of the benchmark is the active part of the strategy which then becomes passive as the fund tracks the benchmark.

2.2 Active Investment Management

In contrast to passive equity management, active equity management seeks to outperform a predetermined benchmark over a specified time period, by employing fundamental and technical analysis to assist in the forecasting of future events and the timing of purchases and sales of securities. Actively managed portfolios can be constructed on either a top-down or a bottom-up basis.

2.2.1 Top-Down Active Management

Top-down active investment management involves three stages:

- asset allocation
- sector selection
- stock selection.

Each of these is considered below.

Asset Allocation

Asset allocation is the result of top-down portfolio managers considering the big picture first, by assessing the prospects for each of the main asset classes, within each of the world's major investment regions, against the backdrop of the world economic, political and social environment.

Within larger portfolio management organisations, this is usually determined on a monthly basis by an asset allocation committee. The committee draws upon forecasts of risk and return for each asset class and correlations between these returns.

It is at this stage of the top-down process that quantitative models are often used, in conjunction with more conventional fundamental analysis, to assist in determining which geographical areas and asset classes are most likely to produce the most attractive, risk-adjusted returns, taking full account of the client's mandate.

Investment Planning

Most asset allocation decisions, whether for institutional or retail portfolios, are made with reference to the peer group median asset allocation. This is known as asset allocation by consensus and is undertaken to minimise the risk of underperforming the peer group.

When deciding if and to what extent certain markets and asset classes should be over- or under-weighted, most portfolio managers set tracking error, or standard deviation of return, parameters against peer group median asset allocations.

Finally, the decision whether to hedge market and/or currency risks must be taken.

Recent academic studies conclude that, over the long term, asset allocation accounts for over 90% of the variation in pension fund returns.

Sector Selection

Once asset allocation has been decided upon, top-down managers then consider the prospects for sectors within their favoured equity markets. Sector selection decisions in equity markets are usually made with reference to the weighting each sector assumes, within the benchmark index against which the performance in that market is to be assessed. Given the strong interrelationship between economics and investment, however, the sector selection process is also heavily influenced by economic factors, notably where in the economic cycle the economy is currently positioned.

Stock Selection

The final stage of the top-down process is deciding which stocks should be selected within the favoured sectors. A combination of fundamental and technical analysis will typically be used in arriving at the final decision.

In order to outperform a predetermined benchmark, usually a market index, the active portfolio manager must be prepared to assume an element of tracking error, more commonly known as active risk, relative to the benchmark index to be outperformed. Active risk arises from holding securities in the actively managed portfolio in differing proportions from that in which they are weighted within the benchmark index. The higher the level of active risk, the greater the chance of outperformance, though the probability of underperformance is also increased.

It should be noted that top-down active management, as its name suggests, is an ongoing and dynamic process. As economic, political and social factors change, so do asset allocation, sector and stock selection.

2.2.2 Bottom-Up Active Management

A bottom-up approach to active management describes one that focuses solely on the unique attractions of individual stocks. Although the health and prospects for the world economy and markets in general are taken into account, these are secondary to factors such as whether a particular company is a possible takeover target or is about to launch an innovative product, for instance.

A true bottom-up investment fund is characterised by significant tracking error as a result of assuming considerable active risk.

Active Share

Active share has emerged in recent years as an alternative method of assessing active fund managers and identifying whether the funds they manage are in fact 'closet-trackers'. Active share focuses on how individual stock weightings differ from the weights in a benchmark and is an improvement on the traditional 'tracking-error' analysis. An academic study of this approach showed a link between outperformance and high active share portfolios.

2.3 Combining Active and Passive Management

Having considered both active and passive management, it should be noted that active and passive investment strategies are not mutually exclusive. Index trackers and actively managed funds can be combined in what is known as core-satellite management. This is achieved by indexing, say, 70% to 80% of the portfolio's value, so as to minimise the risk of underperformance, and then fine-tuning this by investing the remainder in a number of specialist actively managed funds or individual securities. These are known as the satellites.

The core can also be run on an enhanced index basis, whereby specialist investment management techniques are employed to add value. These include stock lending and anticipating the entry and exit of constituents from the index being tracked. In addition, indexation and active management can be combined within index tilts. Rather than hold each index constituent in strict accordance with its index weighting, each is instead marginally overweighted or underweighted, relative to the index based on their perceived prospects.

2.4 Bond Fund Investing

The four principal strategies used to manage bond portfolios are:

- passive, or buy-and-hold
- index-matching, or quasi-passive
- immunisation, or quasi-active
- dedicated and active.

2.4.1 Passive Bond Strategy

The passive buy-and-hold investor is typically looking to maximise the income-generating properties of bonds. The premise of this strategy is that bonds are assumed to be safe, predictable sources of income. Buy-and-hold involves purchasing individual bonds and holding them to maturity. Cash flow from the bonds can be used to fund external income needs or can be reinvested in the portfolio into other bonds or other asset classes.

In a passive strategy, there are no assumptions made as to the direction of future interest rates, and any changes in the current value of the bond due to shifts in the yield are not important. The bond may be originally purchased at a premium or a discount, while assuming that full par will be received upon maturity. The only variation in total return from the actual coupon yield is the reinvestment of the coupons as they occur.

On the surface, this may appear to be a lazy style of investing, but in reality passive bond portfolios provide stable anchors in rough financial storms. They minimise or eliminate transaction costs, and, if originally implemented during a period of relatively high interest rates, they have a decent chance of outperforming active strategies.

2.4.2 Indexing Bond Strategy

Indexing is considered to be quasi-passive by design. The main objective of indexing a bond portfolio is to provide a return and risk characteristic closely tied to the targeted index. While this strategy carries some of the same characteristics of the passive buy-and-hold, it has some flexibility. Just like tracking a specific stock market index, a bond portfolio can be structured to mimic any published bond index.

One also needs to consider the transaction costs associated with not only the original investment, but also the periodic rebalancing of the portfolio to reflect changes in the chosen index.

2.4.3 Immunisation Bond Strategy

This strategy has the characteristics of both active and passive strategies. By definition, pure immunisation implies that a portfolio is invested for a defined return, for a specific period of time, regardless of any outside influences, such as changes in interest rates. Similar to indexing, the opportunity cost of using the immunisation strategy is potentially giving up the upside potential of an active strategy, for the assurance that the portfolio will achieve the intended desired return.

As in the buy-and-hold strategy, by design the instruments best suited for this strategy are high-grade bonds with remote possibilities of default. In fact, the purest form of immunisation is to invest in a zero coupon bond and match the maturity of the bond to the date on which the cash flow is expected to be needed. This eliminates any variability of return, positive or negative, associated with the reinvestment of cash flows.

Duration, or the average life of a bond, is commonly referred to in immunisation, which is sometimes called duration-matching. It is a much more accurate predictive measure of a bond's volatility than maturity. This strategy is commonly used in the institutional investment environment by insurance companies, pension funds and banks to match the time horizon of their future liabilities, with structured cash flows. It is one of the soundest strategies and can be used successfully by individuals. For example, just as a pension fund will use an immunisation to plan for cash flows upon an individual's retirement, that same individual could build a dedicated portfolio for their own retirement plan.

2.4.4 Active Bond Strategy

The goal of active management is maximising total return. Along with the enhanced opportunity for returns obviously comes increased risk. Some examples of active styles include interest rate anticipation, timing, valuation and spread exploitation, and multiple interest rate scenarios. The basic premise of all active strategies is that the investor is willing to make bets on the future rather than settle for what a passive strategy can offer.

2.5 Liability-Driven Investment (LDI)

Liability-driven investment (LDI) is a form of investing in which the main goal is to gain sufficient assets to meet all liabilities, both current and future.

LDIs are most prominent in the funding schemes of defined benefit pension plans, which are designed to provide a predetermined pension upon retirement. The liabilities in these funds arise as a result of the guaranteed pensions they are supposed to provide to members upon retirement. They can often reach into millions of pounds.

In recent years, defined benefit schemes have fallen out of favour due to the significant cost involved in providing benefits to current and future members. The liabilities that the sponsoring companies and plan members must pay for has increased substantially, and this has caused some pension plans to close to new members, reduce benefits to retired members, or even shut down entirely.

2.6 Active Market Timing Strategy

As opposed to a passive buy-and-hold strategy, an active market timing strategy seeks to maximise returns and to minimise volatility by responding to intermediate market moves. Portfolios are positioned to take advantage of both the up-trends and the down-trends, ie, go short or long depending on conditions. Thus in theory, it is possible to make money as long as the markets are trending in one direction for a consistent period of time.

2.7 Long/Short

Long/short equity is an investment strategy generally associated with hedge funds, and more recently certain progressive traditional asset managers. It involves buying long equities that are expected to increase in value and selling short equities that are expected to decrease in value. This is different from the risk reversal strategies when investors will simultaneously buy a call option and sell a put option to simulate being long in a stock.

2.8 Sector-Specific

A common way to diversify is through investment in various sectors of the economy. This is usually accomplished with funds that concentrate in one of the major sectors, such as natural resources or utilities.

2.8.1 What is a Sector Fund?

As the name implies, a sector fund is a collective investment fund that invests in a specific sector of the economy, such as energy or utilities. Sector funds come in many different flavours and can vary substantially in market capitalisation, investment objective (ie, growth and/or income) and class of securities within the portfolio.

- **Natural resources funds** – these funds invest in oil and gas and other energy sources, as well as timber and forestry. These funds are usually appropriate for long-term growth investors.
- **Communications funds** – these funds focus on the telecommunications sector, but can include internet-related companies as well.

- **Utility funds** – these funds invest in securities of utility companies. They are usually designed to pay steady dividends to conservative fixed-income investors, although they may have a growth element as well.
- **Financial funds** – these funds invest in the financial industry. Holdings will include securities of investment, insurance, and banking firms.
- **Health care funds** – these funds can cover any kind of for-profit medical institution, such as pharmaceutical companies. Many of these funds also focus on biotechnology and the companies that make pioneering advances in this industry.
- **Technology funds** – these funds seek to provide exposure in the tech sector. This sector focuses primarily on computers, electronics and other informational technology that is used in a wide range of applications.
- **Precious metals funds** – these funds provide exposure to a variety of metals, such as gold, silver, platinum, palladium and copper.

2.9 Contrarian Investing

A contrarian investor believes that certain crowd behaviour among investors can lead to exploitable mispricings in securities markets. For example, widespread pessimism about a stock can drive a price so low that it overstates the company's risks, and understates its prospects for returning to profitability. Identifying and purchasing such distressed stocks, and selling them after the company recovers, can lead to above-average gains.

Conversely, widespread optimism can result in unjustifiably high valuations that will eventually lead to drops, when those high expectations don't pan out. Avoiding (or short-selling) investments in over-hyped investments reduces the risk of such drops.

These general principles can apply whether the investment in question is an individual stock, an industry sector, or an entire market or any other asset class.

Some contrarians have a permanent bear market view, while the majority of investors bet on the market going up. However, a contrarian does not necessarily have a negative view of the overall stock market, nor do they have to believe that it is always overvalued, or that the conventional wisdom is always wrong. Rather, a contrarian seeks opportunities to buy or sell specific investments when the majority of investors appear to be doing the opposite, to the point where that investment has become mispriced. While more buy candidates are likely to be identified during market declines (and vice versa), these opportunities can occur during periods when the overall market is generally rising or falling.

2.10 Quantitative Investment

Quantitative investing is a technique typically employed by the most sophisticated, technically advanced hedge funds. Computers are used to find predictable patterns within financial data. The process consists of thorough examination of vast databases searching for repeating patterns, typically positive or negative correlations among assets (statistical arbitrage or pairs trading), or price-movement patterns (trend following or mean reversion).

2.11 Trend Investing

Trend investing trading is a strategy that seeks to achieve gains through the analysis of an asset's price momentum either up or down. The trend investor trader enters into a long position when a stock is trending upward with successively higher highs. Vice versa, a short position is taken when the stock is in a down-trend with successively lower highs.

This investing trading strategy assumes that the present direction of the stock will continue into the future. It can be used by short-term, intermediate, or long-term investors. Regardless of their chosen time frame, investor traders will remain in their position until they believe the trend has reversed.

2.12 Costs and Their Impact on Investment

Learning Objective

6.2.2 Analyse and compare charges on the basis of impact, reduction in yield and total expense ratios/ongoing charge and synthetic risk, Sharpe ratio, R-squared and reward indicators

The impact of charges on investment funds is relatively straightforward. Higher charges reduce investment returns. In the case of initial charges, higher charges will reduce the amount of money that is actually invested in the product at the start. In the case of ongoing charges, higher charges lead to a reduction in the value of the product over time.

The higher the charges, the lower the net returns to consumers and therefore the lower the benefits to consumers from making the investment.

This is not to say that other characteristics of the product are not important; simply that, when comparing two identical funds, consumers will be better off selecting the cheaper fund, since this will ultimately lead to their having greater net returns compared with the more expensive fund.

Different types of charges also have different impacts on consumers depending on the length of time that consumers intend to invest their money. Products with high initial charges are likely to be especially costly for those customers who only hold investments for a short period of time. Products with low initial charges but high ongoing charges may end up being particularly costly for customers who hold investments for a long period of time.

Since high charges lead to consumers receiving lower net returns than they otherwise would, a failure to consider the impact of charges is likely to lead consumers to be worse off than otherwise. For these reasons, charges should, ideally, play an important role in the consumer's decision-making process.

2.12.1 Reduction in Yield

The reduction in yield (RIY) is an industry-standard measure of the impact of total charges (takes into account both initial charges and ongoing charges) applied to a policy.

In the UK, the FSA (now superseded by the FCA and the PRA) required mutual funds to disclose more than just their total expense ratios. Mutual funds are required to take into account both the initial charges and ongoing charges and show the effect of their charges on investment over a ten-year workout period. The mutual funds are expected to tabulate results showing the effect of all the charges in £s and also as a RIY in percentage terms.

The disclosure relating to RIY is carried out in a sentence, for example:

Putting it another way, this will have the same effect as bringing investment growth down from 6% a year to 4.1% a year.

The disclosure allows investors to compare the charges of different competing funds in the market so that they can make an informed decision.

If fund providers have disclosure documents that cover multiple funds that they offer, instead of using the RIY sentence they may provide the RIY through a table listing all of the funds covered in that document.

One limitation of the RIY is that it is presented only at one moment in time, normally after ten years. It does not show the impact of the charges over a shorter holding period such as three or even five years. This can cause consumers and advisers to examine charging information at a point of time that does not correspond to their investment horizon.

In addition, the RIY calculation requires assumptions to be made regarding the growth of investments and this may lead some consumers to have a false expectation as to the certainty or level of any returns.

Another requirement with the RIY disclosure in the UK is for funds to provide an effect of charges table. This table is helpful because it reveals the effect of charges at different years and their impact on the terminal wealth at each time.

We have a worked example of a hypothetical fund to demonstrate how the effect of charges information may be tabulated, together with effective RIY values we generate for dates that are for investment periods ranging from one to 10 years. Note that for RIY disclosure purposes only the 10 years' RIY is specified in the prospectus.

Based on our calculations, we reveal that the actual reduction impact of the charges levied can be much higher for lower investment periods. Assuming the fund's growth rate is 5%, then, after deductions, the effective rate actually obtained varies from one period to another.

For example, a £10,000 investment made over one year provides a terminal wealth of £10,026. This is effectively a return of 0.3% only. The 4.7% reduction in the yield reflects the high cost structure in the investment. Over a ten-year period, the effective return after charges is 2.9%, with a reduction from the quoted 5% annual growth rate now coming in at 2.1%.

Effect of Charges Table for Mutual Fund XYZ

At year	Investment (£)	Terminal Wealth (£) @ 5% growth rate	Deductions to date (£)	Terminal Wealth after deductions	Effective RIY (%)
1	10,000	10,500	474	10,026	0.3
3	10,000	11,576	870	10,706	2.3
5	10,000	12,763	1341	11,422	2.7
10	10,000	16,289	2943	13,346	2.9

Source: *CRA International*

The effect of charges table shows information on charges over time – at the end of year one, three, five and ten. This should be useful to a variety of consumers, who can examine the table to see which length of time most closely matches the length of time for which they expect to invest.

The effect of charges table also shows information on charges in pounds sterling rather than in percentages. This should be useful for customers who struggle to understand percentages and find it easier to examine information in monetary terms.

2.12.2 Total Expense Ratios and Ongoing Charges

Under the European Commission's UCITS directive, a simplified prospectus must include disclosure of initial charges and exit charges as well as ongoing fund charges. The European Commission has recommended that the latter are disclosed through the total expense ratio (TER).

This is not a comprehensive measure of charges, since the TER is only a measure of ongoing charges and not initial charges. In addition, showing charges only by means of percentages may make them harder for some consumers to grasp. UK firms are therefore also required to include additional charges disclosures, which in the UK consist of a table showing the effect of charges in monetary terms (see section 2.12.1) and an RIY statistic. Both of these measures were already in place in the UK investment fund market (and the life and pensions market) prior to the introduction of the simplified prospectus for UCITS-regulated funds.

As we discussed earlier in chapter 5, section 2.3, the Retail Distribution Review (RDR) is beginning to have an impact on the fund management expenses for retail collectives. This greater transparency on costs is expected to lead to further fee compression which will obviously have a bearing on future TERs.

The majority of funds must now provide a Key Investor Information Document (KIID) to investors, which displays an ongoing charge figure rather than the total expense ratio, as part of European regulation.

The KIID, which replaces the simplified prospectus, is a two-page document that provides detail about the fund's objective and investment policy, risk and reward, charges and past performance.

Ongoing charges (previously total expense ratios (TERs)) is a figure published annually by an investment company which shows the drag on performance caused by operational expenses. More specifically, it is the annual percentage reduction in shareholder returns as a result of recurring operational expenses assuming markets remain static and the portfolio is not traded. Although the ongoing charges figure is based on historical information, it provides shareholders with an indication of the likely level of costs that will be incurred in managing the fund in the future.

Source: Association of Investment Companies – https://www.theaic.co.uk/sites/default/files/hidden-files/ AICOngoingChargesCalculationMay12.pdf

MiFID, MiFID II and MIFIR

Issued by the European Securities and Markets Authority, MiFID is the Markets in Financial Instruments Directive (2004/39/EC) and has been applicable across the EU since November 2007. It is a cornerstone of the EU's regulation of financial markets; seeking to improve the competitiveness of EU financial markets by creating a single market for investment services and activities and to ensure a high degree of harmonised protection for investors in financial instruments.

MiFID I

MiFID sets out:

- conduct of business and organisational requirements for investment firms
- authorisation requirements for regulated markets
- regulatory reporting to avoid market abuse
- trade transparency obligation for shares
- rules on the admission of financial instruments to trading.

MiFID II and MiFIR

On 20 October 2011, the European Commission adopted a legislative proposal for the revision of MiFID which took the form of a revised Directive and a new Regulation. After more than two years of vigorous debate, the Directive on Markets in Financial Instruments repealing Directive 2004/39/EC and the Regulation on Markets in Financial Instruments, commonly referred to as MiFID II and MiFIR, were adopted by the European Parliament on 15 April 2014, by the Council of the European Union on 13 May 2014 and published in the EU Official Journal on 12 June 2014.

Building on the rules already in place, these new rules are designed to take into account developments in the trading environment since the implementation of MiFID in 2007 and, in light of the financial crisis, to improve the functioning of financial markets, making them more efficient, resilient and transparent.

2.12.3 Synthetic Risk and Reward Indicators

On the 1 July 2012, a set of rules for UCITS-compliant funds came into force in the UK financial services sector. This initiative saw the launch of key investor information documents (KIIDs) and their primary aim was to standardise the data emerging from funds to enable easier comparison by advisers and investor groups.

A major part of the information provided in KIIDs is the synthetic risk and reward indicators (SRRI). Regulations now require all UCITS funds to provide a SRRI score. It is an overall measure of the risk (and reward) of a fund. The risk indicator for any fund can take a value in a range from 1 to 7: the lower part of SRRI corresponds to a low-risk (and typically lower-reward) investment, while the higher value of 7 corresponds to a high-risk (and typically higher-reward) investment. The SRRI is determined from volatility of past returns over a five-year period.

The SRRI may appear as a simple risk measure for a UCITS-compliant fund on the surface, but it is derived from a set of calculations. As indicated earlier, the calculation of SRRI is based on volatility of UCITS past performance. This is the historic volatility of the net asset value (NAV) of the fund. The return measures can be taken on a weekly basis or on a monthly basis if data is not readily available. For a relatively new UCITS, when there is limited data of past performances, the management company will need to identify a representative portfolio model that can be used to simulate the projected volatility.

Guidelines for the determination of the SRRI have been published by the Committee of European Securities Regulators (CESR). The guidelines set out the methodology to be used in the calculation of volatility of a UCITS. In addition, these guidelines include a series of formulae that need to be used to determine the SRRI of absolute return funds, total return funds, life cycle funds and structured funds. For these funds in particular, due to the nature of their characteristic investment strategies, the SRRI calculation incorporates a VAR computation.

The standard approach to calculating SRRI uses weekly standard deviation for a period of 260 weeks with a 16-week buffer.

The results of this calculation then translate into one of the seven risk categories mentioned earlier which are broken down as follows:

Volatility Intervals		Risk Level
0.0%>	<0.5%	1
0.5%>	<2.0%	2
2.0%>	<5.0%	3
5.0%>	<10.0%	4
10.0%>	<15.0%	5
15.0%>	<25.0%	6
25.0%>		7

2.12.4 Sharpe Ratio

The Sharpe ratio uses standard deviation to measure a fund's risk-adjusted returns. The higher a fund's Sharpe ratio, the better a fund's returns have been relative to the risk it has taken on. As it uses standard deviation, the Sharpe ratio can be used to compare risk-adjusted returns across all fund categories.

The Sharpe ratio is a ratio of return versus risk. The formula is:

$(R_p - R_f)/SD$

Investment Planning

where:

Rp = the expected return on the investor's portfolio

Rf = the risk-free rate of return

SD = the portfolio's standard deviation, a measure of risk.

For example, let us assume that you expect a stock portfolio to return 12% next year. If returns on risk-free Treasury notes are, say, 5%, and your portfolio carries a 0.06 standard deviation, from the formula above we can calculate that the Sharpe ratio for your portfolio is:

(0.12 - 0.05)/0.06 = 1.17

This means that for every point of return, you are taking 1.17 units of risk.

2.12.5 R-Squared

R-squared measures the relationship between a portfolio and its benchmark. It can be thought of as a percentage from 1 to 100.

R-squared is not a measure of the performance of a portfolio – a poor portfolio can have a very high R-squared. It is simply a measure of the correlation of the portfolio's returns to the benchmark's returns.

If you want a portfolio that moves like the benchmark, you would want a portfolio with a high R-squared. If you want a portfolio that does not move at all like the benchmark, you would want a low R-squared.

General range for R-squared:

- 70–100% = good correlation between the portfolio's returns and the benchmark's returns
- 40–70% = average correlation between the portfolio's returns and the benchmark's returns
- 1–40% = low correlation between the portfolio's returns and the benchmark's returns.

2.13 Research, Reports and Analysis Methods

Learning Objective

6.2.3 Know the research and reports available to financial advisers: fundamental analysis; technical analysis; fund analysis; fund rating agencies and screening software; broker and distributor reports; sector-specific reports

2.13.1 Fundamental Analysis

Fundamental analysis is about using real data to evaluate a security's value. Although most analysts use fundamental analysis to value stocks, this method of valuation can be used for just about any type of security. Fundamental analysts attempt to study everything that can affect the security's value, including macroeconomic factors (like the overall economy and industry conditions) and company-specific factors (like financial condition and management).

The end goal of performing fundamental analysis is to produce a value that an investor can compare with the security's current price, with the aim of figuring out what sort of position to take with that security (underpriced = buy, overpriced = sell or short). This method of security analysis is considered to be the opposite of technical analysis.

An investor can perform fundamental analysis on a bond's value by looking at economic factors, such as interest rates and the overall state of the economy, and information about the bond issuer, such as potential changes in credit ratings.

When assessing stocks, this method uses revenues, earnings, future growth, return on equity, profit margins and other data to determine a company's underlying value and potential for future growth. In other words, in terms of stocks, fundamental analysis focuses on the financial statements of the company being evaluated.

2.13.2 Technical Analysis

Technical analysis is a method of evaluating securities by analysing the statistics generated by market activity, such as past prices and volume. Technical analysts do not attempt to measure a security's intrinsic value, but instead use charts and other tools to identify patterns that can suggest future activity.

The field of technical analysis is based on three assumptions:

1. The market discounts everything.
2. Prices move in trends.
3. History tends to repeat itself.

Just as there are many investment styles on the fundamental side, there are also many different types of technical traders. Some rely on chart patterns, others use technical indicators and oscillators, and most use some combination of the two. In any case, technical analysts' exclusive use of historical price and volume data is what separates them from their fundamental counterparts. Unlike fundamental analysts, technical analysts don't worry whether a stock is undervalued. The only thing that matters is a security's past trading data and what information this data can provide about where the security might move in the future.

2.13.3 Fund Analysis

Investment fund analysis involves assessing a number of different aspects of the fund to determine whether they are appropriate to include in the portfolio. These include:

- investment objective
- fund manager tenure
- past performance, discrete and cumulative returns
- volatility
- investment philosophy
- investment process
- assets held in the fund
- comparison with benchmark and peers
- initial and ongoing costs
- independent ratings of fund and manager.

A number of independent ratings agencies exist including Morningstar, Lipper and Fitch, which provide analysis and pricing information on investment funds to aid both private investors and investment advisers.

2.13.4 Brokers and Distributor Reports

Research and analysis is available from a vast number of sources including brokers and distributors of funds. This is usually available as periodical updates on fund performance and market commentaries, with input from research analysts and fund managers on market direction.

2.14 Factors to Consider when Selecting Investment Product Providers

Learning Objective

6.2.4 Analyse the factors to consider when selecting investment product providers

When choosing a suitable provider for an investment product, the following factors are worth considering:

- size and position in the market
- administrative efficiency
- competitive on charges
- features and benefits of product compared to peer offerings
- financial rating
- assets.

2.15 Wraps and Other Platforms

Learning Objective

6.2.5 Understand the characteristics, uses, benefits, risks and charges associated with wrap and other platforms

The advantages of wrap platforms are obvious. For the investor they offer an unprecedented overview and control of their investments, savings and pensions; and the possibility of a far greater choice in terms of fund managers, providers and asset classes.

For the adviser and investment adviser, they offer greater automation, much improved efficiency and the potential to offer almost instant valuations, meaning lower costs and the ability to offer a better service. In short, it should mean they can spend more time actually advising their clients and rather less on paperwork. The ability to manage client assets centrally in an administratively efficient way is proving advantageous in the post-RDR world, and enables advisers to offer a transparent fee structure and specific service levels to meet their clients' requirements.

Wraps originated in Australia but have been in use here in the UK for a number of years. Wrap platforms generally offer clients the ability to invest in a variety of different products via a single provider, eg, Transact. The wrap account provides the investor with access to:

- a cash account, used for dealing on purchases and sales, and for the payment of any associated management fees
- a pension account with the usual tax advantages
- an ISA
- an offshore/onshore investment bond.

Benefits to the investor include reduced administration and cost. In most cases, it enables the adviser to offer improved reporting to the client, allowing greater efficiency for their businesses, thereby helping to reduce costs and increase profitability.

In terms of risks, the client's assets are always held separately from those of the wrap provider and so the failure of that business will not affect them. Any assets held in the cash account are covered by the FSCS deposit protection scheme.

Wrap account providers make their money by charging a fee for using the account. Initial costs may also be levied on setting up the account and for any subsequent additional investment. Most platforms have negotiated discounts with fund managers and are able to offer reduced dealing costs on a range of investment funds.

Wraps offer complete transparency and clients can see what they are paying and to whom. Advisers are able to agree a service level and set their charges appropriately.

Key Chapter Points

- Asset allocation is an important component of financial advice, both in terms of meeting investment objectives and of reflecting the client's risk profile.
- Typically, a conservative investor will have a higher exposure to deposit-based and fixed-interest investments, and a more adventurous one will have a higher exposure to equities.
- Individual circumstances including commitments, experience, life cycle stage, age and wealth are factors to consider in designing a portfolio.
- Investment portfolios need to be affordable, taking into account changes in circumstances as far as possible, and they need to be suitable for the client. The level of accessibility must be assessed, to allow liquidity when it is needed.
- Tolerance, attitude and capacity for risk may be graded; for example, using the terms cautious, medium and adventurous. The proportion of risky asset types in a portfolio may be varied according to the desired overall level of risk.
- Risky investments should not generally be undertaken if the investment timescale is short, as short-term fluctuations can lead to losses.

End of Chapter Questions

Think of an answer for each question and refer to the appropriate workbook section for confirmation.

1. What is stochastic modelling?
   Answer reference: Section 1.2

2. What are the advantages of using historical performance data when considering an investment opportunity?
   Answer reference: Section 1.6.4

3. Which form of passive investment management involves the use of computer models to find a representative sample of securities to mimic the performance of an index?
   Answer reference: Section 2.1

4. What are the advantages and disadvantages of using indexation as an investment management strategy?
   Answer reference: Section 2.1

5. What percentage of investment returns are determined by asset allocation?
   Answer reference: Section 2.2.1

6. Explain what is meant by 'active share'.
   Answer reference: Section 2.2.2

7. What are the four principle strategies for managing bond portfolios?
   Answer reference: Section 2.4

8. Explain what synthetic risk reward indicators are.
   Answer reference: Section 2.12.3

9. What three assumptions form the basis of technical analysis?
   Answer reference: Section 2.13.2

10. What advantages do wraps offer investors?
    Answer reference: Section 2.15

Chapter Seven
Investment Advice

1.	Advising Clients	439
2.	The Financial Planning Process	449
3.	Ethically and Socially Responsible Investment Strategies	463
4.	The Advantages of Repaying a Mortgage and Other Borrowings	480
5.	Investment Solutions	482
6.	Presenting Recommendations	487
7.	Consumer Rights and Regulatory Requirements	488
8.	Performance Benchmarks	492

This syllabus area will provide approximately 11 of the 80 examination questions

1. Advising Clients

Learning Objective

7.1.1 Apply a framework for providing financial advice, paying particular attention to: the nature of the client relationship, confidentiality, trust and client protection; the information required from clients and methods of obtaining it; monitoring and review of clients' circumstances; the information clients must be given under the current regulatory requirements; additional requirements needed when advising on unregulated retail products

1.1 The Nature of the Client Relationship

The relationship between a client and financial adviser is very important to the success of the planning process. We could think about this relationship from three different perspectives – the legal, the personal, and the skills which an adviser might need to foster such a relationship:

- **Legal** – in some cases, a financial adviser will be an independent financial adviser (IFA), or part of an IFA firm. The relationship with the customer is that of agent. The adviser acts as the agent of the customer in any transactions they arrange on their behalf, and is responsible for providing them with advice based on a selection of suitable options. In other cases, however, the adviser may be an employee of a single product provider (or of a provider offering its own and a small range of other providers' products) or be restricted and not independent and will disclose how their service is restricted. In this case they act as the agent of the provider(s) and not of the client. These differing legal relationships must be disclosed to the customer, and mean different legal responsibilities to customers.
- **Personal** – in order to provide appropriate advice, financial advisers need a good deal of detailed background information about their clients. This includes not only their current financial situation, but also their plans, hopes and aspirations – and sometimes, some personal and sensitive information about their families. A client will only disclose this sort of information openly and frankly if they trust their adviser's integrity, confidentiality and capabilities.
- **Skills** – clearly, an adviser needs special skills to foster a successful relationship with their client. These include:
  - **Personal** – the adviser needs to create a trusting and open relationship with their client. They may need to be sensitive in questioning the client on personal matters, and conciliatory in persuading them to provide background details which they may not initially wish to divulge (eg, for anti-money laundering purposes).
  - **Organisational** – the busy adviser needs to be able to juggle a full diary of initial contacts and follow-up and repeat meetings. They, therefore, need to be well organised and disciplined in managing their diary and activities, and thorough in completing paperwork promptly.
  - **Technical competence** – they need to have the necessary technical knowledge and skills if they are to gain their client's confidence and provide a competent service.
  - **Integrity** – the client must have absolute confidence in their adviser's integrity; they trust the adviser with a great deal of sensitive financial information, which must not be improperly disclosed or otherwise abused.

1.2 Information Required of Clients and How to Obtain it

To carry out their role in a fiduciary capacity properly, the adviser is duty bound to act in the best interests of the client. In order to be able to provide appropriate advice, the adviser needs a clear picture of the client's current and planned financial situation. To achieve this, information has to be gathered from the client – and, to ensure that this is done in an organised and structured way, this is invariably done by way of a standardised form. Some form of investment policy statement will need to be obtained and maintained by the adviser. Therefore, the adviser in a fiduciary capacity cannot begin the investment management process until the client's objectives and risk parameters are clarified and consistent, and written confirmation has been obtained.

The actual collection of information may be done face-to-face, or at a distance (by telephone or over the internet): this will depend on the adviser's method of delivering services. Face-to-face is still popular for many, especially those dealing with the very wealthy or those who value a high level of personal service.

The document used is often called a fact find or something similar. It will be a fairly lengthy document, which should collect not only the client's basic details – but also their financial background and information to build a picture of their plans and aspirations. Typically, the document will include the following:

Basic Information

- Name, residential and correspondence address of the customer and any spouse/partner, children and other dependants.
- Often, at this point, anti-money laundering information, verifying the customer's identity and address, will be sought.
- Age.
- Occupation – self-employed, employed or unemployed.
- Marital status, number of dependants and their ages.
- Possibly, some basic health information.
- Nationality and domicile (for tax purposes).

Current Financial Situation

This may take the form of a mini-balance sheet for the individual, listing all major financial and other assets (including pensions) and liabilities such as credit card debts, mortgages and overdrafts. It will also identify their tax status – does the individual pay basic rate or higher-rate tax, or are they a non-taxpayer?

Current Income and Outgoings

Income may include such things as:

- Earned income from employment and self-employment.
- Unearned income on investments and deposits.
- Rents on investment property.
- Financial support from others – eg, a former spouse or partner.
- State benefits.

Outgoings may include:

- Rent or mortgage payments.
- Bills for food, heating and electricity.
- Rates/council tax.
- Taxes.
- TV licence.
- Maintenance paid to a former spouse or in respect of a child.
- Credit card and loan outgoings.
- Regular insurance premiums.
- Contributions to regular savings plans and pensions.
- Sums budgeted for holidays, Christmas and the like.

Expected Income and Outgoings

Here the client should list income/outgoings which are not in force at the moment but which are expected in the foreseeable future, such as school fees or a planned holiday.

Aspirations and Goals

In this section the customer should list those of their goals and aspirations which may require some financial planning (for example, early retirement). Examples may include:

- Hopes of retiring some time earlier than the state retirement age.
- A second home abroad.
- A move to a bigger house, or better area, or perhaps putting down a deposit on a first home.
- An expensive cruise to celebrate a significant anniversary.

Together, these elements give the financial adviser a snapshot of where the customer is now; an idea of their current and expected cash flows; and an idea of both their near-term objectives and where they hope to be in some years' time.

1.3 Matching Client Needs with Solutions

This picture of where the client is – or hopes they are – headed is an important area and one where a good adviser can be of considerable help to them.

This is because, before they think about it in any structured way, many clients have a jumble of competing needs and aspirations. Some of these are more important than others, and many may not be able to be realistically achieved at all – or at least not if other aspirations are also to be prioritised. Few clients are lucky enough to have so much money that they can afford to meet all their needs, goals and aspirations immediately.

For example, in terms of importance:

- certain financial outgoings must be paid if the client is to comply with the law – TV licences (assuming the customer has a TV) and taxes, for example
- some are very important – for example, keeping up insurance premiums to protect dependants from risks such as loss of the family breadwinner
- others are less urgent, even if they feel more like needs than wants (an urgent desire for a new car, for example).

So clearly, certain items should be prioritised ahead of others on grounds of their importance. But even then, there may be a number of other things which the client would like to do – but which they cannot afford to do all of, or not all at once. For example, the client may want to:

- trade up to a bigger car
- extend the house to have more space
- take the family abroad on holiday
- cut back on working hours by half a day a week to spend time with the children.

It may be that a financial plan can be arrived at to achieve many of these aims, if only one of them is dropped or postponed. Alternatively, the client may have some aspirations which are simply never going to be achieved in the foreseeable future.

Often, the adviser can help them organise their thoughts and prioritise which of their hopes and aspirations they are going to focus on – and which they will (for now at least) treat as merely a wish list.

1.4　Assessing Affordability and Suitability

Clients expect that their advisers are going to give them appropriate professional advice to help them achieve a sensible financial plan for their current situations, and a roadmap to achieving many of their objectives and aspirations.

They do not benefit from an adviser who simply tells them what they want to hear – for example, that their aims are achievable, if in fact they are not. Nor will they benefit from advice which benefits the adviser more than the customer when in fact there are perhaps better solutions available which would be more cost-effective.

Financial advisers are under strict obligations to ensure that they have given their client suitable advice in light of their stated needs. The rules on this are contained in a part of the FCA's handbook of regulatory rules, called the Conduct of Business Sourcebook (COBS).

Financial advisers should be able to demonstrate this, through the paperwork they complete. This should show how the adviser assessed the client's situation and needs, and the chosen selection of the recommended solutions.

A development that helped to focus advisers' and product providers' attention more closely on the issue of suitability was the FCA's treating customers fairly (TCF) initiative.

1.5　Advising on Unregulated Retail Products

Advisers should note that the RDR has addressed reforms to all retail investment products. The rules apply to a wider range of retail investment products than the pre-RDR packaged product definitions. This was achieved with the introduction of a handbook that the then regulator (the FSA) produced under its definition of 'retail investment product' and this included 'packaged products', unregulated collective investment schemes, all investment in investment trust savings schemes and structured investment products.

One implication of the re-definitions of the 'retail investment product' definition is that advisers may feel that there is now scope to widen promotional efforts to hedge funds and other non-retail schemes to their clients. The IFA is duty bound to perform *a comprehensive and fair analysis of the relevant market*. However, advisers need to be careful as the regulator has already given guidance that IFAs may decide not to include unregulated schemes (unregulated collective investment schemes (UCIS), now referred to as non-mainstream pooled investments (NMPIs)) within their product ranges, on the basis that they are too risky or unsuitable for their clients. Prior to the UK regulator's transformation into the twin peaks regulatory regime, the FSA had already consulted on severely restricting an IFA's ability to promote UCIS/NMPIs.

Before the FCA took over, the FSA had investigated some advisers over unsuitable advice they had given their clients to transfer assets from smaller pension schemes into UCIS held in a SIPP, for example. On the basis of these concerns relating specifically to poor advice and suitability of products recommended, the FSA had secured a variation on their permissions so that IFAs were unable to continue operating in this way. IFAs can consider investment in UCIS, but they need to have undertaken thorough due diligence on the suitability of the investment and the wrapper that it is in.

1.6 Treating Customers Fairly

Learning Objective

7.1.3 Apply the FCA's Fair Treatment of Customers and the six consumer outcomes that firms should aim to achieve in supporting the requirements of Principle 6

Treating Customers Fairly (TCF) aims to support the requirements of the FCA's Principle 6 which states: *'An approved person performing a significant influence function must exercise due skill, care and diligence in managing the business of the firm for which they is responsible in their controlled function'.*

Organisations already have to operate in accordance with a set of principles that include the requirement to act with integrity, consider the information needs of their customers, and other similarly **fair** approaches to doing business. TCF forces providers to demonstrate that they are behaving fairly in all areas of their activities, from the way in which they communicate with their customers, to the quality of their advice.

TCF will, therefore, be an important issue in the ongoing assessment of the suitability of advice, and advisers undertake a thorough assessment of the client's circumstances, taking into account attitude to risk and affordability. It is also more important than ever that the consequences of any recommended plan of action are clearly and properly explained to the customer, in language which they are likely to be able to understand, including the costs and risks involved.

The FCA's retail regulatory agenda aims to ensure an efficient and effective market and thereby help consumers to achieve a fair deal. They aim to achieve this through the use of the TCF initiative. The TCF initiative aims to deliver six improved outcomes for retail consumers, and firms should be focused on trying to achieve these outcomes, which are listed below.

- **Outcome 1** – consumers can be confident that they are dealing with firms where the fair treatment of customers is central to the corporate culture.
- **Outcome 2** – products and services marketed and sold in the retail market are designed to meet the needs of identified consumer groups and are targeted accordingly.
- **Outcome 3** – consumers are provided with clear information and are kept appropriately informed before, during and after the point of sale.
- **Outcome 4** – if consumers receive advice, the advice is suitable and takes account of their circumstances.
- **Outcome 5** – consumers are provided with products that perform as firms have led them to expect, and the associated service is of an acceptable standard and as they have been led to expect.
- **Outcome 6** – consumers do not face unreasonable post-sale barriers imposed by firms to change product, switch provider, submit a claim or make a complaint.

TCF and its six outcomes were introduced in 2006 and the FCA now expects that this is fully embedded in firms. The focus now is on 'conduct risk' which goes further than what was expected of firms in the past. Conduct risk is defined by the regulator as *'the risk that firms' behaviour will result in poor outcomes for customers'*. The regulator's attention is focused on the risks to the delivery of fair customer outcomes in addition to the actual outcomes themselves.

1.7 Paying for Advice

Learning Objective

7.1.2 Understand how financial advice can be paid for: adviser charging; commission; nature and frequency of service to be provided

Regulations laid down by the financial services regulator set out the nature, and usually the content, of information that financial advisers must provide to their clients. These obligations extend not only to the advice the adviser provides – including why they are suitable, and what the benefits, disadvantages, risks and costs are – but also to the adviser's own regulated status, how they work and on what basis charges are paid.

Financial advice can be paid for in one of the following ways:

Adviser Charging

Here the cost of the advice is fully transparent and examples of the types of fees that may be charged are usually provided to the investor at the outset. Hourly rates may be charged, or one-off fees for certain types of work, eg, the arrangement of an investment through a personal pension plan. All work and costs should be agreed in advance and no further fees charged, without prior agreement with the client.

Additional fees may be levied against the value of any funds under the advice or management of the firm, and should be disclosed and agreed prior to engagement.

Under this heading, the regulator has provided guidance on financial adviser charges that conform to the RDR requirement. The requirement applies to: retail advisers (ie, IFA); wealth managers; restricted advisers; private bankers; and stockbrokers. Non-advised services, or execution-only sales, when no advice or recommendation is given, will also fall outside the adviser-charging regime.

Historically, the advice provided by a financial adviser was paid through the receipt of either an upfront commission and/or commission paid from the product during its lifespan; often the latter form of commission was built into investment products and was a percentage of the value of the fund.

New RDR requirements are specifically aimed at addressing the potential for adviser remuneration to change consumer outcomes. In summary these requirements are:

- advisers can set their own charges for their services, since they will no longer be able to receive commission set by product providers
- advisers should have charging structures based on the level of service they provide, rather than the particular provider or product they recommend
- advisers should disclose those charges to consumers up front, using some form of price list or tariff (confirming the specific amount to be paid later on)
- on-going charges should only be levied when an ongoing service has been agreed with the client (except for charges for advice on regular contribution products) and
- product providers will be banned from offering commission to advisers and will also face other requirements if they offer to deduct adviser charges from their product.

Service

The type of service provided may also differ in each scenario. If fees are charged, then it is likely that some form of service agreement will be entered into, in which the person providing the advice agrees to deliver a structured service with frequent reviews. In the commission example, this is less likely to be the case, as the adviser is only remunerated when a product is sold.

1.8 Principles for Businesses

One of the FCA's Principles for Businesses (outlined below) requires a firm to have integrity and take reasonable care to ensure the suitability of its advice and discretionary decisions.

1. Integrity	A firm must conduct its business with integrity.
2. Skill, care and diligence	A firm must conduct its business with due skill, care and diligence.
3. Management and control	A firm must take reasonable care to organise and control its affairs responsibly and effectively, with adequate risk management systems.
4. Financial prudence	A firm must maintain adequate financial resources.
5. Market conduct	A firm must observe proper standards of market conduct.
6. Customers' interests	A firm must pay due regard to the interests of its customers and treat them fairly.
7. Communications with clients	A firm must pay due regard to the information needs of its clients, and communicate information to them in a way which is clear, fair and not misleading.
8. Conflicts of interest	A firm must manage conflicts of interest fairly, both between itself and its customers and between a customer and another client.
9. Customers: relationships of trust	A firm must take reasonable care to ensure the suitability of its advice and discretionary decisions for any customer who is entitled to rely upon its judgement.
10. Clients' assets	A firm must arrange adequate protection for clients' assets when it is responsible for them.
11. Relations with regulators	A firm must deal with its regulators in an open and co-operative way, and must disclose to the FCA appropriately anything relating to the firm of which the FCA would reasonably expect notice.

Source: FCA Handbook

To comply with this, a firm should obtain sufficient information about its private customers to enable it to meet its responsibility to give suitable advice. Similarly, a firm acting as a discretionary investment manager for a private customer should ensure that it has sufficient information to enable it to put suitable investments into the customer's portfolio.

The purpose of gathering information about the client is clearly so that financial plans can be devised and appropriate recommendations made. The types of information that should be gathered include:

- **personal details** – name; address; age; health; family and dependants
- **financial details** – income; outgoings; assets; liabilities; insurance and protection arrangements
- **objectives** – growth; protecting real value of capital; generating income; protecting against future events
- **tolerance and capacity for risk** – cautious; balanced; adventurous
- **liquidity and time horizons** – immediate needs; known future liabilities; need for an emergency reserve
- **tax status** – income; capital gains; inheritance taxes; available allowances
- **investment preferences** – restrictions; ethical considerations.

As we will see in section 2, firms must ensure that any recommendations they make are suitable. To do this, a firm should ensure that the information they gather also includes details about:

- a client's knowledge and experience of the investment or service that will be recommended
- the level of investment risk that the client can bear financially and whether that is consistent with their investment objectives.

1.9 Suitability

Once a clear picture of the customer's requirements and needs is established, the steps expected of the firm to ensure its recommendations are suitable and appropriate will vary depending upon the needs and priorities of the customer, the types of investment or service being offered and the nature of the relationship between the firm and the private customer.

When a firm proposes to offer investment advisory services or discretionary portfolio management, it must first assess whether such services are suitable for a professional or retail client. If the firm intends to offer other investment services, it must ensure that they are appropriate for the client.

The firm should ascertain the:

- client's knowledge and experience of the types of services and transactions
- nature, volume, frequency and time that the client has been involved in such services and transactions
- client's level of education, profession or relevant former profession.

The general requirement is that the firm must take reasonable steps to ensure it makes no personal recommendation to a customer, unless it is suitable for that customer. Suitability will have regard to the facts disclosed by the customer and other facts of which the firm should reasonably be aware.

Having assessed what services and products are suitable and appropriate, the firm should provide the client with a report which should set out, among other things, why the firm has concluded that a recommended transaction is suitable for the client.

If the firm determines after assessment that the service or product is not appropriate for the client, then it should issue a risk warning to the client. If the client still wishes to proceed despite the warning, then it is up to the firm to decide whether it will do so.

If the firm is acting as investment manager for a private customer, there is an ongoing requirement that it must ensure that the portfolio remains suitable. Equally, if a customer has agreed to the firm pooling their funds with those of others, the firm must take reasonable steps to ensure that any discretionary decisions are suitable for the stated objectives of the fund.

1.10 Monitoring and Review

Learning Objective

7.2.1 Analyse the main factors, resources and limitations shaping a client's current and desired financial circumstances: gather appropriate, relevant information about current and projected income, expenditure, debt and savings; consider time horizons and the relative balance of growth versus income; distinguish between what is essential and what is desirable, and prioritise accordingly; agree clear, feasible, prioritised investment objectives

7.4.7 Understand the process of periodic review to meet key criteria: regulatory requirements; appropriate frequency, taking into account client requirements and the chosen investment strategy

Financial planning is not a one-off process. In part, this is because of the possibility of change. A client's plans can change because:

- the environment changes around them – for example:
  - the tax regime changes (and remember, at the least, tax allowances are generally reviewed every year)
  - employment status alters
  - the stock market performs better, or worse, than the client had anticipated or:
- the client's circumstances change or so do their needs, wants and aspirations. For example, when the client marries or divorces, inherits a sum of money or has a child, not only will their needs change but their attitudes to finance may also alter and they may, for example, become more or less risk-averse.

It is important that clients review their plans and monitor progress towards objectives. Without regular updates, it is impossible to know whether the financial goals are likely to be achieved. Quite small changes in financial behaviour can, together, have a big cumulative effect on a client's finances.

So a periodic review can be very helpful in ensuring that the client stays on track. By repeating the planning exercise (say) a year later, both adviser and client can see whether they are making progress towards their goal, or whether they are drifting off-target and needs to use a little financial discipline.

The adviser should agree early on whether ongoing monitoring and review is going to fall within their remit – in many cases, this will be so. If so, the adviser should have advised the customer of how frequently they can expect to see an update of the plan and any new recommendations.

Periodic reviews to clients should include the up-to-date value of the customer's investments. Investments should be valued on a basis which has already been agreed with the client (eg, when stocks and shares are involved, the valuation process should be consistent as to whether bid or mid-prices are used and what exchange rate is used for any foreign assets).

It will also generally include a statement showing any transactions undertaken over the period (including any charges that have been deducted, and any additions to or withdrawals from the customer's portfolio).

If a full periodic review is being carried out, the adviser should re-verify the customer's details and establish whether there have been any changes to their circumstances which might require an amendment to the plan. If this is the case, the adviser should check the new details, and then go through the new recommendations with the customer to ensure they understand their implications in full – just as at the outset.

1.11 Investment and Speculation

There are no universally accepted definitions to differentiate between investment and speculation in a precise scientific manner.

For a wealth/asset manager, it is important to understand the distinction between investment and speculation. Investment can be differentiated from speculation by the time frame adopted and the knowledge and level of risk assumed by the investor. Investment, as a professional activity, is undertaken to yield desired wealth benefits over a much longer time frame. Further, with speculation there may be limited knowledge or no knowledge about the risks borne by an investor. With investment activity, on the other hand, a great deal of resources and knowledge are directed towards understanding the risk factors in each asset class closely and then to managing or mitigating unwanted risks from an investment portfolio systematically. As a result, investment is generally undertaken via a diversified portfolio of assets for the medium to long-term, whereas speculation is based on profiting from the short-term price movements of individual securities or assets. Wealth/asset management can be further differentiated by its structured approach to identifying client needs and developing holistic plans that address the complete range of a client's needs.

2. The Financial Planning Process

Learning Objective

7.2.1 Analyse the main factors, resources and limitations shaping a client's current and desired financial circumstances: gather appropriate, relevant information about current and projected income, expenditure, debt and savings; consider time horizons and the relative balance of growth versus income; distinguish between what is essential and what is desirable, and prioritise accordingly; agree clear, feasible, prioritised investment objectives

The nature of any relationship with a client will depend upon the service being provided. This can range from providing the facilities to execute transactions without any advice, to ongoing relationships that deal with selected financial areas only, investment management only or extend to in-depth wealth management or private banking.

The client relationship can, therefore, be a one-off service to satisfy a client's needs or a long-term relationship where the wealth manager is an integral part of the client achieving their investment objectives. Whatever the service, an adviser has a fiduciary duty to their client that requires them to observe the highest standards of personal conduct and fully respect the confidence and trust implicit in their relationship.

The main responsibilities of the adviser are to:

- help clients to decide on, and prioritise, objectives
- document the client's investment objectives and risk tolerance
- determine, and agree, an appropriate investment strategy
- act in the client's best interest
- if agreed, keep the products under review
- carry out any necessary administration and accounting.

The financial planning process can be divided into five stages, each of which will be considered below.

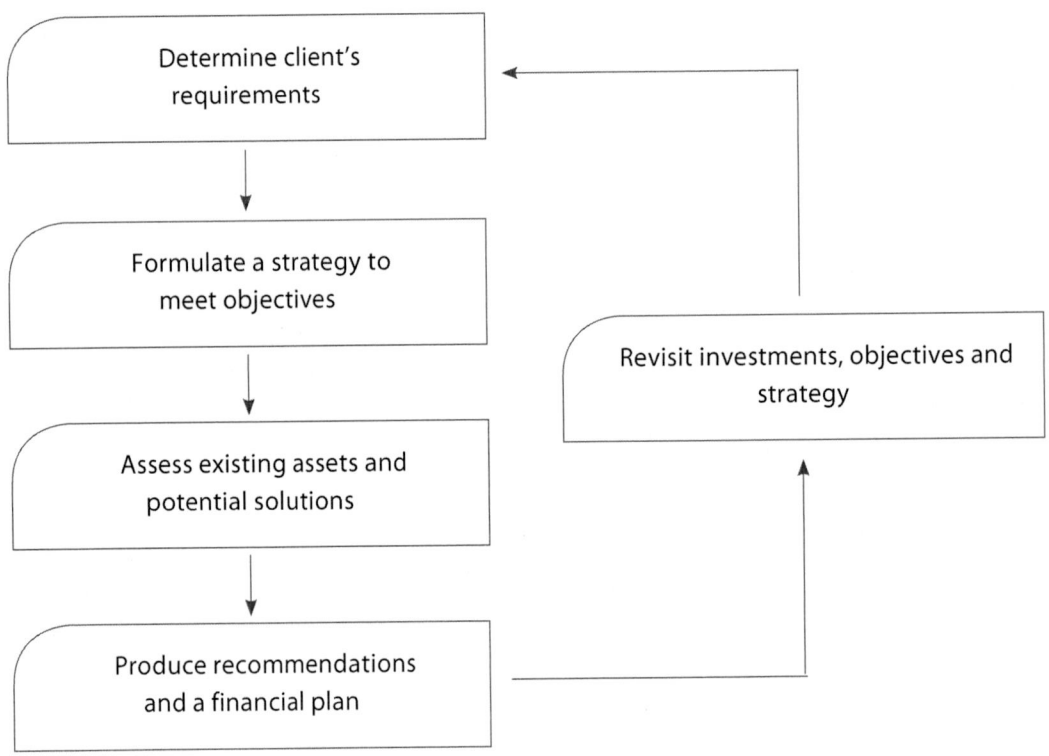

2.1 Determining Client Requirements

Individuals have varying objectives and expectations. Clearly, before advising the client the adviser must be aware of these various needs, preferences, expectations and the financial situation of the client; the adviser must know their clients before being able to provide appropriate advice.

It is essential to establish the fullest details about the client, not only their assets and liabilities but the life assurance or protection products or arrangements that they may have in place. Their family circumstances, health and future plans and expectations are equally important. Clients often approach advisers about investment opportunities, without considering these other factors and it is important that the adviser establishes this so that they can check the suitability of existing and proposed recommendations and prioritise what needs to be dealt with first.

Below, we will consider some of the key client information that an adviser needs to establish.

2.1.1 Information to be Collected

The information that needs to be captured (known as a fact find) can be broken down into the following:

- personal and financial details
- objectives
- risk tolerance
- liquidity and time horizons
- tax status
- investment preferences.

Personal and Financial Details

The adviser will need to establish, among other things:

- personal details
- health status
- details of family and dependants
- details of occupation, earnings and other income sources
- estimates of present and anticipated outgoings
- assets and liabilities
- any pension arrangements
- potential inheritances and any estate planning arrangements, such as a will.

It is essential not to see this as a simple data collection exercise but to see beyond the headings, as to why the information is needed and what this may show about the financial position and needs of the client.

Exercise

Use the following table or a separate piece of paper to record why such information might be needed

Information needed	Why needed?
Personal details	
Health status	
Details of family and dependants	
Details of occupation, earnings and other income sources	
Estimates of present and anticipated outgoings	
Assets and liabilities	
Any pension arrangements	
Potential inheritances and any estate planning arrangements, such as a will	

Be aware that the scale of potential information that will be needed is significant, so there is no simple 'right' answer and it gives an indication as to why the information might be relevant. Everyone is different, so the information needed will vary from person to person.

Objectives

There are a wide range of available investment opportunities and, to understand which might be suitable for a client, an adviser needs to start with understanding what the client's investment or financial objectives are. This requires the client to consider what they are trying to achieve. The answer will determine the overall investment strategy that will drive the investment planning process.

Typical financial objectives include:

- maximising future growth
- protecting the real value of capital
- generating an essential level of income
- protecting against future events.

It is also important to remember that a client may have more than one financial objective, such as funding school fees, while at the same time maximising the growth of their investments to provide the funds needed in retirement.

Having determined the client's overall financial objectives, the adviser also needs to know how this will affect the choice of investments, so investment objectives are often categorised into:

- **Income** – investors seek a higher level of current income at the expense of potential future growth of capital.
- **Income and growth** – investors need a certain amount of current income but also invest to achieve potential future growth in income and capital.
- **Growth** – investors do not seek income and their primary objective is capital appreciation.
- **Outright growth** – the investor is seeking maximum return through a broad range of investment strategies, which generally involve a high level of risk.

Risk Tolerance

Volatility in the prices of investments or the overall value of an investment portfolio is inevitable. At a personal level this translates into the risk that prices may be depressed at the time when an investor needs funds, which will mean that they will not achieve their investment goals.

A client needs to have a very clear understanding of their tolerance to risk, as it is essential to choosing the right investment objectives. In many ways, risk tolerance is subjective and is very dependent upon the emotional make-up of a person. It is also objective, in that age will affect how much risk a client can assume because, as people get older, there is less time to recover from poor investment decisions or market falls and so appetite to take risk may change.

Although risk itself is an emotive subject, the actual establishment of a client's tolerance towards it need not be subjective. Indeed, an objective measure of a client's risk tolerance is provided by the risks that will need to be taken if the client's stated investment aims are to be met. If the client believes these risks are too great, then the client's objective will need to be revised. We will return to the subject of a client's risk profile in section 2.6.

Liquidity and Time Horizons

It is also essential to understand a client's liquidity requirements and the time horizons over which they can invest, as these will also have a clear impact on the selection and construction of any investments.

Liquidity refers to the amount of funds a client might need both in the short and long term. When constructing an investment portfolio, it is essential that an emergency cash reserve is put to one side that the client can access without having to disturb longer-term investments.

If there are known liabilities that may arise in future years, consideration should also be given as to how funds will be realised at that time. Consideration needs to be given as to whether it is sensible to plan on realising profits from equities, as market conditions may be such as to require losses to be established unnecessarily. Instead, conservative standards suggest investing an appropriate amount in bonds that are due to mature near the time needed, so that there is certainty of the availability of funds.

Time horizon refers to the period over which a client can consider investing their funds. Definitions of time horizons vary, but short-term is usually considered to be from one to four years, while medium-term refers to a period from five to ten years and long-term is considered to be for a period of ten years or more.

Time horizon is very relevant when selecting the types of investment that may be suitable for a client. It is generally stated that an investor should only invest in equities if they can do so for a minimum period of five years. This is to make the point that growth from equities comes from long-term investment and the need to have the time perspective that can allow an investor to ride out periods of market volatility.

The lower the client's liquidity requirements and the longer their timescale, the greater will be the choice of assets available to meet their investment objective. The need for high liquidity allied to a short timescale demands that the client should invest in lower-risk assets, such as cash and short-dated bonds, which offer a potentially lower return than equities; if the opposite is true, the portfolio can be more proportionately weighted towards equities.

Whatever their requirements, it is important, however, that the client maintains sufficient liquidity to meet both known commitments and possible contingencies.

2.1.2 Client Information Collection Methods

Learning Objective

7.1.4 Understand the purpose, merits and limitations of using questionnaires and interviews to elicit customer information

There is no simple way of establishing all of this information quickly. The adviser will need to undertake a detailed, and potentially lengthy, interview with the client in order to understand what existing assets and liabilities they have before they can turn to developing a true understanding of what their needs are.

There is also no single correct way of collecting all of the required information. Most firms use a KYC questionnaire that the adviser completes during their interview with the client so that the information is collected in a logical and straightforward manner and is available for later use.

The advantage of this approach is in its consistency, the factual record it creates and the opportunity for quality checking that it provides.

Its disadvantage is the customer's reaction to what they may perceive as a lengthy form-filling exercise, hence the need for communication skills that we will consider in section 6. Only having completed this, can the adviser then start on the next significant exercise: that is, to identify potential solutions and then match these to the client's needs and demands.

2.2 Developing a Strategy

Learning Objective

7.4.1 Apply a strategy and rationale that will meet the client's objectives: highlight the pertinent issues and priorities; formulate a plan to deal with them; offer proposals to achieve these objectives; explain clearly the relative merits and drawbacks of each proposal and combination thereof; agree a strategy that the client understands and accepts

Having established what the needs and objectives of the client are, a thorough assessment of their existing financial position obviously needs to be completed.

An analysis of their assets and liabilities and their income and outgoings needs to be undertaken to establish their true financial position. It is only once this has been done that an assessment can be made of both the affordability and suitability of their existing arrangements.

Once the adviser has a complete financial picture for the client, they can then move on to assess what the client is aiming to achieve and what should be the client's priorities. It needs to be remembered that financial planning is a long-term process and not a one-off exercise. Most clients will need to prioritise their needs and then deal with the most pressing first and others when the constraints of affordability allow.

The development of a strategy will involve:

- assessing where action is needed
- prioritising what should be addressed
- identifying where action should be left until a later date
- developing potential solutions to address the priorities for further investigation.

2.3 Assessing Existing Assets and Potential Products

Having determined a strategy to meet the client's needs, the next stage is to investigate how the potential solutions can be implemented. This will involve assessing the suitability of the client's existing assets and investigating the characteristics of products that can potentially meet their needs.

Existing assets and products will need to be checked for suitability. This will involve determining the details of each product, assessing whether they meet the client's needs and establishing any issues that may arise in moving these to alternative options. There are many factors to consider, and these will be driven by the type of asset, product or arrangement.

Some items to consider include:

- their relevance to the true needs of the client
- whether they are affordable options
- the degree of risk associated with the product considered against the client's risk tolerance
- the extent of any diversification, or lack of
- the level of charges compared to comparable products
- income generation and tax treatment
- performance of investments, growth achieved and any taxation treatment on encashment
- how long any assets need to be retained to earn any bonuses
- any encashment penalties.

This analysis will then provide the basis for continuing the financial planning process. It will identify which assets should be retained and which should be disposed of to finance meeting the client's objectives. The next steps are to identify suitable financial products that can meet the client's requirements and evaluating their features.

This part of the process essentially involves matching the investor's investment and protection objectives with the characteristics of the various financial assets and protection products. For investment-related products, the main characteristics to consider are:

- the risks associated with the investment product
- its liquidity (that is the ease of selling it or otherwise converting it into cash)
- its tax-efficiency
- whether it is income-producing or more suitable for capital growth.

For life assurance and protection products, the process is essentially the same in that it involves identifying the range of potentially suitable products, assessing the key product features against the client's needs and selecting the most suitable option.

2.4 Producing Recommendations and a Financial Plan

So far, we have determined the needs of the client, developed a strategy to meet their needs and identified which assets should be retained and which liquidated to finance the solutions that we have identified as meeting their needs.

The final stage of the process is, therefore, to produce recommendations and a financial plan for presentation to the client. The plan should detail the following:

- Document the client's existing position.
- Identify the areas that require addressing and what the priorities are.
- Detail the recommendations made and the reasons why they are suitable and appropriate.
- Document the areas where action has been deferred until a later date.

2.5 Monitoring and Reviewing Clients' Circumstances

It may be stating the obvious but, after the adviser and client have spent considerable time and effort establishing needs, objectives and plans, why wouldn't they want to make sure that these were checked from time to time to make sure they are still relevant and still meeting their planned objectives?

Whether they do so will depend upon whether the advice has been part of a one-off exercise or an ongoing service. If it is part of an ongoing proposition, such as wealth management, discretionary investment management or private banking, ongoing management of the assets and regular reviews of the client's objectives and strategy will be integral to the service proposition. If it is a one-off transaction, the client should be persuaded of the advantage of regular reviews.

There are often too many issues that arise from the results of the financial planning exercise than can be dealt with at one time. There are many reasons why this may be so, for example, affordability or just what the client is prepared to address at one time.

The adviser may have recommended investment in a range of collective investment schemes and, as economic or market circumstances change, a point will arise where profits need to be taken or investments switched.

Equally, a client's circumstances will change, as few things in life stay still. Further regular meetings to review the client's circumstances are clearly a sensible and practical thing to do, but one that sometimes gets lost in the busy lives that clients and advisers lead.

It is also something that is often forgotten by financial services organisations, which sometimes devote more effort to generating new business than servicing existing business. Sometimes it takes a detailed financial analysis of their performance for them to remember that looking after their existing client base is usually far more profitable than chasing new business.

It is the practice among the better financial advisers to meet regularly with their clients. This is not simple altruism. Experience has shown that a financial adviser with a client base numbering just a few hundred can earn a very acceptable income from repeat business from their clients by ensuring they are always focused on making sure that their objectives are the same as the clients. Best practice, therefore, dictates that an adviser should agree the frequency with which they will meet to undertake a further review of the client's position.

2.6 Risk and Client Suitability

Learning Objective

7.3.1 Analyse a profile of a client's risk exposure and appetite for risk, based on the following objective and subjective factors: level of wealth; timescale; commitments; life cycle; life goals; investment objectives; attitudes; experiences; knowledge; capacity for loss

7.3.2 Apply a client risk profile to the investment selection process

7.3.4 Assess affordability and suitability based on a range of factors including product provider quality, performance, risk, charges and client service

The risk tolerance of a client will have a considerable impact on the financial planning strategy that an adviser recommends. It will exhibit itself in the importance that is given to financial protection and in what is an acceptable selection of investment products.

Attitude to risk and its definitions are constant themes that financial services companies revisit. The reason for this is simple, namely that they want to be able to categorise a client into a risk category and then be able to say which of their products are suitable for clients with that risk profile.

However, definitions of risk profiles are imprecise and, after reviewing the suggested classification in the next section, you will understand why trying to turn this into a mathematical exercise is not straightforward. As a result, advisers need to understand even more about suitability and risk and recognise that it is only with the application of skill and knowledge that solutions can be matched with client needs.

2.6.1 Determining a Client's Risk Profile

Objective Factors

As we have seen above, determining a client's attitude to risk needs to be as accurate as possible as it will drive both priorities and solutions. There are a number of objective factors that can be established that will help define this, including:

- **Timescale** – the timescale over which a client may be able to invest will determine both what products are suitable and what risk should be adopted. For example, there is little justification in selecting a high-risk investment for funds that are held to meet a liability that is due in 12 months' time. By contrast, someone in their 30s choosing to invest for retirement is aiming for long-term growth, and higher-risk investments will then be suitable. As a result, the acceptable level of risk is likely to vary from scenario to scenario.
- **Commitments** – family commitments are likely to have a significant impact on a client's risk profile. For example, if a client needs to support elderly relatives or children through university, this will have a determining influence on what risk they can assume. While by nature they may be adventurous investors, they will want to meet their obligations, which will make higher-risk investments less suitable.

- **Wealth** – wealth will clearly be an important influence on the risk that can be assumed. A client with few assets can ill afford to lose them, while ones whose immediate financial priorities are covered may be able to accept greater risk.
- **Life cycle** – stage of life is equally important. A client in their 30s or 40s who is investing for retirement will want to aim for long-term growth and will be prepared to accept a higher risk in order to see their funds grow. As retirement approaches, this will change as the client seeks to lock in the growth that has been made and, once they retire, they will be looking for investments that will provide a secure income on which they can live.
- **Age** – the age of the client will often be used in conjunction with the above factors to determine acceptable levels of risk, as some of the above examples have already shown.

Individual circumstances may differ widely, but some aspects of common life stages encountered in different typical age groups are described below:

- **Minors (under 18)** – someone who is under 18 may have very little in the way of direct investment needs. They are likely to be dependent on one or two parents, and have no dependants of their own.
- **Single and still young (18 to 35)** – if your client is in their early or mid-20s, they may still not yet have any dependants. They may now be financially independent of their parents, even if they are still living at home. Alternatively, they may be renting a flat or possibly even buying a house. They are unlikely to have accumulated much capital and could be spending everything that they earn. They are also more likely to be an employee than to be self-employed.
- **Married or cohabiting (20 to 30)** – they are likely to have stopped being dependent on parents at this stage and are probably either renting or buying a house.
- **Couple working but no dependants (20 to 30)** – this is the time when a couple will be building up their income at the fastest possible rate, before the expenses of looking after children begin.
- **One of a couple working, with no dependants (20 to 30)** – the client's financial life could be a little bit more fragile. Dependence upon the earnings of one person increases the possibility of difficulties if there is a fall in their earnings.
- **One of a couple working, with dependants (25 to 40)** – with all the earnings concentrated in the hands of one of the couple and with there being both a partner and at least one dependant to look after, the burden of dependency has now begun to reach its maximum.
- **Married or cohabiting, with older children (35 to 50)** – this is the point when the expenses are probably at their highest, even without school fees. Higher education costs can increase the burden – especially if it includes university. However, the couple may again have two incomes (and possibly even have a higher net income despite the higher level of expenses).
- **After children: empty-nesters (45 to 60)** – when children have left home, their parents may have a higher net income as a result of lower expenses relating to children.
- **Retired (60 or 65 plus)** – retirement income may be significantly lower than when working, but there may be savings that have been built up. Investors may now have more free time, which they may or may not wish to devote to managing their own investments.

Subjective Factors

Establishing objective factors is clearly a preferable and more accurate way to help define a client's risk tolerance, but subjective factors also have a part to play.

A client's attitudes and experiences must also play a large part in the decision-making process. A client may be financially able to invest in higher-risk products and these may suit their needs but if they are by nature cautious, they may find the uncertainties of holding volatile investments unsettling, and both the adviser and the client may have to accept that lower-risk investments and returns have to be selected.

Methods of Assessment

As will be clear from the above, establishing an investor's risk profile is not straightforward. Classifications such as cautious, moderate and adventurous, and a detailed understanding of the risks associated with different asset and product types, will clearly help.

Defining risk profiles has limitations, not least trying to help a customer to understand the difference and agree which is applicable. As a result, many financial services companies have different methods of assessment. Some will rely on detailed client/adviser discussions, whereas others produce far more sophisticated versions of the risk classifications, which employ decision trees that require a client to answer a whole series of questions, in order to determine what products will be suitable. Some companies expand this further, by applying the client's responses to sophisticated financial modelling, that aims, based on historic investment performance data, to predict the probability of certain returns, as required by the client, being achieved.

One approach is to have a written questionnaire which the individual is asked to complete. The FCA has alerted the industry to be more diligent in their questionnaires to improve the outcome of investment performance. The different possible answers to questions can be scored, so that someone who has a more conservative or cautious attitude to risk has a low score, while an adventurous or aggressive risk-taker will show a high score.

The questions asked to assess an individual's risk profile could include the following examples:

- How long do you expect to leave your investment in place until you sell it?
- Which outcome is most important to you from an investment portfolio: preserving asset value/generating income/long-term growth?
- Which of the following investments have you owned before or do you now own: bank or building society deposit accounts/government stocks (gilts)/unit trusts or OEICs/investment trusts/individual company shares?
- Which of the following best describes your experience of investment? *'I have little investment experience beyond bank or building society savings accounts'/'I have had some experience of investment (such as unit trusts or individual shares)'/'I am an experienced investor with a portfolio managed by a financial adviser'/'I am an experienced investor and I prefer to manage my own portfolio.'*
- Which of the following best describes your main objective in investing: the education of your children, your retirement, to leave money in your will?
- How large is your investment plan in proportion to your total savings? (Less than 10%; between 10% and 20%; between 20% and 30%; between 30% and 40%; 40% or more.)

The key point is that the adviser needs to understand the client's attitude to risk and the risk characteristics of different assets and products, if the adviser is to match appropriate solutions with the client's needs.

2.6.2 Risk Profiles and Investment Selection

Attitude to risk will affect the investment policy that is implemented. If we look at three simple definitions of risk tolerance – cautious, moderate and adventurous – we can see how these will influence the choice of investments.

Investment Objective	Risk Tolerance	Attitude to Risk and Possible Investments
Income	Cautious	Willing to accept a lower level of income for lower risk Exposure to high-yield bonds and equities will be low
	Moderate	Seeking to balance potential risk with potential for income growth Exposure to high-yield bonds and equities will be higher
	Adventurous	Willing to adopt more aggressive strategies that offer potential for higher income Exposure to high-yield bonds and equities may be substantial
Income and Growth	Cautious	Seeking maximum growth and income consistent with relatively modest degree of risk Equities will form a relatively small percentage of the portfolio
	Moderate	Seeking to balance potential risk with growth of both capital and income Equities will form a significant percentage of the portfolio
	Adventurous	Able to adopt a long-term view that permits the pursuance of a more aggressive strategy Equities will form the principal part of the portfolio
Growth	Cautious	Seeking maximum growth consistent with relatively modest degree of risk Equities will form a significant percentage of the portfolio
	Moderate	Seeking to balance potential risk with growth of capital Equities will form the principal part of the portfolio
	Adventurous	Able to adopt a long-term view that allows them to pursue a more aggressive strategy Equities may form the whole of the portfolio

2.6.3 Affordability and Suitability of Investment Opportunities

Financial advisers need to assess the affordability and suitability of the range of investment opportunities available to them. Although a comprehensive and detailed formula cannot be delivered for every client, there are a series of steps that an adviser takes, based on the objectives in terms of risk and return, that have been agreed with the client, after taking into account their liquidity, constraints and other special needs.

Financial theory has established a linear relationship between risk and return. More simply, as risk taken in investment increases, return has to increase to compensate investors for the additional risk taken. The risk premium required is with the level of risk taken.

Traditionally, in a risk/return space generated by Markowitz, we can visualise the risk axis being split into zones and defined by three major asset classes that are staple products in a conventional mutual fund constructed by a traditional money manager. These zones are defined by: money market-like instruments; bond-like instruments and equity-like instruments; and risk increases from money-market funds through to equity-like funds. Alternative funds are contemporary investments that have increased the risk space further and also bring with them diversification opportunities for traditional funds.

The following is a checklist to assess the suitability of an investment:

- What are you seeking from your investment – income, growth, or both?
- Risk-return trade-off – carry out an assessment for the maximum risk that can be accepted and the tolerance for maximum loss.
- What is the investment term?
- How much money is available for investment every year?
- What are your expectations of investment returns, as a percentage per annum? Is the risk assessed for the client commensurate with this level of return?
- If income is required, what is this as a percentage return from the total return? Breakdown of income and capital appreciation yields.
- How likely is it that you may need access to this capital, either in part or whole, during the next five years? Impacts on liquidity.
- Is the income or growth guaranteed?
- When your investment term is complete, what do you intend to do with the money? Is this matched to a liability falling due at that time?
- What is your view of charges, ie, is the lowest charging company the best for you, or do you seek a company that has been obtaining better consistent returns?
- Do you want the flexibility to move in a charge-efficient manner from fund to fund?
- Are there any market sectors you would (not) like to invest in? Consider ethical investments if required.
- Is simplified administration important to you?
- Is tax efficiency important?
- How much of the ISA allowance is available for this tax year?
- Is your tax position likely to change for any reason in the foreseeable future, or when you retire?
- What are your immediate and future liquidity requirements?
- Do you have any other requirements and investment constraints?
- Carry out due diligence on product providers.
- Which product provider meets all of these client requirements?
- Will client service meet expectations? Are the charges levied by the provider acceptable?
- Performance attribution of product providers and their selection.

The checklist will provide information on the following and will be used to build up an investment policy:

- Objectives – return requirements and risk tolerance.
- Constraints – liquidity, horizon, regulations, taxes and unique needs.

After an assessment of the client needs, the policies will focus mainly on:

- Active or passive management.
- Asset allocation – proportions of the mix in terms of asset classes and their composition.
- Risk positioning.
- Tax positioning.
- Income generation.

An example of a matrix of objectives for a variety of investors is as follows.

Type of Investor	Return Requirement	Risk Tolerance
Individual and personal trusts	Life cycle (education needs, children, retirement)	Life cycle dependent (old more risk averse)
Mutual funds	Variable	Variable
Pension funds	Assumed actuarial rate	Depends on proximity of payouts
Endowment funds	Determined by current income needs and need for asset growth to maintain real value	Generally conservative
Life insurance company	Should exceed new money rate by sufficient margin to meet expenses and profit objectives; also actuarial rates are important	Conservative
Non-life insurance companies	No minimum	Conservative
Banks	Interest rate spread	Variable

Source: Investments 9th Edition

Example

Your neighbours who have learnt that you have successfully passed your CISI examination in Investment, Risk & Taxation have come to you for advice. Your neighbours are married, both are in their early 50s and they have just finished mortgage payments on their house in which they have lived for the last 15 years. Their two children have both completed their university education, have gained employment and have moved out of the family home. Your neighbours are now planning for retirement.

What advice on investing their retirement savings would you give? If they are very risk-averse what would you advise?

This is an open-ended question and you need to be careful in providing advice until you have thoroughly understood the client's needs and current position. Follow the steps outlined in the checklist before drafting an investment policy statement. At a general level, check that they have both used up their tax allowances and invested in tax-efficient schemes. A high level of risk aversion suggests that asset allocation decisions will most likely be tilting in favour of bond-like investments if income and capital protection is necessary over a long term. A risk-tolerant investor on the other hand will prefer investment growth and will not be averse to losing some capital in return for higher returns. The asset allocation decision in this case will tilt towards equity-like investments to achieve growth.

2.6.4 Capacity For Loss

The FSA's own definition in its Guidance Consultation January 2011, states that, *'by 'capacity for loss', we refer to the customer's ability to absorb falls in the value of their investment. If any loss of capital would have a materially detrimental effect on their standard of living, this should be taken into account in assessing the risk that they are able to take.'*

Capacity for loss is a distinct concept, but related to attitude to risk, and should therefore be considered and documented separately. Firms should ensure they have a robust process for assessing the risk a customer is willing and able to take.

It is critical that firms engage customers in a suitability assessment process (including risk profiling) which acts in the best interests of those customers. Detailed questioning is needed to assess the capacity for loss and this includes, but is not limited to, the following:

- Understanding the individual's income and expenditure both now and in the future.
- Understanding the individual's asset profile both now and in the future.
- Understanding if the individual has or will have dependants.

As well as this deep understanding that is needed to assess capacity for loss, it is important to consider the various factors that could affect the client's financial future.

3. Ethically and Socially Responsible Investment Strategies

Learning Objective

7.3.5 Understand the difference between environmental and social governance, and socially responsible investment strategies, their purpose and the circumstances in which it may be appropriate to discuss them

An individual investor or an organisation may wish to make investment decisions that take into account their ethical beliefs or social values. Churches and charities that have funds to invest on stock markets may want to avoid buying shares or bonds issued by companies involved in certain activities – eg, the manufacture or sale of alcohol products, the provision of gambling facilities, arms-dealing.

Indeed, in some cases the investor must avoid certain areas, perhaps because it is written into its constitution that it must do so. This might be the case for a charitable trust set up by a wealthy benefactor, for example, who wanted their values and wishes reflected in the charity's trust deed.

3.1 General Personal Ethical Considerations

Some people want to avoid having investments in their portfolios that fund businesses of which they do not approve; this is generally referred to as ethical investment.

Ethical investment strategies will vary according to the views of the investor (ie, with regard to their own particular ethics) – but may involve screening out investments in companies involved in specific areas. For example, an investor might specify that they wish to avoid any companies which are involved in:

- animal testing
- genetic modification or engineering
- intensive farming
- arms dealing or dealings with the military
- nuclear power
- pornography or other similar industries and/or
- those with a poor record on human rights.

The firm managing their portfolio will need to screen investments for the above negative criteria.

Still others want to ensure that their investments are in areas of which they positively approve; for example, enterprises that exhibit a degree of social responsibility or are proactive in certain desirable activities. This is generally referred to as socially responsible investment (SRI).

Examples of strategies which are SRI-friendly will screen for positive criteria – eg, an investor might require that their portfolio is invested in companies involved in any of the following fields:

- good corporate governance
- a good record of contribution to the community
- equal opportunities
- positive products and services, such as ecologically friendly cleaning products
- sound supply-chain practices, such as ensuring that a fair price is paid to the producers from whom they source raw materials or supplies.

Such investments are possible, whether within a portfolio of individual stocks or collective funds. Indeed, they are common enough that there is now a relatively wide range of product providers, and products, offering bank accounts and packaged investments such as unit trusts which meet certain stated ethical standards. The Ecology Building Society, for example, grants mortgages on properties that help the environment (eg, energy-efficient houses). Its savers know that the money they place on deposit with it is used to make funding available to, for example, projects aimed at low-impact lifestyles.

In addition, for direct investments, there are a small number of indices which measure the performance of companies meeting certain ethical standards. For example, in the FTSE series of indices, the FTSE4Good index covers the performance of stocks meeting certain criteria; it recently began to include factors relating to how much a company contributes to climate change among the matters it considers.

The Ethical Investment Research Service (EIRIS) provides research and guidance to organisations and investors interested in such an investment approach.

3.1.1 Restrictions on Portfolio Construction and Implications for Performance

Depending on the investor's values and expectations, different restrictions may need to be applied to a portfolio constructed to meet ethical or SRI standards. For example, as already explained:

- one investor might just want to avoid areas they saw as harmful
- another might want to be more proactive, and invest in a way that supports activities that are positively helpful to the environment.

Further, investors have different areas of interest. One person might be more interested in helping people in poorer countries, for example, while another might be more interested in projects closer to home, or supportive of animal welfare instead of that of people.

It is therefore important that, when an investor is interested in ethical investment or SRI, they ensure that their wishes are reflected in the portfolio's restrictions and limits so that the manager knows what is expected. If they are investing in a packaged product such as a unit trust, OEIC or life product, then this will not be tailored to their needs. They should read the product literature carefully to ensure that they understand the limits within which the product will be invested, and that these reflect their concerns.

Ethical or SRI-orientated funds generally state explicitly the criteria they use in selecting investments, so that investors can decide if a particular fund meets their needs. Such funds may use either negative criteria or positive criteria in the process of screening the companies they invest in. Once it has been established whether a company meets the criteria of the fund, investment managers can decide whether the company is worth investing in at the current price based on other, more common, investment criteria such as fundamental analysis (see chapter 6, section 2.13).

Portfolios may be constructed to avoid investments that are involved in or have a poor record in some or all of the following areas:

- Alcohol production or sale.
- Animal exploitation.
- Animal testing for cosmetics.
- Animal testing for pharmaceutical products.
- Environmental degradation and damage.
- Gambling.
- Genetic engineering and modern biotechnology.
- Genetically modified organisms (GMOs).
- Health and safety breaches.
- Human rights breaches.
- Intensive farming.
- Military-related enterprises.
- Nuclear power.
- Offensive or misleading advertising.
- Oppressive regimes.
- Pesticides.
- Pollution breaches.
- Pornography.
- Third World exploitation.
- Tobacco production or sale.

- Tropical hardwoods.
- Water pollution.

Examples of positive criteria include:

- Community involvement.
- Training and education policies.
- Full disclosure and openness about activities.
- Good relations with customers and suppliers.
- Equal opportunities.
- Good employment practices.
- Environmental improvement.
- Environmental management; energy and resource conservation.
- Positive goods and services produced.

Ethical and socially aware investors should remember that the more restrictions they place on a portfolio, the more likely they are to limit its potential for good performance; there are just fewer options for its manager to select from.

In addition, by placing restrictive criteria on it, they may inadvertently be increasing the risk within the portfolio – because its investments may be less diversified than would otherwise be the case, and/or because there is a concentration of investment in areas with a strong correlation to one another. Due to their activities, larger companies may be screened out of ethical funds, thereby limiting the overall selection pool to mainly smaller, potentially more risky companies.

Those in favour of ethical and SRI policies sometimes argue that the performance of individual companies selected on ethical grounds tends – over the long term – is better than that of some other companies, in part because they tend to have strong internal governance criteria, which feeds through into better overall management controls. Others argue that the additional restrictions placed on a company complying with SRI or ethical criteria can only limit its abilities to make decisions in the (financial) best interests of its shareholders – so performance must be lower.

In 1999, EIRIS produced some research comparing the performance of ethical/SRI investments against those managed without such limitations. Its conclusion, at the time, was that ethical/SRI criteria can have both a positive and negative influence on a portfolio but that, overall, performance seemed to be broadly similar.

You might want to look at the performance of the FTSE4Good indices yourself to see how performance compares with that of the wider market indices; consider whether current trends – the publicity given to climate change, for example – may be benefiting companies investing in SRI and ethical ways, and, as a consequence, such indices.

3.1.2 Corporate Social Responsibility (CSR)

Corporate social responsibility (CSR), also known as corporate responsibility, corporate citizenship, responsible business and corporate social opportunity, is a form of corporate self-regulation integrated into a business model.

Ideally, CSR policy functions as a built-in, self-regulating mechanism whereby businesses monitor and ensure their adherence to law, ethical standards, and international norms. Businesses embrace responsibility for the impact of their activities on the environment, consumers, employees, communities, stakeholders and all other members of the public sphere.

Furthermore, such businesses proactively promote the public interest by encouraging community growth and development, and voluntarily eliminating practices that harm the public sphere, regardless of legality. Essentially, CSR is the deliberate inclusion of public interest into corporate decision-making, and the honouring of a triple bottom line: people, planet, profit.

The practice of CSR is subject to much debate and criticism. Proponents argue that there is a strong business case for CSR, in that corporations benefit in multiple ways by operating with a perspective broader and longer than their own immediate, short-term profits. Critics argue that CSR distracts from the fundamental economic role of businesses; others argue that it is nothing more than superficial window-dressing; others argue that it is an attempt to pre-empt the role of governments as a watchdog over powerful multinational corporations.

Along with CSR, there has been increasing debate in recent years about including environmental, ecological, social and governance issues in investment and corporate decisions. The recent climatic change and CO_2 concerns, the financial, economic, and debt crisis, the nuclear catastrophe in Japan, and the crisis in the Arab region have all highlighted the fact that CSR policies need to be widened in scope to take into account the global environmental, social and governance (ESG) responsibility. Pressure groups have responded to the recent crises outlined above and state that the global economy has to be aligned with ESG criteria. They argue that measures and ideas need to be geared towards avoiding financial, economic, confidence, social, and ecological crises in the future.

The European Federation of Financial Analysts Societies (EFFAS) Commission on Environmental, Social and Governance (CESG) issues was founded in October 2007 in Vienna. Its main objective is to facilitate the integration aspects of ESG issues in relation to corporate performance into investment processes. Within EFFAS, a committee on ESG issues has been set up and the body comprises investment professionals from leading European and global sell-side and buy-side firms. Members are predominantly fund managers, financial analysts and equity sector specialists and the committee has been considering processes that need to become more and more a part of traditional investment analysis (mainstreaming).

CESG philosophy is aimed at integrating ESG issues into classic investment research and decisions from the perspective of traditional investors and financial analysts. Hence, the CESG fills the gap between political and high-level industry initiatives, supported by many global investment houses on the one hand, and the need of corporates to enhance corporate reporting on the other.

Encouraging other stakeholder groups to enter into dialogue, the CESG does not confine itself to discussions but rather strives to: define positions on extra-financials; produce outcome such as papers and recommendations; and seeks to play an active role in the dialogue with both investment professionals and corporates.

3.1.3 Social, Environmental and Other Ethical Issues

The following covers some of the issues that are commonly of concern to investors seeking to apply social, environmental and ethical principles to their investments.

The first thing you should remember when assessing the social, environmental and overall ethical performance of a company or an ethical fund is that there is no such thing as a perfect company. All are involved in activities that someone somewhere will object to; none goes far enough in terms of positive social and environmental contribution to satisfy all of the people all the time. With that in mind, ethical/SRI is about compromising and prioritising.

Before constructing an ethical portfolio or choosing an ethical fund, the investor should think through their concerns. They should decide what types of corporate activities they are concerned about and how strongly they feel about them. Some of the common issues that are of concern to many ethical investors are described next. Of course they may have other concerns not covered here that they may want to discuss with their financial adviser or broker.

Traditional Ethical Issues

For many, the first introduction to ethical investment came as a response to the human rights abuses in South Africa under apartheid. Since then, investors have extended the boycotting approach to other oppressive regimes. Such negative coverage has given companies an impetus to adopt human rights policies or codes of business conduct.

Policies of this kind are particularly relevant to operations in countries with poor human rights records. While some investors seek to avoid involvement in oppressive regimes altogether, for others it is what the company does in a country that is of interest. Is it an influence for good, or does the business either benefit from or somehow support a climate of repression?

Other, often connected issues, are armaments (production and sales) and corporate activities such as commodity extraction, breast milk substitution, pharmaceutical marketing and holding debt.

Alcohol, gambling and tobacco were the traditional concerns of the temperance movement back in the 1900s, where the origins of ethical investment can be found. For some these are still of significant concern today, particularly with the adverse effects on health; and likewise pornography, animal testing, intensive farming and fur have been longstanding issues for the UK ethical investor in particular. Attitudes vary between different countries and cultures.

Environmental Issues

Public concerns about the degradation of the environment are becoming increasingly widespread. Protests, shareholder actions, boycotts and other campaigns have brought these concerns to the attention of business. Some companies have also started to engage with stakeholders, including employees, communities, shareholders and campaign groups such as Friends of the Earth and Greenpeace. Calls for increased transparency in company activities have led to an increase in reporting on environmental performance. A number of organisations, notably the Global Reporting Initiative (GRI), have published guidance documents in an attempt to standardise the format used. However, many companies have been criticised for publishing greenwash to improve public relations, without including meaningful performance data.

In addition, there are specific environmental issues that continue to be of concern to responsible investors. Examples include: climate change exacerbated by companies' greenhouse gas emissions and use of ozone-depleting chemicals (ODCs); the use of pesticides and genetic engineering; the use of tropical hardwood; (air and water) pollution; and industries associated with nuclear power, mining and quarrying and fossil fuels.

Social Issues

These encompass a wide range of issues related to how a company behaves towards its stakeholders, ie, customers, employees, suppliers, shareholders and the community within which it operates and what standards it might set. For example, when assessing a company's attitude towards its employees EIRIS looks at several areas, including equal opportunities, training and development, and job creation and security.

When looking at a company's standards with regard to suppliers, one might wish to investigate how companies ensure that core labour rights apply throughout their supply chain, particularly if their suppliers are based in countries where child labour is common. Community involvement and charitable giving have also become areas where companies have come under scrutiny, to see if they make a positive effort to contribute to the communities they work in and to society at large, whether via donations or other means.

Positive Products and Services

Knowing whether the product or service provided by a company contributes positively to society is something that has been of interest to many ethical investors for a number of years. Ethical investment is not only about avoiding companies but also about actively supporting companies that are contributing positively to society and/or the environment.

Of course, there will be different views about what products or services should be regarded as positive; and perhaps one can supply a basically 'good' product or service in a way that does not benefit the world.

Products and services that are often identified as positive include basic necessities, environmental products/services and other services which help make the world a safer and better place. Examples include wind power generators, pollution abatement technology, public transport and bicycles, safety and protection systems such as fire alarms, health care including medicines, housing, utilities and educational services.

Governance and Ethics

Concern about the governance of public companies has increased immensely over the last few years, particularly following corporate scandals such as Enron. Corporate governance has been on the SRI agenda for some time and includes issues such as board structure and practices. This encompasses factors such as women on the board and directors' remuneration, the latter having received massive media and public interest in the so-called fat-cat scandals about large pay rises for directors, when shareholders felt they had not done enough to justify these substantial pay increases. Questions such as does the company have a code of ethics and does it make any political donations also come under this umbrella.

Stock Indices that embody CSR Objectives

The FTSE Group publishes the FTSE4Good Index, an evaluation of CSR performance of companies.

The FTSE4Good Index series, launched in July 2001, measures the performance of UK companies that meet globally recognised corporate responsibility standards. It is similar to the FTSE All Share Index, which lists shares according to market capitalisation (price of the share x number of shares in issue), but excludes tobacco, nuclear power and arms industries. Other indices which embody CSR objectives include the FTSE Environmental, Social and Governance (ESG) index and the low carbon index series.

In the UK the FTSE4Good index has criteria for stock selection, including the environment, universal human rights, social issues and stakeholder relations.

The US equivalent is the MSCI KLD 400 Index, which is a socially screened version of the Standard & Poor's 500 Stock Index.

The management and the evolution of the FTSE4Good Index series is placed under the direction of the FTSE4Good policy committee, an independent body of experts from the fields of corporate responsibility, fund management, academia and the business community. The FTSE4Good policy committee's role is to:

- act as an independent judge of the ability of constituent companies to meet the FTSE4Good Index Series criteria
- oversee the consultation process undertaken to develop criteria
- approve criteria revisions or new criteria.

This FTSE KLD Domini 400 Social Index was launched in 1990 and is designed to help socially conscious investors weigh social and environmental factors in their investment choices.

The FTSE KLD 400 social index is designed to provide exposure to the common stocks of companies that it determines have positive ESG characteristics. The KLD400 consists of 400 companies drawn from the universe of the 3,000 largest US public equities as measured by float-adjusted market capitalisation. The index is composed approximately 90% of large-cap companies, 9% mid-cap companies chosen for sector diversification, and 1% small-cap companies with exemplary social and environmental records.

The eligible universe for the KLD 400 is the 3,000 largest US companies (by float-adjusted market capitalisation) in the US equity market. KLD selects the eligible universe index on 15 April (or closest business day) of each year.

KLD defines US equity as follows: *'US headquarters Primary market listing is the NYSE or NASDAQ companies with non-US incorporation for tax or regulatory purposes evaluated on a case-by-case basis.'* KLD follows the rules of the FTSE AWD USA Index. The following types of equities are not eligible for the KLD 400:

- preferred stocks
- limited or other types of partnerships
- royalty trusts
- closed-ended funds.

In the US, the Calvert Responsible Large Cap Core Index is a stock market index created by Calvert Investments, as a benchmark of large companies that are considered socially responsible or ethical. It currently consists of 468 companies, weighted by market capitalisation, selected from approximately 1,000 of the largest publicly traded companies in the US, using Calvert's social criteria. These criteria relate to the environment, workplace issues, product safety, community relations, weapons contracting, international operations, and human rights.

This index was created following the success of the MSCI KLD 400 by KLD Research & Analytics Inc. The Calvert index is used by many so-called socially responsible mutual funds as a benchmark for their performance.

3.2 Islamic Finance

Learning Objective

7.3.6 Understand the main considerations for investing in accordance with Sharia'a law

Islamic banking refers to a system of banking or banking activity that is consistent with the principles of Islamic law (Sharia'a) and its practical application through the development of Islamic economics.

Sharia'a prohibits the payment of fees for the renting of money (*Riba*, usury) for specific terms, as well as investing in businesses that provide goods or services considered contrary to its principles (*Haraam*, forbidden).

The overarching principle of Islamic finance is that all forms of interest are forbidden. The Islamic financial model works on the basis of risk sharing. The customer and the bank share the risk of any investment on agreed terms, and divide any profits between them. The main categories within Islamic finance are: ijara, ijara-wa-iqtina, mudaraba, murabaha and musharaka.

- **Ijara** is a leasing agreement whereby the bank buys an item for a customer and then leases it back over a specific period.
- **Ijara-wa-Iqtina** is a similar arrangement, except that the customer is able to buy the item at the end of the contract.
- **Mudaraba** offers specialist investment by a financial expert in which the bank and the customer share any profits. Customers risk losing their money if the investment is unsuccessful, although the bank will not charge a handling fee, unless it turns a profit.
- **Murabaha** is a form of credit which enables customers to make a purchase without having to take out an interest-bearing loan. The bank buys an item and then sells it on to the customer on a deferred basis.
- **Musharaka** is an investment partnership in which profit-sharing terms are agreed in advance, and losses are pegged to the amount invested.

3.3 Other Faith-Based Investment Products

Learning Objective

7.3.7 Understand the main considerations for investing in accordance with other faith values

A branch of SRI, faith-based investing, has been around for a long time. In the 1800s, the Quakers, who were anti-slavery and anti-war, avoided investing in weapons production. Today, faith-based investing is often a combination of SRI, plus the screening out of several other things germane to a particular religion. Each group decides both what their financial goals are and their strategies to achieve those goals. They also look at their social and religious teachings and that leads them to be willing to hold certain things in their portfolios.

3.4 Investment for Charities

Learning Objective

7.3.8 Understand the main considerations that should be taken into account when investing for charities

3.4.1 Introduction

Many charities have surplus funds not needed to fund their immediate charitable activities; often the trustees invest some or all of this surplus in order to generate extra income to fund future activities. The basic principle governing trustees' decisions about investing their charity's funds is that they must take a prudent approach. When investing charitable funds (especially those which represent permanent endowment), trustees must seek to strike the right balance for their particular charity between the two objectives of:

- providing an income to help the charity carry out its purposes effectively in the short term and
- maintaining and, if possible, enhancing the value of the invested funds, so as to enable the charity to carry out its purposes in the longer term effectively.

In order to discharge the duty to adopt a prudent approach to the investment of the charity's funds, trustees must:

- know their investment powers
- discharge their duties properly when they take decisions about investments
- have proper arrangements in place for holding investments on behalf of the charity
- follow certain legal requirements if they are going to use an institution to manage the charity's investments on their behalf
- know what they can and cannot do if they are going to apply an ethical approach to the charity's investments.

If the size of the funds to be invested justifies it, trustees should decide on a formal investment policy for the charity. This will, of course, vary in the level of detail and complexity depending on the size of the charity, and on whether the function of investment has been delegated.

3.4.2 Definition of an Investment

Conceptions of what constitutes investment vary. In this context it needs to be distinguished from other forms of income-generation, such as trading and gambling. For most trustees, particularly of smaller charities, the examples of what are and are not investments in the following paragraphs should be sufficient as a guide.

Examples of Investments

The term investment is not defined in statute. Instead the courts have interpreted the phrase. While not exhaustive, some common examples of investments include:

- shares in companies
- land rented or leased out by the charity to tenants
- interest-bearing loans by the charity, for example, government bonds, company loan stock, deposits at banks and building societies and
- units in collective investment schemes, such as unit trusts, OEICs or common investment funds.

Examples of What are not Investments

Some examples of what do not constitute investments are:

- Land purchased and developed with a view to sale. This will usually be regarded as trading rather than investment, and hence may attract only limited tax relief.
- Commodities such as gold or vintage wine, acquired with a view to resale in the future at a profit. This is the only prospect of a financial benefit from the transaction. The purchase and sale of such items will also usually be viewed as trading.

3.4.3 Trustees' Powers of Investment

Under the Trustee Act, most trustees will have a very wide power of investment. In practice this means that most trustees are able to invest in almost anything regarded under trust law as an investment. See section 3.4.2 for examples of what falls within the trust law definition.

There are certain circumstances in which trustees do not have the power of investment which the Trustee Act confers, or when certain conditions apply when using powers of investment. These general powers of investment are not available if:

- the charity is a charitable company (except when the company is itself acting as a charity trustee)
- the charity's governing document excludes or restricts the Trustee Act power (although in certain circumstances this statutory power overrides restrictions or exclusions in the governing document); for instance, the governing document may restrict the trustees to investing in certain types of investment (eg, shares traded on the LSE) or prohibit investment in certain industries (eg, armaments or tobacco).

If the Trustee Act powers are not available, trustees must rely on any powers within their governing document when making investments.

3.4.4 Trustees' Duties

When managing a charity's investments, trustees must act according to certain standards as defined in the Trustee Act 2000, whether they are using the investment powers in that Act or not.

First, there is the general duty of care, which is the duty to exercise such care and skill as is reasonable in the circumstances. This applies both to the use of any power of investment and to the discharge of the specific duties which the Act attaches to the use of investment powers. A higher level of care and skill is expected of a trustee who is or claims to be knowledgeable about or experienced in investments, or who is paid.

Secondly, trustees must comply with the following specific duties:

- Trustees must consider the suitability for their charity of any investment. This duty exists at two levels. The trustees must be satisfied that the type of any proposed investment (eg, a common investment fund or a deposit account) is right for their charity (including whether it is consistent with an ethical investment policy if the charity has one). They also have a duty to consider whether a particular investment of that type is a suitable one for the charity to make. Trustees should, at both levels, try to consider the whole range of investment options which are open to them; how far they should go here will, of course, depend on the amount of funds available for investment.
- Trustees must consider the need for diversification, ie, having different types of investment, and different investments within each type. This will reduce the risk of losses resulting from concentrating on a particular investment or type of investment. Again, how far the trustees can go here will depend on the amount of funds available for investment.
- Trustees must periodically review the investments of the charity. The nature and frequency of these reviews is up to the trustees to decide, but the reviews should be proportionate to the nature and size of the charity's investment portfolio. To review too infrequently may result in losses or missed opportunities; changing investments too frequently may incur unnecessarily high levels of transaction charges.
- Before exercising any power of investment, and when reviewing the charity's investments, trustees must obtain and consider proper advice from a suitably qualified adviser (who may be one of the trustees), unless the size of the funds available for investment is so small that seeking investment advice is not cost-effective.

The Trustee Act requires the objective consideration of the points mentioned above. The trustees of charitable companies have similar obligations, even though the Act does not apply to them expressly. All trustees must also take into account any relevant provisions in their charity's governing document.

Trustees of all charities with permanent endowment have a duty to be even-handed between the interests of present and future beneficiaries of the charity. In practice this means that they must consider whether an investment provides a suitable balance between providing income for current needs and preserving or increasing the value of the investments, so that the charity can operate effectively in future.

Some other duties of trustees with respect to investments are to:

- manage the risks their charity faces, balance those risks against the potential returns from particular investments, and be careful to avoid undue risk to their charity's funds
- invest in markets where financial services are closely regulated, and where compensation schemes are in place
- have a suitably diversified investment portfolio
- be particularly wary of making speculative forms of investment.

A charity's annual report must include a description of the policies used by the trustees to select the charity's investments. Larger charities must, as part of their compliance with accounting requirements, also report on the performance of their investments.

Trustees are not liable to make good any loss to the charity incurred simply because an investment made by them is unsuccessful. However, trustees may be liable if, in making or retaining the unsuccessful investment, they have acted outside the scope of their powers, or failed to discharge the duties.

3.4.5 Delegation of Investment Management

Many charity trustees will consider it best to place the management of the charity's investments in the hands of a specialist.

There are two main ways of doing this:

- investing in one or more collective investment schemes, such as unit trusts, OEICs or common investment funds for charities, or
- delegating their investment decisions by appointing an investment manager.

For smaller charities the first option may well be a cost-effective way of achieving a professionally managed and balanced portfolio. But trustees must still fulfil the investment duties described in the paragraphs above and satisfy themselves of the suitability of any collective scheme as an investment vehicle for their charity.

Larger charities with significant funds may consider appointing an investment manager. This is unlikely to be cost-effective for smaller charities. It involves the trustees in a number of extra duties in appointing an investment manager, providing them with direction as to the charity's investment policies, and reviewing their performance.

The advantage of using an investment manager is, of course, that the manager can pursue an investment strategy which is tailor-made to the needs of the particular charity. But this advantage comes at a cost, both in terms of fees charged for the service, and in terms of the trustees having to discharge the extra responsibilities referred to above, in their relationship with the investment manager.

3.4.6 Investment Policy

The charity trustees will decide on an investment policy for their charity, record it clearly in writing, and keep it under regular review. If they have delegated their investment function to an investment manager these are legal requirements. Without an investment policy, trustees are likely to find it difficult to demonstrate that they are making good use of the charity's funds.

Any investment policy should, for example, address the following considerations:

- the need for enough resources for the charity to carry out its present and future activities effectively
- the level of acceptable risk and how to manage it
- the charity's stance on ethical investment.

Ethical Investment

The question of basing an investment policy on ethical considerations can be an important one for charities. The essentials are dealt with briefly here.

If trustees are to adopt an ethical investment policy, or follow one laid down in the charity's governing document, they need to keep in mind their duty to invest in a way that furthers the purpose of the charity. This will normally be achieved by seeking the maximum return from a set of investments which have been selected prudently. An ethical investment policy can be entirely consistent with this duty, but there can also be a risk that the exclusion from consideration, or preference, of certain investment classes or particular investments may detract from the objective of obtaining the best direct financial returns from investment.

Trustees may well consider that the adoption of a particular ethical investment policy does not detract from the objective of obtaining the best direct financial return from investment. They must, of course, then be able to justify their position, through being able to show that they have, in following the policy, fully discharged the investment duties referred to above.

Some trustees may, however, wish to adopt an ethical investment policy even though it does, or may, detract from the objective of obtaining the best direct financial return. The circumstances in which they may wish to do this are outlined in the following paragraph.

Trustees are able to adopt an ethical investment policy which will involve avoiding investments:

- in a particular business that would for practical reasons conflict with the aims of the charity; for example, a charity with objectives for the protection of the environment and wildlife may decide not to invest in businesses which pollute what the charity is trying to protect
- that might hamper a charity's work, either by making potential beneficiaries unwilling to be helped because of the source of the charity's money, or by alienating supporters.

This requires trustees to strike a balance between the likely cost of lost support, if the charity holds the investments, and any risk of financial underperformance if those investments are excluded from its portfolio.

There may be some cases where the two previous statements do not apply, but the trustees will still wish to make investment decisions on moral grounds. This may include using positive or negative criteria, or a combination of both. In all these cases, however, the trustees must be particularly clear that their decisions will not place the charity at risk of significant financial detriment, due to underperformance by the preferred investments or by the exclusion from consideration of forms of investment to which the trustees are opposed.

Trustees are unlikely to be criticised for adopting a particular policy if they have considered the correct issues, taken appropriate advice and reached a rational result.

Note that ethical investment is not the same as social investment. Also known as programme-related investment (PRI), this is an entirely separate concept, and is not investment in the financial sense, as its primary aim is to carry out the objectives of a charity.

Mixed Motive Investments

As you can see, charitable investment generally falls into one of two categories: a normal financial investment that seeks to generate the best possible return for an acceptable level of risk; or a PRI that seeks to further the charity's objectives and potentially deliver a financial return. Both are accepted methods of investment as long as they are undertaken for the charity's best interests.

In 2011, the Charitable Commission published guidance to clarify that trustees could make investments that had a 'mixed motive'. In other words, investments that were designed to achieve the best possible return while seeking to deliver on the charity's objectives, but could not be wholly considered to be for financial gain, or in the furtherance of the charity's objectives.

3.4.7 Tax Implications

Most investments are treated as qualifying investments by HMRC. However, the making of certain types of investment may be treated as non-qualifying investments. This can lead to a restriction of the charity's tax reliefs. Trustees making such investments must be able to satisfy HMRC that the investments are made for the financial benefit of the charity and not for the avoidance of tax, whether by the charity or by any other person.

Guidance on the tax implications of investment by charities can be found at hmrc.gov.uk.

3.5 Investment for Trusts

Learning Objective

7.3.9 Understand the main considerations that should be taken into account when investing for trusts

A personal trust is created for a person or persons. Personal trusts can be used by beneficiaries to accomplish a variety of financial objectives. Personal trusts are separate legal entities that have the authority to buy, sell, hold and manage property for the benefit of their beneficiaries.

There are typically three main parties to a trust:

1. The **trust creator**, sometimes (in Scotland) called the grantor but usually (in England and Wales) the **settlor**, is the person who began as owner of the property that is to be transferred to and held by the trust.
2. The **trustee** is the person or institution (such as a bank or trust company) that holds the legal title to the trust estate. There may be one or more trustees. If a trustee is unwilling or unable to serve, then a successor trustee steps in to hold and manage the trust estate. The trustee is obliged to act in accordance with the terms of the trust for the benefit of the trust beneficiaries.
3. The **beneficiaries** are the persons who the trust creator intended to benefit from the trust estate.

The law in the area of personal trusts is complex. In the sections that follow we present the key guiding principles of the legislation that advisers need to be aware of when investing for trusts. In England and Wales, the legislation covering trusts and trustees is contained in the Trustees Act 2000. It has given professional trustees far greater investment freedom, while making them more accountable. In addition, trustees are now required to seek professional guidance and investment advice. Trustees should take legal advice if uncertain. The Act covers five areas of trust law: the duty of care imposed upon trustees, trustees' power of investment; the power to appoint nominees and agents; the power to acquire land; and the power to receive remuneration for work done as a trustee. It sets a new duty of care, both objective and standard, massively extends the trustees' powers of investment and limits the trustees' liability for the actions of agents, also providing for their remuneration for work done in the course of the trust. The legislation now requires that trustees should ensure that any adviser they are proposing to use is competent to give advice.

There are three main areas of responsibility that a trustee managing investment trusts should be aware of:

1. a statutory duty of care
2. general powers of investment
3. rules on the appointment of nominees, custodians and investment managers.

3.5.1 Duty of Care

This duty for trustees is enshrined in statue law. Trustees have a duty of care under the Trustee Act 2000.

The new uniform statutory duty of care for trustees makes sure that individuals show such skill and care as is reasonable in the circumstances of the case, making allowance for their specialised knowledge, experience or professional status. The Act requires the delivery of a certain standard of consistency and competence expected of trustees. This makes it more difficult to ignore or overlook their overall responsibilities.

The standard of care takes account of the trustees' experience and professional training. For example, in relation to the purchase of stocks and shares, a higher standard may be expected of a trustee who has specialist knowledge in the area of finance (ie, is an investment banker, specialising in equities), other than of a trustee who is, for example, a beekeeper, particularly if the investment banker is acting as a trustee in the course of their investment banking business.

According to Section I of the Act, the duty of care must be exercised when:

- investing trust capital or reviewing investments
- acquiring or managing land
- appointing someone to give proper advice or reviewing/selecting agents to carry out delegated responsibilities
- insuring trust properties
- exercising powers to compound liabilities
- dealing with audits and valuations of trust property.

The trustee may be liable under law for any act or default by their appointed agents, if they fail to deliver the duty of care responsibilities, when drawing up investment policy statements or entering into or reviewing compliance matters. For professional trustees the duty of care is taken further in the sense that they must select investments with the prudent man rule, looking after the interests of others. In addition, when investing trust money, trustees must treat the beneficiaries impartially and seek to balance the interests of providing income and preserving capital value.

The following steps have to be taken by the trustees:

- Review the trusts aims and objectives.
- Decide which responsibilities should be delegated to agents.
- Review and reconcile the investment management, nominee and custodian arrangements with trust rules.
- Trustees of charitable trusts must act in accordance with Charity Commission rules on the selection and appointment of custodians and nominees.
- Check that investment advice and management is provided by qualified professionals.
- Prepare, review and revise the trust's investment policy statement.

3.5.2 Investment Powers

In the Trustee Act 2000, trustees have been given the flexibility to make investments in any asset classes that are expected to produce an income or capital return. The Act refrains from defining the nature of the investment narrowly: it should be in an asset class that is suitable or appropriate for the needs of the trust. The responsibility requires that the trustee employs appropriate skills in stock selection within each asset class. Finally, the investment portfolio should be diversified.

From a practical point of view, this implies that the trustees must engage in the following process:

- Create and review investment objectives and define the requirements precisely. Trustees must continually refer back to the standard investment criteria to check that they are being fulfilled.
- Work with the appointed investment manager to set and review the investment policy statement of the fund. This ensures that the money manager is fully conversant with the plan requirements.
- Agree the terms of the investment engagement with the investment manager and secure a written agreement. The policy must be written so that all the functions are carried out in the best interests of the trust.

Examples of the contents of the investment policy are as follows:

- Frequency of review and performance reporting.
- Overall return expected, minimum yield required and risks.
- Income or capital requirements.
- The ability to distribute capital in the place of income, ie, total return.
- The nature and timing of any liabilities.
- The liquidity requirement, including dates of planned expenditure.
- The marketability of the investments – important if capital needs to be raised quickly.
- The time horizon of the trust – less than five years or long-term.
- Asset allocation considerations.
- Selection of the benchmark.
- The time horizon over which performance will be assessed.
- The base currency of the trust.
- The residence and tax status of the trust and the beneficiaries.
- Any SRI constraints.
- Any other tax and legal constraints.

3.5.3 Appointment of Nominees, Custodians and Investment Managers

Trustees have been given the power under the Act to appoint a nominee to hold the title to the trust's investments and/or a custodian to look after the documents of the title.

These agreements have to be made in writing and trustees have to check that the nominee:

- is separately incorporated from the investment manager
- is a non-trading company
- provides an insurance cover/indemnity over and above the statutory limits.

4. The Advantages of Repaying a Mortgage and Other Borrowings

Learning Objective

7.2.2 Analyse the merits and disadvantages of paying off mortgage or debt compared with investing surplus funds

4.1 The Relationship between Investment and Borrowings

At different points in the investor's financial life cycle, the typical individual will tend to:

- have surplus funds (for example, someone in middle age and middle management, with solid earnings, having paid off the mortgage and seen any children reach adulthood) or
- be cash-poor and tending to have a certain amount of indebtedness (perhaps someone in young adulthood, while in the early stages of a career, with young children to raise and a mortgage).

Of course, these are only stereotypes and not everyone follows such a pattern. In addition, there are times when people have both debt and investable cash.

It may seem irrational to invest money while also paying interest on a loan. After all, loan interest is typically higher than the interest paid on savings accounts of similar size and term. Sometimes, however, it will be appropriate to allow the investor to remain in some debt, and invest any liquid capital they have in the markets. At other times, this may not make financial sense. It may be more prudent to pay off existing debts before risking committing capital to the markets.

In weighing up the merits of repaying debt, against those of investing surplus cash, the factors to be considered include:

- whether the debt is fixed-rate or variable (will the client be able to keep up the repayments if interest rates go up, if their money is tied up in the markets?)
- any penalties on early repayment of the loan
- the likely direction of interest rates
- the nature of the debt (for example, it may be appropriate to allow a fixed-rate, fixed-term mortgage to run rather than paying it off, if the investor has a good deal on it and wishes to begin investing for the future)
- the investor's tax status: if an investment is particularly tax-favourable, then this may be an additional factor to weigh against the disadvantages of carrying a debt burden.

Many people with capital available to invest will also be owner-occupiers (homeowners) with a mortgage. Should such a person use free capital to pay off all or part of their mortgage rather than invest the money? The cost of maintaining the mortgage can be quantified in terms of the interest cost.

Suppose that an individual has a repayment mortgage for £50,000 and also has £50,000 in cash. If the interest rate on the mortgage is 5% and the after-tax rate of interest paid on deposits is 3%, then the net cost of keeping the mortgage, rather than using the money to pay it off, is 2% (£50,000 x 2% = £1,000 per annum).

What if the individual is considering investing the available sum of £50,000 in equities? This obviously involves taking a risk with the money, and the sum could either grow or fall in value.

Generally, it is well worth someone considering paying off part of their mortgage if they can. This will reduce their interest repayments in the future, and may bring forward the day when they are free of mortgage debt. The alternative of investing the money will also be considered by some, and is a valid strategy for someone who is not risk-averse.

It is also worth bearing in mind that a homebuyer who has an interest-only mortgage backed by a repayment vehicle (such as an equity ISA) is effectively choosing to take the risk of investing in equities (through the ISA) rather than withdrawing and using those funds to partially repay the mortgage.

There are various ways that an individual can consider balancing the relationship between borrowings and capital for investing. The availability of offset mortgages which allow the net outstanding borrowing to be set against cash balances has increased the flexibility that can be employed in reaching a balance that suits the individual.

5. Investment Solutions

Learning Objective

7.4.2 Apply an appropriate investment allocation strategy that best meets the following criteria: client's financial objectives and priorities; client's risk tolerance; appropriate fees and charges; portfolio turnover ratio (PTR); client suitability requirements; adequate diversification and correlation benefits; additional risk, timing and liquidity factors where asset accumulation and decumulation are relevant features

5.1 Investor Circumstances

It is possible to identify a typical financial life cycle (and the financial needs that accompany this) – but bear in mind that every case is different, and there may be many variations in individual circumstances, that cannot easily be fitted into standard categories. In any event, we can identify certain factors that affect an investor's circumstances.

When considering an investor's objectives and risk profile, their wealth is an important consideration. If there is free capital to invest, then clearly it is sensible for the individual to take steps to make the best use of that capital.

It is possible, although not generally advisable, for someone with little wealth to gain exposure to investment markets, for example, by borrowing money to invest, or by using investments such as derivatives or spread betting to gain a greater exposure than the individual's free resources. When investing in risky assets such as equities, a good principle is the often-stated one that someone should only invest what they can afford to lose. Someone who borrows to invest, without having other capital to back it up if things go wrong, has the problem that they may end up with liabilities in excess of assets.

An investor who uses instruments such as derivatives to increase their exposure to the markets should maintain other accessible resources (for example, cash on deposit) that can be used to meet losses that may arise. Clearly, it is also important that they understand and accept the risks involved.

The age of an investor, their stage in the life cycle, and their commitments, all affect their risk profile. Adventurous risk-taking may be unwise for someone with heavy financial commitments, for example, to children and other dependants. Further, time can be a factor: someone who works full-time and has a family may have little time left to manage their investments (even if they had the inclination and skills to do so). Their time commitments may mean that they are more likely to use professional financial advice and management.

5.2 Affordability and Suitability

In considering what recommendations to make to an investor, a planner or adviser needs to take into account not just the factors external to that investor – the investment and economic environment – but also those internal to them. These factors include their own financial situation, and psychological factors such as their appetite for risk. They affect what investments will be suitable for them, in their current situation – and what investments they may be able to afford on an ongoing basis.

There is little point in recommending a regular savings product, if the investor is unlikely to be able to keep up the payments.

Whether an investor is making their own financial planning decisions, or is being advised by a financial adviser, it may seem obvious to state that investments chosen should meet a test of suitability. An adviser clearly needs to follow the regulatory KYC principle in order to be able to assess the suitability requirements of a client.

In order to ensure that recommendations meet the test of suitability, client needs should be quantified and the shortfall (if any) between needs and the client's existing arrangements should be assessed.

For each quantified need, the adviser should draw up a list of suitable products and strategies from those available. From the list of suitable products and strategies, the most suitable combination should be identified. This can generally be achieved by a process of elimination, bearing in mind such factors as risk, flexibility, access, cost, complexity, matched with the investor's investment objectives, and charges.

5.3 Investment Allocation Strategy

Asset allocation strategy is the construction stage of the portfolio management process. Bearing in mind the mandate from the investment policy statement, an investment manager gets to work on the selection of assets, processing capital market expectations and developing the model inputs that are required to build a suitable portfolio that meets the client's objectives.

The traditional asset classes from which a portfolio is constructed include the following:

- **Domestic ordinary shares** – market capitalisation is used as a criterion to distinguish among large-cap, intermediate and small-cap issues as distinct sub-asset classes. Moreover, the decision-making may include an element of style that is captured by following value or growth opportunities.
- **Domestic fixed income** – here the focus may be on short, intermediate or long-term maturities. In particular, recently, inflation-protected securities have been used to distinguish between nominal bonds and inflation-protected bonds.
- **Money market securities** – these securities are of a maturity of less than one year and offer the advantages of easy conversion to meet short- or near-term liquidity needs in a portfolio.
- **International equities** – investment in this area may further be sub-divided into developed, emerging and frontier markets, as permitted within the policy statement.
- **International bonds** – as with international equities, the asset class is sub-divided mainly into permitted developed and emerging markets.
- **Real estate and commodities** – the major asset classes above are the primary asset classes used in the construction of financial portfolios. In the recent decade, however, interest in non-financial asset classes has increased, as money managers have sought better diversification opportunities and yield enhancement. Real estate, commodities and private equity all belong to this unique asset class, often called alternative investments.

It is important to note that when investing in international assets, investors will need to consider the following special issues:

- **Currency risk** – exchange rate movements affect both the total return and the volatility of an asset. The currency risk is often of the same order as the equity risk, but it is considerably greater for bond and money market investments. As a result money managers will want to develop capital market expectations about currency movements and then to decide whether the new position will need to be hedged or left unhedged.
- **Stress-induced correlation increase** – investors should be aware that, during episodes of market stress, correlations across international markets will increase, limiting opportunities for diversification.
- **Emerging markets concerns** – a number of issues may be present that fund managers are wary about. These include: political instability; limitations on ownership of securities by international investors; the quality and content of information available on foreign securities; and non-normality of security returns.

5.3.1 Weighting of Asset Classes

In strategic asset allocation, the money manager has to determine the asset allocation or the proportions of weights given to each asset class that is invested in a portfolio. Asset allocation reviews are carried out on a regular basis during the management of a funded portfolio. For each asset class that is considered as a viable class for the portfolio, there will be a comprehensive view of capital market expectations formed over the investment period.

With capital market expectations and the portfolio objectives in hand, the asset allocation decision is then taken. The inputs to this decision are often fed into an optimiser. A large number of fund managers nowadays use established procedures that have a quantitative flavour. The optimisation methodologies are beyond the scope of this syllabus and use variants of the Markowitz mean-variance approach. Some investment advisers on the other hand, particularly those serving individual investor clientele, may use a qualitative approach to allocation, based on their experiences. In actual fact most professional advisers utilise both quantitative and qualitative judgements in making recommendations.

Experience-Based Approaches

Although qualitative approaches offer a disciplined basis to the asset allocation process, there are advisers who prefer an experience-based qualitative method that is also grounded in financial theory. The lengthy training and experience of an adviser adopting a qualitative approach has worked well for some clients in the past.

Some popular experience-based approaches are:

- **A 60/40 stock/bond allocation** – this may be a good starting point for an average investor. This allocation pre-dates modern portfolio theory and has been suggested to be neutral for an average investor under **normal** market conditions. The 60% equity allocation provides the long-term growth to the fund, while the 40% bond weight in the bond portfolio provides the risk-reduction and income contribution.
- **Increase bond weighting as risk aversion increases** – conservative investors value low volatility. Hence, increasing the allocation to bonds should lead to lower portfolio risks.

- **Increase allocation to stocks as the investment time period gets longer** – this is based on an idea called time diversification, which has shown that, over a longer time period stocks are less risky. The rule-of-thumb suggested by some practitioners in the US market is that the allocation to equities could use the following simple formula: % equity allocation = 100 – age of the investor. This view is based on the works of Malkiel (2004), who put forward a life cycle investment guide to asset allocation. For example, as a starting point for the investment allocation decision for a 30-year-old investor, the adviser may start with a 70/30 equity/bond mix. A 60-year-old investor on the other hand will be given a 40/60 equity/bond mix.

5.3.2 Rebalancing

After a portfolio allocation decision has been taken and the fund is fully invested, the portfolio will have to be rebalanced over the investment time period. Rebalancing may be done on a calendar basis (ie, quarterly or semi-annually). In a strategic asset allocation setting, since the time frames are long, the rebalancing is only necessary if underlying asset prices have changed appreciably and have moved the portfolio weights away from target weights past the tolerance limit agreed within the investment policy statement (IPS) frameworks.

Rebalancing may also be done on percentage-of-portfolio basis. This form of rebalancing occurs when an asset-class weight passes a threshold or a trigger point. When this occurs, the asset weight must be rebalanced all the way back to original target weight.

5.4 Identifying Suitable Product Solutions

Learning Objective

7.3.3 Assess the following factors when selecting suitable product solutions: impact of new solutions on existing arrangements; range of solutions available to suit different circumstances; range of criteria for matching solutions to client needs and demands; discounting alternatives

An adviser needs to be able to analyse a wide range of potentially suitable investment products, taking account of the investor's existing arrangements. Depending on the terms of their engagement, they are likely to need to take a comprehensive approach in arriving at the proposed solutions.

The client's needs and demands should be considered in order to match possible appropriate solutions to these needs and demands, in the light of the features of the various investment alternatives. It is not necessarily the case that only one possible solution should be recommended. There may be a number of feasible solutions that can be discussed with the client.

5.4.1 The Impact of New Solutions

It is not always realistic or beneficial to chop and change between different products as they are launched; some products carry penalties for people encashing them early, and others simply need time to deliver their benefits. But in a rapidly evolving and dynamic market such as that which exists in the UK, it is possible for better-value options to be developed into which the investor can switch, in some cases.

Various considerations may be involved when taking over an existing portfolio and reconstructing it, though there will be the usual need to consider the individual's requirement for accessibility and liquidity, income needs, attitude to risk, timescale and tax position. If clients have investments that no longer meet current requirements and circumstances, they should clearly be changed. However, an adviser may face a dilemma if there are existing life assurance policies or products, which could carry heavy surrender penalties on early encashment.

There may also be tax penalties if investments are disposed of, making it hard to carry out a wholesale realignment. For property, shares and collective investments not sheltered within an ISA, there may be a CGT charge. Encashment of a life assurance investment bond may create a chargeable event, resulting in a possible higher-rate tax liability.

5.4.2 Matching Investment Solutions to Client Circumstances

Depending on an adviser's status – independent, tied or multi-tied (restricted) – they may be required to advise their client on solutions from the whole of the market, from just one provider, or from a limited number of providers. It is important that this is made clear to the investor, so that they can consider the effects of this on the advice received.

Advisers need to be able to apply a range of criteria when matching investment solutions to client needs.

The financial adviser must recognise that each client has their own views, goals and attitudes. Attitudes to risk vary widely and, accordingly, investment choices vary widely too. Some individuals will be reluctant to take on any significant risk of loss of their capital, while others are prepared, in effect, to gamble with their savings.

People are likely to take notice of the growth potential of an investment, while some could be less willing to appreciate the risk involved. The adviser needs to take especial care to make such a client aware of risks.

Attitudes to risk vary according to the different objectives of the investor. An investor may have a core holding of deposits that they wish to keep as an emergency fund, while they may be prepared to take greater risks with other funds they hold.

If a client has a specific target for a particular investment – for example, to pay for children's education, or to pay for a vacation – the adviser may choose lower-risk investment solutions for the funds intended to reach that target than they will for the client's other investments. If an individual is prepared to take on risks for a proportion of their savings and does not require those funds for a specific purpose, then equities may be an appropriate choice for that individual.

6. Presenting Recommendations

Learning Objective

7.4.3 Understand the factors which influence the way in which recommendations are presented

Providing a **written report** to clients is an important part of the process of giving financial advice.

A written report provides a way of putting across recommendations that have already been made orally in meetings with clients. The written format makes some aspects of observations and recommendations easier for the client to understand.

Furthermore, providing a written report is clearly an important way of providing a record of what is being recommended, and on what key information it is based. A report in writing should avoid the potential for misunderstandings about the advice that has been given, thus acting as a safeguard for the adviser in justifying their work, as well as a document of record for the client.

The parts of a financial planning report to a client are normally as follows:

- A statement of the client's objectives.
- A summary of the client's income and assets and other relevant circumstances or problems.
- Recommendations, including any proposals for immediate action, as well as longer-term suggestions for the client to consider in the future. These should be backed up by the reasoning behind them – why they are felt to be suitable – and any risks or inflexibilities inherent in the proposed solutions. These recommendations should include timescales for implementation.
- Appendices, including any data that is best presented separately, if appropriate.

Product quotations, illustrations and brochures should be presented in an orderly way, possibly with an index listing the various items being sent to the client. The language in the report should be as concise and clear as possible. The language used should not include jargon, except when necessary to explain points being made.

Following the preparation of a written report, it is often sensible to have a face-to-face meeting with the client, to give them an opportunity to clear up any misunderstandings that may have arisen with regard to their objectives, and to allow them to ask questions where needs be.

6.1 Clients' Understanding

Learning Objective

7.4.4 Understand how to check clients' understanding of recommendations

Firms are required by the FCA to have regard for the information needs of their clients, taking into account the client's level of sophistication and experience. An adviser should not recommend a transaction or act as an investment manager for a customer, unless they have taken reasonable steps to help the customer understand the nature of the risks involved.

In particular, if highly risky investments are involved, specific risk warnings are required; the same applies to investments that are not readily realisable. The adviser should also explain any likely difficulties in establishing a market price.

Following the recording of recommendations in a report, the adviser may be well advised to check whether the client has read and understood the contents of the report, and should ascertain whether they have any questions to ask about it.

7. Consumer Rights and Regulatory Requirements

Learning Objective

7.4.5 Apply consumer rights and the regulatory requirements to the provision of investment advice

7.1 Protection of Consumers of Financial Services

As in other areas of consumer law, the rights of a consumer in financial services are dictated by the terms of the contract drawn up between the client and the financial institution. In the contract, there may be stated and implied terms.

Under the European Communities Legislation (unfair terms in consumer contracts) of 1995 and its subsequent amendments in 2000, any term that is considered to be unfair to the consumer cannot be enforced. From June 2010, the Consumer Credit Directive (2008/48/EC) established common rules on consumer credit aimed at harmonising aspects of the law in the EU. This Directive covers personal loans between €200-75,000 of durations longer than one month.

Before we consider remedies offered to investors under UK law, let us review the UK regulatory regime. Prior to the abolition of the FSA and the formation of the current regulatory framework, the FSA divided its responsibility between monitoring the health of the financial institutions and overseeing the way firms conducted their businesses.

To provide a clearer and stronger mandate for regulation of the financial services, these responsibilities were separated into a 'twin peaks' regulatory structure, comprising the PRA and the FCA.

The PRA is a subsidiary of the BoE and is solely responsible for the authorisation, regulation and the day-to-day supervision of all firms that are subject to prudential regulation. In addition, the Financial Policy Committee (FPC), in the BoE, has responsibility and the tools to maintain financial stability. Further details of the role of the PRA are available on the BoE website (bankofengland.co.uk/pra).

The PRA was created by the Financial Services Act (2012) and works alongside the FCA. The FCA is a separate organisation and is not part of the BoE. It is responsible for promoting effective competition, ensuring that relevant markets function well and for the conduct regulation of all financial services firms. This includes action to prevent market abuse and to ensure that consumers get a fair deal from financial firms. The FCA will regulate the affairs of those firms that are not supervised by the PRA, such as asset managers and independent financial advisers. For detailed information on the role of the FCA, visit fca.org.uk.

On its website, in its responsibilities to consumers the FCA states *'our role is to regulate financial services firms in the UK, including banks and building societies, mortgage and insurance brokers, and financial advisers.'*

As under the previous regime managed by the FSA, consumers who have reasons for complaint in areas where they have been unfairly treated, still have recourse to turn to the two main bodies that underpin the protection provided to consumers under law. The first of these is the FOS and the second is the FSCS. Recall that the FSCS covers all banks and building societies in the UK. As outlined in earlier sections, under UK law, savers get a fair degree of protection from the FSCS scheme if savings firms go out of business.

The FCA website provides detailed guidance for consumers on the following matters:

- complaints, including how to claim for compensation and about any complaints about firms based abroad
- scams and swindles
- protecting themselves from unauthorised firms, unfair contracts and other matters
- financial services products offered by: mortgage providers; banks; investment firms and insurance companies.

In the area of financial services products offered by investment firms, FCA points to the RDR where it is outlined that changes mean that commissions are abolished and *'Financial Advisers must let you (a consumer) know: how much advice costs and exactly what you are paying for.'*

7.2 Complaints and Compensation

7.2.1 The Financial Ombudsman Service (FOS)

The FOS is established under FSMA and is responsible for receiving and investigating complaints against authorised persons, if they cannot be satisfactorily resolved between the two parties directly. All authorised persons come under the FOS's compulsory jurisdiction – that is, they have to co-operate with it when it investigates complaints and they are bound by its decisions. Some other, non-authorised firms are also voluntarily under its jurisdiction.

The FOS's objective is to resolve disputes quickly and effectively. It has a number of advantages over taking a dispute to court:

- It is free to the complainant.
- It is less intimidating than going to court – many individuals will be nervous of approaching a lawyer, quite apart from the time and cost of the legal process.
- It can take into account factors other than the strict letter of the law (eg, what current common market practice was at the time).
- It is private, whereas court actions are often made public.

Authorised firms are required to co-operate fully with the FOS. In reviewing a case, the FOS can require either party to produce information or documents it deems necessary; failure to do so may be treated as contempt of court. It will investigate cases fully and can allow each side the chance to put its side.

The FOS determines complaints on the basis of what is fair and reasonable, meaning it can consider matters other than the strict letter of the law (although of course this is also important). This means that the FOS can sometimes come to a conclusion which is fairer to all sides than the outcome of legal action might have been.

Once it has made a decision, it will write to both parties to tell them the outcome, with its reasoning. The complainant then has a certain time, set by the FOS at that point, to accept or reject the decision:

- If they accept it, the decision will be binding on the firm being complained about.
- If they reject it, they can take the matter to court.
- If they fail to reply to the FOS, the FOS will treat this as a rejection and the firm will not be bound by its decision.

If it finds in favour of a complainant, the FOS can award compensation for any loss they have suffered, and/or require the firm to take remedial action; assuming the complainant has accepted the FOS's decision, the firm must comply.

The maximum the FOS can award, in monetary terms, is:

- £150,000
- plus the complainant's costs
- plus an award for suffering, damage to reputation, distress or inconvenience, if appropriate.

It can recommend an award higher than £150,000, but this is not binding on the firm; therefore a complainant who believes they may deserve more than this may be best advised to take legal action immediately, instead.

7.3 Other Regulations

As set out in the Principles for Businesses, financial advisers – and the providers of the products recommended – are required to communicate information to a customer in a way which is clear, fair and not misleading. They must also communicate in a way which has regard for the customer's knowledge of the business. This implies that firms should be considering their customers' level of financial sophistication, tailoring the language they use accordingly, and ensuring that any matters that may need explanation are made clear.

There are specific and detailed rules in connection with:

- **Financial promotions** – these refer to communications that are or may be inducements to clients, in connection with regulated activities, through any medium. The intention is to ensure that promotions are fair and not misleading, and that their target audience receives clear and adequate information which is appropriate to its level of understanding.
- **Status disclosure** – firms must tell clients and potential clients about their status (independent, or tied) and the way in which they are remunerated, in a prescribed format.
- Terms of business and client agreements – the FCA has rules on when firms must provide their clients with their terms of business, and what these must contain.
- **KYC** – the FCA requires that financial advisers ensure that they have found out enough about their customer to ensure that their advice is appropriate to their circumstances.
- **Execution-only transactions** – refers to a transaction or account when no advice is given, and the provider exercises no discretion. The client makes their own decisions as to what transactions are to be undertaken, and instructs the provider to put them into effect. There are various differences between the regulatory regime for this type of business and for business when the provider gives advice or exercises discretion.
- **Charges, commissions and product disclosure** – advisers have to disclose a considerable amount of information about the way in which they are paid.
- **Cancellation and cooling-off** – provisions apply to a number of packaged products and allow clients, who have bought on the basis of advice, the opportunity to consider what they have done, for a short period after the transaction has been effected – and, if they believe it is appropriate, to change their minds. This period for reflection is known as the cooling-off period. Cancellation notices must be issued in respect of a range of packaged investment and insurance products. They are not applicable to non-packaged investments, such as the purchase of direct shareholdings.

8. Performance Benchmarks

Learning Objective

7.4.6 Assess the factors influencing the choice of benchmark and the basis for review: portfolio's asset allocation; risk/return profile; alternative investments; taxation; peer groups; maintenance of capital value

Once the portfolio has been constructed, the portfolio manager and client need to agree on a realistic benchmark against which the performance of the portfolio can be judged. The choice of benchmark will depend on the precise asset split adopted and should be compatible with the risk and expected return profile of the portfolio. If an index is used, this should represent a feasible investment alternative to the portfolio constructed.

Portfolio performance is rarely measured in absolute terms but in relative terms against the predetermined benchmark and against the peer group. In addition, indexed portfolios are also evaluated against the size of their tracking error, or how closely the portfolio has tracked the chosen index. Tracking error arises from both underperformance and outperformance of the index being tracked.

It is essential that the portfolio manager and client agree on the frequency with which the portfolio is reviewed, not only to monitor the portfolio's performance but also to ensure that it still meets with the client's objectives and is correctly positioned given prevailing market conditions.

Key Chapter Points

- Financial advice extends well beyond investment matters, to areas such as budgeting, borrowing and protection.
- The process of giving financial advice requires that the adviser establishes a sound relationship with their client.
- Financial advice is not usually a one-off process; periodic monitoring and review of a client's arrangements is important.
- The review will lead to the creation of a set of portfolio objectives that will summarise the client's risk and return requirements.
- The process of understanding a client's precise requirements along with the objectives will lead to the development of a comprehensive investment policy statement.
- Investment decisions will take into account investors' unique requirements, including ethical and social considerations.
- Non-financial factors need to be taken into account along with investment decisions that include corporate, social, environmental and governance issues.
- The role of trustees is to have a duty of care over the powers they have been given to look after the financial needs of their beneficiaries. They must act in accordance with the principles of the Trustee Act.
- Investment managers have a duty not only to meet the requirements as set out in an investment policy statement, but to also prepare regular written reports for clients to explain and justify the investment decisions taken as a matter of record-keeping and also to protect the adviser against unwarranted criticism.
- The FSA has been replaced by the PRA/FCA regulatory regime. Consumer complaints can be directed to the FCA. As under the previous regime, the FOS is available to those consumers who are unhappy and still have concerns about their complaints. Authorised firms are required to co-operate fully with the FOS in reviewing a case.
- Performance measurement is a specialised area of portfolio monitoring. Suitable benchmarks need to be identified at early stages of the portfolio management process for both actively and passively managed portfolios. Passive managers seek to minimise tracking error against benchmarks. In their search for alpha, active managers seek to beat benchmark returns.

End of Chapter Questions

Think of an answer for each question and refer to the appropriate workbook section for confirmation.

1. What was the purpose of the TCF initiative introduced by the FSA in 2006?
   Answer reference: Section 1.6

2. Why do regular reviews form an important part of the service that advisers offer clients?
   Answer reference: Section 1.10

3. How is investing differentiated from speculating?
   Answer reference: Section 1.11

4. What is the initial stage in any financial planning process?
   Answer reference: Section 2

5. Why are liquidity and time horizons important considerations when advising clients?
   Answer reference: Section 2.1.1

6. Which asset type is likely to form a large part of a portfolio for a cautious investor seeking growth?
   Answer reference: Section 2.6.2

7. Explain what is meant by ethical investment?
   Answer reference: Section 3.1

8. What is the main principle underlying Islamic finance?
   Answer reference: Section 3.2

9. What is the basic principle governing trustees' decisions about investing their charity's funds?
   Answer reference: Section 3.4.1

10. What specific duties must trustees comply with when managing funds of a charity?
    Answer reference: Section 3.4.4

Chapter Eight
Portfolio Performance and Review

1. Purpose and Concept of Benchmarking   497
2. Portfolio Measurement   504
3. Portfolio Review   513

This syllabus area will provide approximately 5 of the 80 examination questions

1. Purpose and Concept of Benchmarking

Learning Objective

8.1.1 Understand the purpose and limitations of portfolio evaluation

8.1.2 Understand the concept and purpose of benchmarking: global investment performance standards (GIPS); WMA wealth management benchmarks; peer group average (WM and CAPS)

1.1 The Purpose and Limitations of Portfolio Evaluation

Investing involves making decisions that are readily quantifiable in an ex-post analysis of investment performance. The measurement and assessment of outcomes of investment decisions is performance evaluation.

If the performance of an investment fund or investment manager is to be assessed, then the first issue to address is how to measure that performance. Investment performance is usually monitored by comparing it to a relevant benchmark.

Performance benchmarks are important for three reasons: they help to measure the investment performance of institutional fund managers; they provide clients and trustees with a reference point for monitoring performance; and they have the effect of modifying the behaviour of fund managers. It is worth pointing out that benchmarks are important, but so are fee structures. Together, they can either provide the right incentives for fund managers or they can seriously distort their investment behaviour.

Performance evaluation is a relative concept and investment managers need to show how well they have done in their efforts to achieve their investment objectives. As an external measure this benchmark should possess certain basic properties. Some of the main ones are outlined below:

- **Unambiguous** – the identities and weights of the securities or factor exposures constituting the benchmark are clearly defined.
- **Investable** – it is possible to forego active management and hold this benchmark as a passively managed portfolio.
- **Measurable** – the returns and risk of this portfolio can be calculated quickly and frequently.
- **Appropriate** – the benchmark is consistent with the manager's investment style or area of expertise.
- **Specified in advance** – the benchmark is specified in the investment policy statement at the start of the investment process and is known to all parties.

There are three main ways in which portfolio performance is assessed:

- Comparison with a relevant bond or stock market index.
    - An index comparison provides a clear indication of whether the portfolio's returns exceed that of the bond or stock market index that is being used as the benchmark return.
    - As well as the main stock market indices that are generally seen, many sub-indices have been created over the years which allow a precise comparison to be made.
- Comparison with similar funds or a relevant universe comparison.
    - Investment returns can also be measured against the performance of other fund managers or portfolios which have similar investment objectives and constraints.
    - A group of similar portfolios is referred to as an investment universe.

- Comparison with a custom benchmark.
  - Customised benchmarks are often developed for funds with unique investment objectives or constraints.
  - If a portfolio spans several asset classes, then a composite index may need to be constructed by selecting several relevant indices and then multiplying each asset class weighting to arrive at a composite return.

Global Investment Performance Standards (GIPS) represent a great leap forward for the performance measurement industry. They are not a way of benchmarking performance, but are global standards for calculating and presenting performance figures. Originally established in 1999 by the CFA Institute, GIPS were significantly enhanced in 2005 and have been voluntarily adopted by industry representative organisations in over 20 countries in order to help promote best standards. GIPS fulfil an essential role in investment management around the world. They meet the need for consistent, globally accepted standards for investment management firms in calculating and presenting their results to potential clients.

Most pension funds adopt cautious investment policies, and the guidance and benchmarks they set for fund managers means that most schemes keep their asset allocation close to the CAPS or averages provided by other performance measurement firms.

These service providers to investing institutions create universes, which are an aggregation of funds or portfolios with similar investment briefs or types of owner, and are used for peer group comparisons. There are many specialist sub-groups of universe groupings to cater for a wide range of fund structures and investment management styles to provide a relevant and accurate relative comparison.

1.1.1 WMA Wealth Management Benchmarks

The MSCI WMA Private Investor Index Series, a key benchmark for UK private client portfolio performance widely used by investment managers and financial advisers.

The indices, which provide an overview of five distinct investment strategies, were developed by the WMA in conjunction with the new sole authorised index data provider, MSCI.

The asset allocations weightings are reviewed on a quarterly basis under the guidance of the WMA Private Investors Indices Committee. The indices are made up of asset classes, such as equities, bonds, real estate, cash and alternative investments.

To better reflect the requirements of the WMA Indices Committee and the wider wealth management practitioner community, from March 2017 onwards, four of the indices (Growth, Balanced, Income and Conservative) all include an expanded range of fixed-income index allocation options to include gilts, corporate and inflation-linked bonds.

On 1 June 2017, the Association of Professional Financial Adviser (APFA) merged with the WMA to form the Personal Investment Management & Financial Advice Association (PIMFA).

Source: www.thewma.co.uk/news/press-releases/new-msci-wma-private-investor-index-series-now-live

1.2 Stock Market Indices

Learning Objective

8.1.3 Know the construction and weighting methods of the following indices: FTSE 100; FTSE All-Share Index; FTSE Actuaries Government Securities Indices; MSCI World Index; Dow Jones Industrial Average Index; S&P 500 Index; Nikkei 225

Stock market indices have the following uses:

- To act as a market barometer. Most equity indices provide a comprehensive record of historic price movements, thereby facilitating the assessment of trends. Plotted graphically, these price movements may be of particular interest to technical analysts, or chartists, and to momentum investors, by assisting the timing of security purchases and sales, or market timing.
- To assist in performance measurement. Most equity indices can be used as performance benchmarks, against which portfolio performance can be judged.
- To act as the basis for index tracker funds, exchange-traded funds, index derivatives and other index-related products.
- To support portfolio management research and asset allocation decisions.

There are three main types of market index:

- **Price-weighted index** – these are constructed on the assumption that an equal number of shares are held in each of the underlying index constituents. However, as these equal holdings are weighted according to each constituent's share price, those constituents with a high share price, relative to that of other constituents, have a greater influence on the index value. The index is calculated by summing the total of each constituent's share price and comparing this total to that of the base period. Although such indices are difficult to justify and interpret, the most famous of these is the Dow Jones Industrial Average (DJIA).
- **Market value-weighted index** – in these indices, larger companies account for proportionately more of the index as they are weighted according to each company's market capitalisation. The FTSE 100 is constructed on a market-capitalisation-weighted basis.
- **Equal-weighted index** – in certain markets, the largest companies can comprise a disproportionately large weighting in the index, and therefore an index constructed on a market-capitalisation basis can give a misleading impression. An equal-weighted index assumes that equal amounts are invested in each share in the index. The Nikkei 225 is an example of an equal-weighted index.

Most of the major indices used in performance measurement are market-value-weighted indices such as: the S&P 500 and other S&P indices; the Morgan Stanley Capital International (MSCI) Index; and the FTSE 100 and FTSE All-Share indices.

1.2.1 FTSE 100

The FTSE 100 is a market-capitalisation-weighted index, representing the performance of the 100 largest UK-listed blue chip companies. It is free-float weighted to ensure that a true investable opportunity is represented within the index, and screened for liquidity to ensure that the index is tradeable. Capital and total return versions are available. It is reviewed and its components rebalanced every quarter in March, June, September and December. The index represents approximately 80% of the UK's market capitalisation and is used as the basis for investment products, such as funds, derivatives and ETFs.

1.2.2 FTSE All-Share Index

The FTSE All-Share measures the performance of companies listed on the LSE's main market. It covers close to 700 companies representing approximately 98% of the UK's market capitalisation. It is a market-capitalisation-weighted index and screened for size and liquidity. It is considered to be the best performance measure for the overall London equity market and is the basis for a wide range of investment-tracking products.

1.2.3 FTSE Actuaries Government Securities Indices

The FTSE also produces indices based on British government securities. The indices are divided into conventional gilts and index-linked gilts and are also available in maturity bands. There is also a yield index that provides the term structure of the gilt market from one year up to 50 years.

1.2.4 MSCI World Index

The MSCI World index is a free-float-adjusted market-capitalisation-weighted index, that is designed to measure the equity market performance of developed markets. The index includes securities from 23 countries and is calculated on a capital or total return basis and in both dollars and other currencies. It is the common benchmark index used for global funds.

1.2.5 Dow Jones Industrial Average

The Dow Jones Industrial Average was introduced in 1896 and was the first convenient benchmark for comparing individual stocks to the performance of the market and for comparing the market with other indicators of economic conditions.

It is the best-known index in the world and its 30 stocks account for close to 25% of the total US equity market. It was designed in the pre-computer era and is based on a simple price-weighted arithmetic calculation, making it less suitable for index products.

1.2.6 S&P 500 Index

The S&P 500 is regarded as the best indicator of the US equity markets. It focuses on the large cap segment of the US market and provides coverage of approximately 75% of US equities that trade on the NYSE and NASDAQ. It is a market-capitalisation-weighted index that requires a free float of at least 50% and a minimum market capitalisation of US$4 billion. It is widely used as the basis for index products.

1.2.7 Nikkei 225

The Nikkei 225 or Nikkei Stock Average is Japan's most widely watched index of stock market activity and is the oldest and most-watched Asian index. It is an equal-weighting index which is based on each constituent having an equal weighting based on a par value of 50 yen per share. Because it is an equal-weighting index, it needs to be rebalanced periodically. The Nikkei 225 is designed to reflect the overall market, so there is no specific weighting of industries. The 225 components of the Nikkei Stock Average are among the most actively traded issues on the first section of the Tokyo Stock Exchange (TSE).

A new free float adjusted, market cap weighted index, the Nikkei 400, was launched in January 2014 with a base point of 10,000. Constituents are selected based on quantitative criteria such as ROE.

1.2.8 Capped Indices

A capped index is one which sets a limit on the weighting to any particular stock or sector, ie, MSCI Frontier Markets 15% Country Capped Index limits the exposure to any single Frontiers Market to 15% of the index at each quarterly rebalance.

1.3 Composite Benchmarks

Learning Objective

8.1.4 Understand the differences between a single and a composite (synthetic) benchmark

As mentioned in section 1.1, customised benchmarks are often developed for funds with unique investment objectives or constraints. If a portfolio spans several asset classes then a composite index may need to be constructed by selecting several relevant indices and then multiplying each asset class by a weighting to arrive at a composite return.

An example is the private investor indices produced by the MSCI and the Personal Investment Management & Financial Advice Association (PIMFA). The indices provided by PIMFA are based on three portfolios in which each have different asset allocations and are composed of related indices.

The current asset allocations percentages and their respective indices within the PIMFA indices are as follows:

Asset Class	Equities		Bonds			Cash	Real Estate	Alternatives	
Underlying Asset Index	UK Equities [MSCI United Kingdon IMI]	International Equities (MSCI All country World Index (ACWI) ex-UK (in GBP))	Bonds: UK Gilts [Markit iBoxx £ Gilts]	Bonds: Corporates [Markit iBoxx £ Coporate]	Bonds: Inflation-Linked [Markit iBoxx UK Gilt Inflation Linked]	Cash (Cash equivalent) [GBP LIBOR -1% w/ floor 0%]	Commercial Property [MSCI UK IMI Liquid Real EState]	Hedge Funds/ Alternatives [MSCI World DMF 50% + 1 W LIBOR (GBP) 50%]	Total
Conservative	19	13.5	10	25	5	5	5	17.5	100
Income	30	22.5	5	17.5	2.5	5	5	12.5	100
Growth	40	37.5	2.5	5	0	2.5	5	7.5	100
Balanced	32.5	30	5	10	2.5	5	5	10	100
Global Growth	Developed World Equities [MSCI World Index (in GBP)]	Emerging World Equities [MSCI Emerging Market Index (in GBP)]							
	90	5	0	0	0	2.5	0	2.5	100

1.4 Performance Attribution

Learning Objective

8.1.5 Apply suitable benchmarks when measuring and evaluating investment performance

Investors, trustees and plan sponsors will want to assess the returns achieved by a fund manager to determine which elements of the strategy were responsible for results and why.

The process is known as performance attribution and attributes the performance to:

- asset allocation
- sector choice
- security selection.

To determine the returns produced by asset allocation you need to apply the following formula for each asset class:

(fund value at start of period x portfolio manager asset class weightings x benchmark asset class returns)

minus

(fund value at start of period x benchmark asset class weightings x benchmark asset class returns)

This isolates that part of the return attributable to diligent asset allocation, by comparing the portfolio manager's exposure to asset classes and geographical areas to that of the benchmark and then multiplying this difference by the benchmark returns. To determine a portfolio manager's stock selection skill, you need to subtract the fund value resulting from asset allocation from the actual fund value at the end of the period. We will look at how performance is attributed by way of an example.

Example

We will assume that the investment fund we are analysing had a fund value of £20 million at the start of the period we are considering and was valued at £18.75 million at the end, producing a negative return of 6.25%. The asset allocation of the fund was 75% in equities and 25% in gilts.

The benchmark used for the fund assumed an asset allocation of 50% in equities and 50% in gilts. Over the period equities produced a negative return of 10% and gilts a negative return of 5%.

1. Fund performance relative to benchmark performance

Using the figures given above, we can determine the performance of the benchmark as follows:

Benchmark	Asset Allocation	Value at Start of Period	Return	Value at End of Period
Equities	50%	£10m	−10%	£9.0m
Bonds	50%	£10m	−5%	£9.5m
Total		£20m		£18.5m

The fund has therefore outperformed the benchmark by £0.25 million.

The next step is to calculate the absolute outperformance or underperformance of the fund relative to the benchmark attributable to asset allocation.

2. Fund performance attributable to asset allocation

The contribution of asset allocation to fund returns is established by applying the formula referred to above to both the fund's equity and gilt weightings and to the benchmark returns. The benchmark returns are as shown above and the fund's returns are:

Benchmark	Asset Allocation	Value at Start of Period	Return	Value at End of Period
Equities	75%	£15m	−10%	£13.5m
Bonds	25%	£5m	−5%	£4.75m
Total		£20m		£18.25m

Poor asset allocation has caused the fund to underperform the benchmark by £0.25 million.

The final stage is to consider the impact that stock selection has had.

3. Effect of stock selection

The fund value at the end of the period is £18.75 million, while the fund value attributable to asset allocation is £18.25 million. Therefore, good stock selection has added £0.5 million to performance.

The outcome of this performance attribution is summarised in the diagram below.

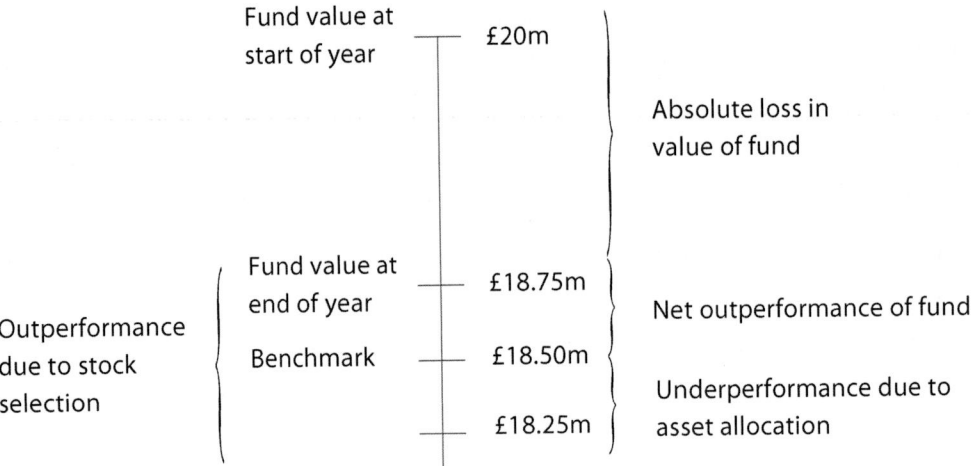

2. Portfolio Measurement

Learning Objective

8.2.1 Analyse portfolio performance in terms of: absolute and relative return; absolute and relative risk; risk-reward ratios; contributions to return arising from asset allocation, currency movements, stock selection and timing; impact of new money and timing factors

2.1 Absolute and Relative Return

Absolute return is a measure of the gain or loss on an investment portfolio expressed as a percentage of invested capital. Relative return is a measure of the return of an investment portfolio, relative to a theoretical passive reference portfolio or benchmark.

There are a number of methods that advisers can use to analyse the performance of an investment portfolio. This next section aims to offer some practical examples to assist you in carrying out this task for your clients.

The effort involved in considering the performance of a large, diverse portfolio may be considerable, and a number of tools are available, which have been specially developed to assist with this task.

Both Lipper and Morningstar provide performance statistics and risk measures for individual funds. Trustnet also provide this information in the form of individual fact sheets available via their website at trustnet.com.

Whichever tool you decide to use, it is important to establish a process for reviewing each component within the portfolio against its sector (or benchmark), and then relating the performance of the portfolio as a whole against its chosen benchmark, while also taking account of the movement of capital into and out of the portfolio.

Let us consider the various performance and volatility measures.

- **Alpha** – a positive alpha is a measure of how much a fund has outperformed its benchmark, and a negative alpha is a measure of how much a fund has underperformed its benchmark. It is often seen as a key measure of the added value of an active fund manager.
- **Beta** – a measure of a fund's sensitivity to market movements. The beta of the market is 1.00 by definition. A beta of 1.10 shows that the fund has performed 10% better than its benchmark index in up markets and 10% worse in down markets, assuming all other factors remain constant. Conversely, a beta of 0.85 indicates that the fund is expected to perform 15% worse than the market's excess return during up markets and 15% better during down markets.
- **Information ratio** – assesses the degree to which a fund manager uses skill and knowledge to enhance returns. This is a versatile and useful risk-adjusted measure of actively managed fund performance, calculated by deducting the returns of the fund benchmark from the returns of the fund and dividing the result by its tracking error. It is generally considered that the higher the number the better, with 0.75 reflecting a very good performance and 1.00 outstanding performance, with the caveat that the R-squared correlation between the fund and its benchmark must be strong if any reliance is to be placed upon the information ratio.
- **R-Squared/R^2** – a measure of the percentage of a fund's movements that can be accounted for by changes in its benchmark index. An R-squared of 100 indicates that a fund's movements are perfectly correlated with its benchmark. Thus, index funds that invest only in S&P 500 stocks typically could have an R-squared close to 100. Conversely, a low R-squared indicates that little of the fund's movements can be explained by movements in its benchmark index. An R-squared measure of 35, for example, means that only 35% of the fund's movements can be explained by movements in the benchmark index. R-squared can be used to ascertain the significance of a particular beta. Generally, a higher R-squared will indicate a more reliable beta. If the R-squared is lower, then the beta is less relevant to the fund's performance.
- **Sharpe ratio** – a risk-adjusted measure developed by Nobel laureate William Sharpe. It is calculated by using standard deviation and excess return to determine reward per unit of risk. The higher the Sharpe ratio, the better the fund's historical risk-adjusted performance. The Sharpe ratio is calculated for the previous 36-month period, by dividing a fund's excess returns by the standard deviation of a fund's excess returns. Since this ratio uses standard deviation as its risk measure, it is most appropriately applied when analysing a fund that is an investor's sole holding. The Sharpe ratio can be used to compare two funds directly on how much risk they had to bear, to earn excess return over the risk-free rate. There is no definition of a good or bad Sharpe beyond the thought that a fund with a negative Sharpe ratio would have been better off investing in risk-free products.
- **Volatility/three-year volatility** – three-year standard deviation is used to represent volatility, and demonstrates a fund's propensity to rise/fall in value over a specified period of time. Standard deviation measures how far actual fund returns have deviated from the sector average. The more a fund's returns have varied from the sector average, the higher the volatility. The volatility of a fund is partly attributable to the assets in which it invests. For example, a fund that invests totally in equities is likely to have a higher volatility than a fund solely invested in cash.
- **Maximum loss/maximum drawdown** – maximum loss (ML) is defined as the maximum loss possible under normal market conditions for a given time period, whereas maximum drawdown (Max DD) is the difference between the peak high and low values of an investment holding over the time period since inception.

Example

Armed with this understanding, we can now analyse the performance of this fund using the information supplied by Trustnet below.

Factsheet as at : August 01, 2010

Jupiter Financial Opportunities

Fund objective

To achieve long-term capital growth principally through investment in equities of financial sector companies on an international basis.

Detailed fund information

Unit name	Jupiter Financial Opportunities
Crown rating	n/a
OBSR rating	AAA
S&P rating	AAA
Sector	Specialist
Launch date	01-Jun-1997
Fund size (as at 31-May-2010)	£ 1,125.5m
Primary asset class	Equity

Price and charges

Bid price	(as at 30-Jul-2010)	GBX 372.71
Offer price	(as at 30-Jul-2010)	GBX 395.48
Initial charge		5.25%
Annual charge		1.50%

Investment

Minimum initial	£500
Minimum additional	£250
Dividend policy	Income distributed 31 December and 30 June.

Codes

Citicode	JU02
SEDOL	0479019

Management information

Address	1 Grosvenor Place, London
Tel	020 7314 7699 (Broker Line)
	020 7314 4933 (Fax Number)
	011 7971 1177 (IFA Support)
	005 0005 0098 (Literature)
	020 7314 7600 (Main Number)
Website	http://www.jupiteronline.co.uk/
Email	brokerdesk@jupiter-group.co.uk

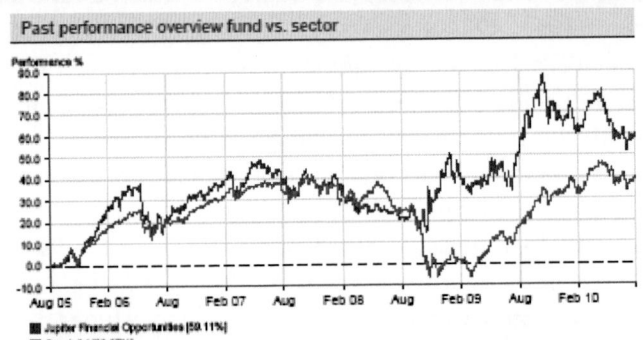

Cumulative performance (%)

	1m	3m	6m	1y	3ys	5ys
Jupiter Financial Opportunities	+3.1	-6.7	-0.9	+6.6	+15.8	+59.1
Specialist	+2.5	-4.0	+5.1	+19.4	+3.7	+39.1

Performance figures are calculated on a bid price to bid price basis. All prices in Pence Sterling (GBX) unless otherwise specified.

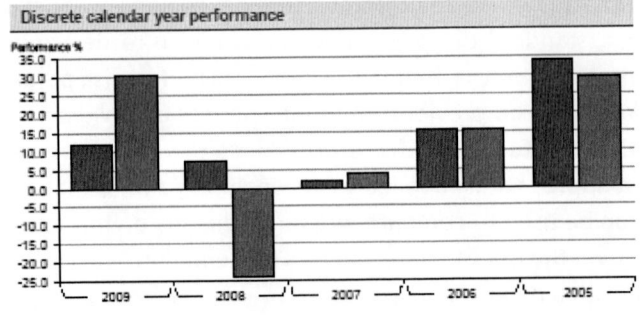

Discrete performance (%)

	YTD	2009	2008	2007	2006	2005
Jupiter Financial Opportunities	-4.5	+11.9	-7.3	+1.9	+15.7	+34.0
Specialist	+2.9	+30.4	-23.8	+3.9	+15.4	+29.4

Performance figures are calculated on a bid price to bid price basis. All prices in Pence Sterling (GBX) unless otherwise specified.

Source: Financial Express. You should not use past performance as a suggestion of future performance. It should not be the main or sole reason for making an investment decision. The value of investments and any income from them can fall as well as rise. You may not get back the amount you invested. Tax concessions are not guaranteed their value will depend on individual circumstances and may change in the future. Fund performance data is based on a (bid to bid) basis and doesn't take into account fees and expenses which are specific to individual plans. Details are available on request.

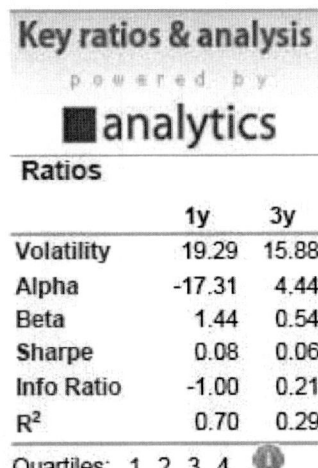

- **Volatility** – if we begin by considering the volatility measure, you can see that the returns achieved by the fund manager deviated from the sector average by some 19.29% over one year and 15.88% over three years.

- **Alpha** – in terms of alpha, it is clear that the fund outperformed its benchmark by –17.31% over one year to 4.44% over three years.

- **Beta** – the beta measure shows that in a climbing market over one year, the fund would have produced a return lower than the index. In a declining market over the same period the fund would have outperformed the index. Over three years the fund would have outperformed the benchmark in a rising market and similarly it would have lost more than the index when the market declined.

- **Sharpe** – the Sharpe ratio is positive, which demonstrates that the investor has benefited from taking the additional risk over investment in risk-free assets such as cash.

- **Information Ratio** – the negative information ratio over one year implies that the fund manager's contribution in terms of skills and knowledge is low. If +1 suggests outstanding performance, then –1 is the opposite end of the spectrum. A positive 0.21 over three years is more encouraging.

- R^2 – R-squared shows that 70% of the fund's performance over one year was down to market movement and followed the benchmark. Over three years, this figure was 29%.

- **Overall View** – it is clear from these figures that the fund manager takes an active approach.

    Given the nature of the underlying assets (financial sector/equities) and the fund's objective (long-term capital growth) this fund can only be viewed as a medium- to long-term investment. As such, the measures discussed above suggest that the investor would benefit from holding the fund rather than the index tracker over a three-year period.

    This view is supported by the cumulative performance figures shown on the fact sheet, which show that the return achieved by the fund exceeded the benchmark over three and five years.

The following is an example of an investment summary from Morningstar, which again shows performance and volatility data, but with some more additional detail to consider.

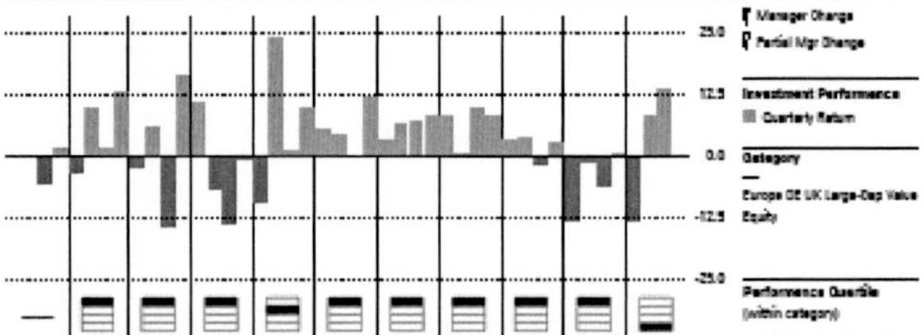

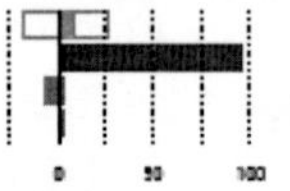

Example

2.2 The Impact of Asset Allocation on the Returns Achieved by the Portfolio

Example

Using the table below, calculate the returns achieved by the following asset allocation models over three years.

AA1	AA2
Cash 10%	Cash 5%
Fixed Interest 20%	Fixed Interest 15%
Commercial Property 30%	Property 50%
Equity 40%	Equity 30%

Asset Class	1-Year Return	3-Year Return
Cash	2%	7%
Fixed Interest	3%	10%
Commercial Property	4%	12%
Equities	5%	15%

AA1	
Cash	10% x 7% = 0.70%
Fixed Interest	20% x 10% = 2.00%
Commercial Property	30% x 12% = 3.60%
Equity	40% x 15% = 6.00%
Total Return	12.30%

AA2	
Cash	5% x 7% = 0.35%
Fixed Interest	15% x 10% = 1.50%
Commercial Property	50% x 12% = 6.00%
Equity	30% x 15% = 4.50%
Total Return	12.35%

As you can see in this example, increasing the portfolio exposure to equities and commercial property by a further 10% has only improved the return by 0.05%.

2.3 The Impact of Currency Movements

Currency fluctuations can have a dramatic impact on investment returns.

Example

Exchange rate at date of investment:		£1.00 – $1.50
Amount invested:		£20,000
Price per unit:		$2.00
Number of units purchased:		15,000
Exchange rate of date of valuation:		£1.00 – $1.90
Price per unit:		$2.50
$ Proceeds:	15,000 x $2.50	$37,500
£ Proceeds:	$37,500/$1.90	£19,737

Although the underlying unit price has increased 25%, the decline of the dollar against sterling has meant that the client is left with a loss of £263 (£20,000–£19,737).

The following is a useful equation that can be used to work out the holding period return to a domestic base currency when an investment is made overseas. Note the equation takes into account the gain (loss) made on the currency exchange and the gain (loss) made on the foreign investment.

$$(1 + R_d) = (1 + R_f)(1 + R_{fx})$$

where:

R_d = the holding period return (annualised) to an investor in a domestic base.

R_f = the holding period return gained on the investment made overseas.

R_{fx} = the holding period return gained on the currency exchange.

Thus:

$$R_d = [(1 + R_f)(1 + R_{fx})] - 1$$

1. In the example above, the UK investor has £20,000 to invest. The investor converts this amount of domestic cash into foreign currency, dollars, and now has $30,000 (ignore the bid-ask spread and commissions).
2. This is invested in US shares priced at $2.00 per share and so 15,000 US stocks are purchased.
3. After one year, the stocks appreciate to $2.50. The holding period return on the foreign stocks, R_f, is ($2.50–$2.00)/$2.00 = 25%.
4. The investor sells the US stocks and receives $37,500 in return.
5. The dollar investment is converted to sterling at 1.90$/£.
6. The investor receives $37,500/$1.90 = £19,737.
7. Over the one year, the dollar investment gained 25% (R_f = 0.25).

8. Over the year, the currency based on a unit of dollar has moved down from $1.50/£1 (or £1/$1.50 = £0.67/$) to $1.90/£1 (£0.53/$).
9. The return on the currency, R_{fx}, in unit dollar terms is (0.53−0.67)/0.67 = −21%.
10. The return to the UK investors from this overseas investment is:
    $R_d = [(1.25)(0.79)] - 1 = 1\%$ loss (or loss of £263 in monetary value).

2.4 What Does Risk/Reward Ratio Mean?

This is a ratio used by many investors to compare the expected returns of an investment to the risk taken. Essentially, an inverse of this ratio is more common as a rule of thumb and is used by many traders to pick profitable trades. A 2:1 or a 3:1 reward ratio is considered an attractive proposition by some traders and may be justification to enter into a deal.

Every deal involves an element of risk and the trade may result in a loss. Hence, the maximum downside loss possible is calculated first and then the trader determines the expected profit. This ratio may also be calculated mathematically as:

$$\text{Reward to Risk Ratio} = \text{Expected Profit/Possible Loss}$$

Example

A trader wishes to buy 100 shares of Topbuy plc at £2.50 each. They will put a stop loss order at £1.50 if the price drops unexpectedly over their holding period. Hence, their maximum loss will be £1.00 per share.

On the upside, the trader's view is that prices will rise to £5.00 but they will actually take profits if prices move up to £4.50: an expected profit of £2.00.

Risk/reward ratio = £1.00/£2.00 = 0.5.

Alternatively, their reward/risk ratio is: £2.00/£1.00 = 2:1.

Many traders may decide to screen off trading opportunities offering a minimum of 2:1 reward ratio over their holding period.

2.5 Performance Measures for Including New Money and Timing Factors

In a performance measurement context, a suitable metric needs to take into account any money that is entering or leaving an investment over its investment period. The TWRR takes account of any new money and the timing of cash flows into and out of an investment.

The TWRR reflects the compound growth over a stated investment period of one unit of money initially invested into an account. Its calculation requires the account to be revalued every time an external cash flow occurs.

The new money and timing aspect can best be demonstrated with the example below:

Example

SII Asset Management manages the institutional and individual accounts, including the account of the Thapar family. The Thapar account was initially valued at £1,000,000 at the start of the month A. It received two cash flows during month A. A contribution of £30,000 was made on day five of this month, followed by another of £20,000 on day 16. Assume that on day five, the value of the investments in the Thapar account was £1,015,000 (just before new money came in) and £1,040,000 on day 16 (before the new injection of money). The fund was valued at £1,080,000 at the end of the month.

New money has come into this account at different times – determine the performance of this account.

The TWRR methodology is to determine the sub-period returns first and then to chain-link them to determine the cumulative wealth relative for the full one-month period.

Sub-period return calculations:

1–5 days return: $\dfrac{(1,015,000 - 1,000,000)}{(1,000,000)} \times 100 = 1.5\%$

6–16 days return: $\dfrac{(1,040,000 - 1,045,000^*)}{(1,045,000^*)} \times 100 = -0.48\%$

* Includes contribution of £30,000 on day five.

17–30 days return: $\dfrac{(1,080,000 - 1,060,000^{**})}{(1,060,000^{**})} = 1.89\%$

** Includes contribution of £20,000 made on day 16.

The three sub-period returns are now converted into wealth return relatives and then chain-linked to determine the final wealth return (R) over the one month holding period as follows:

$R = [(1 + 0.015)(1 + (-0.0048))(1 + 0.0189)] - 1 = 2.92\%$

The TWRR is 2.92% and it accurately reflects how an investors fund would have performed over the investment period if the funds had been placed into the account at the start of the period. The TWRR is adopted as an appropriate measure of account performance. Further, the GIPS generally require that TWRR methodology is adopted.

3. Portfolio Review

Learning Objective

8.3.1 Understand the importance of regularly reviewing the client's portfolio

8.3.2 Apply measures to address the factors that require attention as part of the portfolio review and administration process: changes in client circumstances; changes in the financial environment; new products and services available; administrative changes or difficulties; investment-related changes (eg, credit rating, corporate actions); portfolio rebalancing; benchmark review

3.1 The Importance of Portfolio Reviews

It is important to ensure that the management of a client's portfolio is reviewed regularly. The frequency of review should be agreed with the client and should take into account any changes in the client's circumstances or requirements. For example, the portfolio may have been initially created to generate a capital return, while the client may now require a regular income.

Changes in the performance of the underlying assets may also require a rebalancing of the asset allocation. For example, the outperformance of the equity holding, compared with the other assets such as bonds and property, may alter the risk profile of the overall portfolio.

Various portfolio-balancing techniques can be employed to ensure that the asset allocation is adjusted to remain in line with what was originally agreed.

Regular reviews are also necessary for the purposes of calculating performance and reporting to the client, including the calculation of any performance-related fees.

3.2 Factors Requiring Review

3.2.1 Changes in Client Circumstances

Changes in the client's personal circumstances can have a bearing on the structure of the portfolio and will require a review, eg, a requirement for regular income instead of growth or access to a lump sum to assist with an unplanned expense.

When creating a portfolio it is important to consider the client's requirements and ensure that some tolerance is built in to cope with unforeseen events, ie, ensuring that some capital remains accessible for emergencies.

3.2.2 Changes in the Financial Environment

Economic changes can impact the portfolio and will require a review to assess their impact and determine a strategy for minimising their impact.

Examples include a change to tax laws and rates of taxation of gains or income generated from within an investment portfolio, including amendments to legislation surrounding certain investment vehicles such as pensions, EISs and ISAs.

3.2.3 New Products and Services

The introduction of new products onto the market can also require a review, due to improved charging structures or additional features and benefits that were not offered by the original contract.

3.2.4 Administrative Changes or Difficulties

If the ongoing management of the portfolio is proving difficult, due to issues dealing with a particular platform, technology or provider, which is proving detrimental to the efficient and timely dealing, then a review may be appropriate.

3.2.5 Investment-Related Changes

Changes to the underlying holdings within a portfolio due to a corporate action should trigger a review of the portfolio, to ensure that the level of overall exposure to that particular stock has not been altered significantly.

3.3 Portfolio Rebalancing

Portfolio rebalancing relates to adjustments in the levels of exposure to the various asset classes and should be reviewed as part of the scheduled portfolio review or earlier, if changes in the economic cycle mean that a greater or less exposure is required in other areas.

Various methods are employed in the industry including automatic rebalancing, if assets are sold or purchased continually to ensure that the right balance is maintained.

3.4 Benchmark Review

A review of the benchmark may be required if it is no longer representative of the portfolio objective or contains assets which the portfolio no longer has exposure to.

3.5 The Portfolio Review Process

In practice the adviser should ensure that they have a strict administrative process in place to ensure that the portfolio is reviewed, both at the agreed anniversary dates and during the interim period when any changes occur.

Ensuring reviews are carried out at the agreed points during the year is relatively straightforward, and requires nothing more than a simple diary system that is made available to the adviser and their support team. This should be checked frequently and a list of forthcoming reviews for the next time period shared with the team.

Portfolio Performance and Review

Capturing changes to the client's circumstances is a different matter. Some individuals like to keep their adviser informed and will contact them as and when changes occur, or are anticipated. Indeed, part of the adviser's job should be to encourage this form of regular communication or information-sharing. For those clients who are less forthcoming, the adviser should take steps to incorporate a regular email or phone call into their diary, to ensure that any changes or developments in the client's personal circumstances are known.

The adviser may also consider preparing a cut-down version of a fact find as a review questionnaire to send to the client in advance of the next review, which can incorporate changes to income/expenditure, employment, personal status, assets/liabilities and revised/new financial objectives. The completion of such a questionnaire can then be used to set the agenda for the next review meeting and means the adviser is prepared to discuss in outline what changes they feel may need to be made.

In terms of reviewing the investment portfolio, the adviser will need to consider how to ensure that changes to the following areas are captured, then communicated to the investor and acted upon:

- Asset allocation changes.
- Corporate actions (rights issues).
- Recommended fund switches (if advisory).

Changes to the client's personal circumstances may also require the input of other professionals, such as solicitors or accountants. Most firms have links with firms to whom they are happy to refer their clients for advice on matters relating to divorce, starting a new business or selling an existing business. If these links are not already in place, then it makes good business sense to arrange them and ensure that your clients are aware of these additional services.

Key Chapter Points

- There are three main ways in which portfolio performance is assessed: comparison with a relevant bond or stock market index, comparison to similar funds or a relevant universe comparison, and comparison to a custom benchmark.
- There are three main types of market index: price-weighted index, market value-weighted index, and equal-weighted index.
- The FTSE All-Share index measures the performance of companies listed on the LSE's main market. It covers close to 700 companies representing approximately 98% of the UK's market capitalisation.
- The FTSE 100 is a market-capitalisation-weighted index representing the performance of the 100 largest UK-domiciled blue chip companies.
- The Dow Jones Industrial Average is the best known index in the world and its 30 stocks account for close to 25% of the total US equity market.
- Performance attribution is a process that seeks to attribute investment performance to asset allocation, sector choice and security selection.
- The absolute return is simply a measure of the gain or loss on an investment portfolio expressed as a percentage of invested capital.
- Relative return is a measure of the return of an investment portfolio, relative to a theoretical passive reference portfolio or benchmark.
- Regular portfolio reviews are necessary for the purposes of calculating performance and reporting to the client, including the calculation of any performance-related fees.

End of Chapter Questions

Think of an answer for each question and refer to the appropriate workbook section for confirmation.

1. What are the three main types of market index?
   Answer reference: Section 1.2

2. Explain what is meant by performance attribution.
   Answer reference: Section 1.4

3. Why are performance benchmarks important?
   Answer reference: Section 1.1

4. What are the three main ways in which portfolio performance can be assessed?
   Answer reference: Section 1.1

5. Give an example of a price-weighted index.
   Answer reference: Section 1.2.5

6. How does a composite benchmark differ from a single benchmark?
   Answer reference: Section 1.3

7. What is the formula for calculating the returns produced by asset allocation?
   Answer reference: Section 1.4

8. Explain the term 'maximum drawdown'.
   Answer reference: Section 2.1

9. Explain what is meant by relative return.
   Answer reference: Section 2.1

10. What ratio is used to compare the expected returns on an investment with the level of risk taken?
    Answer reference: Section 2.4

Glossary

Glossary

Active Management

A type of investment approach employed to generate returns in excess of an investment benchmark index. Active management is employed to exploit pricing anomalies in those securities markets that are believed to be subject to mispricing by utilising fundamental analysis and/or technical analysis to assist in the forecasting of future events and the timing of purchases and sales of securities.

Alpha

The return from a security or a portfolio in excess of a risk-adjusted benchmark return.

Alternative Investment Market (AIM)

The London Stock Exchange's (LSE) market for smaller UK public limited companies (plcs). AIM has less demanding admission requirements and places less onerous continuing obligation requirements upon those companies admitted to the market than those applying for a full listing on the LSE.

Annual Equivalent Rate (AER)

AER is a notional rate that is quoted on the interest paid on savings and investments.

Arbitrage

Arbitrage is the process of deriving a risk-free profit from simultaneously buying and selling the same asset in two different markets, where a price difference between the two exists.

Asset Allocation

The process of deciding on the division of a portfolio's assets between asset classes and geographically before deciding upon which particular securities to buy.

Auction

System used to issue securities where the successful applicants pay the price that they bid. Examples of its use include the UK Debt Management Office when it issues gilts. Auctions are also used by the London Stock Exchange to establish prices, such as opening and closing options on SETS.

Authorised Corporate Director (ACD)

Fund manager for an open-ended investment company (OEIC).

Bear Market

A persistent downward trend in equities prices is often called a bear market.

Beneficiaries

The beneficial owners of trust property.

Beta

The relationship between the returns on a stock and returns on the market. Beta is a measure of the systematic risk of a security or a portfolio in comparison to the market as a whole.

Bonus Issue

The free issue of new ordinary shares to a company's ordinary shareholders, in proportion to their existing shareholdings through the conversion, or capitalisation, of the company's reserves. By proportionately reducing the market value of each existing share, a bonus issue makes the shares more marketable. Also known as a capitalisation issue or scrip issue.

Bunds

Bonds issued by the German government, with a maturity of anything up to 30 years.

Call Option

An option that gives the buyer the right, but not the obligation, to buy an underlying asset.

Capital Asset Pricing Model

The CAPM is a multi-factor model that expresses a simple relationship between risk and return. It indicates the expected return from holding an asset, based on a risk-free rate of return plus a risk premium.

Capital and Financial Account

The capital and financial account measures inward investment, foreign investment, foreign currency borrowing by, and deposits with, UK banks, and changes in official reserves.

Capital Gains Tax

Capital gains tax (CGT) is a tax on capital gains made when an asset is disposed of.

Central Bank

Central banks typically have responsibility for setting a country's or a region's short-term interest rate, controlling the money supply, acting as banker and lender of last resort to the banking system and managing the national debt.

Clean Price

The quoted price of a bond. The clean price excludes accrued interest to be added or to be deducted, as appropriate.

Closed-Ended

Organisations such as companies which are a fixed size as determined by their share capital. Commonly used to distinguish investment trusts (closed-ended) from unit trusts and OEICs (open ended).

Commodity

Items including sugar, wheat, oil and copper. Derivatives of commodities are traded on exchanges (eg, oil futures on ICE Futures).

Consumer Prices Index (CPI)

Index that measures the movement of prices faced by a typical consumer.

Convertible Bond

A bond which is convertible, usually at the investor's choice, into a certain number of the issuing company's shares.

Correlation

In investment terms, correlation is the extent to which the values of different types of investments move in tandem with one another in response to changing economic and market conditions.

Counterparty Risk

Counterparty risk (also referred to as credit risk or default risk) is the risk that your counterparty in a transaction cannot honour its obligation to you.

Coupon

The regular amount of interest paid on a bond.

Current Account

The current account measures flows in relation to trade in goods and services, income from investment and compensation of employees and current transfers (eg, private sector gifts to people overseas, or government aid to abroad).

Derivatives

Instruments where the price or value is derived from another underlying asset. Examples include options, futures and swaps.

Dirty Price

The price of a bond inclusive of accrued interest or exclusive of interest to be deducted, as appropriate.

Diversification

Investment strategy that involves spreading risk by investing in a range of investments.

Dividend

Distribution of profits by a company to shareholders.

Dividend yield

Most recent dividend as a percentage of current share price.

Enterprise Investment Scheme (EIS)

The enterprise investment scheme (EIS) is designed to help smaller, higher-risk trading companies to raise finance, by offering a range of tax reliefs to investors who purchase new shares in those companies.

Equities

Another name for shares.

Eurobond

An interest-bearing security issued internationally. More strictly a eurobond is an international bond issue denominated in a currency different from that of the financial centre(s) in which it is issued. Most eurobonds are issued in bearer form through bank syndicates.

Exchange Rate

The rate at which one currency can be exchanged for another.

Exchange Traded Funds (ETFs)

Exchange-traded funds (ETFs) are a type of open-ended investment fund that are listed and traded on a stock exchange. They typically track the performance of an index and trade very close to their NAV.

Ex-Dividend (xd)

The period during which the purchase of shares or bonds (on which a dividend or coupon payment has been declared) does not entitle the new holder to this next dividend or interest payment.

Financial Conduct Authority (FCA)

One of the two regulators of the financial services sector in the UK.

Financial Ombudsman Service (FOS)

The FOS is responsible for receiving and investigating complaints against authorised persons, if they cannot be satisfactorily resolved between the two parties directly.

Financial Services Compensation Scheme (FSCS)

If a UK deposit-taker fails, the depositor will have recourse to the Financial Services Compensation Scheme (FSCS). The scheme, originally administered by the FSA, is now under the supervision of the new UK regulatory regime. The FSCS deals with all claims against authorised firms and is an independent body set up under the Financial Services and Markets Act (2000).

Floating Rate Notes (FRNs)

Debt securities issued with a coupon periodically referenced to a benchmark interest rate such as LIBOR.

FTSE 100

Main UK share index of the 100 largest listed company shares measured by market capitalisation. Also referred to as the 'Footsie'.

FTSE All Share Index

Index comprising more than 90% of UK listed shares by value.

Fundamental Analysis

The calculation and interpretation of yields, ratios and discounted cash flows (DCFs) that seek to establish the intrinsic value of a security or the correct valuation of the broader market.

Fund Manager

Firm or person that makes investment decisions on behalf of clients.

Future

An agreement to buy or sell an item at a future date, at a price agreed today. Differs from a forward in that it is a standardised contract traded on an exchange.

Gearing
Gearing, also known as financial leverage, is the financial ratio of a company's long-term debt to its equity capital.

Gross Domestic Product (GDP)
A measure of a country's output.

Gross Redemption Yield (GRY)
The annual compound return from holding a bond to maturity taking into account both interest payments and any capital gain or loss at maturity. Also referred to as the yield to maturity (YTM). The GRY or YTM is the internal rate of return on the bond based on its trading price.

Hedging
A technique employed to reduce the impact of adverse price movements on financial assets held.

Index-Linked Gilts
Gilts whose principal and interest payments are linked to the retail prices index (RPI).

Individual Savings Accounts (ISAs)
ISAs are tax-assisted savings vehicles.

Inflation
Inflation measures the general rise in prices in an economy.

Information Ratio
The information ratio compares the excess return achieved by a fund over a benchmark portfolio to the fund's tracking error.

Initial Public Offering (IPO)
A new issue of ordinary shares that sees the company gain a stock market listing for the first time, whether made by an offer for sale, an offer for subscription or a placing.

Investment Trust
Despite the name, an investment trust is a company, not a trust, which invests in a diversified range of investments.

Leveraged Buyouts
Leveraged buyouts involve a financial sponsor agreeing to an acquisition without itself committing all the capital required for the acquisition.

Listing
Companies whose securities are listed are available to be traded on an exchange, such as the London Stock Exchange.

Liquidity
Liquidity is the ease and speed with which a holding in a share is turned into cash at the prevailing market price.

London Interbank Offered Rate (LIBOR)
Benchmark money market interest rates published for a number of different currencies over a range of periods.

London Stock Exchange (LSE)
The main UK market for securities.

Maturity
Date when the principal on a bond is repaid.

M0
M0 is the measure of notes and coin in circulation outside the BoE, plus operational deposits at the BoE.

M4
M4 is the measure of notes and coin in circulation with the public, plus sterling deposits held with UK banks and building societies by the rest of the private sector.

NASDAQ
The second-largest stock exchange in the US. NASDAQ lists certain US and international stocks and provides a screen-based quote-driven secondary market that links buyers and sellers worldwide. NASDAQ tends to specialise in the shares of technology companies.

Nominal Value

The amount on a bond that will be repaid on maturity. Also known as face or par value. Also applied to shares in some jurisdictions and representing the minimum that the shares are issued for.

Offer Price

Bond and share prices are quoted as bid and offer. The offer is the higher of the two prices and is the one that would be paid by a buyer.

Open-Ended

Type of investment, such as OEICs or unit trusts, which can expand without limit.

Open-Ended Investment Company (OEIC)

Collective investment vehicle similar to a unit trust. Alternatively described as an ICVC (investment company with variable capital).

Option

A derivative giving the buyer the right, but not the obligation, to buy or sell an asset in the future.

Preference Share

Shares which usually pay fixed dividends but do not have voting rights. Preference shares have preference over ordinary shares in relation to the payment of dividends and in default situations.

Public Sector Net Cash Requirement (PSNCR)

The amount borrowed annually by the UK government is PSNCR (also referred to as the budget deficit). It is equal to the sum of the CGNCR, the local government net cash requirement (LGNCR); and the public corporations net cash requirement (PCNCR).

Put Option

An option that gives the buyer the right, but not the obligation, to sell an underlying asset.

Real Estate Investment Trust (REIT)

An investment trust that specialises in investing in commercial property.

Redemption

The repayment of principal to the holder of a redeemable security.

Retail Prices Index (RPI)

Index that measures the movement of prices faced by retail consumers in the UK.

Rights Issue

The issue of new ordinary shares to a company's shareholders in proportion to each shareholder's existing holding. The issue is made in accordance with the shareholders' pre-emptive rights and the new shares are usually offered at a discounted price to that prevailing in the market. The means that the rights have a value, and can be traded 'nil paid'.

Running Yield

The running yield (also known as the interest yield) on a gilt expresses the income received on it, as a percentage of the investor's outlay.

Stamp Duty Land Tax (SDLT)

Stamp duty land tax (SDLT) is payable by the purchaser on purchases of land and property in the UK for most residential property.

Standard Deviation

The standard deviation of a share measures the average return made on it over a period of time by showing the degree to which its price fluctuates in relation to its mean return.

Stock Exchange Electronic Trading System (SETS)

SETS is the single platform, with an electronic order book, trading constituents of the FTSE All Share Index, ETFs and exchange-traded commodities, along with over 180 of the most traded AIM and Irish securities.

Systematic Risks

These are market risks that cannot be diversified away.

Treasury Bills

Short-term (often three months) borrowings of the government. Issued at a discount to the nominal value at which they will mature. Traded in the money market.

T+2

The two-day rolling settlement period over which all equity deals executed on the London Stock Exchange's (LSE) SETS are settled. This is also a standard settlement period for many international equity markets.

T-Bonds

Bonds with a maturity of ten years or more, issued by the US and Canadian governments.

Unit Trust

A vehicle whereby money from investors is pooled together and invested collectively on their behalf. Unit trusts are open-ended vehicles.

Unsystematic Risk

These are the risks associated with a specific stock and can be diversified away by increasing the number of stocks in a portfolio.

Venture Capital Trusts

Venture capital trusts (VCTs) are companies listed on the LSE and are similar to investment trusts. They are designed to enable individuals to invest indirectly in a range of small higher-risk trading companies, whose shares and securities are not listed on a recognised stock exchange, by investing through VCTs.

Yield

Income from an investment expressed as a percentage of the current price.

Yield Curve

The depiction of the relationship between the yields and the maturity of bonds of the same type.

Zero Coupon Bonds (ZCBs)

Bonds issued at a discount to their nominal value that do not pay a coupon but which are redeemed at par on a pre-specified future date.

Multiple Choice Questions

Multiple Choice Questions

1. A client holds an investment portfolio covering a number of different equities. The client is concerned about the following risks:

   Risk 1 – The risk that inflation will fall sharply

   Risk 2 – The risk that the UK pound will fall significantly against the US dollar

   Risk 3 – The risk that the pharmaceutical industry will sharply decline

   Risk 4 – The risk that a particular company's management team will perform poorly

   Which of the following statements is true?

   A. Only Risks 1 and 2 can be mitigated by using pound cost averaging
   B. Only Risks 2 and 3 can be mitigated by using the efficient market hypothesis
   C. Only Risks 3 and 4 are likely to reduce by using diversification strategies
   D. Only Risks 1 and 4 are likely to reduce by using hedging strategies

2. Four investors, holding different shares, benefit from a rights issue as shown in the following table:

Investor	Shares Held	Current Market Price	Rights Issue Price	Rights Issue Share Price
A	48	220p	1:3	190p
B	48	225p	1:4	180p
C	48	230p	1:3	170p
D	48	235p	1:4	160p

   Which investor will end up with the highest theoretical ex-rights share price?

   A. Investor A
   B. Investor B
   C. Investor C
   D. Investor D

3. Your client is aged 37, has a balanced attitude to risk and wishes to invest for long-term capital growth. Based on the following portfolio, which course of action would you recommend?

Cash	75,000
Fixed-Interest Stocks	95,000
Equities	30,000
Total	200,000

    A. Leave the portfolio unchanged
    B. Reduce the fixed interest and increase cash
    C. Reduce cash and invest in fixed interest
    D. Reduce cash and increase equity investments

4. The time value of money is used to calculate which of the following?

    A. The period an investment will be held for
    B. The amount needed now to produce a future sum
    C. The impact of inflation on a published interest rate
    D. The annual percentage rate on an account

5. An investor is comparing a series of investments that have produced an annual average return of 5% and which have the following standard deviations. Which is most suitable if the investor has a cautious attitude to risk?

    A. Stock A with a standard deviation of 4%
    B. Stock B with a standard deviation of 7%
    C. Stock C with a standard deviation of 9%
    D. Stock D with a standard deviation of 11%

6. During the course of a typical economic cycle, an investment manager made the following strategic switches:

    Switch A – Defensive equities to interest-rate-sensitive equities
    Switch B – Exchange-rate-sensitive equities to basic industry equities
    Switch C – Cyclical consumer equities to commodities
    Switch D – General industrial equities to capital spending equities

Assuming these switches were theoretically sound, which of the following statements is true?

    A. Switch A occurred at the peak of the bull market
    B. Switch B occurred during the early part of the bear market
    C. Switch C occurred as inflation began to cause concern
    D. Switch D occurred as the recession took hold

Multiple Choice Questions

7. Investors A, B, C and D each have a portfolio of government bonds issued in the US, Canada and/or Germany. The respective term of their portfolio is five, 12, 18 and 30 years. Which of the following statements is true?

    A. Investor A holds more T-bonds than investor B
    B. Investor B and investor C could both hold T-notes and Bunds
    C. Investor C could hold fewer T-bonds than Bunds
    D. Investor D must hold both T-bonds and Bunds

8. Jake is a fund manager for an investment house and is responsible for managing the following funds:

    Fund 1 – Smaller Companies Fund

    Fund 2 – FTSE 100 Fund

    Fund 3 – Emerging Markets Fund

    Fund 4 – Ethical Income Fund

    Which of the following statements is true?

    A. Where stochastic modelling is used, this is most likely to apply to Fund 1
    B. Where stratified sampling is used, this is most likely to apply to Fund 2
    C. Where bottom-up active management is used, this is most likely to apply to Fund 3
    D. Where core-satellite management is used, this is most likely to apply to Fund 4

9. Sally has a one-year fixed rate bond with her High Street bank and Julie has a two-year fixed rate bond, at the same annual rate as Sally, with her High Street building society. When comparing the risks associated with these investments:

    A. Sally has a greater capital risk exposure than Julie
    B. Sally has a lower inflation risk exposure than Julie
    C. Sally and Julie have the same interest rate risk exposure
    D. Sally and Julie have both mitigated their operational risk exposure

10. When considering the criteria to be used for the investment strategy under a life office's new ethical growth fund, the following selection criteria were discussed:

    Criteria 1 – Corporate governance

    Criteria 2 – Genetic engineering

    Criteria 3 – Supply-chain practices

    Criteria 4 – Tropical hardwood

Which of the following statements is true?

A. Criteria 1 and 2 are normally designed to operate as methods of positive screening
B. Criteria 2 and 4 are normally designed to operate as methods of negative screening
C. Only Criteria 1 and 3 are examples of corporate social responsibility
D. Only Criteria 3 and 4 are examples of global reporting initiatives

11. A purchase of a UK residential property which is subject to the standard rates of stamp duty land tax (SDLT) who pays a purchase price of £750,000 will pay what amount of SDLT?

    A. £27,500
    B. £30,000
    C. £37,500
    D. £52,500

12. An investment analyst is using a number of indices as performance benchmarks.

    Index 1 – Nikkei 225 Index
    Index 2 – S&P 500 Index
    Index 3 – MSCI World Index
    Index 4 – Dow Jones Industrial Average Index

    Which of the following statements is true?

    A. Only Index 1 is rebalanced quarterly
    B. Only Index 4 is rebalanced half-yearly
    C. Only Indices 1 and 4 are price-weighted
    D. Only Indices 2 and 3 are market capitalisation-weighted

13. Four investment clients recently disposed of their equity-based unit trusts holdings resulting in a significant capital gain.

    Client 1 is a registered charity working with the homeless
    Client 2 is a trust established to provide for the future welfare of the settlor's grandson
    Client 3 was the main beneficiary of his grandfather's significant estate and consequently had a large sum which he invested
    Client 4 was the winner of a national lottery and used the winnings to indirectly invest in the stock market.

    In respect of these gains, only the investment(s) made by:

    A. Client 2 could incur a 28% capital gains tax liability
    B. Client 4 will suffer from a 50% reduction in the standard annual capital gains tax exemption
    C. Clients 1 and 2 will be automatically immune from the impact of capital gains tax
    D. Clients 3 and 4 could incur a 10% capital gains tax liability

14. A governance analyst identified four significant national statistics based on a six-month review period.

    Fact 1 – A 5% increase in income from overseas investment

    Fact 2 – A 3% decrease in the value of M0

    Fact 3 – A 2% decrease in the value of exported goods

    Fact 4 – A 1% increase in foreign currency borrowing

    When considering the UK balance of payments, which of the following statements is true?

    A. Only Facts 1 and 2 will reduce an overall deficit
    B. Only Facts 1 and 3 will affect the current account
    C. Only Facts 2 and 3 will reduce an overall surplus
    D. Only Facts 2 and 4 will affect the capital account

15. A trader currently holds four options.

Option	Type	Premium	Strike price	Current price of underlying asset
1	Call	6p	123p	125p
2	Call	8p	190p	188p
3	Put	4p	140p	141p
4	Put	5p	170p	142p

    Which of these options is currently in-the-money?

    A. Options 1 and 2
    B. Options 1 and 4
    C. Options 2 and 3
    D. Options 2 and 4

16. An investor incurred a range of charges across his portfolio of collective investments.

    Charge 1 was a preliminary charge of £62

    Charge 2 was a dilution levy of £18

    Charge 3 was a performance fee of £620

    Charge 4 was an exit penalty of £120

    Which of the following statements is true?

    A. Only Charge 1 is normally described as a back-end load
    B. Only Charge 3 is normally described as a front-end load
    C. Charge 2 indicates that the related investment is a single-priced fund
    D. Charge 4 indicates that the related investment is an open-ended fund

17. Jack has annual income in excess of £80,000. He has disposed of listed shares, purchased for £40,000, for a sale price of £75,000 in the 2017–18 tax year. What capital gains tax liability has he incurred?

    A. £2,320
    B. £3,300
    C. £4,740
    D. £7,740

18. What is the accrued interest on the purchase of a £100 nominal UK gilt paying a 6% coupon, which settles 36 days after the last coupon date?

    A. £0.59
    B. £1.17
    C. £0.30
    D. £0.00

19. An investigation by the UK regulator indicates that a financial services provider carried out the following four actions:

    Action 1 – withdrew a newly launched and very competitive product before consumers had a chance to purchase it

    Action 2 – sent a mailshot on its latest fixed-rate mortgage product to its home reversion customers

    Action 3 – increased its pension plan charges for new customers by a total of 80% in three separate stages over a 12-month period

    Action 4 – imposed a £10 charge for customers to formally submit a complaint

    Which of the following statements is true?

    A. Actions 1 and 2 are likely to breach the European Savings Directive
    B. Only Actions 1 and 3 could result in disciplinary procedures
    C. Only Actions 2 and 3 may be covered by the provisions of the FSCS
    D. Actions 2 and 4 are likely to breach the TCF Outcome requirements

20. Chris invested £6,000 at 4% pa, compounded quarterly, whereas Michael invested £6,000 at 3.8% pa compounded annually. Based on gross interest, how much more will Chris receive by the end of the first year compared to Michael?

    A. £8.73
    B. £12.00
    C. £12.35
    D. £15.62

21. A portfolio manager is concerned about a number of different risks.

    Risk 1 – Inflation will be greater than currently predicted

    Risk 2 – An industrial sector will suffer as a result of seasonal factors

    Risk 3 – A company's management team will perform poorly

    Risk 4 – The cost of raw materials will significantly rise and affect profitability

    Which of the following statements is true?

    A. Risk 1 is the risk least likely to be reduced by diversification
    B. Risk 2 is the risk most likely to be reduced by pound cost averaging
    C. Only Risks 1 and 3 are examples of systematic risk
    D. Only Risks 2 and 4 are examples of non-systematic risk

22. An investor recently made four purchases.

    Purchase 1 – £10,100 worth of government bonds

    Purchase 2 – £20,100 worth of exchange-traded funds

    Purchase 3 – £30,100 worth of bank shares, processed using CREST

    Purchase 4 – £40,100 worth of engineering company shares, processed using a stock transfer form

    Which of the following statements is true?

    A. Stamp duty will only apply in the case of Purchase 2
    B. Stamp duty reserve tax will only apply in the case of Purchase 3
    C. Only the stamp duty calculation for Purchase 3 needs to be rounded to the nearest £5
    D. Only the stamp duty calculation for Purchase 4 needs to be rounded to the nearest £10

23. The following measurements relate to the performance of a particular investment over a 10-year period.

    Average annual return = 6.60%
    Standard deviation = 2.20%
    Variance = 4.84%

    As a result of this data, an investor can expect that there is a two-thirds chance of the annual return falling within the range of:

    A. 1.76% and 8.80%
    B. 1.76% and 11.44%
    C. 4.40% and 8.80%
    D. 4.40% and 11.44%

24. Sue works full-time overseas and visits the UK for around 30 days, in total, in any tax year. Sue maintains a UK address and remits around £5,000 of her annual income and £3,000 in capital gains to the UK to invest in a qualifying activity. In these circumstances, what, if any, UK tax liability is most likely to arise in respect of these remittances?

    A. None
    B. Capital gains tax only
    C. Income tax only
    D. Both income and capital gains taxes

25. Four clients recently used Sharia'a-compliant Islamic products.

    Client A used an Ijara

    Client B used a Musharaka

    Client C used a Mudaraba

    Client D used an Ijara-wa-Iqtina

    Which of the following statements is true?

    A. Clients A and D both entered into leasing agreements but only Client D is able to buy the product at the end of the contract
    B. Clients B and C both entered into an investment partnership but only client B is deemed to be a majority partner
    C. Only Client B can suffer from a partial loss of the capital initially invested
    D. Only Client D can cancel the contract mid-term

26. What is the industry standard settlement time for gilts?

    A. T+3
    B. T+2
    C. T+1
    D. T+20

27. The following four clients are interested in making regular contributions into a non-stakeholder personal pension.

    Client 1 – age 28, earns £40,000 pa

    Client 2 – age 38, earns £50,000 pa

    Client 3 – age 48, earns £60,000 pa

    Client 4 – age 58, with no earnings for the last eight years

When considering gross tax-relievable annual contributions, which of the following statements is true?

A. Only Clients 1, 2 and 3 are permitted to contribute
B. Client 1's maximum is £36,400 higher than Client 4's maximum
C. Client 2's maximum is £46,000 higher than Client 4's maximum
D. Only Clients 2 and 3 have a maximum which is in excess of £40,000

28. An investor recently purchased four bonds.

Bond	Market Price	Coupon
1	120p	4.1p
2	140p	5.2p
3	172p	5.6p
4	182p	6.1p

This indicates that:

A. Bond 1 has the highest running yield
B. Bond 3 has the lowest running yield
C. Bond 2 has the highest gross redemption yield
D. Bond 4 has the lowest gross redemption yield

29. A portfolio manager is looking at the correlation of performance statistics between six different assets.

	1	2	3	4	5	6
Asset 1	–	–	–	–	–	–
Asset 2	0.65	–	–	–	–	–
Asset 3	0.71	0.91	–	–	–	–
Asset 4	−0.46	0.72	−0.81	–	–	–
Asset 5	−0.12	−0.21	−0.58	−0.61	–	–
Asset 6	−0.32	−0.48	0.79	0.14	−0.42	–

Based solely on this data, which asset combination is likely to be most diversified?

A. Assets 1 and 5
B. Assets 2 and 3
C. Assets 3 and 4
D. Assets 4 and 6

30. Amy, a non-taxpayer, received a payment of £400 per month into her bank account from an accumulation and maintenance trust, set up for her benefit by her grandfather. Assuming the trustees have paid sufficient tax and the trust income is made up of dividends, what gross income and reclaimable tax credit, if any, applies in respect of Amy over the 2017–18 tax year?

    A. £4,000.00 and £400.00
    B. £6,000.00 and £600.00
    C. £8,727.24 and £3,927.24
    D. £10,666.67 and £3,733.33

31. £100 is invested at the start of each year for five years at a fixed rate of interest of 4% per annum compounded annually. What will the accumulated value of these series of payments be at the end of the five-year period?

    A. £563.30
    B. £574.55
    C. £581.61
    D. £599.02

32. The government announces four policy changes.

    Change 1 – An increase in the defence budget
    Change 2 – An increase in the use of means testing for social security benefits
    Change 3 – An increase in the inheritance tax threshold
    Change 4 – An increase in the rate of capital gains tax

    Which of the following statements is true?

    A. Changes 1 and 3 are examples of expansionary fiscal policy
    B. Changes 1 and 4 are examples of contractionary fiscal policy
    C. Changes 2 and 3 are examples of expansionary monetary policy
    D. Changes 1 and 2 are examples of contractionary monetary policy

33. What is the main difference between strategic and tactical asset allocation?

    A. In strategic asset allocation, the decisions on the portfolio mix are taken from a long-term perspective. Tactical asset allocation engages in short-term, tactical deviations from the mix, in order to capitalise on unusual or exceptional investment opportunities
    B. In tactical asset allocation, the decisions on the portfolio mix are taken from a long-term perspective. Strategic asset allocation engages in short-term, tactical deviations from the mix, in order to capitalise on unusual or exceptional investment opportunities
    C. Strategic asset allocation involves timing the market, whereas tactical asset allocation involves taking a long-term view on markets
    D. Strategic asset allocation is an active investment approach, whereas tactical asset allocation is a passive investment strategy

Multiple Choice Questions

34. If it finds in favour of a complainant, what is the maximum the Financial Ombudsman Service (FOS) can award, in monetary terms?

    A. £75,000 plus the complainant's costs, plus an award for suffering, damage to reputation, distress or inconvenience, if appropriate

    B. £100,000 plus the complainant's costs, plus an award for suffering, damage to reputation, distress or inconvenience, if appropriate

    C. £150,000 plus the complainant's costs, plus an award for suffering, damage to reputation, distress or inconvenience, if appropriate

    D. £200,000 plus the complainant's costs, plus an award for suffering, damage to reputation, distress or inconvenience, if appropriate

35. John holds an investment of £50,000 in an income-producing multi-asset fund, which has over 60% of its assets held in fixed-interest stocks and the balance in equities. How are the payments of income taxed?

    A. 20% tax is deducted at source
    B. Income is paid with a 10% tax credit
    C. Income is paid gross
    D. 22.5% tax is deducted at source

36. Which of the following is not a risk associated with holding cash on deposit?

    A. Inflation
    B. Counterparty
    C. Market
    D. Interest rate

37. When compared to a direct investment in property, investment in a real estate investment trust (REIT) offers what tax advantages?

    A. Exemption from withholding tax on distributions only
    B. Exemption from withholding tax on distributions and capital gains tax on investment profits within the REIT
    C. Exemption from corporation tax on property-related income and gains within the REIT and exemption from withholding tax on distributions
    D. Exemption from corporation tax on property-related income and gains and from capital gains tax on investment profits within the REIT

38. John places £10,000 on deposit, earning interest annually at a rate of 3.5%. If the annual rate of inflation is 1.8%, what is the real value of John's investment at the end of two years?

    A. £10,700.00
    B. £10,712.25
    C. £10,525.95
    D. £10,342.89

39. A client requests your advice on holding cash and explains that they are happy to accept an element of illiquidity for a higher rate of interest. Which of the following is likely to offer the best return?

    A. Notice account
    B. Fixed term deposit
    C. Current account
    D. Money market account

40. How is income treated in a constant net asset value money market fund?

    A. It accrues daily and is paid to the investor
    B. It accrues monthly and is rolled-up
    C. It accrues daily and can be reinvested or paid out
    D. It accrues monthly and is reflected in a higher share price

41. When is the state pension age for women expected to increase to age 65?

    A. 2016
    B. 2018
    C. 2020
    D. 2022

42. Which of the following is not one of the factors of production in the economy?

    A. Land
    B. Labour
    C. Capital
    D. Manufacturing

43. An investor proposes to invest £2 million into an enterprise investment scheme this tax year. Taking all sources of income into account, the investor's total income tax liability for this tax year is estimated to be £200,000 plus £100,000 of tax from dividend income. Therefore, what amount of the proposed investment is subject to income tax reliefs in this tax year, and what time window applies in order to defer any qualifying potential capital gains tax liabilities accruing?

    A. £300,000 and four years respectively
    B. £300,000 and three years respectively
    C. £500,000 and one year respectively
    D. £600,000 and nil respectively

44. In 2017–18, the Johnson family discretionary trust elects to distribute capital to one of the beneficiaries to cover their education costs. In order to facilitate the payment, the trustees elect to sell some of the underlying investments to generate cash, which crystallises a capital gain. What rate of tax will the trust pay on the gain?

    A. 18%
    B. 28%
    C. 20%
    D. 50%

45. In 2017–18, the Smithson family discretionary trust receives total interest of £785 on its cash deposit holdings. Assuming no other income is received by the trust, what marginal rate of tax will be charged on this income?

    A. 10%
    B. 20%
    C. 40%
    D. 45%

46. Under the rent-a-room scheme, how much rental income is an individual allowed to receive free of tax each year?

    A. £10,000
    B. £7,500
    C. £3,600
    D. £11,880

47. Which of the following shares offer a predetermined rate of return?

    A. Zero dividend preference shares
    B. 'A' shares
    C. Stepped preference shares
    D. 'C' shares

48. What percentage of its taxable income must a REIT distribute to its shareholders in order to remain exempt from corporation tax on profits and gains?

    A. 80%
    B. 90%
    C. 25%
    D. 10%

49. What additional risk are investors in synthetic ETFs exposed to, compared to investment in a physical ETF?

    A. Interest rate
    B. Liquidity
    C. Counterparty
    D. Currency

50. Max is looking to invest in an ISA in September 2017. What is the maximum possible contribution that he can make?

    A. £11,880
    B. £11,520
    C. £15,240
    D. £20,000

51. The difference in tax treatment between National Savings & Investments guaranteed income bonds and income bonds is that:

    A. Only guaranteed income bond interest is paid net of tax and no capital gains tax is payable
    B. Only income bond interest is paid net of tax and no capital gains tax is payable
    C. Neither bond is subject to tax on income but only the income bond may be subject to capital gains tax on encashment
    D. Neither bond is subject to capital gains tax on encashment but only the guaranteed income bond interest may be subject to higher rate tax in the hands of the investor

52. What is the maximum investment a taxpayer can make in an enterprise investment scheme during 2017–18 ignoring any option to carry back to the previous tax year?

    A. £500,000
    B. £300,000
    C. £1,000,000
    D. £2,000,000

53. Which investment strategy is based on the theory that certain crowd behaviour by investors can lead to exploitable mispricings in securities markets?

    A. Contrarian
    B. Quantitative
    C. Active market timing
    D. Trend investing

54. Which of the following is not one of the FCA's Principles for Businesses?

    A. A firm must maintain adequate financial resources
    B. A firm must observe proper standards for market conduct
    C. A firm must remain competitive in its market at all times
    D. A firm must conduct its business with integrity

55. Meg is aged 69 and still works part-time. Her total annual income is £19,400. What is her liability to income tax in the 2017–18 tax year?

    A. £1,780
    B. £1,580
    C. £1,880
    D. £1,928

56. Which body is responsible for the regulation of building societies and insurance companies?

    A. Financial Conduct Authority
    B. Bank of England
    C. Association of British Insurers
    D. Prudential Regulation Authority

57. If an adviser working in a regulated financial firm suspects a client is involved in an act concerning the proceeds of crime, the Proceeds of Crime Act 2002 requires that:

    A. an immediate report is made to the firm's money laundering reporting officer (MLRO)
    B. firm evidence is collated before the firm's MLRO makes a report to the National Crime Agency (NCA)
    C. confidentiality under the Data Protection Act is honoured until the facts are established
    D. confidential advice on the required procedure is immediately sought from the NCA

58. What is the maximum award available to an individual through the Financial Services Compensation Scheme in the event of a default by their bank?

    A. £50,000
    B. £85,000
    C. £100,000
    D. £150,000

59. How does the calculation of gross national product differ from the calculation of gross domestic product?

    A. It excludes capital consumption
    B. It includes net property income from abroad
    C. It excludes national income
    D. It includes depreciation

60. Bob has withholding tax assessed on a relief at source basis and Mary on a reclaim basis. This indicates that:

    A. Only Bob's residence and tax status have been established in advance
    B. Only Bob is entitled to claim a reduction on the full rate of withholding tax
    C. Only Mary may benefit from a full rebate of the original amount of withholding tax
    D. Only Mary can offset tax withheld against her domestic tax liabilities

61. Bob has withholding tax assessed on a relief at source basis and Mary on a reclaim basis. This indicates that only:

    A. Bob's residence and tax status have been established in advance
    B. Bob is entitled to claim a reduction on the full rate of withholding tax
    C. Mary may benefit from a full rebate of the original amount of withholding tax
    D. Mary can offset tax withheld against her domestic tax liabilities

62. How are capital gains created within a real estate investment trust taxed?

    A. They are taxed at the corporation tax rate of 20%
    B. No tax is payable if at least 90% of profits are distributed to shareholders
    C. They are taxed at the individual's marginal rate of tax (0%, 10%, or 20%)
    D. No tax is payable if at least 50% of profits are distributed to shareholders

63. What is the current maximum contribution an individual can make to a Junior ISA?

    A. £4,128
    B. £15,240
    C. £3,600
    D. £10,000

64. Ria is buying a new main residence but has decided not to sell her current main residence. She will have to pay the higher rates of SDLT for owning an additional property. How long does she have to sell her original main residence to be able to reclaim the difference between the normal rate and the higher rate of SDLT?

    A. 12 months
    B. 24 months
    C. 36 months
    D. 48 months

65. Which of the following is a coincident indicator of economic activity?

    A. Gross domestic product
    B. Unemployment rate
    C. Stock market returns
    D. Money supply

Multiple Choice Questions

66. What information can be gained from considering a fund's information ratio?

    A. The return achieved for the level of risk taken
    B. The fund's sensitivity to market movements
    C. The extent to which the fund has outperformed its benchmark
    D. The degree to which a fund manager uses skill and knowledge to enhance returns

67. Which one of the following is not a key measure of economic activity?

    A. National income
    B. Gross national product
    C. Purchasing managers index
    D. Gross domestic product

68. What percentage of net scheme assets can a small self-administered scheme lend to the sponsoring employer?

    A. 100%
    B. 50%
    C. 25%
    D. 0%

69. What is the amount of remittance basis charge for a non-domicile who has lived here for seven of the last nine years?

    A. £50,000
    B. £30,000
    C. £2,000
    D. £15,000

70. Which of the following is an example of an equal-weighted index?

    A. FTSE All-Share
    B. Nikkei 225
    C. S&P500
    D. Dow Jones Industrial Average

71. If an investment has an average annual return of 7%, and a standard deviation of 4%, what proportion of returns could fall between 11% and 3%?

    A. 50%
    B. 1/3
    C. 2/3
    D. 100%

72. What is the maximum amount of tax relief a seed enterprise investment scheme investor can claim in the current year?

    A. 50%
    B. 40%
    C. 30%
    D. 20%

73. Which body is responsible for handling complaints against authorised persons in the UK?

    A. Financial Services Compensation Scheme
    B. Financial Conduct Authority
    C. Prudential Regulation Authority
    D. Financial Ombudsman Scheme

74. Which of the following criteria must apply in order for a deed of variation to be valid?

    A. Executed within three years of death
    B. Approved by the Court of Protection
    C. Not made for any consideration
    D. Estate valued at less than £325,000

75. How are dividends paid from venture capital trusts taxed in the hands of the original investor?

    A. They are paid gross with no liability to tax
    B. They are paid with an accompanying 10% tax credit with no further liability
    C. They are taxed at the investors highest marginal rate
    D. They are taxed at a fixed rate of 30%

76. What rate of income tax would be levied on dividends received by an investor with earnings of £200,000 in the current tax year?

    A. 40%
    B. 45%
    C. 32.5%
    D. 38.1%

77. Which of the following transactions is liable for stamp duty reserve tax?

    A. A purchase of gilts
    B. The gift of shares between two connected parties
    C. The purchase of a FTSE 100-listed stock
    D. An investment in an exchange-traded fund

78. How much would you need to invest today to have £5,000 in six years' time, assuming a gross interest of 3.5% per annum?

    A. £3,950.00
    B. £4,125.00
    C. £4,067.50
    D. £4,209.87

79. Which form of investment strategy seeks to profit from analysis of a stock's momentum?

    A. Quantitative
    B. Contrarian
    C. Trend
    D. Long/short

80. What is the current maximum amount of National Savings premium bonds that can be purchased by an individual investor?

    A. £15,000
    B. £25,000
    C. £40,000
    D. £50,000

Answers to Multiple Choice Questions

1.   C   Chapter 3, Section 2.2.8

Risks 1 and 2 are examples of systematic risk which affect the financial system as a whole. Risks 3 and 4 are non-systematic risks so can usually be reduced through diversification.

2.   D   Chapter 1, Section 3.5.4

A = (220 x 48) + (16 x 190) / 64 = 212.5p

B = (225 x 48) + (12 x 180) / 60 = 216p

C = (230 x 48) + (16 x 170) / 64 = 215p

D = (235 x 48) + (12 x 160) / 60 = 220p

3.   D   Chapter 6, Section 1

Given the client's age, attitude to risk, investment objective and timescale, increasing the equity allocation is the most appropriate option.

4.   B   Chapter 3, Section 1.1

Time value of money is used to calculate the amount needed now – present value – to produce a future sum.

5.   A   Chapter 3, Section 2.3.3

A low standard deviation implies lower risk.

6.   C   Chapter 2, Section 7.2

Switch A – likely to occur at the start of a bull market

Switch B – likely to occur during the growth phase of a bull market

Switch C – likely to occur when growth decelerates as interest rates rise to suppress inflation

Switch D – likely to occur during the growth phase of a bull market

7.   C   Chapter 1, Section 2.2.2

T-bonds, issued by the US and Canadian governments, have a maturity of ten years or more. T-notes have a maturity of ten years or less. Bunds, issued by the German government, have a maturity of anything up to 30 years. Investor C could hold fewer T-bonds than bonds.

8.   B   Chapter 6, Section 2.1

The FTSE 100 Fund, being a type of tracker fund, will normally operate under a passive management regime, using one of three tracking methods, namely full replication, stratified sampling or optimisation.

Multiple Choice Questions

9. B Chapter 1, Section 1.4

As Sally is locked in for a shorter term, she has a lower inflation risk exposure. Sally and Julie have similar exposure to capital risk if the deposit taker defaults. Their exposure to interest rate risk is different due to their different fixed terms. Poor service from the deposit taker could expose either to operational risk.

10. B Chapter 7, Section 3.1.1

Genetic engineering and tropical hardwood are examples of activities that SRI-friendly organisations might seek to avoid.

11. A Chapter 4, Section 8.2

Stamp duty land tax on UK residential property is charged on each proportion of the purchase price as follows:

- £0 to £125,000 taxed at 0%
- £125,001 to £250,000 taxed at 2%
- £250,001 to £925,000 taxed at 5%
- £925,001 to £1,500,000 taxed at 10%
- £1,500,001 and above taxed at 12%

Therefore, SDLT of £27,500 applies in this case.

12. D Chapter 8, Section 1.2

S&P 500 and MSCI are market capitalisation-weighted. Nikkei is equal-weighted and the Dow Jones is price-weighted.

13. D Chapter 4, Section 5.1.1

Individuals are taxed at 10% or 20% depending on income levels, charities are exempt and trusts are taxed at 20%.

14. B Chapter 2, Section 6.5.1

The current account includes trade in goods and services and income from overseas investment. Foreign currency borrowing relates to the capital account and M0 simply measures circulated notes and coins plus operational deposits at the BoE.

15. B Chapter 5, Section 13.2.1

A call option is in-the-money if the strike price is below the current price and vice versa for put options.

16. C Chapter 5, Section 6.1–6.2.3

Preliminary charges are a type of front-end load and exit penalties are a type of back-end load. Dilution levies only affect single-priced funds whereas exit penalties can apply to both open and closed-ended funds.

17. C Chapter 4, Section 5.3

Shares purchased for £40,000 and sold for £75,000 (assuming these figures include all allowable costs) create a gain of £35,000. The annual CGT allowance is £11,300 so taxable gain is £23,700.

Jack's income level indicates he will pay capital gains tax at the higher rate of 20%. Therefore, tax due is £23,700 at 20% = £4,740.

18. A Chapter 1, Section 2.6.4

36/184 x 6/2 = £0.59

19. D Chapter 7, Section 1.6

TCF Outcome 2 relates to the correct targeting of consumer groups and TCF outcome 6 relates to unreasonable post-sale barriers for making complaints.

20. D Chapter 1, Section 1.2.2

A = (6,000 x 1.04) − 6,000 x 1.0095^4) = 8.73

B = (6,000 x 1.04) − (6,000 x 1.038) = 12.00

C = (6,000 x 1.01^4) − (6,000 x 1.0095^4) = 12.35

D = (6,000 x 1.01^4) − (6,000 x 1.038) = 15.62

21. A Chapter 3, Section 2.2.1

Risks 2, 3 and 4 are examples of non-systematic risk which can usually be reduced through diversification. Risk 1 is a systematic risk which affects the financial system as a whole and is therefore much harder to mitigate with diversification.

22. B Chapter 4, Section 8.1

CREST-based share purchases trigger SDRT whereas stock transfer form purchases trigger SD (rounded to the nearest £5). Purchases of gilts and ETFs do not trigger stamp duty.

23. C Chapter 3, Section 2.3.3

There is a two-thirds chance that annual returns will fall within one standard deviation of the mean, ie, 6.6% plus/minus 2.2%.

24. A Chapter 4, Section 7.1.1

Sue satisfies the automatic overseas test by working full-time overseas and spending less than 90 days in the UK.

As a non-UK domicile, Sue can remit overseas income and capital gains to the UK, free of UK tax, in order to invest in a qualifying activity.

Multiple Choice Questions

25. **A** **Chapter 7, Section 3.2**

An Ijara is a leasing agreement where the bank buys an item for a customer and then leases it back over a specified period. An Ijara-wa-Iqtina is a similar arrangement, except that the customer is able to buy the item at the end of the contract.

26. **C** **Chapter 1, Section 2.6.2**

The standard settlement time for gilts is T+1, ie, trading day plus one day.

27. **B** **Chapter 4, Section 11.1.4**

The maximum tax-relievable gross annual contribution is £3,600 for non-earners and 100% of earnings up to £40,000 for earners.

28. **B** **Chapter 1, Section 2.4.1**

Running yields are coupon/price, ie, 3.42% (1), 3.71% (2), 3.26% (3) and 3.35% (4). GRYs cannot be determined solely from this data.

29. **C** **Chapter 6, Section 1.6.1**

As the correlation gets closer towards –1, the diversification benefits within a portfolio improve.

30. **C** **Chapter 4, Section 2.2.2**

Income is deemed to have already been taxed at the trust rate, currently 45%. Therefore each net monthly payment of £400 equates to £400 ÷ 0.55 = £727.27 gross.

Over one tax year, gross payments = £727.27 x 12 = £8,727.24, and so the amount reclaimable is £8,727.24 – £4,800 = £3,927.24.

31. **A** **Chapter 3, Section 1.3.2**

Future Value:

= £100 [((1.04)^5 – 1)/0.04](1.04)

= £100 [(1.21– 1)/0.04](1.04)

= £100 [(0.21)/0.04](1.04)

= £100 [5.416](1.04)

= £100(5.633)

= £563.30

32. **A** **Chapter 2, Section 6.2**

Fiscal policy is government policy on taxation, public borrowing and public spending. Spending more money or collecting less taxes are examples of an expansionary fiscal stance.

33.   A   Chapter 6, Sections 1.3 and 1.4

In strategic asset allocation, the decisions on the portfolio mix are taken from a long-term perspective. Tactical asset allocation engages in short-term, tactical deviations from the mix, in order to capitalise on unusual or exceptional investment opportunities.

34.   C   Chapter 7, Section 7.2

The maximum the FOS can award, in monetary terms, is £150,000 plus the complainant's costs, plus an award for suffering, damage to reputation, distress or inconvenience, if appropriate.

35.   C   Chapter 4, Section 3.2

The tax treatment of distributions from collectives depends on the type of investments in which the scheme invests. Funds invested mainly in cash deposits and interest-bearing securities pay out distributions which are mostly made up of interest, and the distribution will be paid gross of tax.

36.   C   Chapter 1, Section 1.4

Deposits, as money market products, are generally regarded as low-risk investments, but they are not entirely risk-free. The risks associated with them are: capital risk, inflation risk, interest rate risk and operational risk.

37.   D   Chapter 5, Section 3.2

A REIT offers, within certain criteria, exemptions from corporation and capital gains taxes on property related income and gains. However, distributions are subject to a withholding tax at basic rate income tax unless qualified to receive gross payments. This applies to classes of investor such as charities, UK companies and pension funds.

38.   D   Chapter 1, Section 1.2.4

Interest in real terms is 3.5% – 1.8% = 1.7%.
Compounded for two years = £10,000*(1+0.017)^2 = £10,342.89.

39.   D   Chapter 1, Section 1.7

While a money market account makes a decent low-risk investment, keep in mind that, because it is an investment, there are certain restrictions. Your money will not be as liquid as it is in a regular savings account, and a money market account usually requires a minimum deposit, as well as a minimum balance. While you can make withdrawals from a money market account, there is a limit to how many you can make.

Multiple Choice Questions

40. **C** **Chapter 1, Section 1.8.1**

There are two basic types of money market funds: constant net asset value (CNAV) and accumulating net asset value. Shares in CNAV funds are issued with an unchanging face value (such as £1 per share). Income in the fund is accrued daily and can either be paid out to the investor or used to purchase more units in the fund at the end of the month. Accumulating net asset value funds, known alternatively as roll-up funds, operate under the same investment guidelines as CNAV funds and income is accrued daily. However, unlike CNAV funds, income is not distributed. Instead income is reflected by an increase in the value of the fund shares.

41. **B** **Chapter 2, Section 1.3**

The SPA for women is set to increase from 60 to 65 by 2018, the same as men, and by 2020, the SPA for both sexes will be 66.

42. **D** **Chapter 2, Section 1.8**

Economists identify four factors of production in the economy: land, labour, capital (ie, machinery and plant) and enterprise. These factors are combined in various ways, in order to produce goods and services.

43. **B** **Chapter 5, Section 11.1**

An EIS investor is eligible for 30% of the cost of the shares to be set against income tax liability for the tax year in which the investment was made.

Relief can be claimed for up to £1 million invested in EIS shares, making a maximum tax reduction in that tax year of £300,000.

The investor has £300,000 of a tax liability that can be reclaimed.

Going forward, EIS shares can only qualify for CGT relief provided they have qualified for income tax relief and this relief still applies. EIS shares potentially subject to capital gains tax liabilities may have this liability deferred if the gain is invested in an EIS qualifying company between one year before and three years after the liability arises.

44. **C** **Chapter 4, Section 5.1.3**

Gains of trustees are taxed at the tax rates applicable for trusts, which changed in April 2016 to 20%. Trusts have an annual CGT exemption which depends on the type of trust in question. For personal representatives of deceased persons and trustees of certain settlements for the disabled it is £11,300. For most others it is £5,650 – half the level for individuals of £11,300.

45. **B** **Chapter 4, Section 2.2.2**

In both discretionary trusts and accumulation and maintenance trusts, income is taxed at the special trust rates, apart from the first £1,000 of trust income, which is known as the standard rate band. Income that falls within the standard rate band is taxed at lower rates of 7.5% for dividends and 20% for rental income and savings interest.

46. B Chapter 4, Section 3.1.3

There is an exemption for people renting out a room in their own home, on the rent-a-room scheme, where someone can earn up to £7,500 pa tax-free.

47. A Chapter 5, Section 3.1.1

The final redemption value of the zero at the liquidation date is predetermined, subject to the investment trust actually having enough assets to cover this at that date. Zeros are, therefore, issued at a price which usually rises by a compound growth rate to the final value.

48. B Chapter 5, Section 3.2

Under current law, the holding company of a REIT group must be UK-resident and listed on a recognised stock exchange. REITs are required to distribute at least 90% of their tax exempt income profits to investors.

49. C Chapter 5, Section 7.1

Synthetic ETFs gain their exposure using derivative contracts such as total return swaps, which they negotiate with third party investment banks or counterparties. The ETF provider uses investor cash to purchase securities and create a collateral basket. It then offers the return earned on this collateral to the counterparty, in exchange for a payment equal to the return achieved by the securities that it wishes to track. This strategy presents two risks to investors: the ability of the third party to fulfil their financial obligations, and the quality of the collateral held in the basket. Failure of the counterparty in this scenario will affect their ability to make the required payments to the ETF, while holding poor quality or illiquid securities as collateral could prevent the ETF provider from returning capital to investors.

50. D Chapter 5, Section 8.1

From 6 April 2017, the maximum allowable ISA contribution increased to £20,000.

51. A Chapter 5, Section 8.4

No NS&I product is subject to capital gains tax.

The guaranteed income bond interest is taxable and paid gross.

The income bond interest is taxable and paid gross.

52. C Chapter 5, Section 11.1

Income tax reliefs – the investor is eligible for relief of 30% of the cost of the shares, to be set against his income tax liability for the tax year in which the investment was made. Relief can be claimed up to a maximum of £1,000,000 invested in such shares, which means a maximum tax reduction in any one year of £300,000 (assuming the individual had a big enough income tax liability to cover this). The relief cannot be set off against dividend income, as the tax credit attached to a dividend is not recoverable.

Multiple Choice Questions

53.   **A**   **Chapter 6, Section 2.9**

A contrarian investor believes that certain crowd behaviour among investors can lead to exploitable mispricings in securities markets.

54.   **C**   **Chapter 7, Section 1.8**

A firm must remain competitive in its market at all times is not one of the FCAs Principles for Businesses. See fshandbook.info/FS/html/FCA/PRIN/2/1 for details.

55.   **B**   **Chapter 4, Section 11.3.3**

At age 69, Meg is entitled to a personal allowance of £11,500. No reduction for excess income applies.

Therefore, Meg's taxable income is £19,400 – £11,500 = £7,900.

This is taxable at the basic rate of 20%.

Therefore, Meg's income tax liability is £1,580.

56.   **D**   **Chapter 1, Section 1.3**

The Prudential Regulation Authority is part of the Bank of England and carries the prudential regulatory powers over financial firms, such as banks, building societies, investment and insurance companies.

57.   **A**   **Chapter 4, Section 10.5**

Despite requirements for financial advisers to maintain client confidentiality, any suspicion of possible breaches of the law must be reported to the firm's MLRO who will decide whether or not to report the matter to the NCA. Failure of the adviser to follow this procedure is a criminal offence.

58.   **B**   **Chapter 1, Section 1.5.2**

The FSCS will pay maximum compensation of £85,000 for each account holder who is an eligible claimant, in each of the authorised savings institutions where an account is held, following default by a UK-regulated bank or building society.

59.   **B**   **Chapter 2, Section 3.1.3**

The difference between these items is net property income from abroad. The sum of gross domestic product plus net property income from abroad is the GNP.

60.   **A**   **Chapter 4, Section 7.3.3**

Withholding tax relief at source enables withholding tax to be reduced or not applied based on receipt of a notification of the investor's status.

Where the reclaim basis is used, withholding tax is deducted, but some or all of it may be repaid to the investor upon submission of the appropriate paperwork.

61.   A   Chapter 4, Section 7.3.3

Withholding tax relief at source enables withholding tax to be reduced or not applied based on receipt of a notification of the investor's status.

Where the reclaim basis is used, withholding tax is deducted, but some or all of it may be repaid to the investor upon submission of the appropriate paperwork.

62.   B   Chapter 5, Section 3.2

REITs are required to distribute at least 90% of their tax-exempt income profits to investors who will then pay CGT at a rate of 0%, 10% or 20% depending on their other income and gains.

63.   A   Chapter 5, Section 8.1

Each child can have one cash and one stocks and shares junior ISA at any one time. Anyone can put money into a junior ISA and the total limit is £4,128 per year.

64.   C   Chapter 1, Section 4.6.1

If there is a delay selling her main residence, and it has not been sold on the day she completes her new purchase:, Ria may be able to receive a refund if she sells her previous main home within 36 months.

65.   A   Chapter 2, Section 5.10

Coincident indicators are those which change at approximately the same time as the whole economy, thereby providing information about the current state of the economy. An example is personal income. There are many coincident economic indicators: GDP, industrial production and retail sales are coincident indicators and a coincident index may be used to identify, after the fact, the dates of peaks and troughs in the business cycle.

66.   D   Chapter 8, Section 2.1

The information ratio assesses the degree to which a fund manager uses skill and knowledge to enhance returns. This is a versatile and useful risk-adjusted measure of actively managed fund performance, calculated by deducting the returns of the fund benchmark from the returns of the fund and dividing the result by its tracking error.

67.   C   Chapter 2, Section 3.1

Three key measures of economic activity are national income, gross national product and gross domestic product.

68.   B   Chapter 5, Section 16.2.2

Loans can be made to the sponsoring employer, but are subject to certain conditions set by HMRC. The loan should not exceed 50% of the net market value of the scheme's assets.

Multiple Choice Questions

69. **B** **Chapter 4, Section 7.1.2**

The remittance basis charge was increased to £50,000 for non-domiciles who have been resident in at least 12 of the last 14 years and wish to claim the remittance basis. Anyone resident for seven of the previous nine years would continue to pay a remittance basis charge of £30,000.

70. **B** **Chapter 8, Section 1.2**

In certain markets, the largest companies can comprise a disproportionately large weighting in the index, and therefore an index constructed on a market-capitalisation basis can give a misleading impression. An equal-weighted index assumes that equal amounts are invested in each share in the index, and the Nikkei 225 is an example of such an index.

71. **C** **Chapter 3, Section 2.3.3**

The volatility in the value of an investment can be quantified statistically by calculating the standard deviation of the values. Standard deviation measures how widely the value of an investment is dispersed around its mean or average. There is a chance that 2/3 of the annual return will be between 3% and 11% and there is a chance of 1/3 that the annual return will be below 3% and above 11%.

72. **A** **Chapter 5, Section 11.2**

Investors can get up to 50% tax relief in the tax year the investment is made, regardless of their marginal tax rate.

73. **D** **Chapter 7, Section 7.2.1**

The Financial Ombudsman Service (FOS) is established under FSMA and is responsible for receiving and investigating complaints against authorised persons.

74. **C** **Chapter 4, Section 6.1.8**

For a deed of variation to be valid, it must not be made for any consideration (ie, no one should have received money or value as encouragement for them to sign).

75. **A** **Chapter 5, Section 11.3**

In terms of income tax, investors benefit from an exemption from income tax on dividends from ordinary shares in VCTs (dividend relief).

76. **D** **Chapter 4, Section 3.1.2**

Three different income tax rates apply to UK dividend income and are dependent on the investor's overall tax position, taking account of their allowances and whether they are a basic rate, higher rate or additional rate taxpayer.

Tax rate applied (after deduction of personal allowance/dividend allowance/blind person's allowance). Dividend income falling below the basic rate tax limit	7.5%
Dividend income over the basic rate tax limit and below £150,000	32.5%
Dividend income above £150,000	38.1%

77.   **C**   **Chapter 1, Section 3.7.4**

SDRT of 0.5% is payable on the value of purchases of UK equities settled through CREST, rounded to the nearest penny.

78.   **C**   **Chapter 3, Section 1.2.1**

The amount that needs to be invested today in order to obtain a targeted future sum is determined through discounting. The procedure is a reverse process to compounding. Thus, the future amount required by the rate of interest earned over the period is calculated by rearranging the formula for compound interest as follows:

$$PV = \frac{FV}{(1 + r)^n}$$

79.   **C**   **Chapter 6, Section 2.11**

Trend investing trading is a strategy that seeks to achieve gains through the analysis of an asset's price momentum either up or down.

80.   **D**   **Chapter 1, Section 1.7.1**

The minimum holding is £100 and the maximum is currently £50,000.

Syllabus Learning Map

Syllabus Unit/ Element		Chapter/ Section
Element 1	**Asset Classes**	**Chapter 1**
1.1	**Cash and Cash Equivalents** On completion, the candidate should:	
1.1.1	understand the main types of deposit account: • current • instant access • National Savings & Investment products • notice • fixed rate • term • money market accounts	1.7
1.1.2	analyse the main characteristics, risk and returns of cash deposits: • liquidity • rates of interest • past returns • real returns • deposit takers • statutory protection • risks, inflation risk, interest rate risk and institutional risk • credit risk assessment of deposit taking institutions • foreign currency deposits • costs, charges and penalties • requirement linked accounts • Financial Services Compensation Scheme limits	1
1.1.3	analyse the main characteristics, risks and returns of money market funds • cash assets only • near-cash assets • pricing, liquidity and fair value • costs, charges and penalties • constant NAV • low volatility NAV • variable NAV • fees and gates	1.8
1.1.4	analyse the main characteristics, risks and returns of peer-to-peer lending	1.9
1.1.5	analyse the factors to take into account when selecting between different types of cash deposits, accounts and money market funds: • entry requirements	1

Syllabus Unit/ Element		Chapter/ Section
1.2	**Fixed-Income Securities** On completion, the candidate should be able to:	
1.2.1	know the main issuing institutions and purposes for issuing fixed-income securities: • sovereign states and governments • public authority • corporate • credit institutions • supranational	2
1.2.2	analyse the main sources of investment risk and return associated with fixed-income securities: • capital return • interest or yield • liquidity • rates of interest • real returns • credit ratings • credit enhancements • duration	2.4, 2.5
1.2.3	analyse the characteristics and differences between the main types of fixed income securities: • fixed-rate bonds • floating rate notes • zero coupon bonds • inflation-linked bonds • other index- and asset-linked bonds • asset-backed securities • convertible bonds • subordinated bonds • perpetual bonds • eurobonds and foreign issuer bonds • CoCos	2
1.2.4	understand how fixed-income securities are traded and settled: • primary and secondary markets • decentralised market • retail bond markets • clearing, settlement and safe custody • pricing, liquidity and fair value • coupon • nominal value • market price • clean and dirty prices • redemption date • transaction costs and charges	2.6

Syllabus Learning Map

Syllabus Unit/ Element		Chapter/ Section
1.2.5	understand the purpose and construction of the main bond indices, and the considerations needed for less liquid markets	2.7
1.2.6	analyse the factors to take into account when selecting bonds and bond funds: • bond characteristics • direct bond strategies • indirect investment • investing in bonds through funds • advantages and disadvantages of investing in bonds and bond funds	2.8
1.3	**Equities** On completion, the candidate should be able to:	
1.3.1	understand the characteristics and differences between the main types of shareholder equity: • ordinary • redeemable • non-voting • preference • convertible preference	3.2
1.3.2	understand the characteristics and differences between the main types of private equity share capital	3.3
1.3.3	analyse the main sources of investment risk and return associated with equities: • capital return • dividends • liquidity • credit ratings • corporate actions • company liquidation • market conditions • activist shareholder	3.4, 3.5
1.3.4	understand the issues involved in dealing for clients in equity markets: • regulated and designated investment exchanges • multilateral trading platforms • dark pools • organised trading facilities • OTC trading • access to markets • principal and agency trading • listed and unlisted securities • quoted and unquoted securities • admission to trading	3.6

Syllabus Unit/ Element		Chapter/ Section
1.3.5	understand how equity securities are traded and settled: • liquidity, pricing and fair value • cost of purchase and sale • nominal value • market price • cum- and ex-dividend • transaction costs and charges	3.7
1.3.6	understand the purpose and construction of the main equity indices, and the considerations needed for less liquid markets	3.8
1.3.7	analyse equity securities and equity funds using the following valuation measures: • price earnings (P/E) ratio • earnings per share • dividend yield • dividend cover • gearing • borrowings • net asset value and enterprise value • past performance • price-to-cash flow ratio • price-to-book ratio	3.9
1.3.8	analyse the factors to take into account when selecting equities and equity funds: • equity fund strategies – growth, income, market capitalisation, sector, region, customised • growth/dividend prospects • direct versus indirect investment • advantages and disadvantages of investing in equities • cost, turnover, liquidity and ease of trading	3.10, 3.11
1.4	**Property** On completion, the candidate should be able to:	
1.4.1	understand the differences, characteristics, risks and returns of the main property markets and sectors: • residential • buy-to-let • commercial – retail space, hotel, office, industrial/warehouse	4

Syllabus Learning Map

Syllabus Unit/ Element		Chapter/ Section
1.4.2	analyse the main sources of investment risk and return associated with property investment, both direct and indirect • capital growth • yield • location and quality • occupancy rate • tenant creditworthiness, tenancy and rental agreement • term and structure of lease • asset liquidity • market volatility and risk • sector risk	4
1.4.3	understand how the direct residential and commercial property markets operate: • ownership and lease structures • conveyancing, buying and selling • costs – transactional, management • property valuation • finance and gearing • investment performance measurement and the role of the Investment Property Databank	4
1.4.4	analyse property and property funds using the following valuation measures: • cash flow and average yield • capitalisation rate • rental value, review • reversionary value • comparative analysis • market indices and trends	4.10
1.4.5	analyse the factors to take into account when selecting property and property funds: • property shares, OEICs, REITs, bonds, trusts, funds, fund of funds, limited partnerships • relative merits of investing through open-ended and closed-ended vehicles • property fund strategies • growth/dividend prospects • direct versus indirect investment • pricing, liquidity and fair value • advantages and disadvantages of investing in property • costs and ease of trading	4.11, 4.12

Syllabus Unit/ Element		Chapter/ Section
1.5	**Other Assets** On completion, the candidate should be able to:	
1.5.1	understand the purpose, characteristics, risks and returns of the main types of alternative investments: • gold and other metals • commodities • art • antiques	5
1.5.2	analyse the factors to take into account when investing in alternative investments: • direct versus indirect investment • investment time horizon • features – quality, durability, provenance • transaction, delivery and ongoing costs • pricing, liquidity and fair value • advantages and disadvantages of investing in alternatives	5

Element 2	**The Macroeconomic Environment**	**Chapter 2**
2.1	**Macroeconomic Trends and Indicators** On completion, the candidate should be able to:	
2.1.1	understand the main long-term global trends and the effects of technological changes/advancements: • ageing population • rising living standards • access to education • growth of the service sector • changing patterns of the economy • productivity of capital and labour • wealth and income distribution • growth of developing economies • natural resources	1
2.1.2	understand the impact of the following on global trades and asset classes: • international markets • trade agreements • tariffs • protectionism • globalisation of business and finance • market failures	2

Syllabus Learning Map

Syllabus Unit/ Element		Chapter/ Section
2.1.3	understand the main stages of economic, financial and stock market cycles, including: • trade cycles • business cycles • asset price bubbles • economic shocks • difficulty in forecasting national and international trends	4
2.1.4	interpret key economic and business indicators: • gross domestic product • inflation • interest rates • consumer price and inflation indices • retail sales • unemployment rate • industrial production • stock market indices • money supply changes • foreign exchange indices • leading, lagging and coincident indicators • procyclic, countercyclic and acyclic indicators	5
2.2	**Fiscal and Monetary Policy** On completion, the candidate should be able to:	
2.2.1	understand the role of government and central banks in fiscal and monetary policy: • interest-rate-setting process • quantitative easing • unwinding of central bank balance sheets • money market operations • fiscal stance • other interventions	6
2.2.2	understand how the money supply affects: • inflation, deflation, disinflation • interest rates • exchange rates • relationship between money supply, inflation and employment	6.4
2.2.3	understand the impact of surpluses and deficits on business and the economy	6.5
2.2.4	understand the composition of the balance of payments, and the factors behind and benefits of international trade and capital flows: • current account • imports • exports	6.5

Syllabus Unit/ Element		Chapter/ Section
2.3	**Influences on Asset Classes** On completion, the candidate should be able to:	
2.3.1	Understand the role of financial investment in the economy: • primary markets as introducers of new funds to business and government • secondary markets enabling investors to adjust investments to meet individual needs	1, 7
2.3.2	analyse the impact of macroeconomic influences on each of the following asset classes • fixed income • commodities • cash • property • equities	7.2

Element 3	**Principles of Investment Risk and Return**	Chapter 3
3.1	**The Time Value of Money** On completion, the candidate should be able to:	
3.1.1	understand the effects of compound interest and the time value of money	1.1, 1.4
3.1.2	Calculate the present value of: • lump sums • regular payments	1.2
3.1.3	Calculate the future value of: • lump sums • regular payments	1.3
3.1.4	calculate real and inflation-adjusted returns: • nominal returns • real or inflation-adjusted returns • total returns	1.5
3.2	**Investment Risk and Return** On completion, the candidate should:	
3.2.1	analyse and explain the main types of risk and the implications for investors: • systemic risk • systematic risk • market risk – asset price volatility, currency, interest rates, foreign exchange rates, commodity price volatility • concentration and diversification • long-term investment risk • liquidity, credit risk and default • gearing • country risk • counterparty and institutional risk • market timing • corporate governance risk	2.2

Syllabus Learning Map

Syllabus Unit/ Element		Chapter/ Section
3.2.2	understand the main risk and return measures, and how they are used within asset and portfolio evaluation, and their purposes: • holding period return • total return and its components • standard deviation • volatility • covariance and correlation • risk-adjusted returns • benchmarking	2.3
3.2.3	apply the theory of investment risk and return to the measurement of portfolio performance: • holding period return • relative return • standard deviation • risk-adjusted returns	2.6
3.3	**Models of Investment Theory** On completion, the candidate should be able to:	
3.3.1	understand the main propositions and limitations of the efficient markets hypothesis (EMH) • strong form • semi-strong form • weak form • assumptions and shortcomings	3.1
3.3.2	understand the main principles of modern portfolio theory (MPT), the capital asset pricing model (CAPM), its application and limitations: • risk-free rate of return • risk premium • cost of capital and return on capital • excess returns • correlation measures • systematic and unsystematic risk • risk and diversification • efficient frontier, portfolio optimisation and leverage • assumptions and shortcomings	3.2, 3.3
3.3.3	understand the main principles behind arbitrage pricing theory (APT), its application and limitations: • factor structure and analysis • macroeconomic and market factors • arbitrage theory and mechanics • relationship with CAPM • assumptions and shortcomings	3.4

Syllabus Unit/ Element		Chapter/ Section
3.3.4	understand the principles of behavioural finance: • loss aversion • price reaction and price trends • barriers and biases – practical and psychological • relationship with EMH • assumptions and shortcomings	3.5
3.3.5	understand the types and uses of multi-factor models, their assumptions and limitations	3.6
3.3.6	understand how to reduce portfolio risk through diversification and hedging: • significance of alpha and beta • correlation and relative risk • principles of asset allocation • hedging and immunisation • active and passive strategies	3.7

Element 4	Taxation of Investors and Investments	Chapter 4
4.1	**Income Tax** On completion, the candidate should be able to:	
4.1.1	understand how a private individual's income tax liability is determined using: • tax rates • tax rate bands • personal allowances	1
4.1.2	understand how the income tax liability for a trust is determined based on: • trust type • tax rates • tax rate bands	2
4.1.3	understand the application of income tax in respect of: • individuals • trusts • charities	1, 2
4.2	**Taxation of Investment Income** On completion, the candidate should be able to:	
4.2.1	understand the tax treatment of investment income: • savings income • dividend income • rental income	3.1

Syllabus Learning Map

Syllabus Unit/ Element		Chapter/ Section
4.3	**National Insurance Contributions** On completion, the candidate should be able to:	
4.3.1	understand the basis on which National Insurance contributions (NICs) are levied: • employers • employees • self-employed • voluntary	4
4.4	**Capital Gains Tax** On completion the candidate should be able to:	
4.4.1	understand the application of capital gains tax in respect of: • individuals • trusts • charities	5
4.4.2	understand the application of capital gains tax to the sale of assets, such as: • shares • government bonds • corporate bonds • real estate • chattels	5
4.5	**Inheritance Tax** On completion, the candidate should be able to:	
4.5.1	understand the application of inheritance tax (IHT): • chargeable transfers • potentially exempt transfers • transfers on death • nil-rate band • exemptions and reliefs • gifts with reservation • valuation of assets • deed of variation	6
4.5.2	understand how intestacy rules may apply in England and Wales, and the implications of these rules for estate planning	6.3
4.5.3	understand the application of IHT to: • transfers into trusts • assets held in trusts • transfers out of trusts	6
4.6	**Residence and Domicile** On completion, the candidate should be able to:	
4.6.1	understand the impact of the rules on residency and domicile and the implications for income tax and CGT	7.1
4.6.2	understand the use of double taxation treaties	7.2

Syllabus Unit/ Element		Chapter/ Section
4.6.3	understand how withholding tax is applied based on: • residency • product • tax regime (at source or reclaimable) • beneficiary • European Savings Directive • qualified intermediaries scheme	7.3
4.6.4	know the impact of residency and domicile on the liability to IHT	7.4
4.6.5	understand the reporting requirements for: • FATCA • CDOT	7.5
4.7	**Stamp Duty** On completion, the candidate should be able to:	
4.7.1	understand the application of stamp duty and stamp duty reserve tax (SDRT) to the purchase of securities, including: • company shares • share options • unit trusts and open-ended investment companies (OEICs) • government bonds • corporate bonds • exchange-traded funds (ETFs)	8.1
4.7.2	understand the application of stamp duty land tax (SDLT), including the main reliefs and exemptions, to the purchase of property	8.2
4.8	**Value Added Tax** On completion, the candidate should be able to:	
4.8.1	understand how liability to value added tax (VAT) arises and is charged	9
4.9	**Corporation Tax** On completion, the candidate should be able to:	
4.9.1	understand how liability to corporation tax (CT) arises and is charged: • companies and organisations: trading, non-trading • taxable profits and accounting periods • rates, allowances and reliefs • taxation of franked income	10
4.10	**Tax Compliance** On completion, the candidate should be able to:	
4.10.1	understand how tax is accounted for and an adviser's duties regarding tax compliance, avoidance and evasion	10
4.10.2	understand international disclosure requirements	10.6

Syllabus Learning Map

Syllabus Unit/ Element		Chapter/ Section
4.11	**Tax Planning** On completion, the candidate should be able to:	
4.11.1	apply the key principles of investment tax planning: • use of personal allowances • spouses' personal allowances • children's tax position • pension contributions • use of tax wrappers • use of capital gains tax exemptions • tax deferral • use of life assurance bonds	11.1
4.11.2	analyse the criteria for selecting a tax-planning strategy	11.2
4.11.3	apply the key principles of IHT planning: • lifetime gifts • trusts • transferability of nil rate band	11.3
4.11.4	apply common tax computations for: • an individual's liability to income tax • age allowance • CGT liability on share disposals • IHT liability on lifetime transfers and at death	11.3
4.11.5	apply the above principles to basic recommendations relating to the taxation of investments and pensions	11.4

Element 5	**Investment Products**	Chapter 5
5.1	**Collective Investments** On completion, the candidate should be able to:	
5.1.1	understand the main types, purposes, common investment characteristics and behaviours of funds, collectives and other products	1, 2 & 3
5.1.2	understand the structure of multi-manager and multi-asset funds	1.2
5.1.3	understand the tax treatment within the fund and for UK investors of income arising from collective investments: • open-ended investment companies (OEICs) • investment companies with variable capital (ICVCs) • unit trusts	4
5.1.4	understand the main types, purposes, common investment characteristics and behaviours of: • onshore collective investment funds • offshore collective investment funds	5
5.1.5	understand the tax treatment of UK investors investing in offshore funds, including: • differences between reporting funds and non-reporting funds • taxation of offshore funds	5.1

Syllabus Unit/ Element		Chapter/ Section
5.1.6	analyse the charges and pricing of collective investments: • initial, annual, exit and performance fee charging structures • single pricing • bid/offer pricing • dilution levies • forward pricing	6
5.1.7	analyse the relative merits and limitations of investing in a collective investment fund compared with other forms of direct and indirect investment, in terms of: • risk • return • tax treatment • turnover, liquidity and access • expenses – transaction and ongoing • management and administration	6
5.2	**Exchange-Traded Funds and Exchange-Traded Commodities** On completion, the candidate should be able to:	
5.2.1	understand the main types, purposes, underlying structure, common investment characteristics and behaviours of: • exchange-traded funds (ETFs) • exchange-traded commodities (ETCs)	7
5.2.2	analyse the relative merits and limitations of investing in exchange-traded funds (ETFs) or exchange-traded commodities (ETCs) compared with other forms of direct and indirect investment, in terms of: • risk • return • physical v synthetic • tax treatment • turnover, liquidity and access • expenses – transaction and ongoing • management and administration	7
5.3	**Closed-Ended Funds and Investment Companies** On completion, the candidate should be able to:	
5.3.1	understand the main types, purposes, common investment characteristics and behaviours of: • onshore closed-ended funds and investment companies; investment trusts; real estate investment trusts • offshore closed-ended funds and investment companies	3
5.3.2	understand when and why borrowing/gearing is used by closed ended funds, and the benefits and risks associated with it	3

Syllabus Learning Map

Syllabus Unit/ Element		Chapter/ Section
5.3.3	analyse the relative merits and limitations of investing in closed-ended funds and investment companies compared with other forms of direct and indirect investment, in terms of: • risk • return • tax treatment • premiums and discounts • turnover, liquidity and access • expenses – transaction and administration • management and administration	3
5.4	**Individual Savings Accounts and Child Trust Funds** On completion, the candidate should be able to:	
5.4.1	analyse the key features, restrictions and tax treatment of ISAs, junior ISAs and child trust funds (CTFs): • eligibility • eligible investments • subscriptions and additional subscriptions • transfers • withdrawals • use in investment and tax planning	8.1, 8.2
5.5	**National Savings & Investments** On completion, the candidate should be able to:	
5.5.1	analyse the key features, restrictions and tax treatment of National Savings, premium bonds and investments: • use in investment and tax planning	8.4
5.6	**Life Assurance Based Investments** On completion, the candidate should be able to:	
5.6.1	analyse the key features, relative merits and limitations of investing in onshore and offshore life assurance-based investments compared with other forms of direct and indirect investment: • risk • return • tax treatment (offshore, onshore) • turnover, liquidity and access • expenses – transaction and ongoing • management and administration	9
5.7	**Private Equity Funds** On completion, the candidate should be able to:	
5.7.1	understand the main types, purposes, structures, tax treatment and investment characteristics of private equity funds	10

Syllabus Unit/ Element		Chapter/ Section
5.8	**Venture Capital Trusts and Enterprise Investment Schemes** On completion the candidate should be able to:	
5.8.1	analyse the key features, relative merits and limitations of investing in venture capital trusts (VCTs), enterprise investment schemes (EISs) and seed enterprise investment schemes (SEISs) compared with other forms of direct and indirect investment: • partners/ investors • investment management • tax characteristics • past performance in terms of risk and returns • discounts • premiums • secondary market liquidity	11
5.9	**Distributor Influenced Funds (DIFs)** On completion, the candidate should be able to:	
5.9.1	analyse the key features, relative merits and limitations of investing in a distributor-influenced fund compared with other forms of direct and indirect investment: • roles and responsibilities of underlying parties • fee structure • expenses and commissions • tax characteristics • investment performance and risk • other risks – distributor power and expertise, conflicts of interest, suitability • secondary market liquidity • requirements on avoiding conflicts of interest	12
5.10	**Derivatives** On completion, the candidate should be able to:	
5.10.1	understand the purposes, structure and risk/reward characteristics of the main types of financial derivatives pertaining to each main asset class: • futures • forward contracts • options • warrants • contracts for differences	13

Syllabus Learning Map

Syllabus Unit/ Element		Chapter/ Section
5.10.2	understand the effects of implementing simple derivatives strategies for the purposes of hedging or speculation in terms of: • risk transfer and risk/reward payoff • transaction costs and margin • ease of implementation and unwinding	13
5.11	**Hedge Funds** On completion, the candidate should be able to:	
5.11.1	analyse the key features, relative merits and limitations of investing in hedge funds compared with other forms of direct and indirect investment: • main types of hedge fund • regulatory environment • investment risk • use of short and long positions • custody and safe-keeping practices • limitations in respect of voting capital • funds of hedge funds (FoHFs)	14
5.12	**Absolute Return Funds (ARFs)** On completion, the candidate should be able to:	
5.12.1	analyse the key features, relative merits and limitations of investing in absolute return funds (ARFs) compared with other forms of direct and indirect investment: • structure • income and capital growth • investment risk and return • expenses • capital protection • monitoring performance versus benchmark	14.4
5.13	**Structured Products** On completion, the candidate should be able to:	
5.13.1	analyse the key features, relative merits and limitations of investing in retail structured products and investment notes compared with other forms of direct and indirect investment: • structure (structured deposits and products) • income and capital growth • investment risk and return • expenses • capital protection • American and European soft protection • counterparty risk	15

Syllabus Unit/ Element		Chapter/ Section
5.14	**Pension Arrangements** On completion, the candidate should be able to:	
5.14.1	analyse the main types, purpose, structure and operation, tax treatment and investment characteristics of pension arrangements: • defined benefit • defined contribution • personal pensions • self-invested personal pensions (SIPPs) • small self-administered schemes (SSASs)	16
5.14.2	analyse the key features of pension arrangements: • contributions – sources, level and limits • investment selection and performance • how benefits are provided • annual and lifetime allowances	16

Element 6	**Investment Planning**	**Chapter 6**
6.1	**Asset Allocation** On completion, the candidate should be able to:	
6.1.1	understand the purpose and principles of asset allocation: • relationship with investment theory • achievement of performance objectives • trade-off between risk and return • stochastic modelling • active and passive management • strategic asset allocation (SAA) • tactical asset allocation (TAA)	1
6.1.2	understand how investment theory is applied to the process of portfolio construction	1
6.1.3	understand the basic ways to diversify a portfolio: • asset class • geographical area • sector • currency • maturity	1.5
6.1.4	analyse combinations of asset classes based on: • historical returns • index and benchmark comparisons • correlation of performance between asset classes • advantages and limitations of relying on historical data	1.6

Syllabus Learning Map

Syllabus Unit/ Element		Chapter/ Section
6.2	**Investment Selection** On completion, the candidate should be able to:	
6.2.1	understand the aims and characteristics of the main fund management strategies and styles: • indexing or passive management • active or market timing • passive-active combinations • cash and bond fund strategies • liability-driven investment (LDI) • long, short and geared • sector-specific • contrarian • quantitative, trend and trading strategies	2
6.2.2	analyse and compare charges on the basis of impact, reduction in yield and total expense ratios/ongoing charge and synthetic risk, Sharpe ratio, R-squared and reward indicators	2.12
6.2.3	know the research and reports available to financial advisers: • fundamental analysis • technical analysis • fund analysis • fund rating agencies and screening software • broker and distributor reports • sector-specific reports	2.13
6.2.4	analyse the factors to consider when selecting investment product providers	2.14
6.2.5	understand the characteristics, uses, benefits, risks and charges associated with wrap and other platforms	2.15

Element 7	**Investment Advice**	Chapter 7
7.1	**Advising Clients** On completion, the candidate should be able to:	
7.1.1	apply a framework for providing financial advice, paying particular attention to: • the nature of the client relationship, confidentiality, trust and client protection • the information required from clients and methods of obtaining it • monitoring and review of clients' circumstances • the information clients must be given under the current regulatory requirements • additional requirements needed when advising on unregulated retail products	1

Syllabus Unit/ Element		Chapter/ Section
7.1.2	understand how financial advice can be paid for: • adviser charging • commission • nature and frequency of service to be provided	1.7
7.1.3	apply the FCA's Fair Treatment of Customers and the six consumer outcomes that firms should aim to achieve in supporting the requirements of Principle 6	1.6
7.1.4	understand the purpose, merits and limitations of using questionnaires and interviews to elicit customer information	2.1.2
7.2	**Client Fact Finding** On completion, candidates should be able to:	
7.2.1	analyse the main factors, resources and limitations shaping a client's current and desired financial circumstances: • gather appropriate, relevant information about current and projected income, expenditure, debt and savings • consider time horizons and the relative balance of growth versus income • distinguish between what is essential and what is desirable, and prioritise accordingly • agree clear, feasible, prioritised investment objectives	1.10.2
7.2.2	analyse the merits and disadvantages of paying off mortgage or debt compared with investing surplus funds	4
7.3	**Risk and Client Suitability** On completion, candidates should be able to:	
7.3.1	analyse a profile of a client's risk exposure and appetite for risk, based on the following objective and subjective factors: • level of wealth • timescale • commitments • life cycle • life goals • investment objectives • attitudes • experiences • knowledge • capacity for loss	2.6
7.3.2	apply a client risk profile to the investment selection process	2.6
7.3.3	assess the following factors when selecting suitable product solutions: • impact of new solutions on existing arrangements • range of solutions available to suit different circumstances • range of criteria for matching solutions to client needs and demands • discounting alternatives	5.4

Syllabus Unit/ Element		Chapter/ Section
7.3.4	assess affordability and suitability based on a range of factors including product provider quality, performance, risk, charges and client service	2.6
7.3.5	understand the difference between environmental and social governance, and socially responsible investment strategies, their purpose and the circumstances in which it may be appropriate to discuss them	3, 3.1
7.3.6	understand the main considerations for investing in accordance with Sharia'a law	3.2
7.3.7	understand the main considerations for investing in accordance with other faith values	3.3
7.3.8	understand the main considerations that should be taken into account when investing for charities	3.4
7.3.9	understand the main considerations that should be taken into account when investing for trusts	3.5
7.4	**Planning and Recommendations** On completion, the candidate should be able to:	
7.4.1	apply a strategy and rationale that will meet the client's objectives: • highlight the pertinent issues and priorities • formulate a plan to deal with them • offer proposals to achieve these objectives • explain clearly the relative merits and drawbacks of each proposal and combination thereof • agree a strategy that the client understands and accepts	2.2
7.4.2	apply an appropriate investment allocation strategy that best meets the following criteria: • client's financial objectives and priorities • client's risk tolerance • appropriate fees and charges • portfolio turnover ratio (PTR) • client suitability requirements • adequate diversification and correlation benefits • additional risk, timing and liquidity factors where asset accumulation and decumulation are relevant features	5
7.4.3	understand the factors which influence the way in which recommendations are presented	6
7.4.4	understand how to check clients' understanding of recommendations	6.1
7.4.5	apply consumer rights and the regulatory requirements to the provision of investment advice	7

Syllabus Unit/ Element		Chapter/ Section
7.4.6	assess the factors influencing the choice of benchmark and the basis for review • portfolio's asset allocation • risk/return profile • alternative investments • taxation • peer groups • maintenance of capital value	8
7.4.7	understand the process of periodic review to meet key criteria: • regulatory requirements • appropriate frequency, taking into account client requirements and the chosen investment strategy	1.10

Element 8	Portfolio Performance and Review	Chapter 8
8.1	**Selection and Use of Benchmarks** On completion, the candidate should be able to:	
8.1.1	understand the purpose and limitations of portfolio evaluation	1
8.1.2	understand the concept and purpose of benchmarking • Global investment performance standards (GIPS) • WMA wealth management benchmarks • Peer group average (WM and CAPS)	1
8.1.3	know the construction and weighting methods of the following indices: • FTSE 100 • FTSE All Share Index • FTSE Actuaries Government Securities Indices • MSCI World Index • Dow Jones Industrial Average Index • S&P 500 Index • Nikkei 225	1.2
8.1.4	understand the differences between a single and a composite (synthetic) benchmark	1.3
8.1.5	apply suitable benchmarks when measuring and evaluating investment performance	1.4
8.2	**Portfolio Measurement** On completion, the candidate should be able to:	
8.2.1	analyse portfolio performance in terms of: • absolute and relative return • absolute and relative risk • risk-reward ratios • contributions to return arising from asset allocation, currency movements, stock selection and timing • impact of new money and timing factors	2.1

Syllabus Learning Map

Syllabus Unit/ Element		Chapter/ Section
8.3	**Portfolio Review** On completion, the candidate should be able to:	
8.3.1	understand the importance of regularly reviewing the client's portfolio	3
8.3.2	apply measures to address the factors that require attention as part of the portfolio review and administration process: • changes in client circumstances • changes in the financial environment • new products and services available • administrative changes or difficulties • investment-related changes (eg, credit rating, corporate actions) • portfolio rebalancing • benchmark review	3

Examination Specification

Each examination paper is constructed from a specification that determines the weightings that will be given to each element. The specification is given below.

It is important to note that the numbers quoted may vary slightly from examination to examination as there is some flexibility to ensure that each examination has a consistent level of difficulty. However, the number of questions tested in each element should not change by more than plus or minus 2.

Element Number	Element	Questions
1	Asset Classes	14
2	The Macroeconomic Environment	6
3	Principles of Investment Risk and Return	6
4	Taxation of Investors and Investments	16
5	Investment Products	17
6	Investment Planning	5
7	Investment Advice	11
8	Portfolio Performance and Review	5
Total		80

CISI Chartered MCSI Membership can work for you...

Studying for a CISI qualification is hard work and we're sure you're putting in plenty of hours, but don't lose sight of your goal!

This is just the first step in your career; there is much more to achieve!

The securities and investments sector attracts ambitious and driven individuals. You're probably one yourself and that's great, but on the other hand you're almost certainly surrounded by lots of other people with similar ambitions.

So how can you stay one step ahead during these uncertain times?

Entry Criteria for Chartered MCSI Membership

As an ACSI and MCSI candidate, you can upgrade your membership status to Chartered MCSI. There are a number of ways of gaining the CISI Chartered MCSI membership.

A straightforward route requires candidates to have:
- a minimum of one year's ACSI or MCSI membership;
- passed a full Diploma; Certificate in Private Client Investment Advice & Management or Masters in Wealth Management award;
- passed IntegrityMatters with an A grade; and
- successfully logged and certified 12 months' CPD under the CISI's CPD Scheme.

Alternatively, experienced-based candidates are required to have:
- a minimum of one year's ACSI membership;
- passed IntegrityMatters with an A grade; and
- successfully logged and certified six years' CPD under the CISI's CPD Scheme.

Joining Fee:	Current Grade of Membership	Grade of Chartership	Upgrade Cost
	ACSI	Chartered MCSI	£85.00
	MCSI	Chartered MCSI	£30.00

By belonging to a Chartered professional body, members will benefit from enhanced status in the industry and the wider community. Members will be part of an organisation which holds the respect of government and the financial services sector, and can communicate with the public on a whole new level. There will be little doubt in consumers' minds that chartered members of the CISI are highly regarded and qualified professionals and, as a consequence, will be required to act as such.

The Chartered MCSI designation will provide you with full access to all member benefits, including Professional Refresher where there are currently over 100 modules available on subjects including Anti-Money Laundering, Information Security & Data Protection, Integrity & Ethics, and the UK Bribery Act. CISI TV is also available to members, allowing you to catch up on the latest CISI events, whilst earning valuable CPD.

Revision Express

You've bought the workbook... now test your knowledge before your exam.

Revision Express is an engaging online study tool to be used in conjunction with most CISI workbooks.

Key Features of Revision Express:
- Examination-focused – the content of Revision Express covers the key points of the syllabus
- Questions throughout to reaffirm understanding of the subject
- Special end-of-module practice exam to reflect as closely as possible the standard you will experience in your exam (please note, however, they are not the CISI exam questions themselves)
- Extensive glossary of terms
- Useful associated website links
- Allows you to study whenever you like, and on any device

IMPORTANT: The questions contained in Revision Express products are designed as aids to revision, and should not be seen in any way as mock exams.

Price per Revision Express module: £35
Price when purchased with the corresponding CISI workbook: £105

To purchase Revision Express:

call our Customer Support Centre on:
+44 20 7645 0777

or visit the CISI's online bookshop at:
cisi.org/bookshop

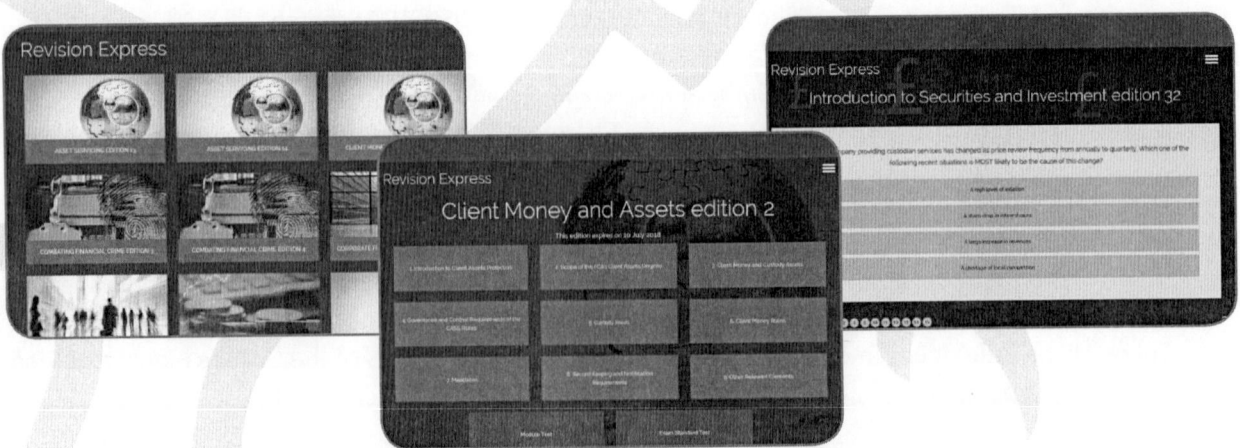

For more information on our elearning products, contact our Customer Support Centre on +44 20 7645 0777, or visit our website at cisi.org/elearning

Professional Refresher

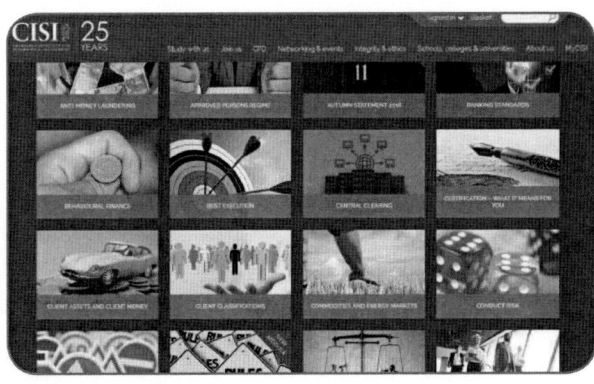

Self-testing elearning modules to refresh your knowledge, meet regulatory and firm requirements, and earn CPD.

Professional Refresher is a training solution to help you remain up-to-date with industry developments, maintain regulatory compliance and demonstrate continuing learning.

This popular online learning tool allows self-administered refresher testing on a variety of topics, including the latest regulatory changes.

There are currently over 100 modules available which address UK and international issues. Modules are reviewed by practitioners frequently and new topics are added to the suite on a regular basis.

Benefits to firms:
- Learning and testing can form part of business T&C programme
- Learning and testing kept up-to-date and accurate by the CISI
- Relevant and useful – devised by industry practitioners
- Access to individual results available as part of management overview facility, 'Super User'
- Records of staff training can be produced for internal use and external audits
- Cost-effective – no additional charge for CISI members
- Available to non-members

Benefits to individuals:
- Comprehensive selection of topics across sectors
- Modules are regularly reviewed and updated by industry experts
- New topics added regularly
- Free for members
- Successfully passed modules are recorded in your CPD log as active learning
- Counts as structured learning for RDR purposes
- On completion of a module, a certificate can be printed out for your own records

The full suite of Professional Refresher modules is free to CISI members, or £250 for non-members. Modules are also available individually. To view a full list of Professional Refresher modules visit:

cisi.org/refresher

If you or your firm would like to find out more, contact our Client Relationship Management team:

+ 44 20 7645 0670
crm@cisi.org

For more information on our elearning products, contact our Customer Support Centre on +44 20 7645 0777, or visit our website at cisi.org/refresher

Professional Refresher

Free to CISI members

Top 5

SCORM COMPLIANT

Integrity & Ethics
- High Level View
- Ethical Behaviour
- An Ethical Approach
- Compliance vs Ethics

Anti-Money Laundering
- Introduction to Money Laundering
- UK Legislation and Regulation
- Money Laundering Regulations 2007
- Proceeds of Crime Act 2002
- Terrorist Financing
- Suspicious Activity Reporting
- Money Laundering Reporting Officer
- Sanctions

Financial Crime
- What Is Financial Crime?
- Insider Dealing and Market Abuse Introduction, Legislation, Offences and Rules
- Money Laundering Legislation, Regulations, Financial Sanctions and Reporting Requirements
- Money Laundering and the Role of the MLRO

Information Security and Data Protection
- Information Security: The Key Issues
- Latest Cybercrime Developments
- The Lessons From High-Profile Cases
- Key Identity Issues: Know Your Customer
- Implementing the Data Protection Act 1998
- The Next Decade: Predictions For The Future

UK Bribery Act
- Background to the Act
- The Offences
- What the Offences Cover
- When Has an Offence Been Committed?
- The Defences Against Charges of Bribery
- The Penalties

Latest Modules

Bonds
- Definition, Key Terms and Characteristics
- The Different Types of Bonds
- The Advantages and Disadvantages of Bonds
- Rating Bonds

General Data Protection Regulation (GDPR)
- Understanding the Terminology
- The Six Data Protection Principles
- Data Subject Rights
- Technical and Organisational Measures

Human Trafficking and the Modern Slavery Act 2015
- Human Trafficking and Modern Slavery
- Definitions and Scale of the Problem
- Detection and Prevention
- Statements

Long-term Care
- Setting the Scene
- State Provision
- Planned Changes
- Funding Your Own Care
- Effective Structuring

Managing in the Regulatory Environment
- Regulatory Framework and Expectations
- The Conduct Rules
- Obligations on Managers
- Personal Responsibilities
- Responsibilities for Managing Others
- If Things Go Wrong

Operations

Best Execution
- What Is Best Execution?
- Achieving Best Execution
- Order Execution Policies
- Information to Clients & Client Consent
- Monitoring, the Rules, and Instructions
- Best Execution for Specific Types of Firms

Approved Persons Regime
- The Basis of the Regime
- Fitness and Propriety
- The Controlled Functions
- Principles for Approved Persons
- The Code of Practice for Approved Persons

Corporate Actions
- Corporate Structure and Finance
- Life Cycle of an Event
- Mandatory Events
- Voluntary Events

Wealth

Client Assets and Client Money
- Protecting Client Assets and Client Money
- Ring-Fencing Client Assets and Client Money
- Due Diligence of Custodians
- Reconciliations
- Records and Accounts
- CASS Oversight

Investment Principles and Risk
- Diversification
- Factfind and Risk Profiling
- Investment Management
- Modern Portfolio Theory and Investing Styles
- Direct and Indirect Investments
- Socially Responsible Investment
- Collective Investments
- Investment Trusts
- Dealing in Debt Securities and Equities

Banking Standards
- Introduction and Background
- Strengthening Individual Accountability
- Reforming Corporate Governance
- Securing Better Outcomes for Consumers
- Enhancing Financial Stability

Suitability of Client Investments
- Assessing Suitability
- Risk Profiling
- Establishing Risk Appetite
- Obtaining Customer Information
- Suitable Questions and Answers
- Making Suitable Investment Selections
- Guidance, Reports and Record Keeping

International

Foreign Account Tax Compliance Act (FATCA)
- Foreign Financial Institutions
- Due Diligence Requirements
- Reporting
- Compliance

MiFID II
- The Organisations Covered by MiFID
- The Products Subject to MiFID's Guidelines
- The Origins of MiFID II
- The Products Covered by MiFID II
- Levels 1, 2, and 3 Implementation

UCITS
- The Original UCITS Directive
- UCITS III
- UCITS IV
- Non-UCITS Funds
- Future Developments

cisi.org/refresher

Feedback to the CISI

Have you found this workbook to be a valuable aid to your studies? We would like your views, so please email us at learningresources@cisi.org with any thoughts, ideas or comments.

Accredited Training Partners

Support for exam students studying for the Chartered Institute for Securities & Investment (CISI) qualifications is provided by several Accredited Training Partners (ATPs), including Fitch Learning and BPP. The CISI's ATPs offer a range of face-to-face training courses, distance learning programmes, their own learning resources and study packs which have been accredited by the CISI. The CISI works in close collaboration with its ATPs to ensure they are kept informed of changes to CISI exams so they can build them into their own courses and study packs.

CISI Workbook Specialists Wanted

Workbook Authors

Experienced freelance authors with finance experience, and who have published work in their area of specialism, are sought. Responsibilities include:
- Updating workbooks in line with new syllabuses and any industry developments
- Ensuring that the syllabus is fully covered

Workbook Reviewers

Individuals with a high-level knowledge of the subject area are sought. Responsibilities include:
- Highlighting any inconsistencies against the syllabus
- Assessing the author's interpretation of the workbook

Workbook Technical Reviewers

Technical reviewers to provide a detailed review of the workbook and bring the review comments to the panel. Responsibilities include:
- Cross-checking the workbook against the syllabus
- Ensuring sufficient coverage of each learning objective

Workbook Proofreaders

Proofreaders are needed to proof workbooks both grammatically and also in terms of the format and layout. Responsibilities include:
- Checking for spelling and grammar mistakes
- Checking for formatting inconsistencies

If you are interested in becoming a CISI external specialist call:
+44 20 7645 0609

or email:
externalspecialists@cisi.org

For bookings, orders, membership and general enquiries please contact our Customer Support Centre on +44 20 7645 0777, or visit our website at cisi.org